THE
BIG BOOK OF JO'S
QUICK & EASY
MEALS

JOANNA CISMARU

AUTHOR OF *30-MINUTE ONE-POT MEALS*
AND CREATOR OF THE
JO COOKS BLOG

PAGE STREET
PUBLISHING CO.

Copyright © 2021 Joanna Cismaru

First published in 2021 by
Page Street Publishing Co.
27 Congress Street, Suite 105
Salem, MA 01970
www.pagestreetpublishing.com

All rights reserved. No part of this book may be reproduced or used, in any form or by any means, electronic or mechanical, without prior permission in writing from the publisher.

Distributed by Macmillan, sales in Canada by The Canadian Manda Group.

25 24 23 22 21   1 2 3 4 5

ISBN-13: 978-1-64567-288-3
ISBN-10: 1-64567-288-3

Library of Congress Control Number: 2020948907

Cover and book design by Laura Benton for Page Street Publishing Co.
Photography by Joanna Cismaru

Printed and bound in China

Page Street Publishing protects our planet by donating to nonprofits like The Trustees, which focuses on local land conservation.

DEDICATION AND ACKNOWLEDGMENTS

I'd like to dedicate this book to you, my readers, without whom this book would not have been possible. Over the years, you have all been right there with me, trying out my recipes and letting me know how much you love them. Your many comments and emails have encouraged me to continue down this path—for that, I love and appreciate you all.

I'd also like to thank my husband, who has been my strength through all this and has always supported and helped me through difficult times. He's my recipe tester, my hand model, the one who always tells me the truth, whether I want to hear it or not. Thank you for putting up with my occasional rants—especially when the blog is down and I lose it—and for always being there for me. I love you and couldn't imagine life without you.

Thank you to everyone at Page Street Publishing, who helped make this book happen.

Thank you to my parents and sister for all your support and love.

Last but not least, to the person reading this book: Thank you!

CONTENTS

Introduction — 7

Chicken — 8

Bruschetta Chicken — 11
Beer Can Chicken — 12
Roasted Chicken and Vegetables — 15
Lemon Chicken Piccata — 16
Spatchcock Chicken — 19
Roasted Cornish Hens — 20
Korean Fried Chicken — 23
Garlic Butter Chicken — 24
Coconut Chicken Curry — 27
Chicken Drumsticks with Beluga Lentils — 28
Oven-Baked Chicken Thighs — 31
Chicken Kiev — 32
Chicken Stroganoff — 35
Chicken Francese — 36
Garlic and Paprika Chicken — 39
Oven-Roasted Chicken Shawarma — 40
Spanish Chicken and Rice — 43
Chicken and Mushrooms in Creamy Dill Sauce — 44
Cheese and Prosciutto–Stuffed Chicken Breasts — 47

Beef — 48

Salisbury Steak — 51
Pan-Seared Steak — 52
Steak Tacos — 55
Easy Swiss Steak — 56
Beef Tips with Gravy — 59
Instant Pot® Beef Burgundy — 60
Easy Beef and Broccoli Stir-Fry — 63
Garlic Butter Steak Bites — 64
Easy Meatloaf — 67
Taco Lasagna — 68
Matambre (Argentinean Stuffed Flank Steak) — 71
Ginger Beef — 72
Blue Cheese Burgers with Crispy Fried Onions — 75
Italian Stuffed Peppers — 76
Carne Asada — 79
Beef Tenderloin — 80
Skillet Lasagna — 83

Pork — 84

Perfect Pork Tenderloin — 87
Baked Honey-Glazed Pork Ribs — 88
Honey Mustard Pork Tenderloin — 91
Mustard-Balsamic Pork Chops — 92
Rosemary-Garlic Pork Roast — 95
Honey-Garlic Pork Loin — 96
Lemon-Garlic Pork Roast — 99
Italian Breaded Pork Chops — 100
Pan-Seared Pork Chops with Gravy — 103
Pork Schnitzel — 104
Ranch Pork Chops and Potatoes — 107
Instant Pot® Barbecue Pork Ribs — 108
Grilled Tomahawk Pork Chops — 111
Quick and Easy Pork Sausages — 112
Pork Fajitas — 115
Braised Pork in Sweet Soy Sauce — 116

Seafood — 118

Cilantro-Lime Salmon — 121
Easy Crab Cakes — 122
Baked Lemon-Garlic Halibut — 125
Honey-Soy Shrimp — 126
Spicy New Orleans Shrimp — 129
Baked Lemon-Pepper Salmon — 130
Honey-Garlic Salmon and Veggies Sheet Pan Dinner — 133
Coconut Shrimp Curry — 134
Easy Tuna Salad — 137
Sole Meunière — 138
Chili-Garlic Shrimp — 141
Lemon-Garlic Scallops — 142
Firecracker Salmon — 145
Lemon-Butter Baked Cod — 146
Honey Mustard Salmon — 149
Maple and Mustard–Glazed Salmon — 150

Vegetarian 152

Tofu Drunken Noodles	155
Easy California Quinoa Salad	156
Grilled Vegetable Quesadillas	159
Sesame Noodles	160
Easy Tomato and Chickpea Salad	163
Chanterelle Mushrooms with Tagliatelle	164
Cheesy Zucchini Quiche	167
Couscous Pilaf with Sautéed Mushrooms	168
Spinach and Ricotta–Stuffed Shells	171
Baked Mac and Cheese	172
Arugula and Basil Pesto Risotto with Sautéed Mushrooms	174

Pasta 176

Creamy Carbonara	179
Creamy Goat Cheese Pasta	180
Cacio e Pepe	183
Pesto Shrimp Asparagus Pasta	184
Aglio e Olio	187
Pasta Primavera	188
Pumpkin and Sausage Pasta	191
Creamy Garlic-Parmesan Orzo	192
Sausage and Leek Ragu Gnocchi	195
Cheesy Chicken and Broccoli Pasta	196
Three-Cheese Hamburger Helper	199
The Best Chili Mac and Cheese	200
Easy Spaghetti Bolognese	203
Spinach-Artichoke Pasta	204

Casseroles 206

Chicken Divan	209
Baked Spaghetti Casserole	210
Cabbage Roll Casserole	213
Tuna Noodle Casserole	214
Chicken Tamale Casserole	217
Chicken Gloria	218
Turkey Tetrazzini	221
Easy Beef Lasagna	222
Chicken-Bacon-Ranch Casserole	225
White Chicken Enchiladas	226
Skillet Shepherd's Pie	229

Breakfast 230

Crescent Bacon Breakfast Ring	233
Dutch Baby Pancake	234
The Best Buttermilk Pancakes	237
Pumpkin-Zucchini Muffins	238
My Favorite Blueberry Muffins	241
Sausage and Egg Breakfast Rolls	242
French Toast	245
Overnight Breakfast Casserole	246
Sheet Pan Pancakes	249
Ham and Cheese Breakfast Muffins	250
Sausage–French Toast Roll-Ups	253
Baked Breakfast Taquitos	254

Lunch 256

Easy Chicken Fajitas	259
Quick and Easy Cobb Salad	260
Thai Chicken Salad	263
Easy Thai Steak Salad	264
Reuben Sandwich	267
Mediterranean Grilled Chicken Salad	268
Quiche Lorraine	271
Vietnamese Fish Tacos	272
Buffalo Chicken Quesadillas	275
Pad Thai	276
Pad See Ew	278
Korean Beef Rice Bowls	281

Soups 282

Chicken and Rice Soup	285
Easy Tortellini Soup	286
Egg Roll Soup	289
Beef Stroganoff Soup	290
Avgolemono Soup	293
Egg Drop Soup	294
Cheesy Chicken Enchilada Soup	297
Italian Wedding Soup	298
Albondigas Soup	301
Beef and Barley Soup	302
Instant Pot® Chicken Noodle Soup	305
Creamy Loaded Potato Soup	306
Sausage and Bean Soup	309
Broccoli-Cheese Soup	310

Starters — 312
Chimichurri Meatballs — 315
Easy Bruschetta — 316
Lasagna Dip — 319
Pico de Gallo — 320
Fried Pickles — 323
Vegetarian Stuffed Mushrooms — 324
Taco Meatball Ring — 327
Avocado-Shrimp Salsa — 328
Olive Tapenade — 331
Chile con Queso — 332
Honey-Garlic Shrimp — 335
Homemade Salsa — 336

Salads — 338
Tabbouleh Salad — 341
Greek Salad — 342
Macaroni Salad — 345
Creamy Cucumber Salad — 346
Greek Pasta Salad — 349
Italian Pasta Salad — 350
Mexican Street Corn Salad — 353
Waldorf Salad — 354
Summer Fruit Salad with Lemon Dressing — 357
Taco Pasta Salad — 358
Kale and Quinoa Salad with Lemon Vinaigrette — 361
Fattoush Salad — 362

Sides — 364
Skillet Green Beans — 367
Perfect Thyme Skillet Potatoes — 368
Instant Pot® Baked Beans — 371
Old-Fashioned Green Beans — 372
White Beans with Bacon and Herbs — 375
Roasted Red Peppers — 376
Brandy-Glazed Carrots — 379
Mushroom Risotto — 380
Mashed Potatoes — 383
Creamy Garlic-Parmesan Mushrooms — 384
Italian Roasted Veggies — 387
Creamy Polenta — 388

Breads and Rolls — 390
White Bread — 393
Two-Ingredient Dough — 394
Raisin Bread — 397
Slow Cooker Bread — 398
Dinner Crescents — 401
Classic Dinner Rolls — 402
Rye Bread — 405
Buttermilk Biscuits — 406
Easy Banana Bread — 409
No-Knead Skillet Bread — 410

Desserts — 412
Churro Apple Pie Cookies — 415
Cinnamon Cream Cheese Pockets — 416
Pumpkin Delight — 419
Mini Blueberry Galettes — 420
Blueberry Cheesecake Cookies — 423
Quick Apple Turnovers — 424
Strawberry Tiramisu Trifle — 427
Blueberry Cake — 428
Cherry Cobbler — 431
Apple Fritters — 432
Best Ever Chocolate Chip Cookies — 435
Angel Berry Trifle — 436

About the Author — 437
Index — 437

INTRODUCTION

IT'S BEEN AN ENTIRE DECADE SINCE I STARTED MY BLOG, JO COOKS. And what a decade it's been. In the beginning, people often asked me if I'd run out of recipes. In my mind, there was no such possibility. How could there be? There are so many different cuisines and so many ingredients to try, the possibilities truly are endless. I've included 200 recipes here to prove that!

So what's this book all about, anyway? Well, let me tell you. As much as I appreciate a good recipe that I could spend hours slaving over in the kitchen, I don't always have the time to do so. I know I'm not alone in this. We all have busy lives—so when it comes to cooking, we like to take the easy way out. But ordering or eating out is not always an option, which is why my blog focuses on quick and easy recipes, many of which are one-pot recipes and can be done in 30 or fewer minutes. So that's what this book is about: quick and easy recipes that don't require you to be a chef or ask you to go hunting for exotic ingredients. Quick, easy, delicious, no-fuss, family-friendly recipes that we all can make. These are recipes that are tried, tested and true, recipes that many of my readers have made and loved.

Over the years, I've also had the pleasure of trying many different cuisines, and I love them all. I guess I'm just not picky when it comes to food. There are some items I won't eat, but I can honestly say that as far as different cuisines go, anything I've tried I've enjoyed. Which is what I tried to bring to this book. I wanted to have recipes from all over the world. I've had the pleasure of trying many different foods, and I've had a lot of fun trying to re-create those recipes or come up with new ones.

Coming from a Romanian background, I have a few Romanian recipes in my repertoire from my mother and mother-in-law. I wanted these recipes to be easily accessible to everyone, without any guesswork. But I don't do this with just my Romanian recipes; I do this with every single recipe I write. I hate taking unnecessary steps when doing something, and my goal is to make things as easy as possible. I always try to follow the principle of KISS: **K**eep **I**t **S**imple, **S**tupid.

One of my favorite chefs is, of course, Julia Child. I love watching her cooking show, and I can spend hours watching her make a recipe and then try to make it myself but in a simpler way. Let's face it, French food is incredibly delicious, but it's not easy. However, I love a challenge. So the next time you crave Quiche Lorraine (page 271) or Lemon Chicken Piccata (page 16), don't worry—I've got you covered.

I've divided this book into chapters such as breakfast, lunch and dinner, but I also wanted to focus on ingredients like poultry, beef, pork, and so on. I felt it was important to give you plenty of options. This book should be your go-to book whenever you need to make a meal—or dessert!—for any time of day. It focuses on meals that are easy or quick to prep, because let's face it, the hardest part about cooking is prepping. I hope you find recipes in here that you and your family will love!

CHICKEN

THIS IS PROBABLY ONE OF THE BIGGEST CHAPTERS IN THIS BOOK.

And that's because I want to prove to you that chicken is *not* boring. Plus I have a lot of chicken recipes on the blog. And I mean a lot. Like more than 350 chicken recipes. But who's counting? It was tough picking out readers' favorites along with my own, such as Beer Can Chicken (page 12), Lemon Chicken Piccata (page 16), Korean Fried Chicken (page 23) or Chicken Francese (page 36), but someone had to do it.

In this chapter, I present to you nineteen chicken recipes that are definitely full of flavor but also easy and simple to make, even for the beginner cook. My goal is to prove to you that cooking chicken can be simple—it truly isn't rocket science. All you need to know are some fundamentals.

Before I get into all these delicious recipes, I want to cover safety first.

THAWING FROZEN CHICKEN

Never thaw frozen chicken on the kitchen counter. I'll be the first to admit that I used to do this all the time, until I learned better. The best way to thaw frozen chicken is to place it in a bowl or shallow pan in the refrigerator or in a pan of cold water, changing the water every hour or so. I usually go the refrigerator route—it's easier and I don't have to worry about changing water. However, you do need to plan ahead, so make sure to take out your chicken the night before to thaw in the refrigerator overnight. This way, when you come home from work the next day, you'll have chicken that's ready to be cooked.

WASHING RAW CHICKEN?

Washing raw chicken can promote cross contamination: The juices can splatter and spread bacteria to other areas around your sink and to your clothes. This can increase your risk of food poisoning from bacteria. I used to wash raw chicken, but I have learned better. If you're worried about bacteria on the chicken, cooking the chicken will kill any bacteria that are present.

COOKING CHICKEN THOROUGHLY

Always make sure to cook chicken thoroughly, until it's no longer pink inside and the juices run clear. When you cut into the thickest part of the meat, make sure it's steaming hot and there's no pink meat. The best and most accurate way to tell when chicken is cooked is to use an instant meat thermometer. When the internal temperature of the thickest part of the chicken reaches 165°F (74°C), your chicken is cooked through.

BRUSCHETTA CHICKEN

PREP TIME: 10 MINUTES
COOK TIME: 10 MINUTES
TOTAL TIME: 20 MINUTES
SERVES: 4

1 cup (180 g) finely cubed tomatoes (I recommend Roma tomatoes)
1 clove garlic, minced
1 shallot, minced
3 leaves fresh basil, finely chopped
½ tsp salt, divided, plus more as needed
½ tsp black pepper, divided, plus more as needed
2 tbsp (30 ml) olive oil, divided
2 boneless, skinless chicken breasts, cut in half lengthwise
4 slices mozzarella cheese
¼ cup (60 ml) balsamic glaze

My recipe for bruschetta chicken is made with melty mozzarella cheese and topped with fresh homemade bruschetta. And it requires only twenty minutes of your time from start to finish! All that with just a few kitchen staples? You'll be welcoming this main event to your weekly rotation.

The reason this takes such little time to cook is because I cut the chicken breasts in half horizontally to create thin pieces of chicken that cook in no time at all! The bruschetta is incredibly simple to make—just chop the ingredients and toss. Cook your chicken, top it with the bruschetta and you've got yourself dinner!

In a medium bowl, toss together the tomatoes, garlic, shallot, basil, ¼ teaspoon of the salt, ¼ teaspoon of the black pepper and 1 tablespoon (15 ml) of the oil. Taste the bruschetta and adjust the seasoning with salt and black pepper if needed. Set the bruschetta aside.

Season both sides of the chicken with the remaining ¼ teaspoon of salt and the remaining ¼ teaspoon of black pepper. Heat the remaining 1 tablespoon (15 ml) of oil in a large skillet over medium heat. Add the chicken breasts to the skillet and cook them for 3 to 4 minutes per side, until they are browned and cooked through. Top each piece of chicken with 1 slice of mozzarella cheese. Cover the skillet with a lid and allow the cheese to melt. Remove the skillet from the heat.

Top each chicken breast with the bruschetta and drizzle it with the balsamic glaze.

RECIPE NOTES

It's best to store the chicken and bruschetta separately. Transfer any leftovers to airtight containers and store them in the fridge for 3 to 4 days.

To reheat the chicken, place the chicken in a baking dish, cover it with foil and bake the chicken at 400°F (204°C) for about 10 minutes, or until it is heated through. Alternatively, you can reheat the chicken in the microwave.

Stored in an airtight container or a large freezer bag, the chicken will last in the freezer for 4 months. The chicken will reheat best when thawed overnight in the fridge.

The bruschetta will not freeze well. It is best kept fresh. When the tomatoes are frozen and thawed, they get quite watery and mushy.

NUTRITION INFORMATION

Serving size: 1 serving; **Calories:** 249; **Carbohydrates:** 10 g; **Protein:** 19 g; **Fat:** 15 g

BEER CAN CHICKEN

This is a great way to roast a chicken because the chicken is standing up, which means that you're roasting it evenly all around—no more soggy skin. We all love crispy skin on our chicken—it's the tastiest part—yet we want the meat to be moist. With this method, you'll end up with juicy, tender chicken every single time, with crispy skin all around.

PREP TIME: 10 MINUTES
COOK TIME: 1 HOUR, 15 MINUTES
REST TIME: 15 MINUTES
TOTAL TIME: 1 HOUR, 40 MINUTES
SERVES: 6

SPICE RUB
1 tbsp (15 g) packed brown sugar
1 tbsp (3 g) dried tarragon
1 tsp salt
1 tsp black pepper
1 tbsp (9 g) smoked paprika
1 tsp garlic powder
½ tsp chili powder

CHICKEN
1 (3- to 4-lb [1.3- to 1.8-kg]) whole chicken
1 (12-oz [360-ml]) can beer (I recommend Sleeman Honey Brown Lager, a pilsner or Coors Light)
3 tbsp (45 ml) olive oil

To make the spice rub, combine the brown sugar, tarragon, salt, black pepper, smoked paprika, garlic powder and chili powder in a small bowl. Set the spice rub aside.

To make the chicken, preheat the oven to 425°F (218°C). Place a small roasting pan in a larger baking dish to prevent making a mess of the oven.

Remove any giblets from the chicken if necessary. Pat it dry with paper towels.

Open the can of beer and pour about one-fourth of it into the roasting pan, and then set the can of beer in the center of the roasting pan.

Drizzle the oil over the chicken and rub it all over, massaging it into the skin. Sprinkle the spice rub over the chicken, and use your hands to massage the rub into all the nooks and crannies of the chicken. Place the chicken upright over the beer can. Use the chicken's legs to support its body, similar to a tripod. This will prevent the chicken from falling over.

Transfer the roasting pan to the oven. Bake the chicken for about 1 hour and 15 minutes, or until it is golden and cooked through. To check for doneness, insert a knife into the thickest part of the chicken thigh—the juices should run clear. In addition, use a meat thermometer to make sure the chicken's internal temperature is 165°F (74°C).

Carefully lift the chicken off the beer can. To make this easier, you can have someone else help you remove the chicken while you hold the beer can. Transfer the chicken to a cutting board and cover it with aluminum foil. Let it rest for 15 minutes before carving it.

RECIPE NOTE
Don't throw away those pan juices—use them to make a delicious gravy. In a small bowl, whisk together 1 tablespoon (9 g) of cornstarch with 1 tablespoon (15 ml) of water. Cook the drippings over medium heat until they are bubbling. Add the cornstarch mixture and bring to a simmer. Cook for about 1 minute, until the gravy thickens. Season the gravy with salt and black pepper as needed.

NUTRITION INFORMATION
Serving size: 1 serving; **Calories:** 374; **Carbohydrates:** 5 g; **Protein:** 24 g; **Fat:** 26 g

ROASTED CHICKEN AND VEGETABLES

This is the kind of dinner my mom used to make often. In fact, she still does, and now so do I. It's easy to make and requires little prep time: combine everything in one big baking dish, bake the mixture and you've got dinner—enough to feed a crowd. The great thing is you can use any part of the chicken for this dish, and while I use potatoes and a bell pepper as the main veggies here, feel free to use up what you have in the fridge. Some great options would be cauliflower, carrots or Brussels sprouts.

PREP TIME: 10 MINUTES
COOK TIME: 1 HOUR
TOTAL TIME: 1 HOUR, 10 MINUTES
SERVES: 6

4 potatoes, peeled and cubed
1 onion, cut into wedges
2 cups (300 g) cherry tomatoes or quartered slicing tomatoes
1 red bell pepper, roughly chopped
1 cup (130 g) Kalamata olives
2 lb (896 g) boneless, skinless chicken breasts, thighs or drumsticks
6 cloves garlic, minced, divided
4 tbsp (60 ml) olive oil, divided
1 tbsp (15 ml) balsamic vinegar, divided
1 tsp smoked paprika, divided
Salt, as needed
Black pepper, as needed
3 leaves fresh basil, chopped

Preheat the oven to 375°F (191°C).

In a large bowl, combine the potatoes, onion, tomatoes, bell pepper and olives. Place the chicken in another large bowl. Add half of the garlic, 2 tablespoons (30 ml) of the oil, ½ tablespoon (7 ml) of the balsamic vinegar, ½ teaspoon of the smoked paprika, salt and black pepper to the vegetable mixture. Add the remaining half of the garlic, remaining 2 tablespoons (30 ml) of the oil, remaining ½ tablespoon (8 ml) of the balsamic vinegar, remaining ½ teaspoon of the smoked paprika, salt and black pepper to the chicken. Toss the vegetables and chicken well to coat them in the seasonings.

Transfer the vegetables to a 9 x 13–inch (27 x 39–cm) baking dish. Arrange the chicken over the vegetables. Roast the chicken and vegetables for 1 hour, or until the chicken is cooked through and the potatoes are fork-tender.

Sprinkle the basil all over the chicken and vegetables. Drizzle some of the pan juices over each serving of chicken.

RECIPE NOTES

Store any leftovers in an airtight container in the fridge for 4 days. You can store the veggies and chicken separately if you prefer, but I just toss everything together.

Reheat the chicken and vegetables in the microwave. Or transfer the leftovers to a baking dish, cover the dish with foil and reheat the leftovers in the oven at 375°F (191°C) for about 10 minutes, or until they are warmed through.

If you want to freeze your leftovers, they will last up to 4 months stored in an airtight container or large freezer bag. Keep in mind that the veggies, after being cooked and frozen, will soften quite a bit.

NUTRITION INFORMATION

Serving size: 1 serving; **Calories:** 370; **Carbohydrates:** 22 g; **Protein:** 18 g; **Fat:** 24 g

LEMON CHICKEN PICCATA

This lemon chicken piccata is one of my most popular recipes on the blog. It really is a crowd favorite, and that's because of its simplicity and deliciousness. I love to serve this over buttered egg noodles, rice or even some Mashed Potatoes (page 383). It's the perfect dish for a weeknight meal, but it's fancy enough for a special occasion, like a romantic dinner with your partner. After all, I always say that the way to a loved one's heart is through their stomach.

PREP TIME: 15 MINUTES
COOK TIME: 25 MINUTES
TOTAL TIME: 40 MINUTES
SERVES: 4

2 boneless, skinless chicken breasts, cut in half lengthwise
¼ tsp salt, plus more as needed
½ tsp black pepper, plus more as needed
¼ cup (30 g) all-purpose flour
4 tbsp (60 g) unsalted butter, divided
2 tbsp (30 ml) olive oil
⅓ cup (80 ml) fresh lemon juice
½ cup (120 ml) dry white wine (see Recipe Note)
¼ cup (35 g) capers in brine, drained
⅓ cup (16 g) chopped fresh parsley

Season the chicken with the salt and black pepper.

Place the flour in a shallow dish. Dredge the chicken in the flour and shake off any excess.

In a large skillet over medium-high heat, melt 2 tablespoons (30 g) of the butter with the oil.

Add the chicken breasts to the skillet and cook them for 3 to 4 minutes per side, until they are browned. Remove the chicken from the skillet.

Remove the skillet from the heat. Add the lemon juice, wine and capers. Scrape up the brown bits from the bottom of the skillet for extra flavor.

Return the skillet to the heat and bring the lemon juice mixture to a boil. Taste the sauce and season it with additional salt and black pepper if needed. Add the chicken back to the skillet and cook it in the sauce for about 5 minutes.

Transfer the chicken to a platter. Add the remaining 2 tablespoons (30 g) of butter to the skillet and whisk the sauce for about 1 minute. The sauce will thicken a bit.

You can return the chicken to the skillet and garnish it with the parsley. Alternatively, you can pour the sauce over the chicken and garnish it with the parsley.

RECIPE NOTE
Chicken broth would be a good substitute for the white wine.

NUTRITION INFORMATION
Serving size: 1 serving; **Calories:** 290; **Carbohydrates:** 9 g; **Protein:** 13 g; **Fat:** 20 g

SPATCHCOCK CHICKEN

To spatchcock a chicken basically means to butterfly a chicken and remove the backbone. It's simple to do, especially if you have a good pair of kitchen shears. Spatchcocking also cuts the roasting time by quite a bit. The great thing about this method is that you can also cook the chicken on a grill for 15 to 20 minutes per side, which is perfect for those summer barbecues.

PREP TIME: 15 MINUTES
COOK TIME: 45 MINUTES
REST TIME: 15 MINUTES
TOTAL TIME: 1 HOUR, 30 MINUTES
SERVES: 6

CHICKEN
½ cup (120 g) unsalted butter, softened
¼ cup (12 g) chopped fresh poultry herb blend
3 cloves garlic, minced
1 tbsp (6 g) lemon zest
1 tbsp (9 g) smoked paprika
½ tsp salt, plus more as needed
½ tsp black pepper, plus more as needed
1 (4-lb [1.8-kg]) whole chicken

GRAVY
1 tbsp (9 g) cornstarch
1 cup (240 ml) low-sodium or unsalted chicken broth or water
Salt, as needed
Black pepper, as needed

To make the chicken, preheat the oven to 425°F (218°C). Spray a 12-inch (36-cm) oven-safe skillet with cooking spray. See the Recipe Notes if you don't have a 12-inch (36-cm) skillet.

In a small bowl, combine the butter, poultry herb blend, garlic, lemon zest, smoked paprika, salt and black pepper. Stir or mash the ingredients with a spatula until they are well combined.

Place the chicken breast side down with the legs toward you. Use a pair of kitchen shears to cut along each side of the backbone, cutting through the ribs as you go. Open the chicken, turn it over and then flatten the breastbone with the heel of your hand by pressing down, so that all the meat is of the same thickness. Cut the wing tips off. Season the inside of the chicken generously with additional salt and black pepper, then flip it over so that the breast side is up. Run your fingers under the chicken's breast and thigh skin, and then rub half of the compound butter under the skin. Spread the rest of the compound butter over the top of the bird.

Place the chicken in the prepared skillet and bake the chicken, uncovered, for 45 minutes, or until it registers 165 to 170°F (74 to 77°C) on an instant-read thermometer. The baking time can vary if you are using a larger or smaller chicken. Do not drain the fat drippings from the skillet. Let the chicken rest at room temperature for about 15 minutes before carving and serving it.

To make the gravy, transfer the fat drippings from the skillet to a small saucepan over medium heat. Cook the drippings until they are bubbling. Stir in the cornstarch and broth. Bring the gravy to a boil, whisking it constantly, and cook it for 1 minute. Taste the gravy and adjust the seasonings with salt and black pepper as needed.

NUTRITION INFORMATION
Serving size: 1 serving; **Calories:** 466; **Carbohydrates:** 3 g; **Protein:** 28 g; **Fat:** 37 g

RECIPE NOTES

If you don't have a skillet large enough to roast the chicken, you can use a baking sheet. Line a large baking sheet with aluminum foil, then place a baking rack on the baking sheet. Spray the rack with cooking spray and proceed with the directions.

If your oven has a Roast function, preheat it to 375°F (191°C). Roast the chicken for 35 minutes, or until it registers 165 to 170°F (74 to 77°C) on an instant-read thermometer.

ROASTED CORNISH HENS

Cornish hens, sometimes referred to as Cornish game hens, are a smaller variety of chicken, weighing just 1 to 2 pounds (448 to 896 g) each. Whenever I see them at the grocery store, I always pick up a few. I can't help myself—they're perfect for Sunday night suppers, romantic date nights or impressing your dinner party guests. They're simple and elegant and turn out perfect every single time.

PREP TIME: 10 MINUTES
COOK TIME: 1 HOUR
REST TIME: 20 MINUTES
TOTAL: 1 HOUR, 30 MINUTES
SERVES: 4

DRY RUB
1 tsp salt
1 tsp black pepper
1 tbsp (3 g) Italian seasoning
2 tsp (6 g) smoked paprika
1 tsp garlic powder
¼ tsp red pepper flakes

CORNISH HENS
2 (1½-lb [672-g]) whole Cornish hens
2 sprigs fresh rosemary, plus more as needed
4 sprigs fresh thyme, plus more as needed
1 onion, quartered
6 cloves garlic
1 lemon, sliced, divided
2 tbsp (30 ml) olive oil
Mashed Potatoes (page 383), for serving

To make the dry rub, combine the salt, black pepper, Italian seasoning, smoked paprika, garlic powder and red pepper flakes in a small bowl. Set the dry rub aside.

To make the Cornish hens, preheat the oven to 425°F (218°C).

Pat the hens dry with paper towels. Generously season them inside and outside with the dry rub.

In a 9 x 13–inch (27 x 39–cm) roasting pan, combine the rosemary, thyme, onion, garlic and half of the lemon slices. Place the hens in the roasting pan on top of the herb mixture and drizzle the oil over the hens.

Roast the Cornish hens for 50 to 60 minutes, or until an instant-read thermometer inserted into the thickest part of the breast registers at 165°F (74°C).

Remove the hens from the oven and let them rest for 20 minutes. Garnish them with the remaining lemon slices and additional rosemary and thyme. Serve the hens over the Mashed Potatoes.

RECIPE NOTES
Leftover roasted Cornish hens will last 3 to 4 days in the fridge or 1 to 3 months in the freezer. They reheat well in the microwave. You can also keep some of the pan drippings and reheat the hens in a skillet with the drippings to prevent them from drying out.

NUTRITION INFORMATION
Serving size: ½ hen; **Calories:** 783; **Carbohydrates:** 10 g; **Protein:** 60 g; **Fat:** 55 g

KOREAN FRIED CHICKEN

PREP TIME: 15 MINUTES
COOK TIME: 15 MINUTES
TOTAL: 30 MINUTES
SERVES: 6

FRIED CHICKEN
2 lb (896 g) boneless, skinless chicken breasts, cut into 1" (3-cm) pieces
1 large egg, beaten
½ cup (72 g) cornstarch
Vegetable oil, as needed

KOREAN SAUCE
3 tbsp (45 g) unsalted butter
4 cloves garlic, minced
1 tbsp (9 g) minced fresh ginger
¼ cup (60 ml) honey
¼ cup (60 g) brown sugar
2 tbsp (30 ml) low-sodium soy sauce
1 tbsp (15 ml) rice vinegar
1 tbsp (15 ml) sesame oil
2 tbsp (36 g) gochujang

GARNISHES
Chopped green onions
Toasted sesame seeds
Sliced red chilis

NUTRITION INFORMATION
Serving size: 1 serving; **Calories:** 466; **Carbohydrates:** 33 g; **Protein:** 34 g; **Fat:** 22 g

I first had this dish not too long ago when my husband, Remo, and I started going to this local restaurant. They offered Korean fried chicken as an appetizer, and once I ordered it, we both fell in love with the flavors. Being the food blogger that I am, I had to come home and re-create the flavors myself. I will be bold and say that I came pretty close. Since then, I've made this recipe often, but I don't serve it as an appetizer; rather, I serve it as a main along with some rice and steamed veggies. It's one of my favorite chicken recipes, and it's incredibly easy to make.

To make the fried chicken, combine the chicken pieces and egg in a large bowl. Toss the chicken pieces to ensure they are well coated with the egg.

Place the cornstarch in a large bowl. Dredge the chicken pieces in the cornstarch.

Add about 3 inches (9 cm) of the vegetable oil to a heavy-bottomed pan. Heat the oil to 375°F (191°C).

Working in batches, add the chicken to the oil and fry it for 3 to 4 minutes per batch. Transfer the chicken to a plate lined with paper towels.

To make the Korean sauce, melt the butter in a large skillet over medium heat. Add the garlic and ginger and cook them for 30 seconds, or until they are aromatic. Stir in the honey and brown sugar and cook the mixture for about 1 minute, until the brown sugar dissolves. Add the soy sauce, rice vinegar, sesame oil and gochujang and stir the ingredients together. Cook the sauce for 30 seconds, then add the chicken to the skillet and toss it until it is well coated with the sauce.

Garnish the Korean fried chicken with the green onions, sesame seeds and red chilis prior to serving it.

RECIPE NOTES

Store leftovers in an airtight container in the fridge for 3 to 4 days. Cooked chicken will start to grow bacteria, so don't leave it sitting at room temperature for longer than 1 hour.

If you want to extend the shelf life of cooked chicken, you can freeze it in a covered airtight container or in heavy-duty freezer bags. Or you can wrap it tightly with aluminum foil or freezer wrap. Keep in mind that you may lose some quality if you freeze the chicken.

To reheat leftovers, pop them in the microwave or back into a skillet or wok until they are heated through.

GARLIC BUTTER CHICKEN

I can't get over how simple this recipe is: It requires minimal effort and prep time, it calls for simple ingredients that you're likely to already have and it cooks fast. This chicken dish is also super versatile. You can serve it with anything you like—rice, Mashed Potatoes (page 383), steamed veggies, noodles, you name it.

PREP TIME: 10 MINUTES
COOK TIME: 10 MINUTES
TOTAL TIME: 20 MINUTES
SERVES: 4

1½ lb (672 g) boneless, skinless chicken breasts, cut into strips
¼ tsp salt, or as needed
½ tsp black pepper, or as needed
4 tbsp (60 g) butter
4 cloves garlic, minced
¼ tsp red pepper flakes
1 tsp smoked paprika
1 tbsp (15 ml) Sriracha sauce
½ cup (120 ml) low-sodium or unsalted chicken broth
2 tbsp (6 g) chopped fresh parsley
Lemon slices, as needed

Season the chicken with the salt and black pepper.

Melt the butter in a large skillet over medium heat. Add the chicken strips and cook them for 3 to 4 minutes on each side. Remove the chicken from the skillet.

In the same skillet, combine the garlic, red pepper flakes, smoked paprika and Sriracha sauce. Sauté the mixture for 30 seconds, until the garlic is aromatic. Finally, deglaze the skillet with the chicken broth and bring the sauce to a simmer.

Add the chicken back to the skillet and gently toss the chicken, so that each piece of chicken is coated with the sauce.

Remove the skillet from the heat. Garnish the chicken with the parsley and lemon slices. Serve the garlic butter chicken hot or warm.

RECIPE NOTES

This garlic butter chicken will last in the fridge for up to 3 days if it's wrapped well or stored in an airtight container.

To extend the shelf life of this dish, I recommend freezing it, wrapped well or stored in an airtight container. It will last from 4 to 6 months.

NUTRITION INFORMATION

Serving size: 1 serving; **Calories:** 307; **Carbohydrates:** 2 g; **Protein:** 37 g; **Fat:** 16 g

COCONUT CHICKEN CURRY

This recipe came to be because of the many requests from my readers who loved my Coconut Shrimp Curry (page 134) so much that they asked me to come up with a similar recipe using chicken. Of course, it didn't take much convincing, especially since I had become allergic to shrimp. So I was more than happy and ready to comply. Don't be afraid of curry—this dish really is simple and quick, with just a few ingredients.

PREP: 5 MINUTES
COOK: 30 MINUTES
TOTAL: 35 MINUTES
SERVES: 6

2 tbsp (30 ml) olive oil
2 lb (896 g) boneless, skinless chicken breasts, cut into bite-sized pieces
½ tsp salt, or as needed
½ tsp black pepper, or as needed
1 onion, chopped
3 cloves garlic, minced
2 tbsp (18 g) curry powder
1 cup (240 ml) low-sodium chicken broth
1 (14-oz [420-ml]) can coconut milk
1 (15-oz [420-g]) can diced tomatoes, undrained
2 tbsp (30 g) tomato paste
2 tbsp (24 g) sugar
2 tbsp (6 g) chopped fresh parsley
Cooked rice, for serving

Heat the oil in a large skillet or Dutch oven over medium heat. Add the chicken to the skillet and season it with the salt and black pepper. Cook the chicken for about 5 minutes, stirring it occasionally, or until it is no longer pink.

Add the onion, garlic and curry powder and stir to combine the ingredients. Cook the mixture for 2 minutes, then add the chicken broth, coconut milk, diced tomatoes and their juice, tomato paste and sugar. Stir everything together. Bring the curry to a boil, then cover the skillet with a lid. Reduce the heat to low and simmer the curry for 15 to 20 minutes to develop its flavors.

Garnish the curry with the parsley and serve it over the rice.

RECIPE NOTES

The curry should be stored in an airtight container in the refrigerator for 3 days.

If you want this curry to last, my advice is to freeze it. Ensure that it is fully cooled before transferring it to a shallow container to ensure even freezing. Stir it well while you are reheating it.

NUTRITION INFORMATION

Serving size: 1 serving; **Calories:** 396; **Carbohydrates:** 13 g; **Protein:** 35 g; **Fat:** 23 g

CHICKEN DRUMSTICKS WITH BELUGA LENTILS

Beluga lentils may sound fancy, but any type of lentils will work for this recipe. Beluga lentils are said to resemble beluga caviar because they tend to glisten when they cook, so that's how they got their name. However, if you've got red or green lentils in your pantry, use those. The color doesn't matter, because this dish is loaded with flavor. If there's one ingredient I urge you to use and not substitute with anything else, it's the fire-roasted tomatoes—they are so good and provide a subtle smoky flavor to this wonderful dish.

PREP TIME: 10 MINUTES
COOK TIME: 1 HOUR, 20 MINUTES
TOTAL TIME: 1 HOUR, 30 MINUTES
SERVES: 4

3 tbsp (45 ml) olive oil
8 skin-on chicken drumsticks (see Recipe Notes)
½ tsp seasoning salt, or as needed
½ tsp red pepper flakes
1 cup (89 g) sliced leeks
5 cloves garlic, minced
1 tbsp (9 g) smoked paprika
1 cup (192 g) beluga lentils
1 cup (240 ml) white wine (I recommend sauvignon blanc)
1 (15-oz [420-g]) can fire-roasted tomatoes, undrained
2 cups (480 ml) low-sodium chicken broth
1 tbsp (15 ml) Sriracha sauce (optional)
½ tsp salt, or as needed
¼ tsp black pepper, or as needed
1 zucchini, sliced into half-moons
1 tbsp (3 g) fresh thyme leaves

Heat the oil in a large oven-safe Dutch oven or casserole dish over medium-high heat.

Season the chicken drumsticks with the seasoning salt and red pepper flakes. Add the drumsticks to the Dutch oven and brown them on all sides, about 5 minutes total. The chicken won't be cooked through, but we will finish cooking it in the oven. Transfer the chicken drumsticks to a plate and set it aside.

Reduce the heat to medium and add the leeks and garlic to the Dutch oven. Cook them, stirring frequently, for about 3 minutes, or until the leeks soften and become translucent.

Stir in the smoked paprika, then add the beluga lentils, wine and tomatoes and their juice.

Add the broth and Sriracha sauce, if using. Stir everything together and taste the mixture. Adjust the seasonings with the salt and black pepper as necessary.

Preheat the oven to 375°F (191°C).

Cook the lentils for about 10 minutes. Add the zucchini to the Dutch oven. Stir it into the mixture, then place the chicken on top of everything.

Transfer the Dutch oven to the oven and cook the chicken and lentils for about 1 hour, or until the lentils are cooked through.

Garnish the chicken and lentils with the thyme and serve them immediately.

RECIPE NOTES

You can use chicken breasts in this recipe if you prefer. Or, if you prefer red meat, you could use stewing beef.

You can also cook this in an Instant Pot® on high pressure for 15 minutes.

NUTRITION INFORMATION

Serving size: 1 serving; **Calories:** 612; **Carbohydrates:** 40 g; **Protein:** 43 g; **Fat:** 26 g

OVEN-BAKED CHICKEN THIGHS

PREP TIME: 5 MINUTES
COOK TIME: 35 MINUTES
REST TIME: 10 MINUTES
TOTAL TIME: 50 MINUTES
SERVES: 6

SAUCE
2 tbsp (30 ml) olive oil
1 tbsp (15 g) whole-grain Dijon mustard
1 tbsp (15 g) yellow mustard
2 tbsp (30 ml) honey
6 cloves garlic, minced
¼ tsp red pepper flakes

CHICKEN
2 lb (896 g) bone-in, skin-on chicken thighs (see Recipe Notes)
1 tsp salt, or as needed
1 tsp black pepper, or as needed
1 tbsp (10 g) parsley, chopped

This recipe for baked chicken thighs is a force to be reckoned with. It's easy to prep, with a simple and delicious mustard and honey sauce that coats the chicken thighs before they are baked to perfection. That's all there is to it, and you know it's good because this has been the top recipe on my blog since I published it.

To make the sauce, whisk together the oil, Dijon mustard, yellow mustard, honey, garlic and red pepper flakes in a small bowl. Set the sauce aside.

To make the chicken, preheat the oven to 425°F (218°C).

Place the chicken thighs in a large bowl and season them with the salt and black pepper.

Pour the sauce over the thighs and toss to coat them well.

Transfer the chicken thighs and sauce to a 9 x 13–inch (27 x 39–cm) baking dish.

Bake the chicken for about 35 minutes, or until the thighs reach an internal temperature of 165°F (74°C) and the skin is crispy.

Transfer the chicken to a serving plate, cover the plate with aluminum foil and let the thighs rest for 10 minutes before serving them garnished with parsley.

RECIPE NOTES

Boneless, skinless chicken thighs can also be used, but they will bake fast—they should require only 20 to 25 minutes in the oven.

The honey mustard sauce is completely optional. For a simpler chicken thigh recipe, simply season the thighs with salt and black pepper, drizzle 2 tablespoons (30 ml) of olive oil in the baking dish and bake the thighs as instructed.

When stored or wrapped well, this oven-baked chicken will last in the fridge for up to 3 days. I recommend freezing it to extend its shelf life. When stored in an airtight container, the chicken will last in the freezer for 4 to 6 months.

NUTRITION INFORMATION

Serving size: 1 thigh; **Calories:** 403; **Carbohydrates:** 8 g; **Protein:** 25 g; **Fat:** 30 g

CHICKEN KIEV

Chicken Kiev is a scrumptious chicken dish straight from Eastern Europe. You wrap chicken around a delectable garlic butter interior before dredging it in breadcrumbs and flour, ensuring the perfect crispy exterior. I love to serve this with Mashed Potatoes (page 383), scalloped potatoes or even Creamy Polenta (page 388).

PREP TIME: 30 MINUTES
COOK TIME: 40 MINUTES
CHILLING TIME: 2 HOURS, 30 MINUTES
TOTAL TIME: 3 HOURS, 40 MINUTES
SERVES: 4

GARLIC BUTTER

½ cup (120 g) unsalted butter, softened
6 cloves garlic, minced
½ cup (24 g) chopped fresh parsley
¼ cup (12 g) chopped fresh dill
½ tsp salt, or as needed
½ tsp black pepper, or as needed
2 tbsp (30 ml) fresh lemon juice

CHICKEN KIEV

4 boneless, skinless chicken breasts
½ tsp salt
½ tsp black pepper
½ cup (60 g) all-purpose flour
2 large eggs, beaten
1½ cups (90 g) panko breadcrumbs
Vegetable oil, as needed

To make the garlic butter, use a fork or spatula to mix together the butter, garlic, parsley, dill, salt, black pepper and lemon juice. Place the garlic butter on a piece of plastic wrap and roll it into a log. Place it in the freezer to chill for 30 minutes, or until it is firm enough to slice.

To make the chicken Kiev, lay each chicken breast on a work surface. Butterfly each chicken breast by slicing it horizontally. Place each butterflied chicken breast between 2 pieces of parchment paper or plastic wrap and then flatten the chicken breast using a meat mallet. If you don't have a meat mallet, you can use the back of a heavy skillet. Season each breast on both sides with the salt and black pepper.

Cut the frozen butter into 4 equal pieces. Place a frozen piece of garlic butter in the center of a chicken fillet. Fold the chicken over the garlic butter, gathering the sides to the center to form either a ball or a log. Wrap each chicken piece in plastic wrap and twist the ends to make sure it's wrapped tightly. Place the wrapped chicken pieces in the freezer for about 2 hours, until the seams have frozen.

Place the flour on a shallow plate. Place the eggs on a second shallow plate. Place the breadcrumbs in a shallow bowl.

Roll each frozen chicken breast in the flour and make sure it is coated evenly, then roll it in the eggs and finally roll it through the breadcrumbs.

In a large pot or Dutch oven, heat about 2 inches (6 cm) of the oil to 350°F (177°C). Preheat the oven to 400°F (204°C). Set a 9 x 13–inch (27 x 39–cm) baking dish next to the pot of oil.

Working in batches, deep-fry each piece of chicken for 2 to 3 minutes, until it is golden brown on all sides. Transfer the fried chicken to the baking dish. Bake the chicken Kiev for 20 to 25 minutes, or until its internal temperature reaches 165°F (74°C).

NUTRITION INFORMATION

Serving size: 1 breast; **Calories:** 497; **Carbohydrates:** 25 g; **Protein:** 32 g; **Fat:** 30 g

RECIPE NOTES

Store any leftover chicken Kiev in an airtight container in the refrigerator for 3 to 4 days. Keep in mind that the breading will become soggier the longer it's kept in the fridge.

Freeze chicken Kiev in an airtight container for up to 3 months. Allow the chicken to thaw overnight in the fridge before heating it in the oven, on the stove or in the microwave.

CHICKEN STROGANOFF

We all know and love beef stroganoff, but this is my chicken version. Tender pieces of chicken and hearty mushrooms are smothered in a rich sauce made from sour cream and white wine. The best way to serve this is over Mashed Potatoes (page 383), noodles or cooked rice.

PREP TIME: 10 MINUTES
COOK TIME: 25 MINUTES
TOTAL TIME: 35 MINUTES
SERVES: 4

CHICKEN

1 tbsp (15 ml) olive oil
1 lb (448 g) boneless, skinless chicken thighs, cut into bite-sized pieces
½ tsp salt, or as needed
½ tsp black pepper, or as needed

STROGANOFF SAUCE

2 tbsp (30 ml) olive oil
1 onion, chopped
4 cloves garlic, minced
1 lb (448 g) white button or cremini mushrooms, sliced
1 tsp Italian seasoning
1 tsp paprika
¼ tsp salt
½ tsp black pepper
1 tsp Worcestershire sauce
¼ cup (60 ml) dry white wine
1 tbsp (8 g) all-purpose flour
2 cups (480 ml) low-sodium or unsalted chicken broth
¾ cup (90 g) sour cream

2 tbsp (6 g) chopped fresh parsley, for garnish

To make the chicken, heat the oil in a large skillet over medium heat. Add the chicken thighs and season them with the salt and black pepper. Cook the chicken for about 5 minutes, or until it is cooked through. Transfer the chicken to a plate and set it aside.

To make the stroganoff sauce, heat the oil in the same skillet over medium-high heat. Add the onion and sauté it for 3 minutes, or until it is transparent and has softened. Stir in the garlic and sauté the mixture for 30 seconds, until the garlic is fragrant.

Add the mushrooms and cook the mixture for about 5 minutes, until the mushrooms start to brown. Add the Italian seasoning, paprika, salt and black pepper and stir to combine the ingredients. Add the Worcestershire sauce and wine to deglaze the skillet. Cook the mixture for 2 to 3 minutes, until the alcohol has cooked off.

Add the flour and stir it into the mixture. Cook the mixture for 1 minute, then add the broth. The sauce should begin to thicken a bit. Reduce the heat to low and stir in the sour cream. Let the sauce simmer for about 5 minutes, until it is smooth and creamy.

Add the cooked chicken to the skillet and cook the stroganoff for 2 minutes, until the chicken is heated through.

Garnish the chicken stroganoff with the parsley and serve it.

RECIPE NOTES

The best place to keep your leftover stroganoff is in the coldest area in your fridge—usually near the back corners of the bottom shelf, because that's where the cold air naturally settles. Store your stroganoff in airtight containers in the fridge for 3 to 4 days. If you have any uneaten stroganoff after that time, store it in the freezer.

NUTRITION INFORMATION

Serving size: 1 serving; **Calories:** 509; **Carbohydrates:** 13 g; **Protein:** 26 g; **Fat:** 39 g

CHICKEN FRANCESE

Talk about an impressive chicken dish! This is a classic Italian American dish, incredibly easy to prepare and cook. If you love lemony chicken, this dish is for you. It's great served over Mashed Potatoes (page 383) or noodles or with a side of roasted broccoli.

PREP TIME: 10 MINUTES
COOK TIME: 20 MINUTES
TOTAL TIME: 30 MINUTES
SERVES: 4

CHICKEN
½ cup (60 g) all-purpose flour
1 tsp salt, or as needed
½ tsp black pepper, or as needed (see Recipe Notes)
3 large eggs
4 boneless, skinless chicken breasts, cut in half lengthwise
¼ cup (60 ml) vegetable oil

SAUCE
1 lemon, sliced into thin rounds and seeds removed
2 tbsp (30 g) unsalted butter
1 tbsp (8 g) all-purpose flour
1 cup (240 ml) low-sodium chicken broth
½ cup (120 ml) dry white wine
1 tbsp (15 ml) fresh lemon juice
½ tsp salt
Black pepper, as needed

2 tbsp (6 g) chopped fresh parsley

To make the chicken, whisk together the flour, salt and black pepper on a shallow plate. In a shallow bowl, whisk the eggs.

Place each piece of chicken between 2 pieces of parchment paper and lightly pound it with the flat side of a meat mallet until it's about ¼ inch (6 mm) thick.

Dredge the chicken cutlets in the flour mixture, fully coating both sides and shaking off any excess. Next, coat the chicken in the eggs.

Heat the oil in a 12-inch (36-cm) skillet over medium-high heat until it is shimmering. Add 3 or 4 chicken cutlets (or as many as you can fit) to the skillet. Cook the chicken for about 3 minutes per side, until it is lightly browned. Transfer the chicken to a plate lined with paper towels. Repeat this process with the remaining chicken.

To make the sauce, clean the skillet of any excess oil, then add the lemon slices and cook them for about 30 seconds per side, until they are fragrant and slightly charred. Add the butter to the skillet and allow it to melt. Whisk in the flour and cook the mixture for 30 seconds to cook off the flour taste. Whisk in the broth, wine, lemon juice, salt and black pepper. Simmer the sauce for about 2 minutes, until it has slightly reduced.

Transfer the chicken to the skillet and cook it for 3 to 4 minutes, until it is heated through.

Garnish the chicken with the parsley before serving it.

RECIPE NOTES
Freshly ground black pepper is best in this dish.

Leftovers can be refrigerated for up to 5 days or frozen in an airtight container for up to 3 months.

NUTRITION INFORMATION
Serving size: 2 cutlets; **Calories:** 466; **Carbohydrates:** 18 g; **Protein:** 33 g; **Fat:** 27 g

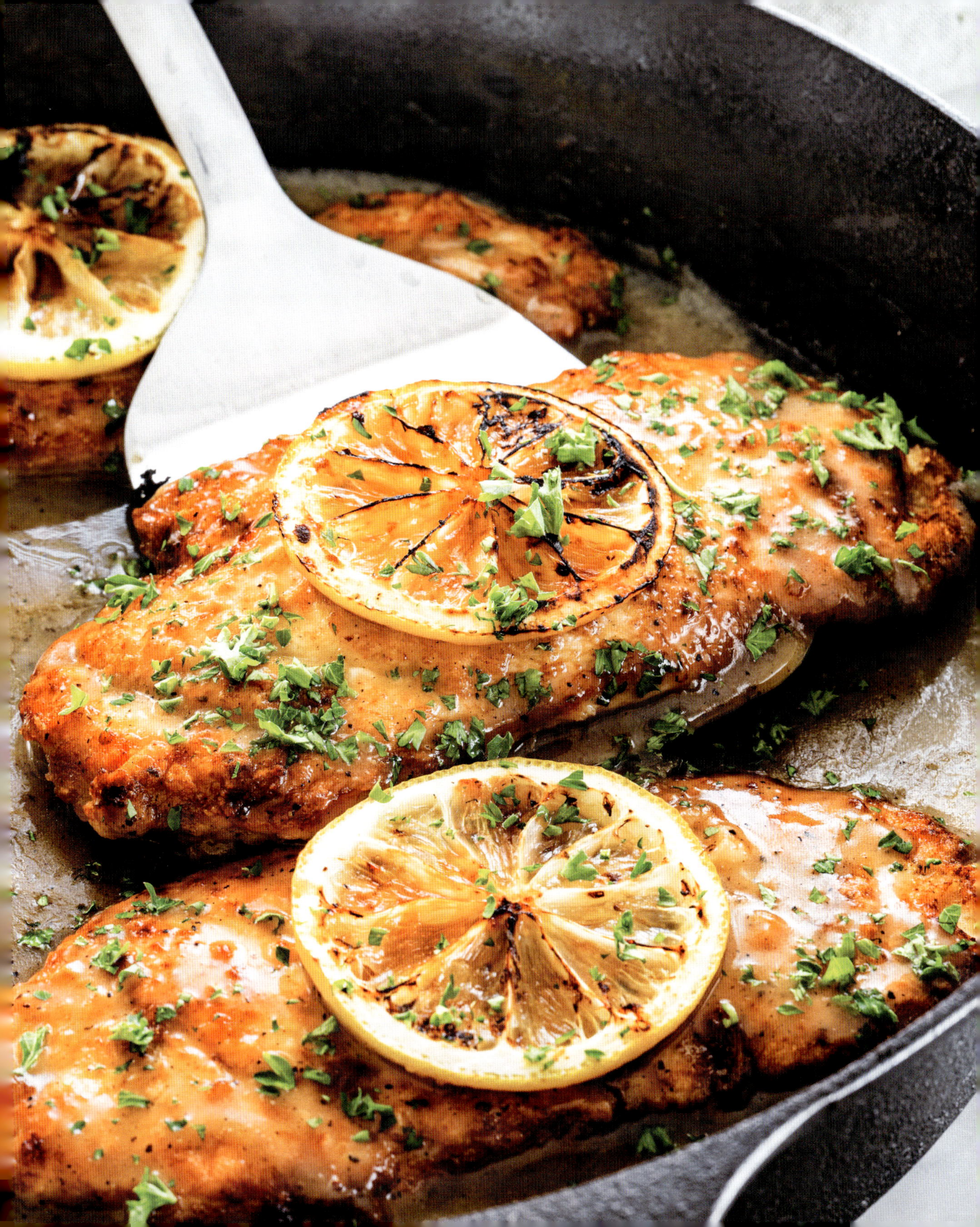

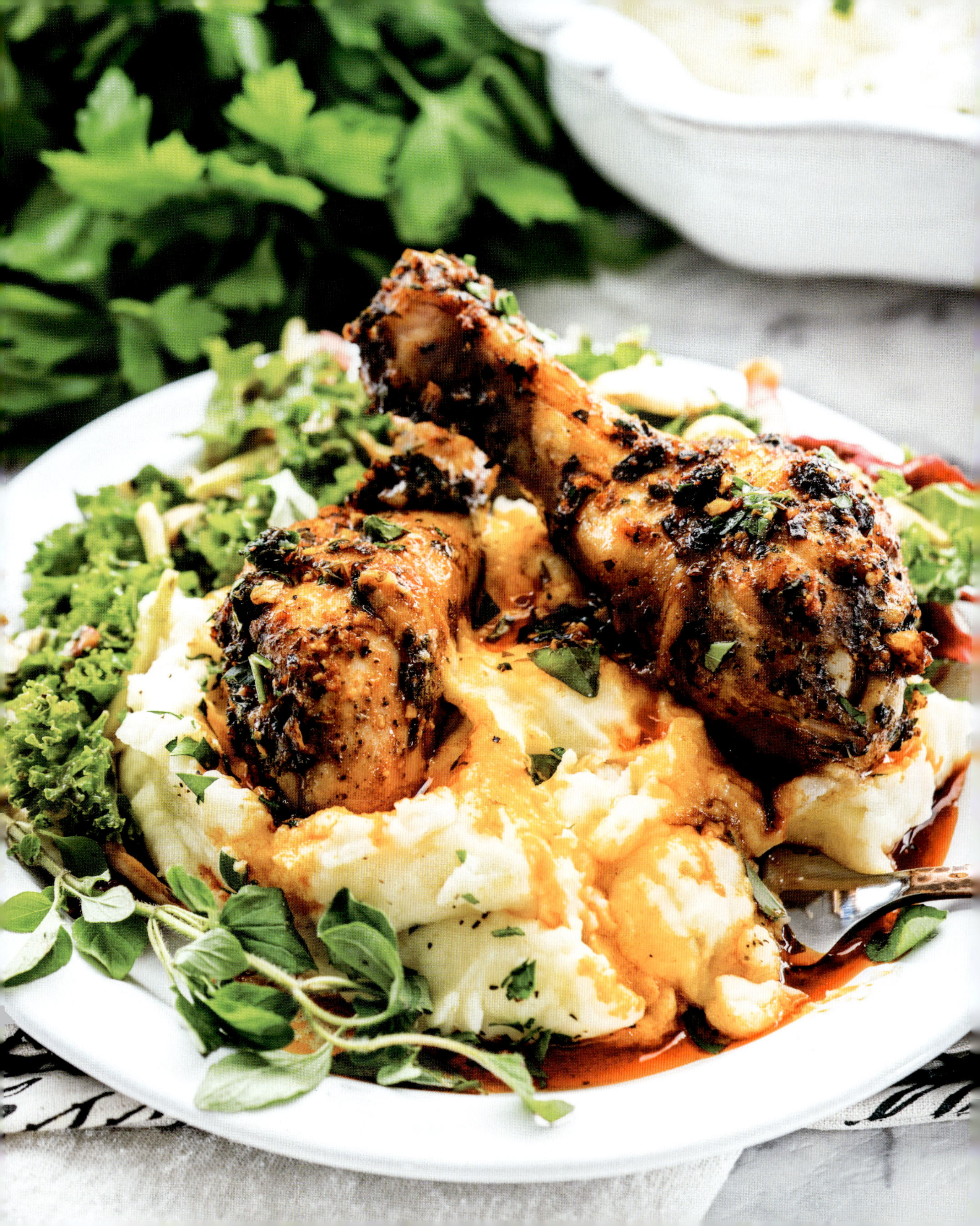

GARLIC AND PAPRIKA CHICKEN

This is one of my most popular chicken dishes on the blog. Crispy, juicy and tender chicken drumsticks are baked in a garlic and smoked paprika sauce. But learn from my mistake: Be sure to use smoked paprika and not cayenne pepper like I once did because I refused to wear my glasses and couldn't read the label on the spice jar. Needless to say, that chicken was so spicy nobody could eat it. If you do make this recipe the correct way, you'll love it.

PREP TIME: 5 MINUTES
COOK TIME: 50 MINUTES
TOTAL TIME: 55 MINUTES
SERVES: 12

½ cup (120 ml) olive oil
8 cloves garlic, minced
2 tbsp (18 g) smoked paprika (see Recipe Notes)
½ tsp red pepper flakes
¼ cup (12 g) chopped fresh parsley
2 tbsp (6 g) chopped fresh oregano
12 chicken drumsticks
½ tsp salt, or as needed
½ tsp black pepper, or as needed

Preheat the oven to 425°F (218°C).

Heat the oil in a small skillet over medium heat. Add the garlic, smoked paprika, red pepper flakes, parsley and oregano. Cook this mixture for about 1 minute, being careful not to burn the garlic.

Pat the chicken drumsticks dry and season them with the salt and black pepper. Place the drumsticks in a 9 x 13–inch (27 x 39–cm) baking dish.

Pour the oil mixture over the drumsticks and make sure they are coated thoroughly.

Bake the drumsticks for about 45 minutes, or until they are cooked through.

Serve the drumsticks with your favorite side dish and salad.

RECIPE NOTES

If you can't find smoked paprika, sweet paprika will work as well.

The spice blend can be used on any type of chicken. The cooking time will be the same for breasts and leg quarters.

Stored in an airtight container after it has cooled, this chicken dish will keep for 3 to 4 days in the fridge. Reheat it in the microwave or the oven.

To freeze the drumsticks, place them on a baking sheet and allow them to freeze solid. Place the drumsticks in a freezer bag or an airtight container afterward. This method will allow them to keep for 4 to 6 months in the freezer. Remove them from the freezer and allow them to thaw in the fridge overnight. Reheat the drumsticks in a 350°F (177°C) oven until they are warmed through.

NUTRITION INFORMATION

Serving size: 1 drumstick; **Calories:** 209; **Carbohydrates:** 2 g; **Protein:** 14 g; **Fat:** 16 g

OVEN-ROASTED CHICKEN SHAWARMA

PREP TIME: 25 MINUTES
MARINATING TIME: 1 HOUR
REST TIME: 5 MINUTES
COOK TIME: 50 MINUTES
TOTAL: 2 HOURS, 20 MINUTES
SERVES: 8

CHICKEN SHAWARMA
¼ cup (60 ml) fresh lemon juice
½ cup (120 ml) olive oil
1 tsp salt
2 tsp (6 g) ground cumin
2 tsp (6 g) black pepper
2 tsp (6 g) smoked paprika
½ tsp ground turmeric
1 tsp red pepper flakes
½ tsp ground cinnamon
4 cloves garlic, minced
3 boneless, skinless chicken breasts
1 onion, sliced
2 tbsp (6 g) chopped fresh parsley

GARLIC SAUCE
1 cup (240 ml) vegetable oil
⅓ cup (80 ml) fresh lemon juice
6 cloves garlic, peeled
1 large egg white
1 tsp salt

With just a handful of everyday spices, you can turn plain chicken into an exotic meal of chicken shawarma that's been infused with Middle Eastern flavors. The garlic sauce is a must if you're making this chicken dish.

CHICKEN SHAWARMA WRAPS
Pita wraps, as needed
Hummus, as needed
Tabbouleh Salad (page 341), as needed

To make the chicken shawarma, combine the lemon juice, olive oil, salt, cumin, black pepper, smoked paprika, turmeric, red pepper flakes, cinnamon and garlic in a large bowl. Whisk the ingredients well. Add the chicken, making sure it is well coated in the marinade. Cover the bowl with plastic wrap or foil and refrigerate the chicken for at least 1 hour. The longer the meat marinates, the more flavor it will have.

Preheat the oven to 425°F (218°C).

Add the onion to the bowl of chicken and toss the mixture well, so that the onion is fully coated in the marinade. Transfer the chicken, onion and marinade to a 9 x 13–inch (27 x 39–cm) baking dish. Spread out everything evenly in the baking dish.

Bake the chicken shawarma for 40 to 45 minutes, until the chicken is browned and crisp on the edges. If you want the chicken to be crispier on top, turn on the broiler to high and broil the chicken for 3 minutes, until it is very crispy.

Let the chicken rest for about 5 minutes, then cut it into bite-sized pieces.

To make the garlic sauce, combine the vegetable oil, lemon juice, garlic, egg white and salt in a blender. Blend the ingredients for 1 to 2 minutes, until they form a smooth sauce. This recipe will make about 1½ cups (360 ml) of sauce. Refrigerate any leftover sauce for up to 1 month.

To make the chicken shawarma wraps, warm the pita wraps in the microwave for about 30 seconds. Spread some of the hummus over each wrap. Spoon 2 to 3 tablespoons (30 to 45 g) of the Tabbouleh Salad over the hummus, add some of the chicken shawarma, drizzle the chicken with the garlic sauce, garnish with the parsley and serve the wraps.

NUTRITION INFORMATION
Serving size: 1 serving; **Calories:** 460; **Carbohydrates:** 5 g; **Protein:** 10 g; **Fat:** 46 g

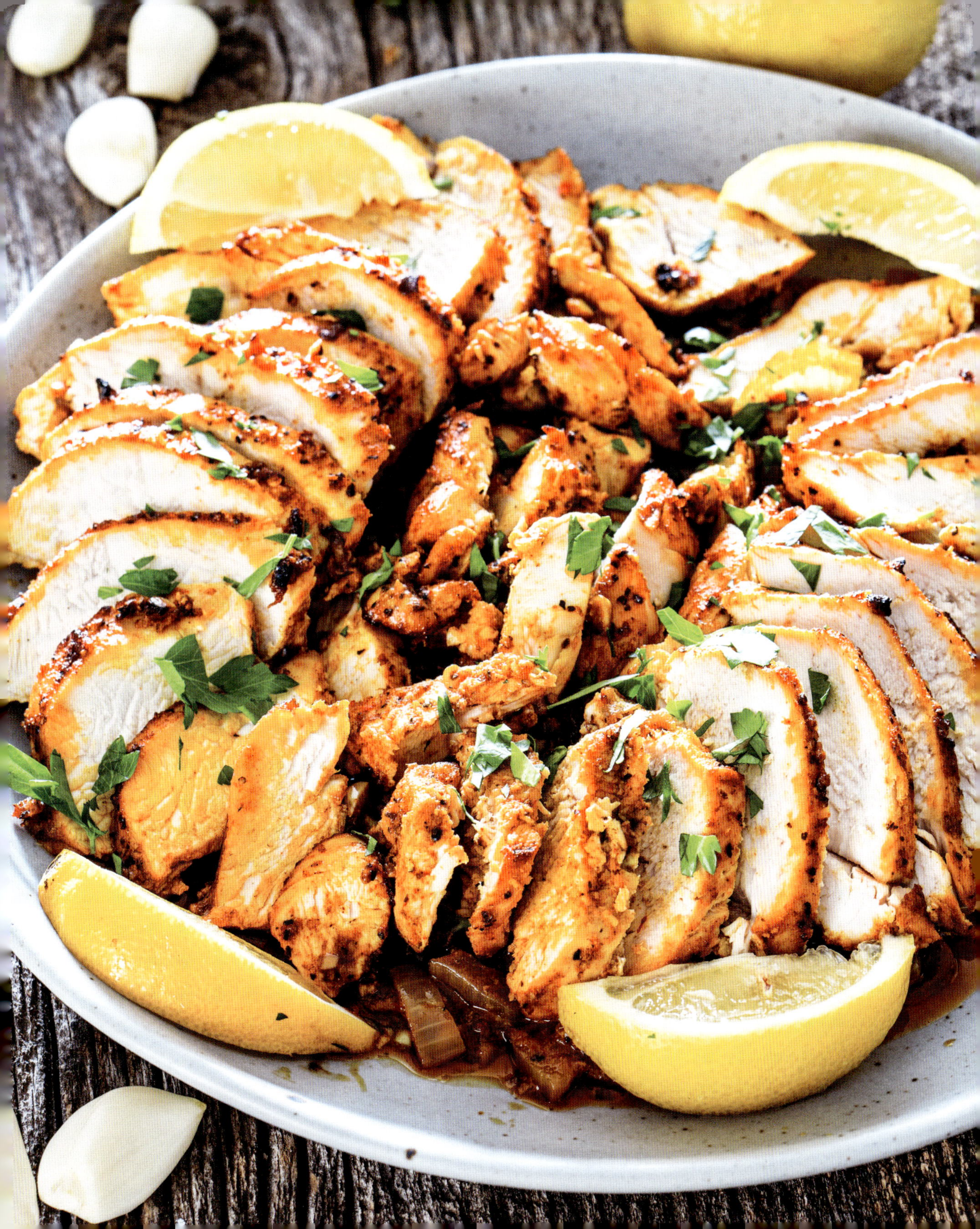

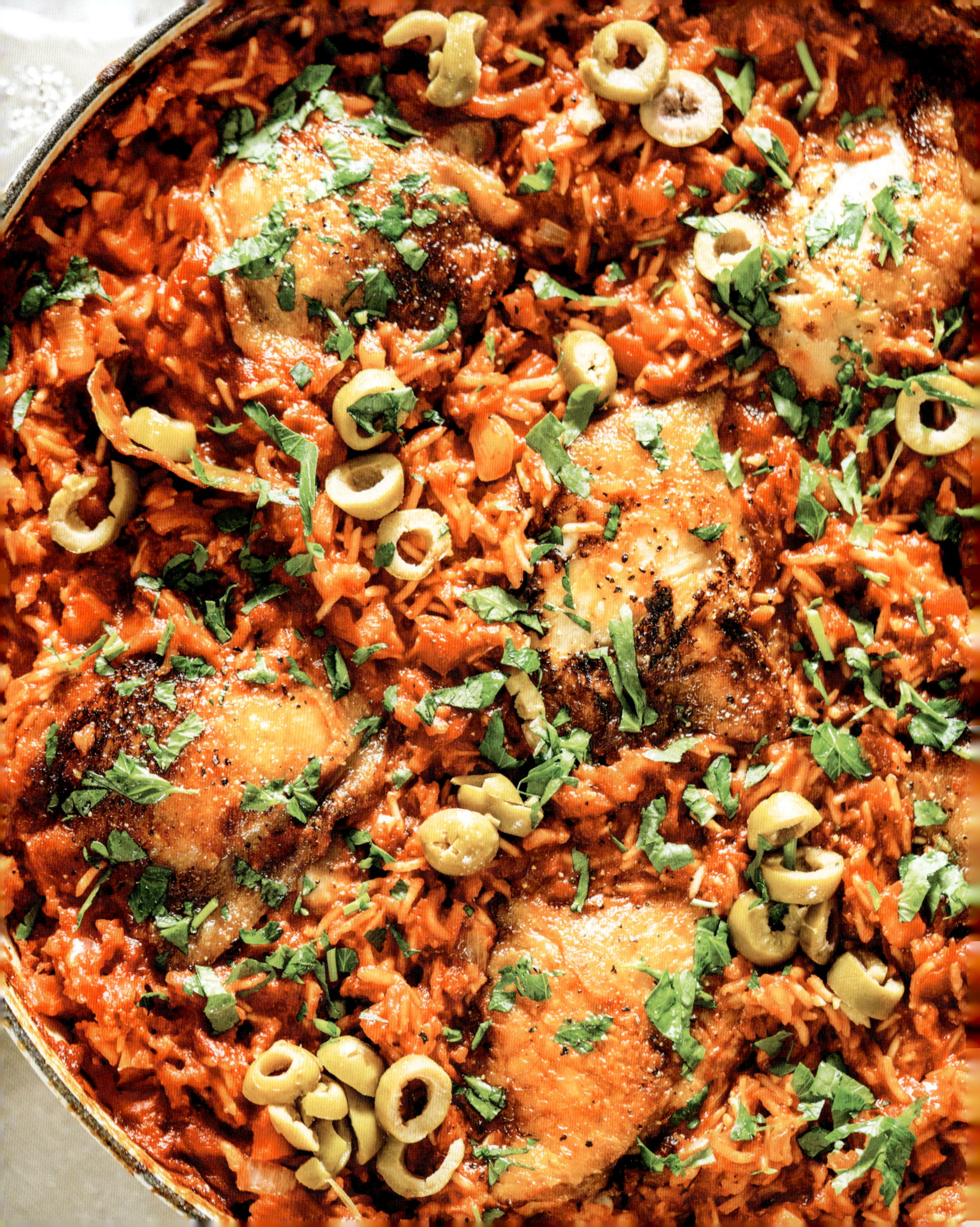

SPANISH CHICKEN AND RICE

PREP TIME: 10 MINUTES
COOK TIME: 1 HOUR
TOTAL TIME: 1 HOUR, 10 MINUTES
SERVES: 6

2 tbsp (30 ml) olive oil
6 bone-in, skin-on chicken thighs
½ tsp salt, plus more as needed
¼ tsp black pepper, plus more as needed
1 onion, chopped
6 cloves garlic, minced
2 red bell peppers, chopped
¼ tsp red pepper flakes
1 tsp smoked paprika
1 dried bay leaf
2 tbsp (30 g) tomato paste
1½ cups (315 g) long-grain rice (see Recipe Notes)
1 (28-oz [784-g]) can crushed tomatoes
2 cups (480 ml) low-sodium chicken broth
½ cup (65 g) green olives, pitted and sliced
1 tbsp (3 g) chopped fresh parsley

This chicken and rice dish is packed with great flavors and vibrant colors. While it may take a bit longer to cook, it really is easy and quick to put together. Here I'm using some common Spanish spices, olives and lots of fresh garlic for flavor and fragrance.

Preheat the oven to 400°F (204°C).

Heat the oil in a large Dutch oven or oven-safe skillet over medium heat. Add the chicken thighs skin side down and cook them for 5 to 7 minutes, until they are crispy and golden brown. Season the chicken with the salt and black pepper. Turn the thighs over and cook them for 5 minutes, until they are golden on the opposite side. Transfer the thighs to a plate and set the plate aside.

Add the onion, garlic and bell peppers to the skillet. Cook the vegetables for 3 to 5 minutes, until the onion and bell peppers are soft.

Add the red pepper flakes, smoked paprika, bay leaf and tomato paste and stir the ingredients together. Season the mixture with additional salt and black pepper as needed. Stir in the rice, tomatoes and broth. Bring the mixture to a boil.

Transfer the chicken back to the skillet, placing the thighs on top of the rice. Bake the chicken and rice for about 45 minutes, or until the rice is tender. To prevent the rice from becoming too crispy on top, you can cover the skillet for the first 30 minutes and then remove the lid for the last 15 minutes if desired.

Discard the bay leaf. Garnish the chicken and rice with the green olives and parsley and serve the dish warm.

RECIPE NOTES

If you use brown rice, cook the dish for an additional 15 to 20 minutes, or until the rice is tender.

You can use any type of chicken you prefer. If you're using chicken breasts, cook them in the oven for an additional 10 minutes.

Be sure to store this dish as soon as it's cooled, as rice is a breeding ground for bacteria. Store leftovers in an airtight container in the fridge for 3 to 4 days. If you decide to freeze leftovers, store this dish in a freezer bag with the air pressed out. Thaw it overnight in the fridge and fluff the rice before reheating. This dish will last for 3 months in the freezer.

NUTRITION INFORMATION

Serving size: 1 serving; **Calories:** 444; **Carbohydrates:** 29 g; **Protein:** 24 g; **Fat:** 26 g

CHICKEN AND MUSHROOMS IN CREAMY DILL SAUCE

PREP TIME: 10 MINUTES
COOK TIME: 20 MINUTES
TOTAL TIME: 30 MINUTES
SERVES: 4

1 tbsp (15 ml) olive oil
1 lb (448 g) boneless, skinless chicken thighs, cut into 1" (3-cm) cubes (see Recipe Notes)
½ tsp salt, plus more as needed
¼ tsp black pepper, plus more as needed
1 onion, chopped
2 cloves garlic, minced
12 oz (336 g) white button mushrooms, halved
½ cup (120 ml) white wine (I recommend sauvignon blanc)
1 cup (240 ml) low-sodium chicken broth
2 tbsp (6 g) chopped fresh dill, plus more as needed
½ cup (60 g) sour cream
2 tbsp (30 g) unsalted butter
1 tbsp (8 g) all-purpose flour
Cooked rice, cooked pasta, Mashed Potatoes (page 383) or Creamy Polenta (page 388), for serving

If you're looking for a quick yet mouthwatering dish loaded with chicken and mushrooms in a smooth, rich and creamy sauce, look no further: This is an easy recipe that comes together in just 30 minutes!

Heat the oil in a large skillet over medium-high heat. Season the chicken with the salt and black pepper. Add the chicken to the skillet and cook it for about 5 minutes, until it is no longer pink.

Add the onion and garlic and cook the mixture for 2 minutes, until the onion is soft. Add the mushrooms and cook the mixture for 5 to 7 minutes, stirring it occasionally, until the mushrooms soften and are golden brown.

Stir in the white wine and broth. Bring the mixture to a boil. Add the dill and sour cream and stir to combine the ingredients. Add the butter and stir it into the mixture until it melts.

Transfer ½ cup (120 ml) of the broth from the skillet to a small bowl. Add the flour and whisk to combine it with the broth.

Pour this broth-flour mixture back into the skillet. Stir the sauce well and let it simmer for 5 minutes. Taste the sauce and adjust the seasoning with additional salt and black pepper as needed.

Garnish the chicken with additional dill (if desired). Serve the chicken and sauce over cooked rice, pasta, Mashed Potatoes or Creamy Polenta.

RECIPE NOTES

You can use chicken breasts or drumsticks if you prefer.

This recipe will work for any type of cubed protein you like. Or it can be made vegetarian by omitting the meat and using extra mushrooms. Swap out the chicken broth for vegetable broth.

I used white button mushrooms in this dish, but you can use whichever type you like most. Hardier varieties like cremini work best.

NUTRITION INFORMATION

Serving size: 1 serving; **Calories:** 458; **Carbohydrates:** 10 g; **Protein:** 23 g; **Fat:** 34 g

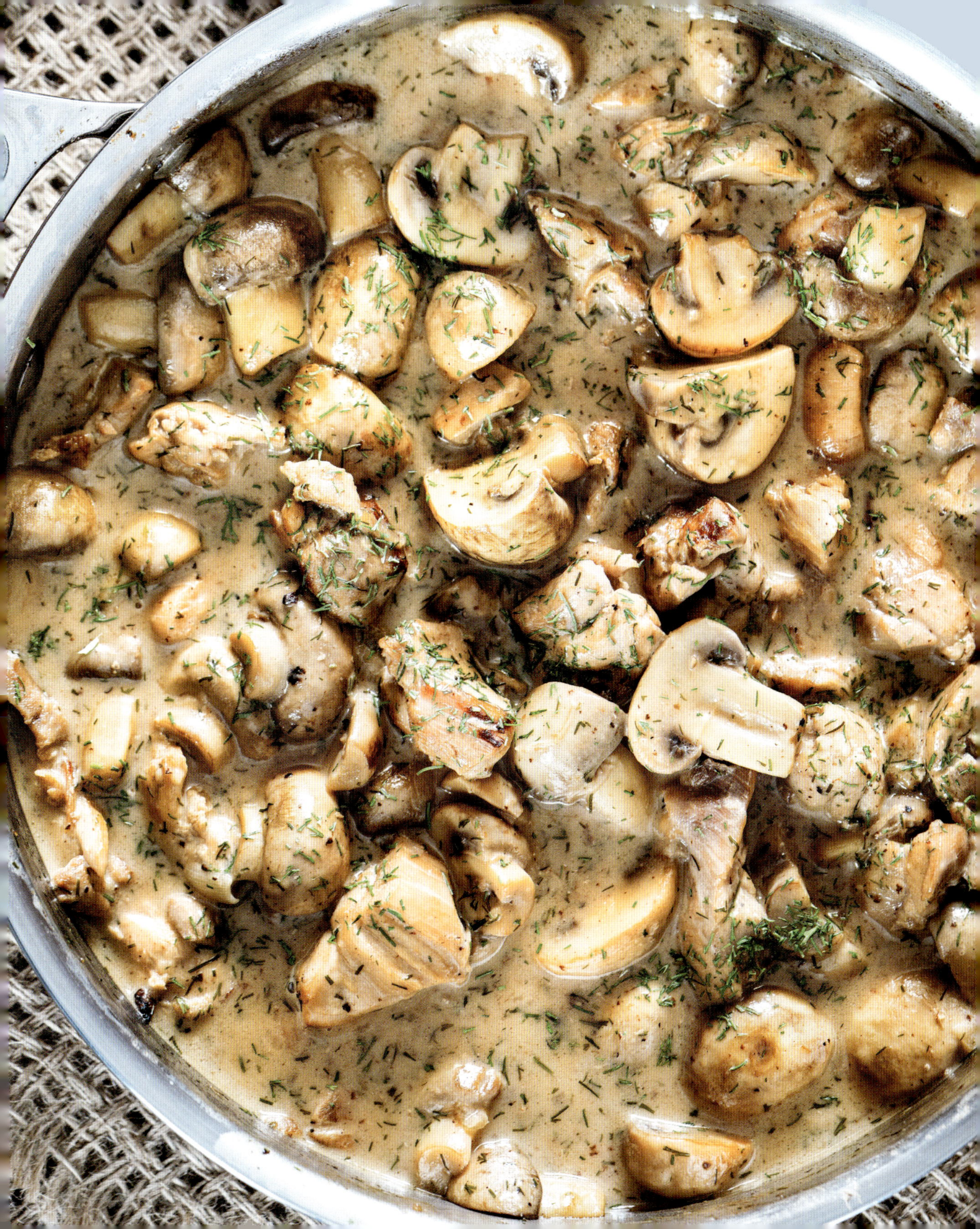

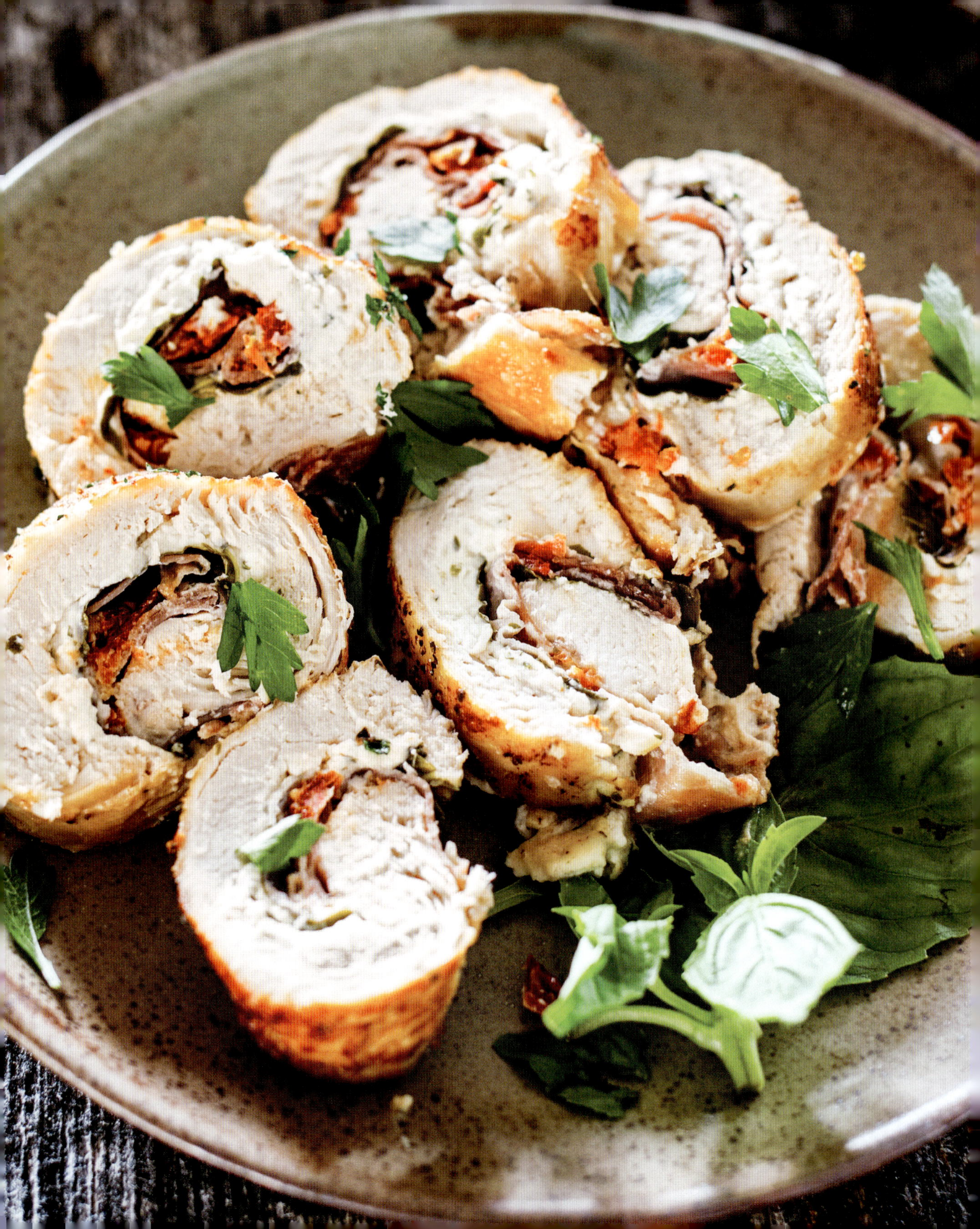

CHEESE AND PROSCIUTTO-STUFFED CHICKEN BREASTS

PREP TIME: 20 MINUTES
COOK TIME: 35 MINUTES
REST TIME: 15 MINUTES
TOTAL TIME: 1 HOUR, 10 MINUTES
SERVES: 2

2 boneless, skinless chicken breasts

¼ cup (60 g) cream cheese (I recommend spreadable garlic and herb cream cheese)

6 to 12 leaves fresh basil

4 thin slices prosciutto

2 tbsp (30 g) chopped oil-packed sun-dried tomatoes

¼ tsp salt, or as needed

½ tsp black pepper, or as needed

2 tbsp (30 ml) olive oil

Stuffed with cheese, prosciutto, basil and sun-dried tomatoes, these chicken breasts are an impressive dish for a Sunday night dinner or a holiday.

Preheat the oven to 450°F (232°C).

Pound the chicken breasts with a meat mallet until they are ¼ to ½ inch (6 to 13 mm) thick.

Spread half of the cream cheese on each chicken breast. Top the cream cheese with half of the basil, 2 slices of the prosciutto and 1 tablespoon (15 g) of the tomatoes. Carefully roll up the breasts and secure them with toothpicks. Season the chicken with the salt and black pepper.

Heat the oil in an oven-safe skillet over medium-high heat. Add the chicken seam side down and cook it for 5 to 7 minutes per side, until it is just slightly golden brown. You may need to remove the toothpicks to brown the chicken on all sides. Once the chicken is browned, remove all the toothpicks.

Place the skillet in the oven and bake the chicken for 20 minutes, until it is cooked through.

Transfer the chicken to a cutting board and let it rest for about 15 minutes before slicing it.

RECIPE NOTES

Store any leftover chicken in an airtight container in the refrigerator for 3 to 4 days.

Freeze this chicken stored in airtight containers for up to 3 months. Allow the chicken to thaw overnight in the fridge before heating it in the oven, on the stove or in the microwave.

NUTRITION INFORMATION

Serving: 1 breast; **Calories:** 394; **Carbohydrates:** 6 g; **Protein:** 29 g; **Fat:** 28 g

BEEF

BEFORE WE MOVED TO ALBERTA, more than ten years ago, I didn't enjoy or appreciate beef. Once we moved here and learned that Alberta is known for its beef, I knew I had to change my perspective—or at least give beef another try.

Once I had top-quality steak at a barbecue at my sister's house, I knew what I had been missing. It's a fact that Alberta beef is graded AA or higher because the farmers take extra steps to ensure quality. Every guest I've served my beef recipes to, such as my Pan-Seared Steak (page 52) or Steak Tacos (page 55), has said that the beef here in Alberta is amazing. When cooked right, good beef practically melts in your mouth.

For the past ten years, I have enjoyed a lot of great beef and have come up with lots of mouthwatering beef recipes. I love a good strip loin, like I use in my Garlic Butter Steak Bites (page 64), but I realize that good beef is not always economical. In this chapter, I want to show you many recipes that use the less expensive option of ground beef, such as Salisbury Steak (page 51) or Italian Stuffed Peppers (page 76). Even though ground beef is more economical than steak, you can still end up with a delicious meal—because with the right spices and herbs, you can make even ground beef shine.

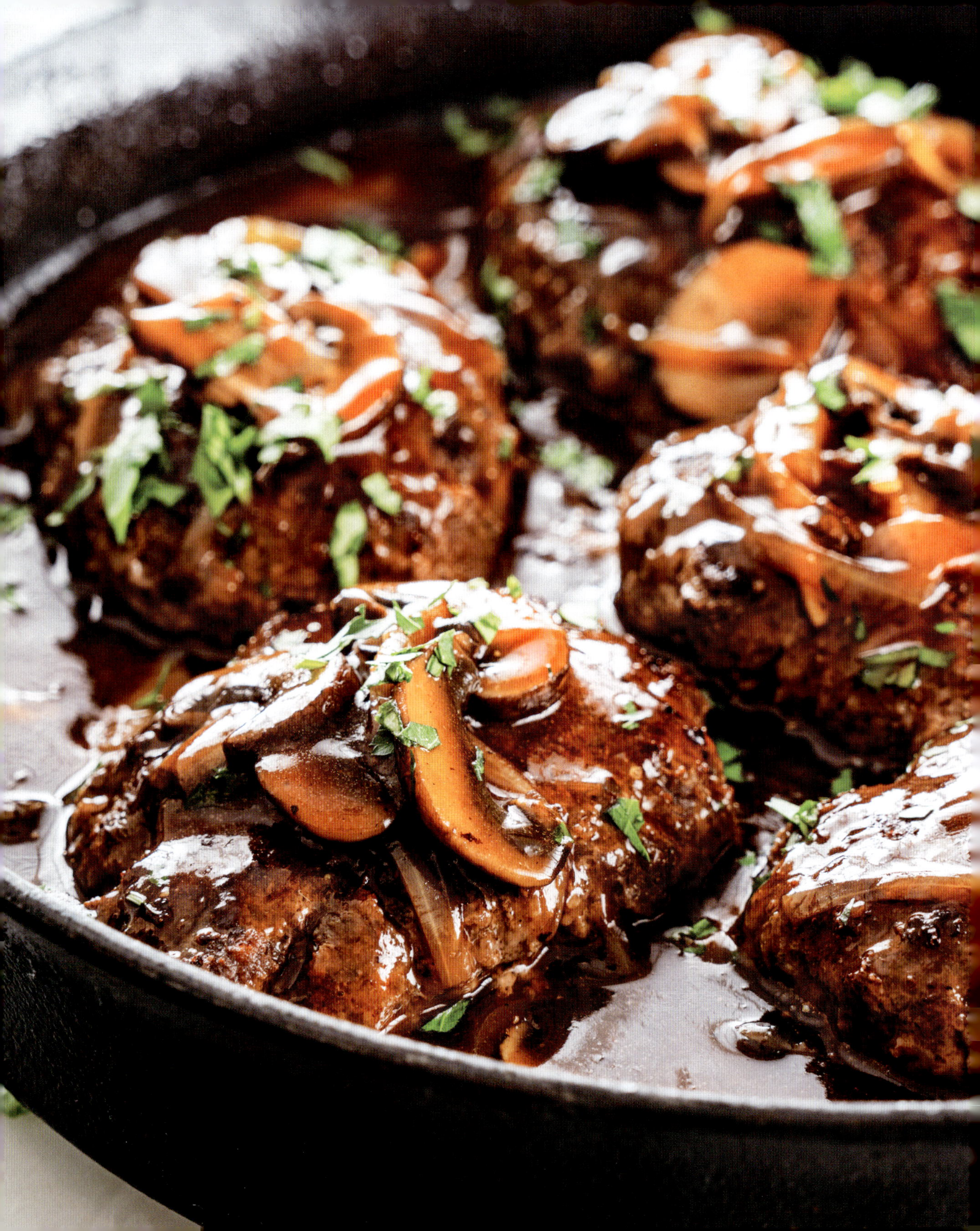

SALISBURY STEAK

Talk about an American classic! This Salisbury steak is ready in just 35 minutes, but tastes as if it took hours to make. This dish comes complete with a special onion-mushroom gravy that's so good over the steak, it will surely become your family's favorite.

PREP TIME: 15 MINUTES
COOK TIME: 25 MINUTES
TOTAL TIME: 35 MINUTES
SERVES: 6

SALISBURY STEAK
2 lb (896 g) extra lean ground beef
½ cup (75 g) breadcrumbs
1 large egg
½ tsp Worcestershire sauce
½ tsp salt
½ tsp black pepper
1 tbsp (15 ml) olive oil
1 tbsp (15 g) butter

ONION-MUSHROOM GRAVY
1 onion, halved and thinly sliced
8 oz (224 g) cremini mushrooms, sliced
¼ tsp salt, or as needed
¼ tsp black pepper, or as needed
2 cups (480 ml) low-sodium beef broth
1 tbsp (15 g) tomato paste
1 tbsp (15 ml) soy sauce
1 tsp Worcestershire sauce
2 tsp (6 g) cornstarch
2 tsp (10 ml) water

1 tbsp (3 g) chopped fresh parsley
Mashed Potatoes (page 383), for serving

To make the Salisbury steak, use clean hands to combine the beef, breadcrumbs, egg, Worcestershire sauce, salt and black pepper in a large bowl. Divide the meat mixture into 6 equal pieces and form them into oval patties.

Heat the oil and butter in a large skillet over medium-high heat. Add the meat patties and fry them for about 5 minutes per side, until they are no longer pink in the middle. Transfer the patties to a plate.

To make the onion-mushroom gravy, reduce the heat to medium and add the onion. Cook the onion for about 6 minutes, until it has softened. Add the mushrooms, then add the salt and black pepper and stir to combine the ingredients. Cook the vegetables for 5 minutes, until the onions are golden brown.

Add the broth, tomato paste, soy sauce and Worcestershire sauce and stir to combine the ingredients. In a small bowl, whisk the cornstarch and water to create a slurry. Add the slurry to the skillet. Whisk the sauce for about 2 minutes, until it thickens.

Transfer the Salisbury steaks back to the skillet and spoon the gravy over the tops of the steaks. Cook the steaks for 1 minute, until they are warmed through.

Garnish the Salisbury steaks with the parsley. Serve them with the gravy over the Mashed Potatoes.

RECIPE NOTES
Transfer your leftovers to an airtight container and store them in the fridge for 3 to 4 days. Since the beef is fully cooked and you don't have to worry about overcooking it, you can reheat it in the microwave in 20-second intervals until it is hot.

NUTRITION INFORMATION
Serving size: 1 steak; **Calories:** 382; **Carbohydrates:** 12 g; **Protein:** 35 g; **Fat:** 21 g

PAN-SEARED STEAK

This pan-seared steak with herbed brown butter is about to become your favorite way to enjoy a perfect cut of steak. It certainly is mine. You might just prefer this method over your grill! With the perfect crust on the meat and the flavors of fresh herbs, this recipe will transport you straight to a high-end steak house.

PREP TIME: 5 MINUTES
REST TIME: 35 MINUTES
COOK TIME: 15 MINUTES
TOTAL TIME: 55 MINUTES
SERVES: 2

2 (8-oz [224-g]) rib eye steaks
½ tsp salt, or as needed
½ tsp black pepper, or as needed
8 tbsp (120 g) unsalted butter
1 sprig fresh rosemary
3 sprigs fresh thyme

Let the steaks rest at room temperature for 20 to 30 minutes prior to cooking them. Season them with the salt and black pepper.

In a 1-quart (960-ml) saucepan over medium heat, combine the butter, rosemary and thyme. Stir the butter constantly. Once the butter has melted, it will start to sizzle. Continue stirring the butter for 3 to 5 minutes, or until the butter turns golden brown. Remove the saucepan from the heat.

Add 2 tablespoons (30 ml) of the brown butter to a large skillet or grill skillet over medium-high heat. Once the butter is hot, add the steaks. Sear the steaks for 3 to 4 minutes on one side, then flip them. Cook the steaks for 2 minutes on the opposite side, then drizzle some more brown butter over the steaks.

Carefully tilt the skillet to allow the butter to pool to one side. Baste the steaks by using a 1-tablespoon (15-ml) spoon to drizzle the brown butter over the steaks. Repeat this step for 1 to 2 minutes, then remove the steaks from the skillet.

Let the steaks rest for 5 minutes before serving them.

RECIPE NOTES

To save on cleanup, you can use the same skillet for browning the butter and searing the steaks. You'll just need to remove most of the brown butter from the skillet before pan-searing the steaks.

Transfer the steaks to an airtight container and keep them in the fridge for 3 to 4 days. You can eat the steak cold, sliced and tossed into a salad. You can also reheat it, but keep in mind the internal temperature of the steak will increase during the reheating process and reduce the pinkness in the middle.

NUTRITION INFORMATION

Serving size: 1 steak; **Calories:** 911; **Carbohydrates:** 1 g; **Protein:** 49 g; **Fat:** 80 g

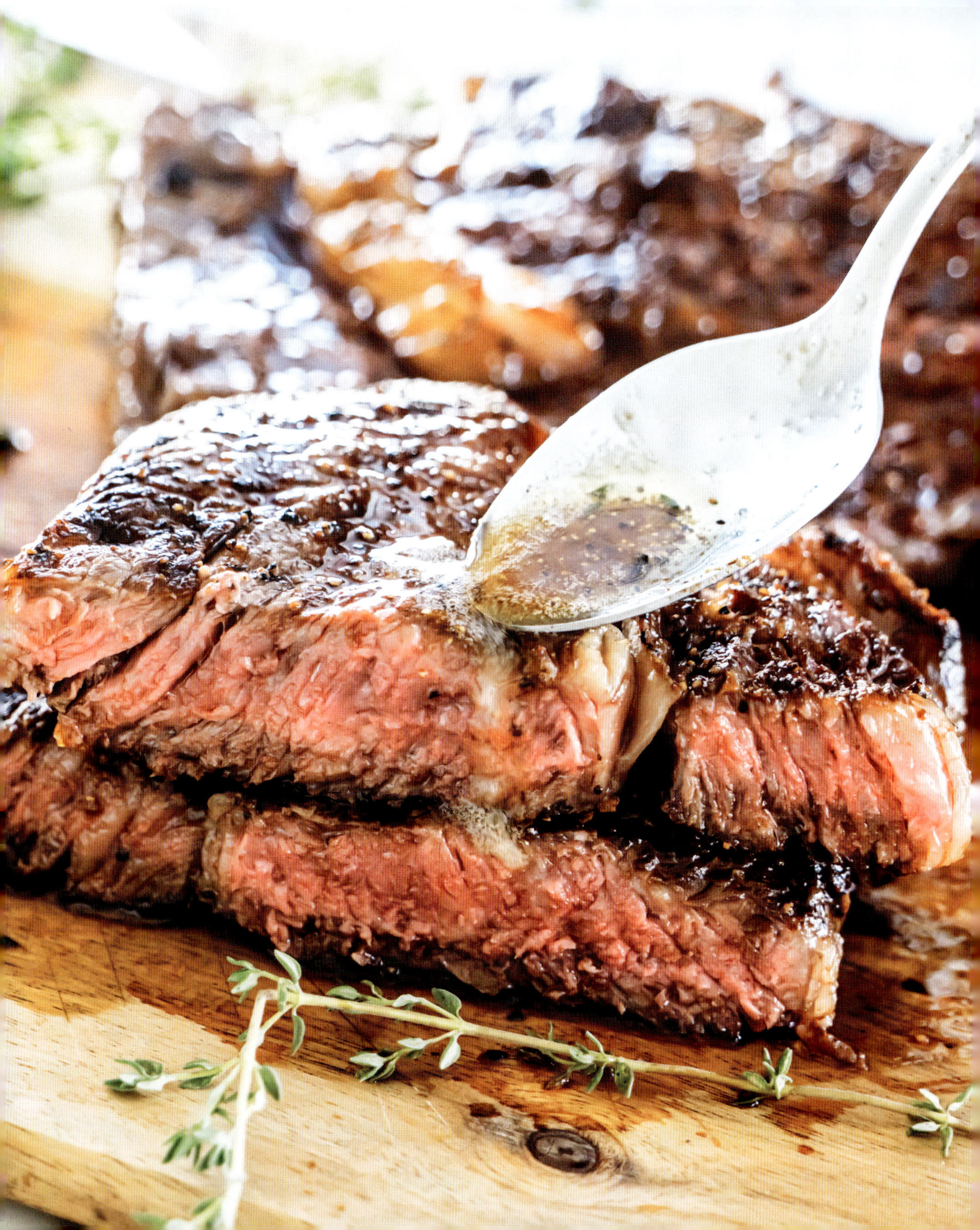

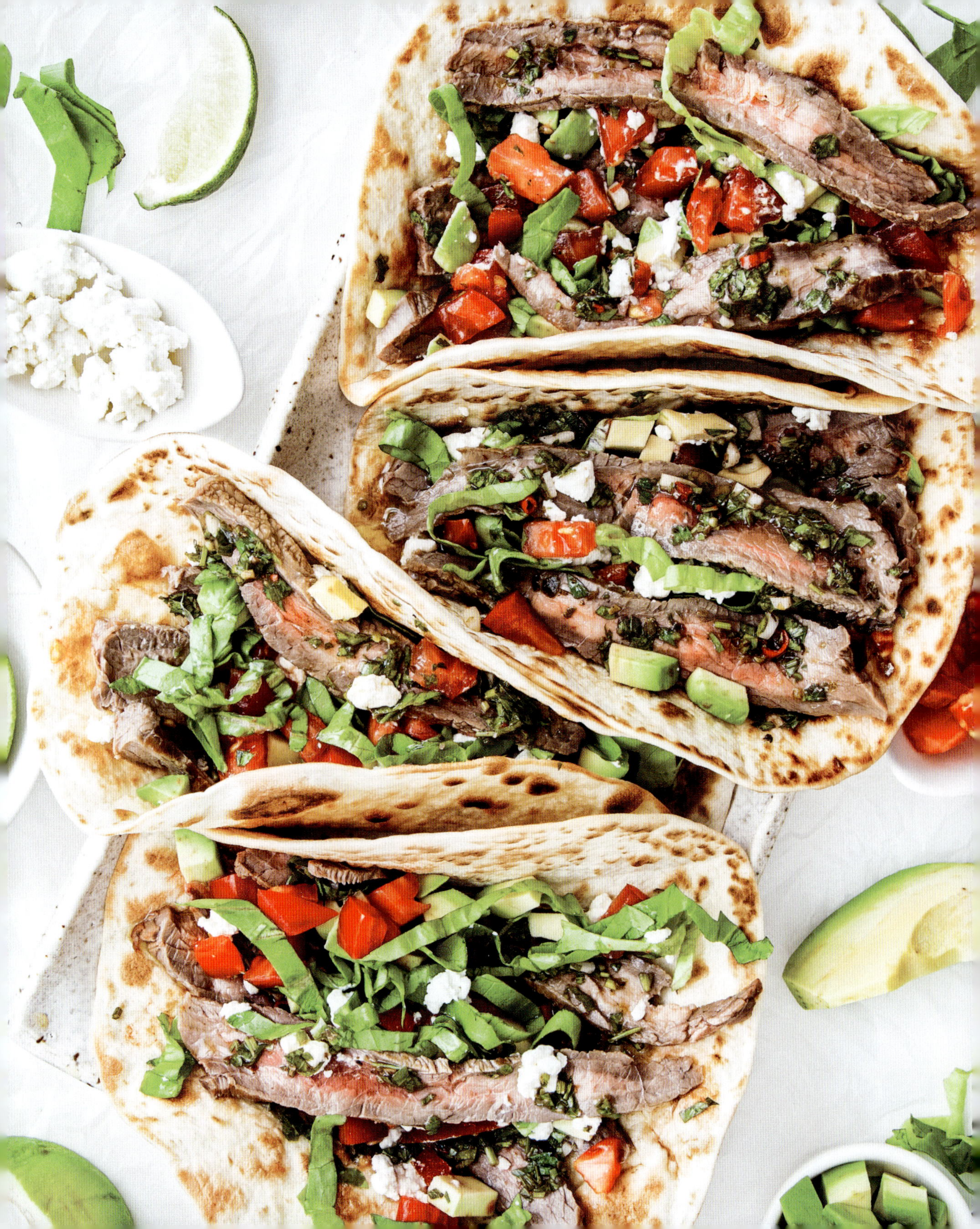

STEAK TACOS

These steak tacos are perfect for lunch or dinner. Tender steak cooked to medium-rare perfection, piled into soft tortillas and topped with chimichurri sauce and your favorite taco toppings—dinner is served!

PREP TIME: 10 MINUTES
REST TIME: 10 MINUTES
COOK TIME: 15 MINUTES
TOTAL TIME: 35 MINUTES
SERVES: 8

2 sirloin steaks
8 medium tortillas
½ cup (120 ml) Chimichurri Sauce (page 315)
1 avocado, finely chopped
1 cup (180 g) chopped tomatoes
1 cup (47 g) roughly chopped lettuce
½ cup (75 g) crumbled feta cheese
1 lime, cut into wedges

In a large skillet or on a grill, cook the steaks to your preferred doneness. Let them rest for 10 minutes.

Toast the tortillas in a hot skillet for about 30 seconds per side, or until they start to brown and become golden. I do not use any olive oil or butter, but you can brush a bit of olive oil or butter in the skillet if you prefer.

Slice the steak into thin strips. Place a few steak strips on a tortilla, then drizzle the Chimichurri Sauce over the tacos. Top the tacos with the avocado, tomatoes, lettuce and feta cheese. Serve the tacos with lime wedges on the side.

RECIPE NOTES

Leftover steak will last 3 to 4 days in the fridge. You can enjoy the leftover steak cold in future tacos if you don't want to lose the pink. You can reheat the meat in the microwave or in a skillet, but keep in mind you will likely lose the pink color.

Cooked steak will last 2 to 3 months in the freezer. Let it thaw overnight in the fridge before reheating it.

If you'd like to store the Chimichurri Sauce, it will last for 3 weeks in the fridge or 3 months in the freezer.

NUTRITION INFORMATION

Serving size: 1 taco; **Calories:** 340; **Carbohydrates:** 21 g; **Protein:** 17 g; **Fat:** 21 g

EASY SWISS STEAK

This Swiss steak recipe is made with inexpensive beef, which is cooked until it's tender in a flavorful tomato sauce. Made in one pot, this impressive steak dinner doesn't have to cost you much money or effort!

PREP TIME: 30 MINUTES
COOK TIME: 2 HOURS
TOTAL: 2 HOURS, 30 MINUTES
SERVES: 6

1 (2-lb [896-g]) bottom round roast, cut into ½" (13-mm)-thick slices
1 tsp salt, plus more as needed
1 tsp black pepper, plus more as needed
½ cup (60 g) all-purpose flour
3 tbsp (45 ml) olive oil, divided
1 onion, sliced
4 cloves garlic, minced
1 tbsp (15 g) tomato paste
1 (15-oz [420-g]) can diced tomatoes, undrained
2 cups (480 ml) low-sodium beef broth
2 tsp (2 g) Italian seasoning
1 tbsp (15 ml) Worcestershire sauce
1 tbsp (3 g) chopped fresh parsley

Use a meat tenderizer mallet to poke holes into each slice of steak on both sides. You can also do this with a fork or paring knife.

Season the beef slices with the salt and black pepper. Add the flour to a shallow bowl. Dredge each piece of beef well in the flour.

Heat 2 tablespoons (30 ml) of the oil in a large, deep skillet over medium-high heat. Add the beef to the skillet and cook it for 4 to 5 minutes per side, or until it is seared and well browned. Remove the beef from the skillet and set it aside.

Heat the remaining 1 tablespoon (15 ml) of oil in the skillet. Add the onion and cook it for 3 to 4 minutes, until it is soft and translucent. Add the garlic and cook it for 30 seconds, or until it is aromatic.

Stir in the tomato paste and cook the mixture for 1 minute. Add the tomatoes and their juice, broth, Italian seasoning and Worcestershire sauce. Stir everything together well.

Bring the sauce to a boil, then reduce the heat to low and bring the sauce to a simmer. Transfer the beef back to the skillet, making sure it's fully submerged in the sauce. Cover the skillet and cook the Swiss steak for 1½ hours, stirring it occasionally, or until the sauce has reduced to your liking and the beef is tender.

Taste the Swiss steak for seasoning and add additional salt and black pepper if needed. Garnish the Swiss steak with the parsley and serve it.

RECIPE NOTES

Transfer leftovers to an airtight container and store them in the fridge for 3 to 4 days.

You can reheat the Swiss steak in the microwave or in a skillet over medium heat, stirring it occasionally. If you find the sauce has reduced too much, you can add a splash of water or broth to thin it.

You can also store leftovers in the freezer for 2 to 3 months. It'll be much easier to let the leftovers thaw overnight in the fridge before using one of the reheating methods just detailed. This will ensure you can reheat the meat carefully without breaking it apart.

NUTRITION INFORMATION

Serving size: 1 serving; **Calories:** 345; **Carbohydrates:** 15 g; **Protein:** 37 g; **Fat:** 15 g

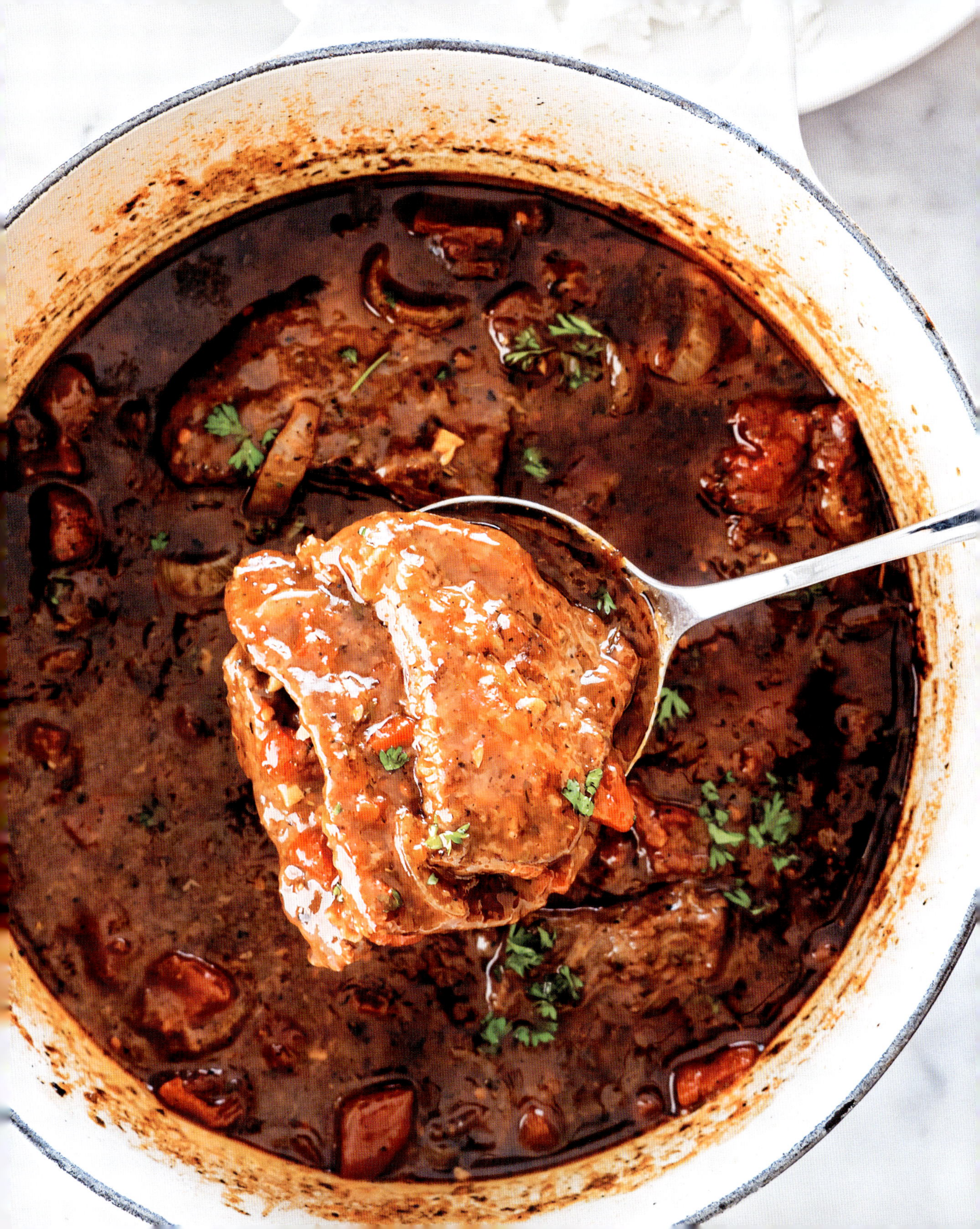

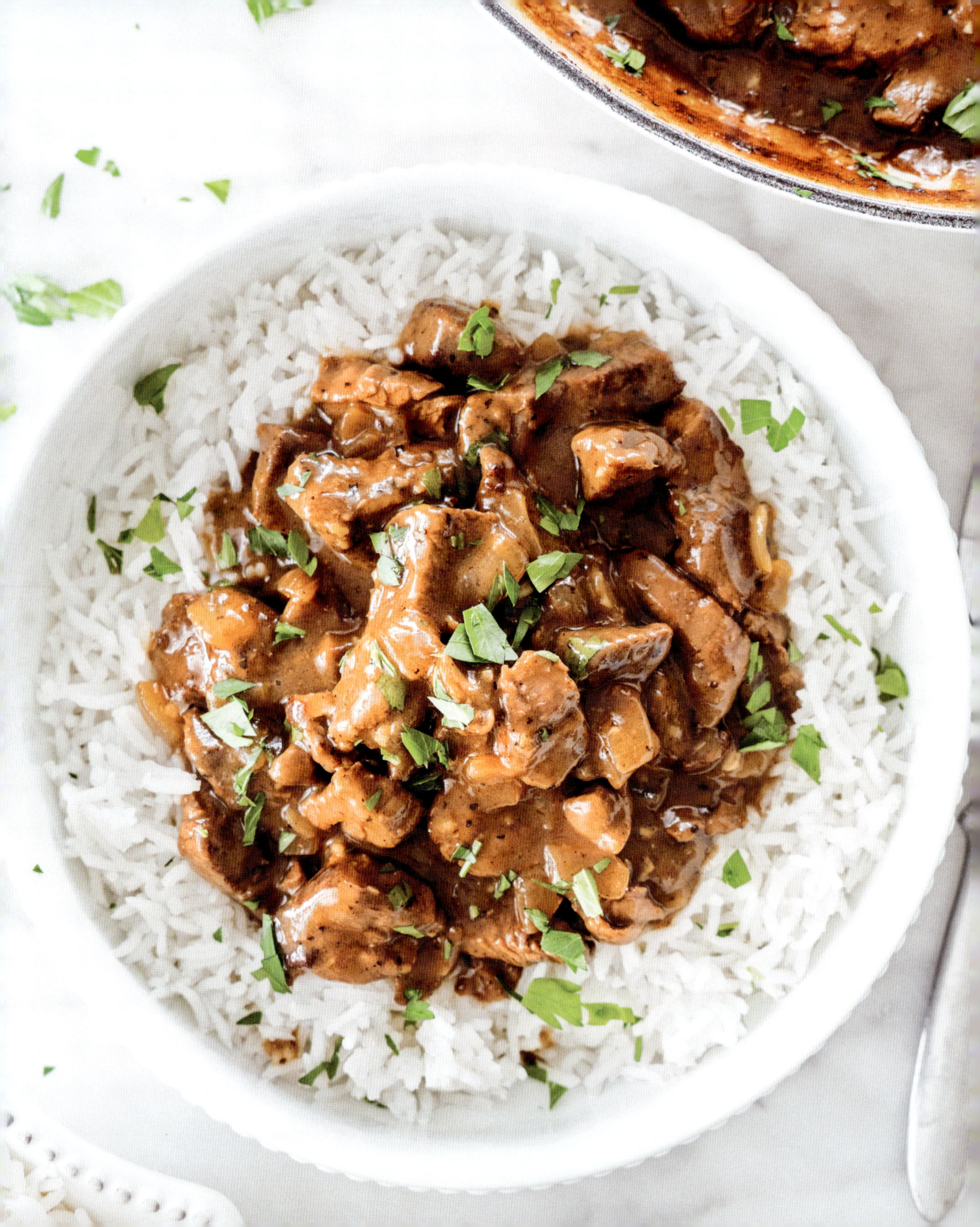

BEEF TIPS WITH GRAVY

This is my go-to recipe for beef tips! Made with staples from your kitchen and using only one pot, this dish is a favorite comfort meal that all ages will crave.

PREP TIME: 15 MINUTES
COOK TIME: 45 MINUTES
TOTAL TIME: 1 HOUR
SERVES: 6

2 lb (896 g) cubed beef chuck roast, sirloin or another type of stewing beef
1 tsp salt, plus more as needed
1 tsp black pepper, plus more as needed
1 tbsp (15 ml) olive oil
3 tbsp (45 g) unsalted butter
1 onion, diced
3 cloves garlic, minced
¼ cup (30 g) all-purpose flour
4 cups (960 ml) low-sodium beef broth
2 tbsp (30 ml) soy sauce
2 tbsp (30 ml) Worcestershire sauce
2 sprigs fresh thyme
1 dried bay leaf
1 tbsp (3 g) chopped fresh parsley

Season the beef cubes with the salt and black pepper.

Heat the oil in a large Dutch oven over medium-high heat. Add the beef cubes and sear them on all sides, 3 to 5 minutes total. Remove the cubes from the Dutch oven and set them aside.

Add the butter to the Dutch oven and let it melt. Add the onion and cook it for 3 to 4 minutes, or until it is soft and translucent.

Add the garlic and cook it for 30 seconds, then sprinkle the flour over the onion and garlic. Stir well to incorporate the ingredients and cook them for 1 to 2 minutes. Add the broth and whisk the mixture well. Add the soy sauce, Worcestershire sauce, thyme, bay leaf and seared beef.

Bring the mixture to a boil, then reduce the heat to low and bring the mixture to a simmer. Let the beef tips and gravy simmer for 30 minutes, stirring them occasionally, until the gravy has thickened and the beef is tender.

Remove the thyme sprigs and bay leaf. Taste the gravy and adjust the seasoning with additional salt and black pepper if needed. Garnish the beef tips and gravy with the parsley and serve.

RECIPE NOTE

Transfer leftovers to an airtight container and store them in the fridge for 3 to 4 days. You can reheat them in the microwave or on the stove.

NUTRITION INFORMATION

Serving size: 1 serving; **Calories:** 401; **Carbohydrates:** 8 g; **Protein:** 35 g; **Fat:** 25 g

INSTANT POT® BEEF BURGUNDY

This Instant Pot recipe features a full bottle of red wine and fall-apart tender morsels of savory beef. Gourmet dinner is served in just over an hour! Try it over noodles, rice or creamy Mashed Potatoes (page 383).

PREP TIME: 15 MINUTES
COOK TIME: 55 MINUTES
NATURAL PRESSURE RELEASE: 10 MINUTES
TOTAL TIME: 1 HOUR, 20 MINUTES
SERVES: 6

2 tbsp (30 ml) olive oil
2 lb (896 g) cubed beef chuck roast or other stewing beef
1 tsp salt, plus more as needed
1 tsp black pepper, plus more as needed
2 tbsp (30 g) unsalted butter
8 oz (224 g) cremini mushrooms, halved
1 white onion, diced
4 cloves garlic, minced
2 tbsp (30 g) tomato paste
1 (25-oz [750-ml]) bottle Burgundy, Cabernet Sauvignon, Pinot Noir or zinfandel wine
1 cup (240 ml) low-sodium beef broth
2 dried bay leaves
2 sprigs fresh thyme
1 tbsp (9 g) cornstarch
1 tbsp (15 ml) water
1 tbsp (3 g) chopped fresh parsley
Mashed Potatoes (page 383) or cooked noodles, for serving

Heat the oil in the Instant Pot on the Sauté setting. Season the beef cubes with the salt and black pepper. Add the beef to the Instant Pot and sear it for 3 to 5 minutes, until it is browned on all sides. Remove the beef from the pot and set it aside.

Melt the butter in the pot. Add the mushrooms and onion. Cook the vegetables for 4 to 5 minutes, stirring them occasionally, until the onion softens and the mushrooms begin to brown. Add the garlic and cook it for 30 seconds, then mix in the tomato paste. Cook the mixture for 1 to 2 minutes.

Add the wine, broth, bay leaves and thyme. Stir everything together well. Transfer the beef back to the pot. Secure the lid of the Instant Pot and turn the valve from Vent to Seal. Cook the beef for 25 minutes on high pressure, then let the pressure release naturally for 10 minutes. Quick-release the remaining pressure.

Set the Instant Pot to the Sauté setting and bring the beef mixture to a bubble. Let it simmer for 10 to 15 minutes to reduce the sauce slightly.

In a small bowl, whisk together the cornstarch and water to create a slurry. Add the slurry to the Instant Pot. Mix the slurry into the sauce and cook it for 1 to 2 minutes to allow the sauce to thicken. You can add more slurry if you'd like a thicker sauce.

Taste the beef Burgundy and adjust the seasoning with additional salt and black pepper as needed. Discard the bay leaves and thyme. Garnish the beef with the parsley and serve it over Mashed Potatoes or noodles.

RECIPE NOTES

Transfer any leftovers to an airtight container and store them in the fridge for 3 to 4 days. This dish will reheat well either in the microwave or on the stove. In a saucepan or a skillet, bring the leftovers to a boil over high heat, then reduce the heat to low and bring them to a simmer. Cook the beef and sauce for 10 minutes, or until they are fully heated through. You may have to shred a piece of beef to make sure it's not cold in the center. Feel free to add a splash of water or broth if the sauce gets too thick.

Your beef Burgundy will last in the freezer for 4 to 6 months. Reheating will be much easier if you let the leftovers thaw overnight, but it isn't completely necessary.

NUTRITION INFORMATION

Serving size: 1 serving; **Calories:** 496; **Carbohydrates:** 10 g; **Protein:** 34 g; **Fat:** 25 g

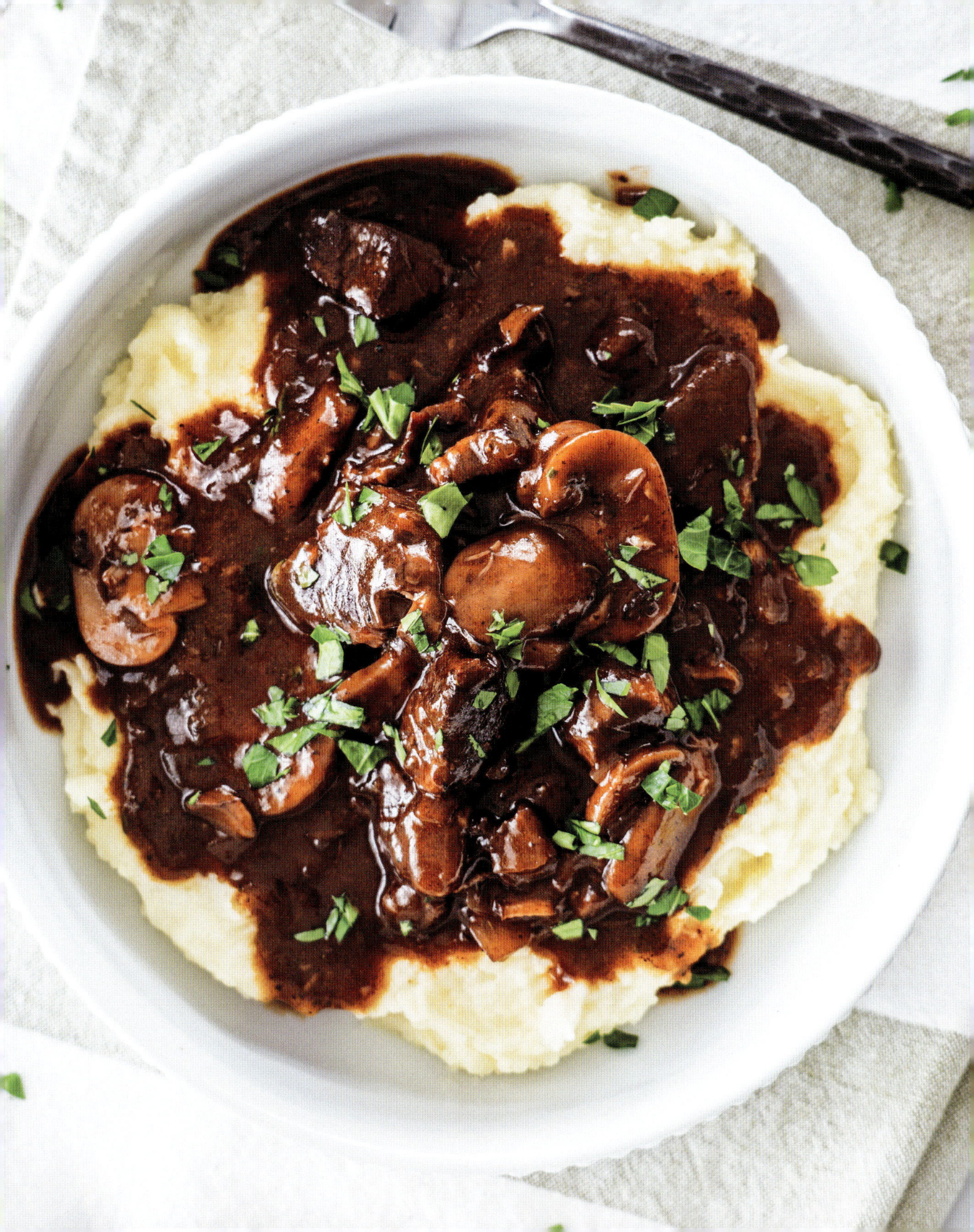

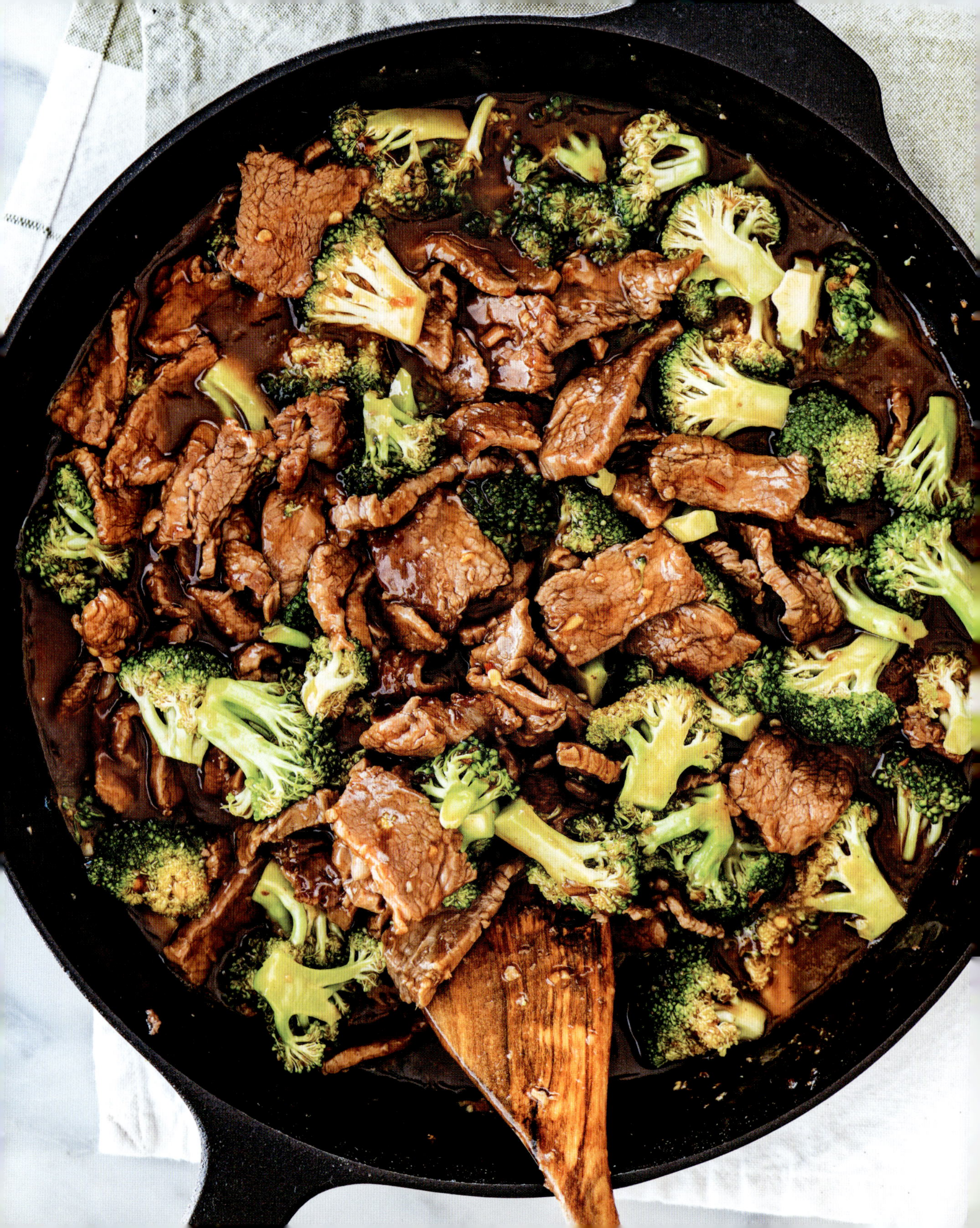

EASY BEEF AND BROCCOLI STIR-FRY

This is a classic Chinese American dish that is one of my favorites, one that I always order whenever I eat at a Chinese restaurant. Believe it or not, this stir-fry really is ready in just fifteen minutes—the secret is to prepare everything beforehand, then just dump and cook. Easy as pie!

PREP TIME: 5 MINUTES
COOK TIME: 10 MINUTES
TOTAL TIME: 15 MINUTES
SERVES: 4

SAUCE

½ cup (120 ml) low-sodium soy sauce

2 tbsp (18 g) cornstarch

3 cloves garlic, minced

3 tbsp (45 ml) cooking wine (see Recipe Note)

3 tbsp (45 ml) honey

1 tsp minced fresh ginger

2 tbsp (30 ml) sesame oil

¼ tsp red pepper flakes

1 tbsp (15 ml) Sriracha sauce, or as needed

½ cup (120 ml) low-sodium or unsalted beef or chicken broth

BEEF AND BROCCOLI

1 tbsp (15 ml) olive oil

1 lb (448 g) flank steak, trimmed of fat and thinly sliced against the grain

1 head broccoli, cut into small florets

Cooked rice or noodles, for serving

To make the sauce, whisk together the soy sauce, cornstarch, garlic, wine, honey, ginger, sesame oil, red pepper flakes, Sriracha sauce and broth. Set the sauce aside.

To make the beef and broccoli, heat the olive oil in a large skillet over medium-high heat. Add the steak and cook it for 4 to 5 minutes, until it starts to brown. Add the sauce and stir to coat the steak with the sauce. The sauce should start to thicken immediately.

Add the broccoli and cook the stir-fry for 2 minutes, until the broccoli is tender and the sauce is thick.

Serve the stir-fry over rice or noodles.

RECIPE NOTE

A good substitute for the cooking wine would be apple cider.

NUTRITION INFORMATION

Serving size: 1 serving; **Calories:** 395; **Carbohydrates:** 30 g; **Protein:** 30 g; **Fat:** 16 g

GARLIC BUTTER STEAK BITES

These steak bites are everything you love about a big steak dinner without all the work. Ready in only fifteen minutes, these steak bites pack so much flavor and are easy to prepare. They're perfect for a fancy party appetizer. Or serve them alongside some creamy Mashed Potatoes (page 383) for an easy and delicious weeknight dinner.

PREP TIME: 5 MINUTES
COOK TIME: 10 MINUTES
TOTAL TIME: 15 MINUTES
SERVES: 4

- 1 tbsp (15 ml) olive oil
- 1½ lb (672 g) sirloin, strip loin, tenderloin or rib eye steak, cut into bite-sized pieces
- ½ tsp salt, or as needed
- ½ tsp black pepper, or as needed
- 2 tbsp (30 g) unsalted butter
- 4 cloves garlic, minced
- ¼ tsp red pepper flakes
- 1 tbsp (3 g) chopped fresh parsley, for garnish

Heat the oil in a large skillet over high heat. Add the steak pieces, working in batches if necessary. Season them with the salt and black pepper.

Cook the steak pieces for at least 2 minutes before stirring them to ensure a good sear. Stir the steak pieces and cook them for another 2 minutes, until they're golden brown on all sides.

Transfer the steak bites to a plate. Add the butter to the skillet and allow it to melt. Reduce the heat to medium. Add the garlic and red pepper flakes. Cook them for about 30 seconds, stirring them constantly, just until the garlic becomes aromatic and starts to brown.

Pour the garlic butter over the steak bites and toss them well. Garnish the steak bites with the parsley and serve them.

NUTRITION INFORMATION

Serving size: 1 serving; **Calories:** 316; **Carbohydrates:** 1 g; **Protein:** 37 g; **Fat:** 17 g

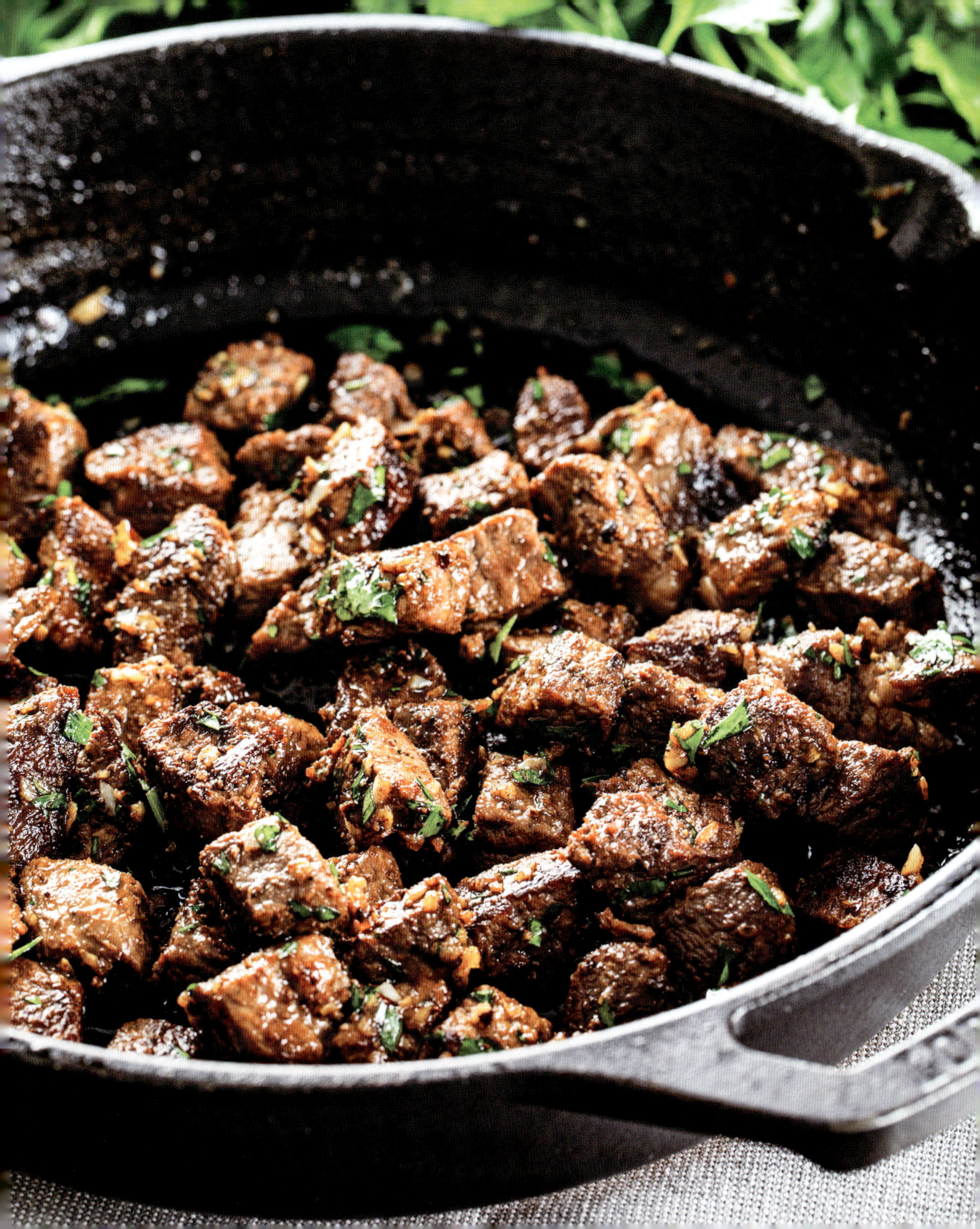

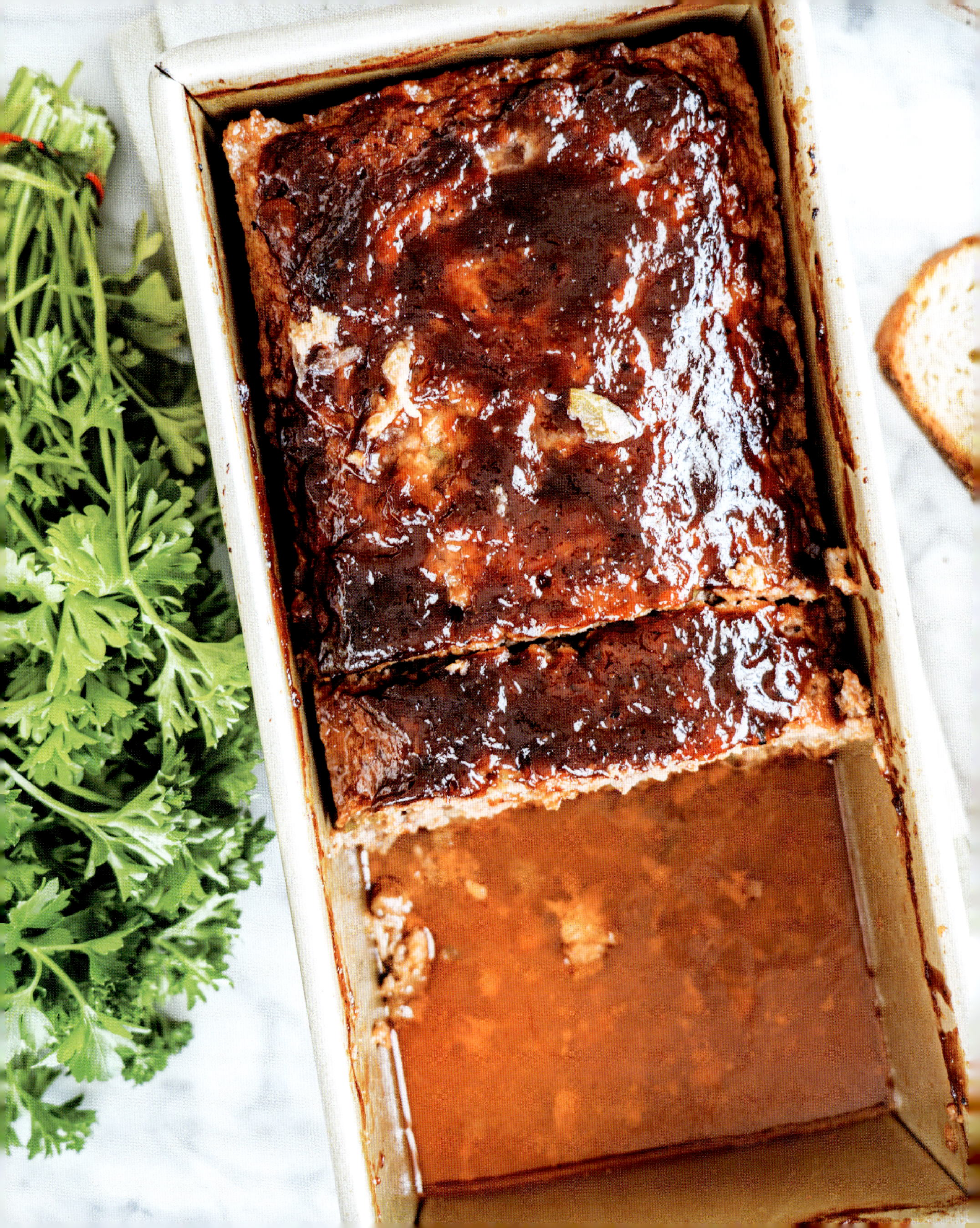

EASY MEATLOAF

PREP TIME: 10 MINUTES
COOK TIME: 1 HOUR, 20 MINUTES
REST TIME: 10 MINUTES
TOTAL TIME: 1 HOUR, 40 MINUTES
SERVES: 8

1 onion, finely chopped or grated
1 cup (60 g) panko breadcrumbs
¼ cup (60 ml) milk
1 lb (448 g) ground pork
1 lb (448 g) ground beef
½ green bell pepper, finely chopped
1 large egg
1 cup (240 ml) barbecue sauce, divided (I recommend Guy Fieri Kansas City Smokey & Sweet barbecue sauce)
1 tsp Worcestershire sauce
1 tsp salt, or as needed
½ tsp black pepper, or as needed

Pretty much everyone has their favorite meatloaf recipe that's been passed down to them, but here's my recipe that will give you a meatloaf that's tender, super moist and delicious. It's a great comfort food, plus it's super economical. This is what Sunday suppers are all about.

Preheat the oven to 350°F (177°C). Spray a 5 x 9–inch (15 x 27–cm) loaf pan with cooking spray.

In a large bowl, stir together the onion, breadcrumbs and milk. Add the pork, beef, bell pepper, egg, ¾ cup (180 ml) of the barbecue sauce, Worcestershire sauce, salt and black pepper. Mix the meat mixture well using your hands or a spoon.

Transfer the meat mixture to the prepared loaf pan and pat it into a loaf. Brush the top of the loaf with the remaining ¼ cup (60 ml) of barbecue sauce.

Bake the meatloaf for 60 to 80 minutes, or until its internal temperature reaches 165°F (74°C).

Let the meatloaf rest for 10 minutes before slicing it.

RECIPE NOTE

Place the loaf pan on a baking sheet before you bake the meatloaf so as not to get your oven dirty.

NUTRITION INFORMATION

Serving size: 1 serving; **Calories:** 386; **Carbohydrates:** 27 g; **Protein:** 24 g; **Fat:** 19 g

TACO LASAGNA

PREP TIME: 10 MINUTES
COOK TIME: 40 MINUTES
TOTAL TIME: 50 MINUTES
SERVES: 8

TACO LASAGNA
1 lb (448 g) ground beef
1 onion, chopped
1 green bell pepper, chopped
7 oz (210 ml) jarred taco sauce
1 (10-oz [300-ml]) can enchilada sauce
15 oz (420 g) ricotta cheese
1 large egg
2½ cups (300 g) shredded Cheddar cheese or Mexican cheese blend, divided
9 no-boil lasagna noodles

TOPPINGS
½ cup (75 g) cherry tomatoes, chopped
2 green onions, chopped
2 tbsp (6 g) chopped fresh cilantro
1 avocado, sliced

There are lots of taco lasagna recipes out there, but I'm biased toward mine because my lasagna is made with no-boil lasagna noodles—not tortillas—to give it that lasagna feel. This is an actual lasagna but with the Mexican-inspired flavors we all know and love.

Preheat the oven to 375°F (191°C).

Heat a large skillet over medium-high heat. Add the beef and cook it for 5 minutes, breaking it up as it cooks, until it is no longer pink.

Add the onion and bell pepper to the beef and cook the mixture for about 3 minutes, until the onion is translucent and the bell pepper is tender.

Stir in the taco sauce and enchilada sauce. Bring the mixture to a boil. Remove the skillet from the heat.

In a medium bowl, stir together the ricotta cheese, egg and ½ cup (60 g) of the Cheddar cheese.

Place 3 lasagna noodles in the bottom of a 9 x 13–inch (27 x 39–cm) baking dish. Spoon half of the meat sauce over the noodles. Add 3 more lasagna noodles, then spread the ricotta mixture over the noodles. Add 3 more lasagna noodles, then top them with the remaining meat sauce. Top the sauce with the remaining 2 cups (240 g) of Cheddar cheese.

Bake the lasagna, uncovered, for 30 minutes, or until the cheese melts and is bubbly and the noodles are cooked through.

Let the lasagna cool for about 10 minutes before slicing it. Top the lasagna with the tomatoes, green onions, cilantro and avocado.

RECIPE NOTES

To freeze leftover lasagna, cut it into individual servings first, then wrap each serving tightly in plastic wrap. Place all the individually wrapped pieces in a large freezer-safe bag. Lasagna will last for several months in the freezer.

To store leftovers in the refrigerator, place the lasagna in an airtight container and refrigerate it for 5 to 7 days.

NUTRITION INFORMATION

Serving size: 1 serving; **Calories:** 536; **Carbohydrates:** 35 g; **Protein:** 32 g; **Fat:** 29 g

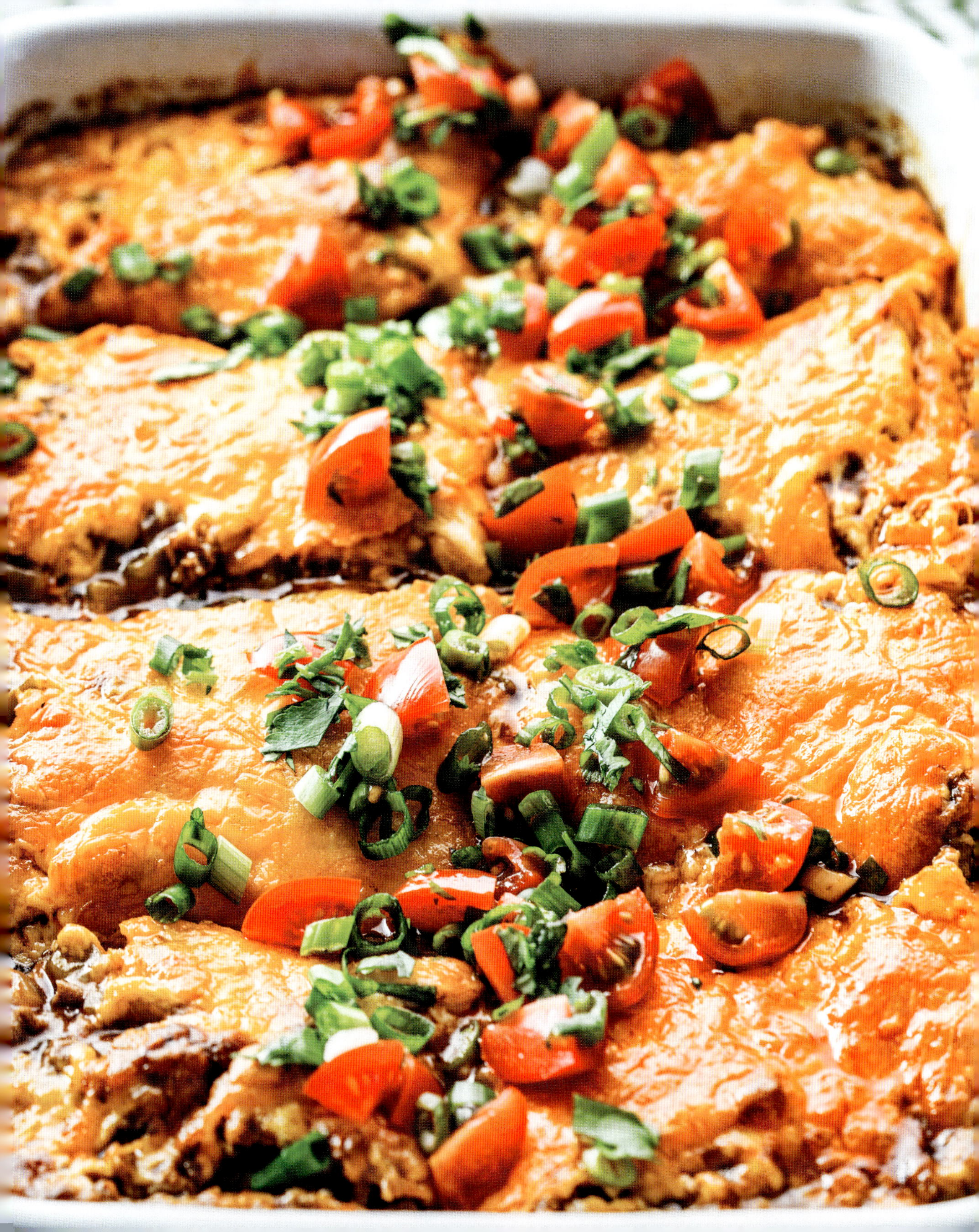

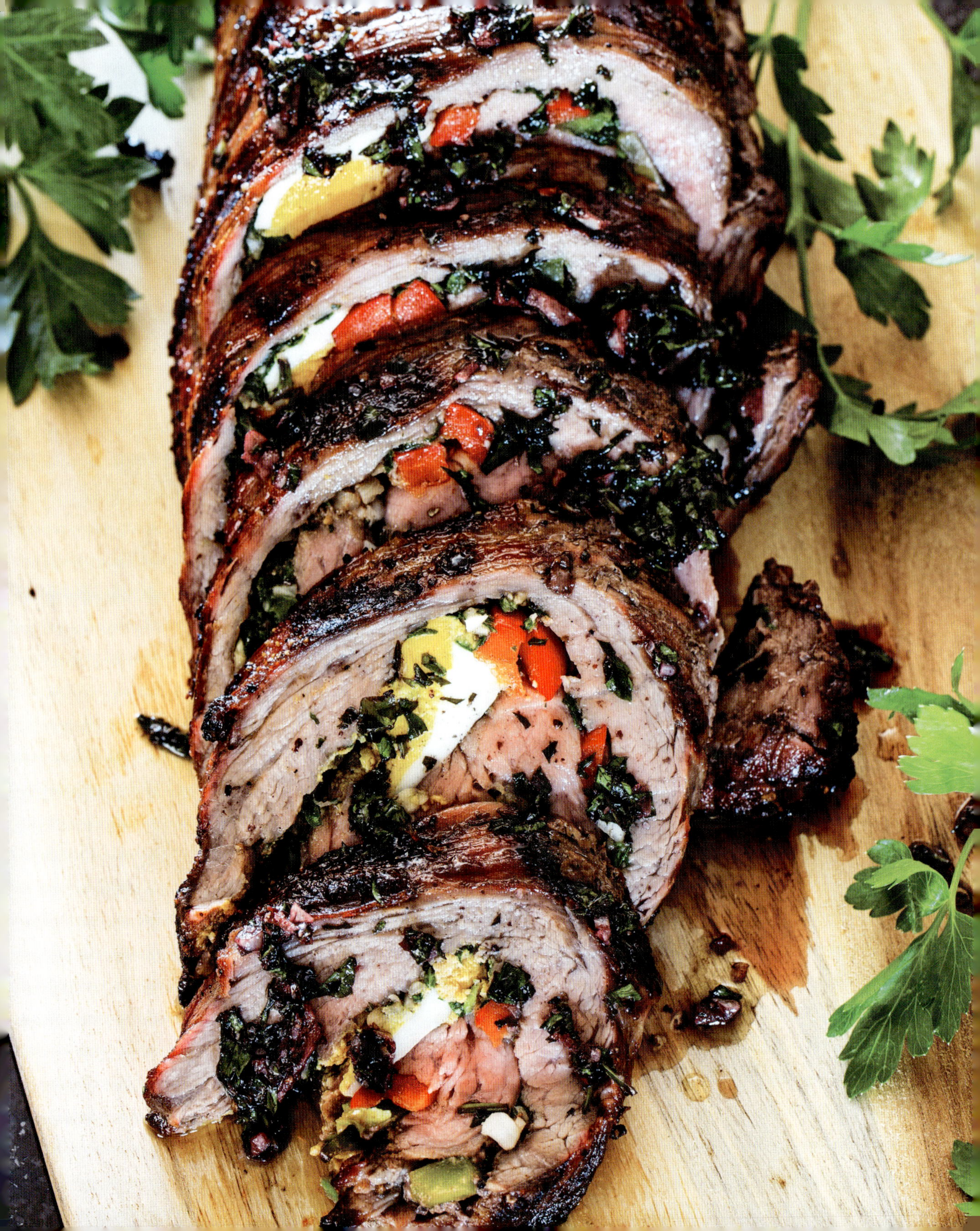

MATAMBRE (ARGENTINEAN STUFFED FLANK STEAK)

PREP TIME: 15 MINUTES
COOK TIME: 20 MINUTES
REST TIME: 15 MINUTES
TOTAL TIME: 50 MINUTES
SERVES: 4

1 (2-lb [896-g]) flank steak
¼ cup (60 ml) olive oil
5 cloves garlic, minced
¼ cup (12 g) chopped fresh cilantro
¼ cup (12 g) chopped fresh parsley
½ tsp salt, plus more as needed
½ tsp black pepper, plus more as needed
⅛ tsp red pepper flakes
2 large hard-boiled eggs, quartered
½ green bell pepper, sliced
½ red bell pepper, sliced

NUTRITION INFORMATION

Serving size: 1 serving; **Calories:** 484; **Carbohydrates:** 3 g; **Protein:** 52 g; **Fat:** 27 g

If you've never tried this Argentinean dish, you're in for a treat. It's basically a flank steak stuffed with hard-boiled eggs, bell peppers and a chimichurri-like paste, all rolled up and cooked to perfection. You can either grill this steak or cook it in the oven. When it's sliced prior to serving, you'll be amazed at how gorgeous the inside looks.

Prepare the grill for cooking over direct medium heat, or about 400°F (204°C).

Using a sharp knife, slice the steak and open it up like a book (see instructions in the Recipe Notes for how to butterfly a flank steak). If you want to make the meat thinner, you can pound it with a meat mallet to flatten and even out the thickness.

In a small bowl, mix together the oil, garlic, cilantro, parsley, salt, black pepper and red pepper flakes. Spread the cilantro and parsley mixture over the flank steak and brush it evenly over the entire surface of the steak.

Arrange the quartered eggs in 3 rows across the flank steak at different intervals. Repeat this process with the green bell pepper and red bell pepper. Carefully roll the meat over the filling left to right, across the grain, jelly-roll style. Tie the steak with butcher twine to hold it together. Season the outside of the roll generously with additional salt and black pepper.

Place the roll on the grill and grill it for 4 or 5 minutes per side, or about 20 minutes total. Let the roll rest for 15 minutes before slicing it.

RECIPE NOTES

To butterfly a flank steak, lay the steak flat on a cutting board. Use a sharp knife to cut into the steak from top to bottom, keeping the knife level with the cutting board. Keep your other hand flat on top of the knife to keep it secure. Fold the top half of the meat back and continue cutting the top half away from the bottom half, working slowly. Continue cutting until the steak opens up flat. Do not cut all the way through the steak. If your cut isn't even, don't worry. You can always pound it with a meat mallet to make it more even. In the end it really doesn't matter, because you'll be filling it and rolling it up.

If the inside of the matambre is not done to your liking and you prefer the meat more well done, place the roll in a baking dish and roast the meat in an oven preheated to 400°F (204°C) for 20 minutes. You can also put it back on the grill, cover it with aluminum foil so it doesn't burn and continue grilling it until it is done to your liking.

If you prefer to roast the matambre, preheat the oven to 350°F (177°C). Place the roll seam side down on a large baking sheet lined with aluminum foil. Bake the matambre for 1 hour. Remove it from the oven and let it rest for 10 minutes before slicing it.

GINGER BEEF

This is a very special recipe for me, because it originated in Calgary, Alberta! It's a dish made of crispy fried strips of beef tossed in a sweet and spicy sauce flavored with lots of ginger and garlic. It's delicious and quite addictive.

PREP TIME: 15 MINUTES
COOK TIME: 15 MINUTES
TOTAL TIME: 30 MINUTES
SERVES: 4

BATTER
1 cup (144 g) cornstarch
¼ cup (30 g) all-purpose flour
1 tsp white pepper
¾ cup (180 ml) water
1 large egg

BEEF
1 lb (448 g) flank steak, cut against the grain into ¼" (6-mm) strips
Vegetable oil, as needed

SAUCE
⅓ cup (80 ml) low-sodium soy sauce
¼ cup (60 ml) water
2 tbsp (30 ml) dark soy sauce
2 tbsp (30 ml) rice vinegar
⅓ cup (80 g) packed brown sugar
1 tsp red pepper flakes

STIR-FRY
1 tbsp (15 ml) sesame oil
5 cloves garlic, minced
1 tbsp (9 g) minced fresh ginger

1 tbsp (9 g) sesame seeds
2 green onions, thinly sliced

To make the batter, whisk together the cornstarch, flour and white pepper in a large bowl. Add the water and egg and whisk until the batter is smooth.

To make the beef, toss the beef strips with the batter until they are fully coated.

Fill a large pot with 2 to 3 inches (6 to 9 cm) of the oil. Heat the oil to 350°F (177°C).

Working in batches, add the beef strips to the oil. Use a fork to stir and break them apart as they cook. Fry the beef strips for 3 to 4 minutes, or until they are golden brown. Remove the beef strips with a slotted spoon and let them drain on a plate lined with paper towels.

To make the sauce, whisk together the low-sodium soy sauce, water, dark soy sauce, vinegar, brown sugar and red pepper flakes in a medium bowl. Set the sauce aside.

To make the stir-fry, heat the sesame oil in a large skillet over medium-high heat. Add the garlic and ginger and cook them for 1 minute, or until they are fragrant. Add the sauce to the skillet and cook it, stirring it constantly, for 1 to 2 minutes, until it has slightly thickened.

Add the fried beef strips to the skillet and toss to coat them in the sauce. Cook the beef and sauce for 1 to 2 minutes, until the sauce is thick and fully coats each beef strip. Garnish the beef with the sesame seeds and green onions.

RECIPE NOTES

Transfer any leftovers to an airtight container and store them in the fridge for 3 to 4 days. You can reheat them in the microwave, or in a skillet over medium heat. If you are using a skillet, add a splash of beef broth or water to keep the sauce from drying out too much as the leftovers reheat.

You can freeze leftovers if you'd like. They'll last in the freezer for 2 to 3 months. You can reheat frozen leftovers in the microwave or in a skillet. If you choose to reheat them in a skillet, let the ginger beef thaw overnight in the fridge.

NUTRITION INFORMATION

Serving size: 1 serving; **Calories:** 582; **Carbohydrates:** 59 g; **Protein:** 30 g; **Fat:** 25 g

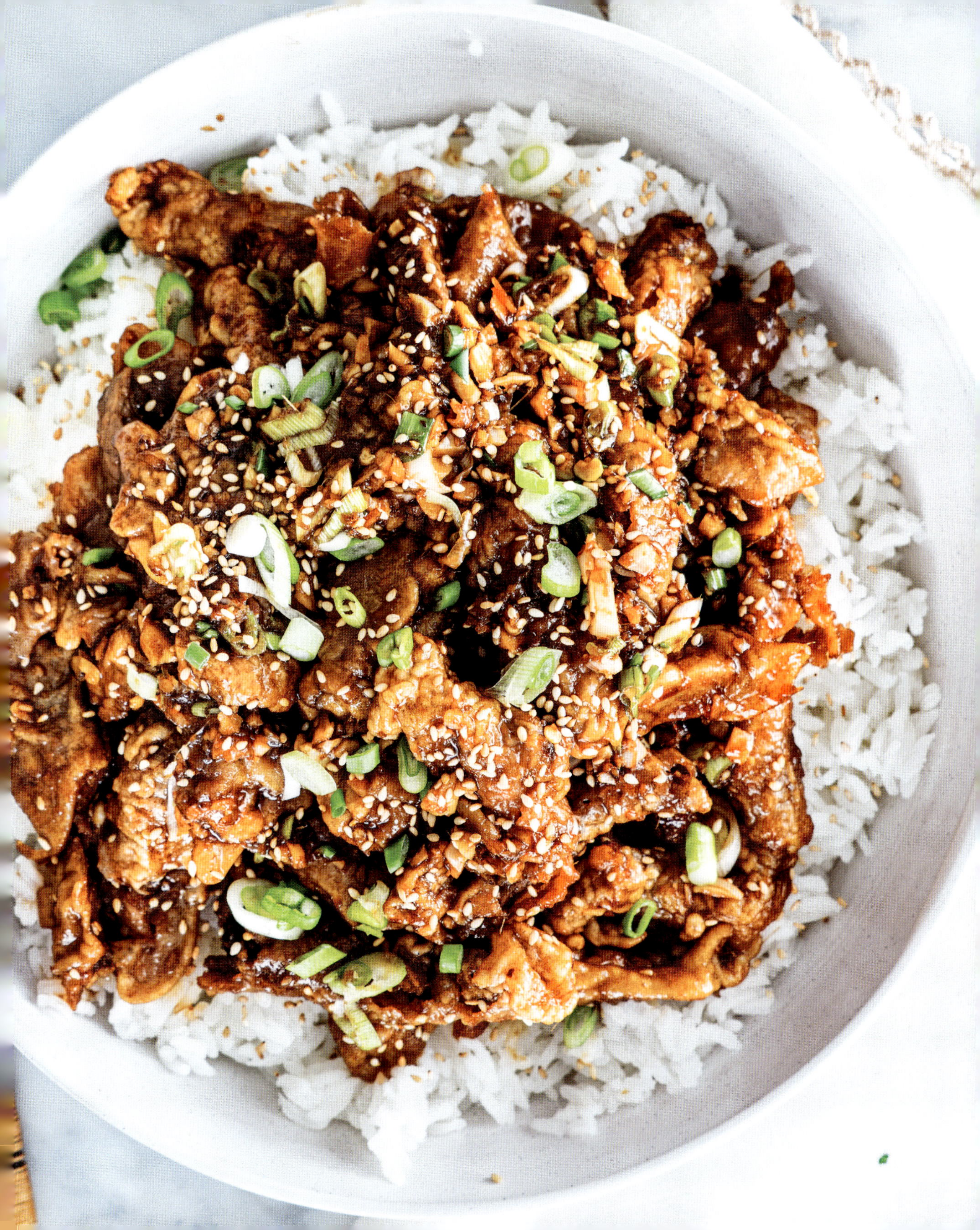

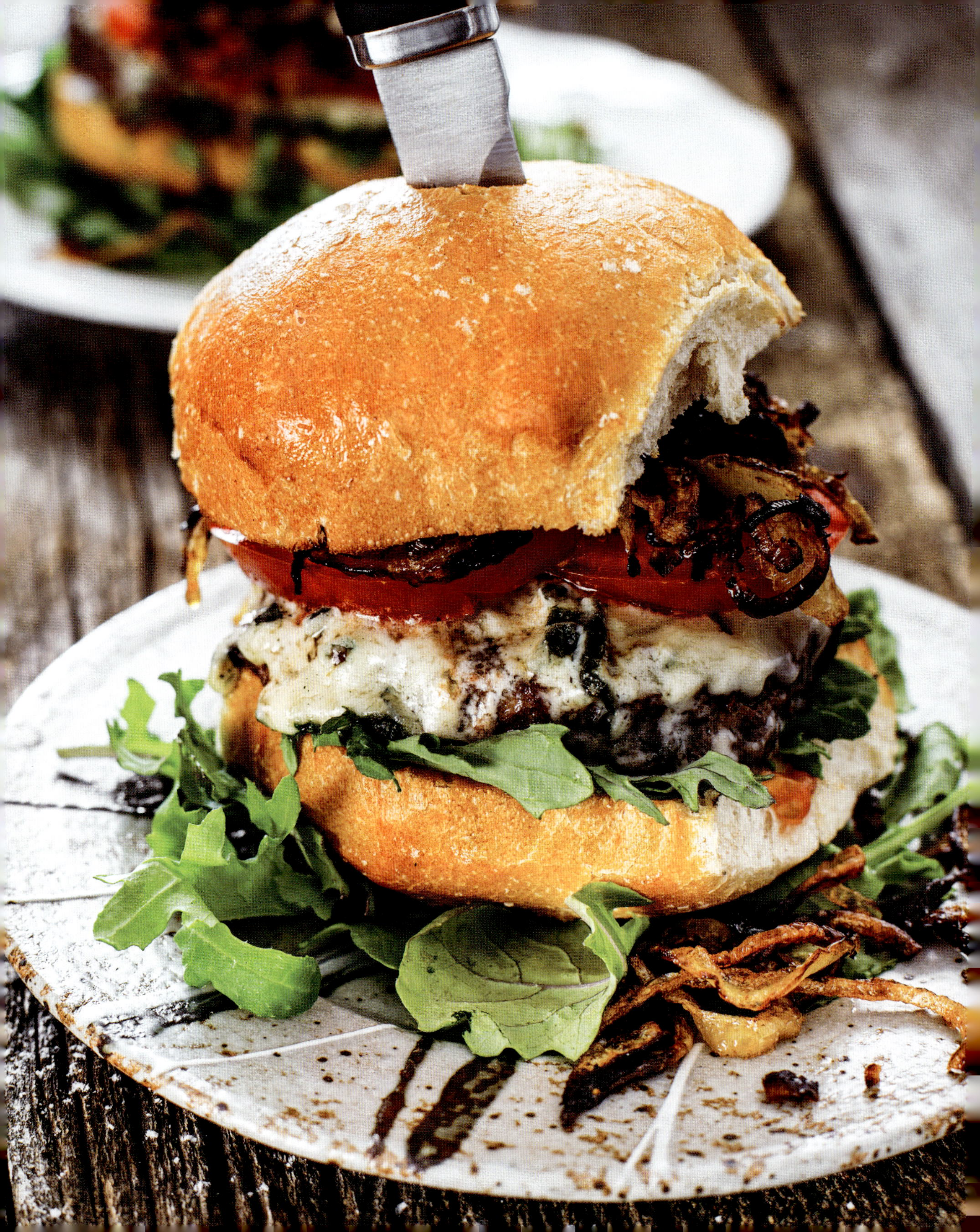

BLUE CHEESE BURGERS WITH CRISPY FRIED ONIONS

PREP TIME: 5 MINUTES
COOK TIME: 15 MINUTES
TOTAL TIME: 20 MINUTES
SERVES: 4

2 tbsp (30 g) butter
2 onions, sliced
1 tsp salt, divided
1 tsp black pepper, divided
4 burger patties
4 slices blue cheese
4 burger buns
4 tbsp (60 g) sweet and spicy mustard
Baby arugula or baby kale
2 tomatoes, sliced

Talk about a mouthful! These are my favorite burgers in the world. They are topped with tangy, creamy, melty blue cheese and crispy onions fried in butter. I'll tell you a little secret: The first time I made these burgers, I wanted caramelized onions, but I forgot about the onions as they cooked and they turned crispy, so I changed the recipe. The recipe is much better with crispy fried onions, in my opinion!

Preheat the grill for cooking over direct high heat.

Melt the butter in a large skillet over medium-high heat. Add the onions and season them with ½ teaspoon of the salt and ½ teaspoon of the black pepper. Cook the onions for 3 to 5 minutes, until they are crispy.

Make sure the grill is cleaned, oiled (if necessary) and hot before cooking the patties.

Season the burger patties with the remaining ½ teaspoon of salt and ½ teaspoon of black pepper. Add the patties to the grill and cook them for about 5 minutes per side. *Do not* press on the patties while they cook.

Lay 1 slice of blue cheese over each patty for the last 2 minutes of cooking. If you want to grill the burger buns, add them to the grill and toast them for no more than 30 seconds.

Remove everything from the grill and assemble the burgers. Spread 1 tablespoon (15 g) of the mustard on the bottom burger bun. Top the mustard with some of the baby arugula. Then add the burger patty, tomato slices, crispy onions and top bun.

RECIPE NOTES

Leftovers are best stored separately. Leave the burger assembly for when you're ready to enjoy your burgers. The arugula, tomatoes and buns are best fresh. The patties will keep in an airtight container in the refrigerator for 3 to 4 days.

To reheat the patties, you can microwave them in 30-second intervals until they're heated through. You can also place them in a skillet, covered, over medium heat until they're warm.

You can enjoy the onions cold on your burger. If you prefer them hot, you can reheat them in the microwave or in a skillet. If you microwave them, I suggest lining your plate with paper towels. This will keep the onions as crispy as possible.

NUTRITION INFORMATION

Serving size: 1 burger; **Calories:** 551; **Carbohydrates:** 32 g; **Protein:** 29 g; **Fat:** 34 g

ITALIAN STUFFED PEPPERS

Stuffed peppers are what my food dreams are made of—they are a dish I grew up with, so these peppers are my idea of comfort food. These peppers are filled with classic Italian ingredients and are quick to prepare: just pop them in the oven and forget about them until they're ready to devour!

PREP TIME: 15 MINUTES
COOK TIME: 2 HOURS, 30 MINUTES
TOTAL TIME: 2 HOURS, 45 MINUTES
SERVES: 12

12 bell peppers (any colors)
1 lb (448 g) ground beef
1 onion or 3 medium shallots, chopped or shredded
1 carrot, shredded
3 cloves garlic, minced
1 tbsp (3 g) Italian seasoning
1 cup (210 g) cooked rice
2 tbsp (30 g) tomato paste
1 tsp salt, or as needed
1 tsp black pepper, or as needed
2 cups (480 ml) low-sodium chicken or beef broth
1 cup (240 ml) tomato sauce
1 tbsp (3 g) chopped fresh parsley, for garnish (optional)

Set a rack in the middle of the oven. Preheat the oven to 375°F (191°C).

Cut the tops off of the bell peppers. Remove and discard any seeds and membranes from the insides of the peppers. To keep the peppers from falling over while they are cooking, cut a small, even piece from the bottom of each pepper to create a flatter bottom.

In a large bowl, combine the beef, onion, carrot, garlic, Italian seasoning, rice, tomato paste, salt and black pepper. Mix the ingredients well. Stuff each pepper full with the beef mixture. Arrange the peppers standing up in a large pot, such as an oval 5-quart (4.8-L) Dutch oven.

In a medium bowl, mix together the broth and tomato sauce. Pour this mixture over the peppers. The liquid needs to come about halfway up the peppers—if needed, add some water to the pot.

Cover the pot with its lid or aluminum foil. Bake the stuffed peppers for 1½ hours. Remove the lid or foil and bake the peppers for 45 to 60 minutes, until the peppers and meat are fork-tender and the rice is fully cooked.

Garnish the stuffed peppers with the parsley (if using) and serve.

RECIPE NOTES

These stuffed peppers will keep in an airtight container in the fridge for 3 to 5 days.

Be sure the meat is cooked all the way through and the bell peppers are entirely cool before placing them in the freezer. Put the peppers in a freezer-safe container or wrap them individually with plastic wrap before placing them in a freezer bag. They will keep for 6 to 8 months in the freezer. Allow the peppers to thaw completely in the fridge before reheating them in the oven at 350°F (177°C).

NUTRITION INFORMATION

Serving size: 1 pepper; **Calories:** 169; **Carbohydrates:** 22 g; **Protein:** 11 g; **Fat:** 4 g

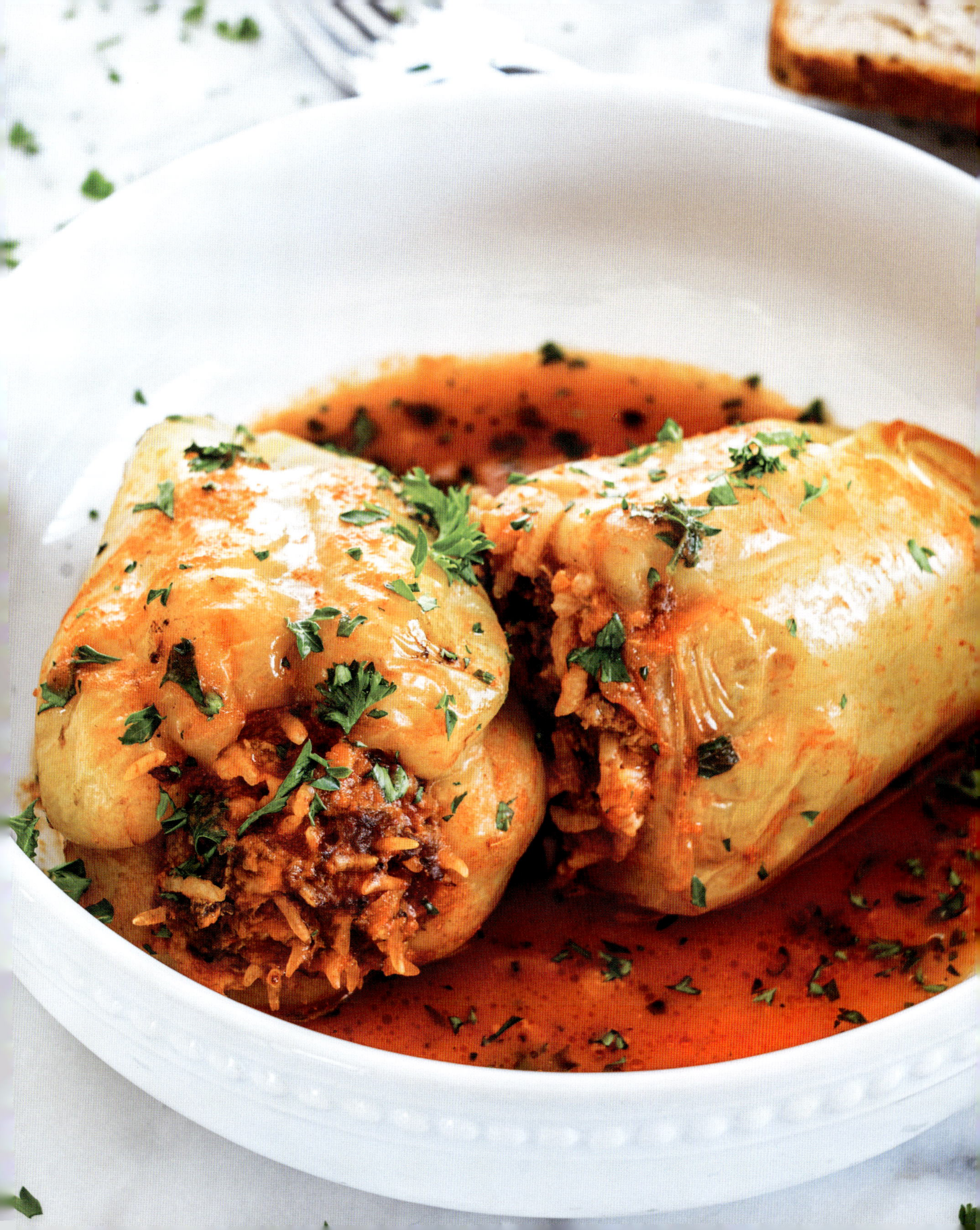

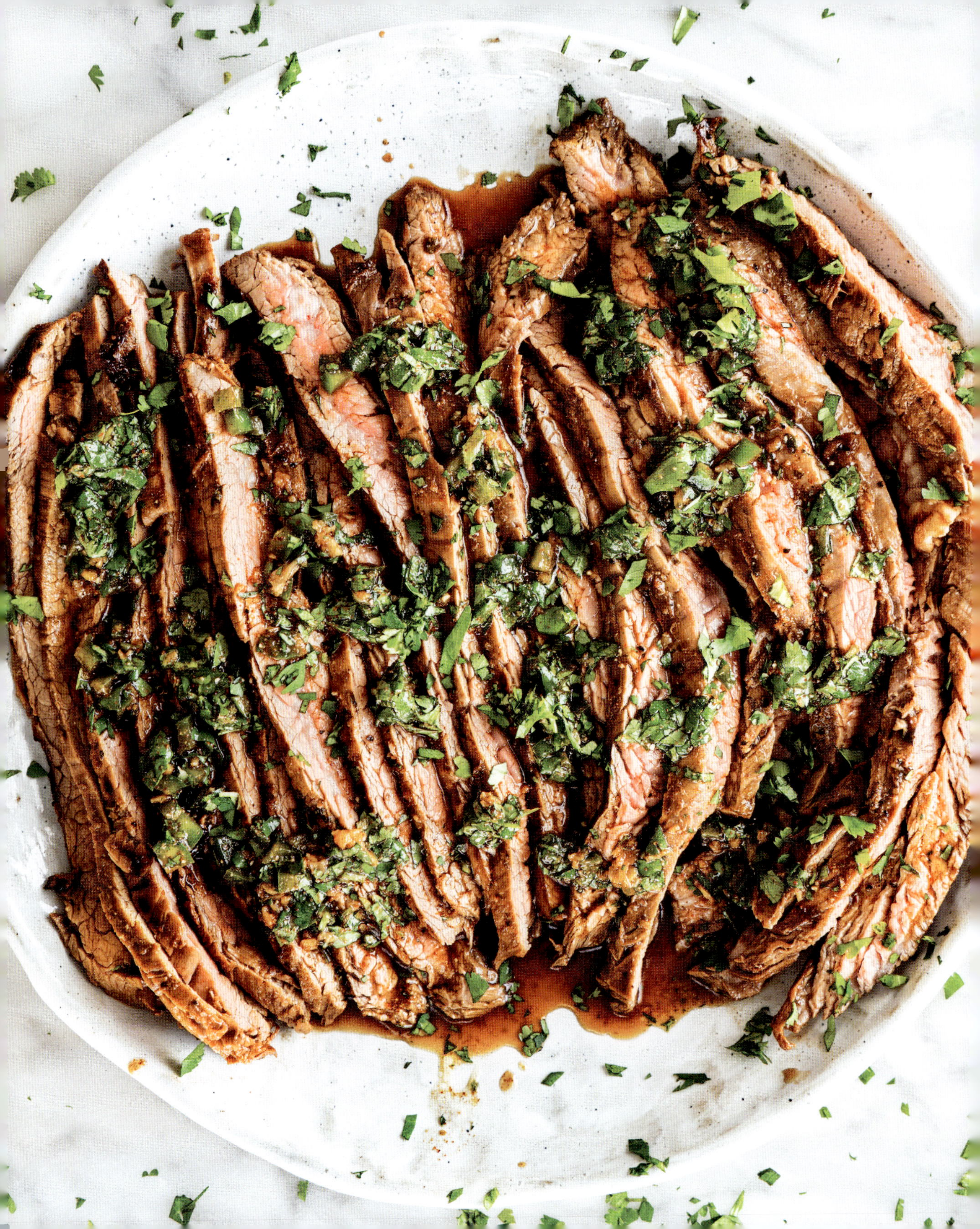

CARNE ASADA

Here is another flank steak recipe, but this time the steak is marinated with flavorful and fresh ingredients then grilled to perfection. This carne asada is perfect for tacos, served with your favorite toppings.

PREP TIME: 15 MINUTES
MARINATING TIME: 2 HOURS
COOK TIME: 15 MINUTES
REST TIME: 5 MINUTES
TOTAL: 2 HOURS, 35 MINUTES
SERVES: 10

3 tbsp (45 ml) olive oil
¼ cup (60 ml) fresh lime juice
½ cup (120 ml) fresh orange juice
¼ cup (60 ml) low-sodium soy sauce
3 cloves garlic, minced
1 jalapeño, minced
1 tsp ground cumin
1 tsp chili powder
½ cup (24 g) chopped fresh cilantro
½ tsp salt, or as needed
½ tsp black pepper, or as needed
1 (2-lb [896-g]) flank steak

In a large ziplock bag, combine the oil, lime juice, orange juice, soy sauce, garlic, jalapeño, cumin, chili powder, cilantro, salt and black pepper. Reserve ¼ cup (60 ml) of the marinade in a small bowl and set it aside in the fridge. Add the flank steak to the bag, close the bag and shake it a bit, making sure the steak is covered in the marinade. Place the bag in the fridge and let the steak marinate for at least 2 hours or up to 4 hours.

Preheat the grill to about 400°F (204°C).

Grill the steak for 5 to 7 minutes per side, or until it is done to your liking. Transfer it to a plate and cover it with aluminum foil. Let the steak rest for about 5 minutes before slicing it into thin strips against the grain. If you slice it right away, all the juices will be released and the steak will be dry.

Serve the carne asada immediately with the reserved marinade.

RECIPE NOTES

Store the cooked carne asada in airtight containers in the refrigerator for up to 3 days. The reserved marinade will last about 1 week.

You can freeze the marinated steak in an airtight container or in freezer bags for 3 to 4 months, but keep in mind that you don't want to refreeze beef after it's thawed, so plan ahead. Allow the beef to thaw at room temperature before carrying on with the recipe.

NUTRITION INFORMATION

Serving size: 1 serving; **Calories:** 175; **Carbohydrates:** 3 g; **Protein:** 20 g; **Fat:** 9 g

BEEF TENDERLOIN

This roasted, melt-in-your-mouth beef tenderloin is a classic celebratory dish! Make that special occasion even more memorable with beautifully cooked medium-rare beef from edge to center with a perfectly browned and flavorful crust!

PREP TIME: 10 MINUTES
COOK TIME: 30 MINUTES
REST TIME: 10 MINUTES
TOTAL: 50 MINUTES
SERVES: 6

BEEF
- 1 (3-lb [1.3-kg]) beef tenderloin
- 1 tsp salt
- 1 tsp black pepper
- 1 tbsp (15 ml) olive oil
- 3 tbsp (45 g) unsalted butter, melted
- 2 tbsp (30 ml) balsamic vinegar
- 1 tsp Dijon mustard
- 4 cloves garlic, minced
- 3 sprigs fresh thyme

YOGURT SAUCE
- ½ cup (143 g) plain Greek yogurt
- ¼ cup (30 g) sour cream
- 2 tbsp (30 ml) fresh lemon juice
- 2 tsp (10 g) horseradish
- ¼ tsp salt, or as needed

To make the beef, trim the silver skin from the tenderloin if needed. Season the beef with the salt and black pepper.

Preheat the oven to 450°F (232°C).

Heat the oil in a large oven-safe skillet over medium-high heat. Add the tenderloin and sear it for 2 minutes per side, until it is browned.

In a small bowl, combine the butter, vinegar, mustard, garlic and thyme. Brush this sauce over the tenderloin, ensuring that all sides are evenly covered in the sauce.

Transfer the skillet to the oven. Roast the tenderloin for about 25 minutes for medium-rare, or until a meat thermometer inserted into the thickest part of the tenderloin reads 130°F (54°C).

In the meantime, make the yogurt sauce. In a small bowl, mix together the yogurt, sour cream, lemon juice, horseradish and salt. Chill the sauce until you are ready to serve the tenderloin.

Place the tenderloin on a cutting board and cover it with aluminum foil. Let the tenderloin rest for about 10 minutes, then slice it and serve it with the yogurt sauce.

RECIPE NOTES

A thermometer is the only way to guarantee a perfectly cooked beef tenderloin. Use the following temperatures to gauge the meat's doneness.

Rare: 120 to 125°F (49 to 52°C)

Medium-rare: 130 to 135°F (54 to 57°C)

Medium: 140 to 145°F (60 to 63°C)

Well done: 150°F (66°C)

Beef tenderloin will last in the fridge for 3 to 4 days when stored properly in an airtight container.

To extend its shelf life, I recommend freezing the tenderloin for up to 3 months. Be sure to thaw it in the fridge overnight before warming it in the oven at 325°F (163°C).

NUTRITION INFORMATION
Serving size: 1 serving; **Calories:** 732; **Carbohydrates:** 3 g; **Protein:** 43 g; **Fat:** 60 g

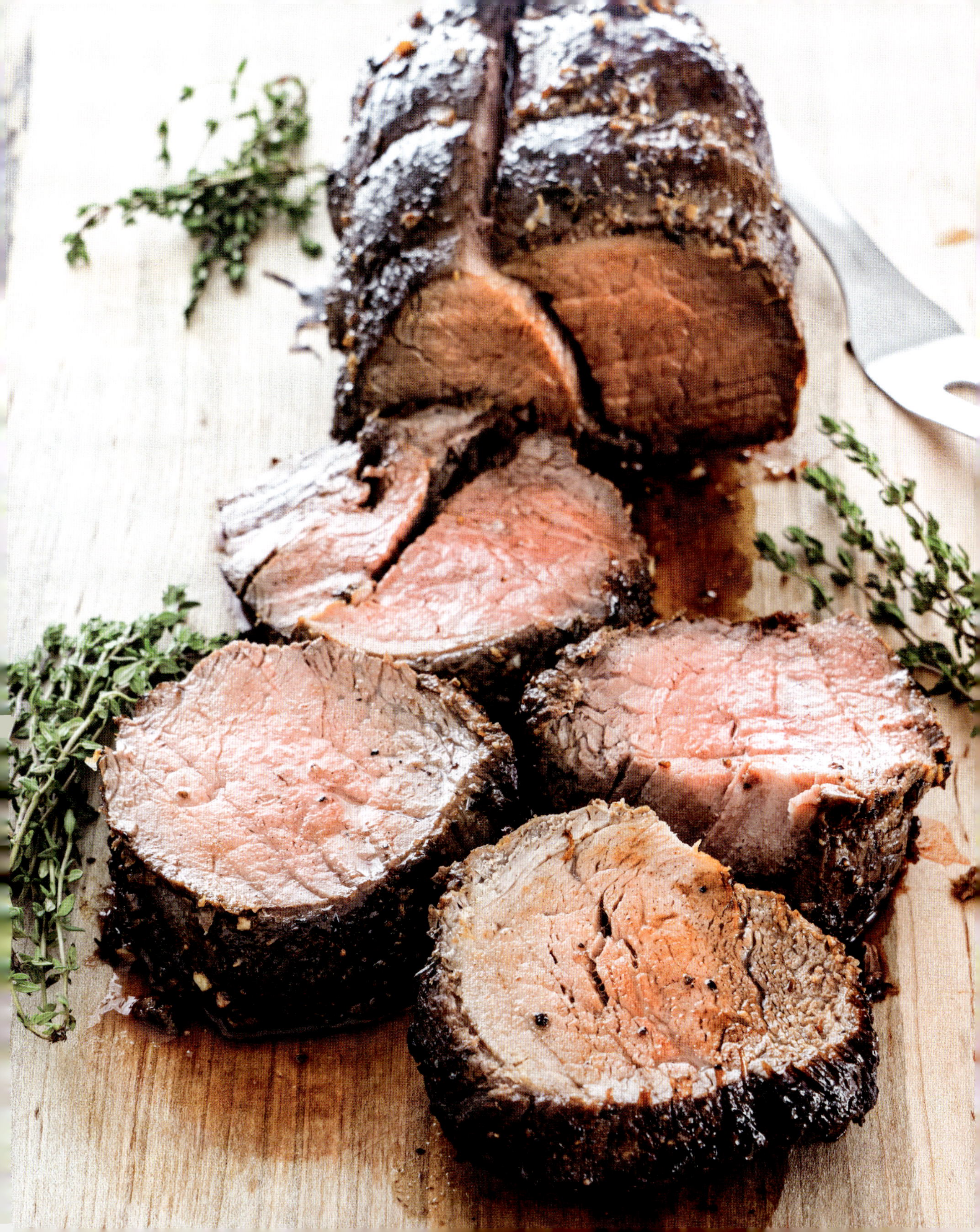

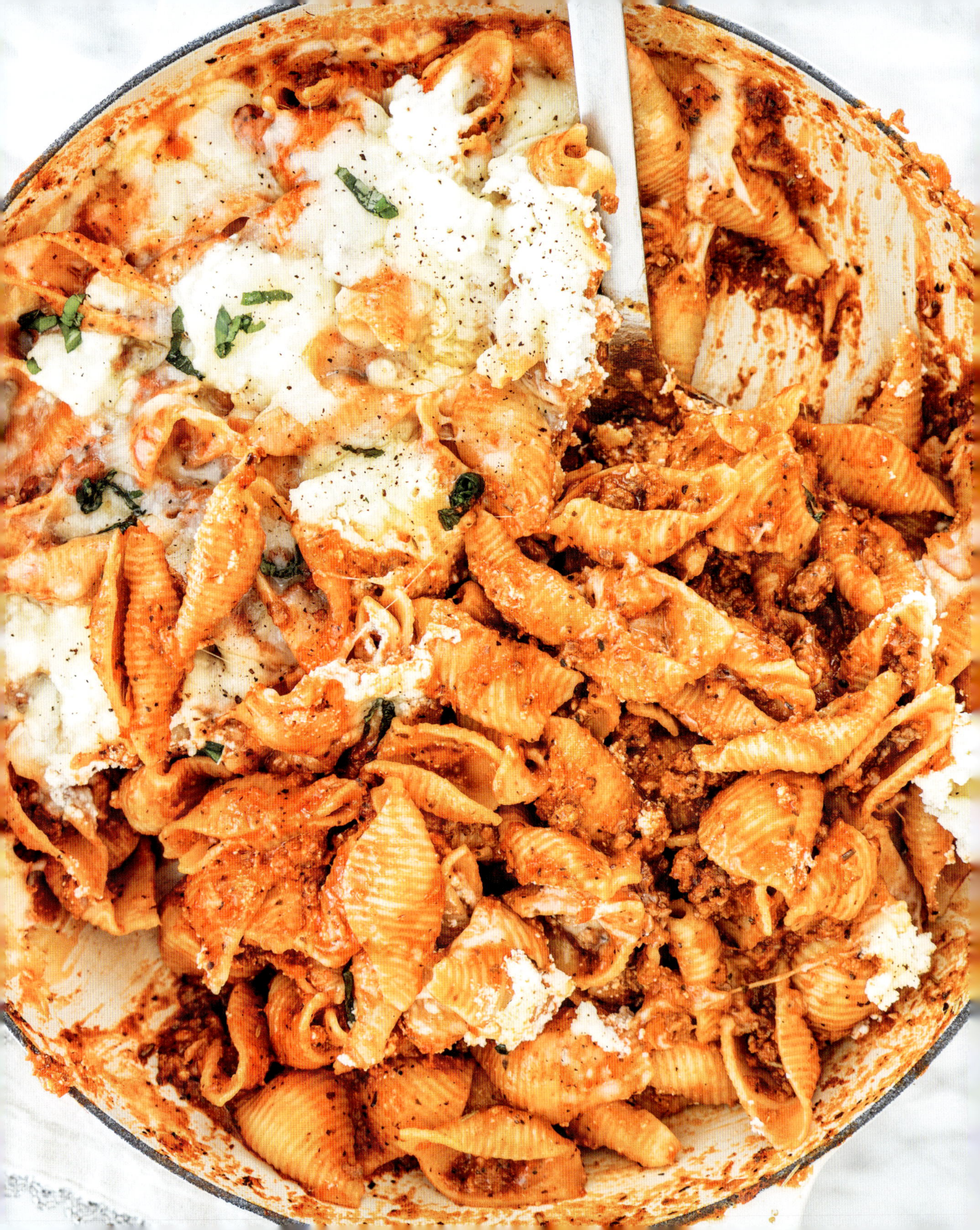

SKILLET LASAGNA

We're back to my roots with this dish. This skillet lasagna is cooked in one pot and in only 30 minutes! This recipe is a favorite of mine and a dish that I could eat daily and never tire of. Lasagna really is the epitome of Italian comfort food, and with this recipe you get all that comfort with minimal effort.

PREP TIME: 5 MINUTES
COOK TIME: 30 MINUTES
TOTAL TIME: 35 MINUTES
SERVES: 8

- 1 lb (448 g) extra lean ground beef
- 5 cloves garlic, minced
- ¼ tsp salt, or as needed
- ½ tsp black pepper, or as needed
- 2 tsp (2 g) dried oregano
- 1 tsp dried basil
- 1 tsp dried rosemary
- 1 (28-oz [784-g]) can crushed tomatoes
- 4 cups (960 ml) water
- 1 lb (448 g) pasta (I recommend shells)
- ½ cup (62 g) ricotta cheese
- 4 oz (112 g) grated Parmesan cheese
- 1 cup (112 g) shredded mozzarella cheese
- 1 tbsp (3 g) chopped fresh basil

Preheat the oven to 450°F (232°C).

In a large oven-safe skillet over medium heat, cook the beef for 5 to 7 minutes, until it is no longer pink. Drain the meat if needed. Add the garlic, salt, black pepper, oregano, basil and rosemary. Stir to combine the ingredients and cook the mixture for 30 seconds.

Add the tomatoes, water and pasta. Make sure there is enough water to fully submerge the pasta. Cook the mixture for 10 to 12 minutes, stirring it occasionally, until the pasta is al dente.

Remove the skillet from the heat. Dollop the ricotta cheese over the top of the lasagna, then top it with the Parmesan cheese and mozzarella cheese. Transfer the skillet to the oven and bake the lasagna for 5 to 10 minutes, until the cheeses have melted and are slightly golden.

Garnish the lasagna with the fresh basil.

RECIPE NOTES

Let any leftover lasagna cool completely, then cover the skillet with aluminum foil or plastic wrap. Store the lasagna in the refrigerator for 3 to 5 days.

NUTRITION INFORMATION

Serving size: 1 serving; **Calories:** 470; **Carbohydrates:** 51 g; **Protein:** 30 g; **Fat:** 15 g

PORK

I LOVE USING PORK IN MANY OF MY RECIPES because not only is pork relatively healthy, but it's inexpensive and quite versatile. There really is no end to what you can do with pork. You can fry it, braise it, roast it, stir-fry it, make sausages from it—the possibilities are endless.

The recipes I included in this chapter are specifically for the everyday home cook. They're not complicated to make at all, yet the results are always impressive enough for dinner parties or special occasions—while still being great options for regular weeknight dinners.

My goal is to teach you how to make simple, basic recipes that are loaded with tons of flavor, like my Perfect Pork Tenderloin (page 87) or Honey-Garlic Pork Loin (page 96). I'll also show you how to make perfect pork chops, such as Mustard-Balsamic Pork Chops (page 92), which are a favorite on the blog. Finally, I want to share with you a recipe that is a favorite in my household: Pork Schnitzel (page 104). It's a simple recipe to make with just a few ingredients. So let's celebrate the pig, because pork is extremely versatile and delicious!

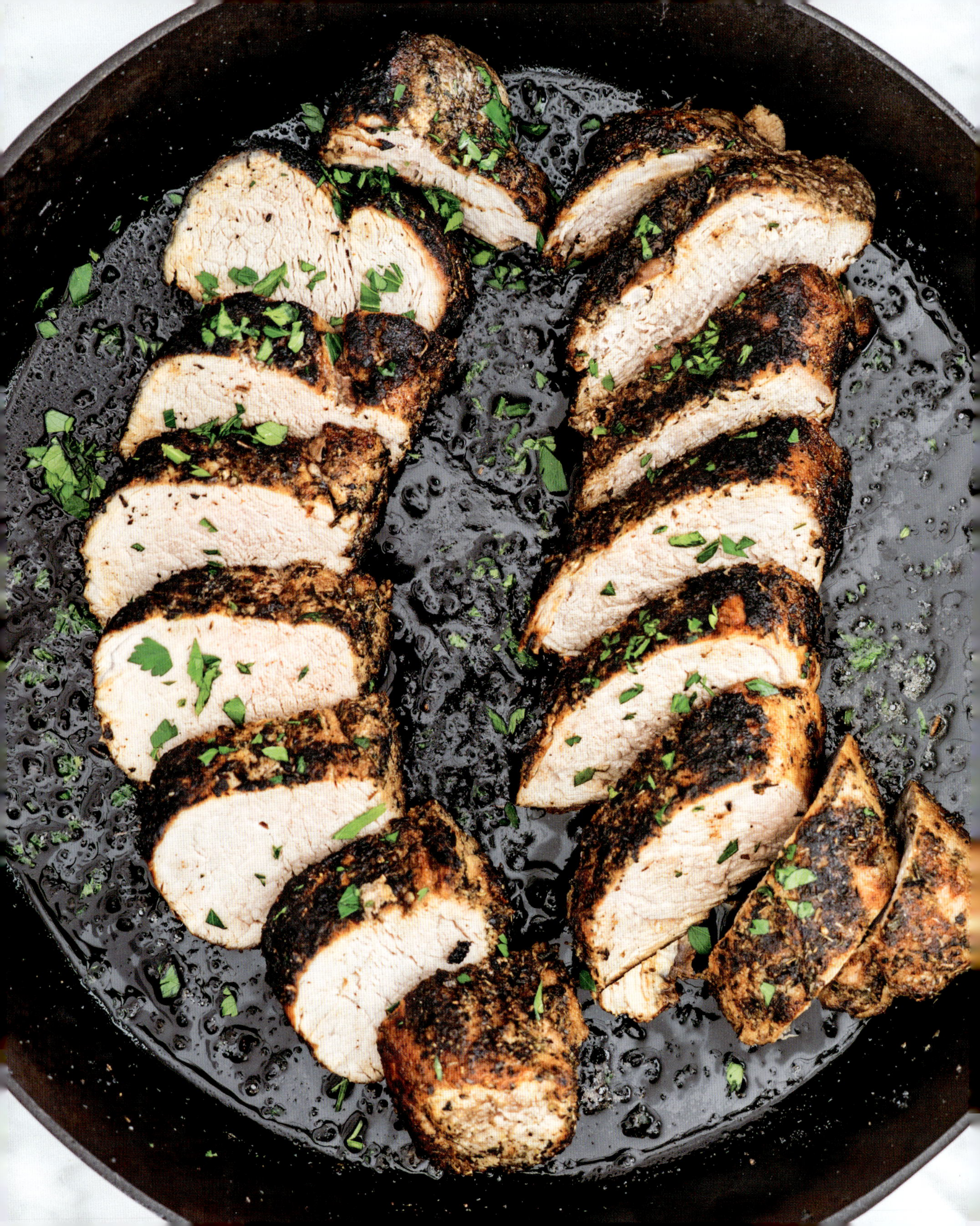

PERFECT PORK TENDERLOIN

I used to dislike pork tenderloin because my mom cooked it for a really long time—it was always dry and chewy. I took it upon myself to learn to make perfectly cooked pork tenderloin that is juicy, flavorful and utterly delicious. In just about 40 minutes, you can have this incredible dish on your dinner table.

PREP TIME: 5 MINUTES
COOK TIME: 25 MINUTES
REST TIME: 10 MINUTES
TOTAL TIME: 40 MINUTES
SERVES: 6

½ tsp salt, or as needed
½ tsp black pepper, or as needed
1 tbsp (3 g) Italian seasoning
1 tsp garlic powder
1 tsp onion powder
2 (1-lb [448-g]) pork tenderloins
1 tbsp (15 ml) olive oil
1 tbsp (15 g) unsalted butter
2 tbsp (6 g) chopped fresh parsley (optional)

Preheat the oven to 400°F (204°C). Place the rack in the middle of the oven.

In a small bowl, combine the salt, black pepper, Italian seasoning, garlic powder and onion powder.

Sprinkle the seasoning over the pork tenderloins and use your hands to rub the spices over the entire surface of the tenderloins, until they are evenly coated.

Heat the oil and butter in a large oven-safe skillet over medium-high heat. Once the oil is hot, add the tenderloins and brown them on all sides, about 6 minutes total.

Transfer the skillet to the oven and bake the tenderloins, uncovered, for 13 to 15 minutes. Halfway through the cooking time, flip the tenderloins over. Bake the tenderloins until the centers register at least 150°F (66°C) on a meat thermometer.

Transfer the tenderloins to a cutting board, cover them with aluminum foil and let them rest for at least 10 minutes before slicing them.

Garnish the tenderloins with the parsley (if using) and serve them.

RECIPE NOTES

Cooked pork tenderloin will keep in an airtight container in the fridge for 3 to 4 days. Be sure to freeze your pork within 2 hours of cooking to limit bacteria growth—it'll last for up to 3 months in the freezer.

NUTRITION INFORMATION

Serving size: 1 serving; **Calories:** 225; **Carbohydrates:** 1 g; **Protein:** 31 g; **Fat:** 10 g

BAKED HONEY-GLAZED PORK RIBS

This easy recipe for pork ribs results in the most incredible pork ribs ever. Finger-licking, smack-your-lips delicious! With this recipe, you can enjoy a barbecue favorite any time of the year! These ribs will give you sticky, sweet, savory, caramelized, smoky goodness in every bite.

PREP TIME: 15 MINUTES
COOK TIME: 1 HOUR, 30 MINUTES
REST TIME: 10 MINUTES
TOTAL TIME: 1 HOUR, 55 MINUTES
SERVES: 6

2 (1½- to 2-lb [672- to 896-g]) racks pork ribs
2 tbsp (30 ml) honey
2 tsp (10 g) brown sugar
⅓ cup (80 ml) olive oil
2 tbsp (30 ml) fresh lemon juice
2 tsp (10 g) salt
1 tsp black pepper
4 cloves garlic, crushed
2 tsp (6 g) paprika
2 tbsp (6 g) dried oregano
1 tbsp (15 g) yellow mustard
2 tsp (10 ml) Sriracha sauce
1 tsp liquid smoke

Remove the silver skin from the bottom side of the ribs: Flip each rib rack over, so that you are looking at the meatless bottom side. Go to one end of the rib rack and slide a knife under the silver skin and pull. It should peel right off in one swipe. Set the ribs aside.

Preheat the oven to 375°F (191°C). Fill a large roasting pan with ½ inch (13 mm) of water. Fit the roasting pan with a roasting rack.

In a large bowl, mix together the honey, brown sugar, oil, lemon juice, salt, black pepper, garlic, paprika, oregano, mustard, Sriracha sauce and liquid smoke. Set the glaze aside.

Place the ribs on the roasting rack, and then thoroughly brush the glaze all over the pork ribs on both sides. If there is any of the glaze left over, pour it over the ribs.

Bake the ribs for 1½ hours. Every 20 minutes, baste the ribs with the drippings from the pan. If the ribs start to brown too much, cover them with foil.

Let the ribs rest for 5 to 10 minutes before serving them.

RECIPE NOTES

Transfer any leftovers to an airtight container or large freezer bag. You may have to cut the ribs so that they'll fit. The ribs will last for 3 to 4 days in the fridge.

To freeze the ribs, transfer the completely cooled ribs to an airtight container or sealable freezer bag. They will last in the freezer for 2 to 3 months.

NUTRITION INFORMATION

Serving size: 1 serving; **Calories:** 629; **Carbohydrates:** 10 g; **Protein:** 28 g; **Fat:** 53 g

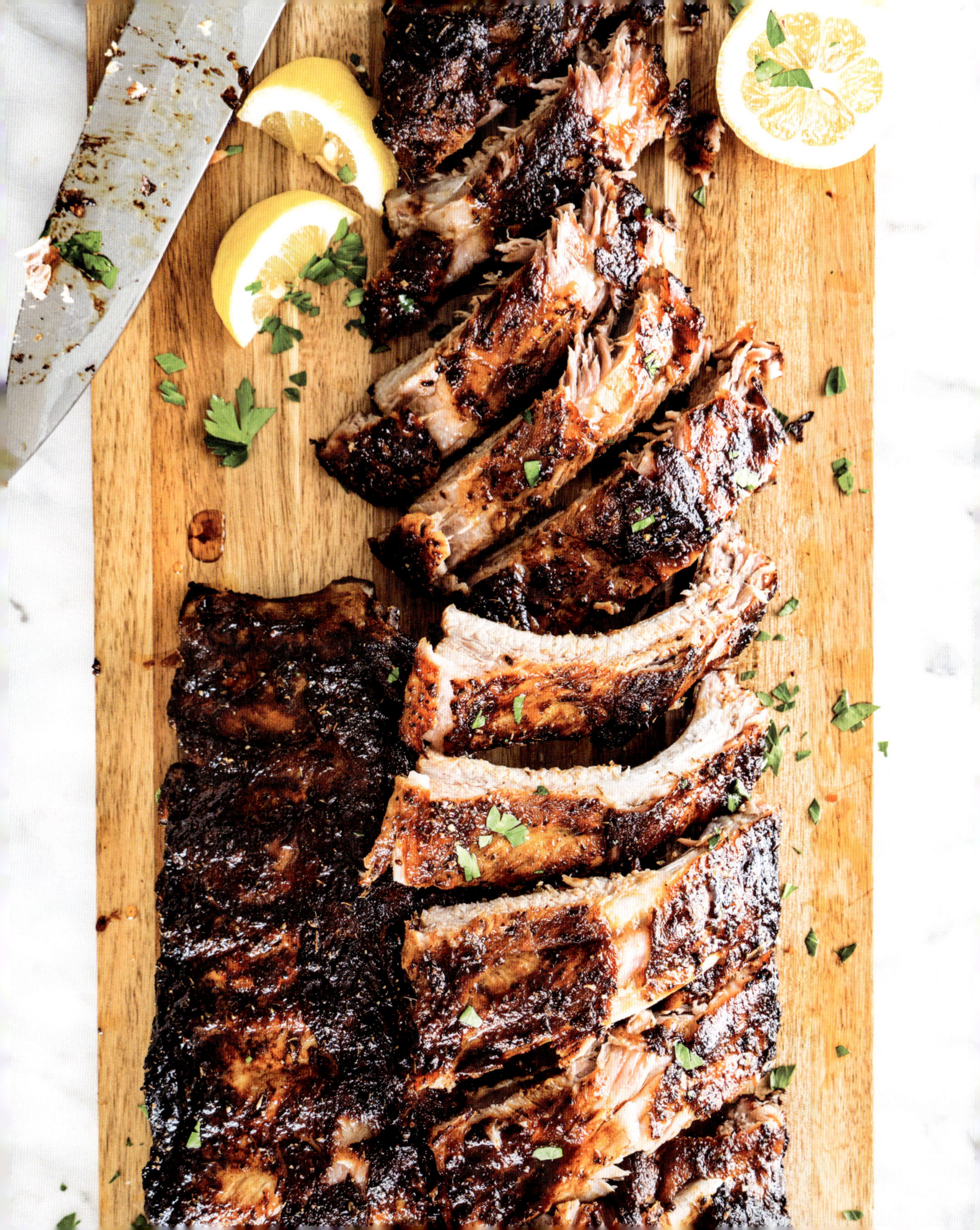

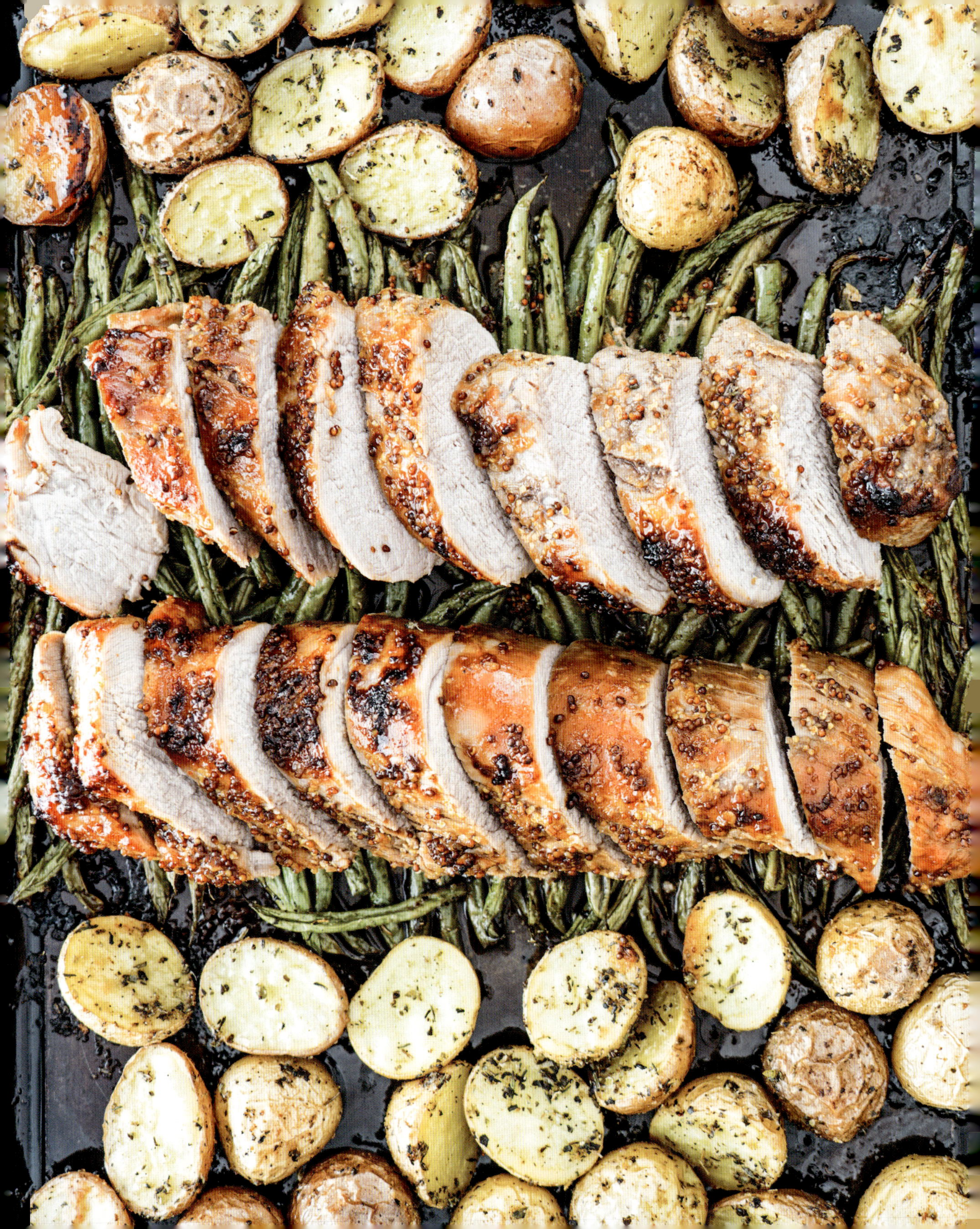

HONEY MUSTARD PORK TENDERLOIN

This honey mustard pork tenderloin is baked to perfection with green beans and potatoes, and it's ready in less than an hour. This recipe is a must for your busy weeknights!

PREP TIME: 10 MINUTES
COOK TIME: 30 MINUTES
REST TIME: 15 MINUTES
TOTAL TIME: 55 MINUTES
SERVES: 6

SAUCE

2 tbsp (30 g) grainy mustard
2 tbsp (30 g) honey
2 tbsp (30 ml) soy sauce
3 cloves garlic, minced
1 tbsp (15 ml) Sriracha sauce or hot sauce of choice

PORK

2 (1-lb [448-g]) pork tenderloins (see Recipe Notes)
2 lb (896 g) baby potatoes
1 lb (448 g) fresh green beans
3 tbsp (45 ml) olive oil, divided
½ tsp garlic powder, divided
1 tbsp (3 g) Italian seasoning, divided
½ tsp salt, divided
¼ tsp black pepper, divided

NUTRITION INFORMATION

Serving size: 1 serving; **Calories:** 413; **Carbohydrates:** 38 g; **Protein:** 36 g; **Fat:** 12 g

To make the sauce, combine the mustard, honey, soy sauce, garlic and Sriracha sauce in a small bowl. Set the sauce aside.

To make the pork, preheat the oven to 450°F (232°C).

Wash the pork tenderloins and pat them dry with paper towels. Brush or spoon the sauce over the pork tenderloins and set them aside.

Place the potatoes in a large bowl. Place the green beans in another large bowl.

Season the potatoes with 1½ tablespoons (23 ml) of the oil, ¼ teaspoon of the garlic powder, ½ tablespoon (2 g) of the Italian seasoning, ¼ teaspoon of the salt and ⅛ teaspoon of the black pepper. Toss the potatoes to coat them evenly.

Season the green beans with the remaining 1½ tablespoons (22 ml) of oil, ¼ teaspoon of garlic powder, ½ tablespoon (1 g) of Italian seasoning, ¼ teaspoon of salt and ⅛ teaspoon of black pepper. Toss the green beans to coat them evenly.

Arrange the green beans down the middle of a large baking sheet. Arrange the potatoes along the sides of the baking sheet. Lay the pork tenderloins on top of the green beans. Brush or spoon more sauce over the pork.

Bake the pork and vegetables for 25 to 30 minutes, making sure to brush or spoon more sauce over the pork halfway through the cooking time, until the thickest part of the pork registers 145°F (63°C) on an instant-read thermometer.

Cover the pork with foil and allow it to rest for 15 minutes before serving.

RECIPE NOTES

One pork tenderloin usually feeds 3 people and usually weighs about 1 pound (448 g).

This honey mustard pork will keep in an airtight container in the fridge for 3 to 4 days. You can reheat it using the microwave, or cut the pork into slices and heat them up in a skillet.

You can freeze this recipe too, if you wish. Be aware that freezing cooked pieces of meat can impact their texture once they have thawed. You can thaw the pork in the microwave, or you can let it thaw out in your fridge overnight.

MUSTARD-BALSAMIC PORK CHOPS

This recipe is a favorite on the blog, and that's because these chops are loaded with the delicious flavors of mustard and balsamic vinegar. When these two ingredients are mixed together, they create a perfect glaze and marinade for these chops.

In a medium bowl, combine the oil, mustard, vinegar, rosemary, salt and black pepper. Whisk the ingredients until the mixture begins to emulsify.

Place the pork chops in a 9 x 13–inch (27 x 39–cm) baking dish and pour the marinade over them. Rub the marinade all over the pork chops.

Cover the baking dish with plastic wrap and refrigerate it for at least 1 hour or up to overnight.

Preheat the oven to 425°F (218°C).

Remove the plastic wrap from the baking dish. Bake the pork chops for 20 to 30 minutes, or until their internal temperature reaches 145°F (63°C).

PREP TIME: 5 MINUTES
MARINATING TIME: 1 HOUR
COOK TIME: 30 MINUTES
TOTAL: 1 HOUR, 35 MINUTES
SERVES: 6

¼ cup (60 ml) olive oil
2 tbsp (30 g) grainy mustard (I recommend Dijon whole-grain mustard)
¼ cup (60 ml) balsamic vinegar
1 tbsp (3 g) roughly chopped fresh rosemary or 1 tsp dried rosemary
Salt, as needed
Black pepper, as needed
6 pork chops

RECIPE NOTES

You can prepare these pork chops the night before and bake them when you come home from work.

All ovens are different, so you should start checking on your pork chops after 20 minutes to make sure they don't overcook.

Store cooled leftovers in an airtight container or ziplock bag. They will last for 3 to 4 days in the fridge or for 2 to 3 months in the freezer. To reheat the pork chops, you can either heat them in a skillet over medium heat or in the oven at 375°F (191°C). Keep in mind that reheating cooked pork will cause it to dry out; it is best served fresh.

NUTRITION INFORMATION

Serving size: 1 pork chop; **Calories:** 300; **Carbohydrates:** 2 g; **Protein:** 29 g; **Fat:** 19 g

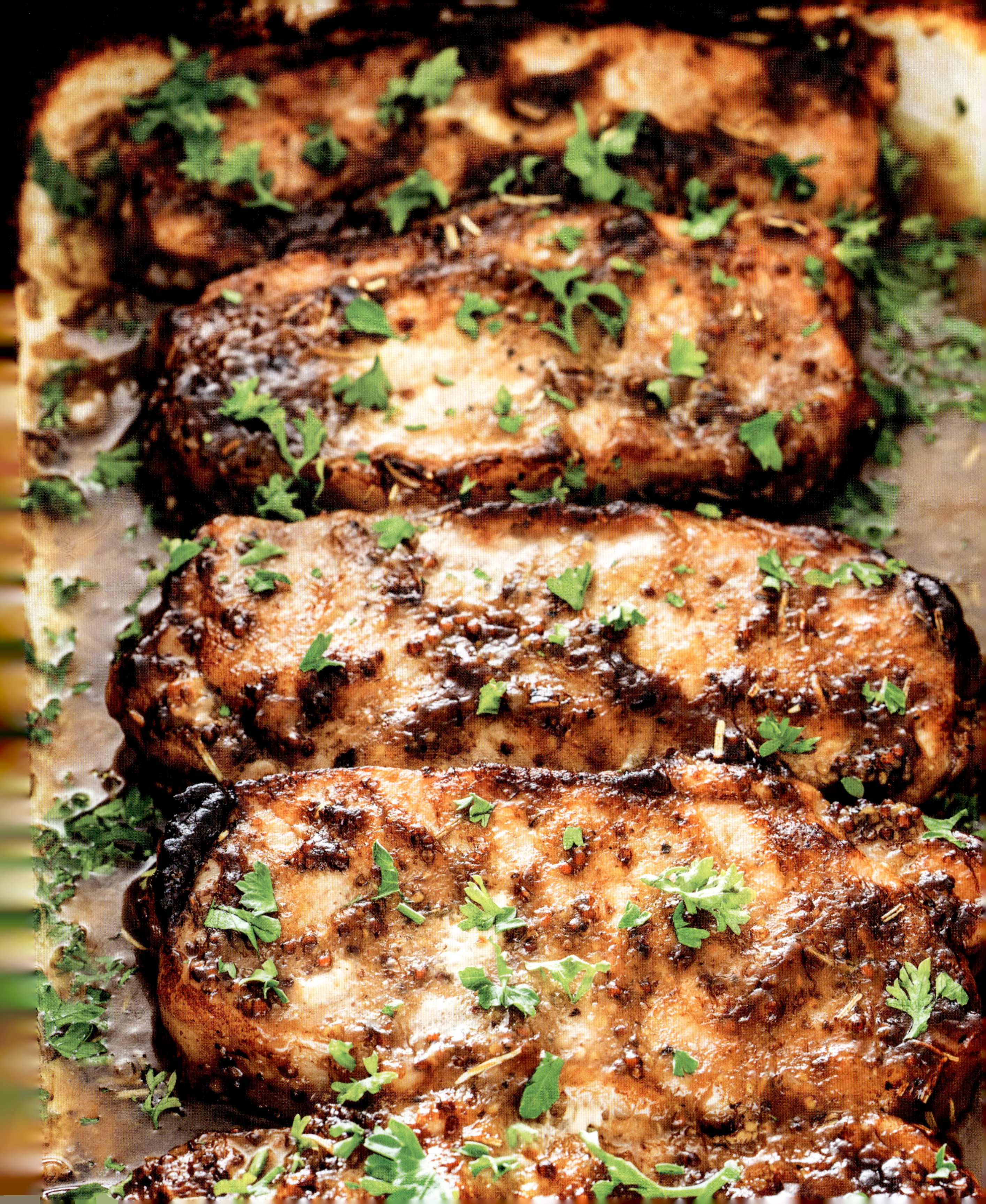

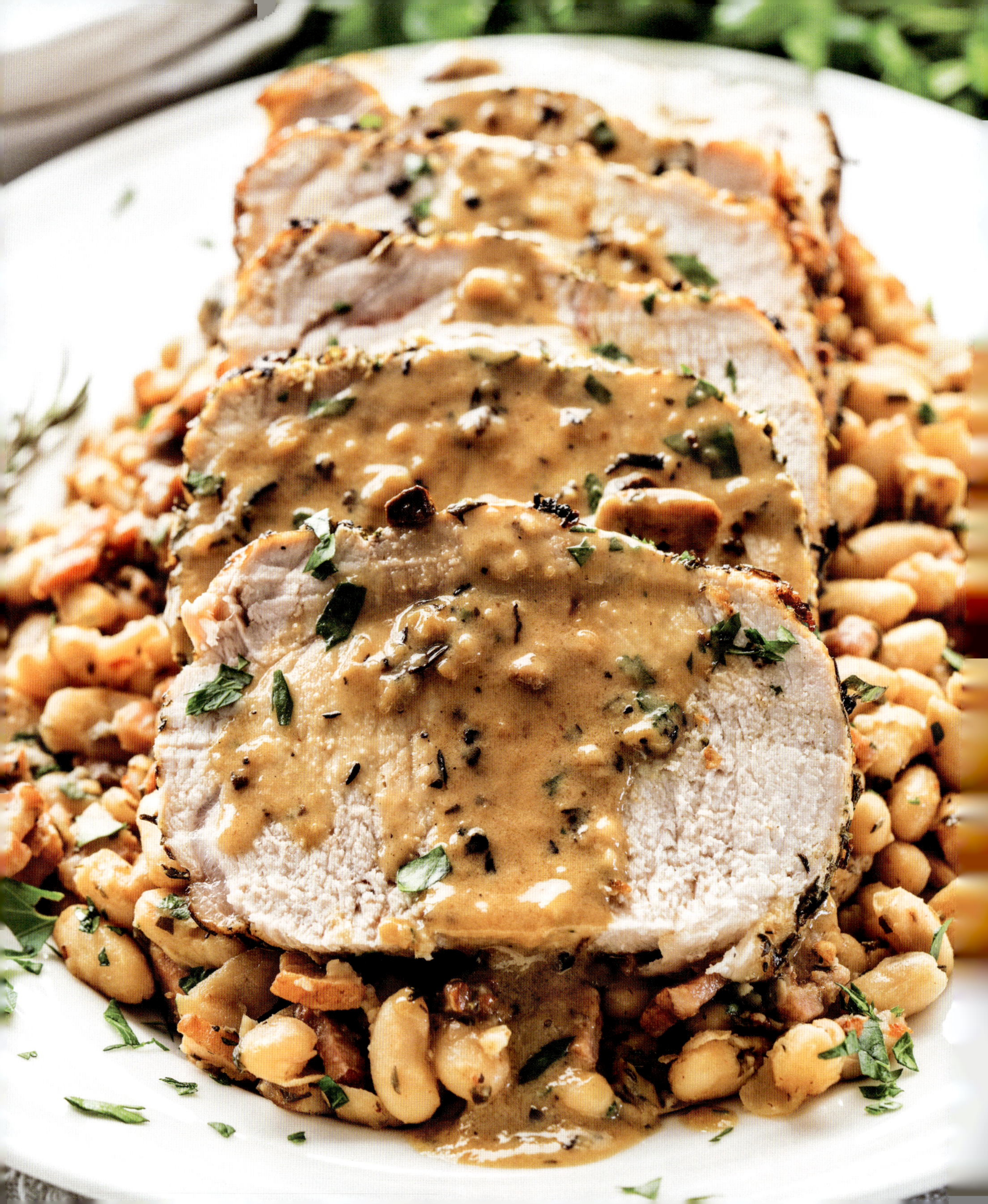

ROSEMARY-GARLIC PORK ROAST

Is there anything quite like pork roast—the way it melts in your mouth and fills your house with the most delicious aroma? This succulent rosemary-garlic pork roast is perfect for a Sunday dinner or a special occasion. It's delicious, quick to prepare and comes complete with a made-from-scratch gravy.

Note that you can strain the gravy to remove the herbs and garlic for a smoother consistency, but I prefer the leftover herbs and garlic in the gravy for extra flavor; if you choose to cook the gravy with the leftover herbs and garlic, remove the garlic prior to serving the gravy.

PREP TIME: 5 MINUTES
COOK TIME: 1 HOUR, 35 MINUTES
REST TIME: 15 MINUTES
TOTAL TIME: 1 HOUR, 55 MINUTES
SERVES: 8

PORK ROAST
¼ cup (60 ml) olive oil
1 tbsp (3 g) fresh thyme leaves or 1 tsp dried thyme
1 tbsp (3 g) chopped fresh rosemary or 1 tbsp (3 g) dried rosemary
4 cloves garlic, minced, plus more as needed
½ tsp red pepper flakes
2 tbsp (6 g) chopped fresh parsley
1 tsp salt, or as needed
1 tsp black pepper, or as needed
1 (4-lb [1.8-kg]) pork loin (see Recipe Notes)
2 bulbs garlic, halved

GRAVY
2 tbsp (30 g) butter
2 tbsp (16 g) all-purpose flour
¾ cup (180 ml) chicken broth
½ cup (120 ml) heavy cream

To make the pork roast, preheat the oven to 375°F (191°C).

In a small bowl, whisk together the oil, thyme, rosemary, garlic, red pepper flakes, parsley, salt and black pepper. Set the oil mixture aside.

Spray a large oven-safe skillet with cooking spray. Place the pork loin in the skillet and rub the pork with the oil mixture. Place the skillet over high heat and sear the pork for 3 minutes per side, for a total of 12 minutes, until it is browned. Top it with more minced garlic if desired and add the garlic bulbs to the skillet.

Roast the pork, uncovered, for 70 to 80 minutes, or until the center of the pork loin reaches between 145 and 155°F (63 and 68°C). Remove the skillet from the oven and place the pork on a cutting board. Cover the meat completely with aluminum foil and let it rest for 15 minutes.

Meanwhile, make the gravy. Remove the garlic bulbs from the skillet. Melt the butter in the skillet over medium-high heat. Sprinkle the flour over the butter and whisk the two together. Pour the broth into the skillet. Bring the mixture to a boil, whisking until it is smooth, and cook it for about 2 minutes. Stir in the heavy cream and cook the gravy for about 2 minutes.

Serve with White Beans with Bacon and Herbs (page 375) as seen in the photo or over Mashed Potatoes (page 383).

RECIPE NOTES
You can use a bone-in pork loin, or you can use one that is boneless as I do. If your pork is on the bigger side, you might need to cook it a bit longer.

If you don't own a meat thermometer, pierce the pork in the middle with a fork. If the juices run clear, the meat is done.

NUTRITION INFORMATION
Serving size: 1 serving; **Calories:** 364; **Carbohydrates:** 1 g; **Protein:** 51 g; **Fat:** 16 g

HONEY-GARLIC PORK LOIN

Forget the days of bland and dry pork. This pork loin is perfectly seasoned, wonderfully moist and coated in a finger-licking honey-garlic glaze.

PREP TIME: 15 MINUTES
COOK TIME: 1 HOUR, 35 MINUTES
REST TIME: 10 MINUTES
TOTAL TIME: 2 HOURS
SERVES: 6

SPICE RUB
1 tsp garlic powder
1 tsp onion powder
1 tbsp (3 g) Italian seasoning
1 tsp smoked paprika
1 tsp salt
1 tsp black pepper

PORK
1 (3-lb [1.3-kg]) pork loin
2 tbsp (30 g) unsalted butter

HONEY-GARLIC GLAZE
2 tbsp (30 g) butter
6 cloves garlic, minced
½ cup (120 ml) honey
¼ cup (60 g) brown sugar
¼ cup (60 ml) soy sauce
½ cup (120 ml) pineapple juice or orange juice
1 tbsp (9 g) cornstarch
2 tbsp (30 ml) water

NUTRITION INFORMATION
Serving size: 1 serving; **Calories:** 521; **Carbohydrates:** 40 g; **Protein:** 52 g; **Fat:** 17 g

Preheat the oven to 375°F (191°C).

To make the spice rub, whisk together the garlic powder, onion powder, Italian seasoning, smoked paprika, salt and black pepper in a small bowl.

To make the pork, sprinkle the spice rub over the entire surface of the pork, pressing firmly to ensure the rub adheres to the meat.

Melt the butter in a large oven-safe skillet over high heat. Place the pork loin in the skillet and sear it on all sides for 3 minutes per side, for a total of 12 minutes, until it is browned.

Transfer the skillet to the oven and roast the pork, uncovered, for 70 to 80 minutes, or until the internal temperature of the pork reaches between 145 and 150°F (63 and 68°C).

Meanwhile, make the honey-garlic glaze. Melt the butter in a small saucepan over medium heat. Add the garlic and cook it for 30 seconds, until it is aromatic. Add the honey, brown sugar, soy sauce and pineapple (or orange) juice. Whisk the ingredients well and bring the mixture to a gentle boil.

In a small bowl, whisk together the cornstarch and water to create a slurry. Add the slurry to the saucepan. Whisk the glaze until it has thickened slightly. Remove the glaze from the heat and set it aside.

When the pork has reached a safe internal temperature, carefully remove the skillet from the oven and baste the pork with the honey-garlic glaze. Do not discard the remaining glaze.

Set the oven to broil. Place the skillet back in the oven and broil the pork for 3 minutes, or until the glaze caramelizes.

Let the pork loin rest for 5 to 10 minutes before slicing and serving it. Serve the pork with the reserved honey-garlic glaze.

RECIPE NOTES

To keep this pork loin fresh in the fridge, store it in a shallow airtight container or wrapped tightly in aluminum foil. It will keep for 3 to 4 days.

If you'd like to make this pork loin ahead of time, you can freeze it, store it in an airtight container or in freezer bags with the air pressed out, for 4 to 6 months. Allow the roast to thaw in the fridge overnight before reheating it in the oven at 350°F (177°C), until the pork is heated through.

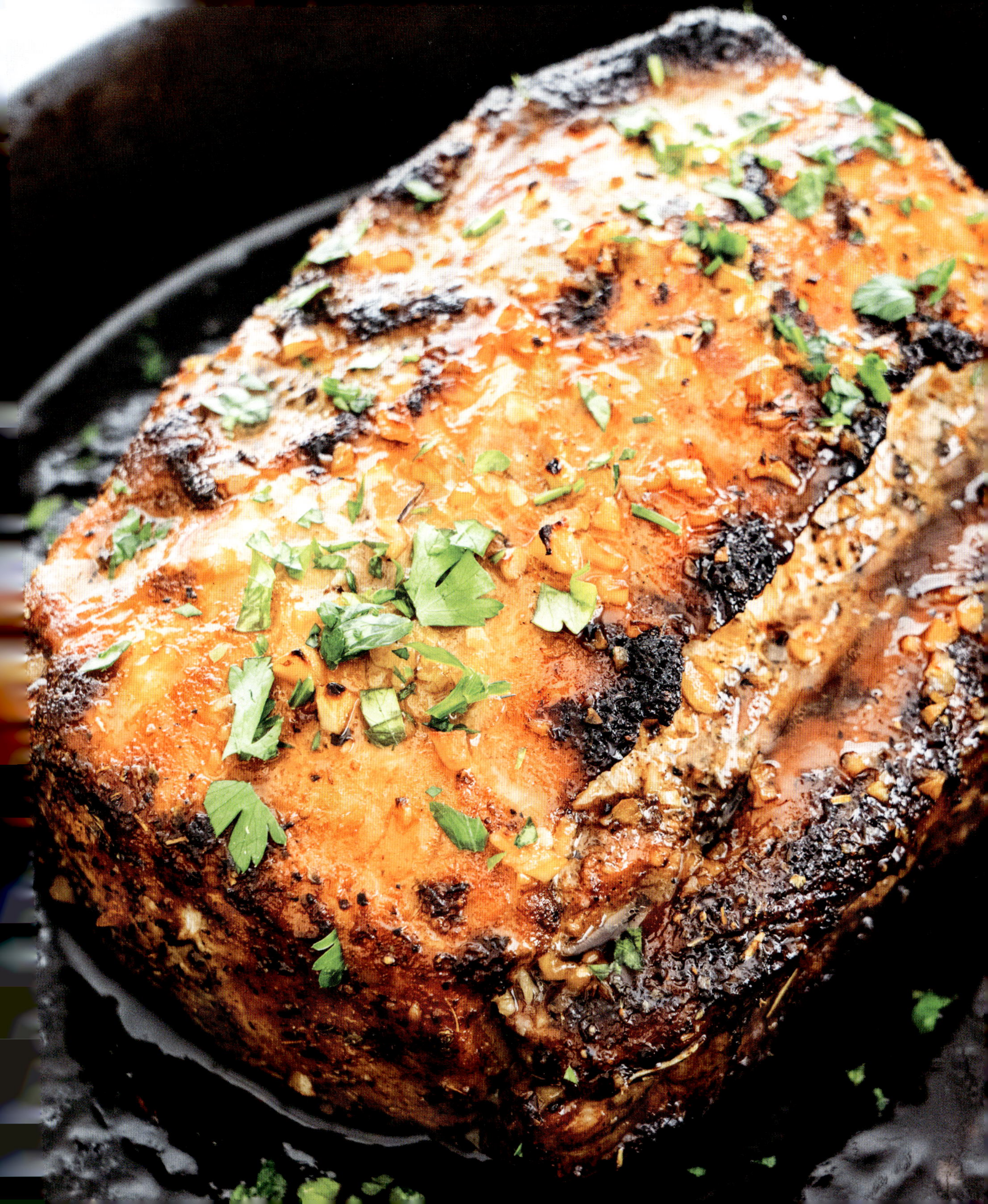

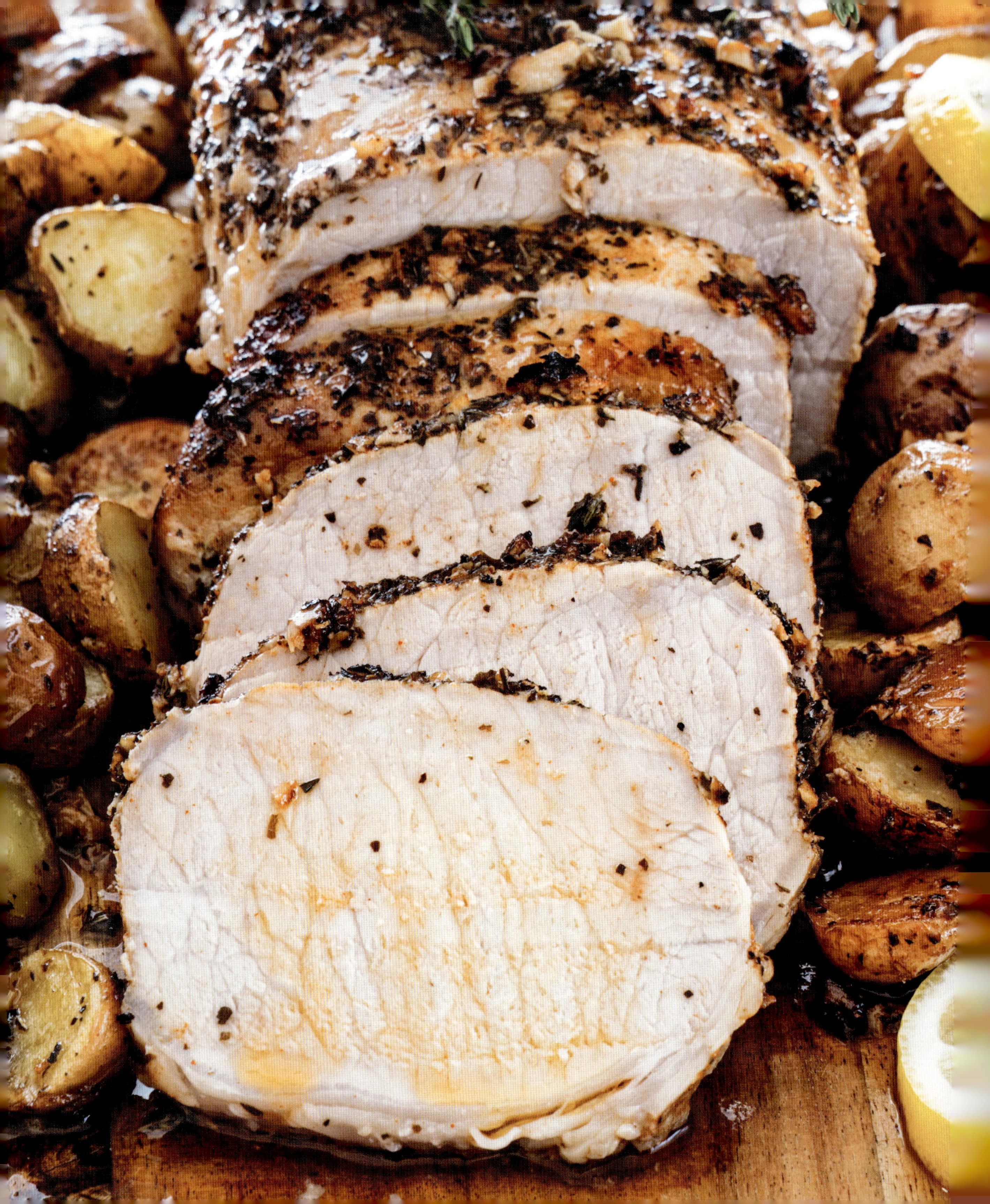

LEMON-GARLIC PORK ROAST

This lemon-garlic pork roast is one of my favorite dishes to make for Sunday night dinners. The marinade, made with lots of garlic and fresh lemon, is tantalizingly aromatic and the secret to creating a restaurant-quality pork loin.

PREP TIME: 15 MINUTES
MARINATING TIME: 1 HOUR
COOK TIME: 1 HOUR
REST TIME: 10 MINUTES
TOTAL: 2 HOURS, 25 MINUTES
SERVES: 6

5 cloves garlic, chopped
½ cup (120 ml) olive oil
1 tbsp (3 g) dried oregano
1 tbsp (3 g) chopped fresh thyme
1 tsp paprika
½ tsp salt, or as needed
½ tsp black pepper, or as needed
2 tbsp (30 ml) fresh lemon juice
1 tbsp (6 g) lemon zest
1 (2-lb [896-g]) pork loin
2 lb (896 g) baby potatoes, halved

In a large ziplock bag, combine the garlic, oil, oregano, thyme, paprika, salt, black pepper, lemon juice and lemon zest. Reserve ½ cup (120 ml) of the marinade for the potatoes.

Place the pork loin in the ziplock bag and make sure the pork is fully covered in the marinade. Close the bag, transfer it to the refrigerator and allow the pork to marinate for at least 1 hour.

Preheat the oven to 375°F (191°C).

Place the potatoes in a large roasting pan. Pour the reserved marinade over the potatoes and toss them in the marinade. Arrange the potatoes around the sides of the roasting pan, making a hole in the middle. Place the pork loin in the center of the roasting pan. Pour the remaining marinade over the pork.

Bake the pork and potatoes for about 1 hour, or until the meat registers 145°F (63°C) on an instant-read thermometer. Remove the roasting pan from the oven. Let the pork rest, covered with foil, for 10 minutes before slicing it.

RECIPE NOTES

Leftover pork roast can be stored in an airtight container in the fridge for 3 to 4 days. Leftovers will also last in the freezer for 2 to 3 months. It's best to reheat leftovers in the microwave to avoid drying out the pork.

You can also reheat the pork in the oven. I suggest pre-slicing the pork, so that it can reheat as fast as possible. Place the pork in a baking dish, add a splash of broth, cover the baking dish with foil and bake the pork at 325°F (163°C) until it is heated through.

NUTRITION INFORMATION

Serving size: 1 serving; **Calories:** 485; **Carbohydrates:** 29 g; **Protein:** 37 g; **Fat:** 24 g

ITALIAN BREADED PORK CHOPS

Golden brown and crispy on the outside but moist and packed full of flavor on the inside, these breaded pork chops are perfect for a quick dinner!

PREP TIME: 10 MINUTES
COOK TIME: 15 MINUTES
REST TIME: 10 MINUTES
TOTAL TIME: 35 MINUTES
SERVES: 4

2 large eggs
2 tbsp (30 ml) milk
1 tsp salt, divided
1 tsp black pepper, divided
1 cup (150 g) Italian breadcrumbs
½ cup (90 g) grated Parmesan cheese
1 tbsp (3 g) Italian seasoning
1 tsp garlic powder
2 tbsp (6 g) chopped fresh parsley
2 tbsp (30 ml) olive oil
4 (1" [3-cm]-thick) boneless pork chops (see Recipe Notes)

In a small bowl, beat together the eggs, milk, ½ teaspoon of the salt and ½ teaspoon of the black pepper. In a separate small bowl, mix together the breadcrumbs, Parmesan cheese, Italian seasoning, garlic powder, parsley and remaining ½ teaspoon of salt and ½ teaspoon of black pepper.

Heat the olive oil in a large oven-safe skillet over medium heat. Meanwhile, dip each pork chop into the egg mixture, then into the breadcrumb mixture, coating the meat evenly. Place the coated pork chops in the skillet and cook them for 4 to 6 minutes on each side, until they are browned and their internal temperature reaches 135°F (57°C).

Transfer the pork chops to a cutting board and let them rest for 10 minutes before slicing them. The residual heat will bring the temperature up to 145°F (63°C).

RECIPE NOTES

If your pork chops are thicker, you may need to finish cooking them in the oven: Preheat the oven to 350°F (177°C). Transfer the skillet to the oven and cook the pork chops for 15 to 20 minutes, or to an internal temperature of 135°F (57°C). Transfer the pork chops to a cutting board and let them rest for 10 minutes before slicing them. The residual heat will bring the temperature up to 145°F (63°C).

Store cooled leftover pork chops in an airtight container or ziplock bag. They will last for 3 to 4 days in the fridge or for 2 to 3 months in the freezer. To reheat the pork chops, you can either heat them in a skillet over medium heat or in the oven at 375°F (191°C). Keep in mind that reheating cooked pork will cause it to dry out; it is best served fresh.

NUTRITION INFORMATION

Serving size: 1 pork chop; **Calories:** 419; **Carbohydrates:** 12 g; **Protein:** 39 g; **Fat:** 23 g

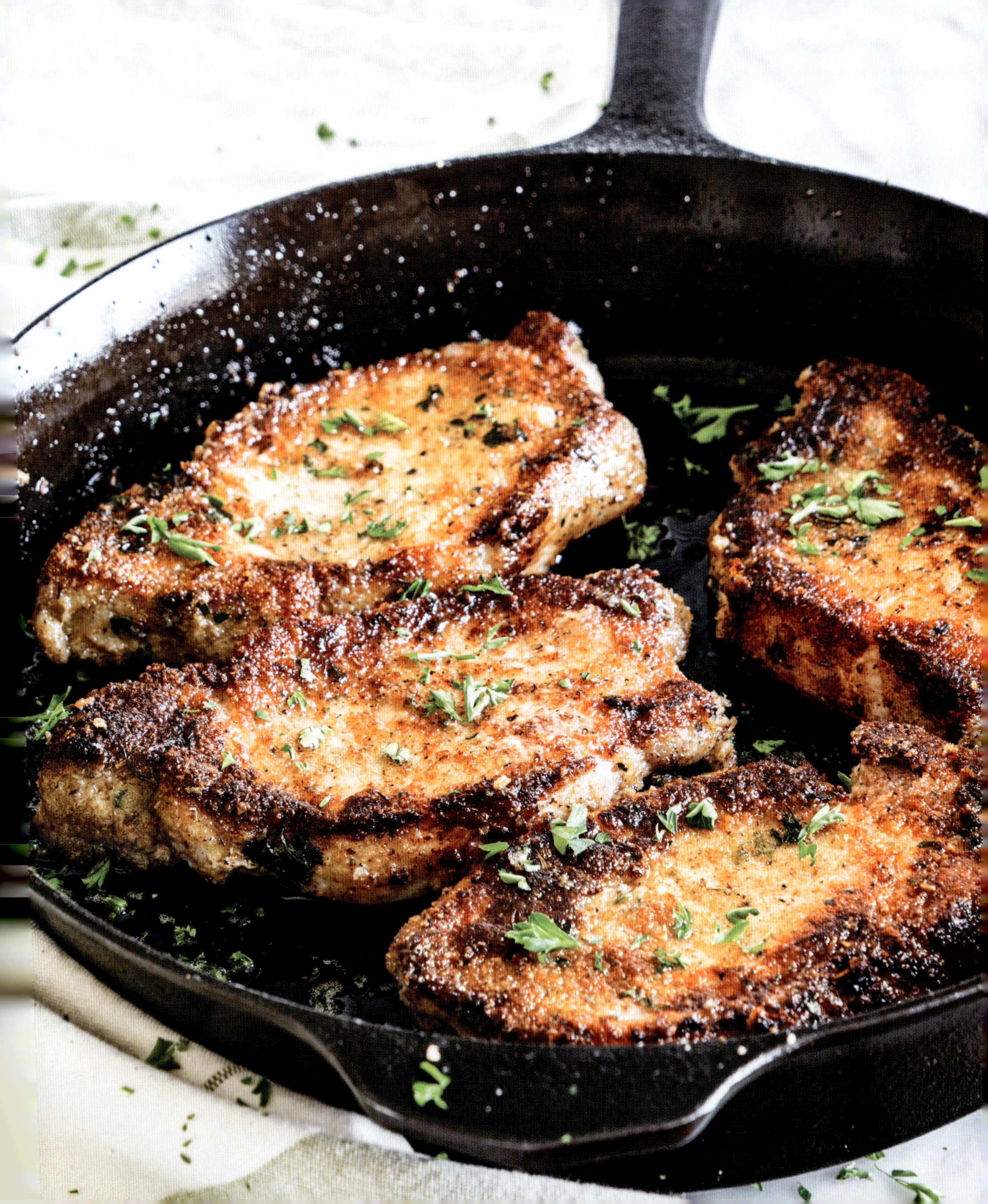

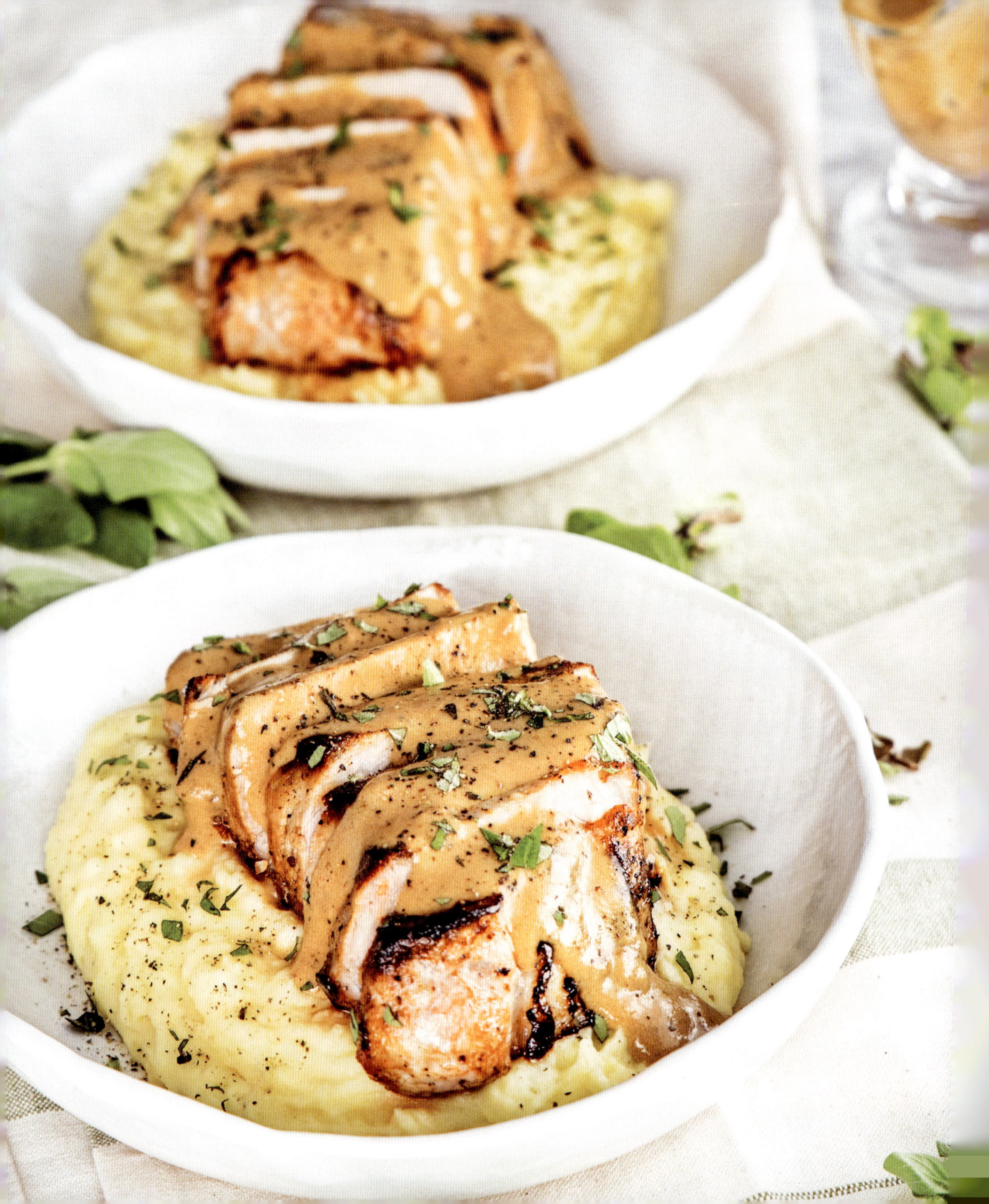

PAN-SEARED PORK CHOPS WITH GRAVY

PREP TIME: 10 MINUTES
COOK TIME: 15 MINUTES
REST TIME: 10 MINUTES
TOTAL TIME: 35 MINUTES
SERVES: 4

PORK CHOPS
1 tbsp (15 g) unsalted butter
1 tbsp (15 ml) olive oil
4 boneless thick-cut pork chops
½ tsp salt, or as needed
½ tsp black pepper, or as needed

GRAVY
1 tbsp (15 g) unsalted butter
1 tbsp (8 g) all-purpose flour
¾ cup (180 ml) half-and-half (see Recipe Notes)
½ cup (120 ml) low-sodium or unsalted chicken broth
¼ tsp salt, or as needed
¼ tsp black pepper, or as needed

Mashed Potatoes (page 383), for serving

If you're looking for restaurant-quality pork chops, then this is the recipe for you. These chops are perfectly pan-seared and served with a homemade gravy.

To make the pork chops, heat the butter and oil in a large skillet over medium-high heat. Season the pork chops with the salt and black pepper. Add the pork chops to the skillet and sear them for 4 to 6 minutes per side, until their internal temperature reaches 135°F (57°C) and the meat has developed a golden-brown crust.

Transfer the pork chops to a cutting board and let them rest for 10 minutes before slicing them. The residual heat will bring the temperature up to 145°F (63°C).

Meanwhile, make the gravy. Reduce the heat to medium and add the butter to the skillet. When the butter has melted, whisk in the flour and cook the mixture for about 1 minute, whisking continuously, to remove the raw flour taste.

Whisk in the half-and-half and broth, whisking until the mixture is smooth. Cook the gravy for about 2 minutes, until it thickens. Season the gravy with the salt and pepper.

Serve the pork chops with the gravy and Mashed Potatoes.

RECIPE NOTES

Half-and-half can be found near the milk and cream in the dairy section of your local grocery store. Half-and-half is a blend of equal parts whole milk and light cream. It averages 10 to 12 percent fat.

If you would prefer to bake the pork chops, preheat the oven to 400°F (204°C). In a large oven-safe skillet over medium-high heat, sear the pork chops on all sides for 2 minutes, just until they are golden. Transfer the skillet to the oven and bake the pork chops for 15 minutes, or until their internal temperature reaches 135°F (57°C). Let them rest for 10 minutes before slicing and serving them. The residual heat will bring the temperature up to 145°F (63°C).

NUTRITION INFORMATION

Serving size: 1 serving; **Calories:** 361; **Carbohydrates:** 3 g; **Protein:** 31 g; **Fat:** 23 g

PORK SCHNITZEL

PREP TIME: 15 MINUTES
COOK TIME: 30 MINUTES
TOTAL TIME: 45 MINUTES
SERVES: 10

10 pork cutlets
1 tsp salt, or as needed
1 tsp black pepper, or as needed (see Recipe Notes)
Vegetable oil, as needed
1 cup (120 g) all-purpose flour
2 large eggs, beaten
1 cup (60 g) panko breadcrumbs (see Recipe Notes)
Mashed Potatoes (page 383), for serving

If you were to ask me which recipe from my blog I make the most at home, it would be this one. It's my husband's favorite meal ever: pork chops with Mashed Potatoes (page 383). If I were to make this dish every single day, he'd never get bored of it. Whenever I want to treat him to a nice dinner, I always know what to make.

While schnitzel is traditionally made with veal, pork or chicken are also quite common since they are more readily available. If your schnitzel is done right, you won't care that it's pork or chicken or veal. It'll taste superb! The secret is to pound your chops nice and thin.

Using the flat side of a meat mallet, pound each pork chop until it is ¼ inch (6 mm) thick. Season both sides of the pork with the salt and black pepper.

Fill a large skillet with about ½ inch (13 mm) of the oil. Set the skillet over medium-high heat and bring the oil to 350°F (177°C).

Create a breading station by setting 3 shallow bowls in a row. Place the flour in the first bowl. Place the eggs in the second bowl. Place the breadcrumbs in the third bowl. Dip the chops in the flour, the egg and then the breadcrumbs, coating both sides.

Working in batches, fry the schnitzels for 2 to 3 minutes on both sides, until they are a deep golden brown. Transfer the pork schnitzel to a plate lined with paper towels.

Serve the pork schnitzel immediately over the Mashed Potatoes.

RECIPE NOTES

Freshly ground black pepper is best in this dish.

I usually use panko breadcrumbs because I find that the pork schnitzel comes out crispier; but Italian breadcrumbs work just as well.

I use boneless pork cutlets because I find they are easier to work with and pound. But pork chops work as well, although you will need to remove the bones first.

NUTRITION INFORMATION

Serving size: 1 pork chop; **Calories:** 320; **Carbohydrates:** 17 g; **Protein:** 34 g; **Fat:** 11 g

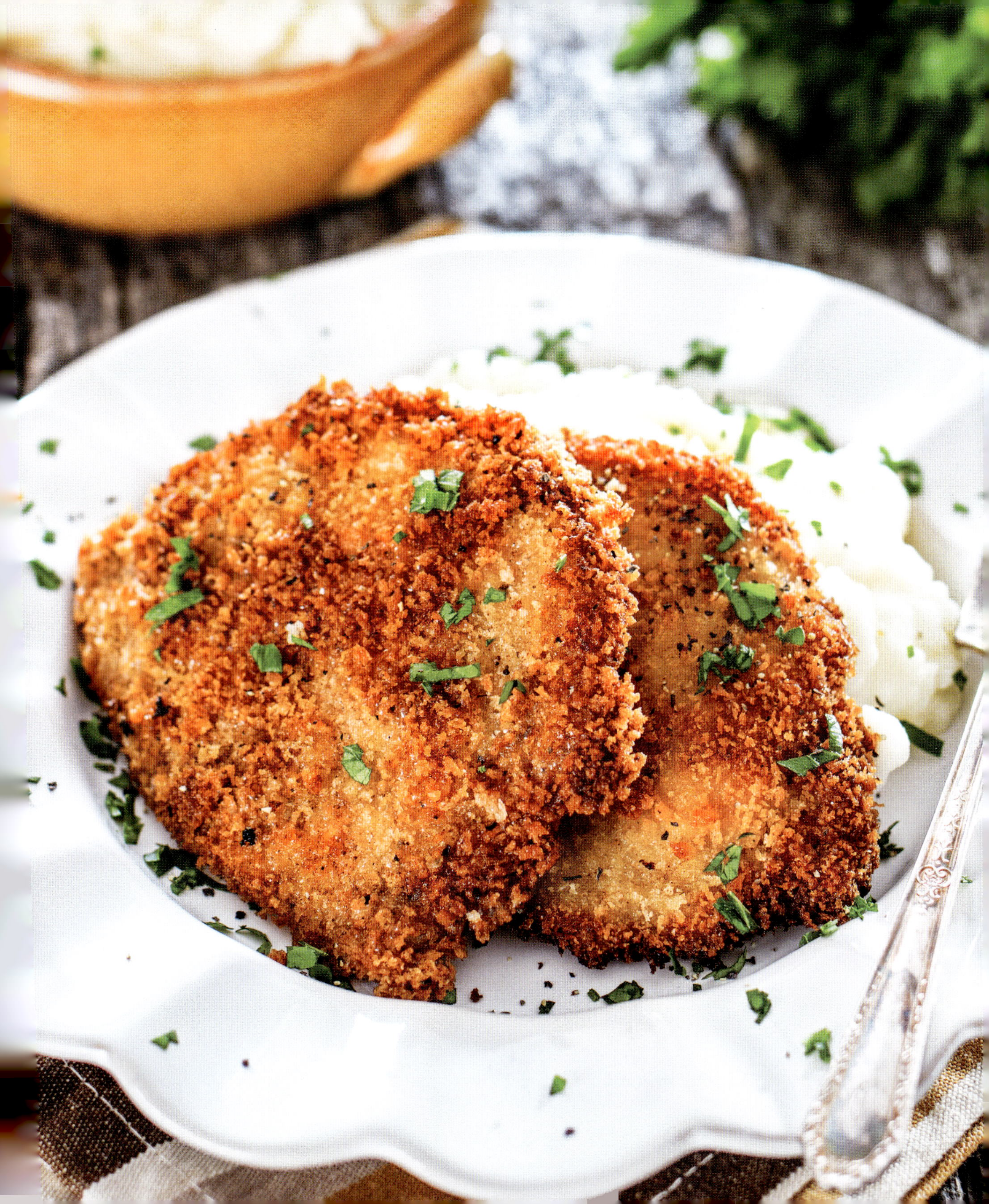

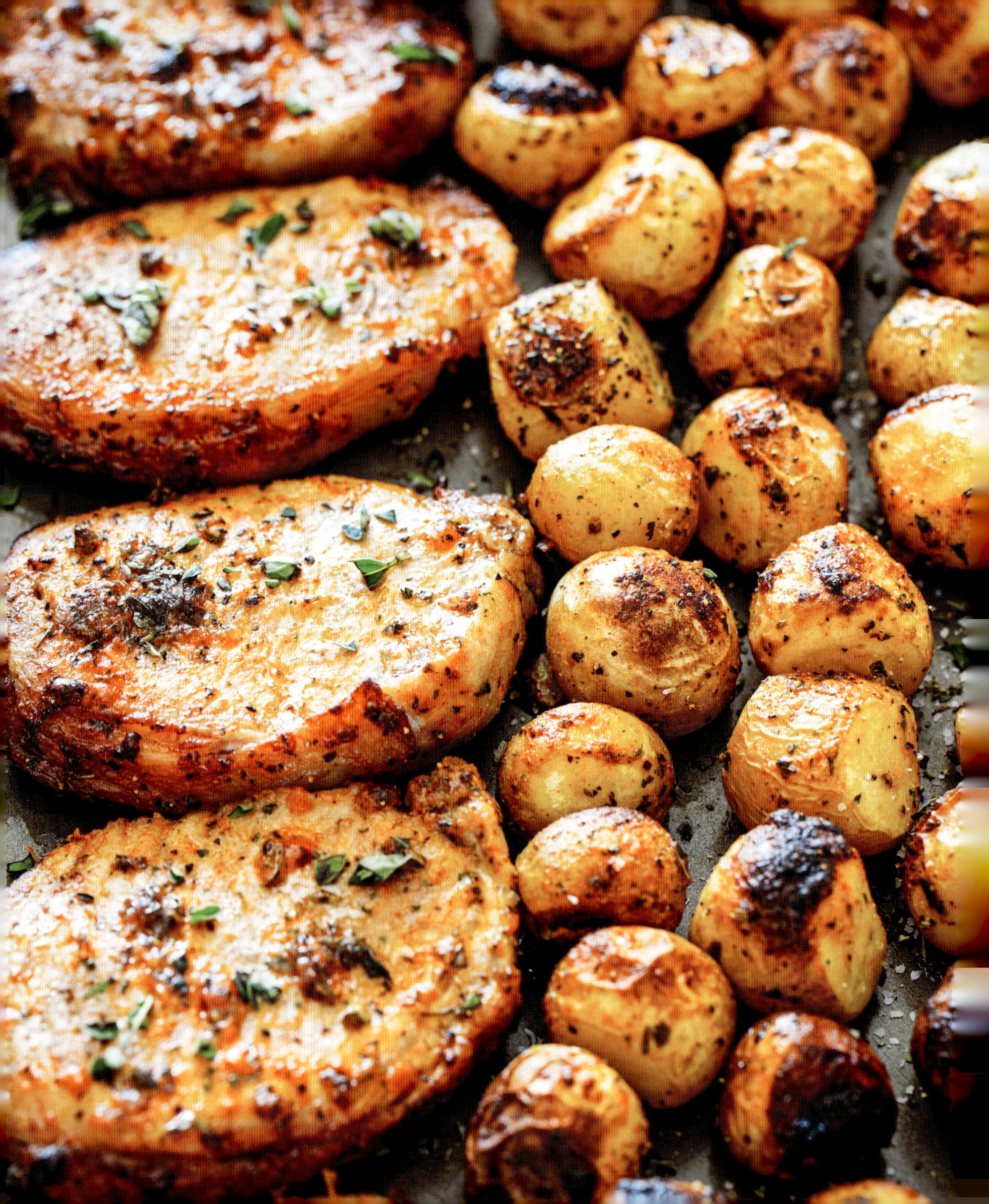

RANCH PORK CHOPS AND POTATOES

PREP TIME: 5 MINUTES
COOK TIME: 30 MINUTES
TOTAL TIME: 35 MINUTES
SERVES: 6

6 (1" [3-cm]-thick) boneless or bone-in pork chops
2 lb (896 g) baby potatoes (see Recipe Note)
3 tbsp (45 ml) olive oil
1 (1-oz [28-g]) package ranch seasoning and salad dressing mix
1 tsp smoked paprika
1 tbsp (3 g) dried oregano
1 tsp black pepper
1 tbsp (3 g) chopped fresh parsley

Here's another extremely popular recipe from the blog that's a super quick, full dinner that's ready in just 35 minutes. Get ready for delicious roasted potatoes with ranch pork chops, all cooked in one pan.

Preheat the oven to 400°F (204°C). Spray a large baking sheet with cooking spray.

Place the pork chops and potatoes on the prepared baking sheet. Drizzle the oil over the pork chops and potatoes and ensure everything is coated well.

In a small bowl, mix together the ranch seasoning, smoked paprika, oregano and black pepper. Rub the seasoning over the pork chops and potatoes.

Roast the pork chops and potatoes for about 30 minutes, or until the internal temperature of the pork chops reaches 145°F (63°C) and the potatoes are fork-tender.

Garnish the pork chops and potatoes with the parsley, then serve them immediately.

RECIPE NOTE

Although I use baby potatoes, you can use regular potatoes cut into cubes. I prefer Yukon gold potatoes, but red potatoes work as well. Another option is fingerling potatoes, but they can be hard to find in the grocery store.

NUTRITION INFORMATION

Serving size: 1 serving; **Calories:** 403; **Carbohydrates:** 30 g; **Protein:** 32 g; **Fat:** 16 g

INSTANT POT® BARBECUE PORK RIBS

PREP TIME: 10 MINUTES
COOK TIME: 45 MINUTES
NATURAL PRESSURE RELEASE: 15 MINUTES
TOTAL TIME: 1 HOUR, 10 MINUTES
SERVES: 8

DRY RUB
1 tbsp (9 g) mustard powder
1½ tbsp (14 g) smoked paprika
1 tbsp (9 g) onion powder
½ tsp cayenne pepper
1 tsp ground cumin
1 tsp garlic powder
1 tbsp (15 g) brown sugar
1 tsp black pepper
2 tsp salt

RIBS
2 (1½- to 2-lb [372- to 896-g]) racks baby back pork ribs
4 cups (960 ml) apple juice
¼ cup (60 ml) apple cider vinegar
2 tbsp (30 ml) liquid smoke

BARBECUE SAUCE
½ cup (120 ml) store-bought barbecue sauce
½ cup (120 g) ketchup
¼ cup (60 ml) whiskey
¼ cup (60 g) brown sugar
2 tbsp (30 ml) Worcestershire sauce
1 tbsp (15 ml) liquid smoke

Making pork ribs is a great use of your Instant Pot. You end up with fall-off-the-bone tender ribs that are always delicious and super sticky from my made-from-scratch whiskey barbecue sauce—and the best part is that it's ready in about an hour.

To make the dry rub, combine the mustard powder, smoked paprika, onion powder, cayenne pepper, cumin, garlic powder, brown sugar, black pepper and salt in a small bowl. Set the dry rub aside.

To make the ribs, remove the membrane from the back of the ribs with a paper towel. Generously season both sides of the ribs with the dry rub. Place the ribs in the Instant Pot, standing up and wrapping around the inside of the Instant Pot. Pour the apple juice, vinegar and liquid smoke in the Instant Pot; there is no need to stir the ingredients. Secure the lid of the Instant Pot and turn the valve from Vent to Seal. Set the Instant Pot to the Meat/Stew setting and set the timer for 20 minutes.

Once the Instant Pot's cycle is complete, wait for about 15 minutes to allow the pressure to release naturally. If you are in a rush, follow the manufacturer's instructions for a quick release. Carefully unlock and remove the lid from the Instant Pot.

While the ribs are cooking, prepare the barbecue sauce. In a small saucepan over low heat, combine the store-bought barbecue sauce, ketchup, whiskey, brown sugar, Worcestershire sauce and liquid smoke. Stir to combine the ingredients. Simmer the sauce for 20 to 25 minutes, until it has reduced a bit.

Preheat the oven to broil. Carefully remove the ribs from the Instant Pot and place them on a large baking sheet. Brush them generously on both sides with the prepared barbecue sauce. Place the ribs under the broiler for about 5 minutes. Keep the oven door open while broiling the ribs and keep an eye on them because they could burn quickly. Serve the ribs with the remaining barbecue sauce.

RECIPE NOTES
If stored in an airtight container or wrapped tightly in aluminum foil, these ribs will last for 3 to 4 days in the fridge. You can also freeze this recipe, wrapped tightly in foil, for 2 to 3 months. Thaw the ribs in the microwave or in cold water. Reheat them in the oven at 350°F (177°C) and slather them with the barbecue sauce.

NUTRITION INFORMATION
Serving size: 1 serving; **Calories:** 491; **Carbohydrates:** 36 g; **Protein:** 33 g; **Fat:** 20 g

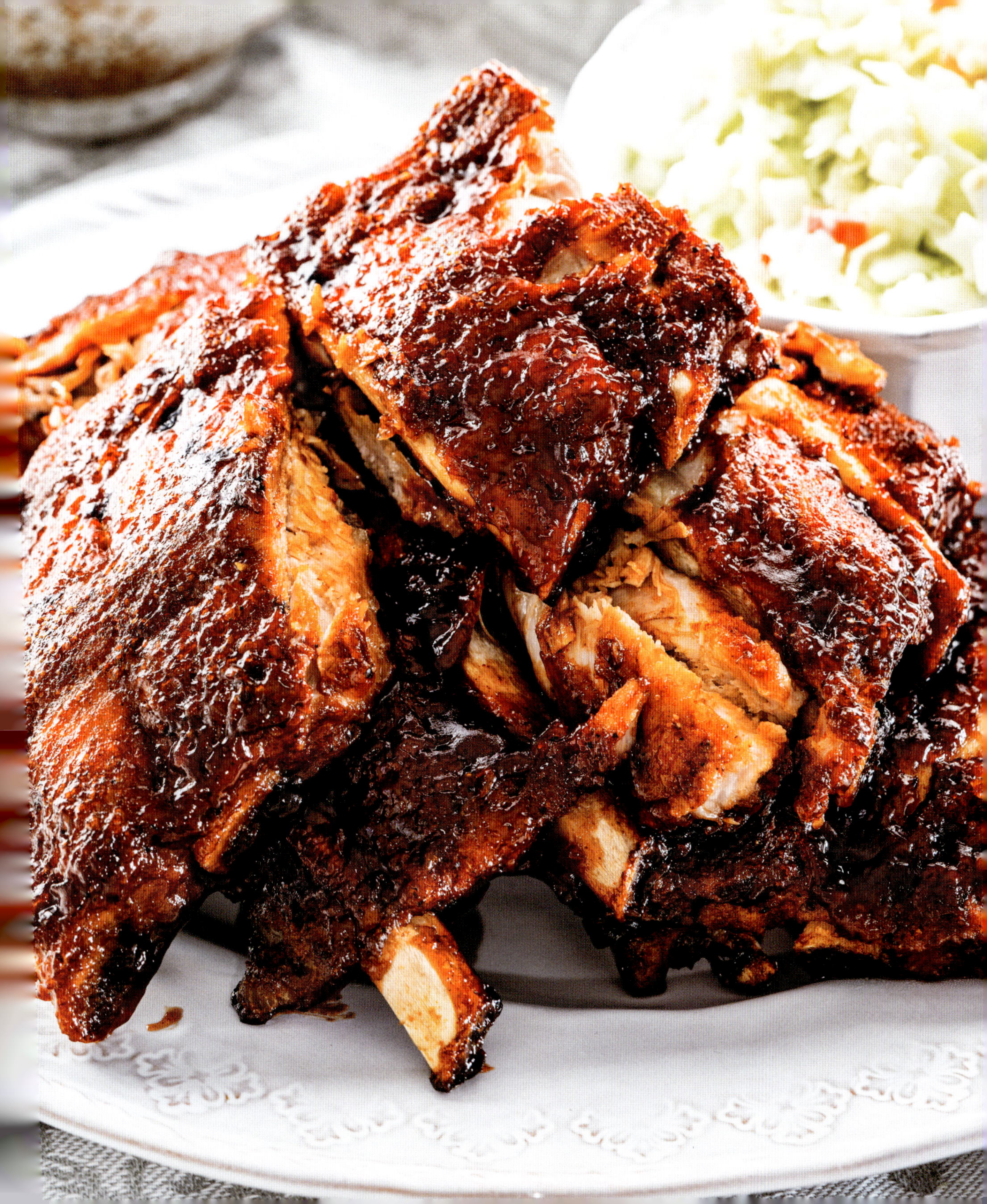

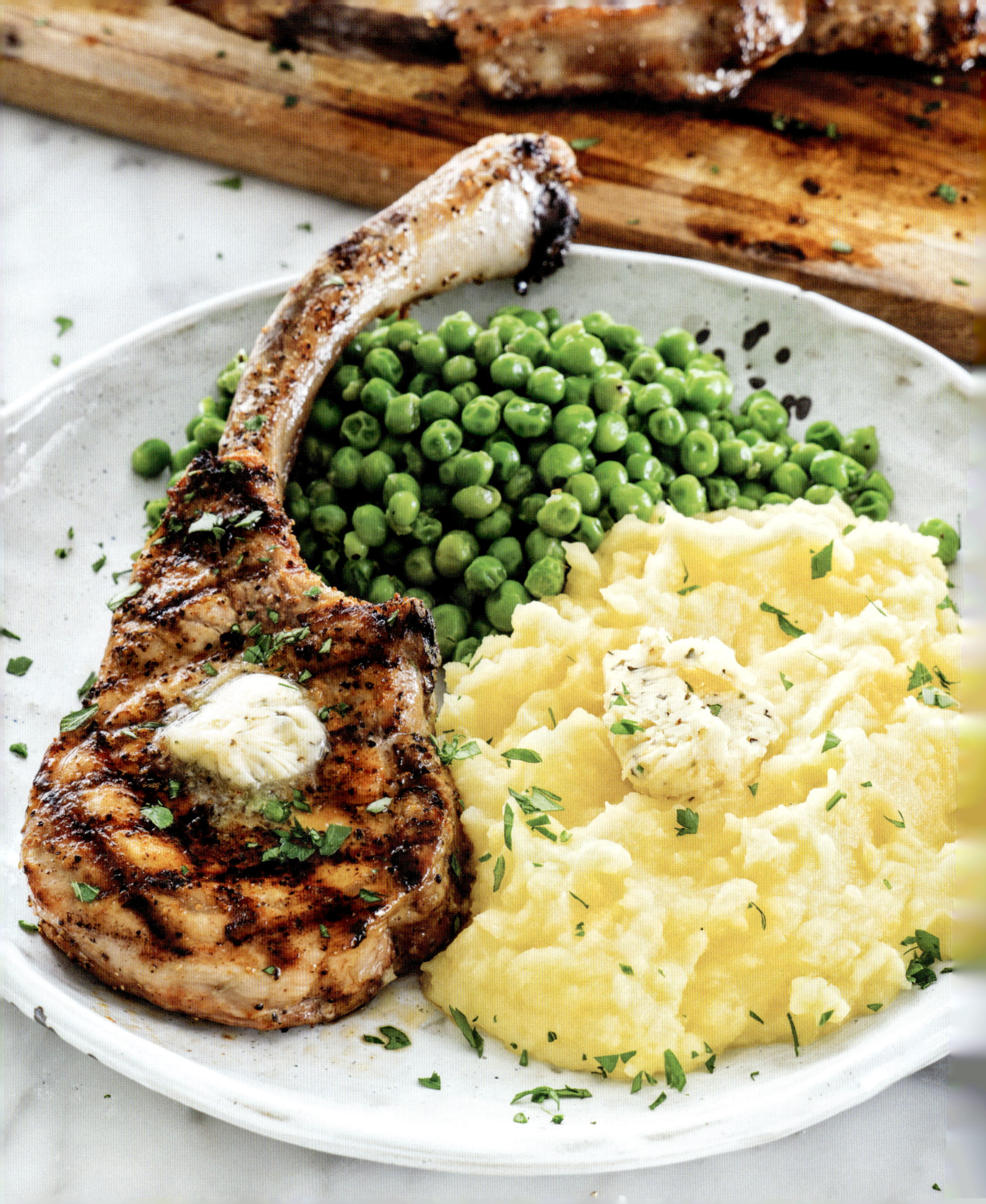

GRILLED TOMAHAWK PORK CHOPS

PREP TIME: 5 MINUTES
MARINATING TIME: 2 HOURS, 20 MINUTES
COOK TIME: 15 MINUTES
REST TIME: 15 MINUTES
TOTAL: 2 HOURS, 55 MINUTES
SERVES: 4

1 tbsp (18 g) kosher salt, or as needed

2 tsp (6 g) black pepper, or as needed

1 tsp chili powder

1 tsp onion powder

½ tsp sugar

4 (12-oz [336-g]) tomahawk pork chops

Butter, for serving

Mashed Potatoes (page 383), for serving

Cooked peas, for serving

This stunning cut of pork deserves the royal treatment. Using a simple five-ingredient dry rub and a compound butter to seal the deal, every bite of this easy recipe feels gourmet. But it's simple enough to make any night of the week!

In a small bowl, combine the kosher salt, black pepper, chili powder, onion powder and sugar. Generously rub half of the spice mixture over both sides of the pork chops. Refrigerate the pork chops for 2 hours before grilling them.

Preheat the grill to medium heat, about 350°F (177°C).

Meanwhile, remove the pork chops from the fridge and let them sit at room temperature, covered, for about 20 minutes. Pat the chops dry with paper towels and reseason them with the remaining half of the spice mixture.

Lightly spray the pork chops with cooking spray and place them on the grill. Grill them on both sides until their internal temperature reaches between 145 and 150°F (63 and 66°C).

Transfer the pork chops to a cutting board and let them rest for 15 minutes before slicing them. Serve them with the butter, Mashed Potatoes and peas.

RECIPE NOTES

Grilling time can vary depending on the thickness of the chop. A 1-inch (3-cm)-thick pork chop can take 12 to 14 minutes, a 1½-inch (4-cm)-thick pork chop can take about 20 minutes. The best way to tell if your chops are done is to use an instant meat thermometer.

Transfer the pork chops to an airtight container and store them for 3 to 4 days in the fridge. You can also keep pork chops in the freezer for 2 to 3 months. I suggest letting the frozen pork thaw fully in the fridge overnight before reheating it.

NUTRITION INFORMATION

Serving size: 1 pork chop; **Calories:** 536; **Carbohydrates:** 2 g; **Protein:** 74 g; **Fat:** 24 g

QUICK AND EASY PORK SAUSAGES

PREP TIME: 15 MINUTES
COOK TIME: 30 MINUTES
TOTAL TIME: 45 MINUTES
SERVES: 16

1 lb (448 g) ground pork
¼ cup (15 g) panko breadcrumbs
1 large egg
2 cloves garlic, minced
½ tsp dried thyme
1 tbsp (3 g) chopped fresh parsley
1 tsp salt, or as needed
½ tsp black pepper, or as needed
2 tbsp (30 ml) olive oil

Did you know that making pork sausages is quite simple? All you need are a few everyday ingredients. These sausages are even easier than you might imagine because I use no casings—just a simple meat mixture, formed by hand into delicious little sausages.

In a large bowl, mix together the pork, breadcrumbs, egg, garlic, thyme, parsley, salt and black pepper. Make sure the ingredients are well incorporated. Divide the mixture into 16 equal portions and shape each portion into a sausage.

Heat the oil in a large skillet over medium-low heat. Working in batches, gently fry the sausages for 12 to 15 minutes, until they are golden on all sides and cooked on the inside.

RECIPE NOTES

You can chill the uncooked sausages in the fridge for 1 to 2 days, or you can freeze them.

Transfer any leftover sausages to an airtight container or sealable freezer bag. They'll last for 3 to 4 days in the fridge. You can reheat them in the microwave, in a skillet over medium-low heat or in the oven at 400°F (204°C) for 10 to 15 minutes.

NUTRITION INFORMATION

Serving size: 1 sausage; **Calories:** 103; **Carbohydrates:** 1 g; **Protein:** 5 g; **Fat:** 8 g

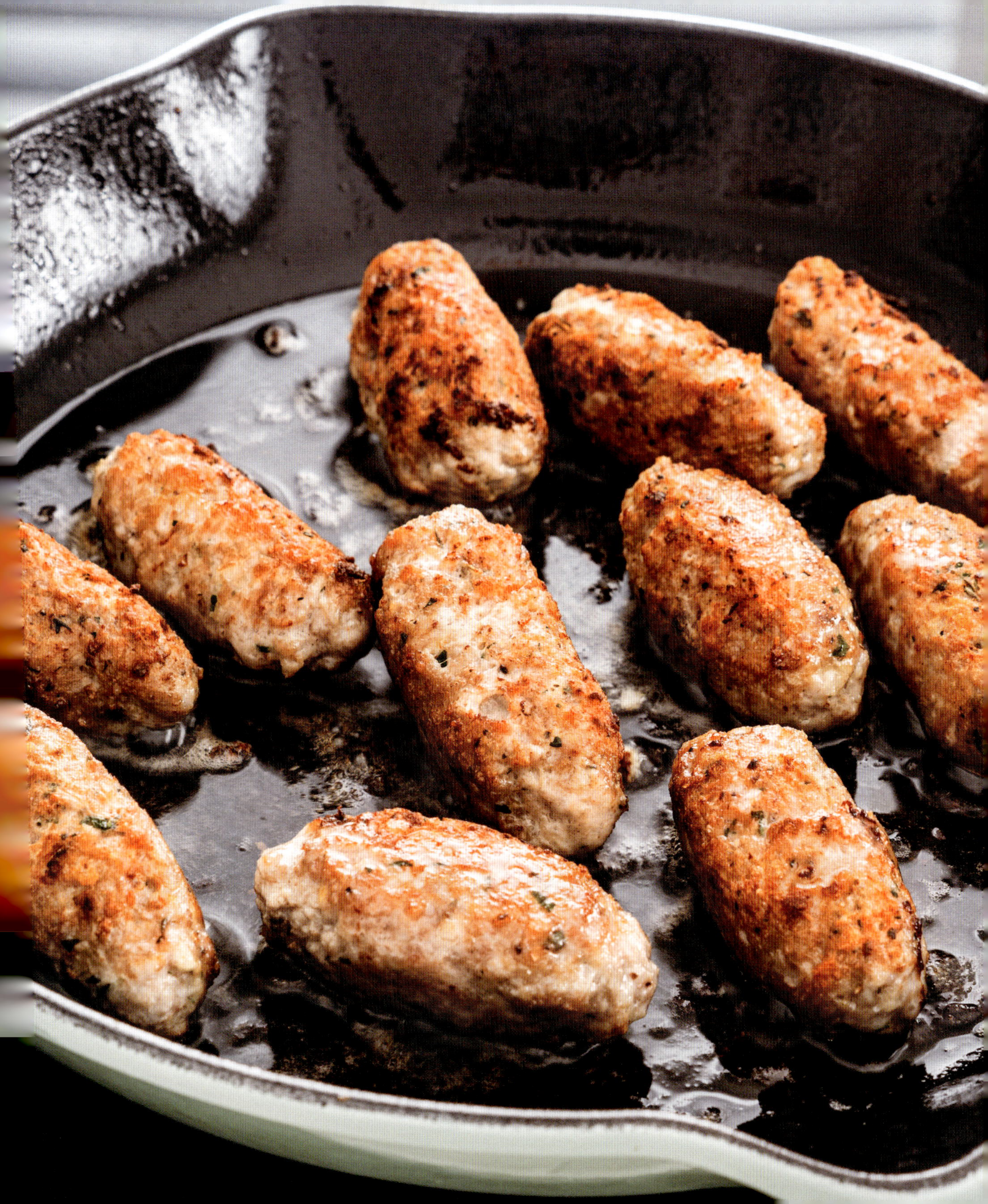

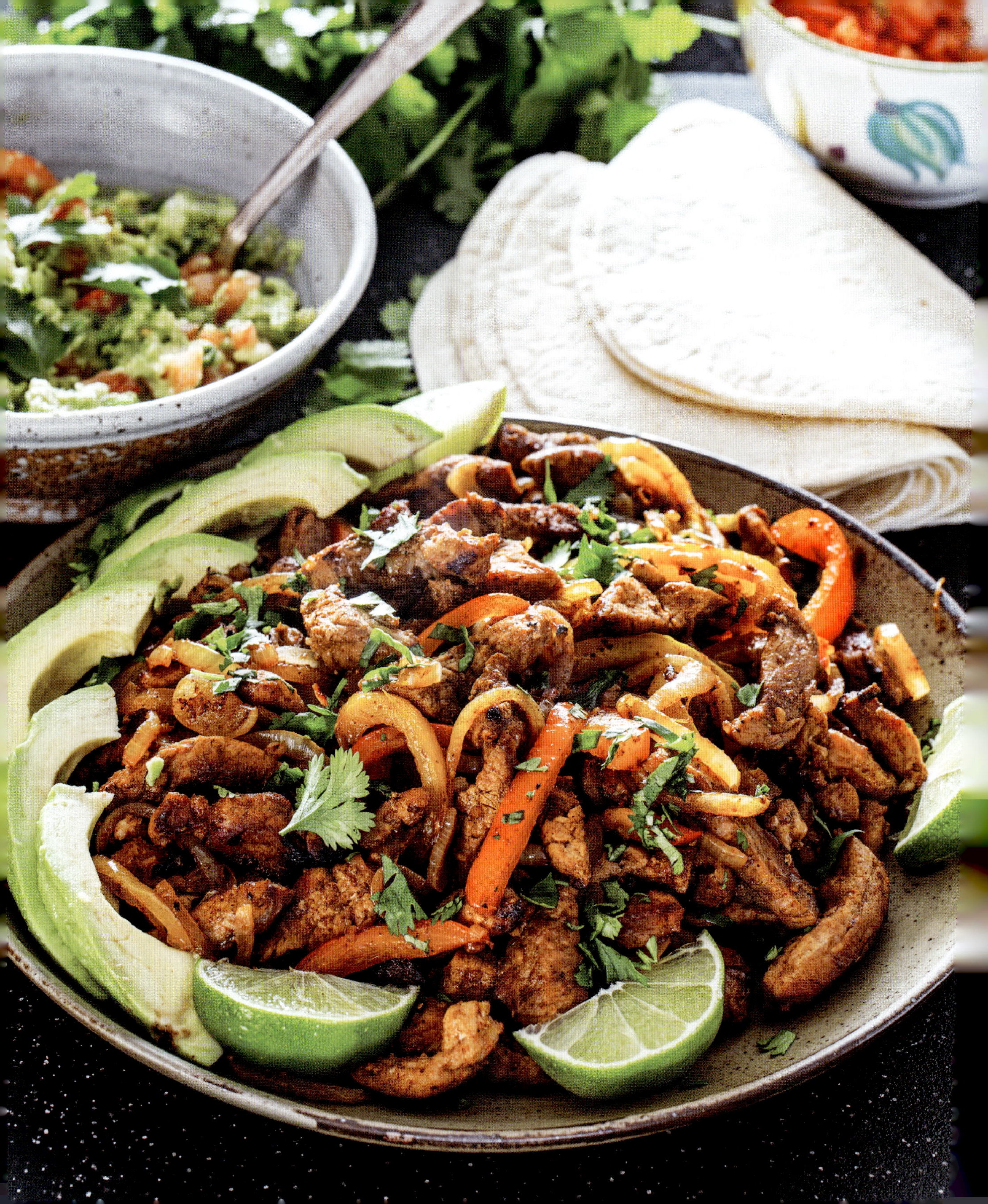

PORK FAJITAS

This recipe is full of zesty ingredients that come together to create delicious one-pan pork fajitas, which are better than anything you can order in a restaurant.

PREP TIME: 20 MINUTES
COOK TIME: 20 MINUTES
TOTAL TIME: 40 MINUTES
SERVES: 8

FAJITAS
2 onions, sliced into long strips
1 red bell pepper, sliced into long strips
1 yellow bell pepper, sliced into long strips
3 tbsp (27 g) fajita seasoning, divided, or as needed (see Recipe Note)
1 (2-lb [896-g]) pork tenderloin
2 tbsp (30 ml) olive oil, divided
8 small tortillas
Roughly chopped fresh cilantro (optional)
1 lime, cut into wedges

GUACAMOLE
2 avocados
2 tbsp (30 ml) fresh lime juice
1 tomato, diced
3 green onions, chopped
½ tsp salt, or as needed
¼ tsp black pepper, or as needed

To make the fajitas, place the onions, red bell pepper and yellow bell pepper in a large bowl. Sprinkle 1½ tablespoons (14 g) of the fajita seasoning over the onions and bell peppers and toss to coat them in the seasoning.

Clean and slice the pork tenderloin into long strips. Place the strips in a large bowl. Sprinkle the remaining 1½ tablespoons (13 g) of fajita seasoning over the pork and stir to make sure each piece of pork is seasoned well.

Heat 1 tablespoon (15 ml) of the oil in a large skillet over medium-high heat. Add the pork and cook it for 5 to 10 minutes, until it's fully cooked and slightly charred but not burned.

Remove the pork from the skillet and wipe the skillet clean.

Heat the remaining 1 tablespoon (15 ml) of oil in the skillet. Add the onion and bell pepper mixture and cook the vegetables for about 5 minutes, until the onions are caramelized and the bell peppers are soft. Add the pork back to the skillet, stir to combine the ingredients and cook them for 1 minute.

To make the guacamole, mash the avocados in a small bowl. Add the lime juice, tomato, green onions, salt and black pepper and stir to combine the ingredients.

To assemble the fajitas, arrange some of the pork, onions, bell peppers and guacamole on the tortillas. Garnish each serving with the cilantro (if using) and serve the lime wedges on the side.

RECIPE NOTE
If you can't find fajita seasoning, you can make your own—recipes abound online—or use taco seasoning.

NUTRITION INFORMATION
Serving size: 1 serving; **Calories:** 367; **Carbohydrates:** 27 g; **Protein:** 28 g; **Fat:** 17 g

BRAISED PORK IN SWEET SOY SAUCE

PREP TIME: 10 MINUTES
COOK TIME: 35 MINUTES
TOTAL TIME: 45 MINUTES
SERVES: 4

2 tbsp (30 ml) vegetable oil
1 (2-lb [896-g]) pork loin, cut into 1" (3-cm) pieces
1 tbsp (15 g) garlic and ginger paste
1 tbsp (15 ml) olive oil
1 tbsp (15 ml) sesame oil
½ cup (120 ml) soy sauce
¼ cup (48 g) sugar
1½ cups (360 ml) water
1 tbsp (15 ml) chili-garlic sauce
2 green onions, chopped (optional)
Cooked noodles or steamed rice, for serving

This is one of my oldest recipes and a reader favorite: tender pieces of pork braised in a flavorful sauce with just a touch of heat. This dish requires few ingredients and just one pan, and it's a great way to switch up your weekly rotation.

Heat the vegetable oil in a large skillet over medium-high heat. Add the pork and sauté it for about 3 minutes, until it is no longer pink and is beginning to brown.

In a medium bowl, combine the garlic and ginger paste, olive oil, sesame oil, soy sauce, sugar, water and chili-garlic sauce. Pour this mixture over the pork and bring it to a boil. Reduce the heat to low and let the pork and sauce simmer for about 30 minutes, uncovered, stirring them occasionally, or until there's about 3 tablespoons (45 ml) of sauce left in the skillet.

Garnish the pork with the green onions (if using). Serve the pork over the noodles or steamed rice.

RECIPE NOTES

Store any leftovers in an airtight container in the fridge for 3 to 4 days. If you made a carb like noodles or rice, you can store the leftover pork in the same container or separately.

NUTRITION INFORMATION

Serving size: 1 serving; **Calories:** 494; **Carbohydrates:** 16 g; **Protein:** 53 g; **Fat:** 23 g

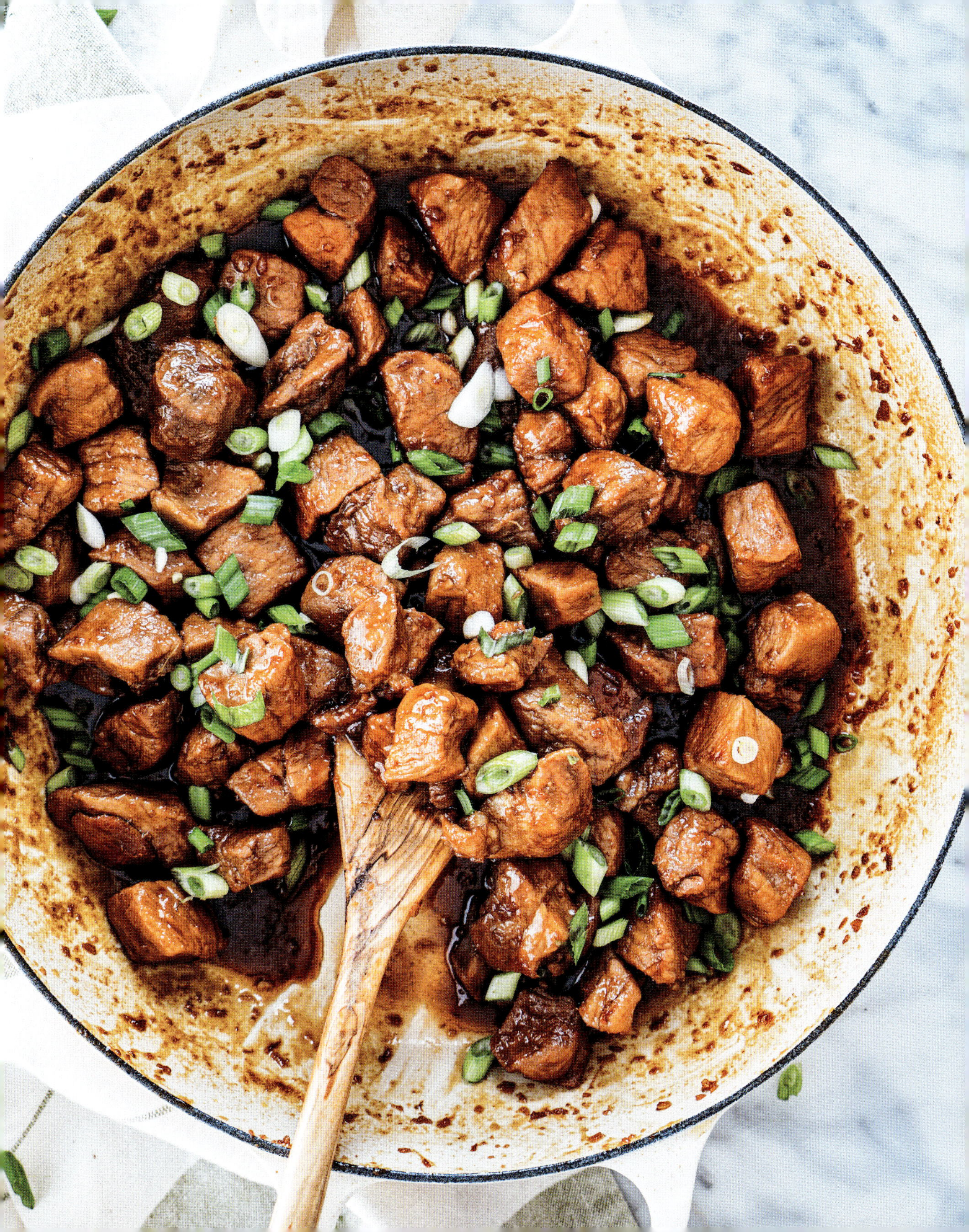

SEAFOOD

FISH IS GOOD FOR US, it's delicious and it's one of the healthiest proteins you can add to your diet. Fish is something we should all cook and eat more often. At least that's what I tell myself all the time. I have quite a few fish recipes on the blog, which is why I want to share some of my favorites and some of my readers' favorites in this book.

My goal for this chapter is to bring variety to your table and allow you to have a few great seafood recipes whenever you're in the mood for it, such as my Firecracker Salmon (page 145) or Lemon-Butter Baked Cod (page 146). If you're just starting to introduce seafood into your diet, you'll love my easy Coconut Shrimp Curry (page 134).

Eating fish once or twice a week—especially fattier fish like salmon, trout or tuna, which are high in omega-3 fatty acids—can be good for your health. So try my Cilantro-Lime Salmon (page 121). It has many health benefits, such as lowering your risk of developing cardiovascular disease and lowering your blood pressure.

One thing to keep in mind is that buying fresh fish can be quite expensive, especially when you're buying wild-caught fish. However, frozen seafood can be an affordable option—try frozen varieties in recipes like the Sole Meunière (page 138) and Chili-Garlic Shrimp (page 141) without compromising on taste.

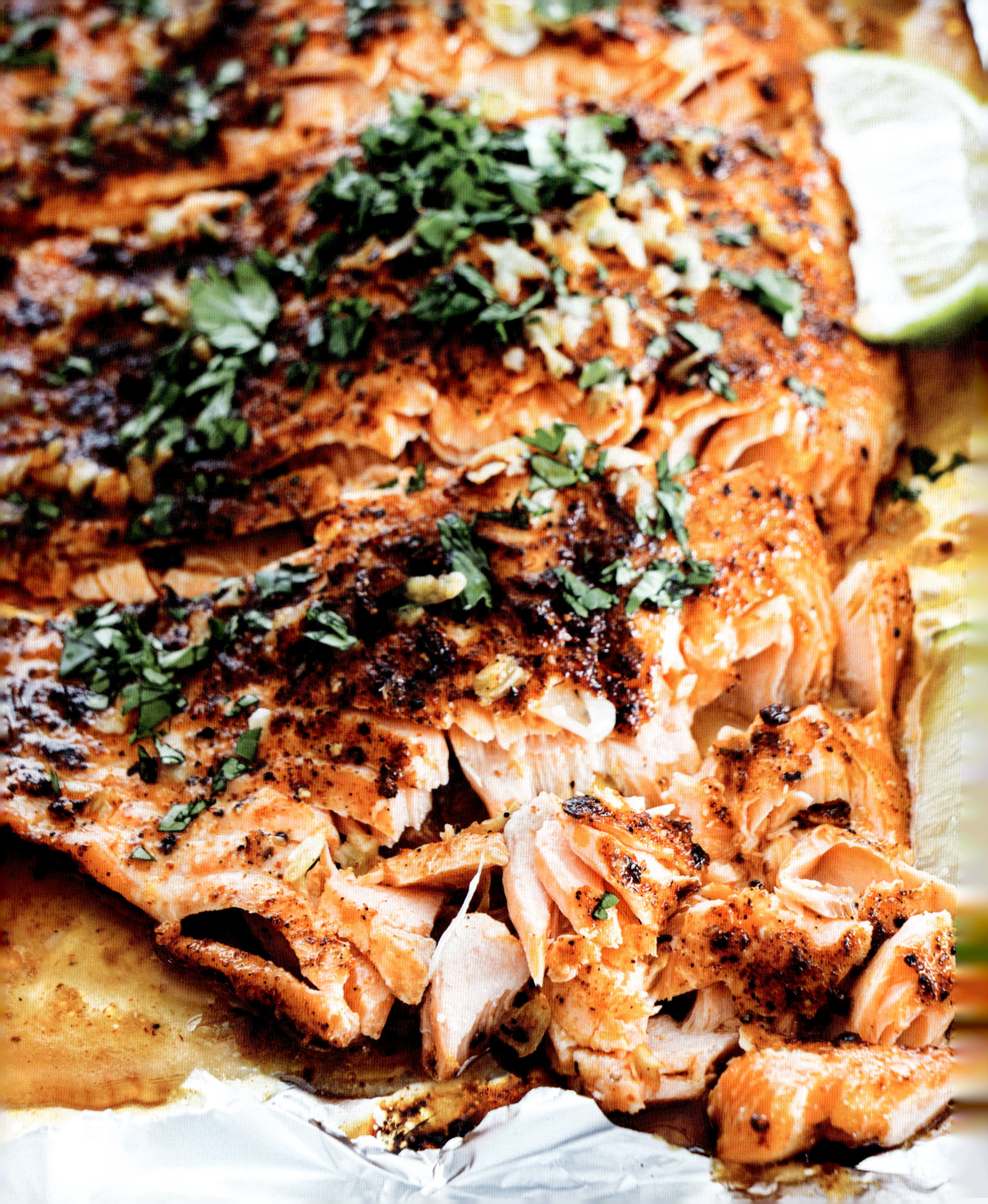

CILANTRO-LIME SALMON

I love this salmon because it's fresh and bright with the flavors of lime, cilantro and a buttery honey sauce. It also makes for a healthy, low-calorie dinner. Best of all, it's ready in only 30 minutes!

PREP TIME: 5 MINUTES
COOK TIME: 25 MINUTES
TOTAL TIME: 30 MINUTES
SERVES: 4

1 lime, sliced
1 tsp smoked paprika
1 tsp chili powder
½ tsp salt
½ tsp black pepper
¼ cup (60 g) unsalted butter, melted
Juice of 2 limes
2 tbsp (30 ml) honey
4 cloves garlic, minced
1 (2-lb [896-g]) skinless or skin-on salmon fillet
¼ cup (12 g) chopped fresh cilantro

Preheat the oven to 350°F (177°C). Line a large baking sheet with aluminum foil. Place the lime slices on baking sheet in a long line; we will place the salmon on top of them.

In a small bowl, whisk together the smoked paprika, chili powder, salt and black pepper. In another small bowl, stir together the butter, lime juice, honey and garlic.

Rub both sides of the salmon with the spice mixture, then lay the salmon on top of the lime slices on the baking sheet. Pour the butter mixture evenly over the salmon. Fold the sides of foil up over the salmon, but do not cover the salmon—this step is just meant to keep the sauce from spilling over.

Bake the salmon for 15 to 20 minutes. Turn the oven to broil and broil the salmon for 5 minutes. Sprinkle the cilantro over the salmon and serve it.

RECIPE NOTES

Salmon will keep in an airtight container in the fridge for up to 3 days; just be sure it has fully cooled before transferring it to the fridge.

You can also freeze this recipe! Place the salmon in an airtight container and freeze it for 4 to 6 months. Allow it to thaw in the fridge overnight and reheat it in the oven at 350°F (177°C).

NUTRITION INFORMATION

Serving size: 1 serving; **Calories:** 471; **Carbohydrates:** 13 g; **Protein:** 46 g; **Fat:** 26 g

EASY CRAB CAKES

My readers love these crab cakes simply because they're delicious, quick and easy to make and use canned crabmeat. These succulent pan-fried crab cakes are crispy on the outside and tender on the inside, loaded with flavor and won't crumble when you fry them!

PREP TIME: 15 MINUTES
COOK TIME: 20 MINUTES
TOTAL TIME: 35 MINUTES
SERVES: 10

12 oz (336 g) canned crabmeat, drained
1 large egg
2 tsp (10 ml) fresh lemon juice
3 tbsp (45 g) mayonnaise
1 tsp Sriracha sauce
2 tbsp (6 g) chopped fresh parsley
3 green onions, chopped
½ cup (30 g) panko breadcrumbs
½ tsp salt, or as needed
¼ tsp black pepper, or as needed
1 tbsp (15 ml) olive oil

In a large bowl, gently combine the crabmeat, egg, lemon juice, mayonnaise, Sriracha sauce, parsley, green onions, breadcrumbs, salt and black pepper.

Form the crab mixture into patties of the desired size; I usually get 10 patties from my mixture.

Heat the oil in a large skillet over medium heat. Working in batches, place the patties in the skillet and cook them for about 5 minutes per side, until they are golden brown.

Serve the crab cakes with your favorite side dish.

RECIPE NOTE

You can bake these crab cakes as well. Preheat the oven to 375°F (191°C). Spray a large baking sheet with cooking spray and place the crab cakes on it. Bake the crab cakes for about 15 minutes, or until they are golden brown.

NUTRITION INFORMATION

Serving size: 1 crab cake; **Calories:** 98; **Carbohydrates:** 4 g; **Protein:** 7 g; **Fat:** 5 g

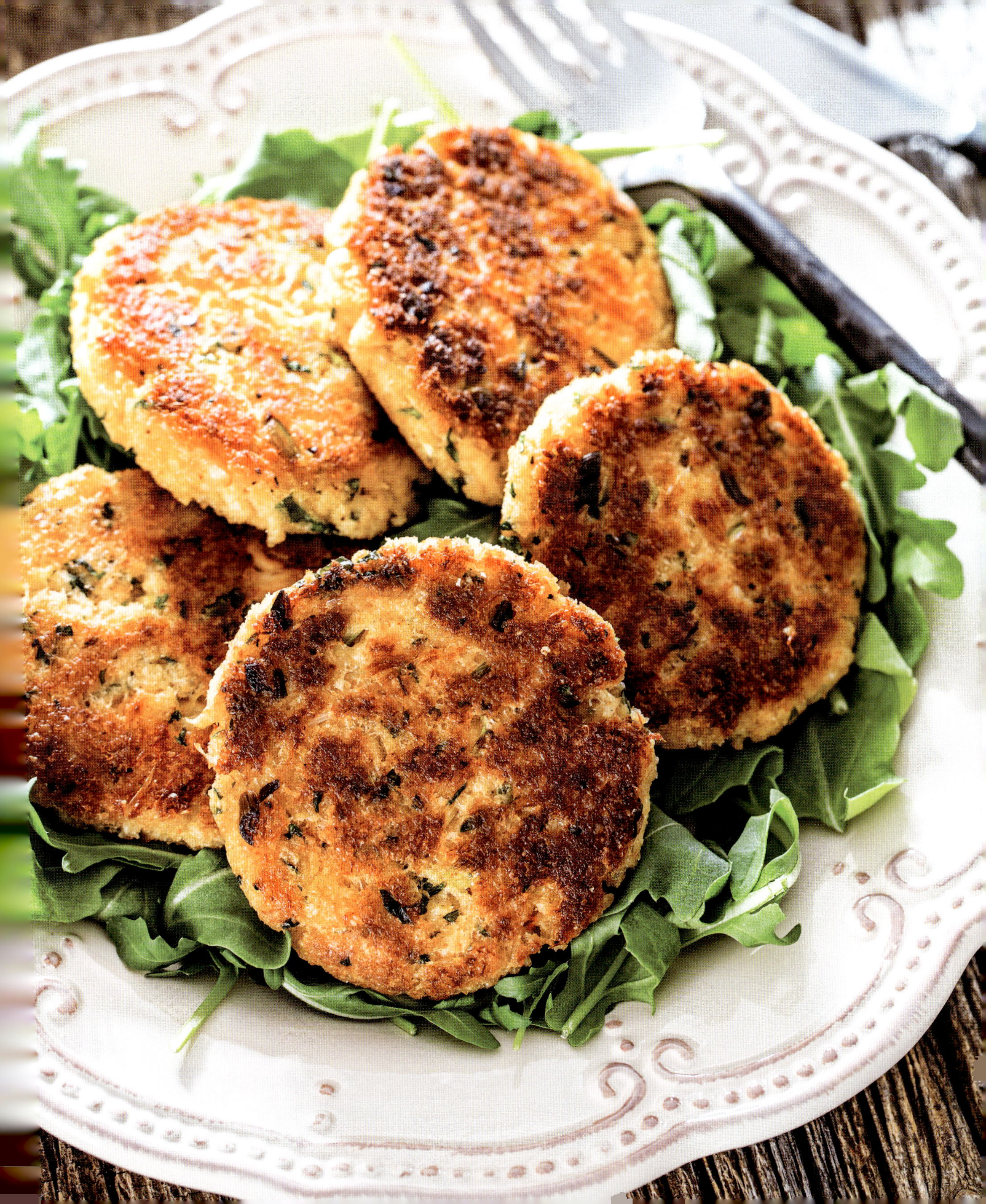

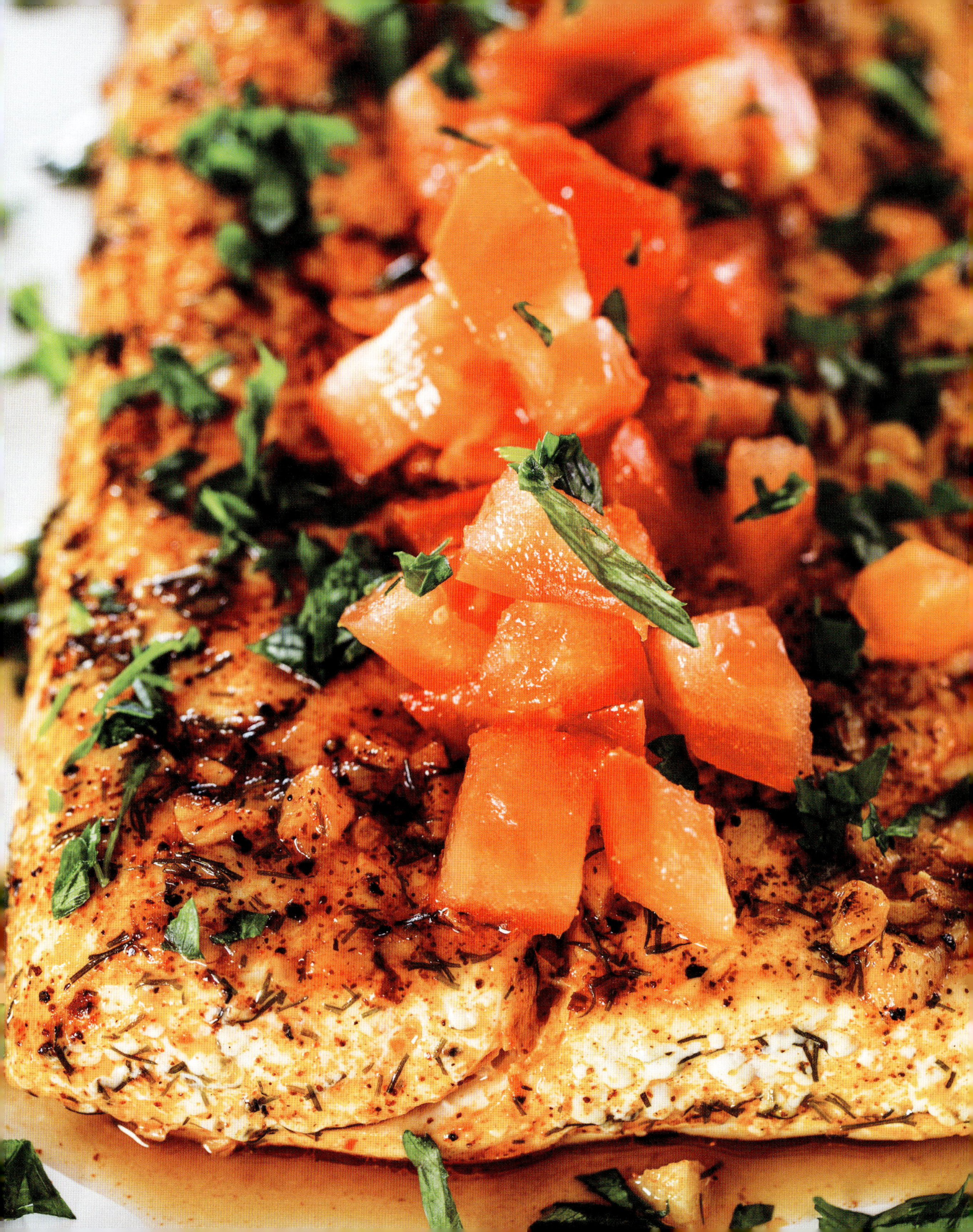

BAKED LEMON-GARLIC HALIBUT

Clean eating has never been any easier: In 55 minutes, you've got yourself a delicious piece of halibut baked to perfection in a lemon and garlic marinade. This is a simple halibut recipe, but I spiced it up a bit with some red pepper flakes and smoked paprika.

PREP TIME: 5 MINUTES
MARINATING TIME: 30 MINUTES
COOK TIME: 20 MINUTES
TOTAL TIME: 55 MINUTES
SERVES: 4

3 tbsp (45 ml) olive oil
⅓ cup (80 ml) fresh lemon juice
1 tsp smoked paprika
½ tsp red pepper flakes
6 cloves garlic, minced
½ tsp black pepper
1 tsp sea salt
1 tsp dried dill
1 (1-lb [448-g]) skinless halibut fillet
1 tomato, diced
2 tbsp (6 g) chopped fresh parsley

In a 9 x 13–inch (27 x 39–cm) baking dish, whisk together the oil, lemon juice, smoked paprika, red pepper flakes, garlic, black pepper, sea salt and dill.

Place the halibut fillet in the baking dish, then flip it over to get some of the marinade on both sides. At this point, you can cut the halibut fillet into smaller individual pieces if desired. Cover the baking dish with plastic wrap and allow the fish to marinate for at least 30 minutes or up to 2 hours in the fridge.

Preheat the oven to 350°F (177°C).

Remove the plastic wrap from the baking dish and transfer it to the oven. Bake the halibut for 20 minutes, or until it is cooked through.

Garnish the halibut with the tomato and parsley, then serve it immediately.

RECIPE NOTES

The baking time should be adjusted based on the thickness of the halibut.

You can use any type of white fish that you prefer. Tilapia is one example.

NUTRITION INFORMATION

Serving size: 1 serving; **Calories:** 216; **Carbohydrates:** 4 g; **Protein:** 21 g; **Fat:** 12 g

HONEY-SOY SHRIMP

Find yourself some plump jumbo shrimp for the ultimate seafood experience: Bite into one of these honey-soy shrimp and you'll taste the juicy meat of the shrimp loaded with garlic, ginger and a bit of heat from the Sriracha!

PREP TIME: 5 MINUTES
COOK TIME: 10 MINUTES
TOTAL TIME: 15 MINUTES
SERVES: 4

⅓ cup (80 ml) low-sodium soy sauce
2 tbsp (30 ml) honey
3 cloves garlic, minced
1 tsp minced fresh ginger
1 tsp Sriracha sauce
1 lb (448 g) tail-on jumbo shrimp, peeled and deveined (see Recipe Notes)
2 tbsp (6 g) chopped fresh parsley

In a medium bowl, whisk together the soy sauce, honey, garlic, ginger and Sriracha sauce.

Add the shrimp to the bowl and toss them well, making sure the shrimp are coated in the sauce.

Heat a large skillet over medium-high heat. Add the shrimp to the skillet, being sure to reserve the sauce in the bowl. Cook the shrimp for 2 to 3 minutes per side, until they start to turn pink and are cooked through. Garnish the shrimp with the parsley. Remove the shrimp from the skillet and set them aside.

Pour the reserved sauce into the skillet and cook it for 2 minutes, until it thickens. Serve the sauce as a dip for the shrimp.

RECIPE NOTES

You can use any type of shrimp that is most convenient for you, as long as it totals 1 pound (448 g).

This recipe can also be made with chicken or veggies like broccoli and carrots.

You can adjust the amount of Sriracha to suit how spicy you'd like the dish to be. If you don't like spice, you can omit it entirely.

You can bake these shrimp at 425°F (218°C) for 10 to 15 minutes, or until they turn pink.

This recipe will keep in an airtight container in the fridge for 3 to 4 days, so feel free to make it ahead of time. You can freeze the shrimp from this recipe for up to 3 months in an airtight container. Just allow the dish to thaw overnight in the fridge before cooking the shrimp.

NUTRITION INFORMATION

Serving size: 1 serving; **Calories:** 161; **Carbohydrates:** 11 g; **Protein:** 25 g; **Fat:** 2 g

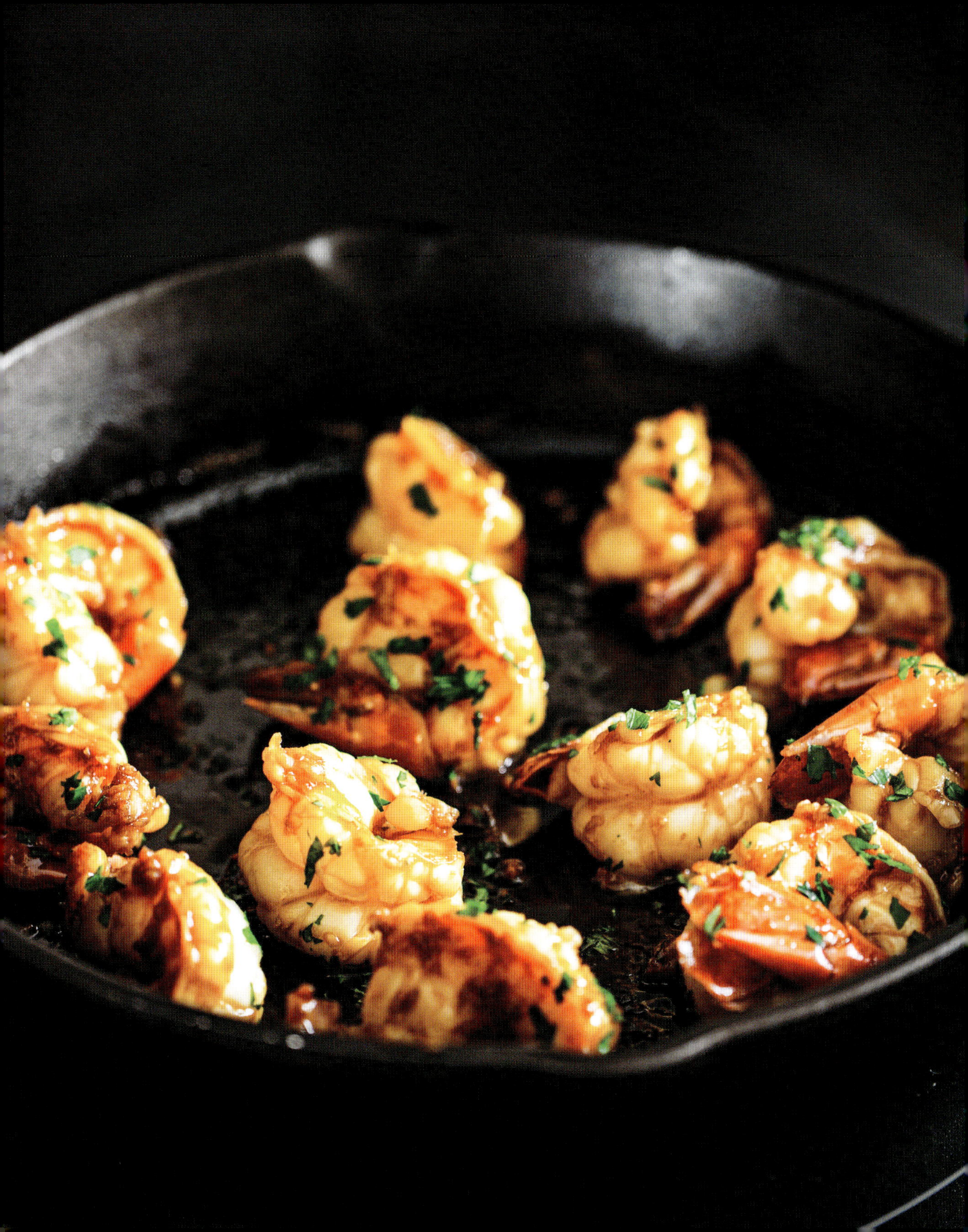

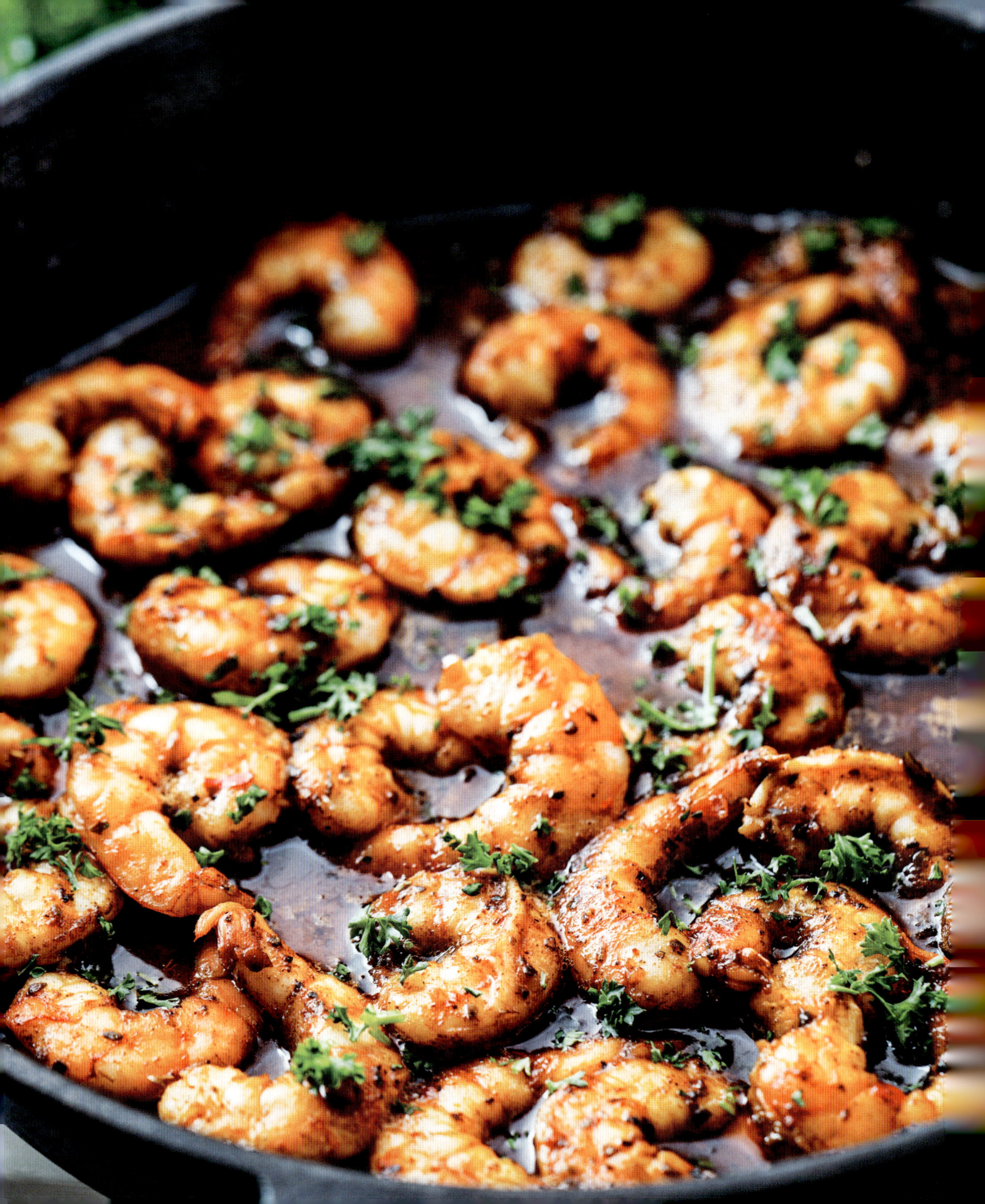

SPICY NEW ORLEANS SHRIMP

A few short years ago, I wasn't a fan of spicy food—but I wanted to be able to eat spicier and spicier foods. Over the past few years, I've trained myself to enjoy a little more spice in my dishes.

This shrimp recipe is one of my favorites, and one of my readers' favorite recipes as well. The shrimp are spicy and decadent. Make sure you have a French baguette to dip into that sauce and soak it all up—that's where all the flavor is!

PREP TIME: 5 MINUTES
COOK TIME: 25 MINUTES
MARINATING TIME: 30 MINUTES
TOTAL TIME: 1 HOUR
SERVES: 2

2 tbsp (30 g) unsalted butter
2 tbsp (30 ml) olive oil
2 tbsp (30 ml) sweet chili sauce
1 tbsp (15 ml) Worcestershire sauce
1 tsp chili powder
1 tsp liquid smoke
1 tsp smoked paprika
1 tsp dried oregano
1 tsp Sriracha sauce or Tabasco® sauce
4 cloves garlic, minced
Juice from ½ lemon, plus more as needed
Salt, as needed
Black pepper, as needed
2 tbsp (6 g) chopped fresh parsley
1 lb (448 g) jumbo shrimp, peeled and deveined
French bread, for serving

In a large oven-safe skillet over low heat, combine the butter, oil, sweet chili sauce, Worcestershire sauce, chili powder, liquid smoke, smoked paprika, oregano, Sriracha sauce, garlic, lemon juice, salt, black pepper and parsley. Stir the mixture and simmer it for 5 to 10 minutes.

Remove the skillet from the heat and let the sauce cool for 2 minutes.

Add the shrimp and toss them in the sauce, so that they are fully immersed.

Cover the skillet with foil and refrigerate it for at least 30 minutes, or up to 4 hours, to allow the shrimp to marinate in the sauce.

Preheat the oven to 400°F (204°C).

Bake the shrimp for 10 to 15 minutes, until it is opaque.

Serve the shrimp immediately with crusty French bread and a drizzle of additional lemon juice as needed.

RECIPE NOTES

This recipe will keep stored in an airtight container in the fridge for 3 to 4 days, so feel free to make it ahead of time. You can freeze the shrimp in an airtight container for up to 3 months. Just allow the dish to thaw overnight in the fridge before cooking the shrimp.

NUTRITION INFORMATION

Serving size: 1 serving; **Calories:** 443; **Carbohydrates:** 15 g; **Protein:** 32 g; **Fat:** 28 g

BAKED LEMON-PEPPER SALMON

PREP TIME: 5 MINUTES
COOK TIME: 30 MINUTES
TOTAL TIME: 35 MINUTES
SERVES: 4

POTATOES

1 lb (448 g) fingerling potatoes, halved

1½ tsp (5 g) lemon-pepper seasoning, or as needed

2 tbsp (30 ml) olive oil

SALMON

3 cloves garlic, minced

2 tbsp (18 g) lemon-pepper seasoning, or as needed

2 tbsp (30 ml) fresh lemon juice

¼ cup (60 g) unsalted butter, melted

1 (2-lb [896-g]) skinless or skin-on salmon fillet

This is a complete dinner, baked on just one baking sheet and featuring roasted potatoes and the most amazing garlic and lemon butter sauce. This recipe requires few ingredients and minimal prep, but it yields big flavor!

Preheat the oven to 425°F (218°C).

To make the potatoes, place the potatoes on a 9 x 13–inch (27 x 39–cm) baking sheet. Add the lemon-pepper seasoning and oil, then toss the potatoes to coat them thoroughly. Spread the potatoes evenly across the baking sheet. Bake them for 10 minutes.

To make the salmon, mix together the garlic, lemon-pepper seasoning, lemon juice and butter in a small bowl. Set the sauce aside.

Once the potatoes have baked for 10 minutes, use a spatula to move the potatoes to the side of the baking sheet; you need just enough room for the salmon to fit on the baking sheet lengthwise. Transfer the salmon to the baking sheet and spoon the prepared sauce over both sides of the salmon.

Bake the salmon and potatoes for 15 minutes, or until the salmon is fully cooked through and the potatoes are tender. Optionally, after the initial 15 minutes have elapsed, increase the oven's temperature to broil and broil the salmon and potatoes for 2 to 5 minutes to make them crispy. If you decide to broil, keep an eye on the salmon and potatoes the entire time to prevent burning them.

RECIPE NOTES

Store any leftover salmon in an airtight container in the fridge for up to 3 days. You can reheat it in 30-second intervals in the microwave or in the oven at 450°F (232°C) for 5 to 7 minutes.

If you choose to freeze your leftovers, they will last for 4 to 6 months. It's best to let the salmon thaw overnight in the fridge before reheating it.

NUTRITION INFORMATION

Serving size: 1 serving; **Calories:** 587; **Carbohydrates:** 23 g; **Protein:** 48 g; **Fat:** 33 g

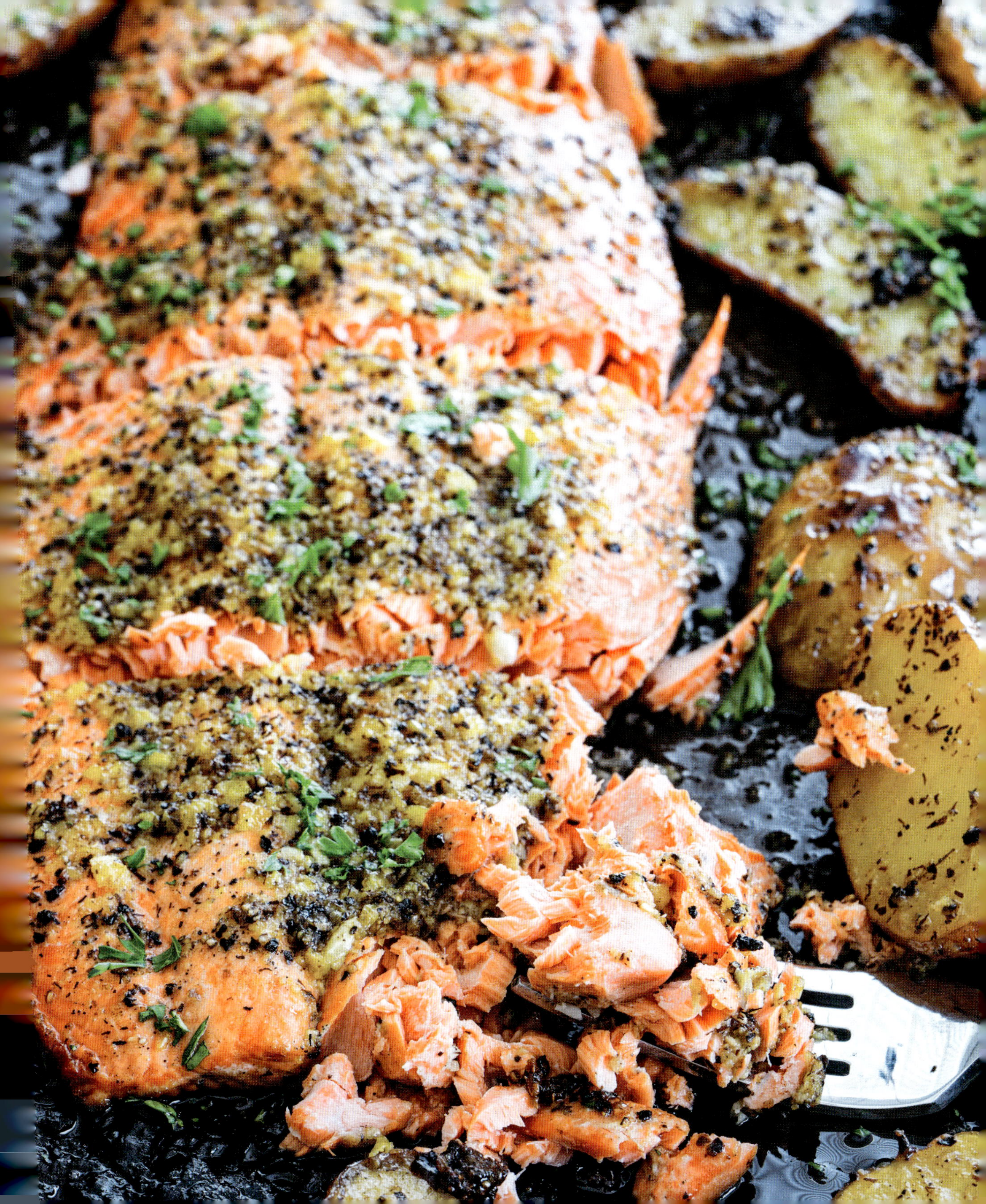

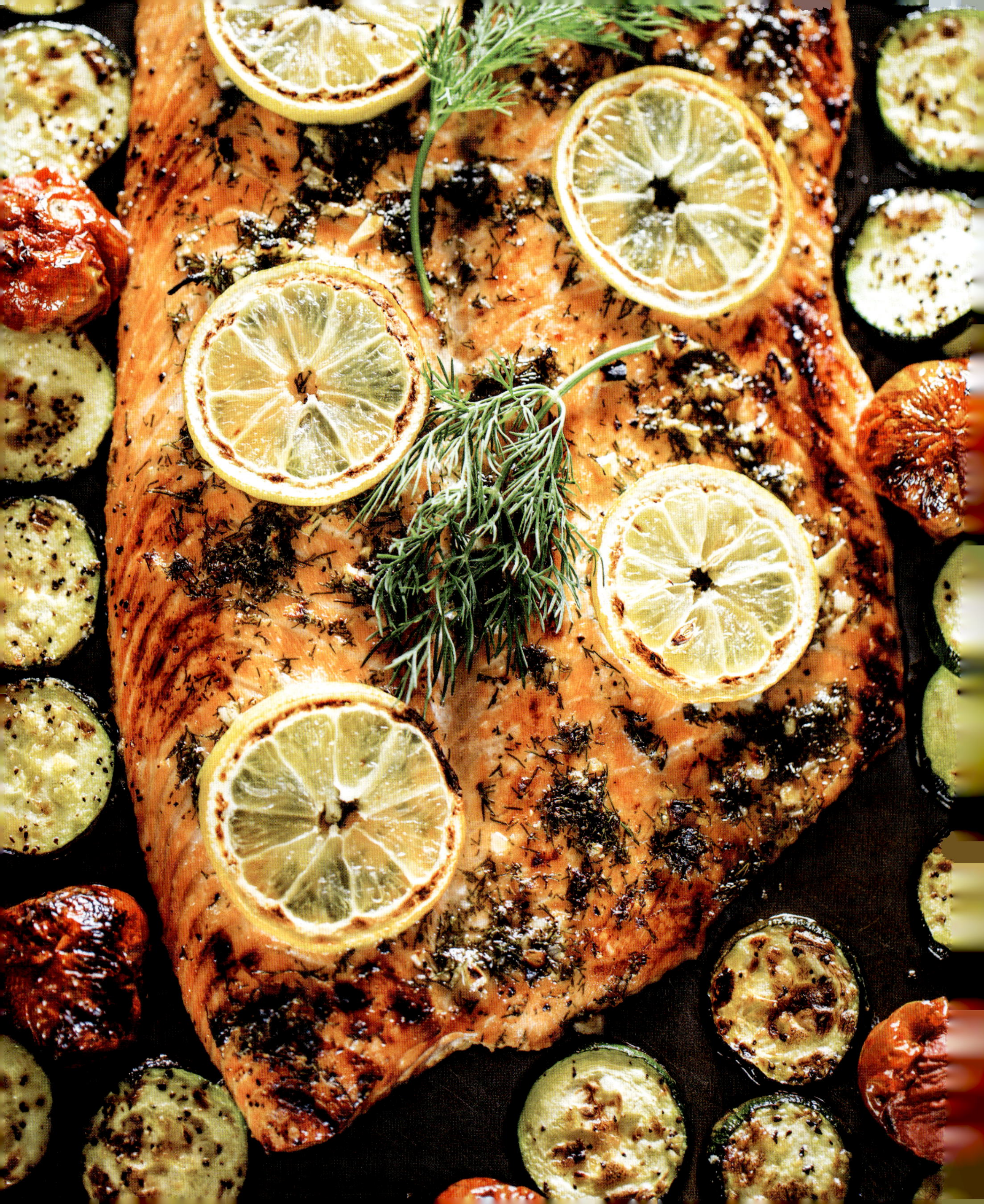

HONEY-GARLIC SALMON AND VEGGIES SHEET PAN DINNER

PREP TIME: 5 MINUTES
COOK TIME: 20 MINUTES
TOTAL TIME: 25 MINUTES
SERVES: 4

2 tbsp (30 ml) honey
3 cloves garlic, minced
¼ cup (60 ml) fresh lemon juice
¼ cup (12 g) chopped fresh dill
½ tsp salt, divided
½ tsp black pepper, divided
1 (2-lb [896-g]) skinless or skin-on salmon fillet
1 lemon, sliced (optional)
2 zucchinis, sliced (see Recipe Notes)
12 cocktail tomatoes
1 tbsp (15 ml) olive oil

Here is another great sheet pan dinner featuring honey-garlic salmon and roasted zucchini and tomatoes. But don't stop there—this recipe is versatile! You can add other veggies to your sheet pan, such as asparagus, green beans, broccoli, mushrooms, carrots, Brussels sprouts, you name it. Use your favorite veggies and in just 25 minutes, dinner is served.

Preheat the oven to 400°F (204°C). Spray a large baking sheet with cooking spray.

In a small bowl, whisk together the honey, garlic, lemon juice, dill, ¼ teaspoon of the salt and ¼ teaspoon of the black pepper. Pour the sauce over the salmon and spread on both sides of the fillet. Place the salmon in the middle of the prepared baking sheet. Place some lemon slices on top of the salmon (if using).

Season the zucchini and tomatoes with the remaining ¼ teaspoon of salt and ¼ teaspoon of black pepper. Drizzle the oil over them and arrange on the baking sheet around the salmon.

Bake the salmon and vegetables for 15 minutes. Increase the oven's temperature to broil and broil them for 3 to 5 minutes, or just until the top of the salmon browns a bit. Make sure you watch it closely, as it can burn quickly.

Serve the salmon and vegetables immediately.

RECIPE NOTES

If you don't like zucchini, you can use any vegetables that you like. For example, broccoli, cauliflower, Brussels sprouts and potatoes are all excellent options.

Salmon can be stored in an airtight container in the fridge for up to 3 days. You can freeze cooked salmon for 2 to 3 months to ensure freshness. Allow it to thaw completely in the fridge before reheating it in the oven at 350°F (177°C).

NUTRITION INFORMATION

Serving size: 1 serving; **Calories:** 427; **Carbohydrates:** 18 g; **Protein:** 47 g; **Fat:** 18 g

COCONUT SHRIMP CURRY

This recipe is not only popular on the blog but it's also one that I am most often requested to share with friends who come over, which boggles my mind because it's such an easy recipe—anyone can make it in just 35 minutes. This curry is packed full of aromatic spices and delicious, plump shrimp.

PREP TIME: 10 MINUTES
MARINATING TIME: 10 MINUTES
COOK TIME: 15 MINUTES
TOTAL TIME: 35 MINUTES
SERVES: 4

SHRIMP AND MARINADE
1 lb (448 g) jumbo shrimp, peeled and deveined
¼ tsp salt
¼ tsp black pepper (see Recipe Notes)
¼ tsp cayenne pepper
2 tbsp (30 ml) fresh lemon juice

CURRY SAUCE
1 tbsp (15 g) coconut oil
1 onion, chopped
3 cloves garlic, minced
1 tbsp (9 g) minced fresh ginger
½ tsp black pepper
½ tsp salt, or as needed
½ tsp ground turmeric
2 tsp (6 g) ground coriander
1 tsp curry powder
1 (15-oz [420-g]) can diced tomatoes, undrained
1 (14-oz [420-ml]) can coconut milk
Cooked rice, for serving
2 tbsp (6 g) chopped fresh cilantro or parsley

To make the shrimp and marinade, place the shrimp in a small bowl. Add the salt, black pepper, cayenne pepper and lemon juice. Toss the shrimp in the marinade to coat them. Cover the bowl with plastic wrap and refrigerate it for 10 minutes.

While the shrimp are marinating, make the curry sauce. Heat the oil in a medium skillet over medium heat. Add the onion and cook it for 2 to 3 minutes, until it softens and becomes translucent. Stir in the garlic, ginger, black pepper, salt, turmeric, coriander and curry powder. Cook the mixture for 1 minute.

Add the tomatoes and their juice and the coconut milk. Stir the sauce and bring it to a boil. Cook the sauce for about 5 minutes, stirring it occasionally. Add the shrimp with the accumulated juices from the marinade and cook them in the sauce for 2 minutes, or until the shrimp are pink and cooked through.

Serve the curry over the rice and garnish the dish with the cilantro.

RECIPE NOTES

Freshly ground black pepper is best in this dish.

The curry should be safely sealed in an airtight container and refrigerated for up to 3 days. If you want this curry to last, you can freeze it for up to 3 months. Ensure that it is fully cooled before sealing it in a shallow container to ensure even freezing. Stir the curry well while reheating it.

NUTRITION INFORMATION

Serving size: 1 serving; **Calories:** 371; **Carbohydrates:** 12 g; **Protein:** 27 g; **Fat:** 26 g

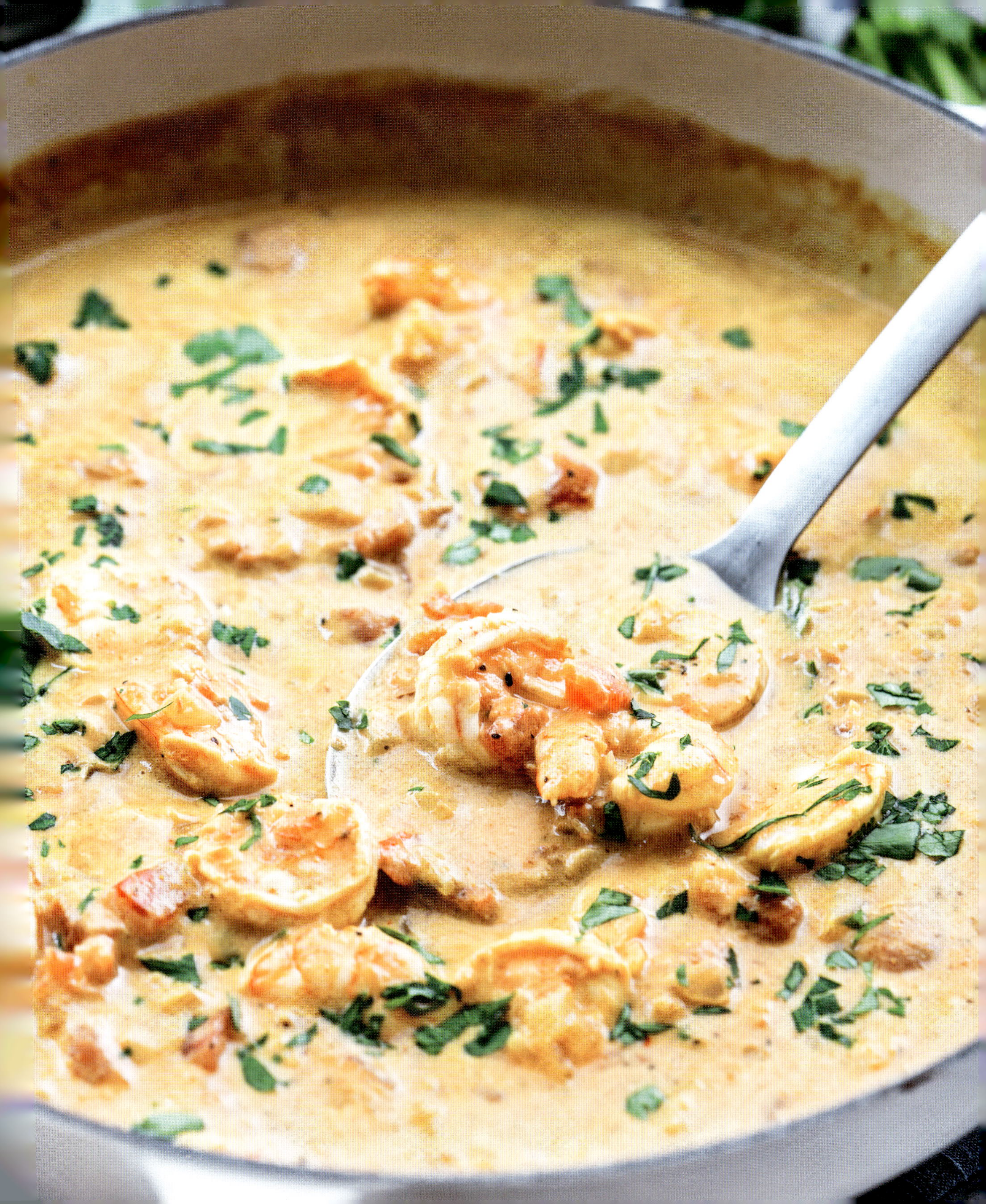

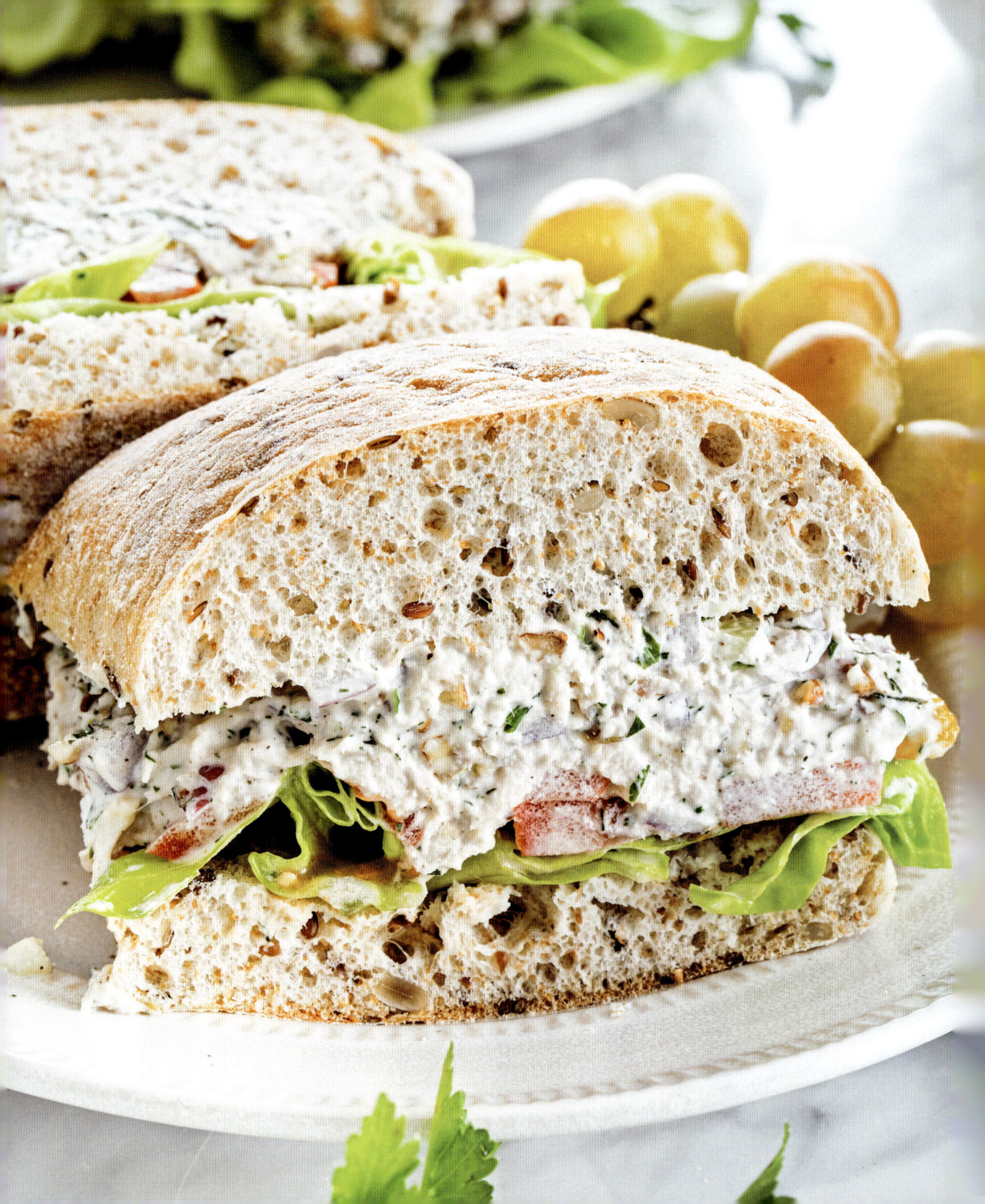

EASY TUNA SALAD

PREP TIME: 15 MINUTES
COOK TIME: NONE
TOTAL TIME: 15 MINUTES
SERVES: 4

½ cup (75 g) chopped red onion
⅓ cup (33 g) chopped celery
1 cup (120 g) pecans, chopped
2 tbsp (6 g) chopped fresh parsley
½ tbsp (2 g) dried dill or 2 tbsp (6 g) chopped fresh dill
½ cup (75 g) raisins
1 cup (240 g) mayonnaise
12 oz (336 g) tuna in water, drained
¼ tsp salt, or as needed
¼ tsp black pepper, or as needed
2 tomatoes, sliced

I have to give credit where credit is due: to my husband. He's the one who came up with this delicious tuna salad. When I worked late nights at my job, he'd often wait for me with dinner on the table, and one night he made me this delicious dish. It's become our go-to tuna salad.

This recipe uses such simple ingredients and tastes so fresh. It's perfect for lunch or dinner! One of my favorite ways to serve it is to make salad wraps with it—I use butter lettuce, which is my favorite lettuce for salad wraps. Just load up each salad wrap and eat as many as you want, guilt-free.

In a medium bowl, combine the onion, celery, pecans and parsley.

Add the dill, raisins, mayonnaise, tuna, salt and black pepper. Stir to combine the ingredients.

Serve the tuna salad with the tomatoes on sandwiches, on top of green salads, in wraps or in pasta salads.

RECIPE NOTES

Refrigerate your tuna salad in an airtight container for 3 to 5 days. You can freeze tuna salad too! It will stay fresh for only 1 week, and it must be stored in small batches in airtight containers.

NUTRITION INFORMATION

Serving size: 1 serving; **Calories:** 700; **Carbohydrates:** 23 g; **Protein:** 21 g; **Fat:** 61 g

SOLE MEUNIÈRE

Sole meunière is a classic French dish—a Julia Child classic to be exact—that's ready in just twenty minutes. I'm talking crispy sole fillets, dripping with butter and studded with capers, parsley and lemon. Totally delicious!

PREP TIME: 10 MINUTES
COOK TIME: 10 MINUTES
TOTAL TIME: 20 MINUTES
SERVES: 6

6 skinless sole fillets (see Recipe Notes)
¼ tsp salt, or as needed
¼ tsp black pepper, or to taste
½ cup (60 g) all-purpose flour
6 tbsp (90 g) unsalted butter, divided
⅓ cup (46 g) capers, drained
3 tbsp (9 g) chopped fresh parsley
Lemon wedges, for serving

Season the sole fillets on both sides with the salt and black pepper.

Place the flour in a shallow dish. Dredge the sole fillets through the flour to coat them on both sides; shake off any excess flour.

Heat a large skillet over medium-high heat until it is very hot. Add 1 tablespoon (15 g) of the butter to the skillet. Heat the butter until brown specks begin to form at the bottom of the skillet and the butter has a nutty aroma; be careful not to burn the butter. Place as many sole fillets as you can in the skillet. Sauté the fish fillets for 1 to 2 minutes per side, or until they are golden brown.

Transfer the fish to an oven-safe platter and repeat the preceding step with the remaining fish fillets. If your oven has a warming drawer, keep the platter of cooked fish in the warming drawer until the butter sauce is ready; otherwise, preheat the oven to 200°F (93°C), then turn the oven off and place the platter in the oven to keep the fillets warm.

Wipe the skillet clean and add the remaining 5 tablespoons (75 g) of butter. Heat the butter until it is bubbling, then add the capers and cook them for about 5 minutes, until the butter starts to brown.

Garnish the fish fillets with the parsley, then immediately pour the butter sauce over the fillets; the parsley should fry in the hot sauce and become crispy.

Garnish the sole with the lemon wedges and serve it at once.

NUTRITION INFORMATION

Serving size: 1 fillet; **Calories:** 267; **Carbohydrates:** 10 g; **Protein:** 22 g; **Fat:** 15 g

RECIPE NOTES

If you prefer, you can use another variety of thin fish fillets, like flounder. Regardless of the type of fish you use, the total weight of the fillets should come to about 1 pound (448 g).

I often serve these fillets with grilled asparagus, but potatoes would also work. Or try serving the fish over rice.

Capers are not traditionally used in this recipe. If you'd prefer not to use capers, it is okay to omit them.

You can store this recipe in an airtight container in the fridge for 3 to 4 days. Unfortunately, this recipe doesn't freeze well, but it's so easy that it's no hassle to make it the day you wish to serve it!

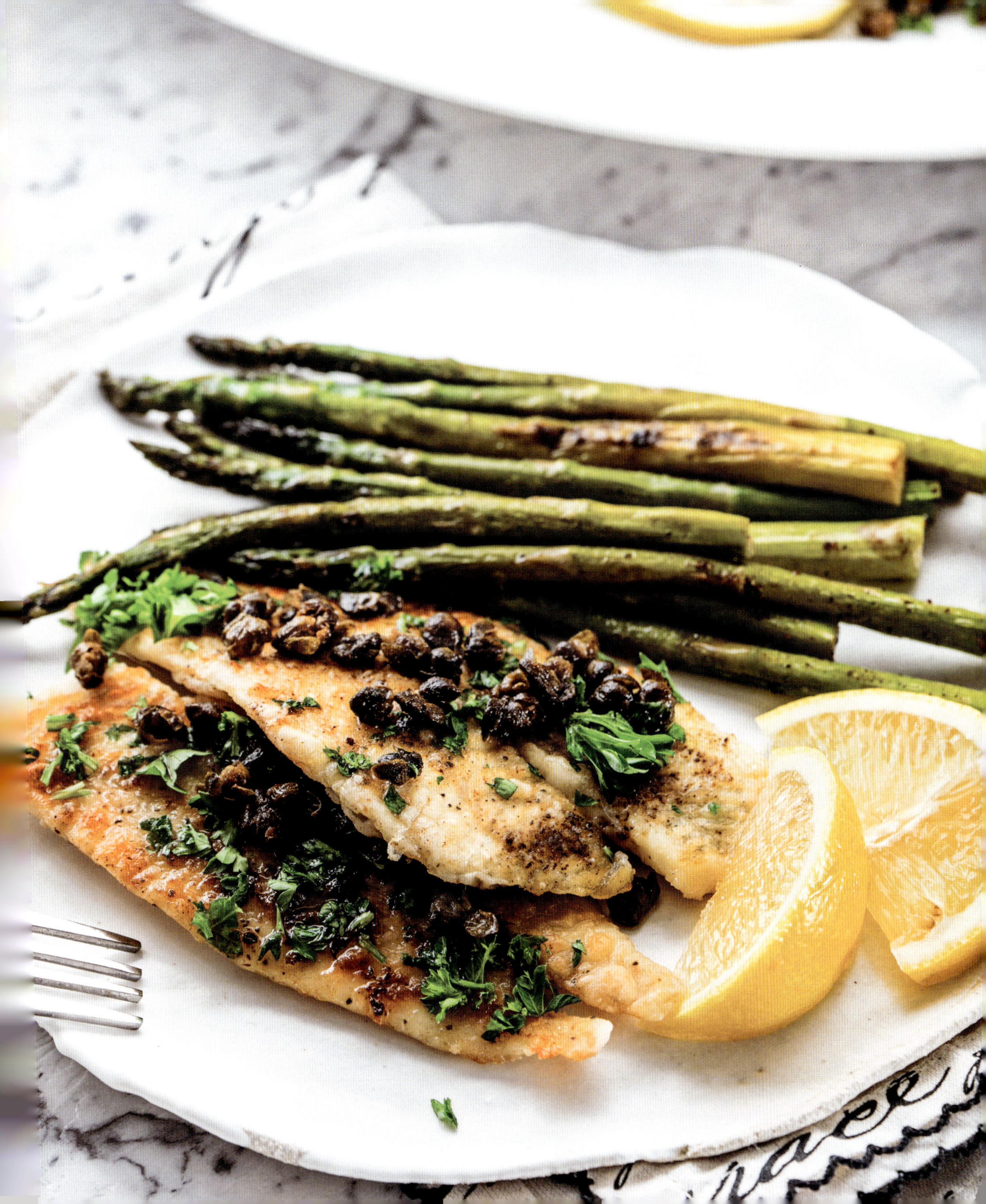

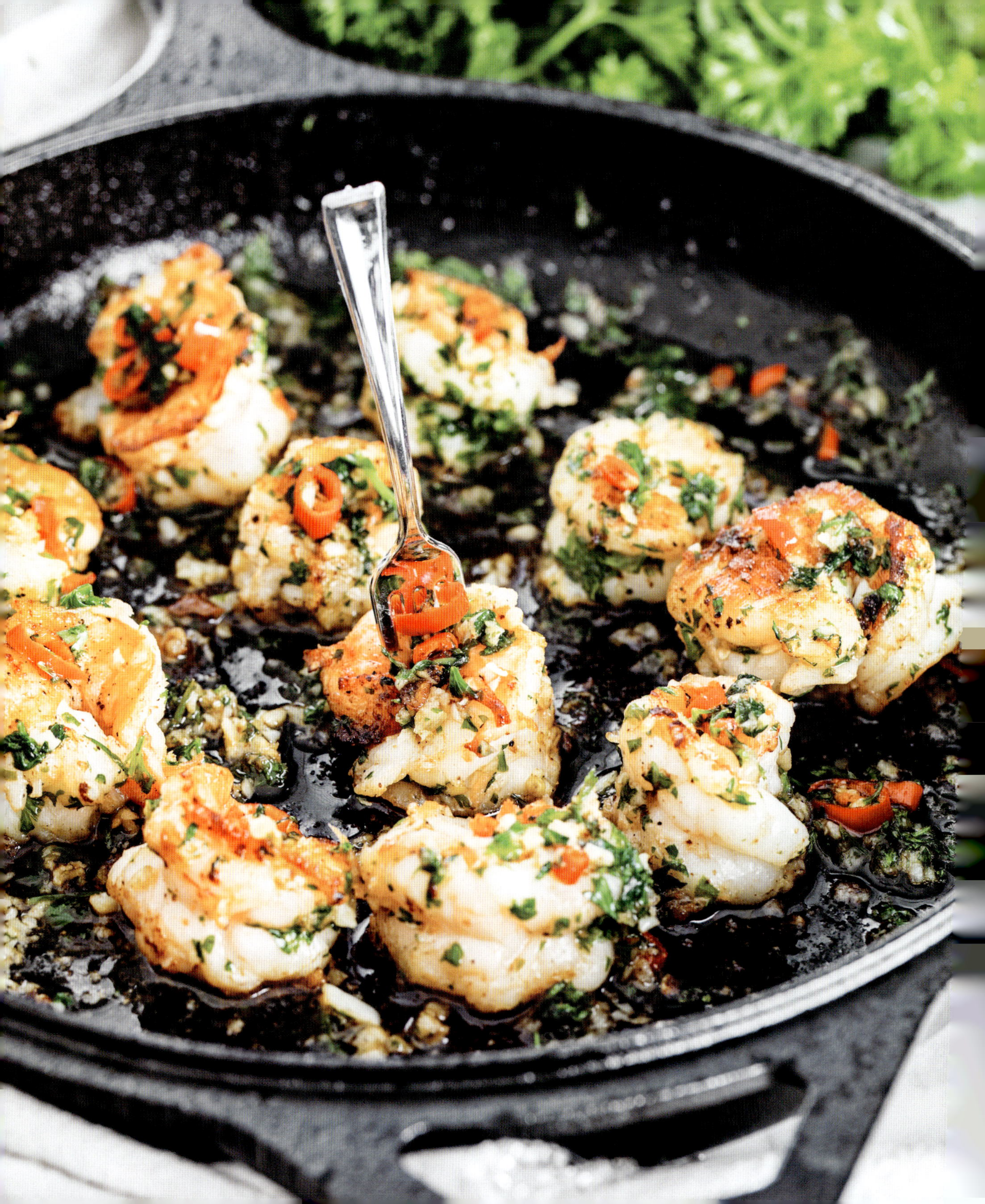

CHILI-GARLIC SHRIMP

Talk about plump and juicy shrimp! If you like a little heat and a lot of garlic on your shrimp, then you'll love this recipe. Ready in just fifteen minutes, these shrimp are perfect as an appetizer or a main dish alongside some steamed veggies.

PREP TIME: 5 MINUTES
COOK TIME: 10 MINUTES
TOTAL TIME: 15 MINUTES
SERVES: 4

2 tbsp (30 ml) olive oil
2 tbsp (30 g) unsalted butter
1 lb (448 g) large or jumbo shrimped, peeled and deveined
½ tsp sea salt, divided
½ tsp black pepper, divided
5 cloves garlic, minced
2 red chili peppers, chopped (see Recipe Note)
¼ cup (14 g) chopped fresh parsley

Heat a large skillet over high heat. Add the oil and butter and allow the butter to melt.

Add the shrimp to the skillet and arrange them in a single layer. Season them with ¼ teaspoon of the salt and ¼ teaspoon of the black pepper. Cook the shrimp for 2 to 3 minutes, until they turn pink, golden and crispy. Flip the shrimp over and sear them for 2 minutes on the opposite side. Season this side with the remaining ¼ teaspoon of salt and ¼ teaspoon of black pepper.

Add the garlic, chili peppers and parsley. Stir everything together. Cook the mixture for 30 seconds, or until the garlic is aromatic.

Serve the chili-garlic shrimp warm on its own, over rice or with steamed veggies.

RECIPE NOTE

Use fresh chilies here—if you use the dried chilies, the heat levels of the dish will be different.

NUTRITION INFORMATION

Serving size: 1 serving; **Calories:** 242; **Carbohydrates:** 3 g; **Protein:** 24 g; **Fat:** 14 g

LEMON-GARLIC SCALLOPS

Scallops are probably my favorite seafood—if they are cooked perfectly, that is. They're a memorable dish for a special occasion. These simple scallops are tender, succulent and served with a lemon-garlic sauce that's perfect over pasta.

PREP TIME: 5 MINUTES
COOK TIME: 10 MINUTES
TOTAL TIME: 15 MINUTES
SERVES: 4

SCALLOPS
1¼ lb (560 g) scallops
2 tbsp (30 ml) olive oil
¼ tsp salt, divided
¼ tsp black pepper, divided
2 tbsp (30 g) butter
Cooked pasta, for serving

LEMON-GARLIC SAUCE
2 tbsp (30 ml) olive oil
2 tbsp (30 g) butter
5 cloves garlic, minced
¼ cup (60 ml) white wine (see Recipe Notes)
2 tbsp (30 ml) fresh lemon juice
¼ tsp salt, or as needed
¼ tsp black pepper, or as needed

To make the scallops, remove the side muscle from the scallops. Pat them dry with paper towels.

Heat the oil in a large skillet over high heat. Working in batches if necessary, gently add the scallops to the skillet, making sure they are not touching one another. Season them with ⅛ teaspoon of the salt and ⅛ teaspoon of the black pepper, then add the butter to the skillet. Sear the scallops for 2 minutes, then flip them over and cook them for 2 to 3 minutes on the other side, or until both sides have a golden-brown crust. Season the other side of the scallops with the remaining ⅛ teaspoon of salt and ⅛ teaspoon of black pepper. Transfer the scallops to a plate.

To make the lemon-garlic sauce, heat the oil in another large skillet over high heat (see Recipe Notes). Add the butter and allow it to melt. Add the garlic and sauté it for 20 to 30 seconds, until it becomes aromatic. Be careful not to burn it.

Add the wine and lemon juice and season the sauce with the salt and black pepper. Cook the sauce for 1 minute, then turn off the heat. Add the scallops and the accumulated juices to the skillet.

Serve the lemon-garlic scallops over the pasta immediately.

RECIPE NOTES
I use a pinot grigio for this recipe, which is also a great wine to serve with this dish.

While I use a different skillet to make a clearer sauce, you could certainly use the same skillet and scrape the brown bits from the bottom to include in the sauce.

NUTRITION INFORMATION
Serving size: 1 serving; **Calories:** 343; **Carbohydrates:** 6 g; **Protein:** 17 g; **Fat:** 26 g

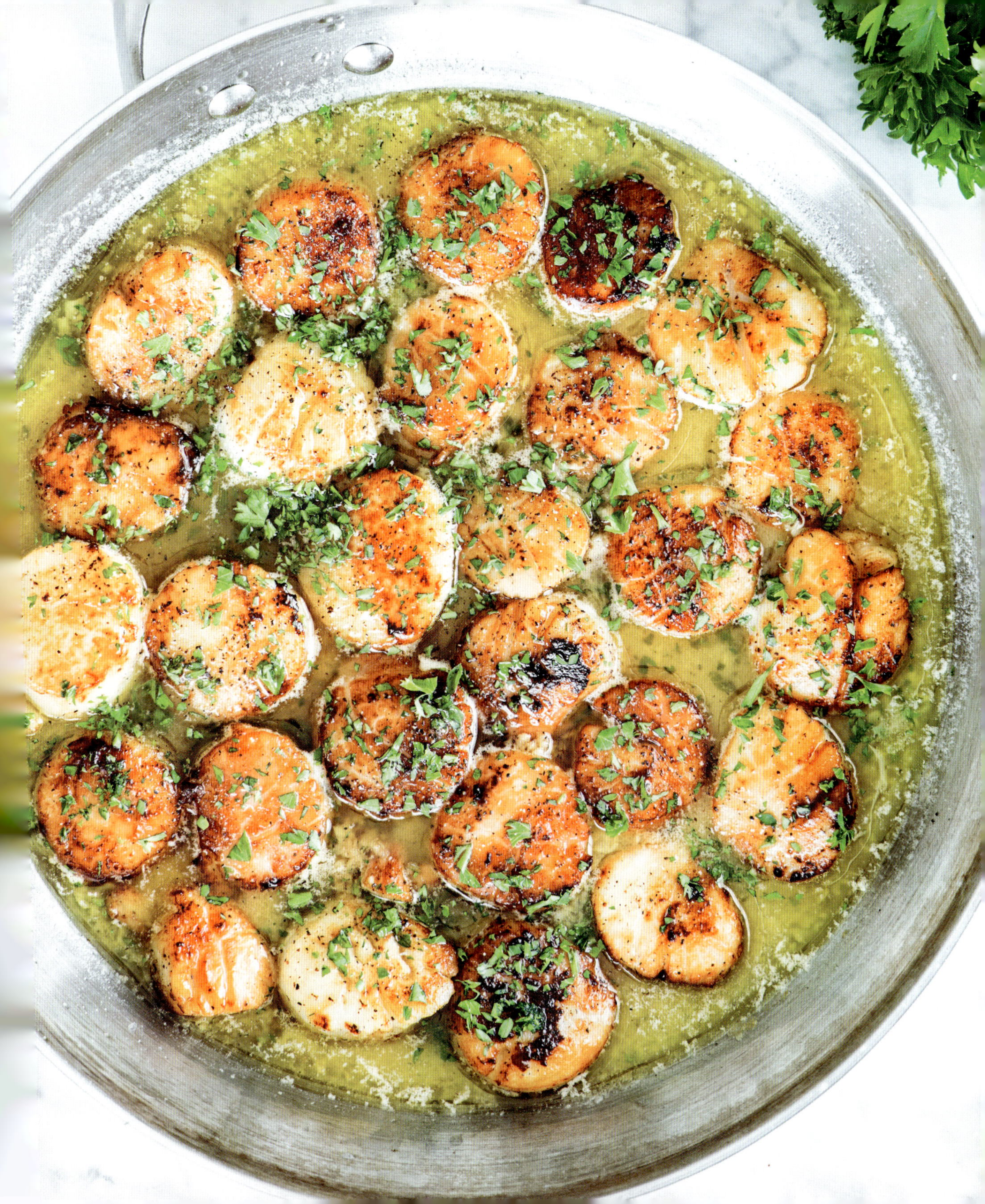

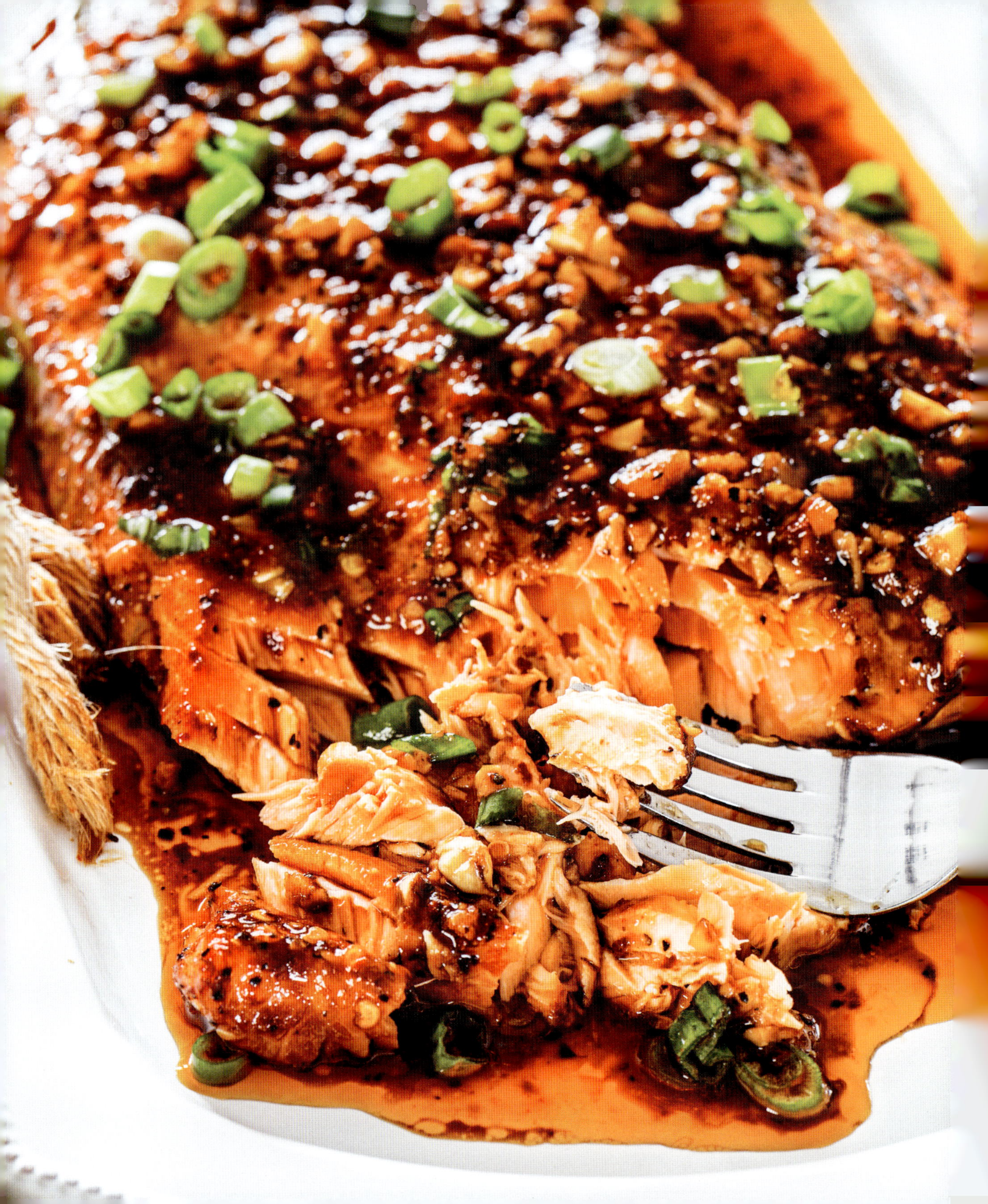

FIRECRACKER SALMON

This salmon is out of this world! Red pepper flakes and Sriracha provide salmon with the fiery flavors that give this dish its name. The sauce is incredible not only on salmon but it's also excellent on chicken.

PREP TIME: 5 MINUTES
MARINATING TIME: 2 HOURS
COOK TIME: 20 MINUTES
TOTAL TIME: 2 HOURS, 25 MINUTES
SERVES: 4

FIRECRACKER SAUCE
3 cloves garlic, minced
1 tsp minced fresh ginger
¼ cup (60 ml) olive oil
¼ cup (60 ml) low-sodium soy sauce
2 tbsp (30 g) brown sugar
1 tsp red pepper flakes (see Recipe Notes)
1 tbsp (15 ml) Sriracha sauce (see Recipe Notes)
1 tsp black pepper

SALMON
1 (1½-lb [372-g]) skinless salmon fillet
2 green onions, chopped

To make the firecracker sauce, whisk together the garlic, ginger, oil, soy sauce, brown sugar, red pepper flakes, Sriracha sauce and black pepper in a small bowl.

To make the salmon, place the salmon in a 9 x 13–inch (27 x 39–cm) baking dish and pour the firecracker sauce over the salmon. Rub or brush the sauce over both sides of the fillet, making sure it is entirely covered. Cover the baking dish with plastic wrap and let the salmon marinate in the fridge for at least 2 hours, or up to 24 hours.

Preheat oven to 375°F (191°C).

Remove the plastic wrap from the baking dish. Bake the salmon for 15 to 20 minutes, until it flakes easily with a fork. Note that the baking time could vary depending on the thickness of the salmon.

Garnish the salmon with the green onions and serve it immediately.

RECIPE NOTES
Feel free to adjust the amount of Sriracha and red pepper flakes to your preference.

You can use skin-on salmon if that's what's available to you.

NUTRITION INFORMATION
Serving size: 1 serving; **Calories:** 394; **Carbohydrates:** 8 g; **Protein:** 34 g; **Fat:** 26 g

LEMON-BUTTER BAKED COD

PREP TIME: 5 MINUTES
COOK TIME: 20 MINUTES
TOTAL TIME: 25 MINUTES
SERVES: 3

COD
1 lb (448 g) skinless cod fillets (see Recipe Notes)
¼ tsp salt, or as needed
¼ tsp black pepper, or as needed
1 tbsp (15 ml) olive oil

LEMON-BUTTER SAUCE
4 tbsp (60 g) unsalted butter
3 cloves garlic, minced (see Recipe Notes)
¼ tsp red pepper flakes
¼ tsp salt, or as needed
¼ tsp black pepper, or as needed
¼ cup (60 ml) dry white wine (see Recipe Notes)
2 cups (300 g) cherry tomatoes
½ cup (65 g) Kalamata olives
¼ cup (60 ml) fresh lemon juice
2 tbsp (6 g) chopped fresh parsley
2 sprigs fresh thyme

This lemon-butter baked cod has a sort of Tuscan vibe with all the olives and tomatoes. But don't be afraid of cooking with cod—while cod on its own can be quite boring, if you use the right ingredients, you will be pleasantly surprised. The lemon-butter sauce in this recipe makes the cod shine. I love to serve this over some steamed veggies, like asparagus, or alongside a garden salad.

To make the cod, preheat the oven to 400°F (204°C).

Season both sides of the cod fillets with the salt and black pepper. Drizzle the oil in a large baking dish. Place the fillets in the baking dish. Cover the baking dish with aluminum foil and bake the cod for 12 minutes.

Meanwhile, make the lemon-butter sauce. Melt the butter in a large skillet over medium-high heat. Add the garlic and red pepper flakes and cook them for 30 seconds. Season the mixture with the salt and black pepper, then pour in the wine. Bring the sauce to a boil and cook it for 1 to 2 minutes.

Add the tomatoes, olives and lemon juice. Reduce the heat to low and simmer the sauce for 5 to 10 minutes, or until the tomatoes begin to burst. Add the parsley and thyme, stirring to incorporate them into the sauce.

Remove the foil from the baking dish and pour the sauce over the cod. Spread the tomatoes and olives evenly around the fillets. Bake the cod and sauce for 5 minutes, until the cod flakes easily with a fork.

RECIPE NOTES

Note that 1 pound (448 g) of cod will be about 3 fillets, which is the number of servings for this recipe. This recipe will also work with other types of mild-flavored whitefish, such as tilapia, bass, halibut and sole.

You can use more or less garlic depending on your preference.

Dry white wines work best for this recipe. These include chardonnay, pinot grigio and sauvignon blanc. If you don't want to use wine, you can use ¼ cup (60 ml) of chicken broth with 1 teaspoon of vinegar.

NUTRITION INFORMATION

Serving size: 1 fillet; **Calories:** 379; **Carbohydrates:** 8 g; **Protein:** 28 g; **Fat:** 24 g

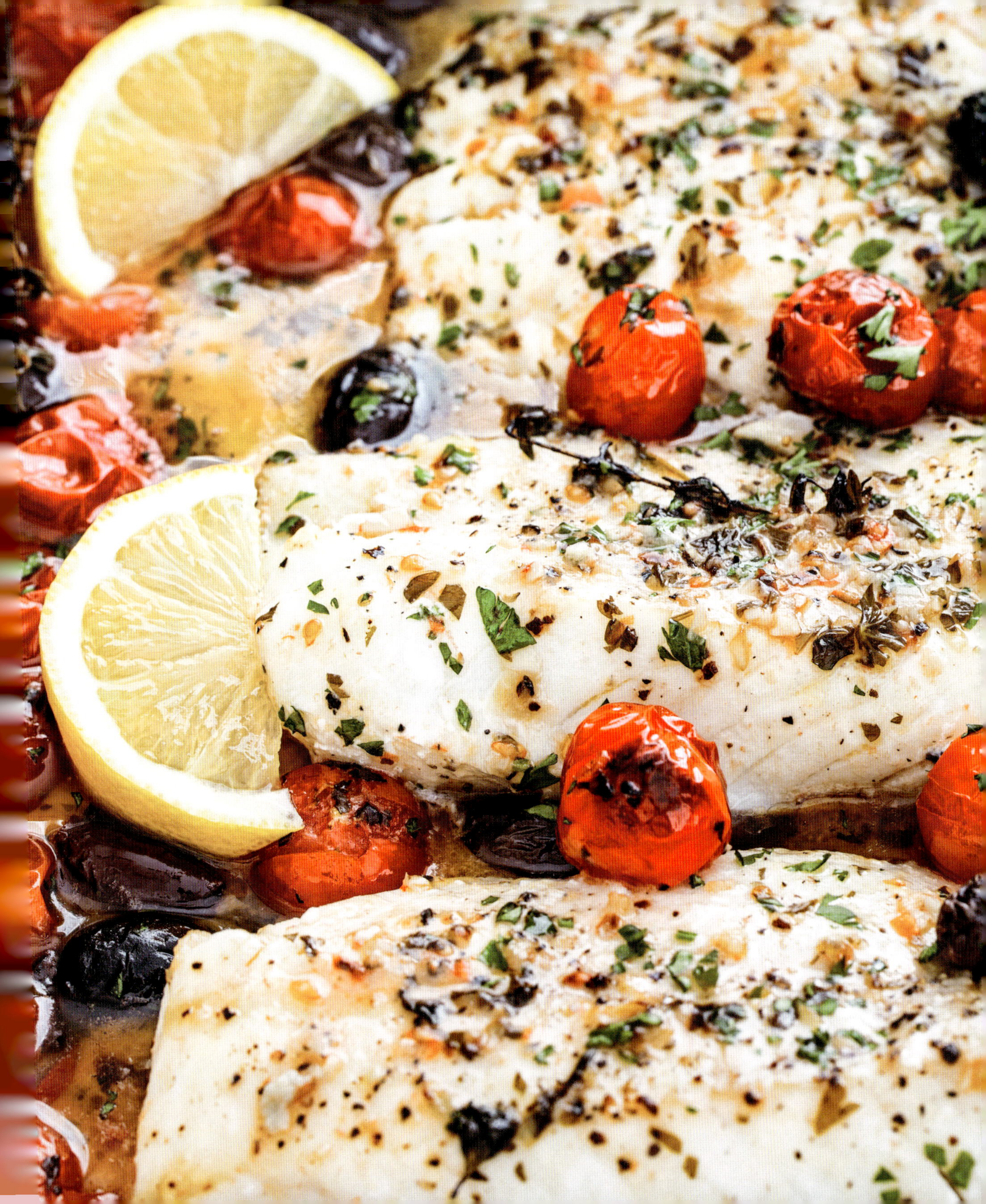

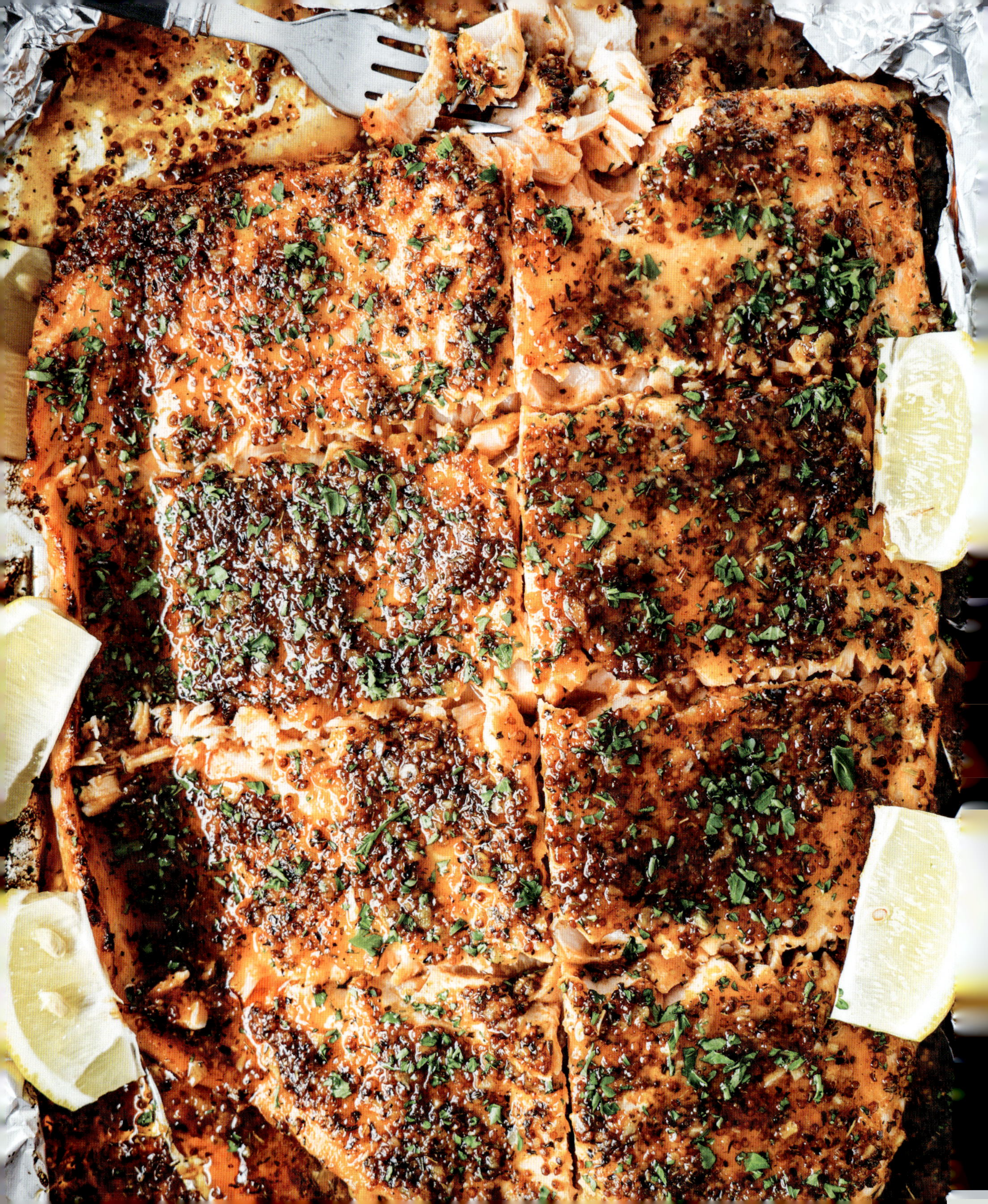

HONEY MUSTARD SALMON

Here's another salmon recipe that is quick and easy to make: You basically pour the delicious honey mustard sauce over a whole salmon fillet and bake it in foil to flaky perfection!

PREP TIME: 5 MINUTES
COOK TIME: 25 MINUTES
TOTAL TIME: 30 MINUTES
SERVES: 8

HONEY MUSTARD SAUCE
⅓ cup (80 ml) honey
¼ cup (60 g) whole-grain mustard
1 tbsp (15 g) Dijon mustard
1 tbsp (15 ml) fresh lemon juice
1 tsp lemon zest
4 cloves garlic, minced
1 tbsp (3 g) Italian seasoning
1 tsp smoked paprika
¼ cup (60 g) unsalted butter, melted
½ tsp salt
½ tsp black pepper

SALMON
1 (3-lb [1.3-kg]) boneless, skinless salmon fillet (see Recipe Note)
1 tbsp (3 g) chopped fresh parsley

To make the honey mustard sauce, whisk together the honey, grainy mustard, Dijon mustard, lemon juice, lemon zest, garlic, Italian seasoning, smoked paprika, butter, salt and black pepper in a medium bowl. Set the bowl aside.

To make the salmon, preheat the oven to 400°F (204°C). Line a large baking sheet with aluminum foil and lightly spray the foil with cooking spray.

Place the salmon in the middle of the prepared baking sheet. Spoon the honey mustard sauce over the salmon.

Fold the aluminum foil over the top of the salmon to completely enclose it.

Bake the salmon for 15 to 20 minutes, or until the salmon is almost cooked through. Remove the baking sheet from the oven and carefully pull back the aluminum foil to completely expose the top of the salmon. Transfer the baking sheet back to the oven, increase the oven's temperature to broil and broil the salmon for about 2 minutes. Keep a close eye on the salmon, as it can burn quickly.

Remove the salmon from the oven and garnish it with the parsley. Serve the salmon immediately.

RECIPE NOTE
The cooking time will vary according to the thickness of the salmon. Thicker pieces will take longer to cook than thinner pieces. My salmon was a little more than 1 inch (3 cm) thick, so it took the entire 20 minutes to cook.

NUTRITION INFORMATION
Serving size: 1 serving; **Calories:** 347; **Carbohydrates:** 13 g; **Protein:** 34 g; **Fat:** 17 g

MAPLE AND MUSTARD–GLAZED SALMON

PREP TIME: 5 MINUTES
COOK TIME: 20 MINUTES
TOTAL TIME: 25 MINUTES
SERVES: 6

1 (1½-lb [672-g]) skinless salmon fillet, cut into 6 equal pieces (see Recipe Notes)

¼ cup (60 g) unsalted butter, melted

¼ cup (60 ml) pure maple syrup

2 tbsp (30 g) whole-grain mustard (I recommend whole-grain Dijon mustard)

2 tbsp (30 ml) soy sauce

Black pepper, as needed (optional; see Recipe Notes)

This maple and mustard–glazed salmon requires just four ingredients that turn ordinary salmon into a superstar. It's a healthy and delicious recipe of salmon glazed with maple syrup and grainy mustard that's ready in only 25 minutes.

Preheat the oven to 425°F (218°C).

Arrange the salmon fillets in a 9 x 13–inch (27 x 39–cm) baking dish.

In a small bowl, whisk together the butter, maple syrup, mustard and soy sauce. Pour the glaze over the salmon. Season the salmon with the black pepper (if using).

Bake the salmon for 15 to 20 minutes, or until it flakes with a fork.

RECIPE NOTES

The sauce in this recipe would also work with other types of fish, such as red snapper or cod.

Freshly ground black pepper is best in this dish.

Salmon doesn't have a very long shelf life, so be sure to eat it quickly. In the fridge, it will keep in an airtight container for up to 2 days. In the freezer, this dish will last in an airtight container for 3 to 4 months. Allow it to thaw in its container overnight in the fridge or in cold water.

NUTRITION INFORMATION

Serving size: 1 fillet; **Calories:** 271; **Carbohydrates:** 9 g; **Protein:** 23 g; **Fat:** 15 g

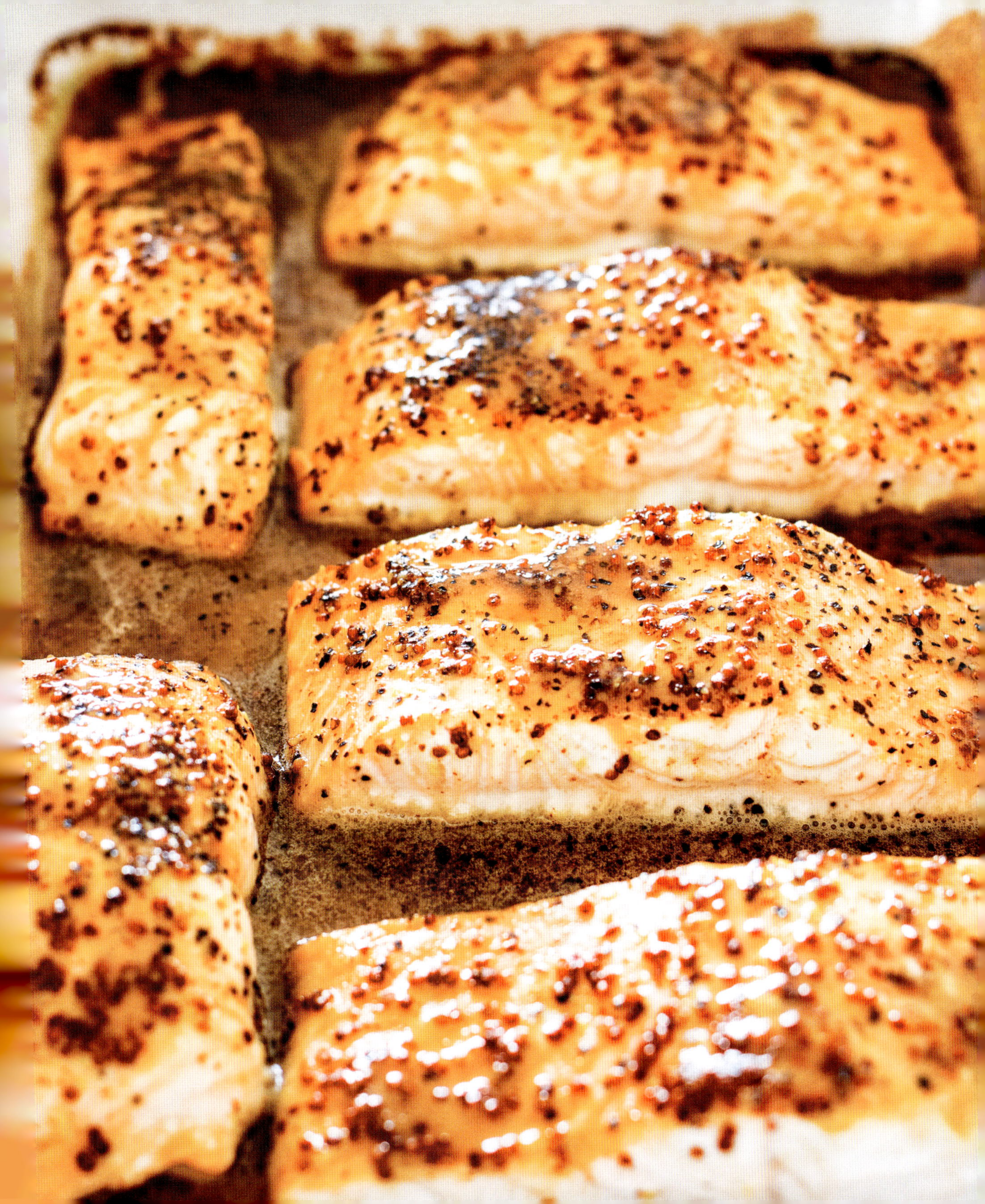

VEGETARIAN

I LOVE TO DABBLE IN VEGETARIAN COOKING because I don't always feel like eating meat, and some dishes—like my Spinach and Ricotta–Stuffed Shells (page 171) and Tofu Drunken Noodles (page 155)—are too good to pass up.

When it comes to vegetarianism, there are many different types. I usually consider meals vegetarian when I simply don't cook with red meat, white meat or fish; but I do use dairy and egg products. For these types of comforting dishes, try my Chanterelle Mushrooms with Tagliatelle (page 164) or the ever-popular Baked Mac and Cheese (page 172).

I hope you love the recipes I have chosen for this chapter, especially if you're looking to enjoy vegetables more often. Even if you love meat like I do, when you have dishes like the ones in this chapter—such as my Easy California Quinoa Salad (page 156) or Cheesy Zucchini Quiche (page 167)—you won't even miss the meat. I hope you'll be inspired to try some of these vegetarian recipes.

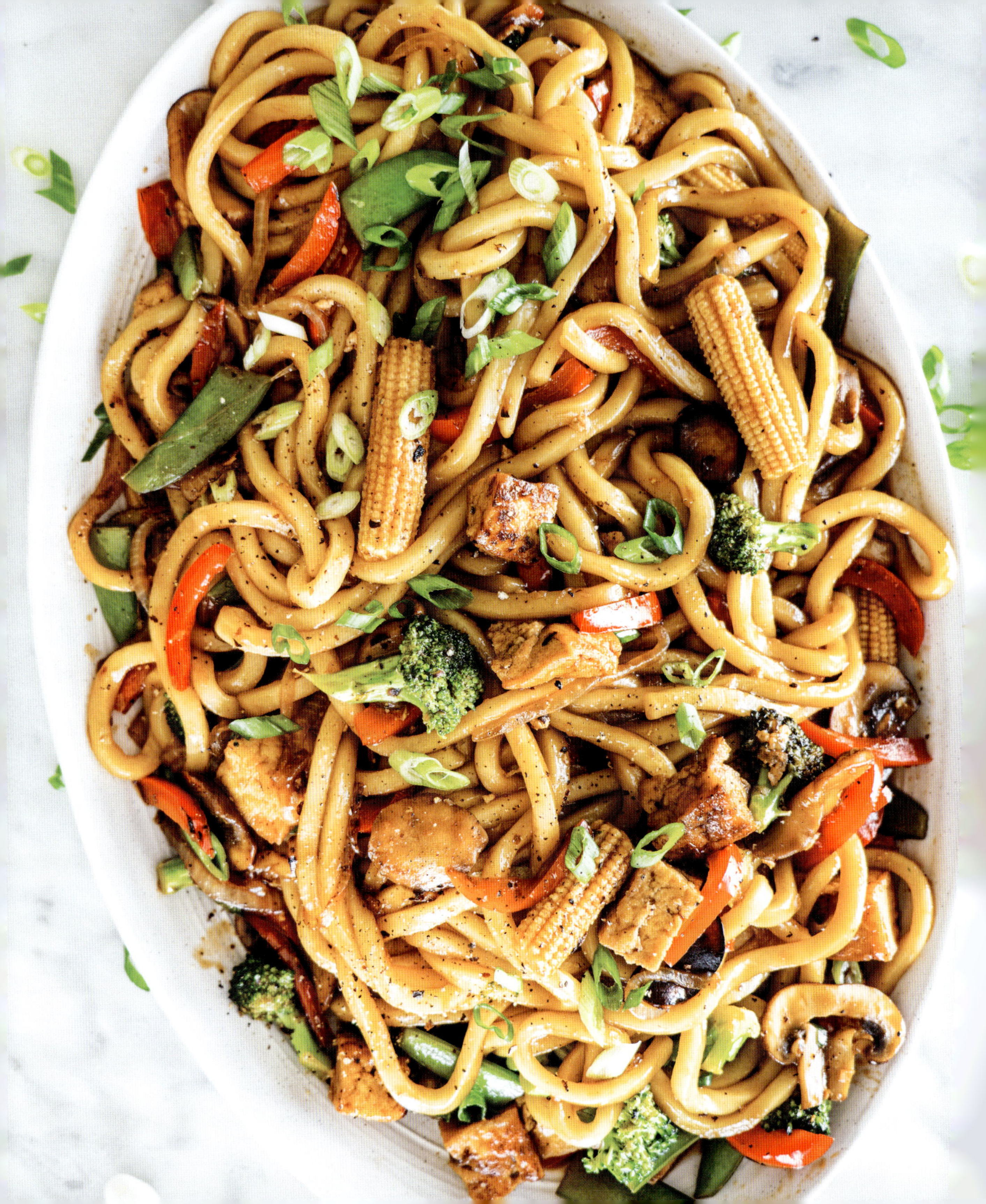

TOFU DRUNKEN NOODLES

Spicy, succulent udon noodles made with tofu and an array of bright veggies means an easy and addictive meal! The secret to this dish is to prep all your ingredients first, because once you start cooking it goes very fast.

PREP TIME: 20 MINUTES
COOK TIME: 20 MINUTES
TOTAL TIME: 40 MINUTES
SERVES: 4

SAUCE

1 tbsp (15 ml) sesame oil
¼ cup (60 ml) low-sodium soy sauce
1 tbsp (15 ml) fish sauce
1 tbsp (15 g) brown sugar
1 tbsp (15 ml) honey
1 tbsp (15 ml) Sriracha sauce
1 tbsp (15 ml) dark soy sauce
2 tbsp (30 ml) oyster sauce
3 cloves garlic, minced
½ cup (120 ml) water

STIR-FRY

1 tbsp (15 ml) sesame oil
1 tbsp (15 ml) olive oil
12 oz (336 g) firm tofu, cut into 1" (3-cm) pieces (see Recipe Notes)
1 onion, thinly sliced
1 red bell pepper, thinly sliced
1 cup (66 g) sliced cremini mushrooms
2 cups (170 g) broccoli florets
½ cup (110 g) baby corn
½ cup (32 g) snap peas
3 (7-oz [196-g]) packages udon noodles, cooked

2 green onions, chopped

To make the sauce, whisk together the sesame oil, low-sodium soy sauce, fish sauce, brown sugar, honey, Sriracha sauce, dark soy sauce, oyster sauce, garlic and water in a small bowl. Set the sauce aside.

To make the stir-fry, heat the sesame oil and olive oil in a large skillet or wok over medium-high heat. Working in batches if necessary, add the tofu to the skillet and cook it for 3 to 5 minutes, until it is browned on all sides.

Add the onion and cook the mixture for 2 to 3 minutes, until the onion begins to soften. Add the bell pepper and mushrooms and sauté the mixture for about 5 minutes, stirring it occasionally, until the bell pepper starts to soften and the mushrooms begin to brown. Add the broccoli, baby corn and snap peas. Toss everything together and cook the stir-fry for 5 minutes.

Add the udon noodles to the skillet and pour in the sauce. Toss and cook the noodles for 2 to 3 minutes, then remove the skillet from the heat. Sprinkle the drunken noodles with the green onions and serve them.

RECIPE NOTES

If you would prefer a nonvegetarian version of this dish, you can substitute the tofu with chicken, shrimp, beef or pork.

Store any leftovers in an airtight container in the fridge for 3 to 5 days. To reheat the noodles, microwave them or cook them in a skillet or wok until they are heated through.

You can freeze your leftover noodles to store them longer, but keep in mind they might decrease in quality and are best served fresh.

NUTRITION INFORMATION

Serving size: 1 serving; **Calories:** 497; **Carbohydrates:** 69 g; **Protein:** 23 g; **Fat:** 17 g

EASY CALIFORNIA QUINOA SALAD

Here's a gorgeous salad, full of bright ingredients such as edamame, mango, bell pepper and cilantro, that's not only delicious but also healthy. It's comfort food that is actually good for you.

PREP TIME: 20 MINUTES
COOK TIME: 10 MINUTES
TOTAL TIME: 30 MINUTES
SERVES: 4

SALAD
½ cup (85 g) uncooked quinoa
1 cup (240 ml) water
1 mango, finely chopped
¼ red onion, chopped
½ red bell pepper, chopped
¾ cup (56 g) shredded unsweetened coconut
¾ cup (83 g) sliced or slivered almonds, toasted if preferred
1 cup (150 g) raisins
1 cup (155 g) shelled edamame, thawed if frozen
¼ cup (12 g) chopped fresh cilantro or parsley

DRESSING
¼ cup (60 ml) fresh lime juice
2 tbsp (30 ml) balsamic vinegar
1 tbsp (15 ml) honey
1 tbsp (15 ml) olive oil
Salt, as needed
Black pepper, as needed

To make the salad, cook the quinoa in the water according to the package's instructions, usually about 10 minutes. Let it cool.

Meanwhile, make the dressing. In a small bowl, whisk together the lime juice, vinegar, honey, oil, salt and black pepper.

To assemble the salad, combine the quinoa, mango, onion, bell pepper, coconut, almonds, raisins, edamame and cilantro in a large bowl. Add the dressing. Toss the salad well and serve it cold.

RECIPE NOTE
Unlike salads that are made with lettuce, spinach, kale and other leafy greens, there is nothing in this recipe that will wilt. It'll stay fresh in an airtight container in the refrigerator for 3 to 4 days.

NUTRITION INFORMATION
Serving size: 1 serving; **Calories:** 524; **Carbohydrates:** 73 g; **Protein:** 14 g; **Fat:** 23 g

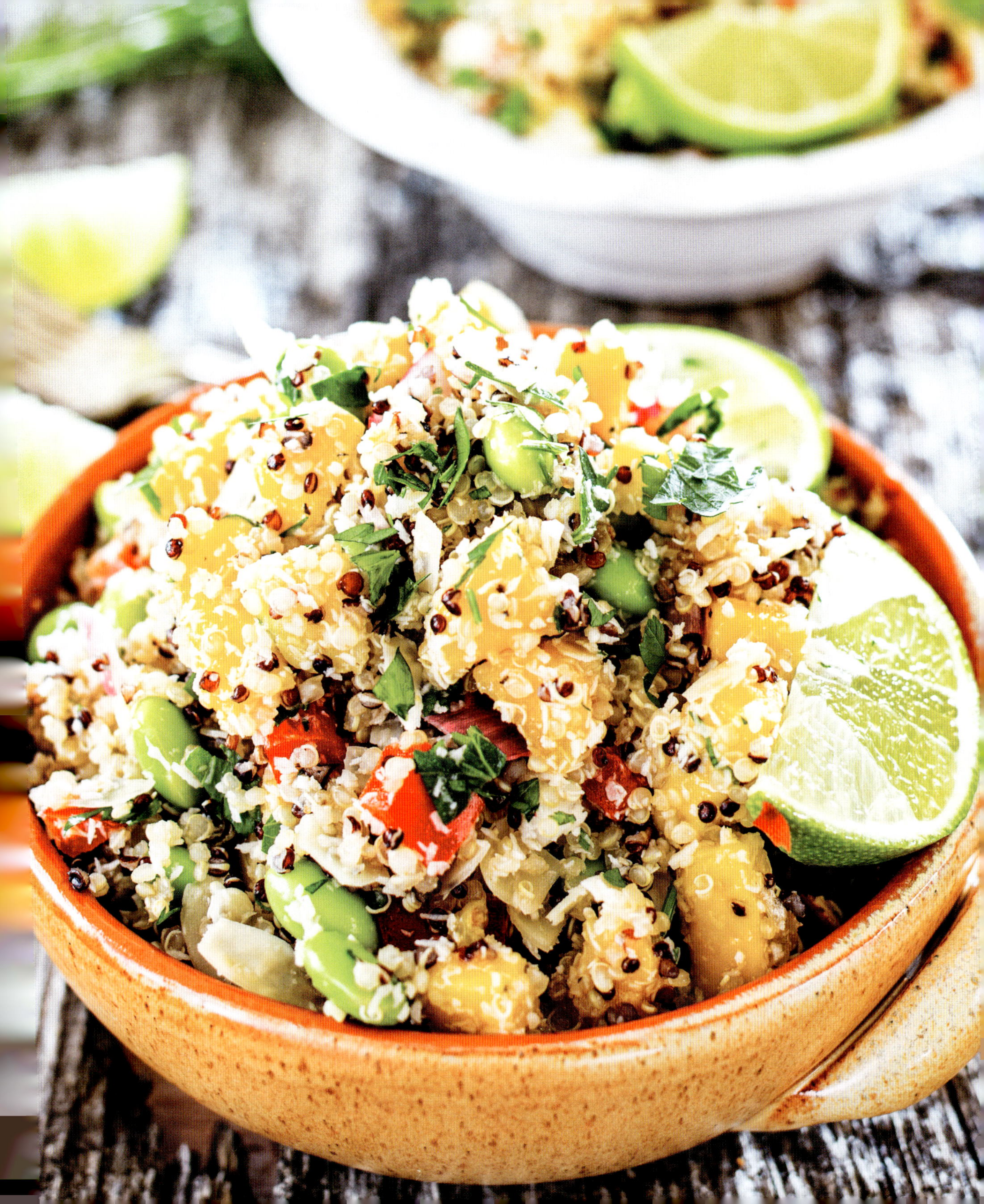

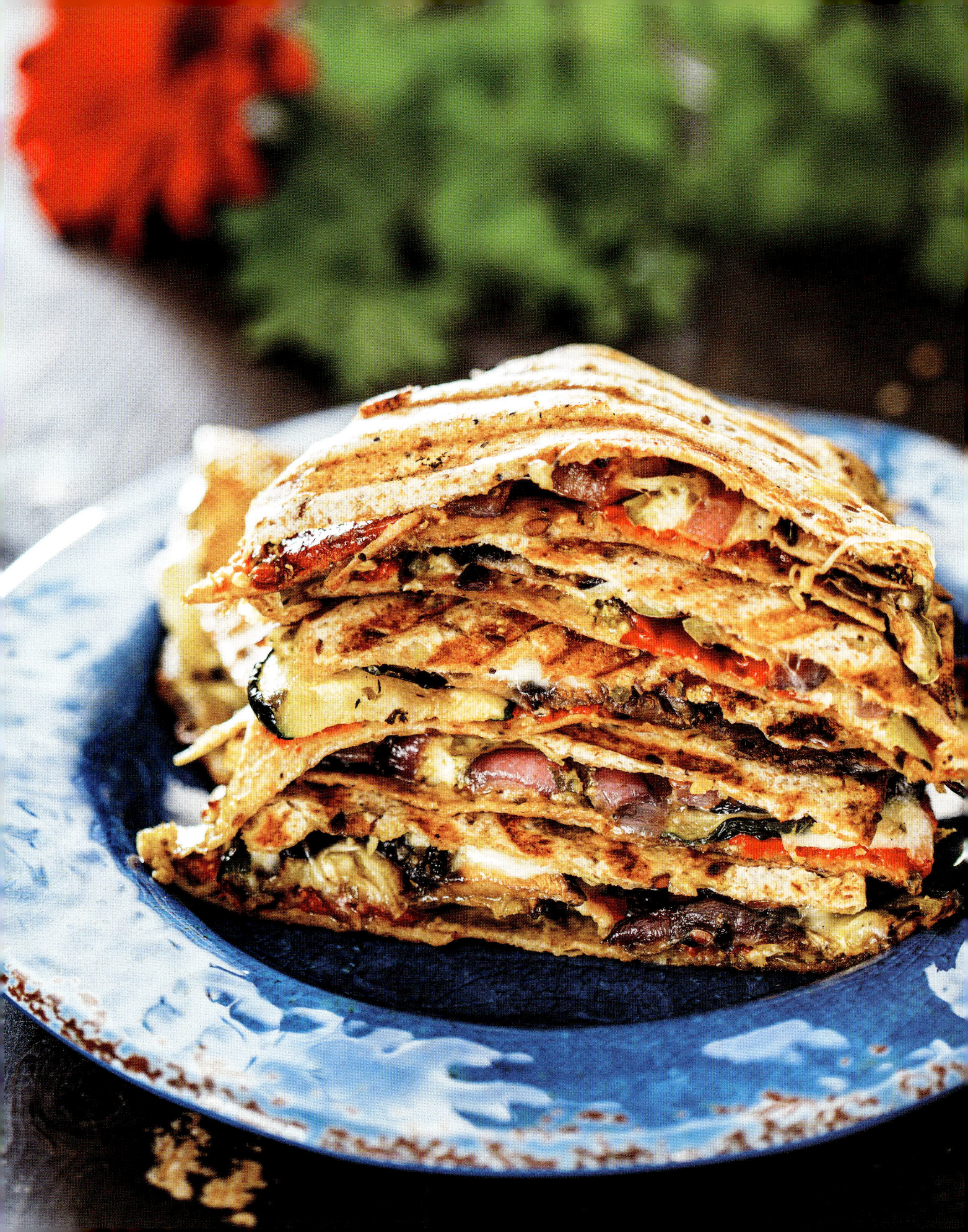

GRILLED VEGETABLE QUESADILLAS

PREP TIME: 20 MINUTES
COOK TIME: 30 MINUTES
TOTAL TIME: 50 MINUTES
SERVES: 4

2 zucchinis, cut into ¼" (6-mm)-thick slices

2 squash (such as cousa squash or yellow squash), cut into ¼" (6-mm)-thick slices

4 portobello mushrooms, sliced

¼ tsp salt, or as needed

½ tsp black pepper, or as needed

1 red onion, sliced

4 red bell peppers or sweet pointed red peppers

8 tbsp (120 g) store-bought pesto

4 large tortillas (I recommend ancient grain tortillas)

2 cups (224 g) shredded mozzarella cheese

Quesadillas are one of my favorite things to have for lunch, and these quesadillas don't disappoint. They're loaded with mozzarella cheese, pesto and lots of fresh veggies like zucchini, mushrooms and bell peppers.

Preheat the grill to between 300 and 350°F (149 and 177°C).

Season the zucchini, squash and mushrooms with the salt and black pepper.

Grill the zucchini, squash, mushrooms, onion and bell peppers for about 3 minutes per side, for a total of 5 to 7 minutes, until grill marks form and the bell peppers are charred. The bell peppers may take up to 8 minutes total. Remove the vegetables from the grill and set them aside.

Let the bell peppers cool, then carefully remove their skin and seeds. Rinse out the bell peppers.

Spread 2 tablespoons (30 g) of the pesto on the top of a tortilla. Arrange some of the grilled vegetables on one side of the tortilla on top of the pesto. Top the vegetables with about ½ cup (56 g) of the mozzarella cheese, although you may use less if you prefer. Fold over the other half of the tortilla to form a half-circle and press down.

You can use a panini press to grill the quesadilla, or you can use a large skillet. If you are using a panini press, grill each quesadilla per the manufacturer's instructions. If you're using a skillet, spray the bottom of the skillet with cooking spray and set the skillet over medium-high heat. Place the quesadilla in the skillet and grill it for 3 minutes per side, until it is golden brown.

Repeat the preceding step with the remaining pesto, tortillas, grilled vegetables and mozzarella cheese.

Cut each quesadilla into 4 pieces and serve them.

RECIPE NOTES

Store leftover quesadillas in an airtight container in the fridge for up to 3 days. Be sure to reheat them on the stove if you want to prevent the tortillas from getting soggy.

If you'd rather freeze the quesadillas, be sure to wrap them individually in parchment paper and freeze them for up to 4 months.

NUTRITION INFORMATION

Serving size: 1 quesadilla; **Calories:** 637; **Carbohydrates:** 81 g; **Protein:** 25 g; **Fat:** 27 g

SESAME NOODLES

These sesame noodles are made with just a handful of simple ingredients and ten minutes of your time. Boil your noodles, mix the sauce, toss and enjoy! This recipe is a great way to put together a fast snack, side or even a meal.

PREP TIME: 5 MINUTES
COOK TIME: 5 MINUTES
TOTAL: 10 MINUTES
SERVES: 6

1 lb (448 g) ramen noodles
¼ cup (60 ml) low-sodium soy sauce
2 tbsp (30 ml) dark soy sauce
2 tbsp (30 ml) rice vinegar
2 tbsp (30 ml) sesame oil
2 cloves garlic, minced
1 tsp minced fresh ginger
1 tsp chili-garlic sauce or sambal oelek
1 tbsp (12 g) peanut butter
2 green onions, chopped
1 tbsp (9 g) sesame seeds
2 tbsp (18 g) peanuts, crushed

Cook the ramen noodles according to the package's instructions, usually about 5 minutes.

Meanwhile, in a medium bowl, whisk together the low-sodium soy sauce, dark soy sauce, vinegar, oil, garlic, ginger, chili-garlic sauce and peanut butter.

Drain the noodles and immediately toss them with the sauce.

Garnish the noodles with the green onions, sesame seeds and peanuts and serve them immediately.

RECIPE NOTE

Store any leftovers in an airtight container in the refrigerator for up to 4 days.

NUTRITION INFORMATION

Serving size: 1 serving; **Calories:** 428; **Carbohydrates:** 51 g; **Protein:** 11 g; **Fat:** 20 g

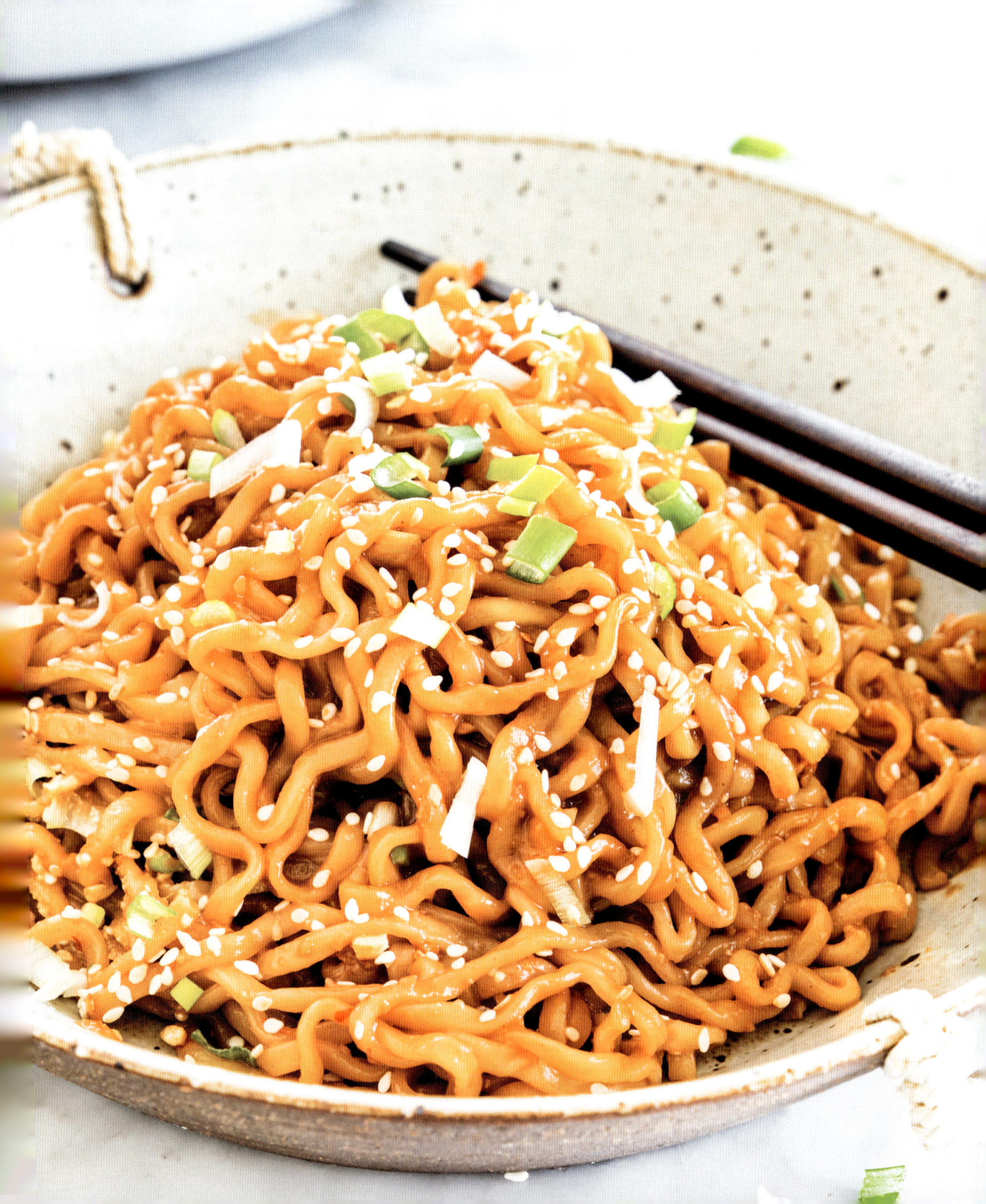

Linguine
Capellini
Fusilli
Vermicelli
Orzo
Rigatoni
Ziti
Penne

EASY TOMATO AND CHICKPEA SALAD

PREP TIME: 15 MINUTES
COOK TIME: NONE
TOTAL TIME: 15 MINUTES
SERVES: 6

1 (19-oz [532-g]) can chickpeas, drained and rinsed
3 tomatoes, chopped
½ English cucumber, chopped
1 red bell pepper, diced
4 green onions, chopped
1 cup (85 g) pea shoots
6 leaves fresh basil, chopped
2 tbsp (30 ml) olive oil
2 tbsp (30 ml) fresh lemon juice
1 cup (150 g) cubed feta cheese
Salt, as needed
Black pepper, as needed

How gorgeous is this salad? It is an excellent source of protein that's perfect for vegetarians. It's super easy to make and ready in just fifteen minutes.

In a large salad bowl, combine the chickpeas, tomatoes, cucumber, bell pepper, green onions, pea shoots, basil, oil, lemon juice, feta cheese, salt and black pepper. Toss the salad well to coat it in the dressing.

Serve the salad immediately.

RECIPE NOTES

Transfer your leftovers to an airtight container and store them in the fridge for 3 to 5 days.

You may find that the salt in the dressing pulls moisture from the veggies in the salad. If you plan on having leftovers, you can prepare the dressing separately and toss it with the salad as you enjoy it.

NUTRITION INFORMATION

Serving size: 1 serving; **Calories:** 292; **Carbohydrates:** 32 g; **Protein:** 14 g; **Fat:** 13 g

CHANTERELLE MUSHROOMS WITH TAGLIATELLE

With a few basic ingredients, you can have this restaurant-worthy dish on your dinner table in just 30 minutes! Fresh chanterelle mushrooms, some Parmesan cheese and a sauce made with olive oil, white wine and lots of garlic never fails to impress.

PREP TIME: 10 MINUTES
COOK TIME: 20 MINUTES
TOTAL TIME: 30 MINUTES
SERVES: 4

12 oz (336 g) tagliatelle (see Recipe Notes)
8 oz (224 g) chanterelle mushrooms
2 tbsp (30 ml) olive oil
½ onion, chopped
4 cloves garlic, minced
½ tsp salt, or as needed
½ tsp black pepper, or as needed
½ cup (120 ml) white wine (such as sauvignon blanc or pinot grigio)
¼ cup (12 g) chopped fresh parsley
1 cup (180 g) grated Parmesan cheese, plus more as needed
Extra virgin olive oil, as needed

Boil the tagliatelle in salted water according to the package's instructions. Reserve 1 cup (240 ml) of the pasta water.

While the pasta is cooking, clean the mushrooms and slice them lengthwise. Set them aside.

Heat the olive oil in a large skillet over medium-high heat. Add the onion and cook it for 3 to 4 minutes, until it is translucent. Add the garlic and cook it for 30 seconds, or until it is fragrant. Add the mushrooms and cook the mixture for about 10 minutes, until the mushrooms begin to shrink and their moisture evaporates. Season the vegetables with the salt and black pepper.

Pour in the wine, stir to combine it with the other ingredients and cook the mixture for about 5 minutes. Add the tagliatelle and ½ cup (120 ml) of the pasta water. Toss everything to coat it in the sauce and add more pasta water if needed. Add the parsley and Parmesan cheese, then toss until everything is mixed well.

Serve the tagliatelle topped with additional Parmesan cheese and a drizzle of the extra virgin olive oil.

RECIPE NOTES

If you like, you can use other varieties of long pasta, like fettuccine.

Store any leftovers in an airtight container in the fridge for 3 to 5 days. To reheat the leftovers, use either the microwave or reheat them in a skillet over medium heat.

NUTRITION INFORMATION

Serving size: 1 serving; **Calories:** 545; **Carbohydrates:** 69 g; **Protein:** 22 g; **Fat:** 18 g

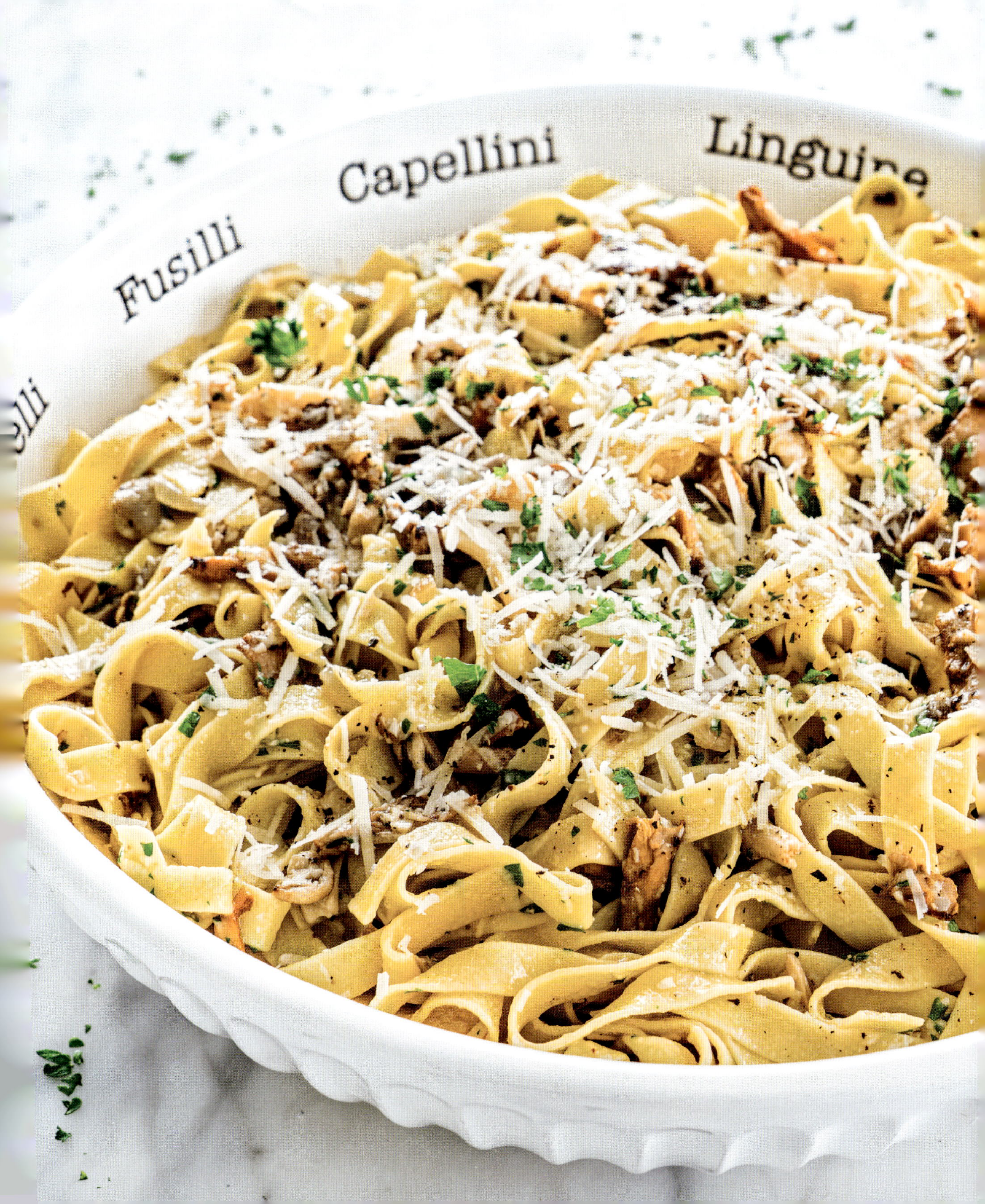
Fusilli
Capellini
Linguine

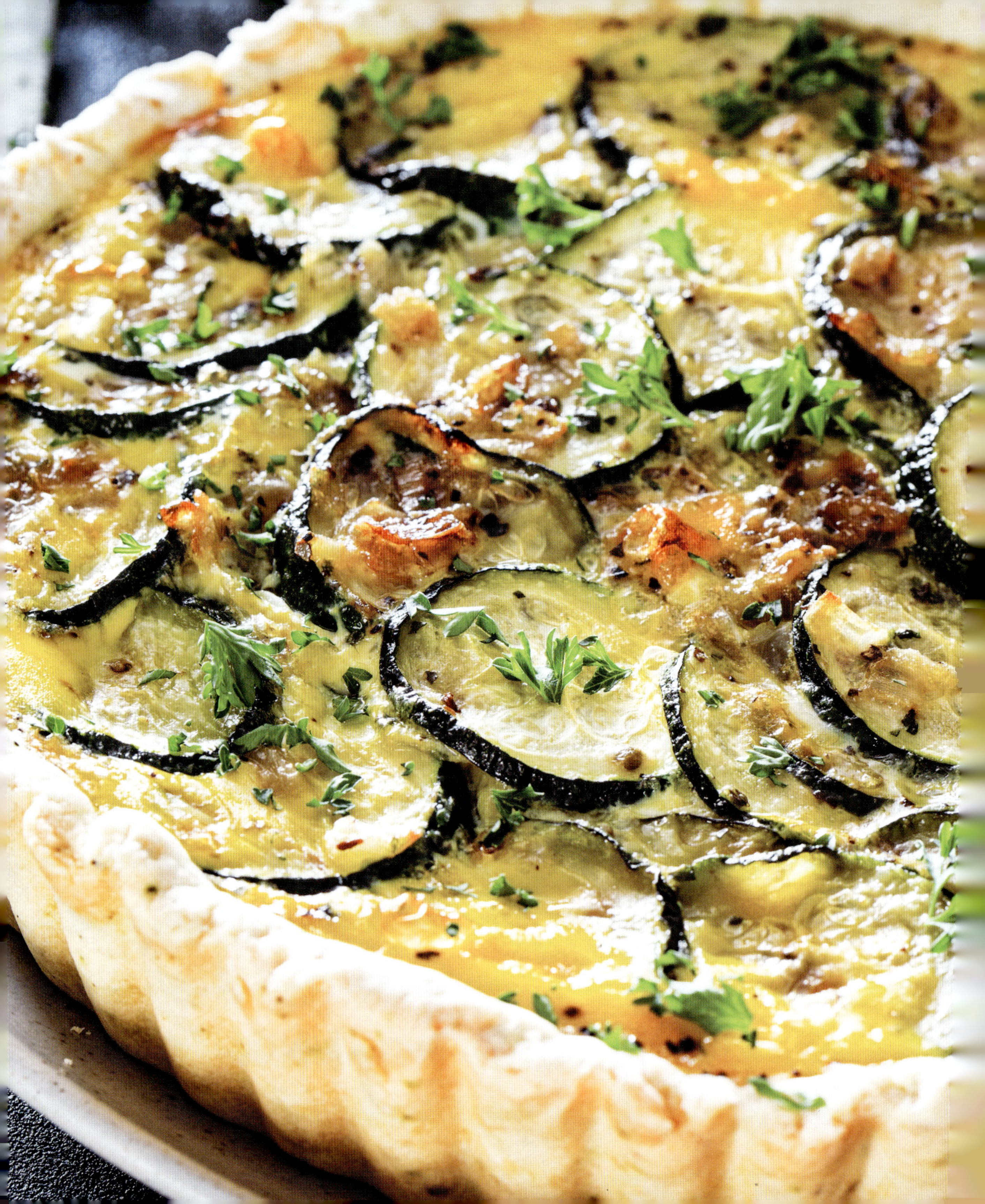

CHEESY ZUCCHINI QUICHE

Here's a simple vegetarian quiche that's cheesy and makes great use of any extra zucchini you have. It's such a simple dish to prepare, and you can make it to suit your own taste.

PREP TIME: 25 MINUTES
CHILLING TIME: 30 MINUTES
COOK TIME: 50 MINUTES
TOTAL: 1 HOUR, 40 MINUTES
SERVES: 8

CRUST
1½ cups (180 g) all-purpose flour, plus more as needed
½ tsp salt
½ tsp dried oregano
1 tsp dried basil
½ tsp black pepper
½ cup (120 g) cold unsalted butter, cut into cubes
3 tbsp (45 ml) ice water

FILLING
3 tbsp (45 g) unsalted butter
1 onion, chopped
1 tsp dried basil
1 tsp dried oregano
Salt, as needed
Black pepper, as needed
3 cups (339 g) sliced zucchini
½ cup (120 ml) milk
3 large eggs
2 cups (224 g) shredded mozzarella cheese

To make the crust, combine the flour, salt, oregano, basil and black pepper in a food processor. Add the butter and pulse until the mixture resembles peas. Continue pulsing while adding the ice water. The dough will begin to stick together.

Flour a work surface and roll out the dough, then knead it until it comes together—do not knead it too much. Form the dough into a disk shape, wrap it in plastic wrap and put in the fridge for 30 minutes to chill.

Preheat the oven to 400°F (204°C).

To make the filling, melt the butter in a medium skillet over medium heat. Add the onion, basil, oregano, salt and black pepper and sauté the mixture for 3 to 4 minutes, until the onion is soft and translucent. Add the zucchini and cook the mixture for about 3 minutes, until the zucchini has softened.

In a small bowl, whisk together the milk and eggs. Set the bowl aside. Dust a work surface with flour. Set a 9-inch (27-cm) pie dish or quiche pan next to the work surface. On the prepared work surface, roll out the dough disk until it is about 12 inches (36 cm) in diameter. Roll the dough around the rolling pin, then lift the rolling pin over the pie dish and unroll the dough into the pie dish. Flute the edges of the crust: Working around the perimeter, pinch sections of the dough with one hand while pushing against it with the index finger of the opposite hand to create a scalloped pattern. Sprinkle the mozzarella cheese over the pastry. Top the cheese with the sautéed zucchini, then carefully pour the egg mixture over the zucchini.

Bake the quiche on the lower rack of the oven for 30 to 40 minutes, or until a knife inserted near the center comes out clean and the crust is golden brown. To avoid overbrowning the quiche, cover the edges loosely with foil for the last 15 minutes of cooking time. Let the quiche cool for 10 minutes before serving it.

RECIPE NOTES

The quiche will last in an airtight container in the fridge for 3 to 4 days. It can also be frozen for 2 to 3 months. Because quiche is a custard, it needs to be refrigerated within 2 hours of cooling.

NUTRITION INFORMATION

Serving size: 1 slice; **Calories:** 356; **Carbohydrates:** 22 g; **Protein:** 12 g; **Fat:** 25 g

COUSCOUS PILAF WITH SAUTÉED MUSHROOMS

PREP TIME: 10 MINUTES
COOK TIME: 20 MINUTES
TOTAL TIME: 30 MINUTES
SERVES: 4

3 tbsp (45 ml) olive oil, divided
14 oz (392 g) sliced mushrooms (I recommend cremini)
1 onion, chopped
2 ribs celery, chopped
1 carrot, chopped
½ tsp ground coriander
½ tsp ground cumin
½ tsp onion powder
¼ cup (60 ml) white wine (I recommend pinot grigio)
1 cup (173 g) uncooked pearl couscous (I recommend Israeli couscous; see Recipe Notes)
2 cups (480 ml) vegetable broth
½ tsp salt, or as needed
¼ tsp black pepper, or as needed
1 tbsp (15 ml) hot sauce (optional; I recommend Sriracha)
¾ cup (101 g) frozen peas
1 tbsp (3 g) chopped fresh parsley

This couscous is delectable and full of complex, savory flavors. It features peas, mushrooms, white wine and a blend of spices. It's perfect as a meal on its own or as a side dish.

Heat 1 tablespoon (15 ml) of the oil in a large skillet over medium-high heat. Add the mushrooms and sauté them for 3 to 5 minutes, until they start to brown. Remove the mushrooms from the skillet and set them aside.

Heat the remaining 2 tablespoons (30 ml) of oil in the same skillet over medium-high heat. Add the onion, celery and carrot and cook the vegetables for 3 to 5 minutes, until the onion is translucent and the celery is tender.

Add the coriander, cumin and onion powder. Stir in the wine. Add the couscous and broth. Season the mixture with the salt and black pepper and stir it well. Reduce the heat to low and cook the couscous for about 7 minutes. At this point, most of the liquid should be absorbed.

Add the hot sauce (if using) and peas and cook the couscous for 2 to 3 minutes, until the remainder of the liquid is absorbed. Stir in the mushrooms.

Garnish the couscous and mushrooms with the parsley and serve the dish warm.

RECIPE NOTES

Couscous is small balls of pasta. You can find it at your local grocery store. If you can't find Israeli couscous, regular couscous will also work.

This recipe will last in an airtight container in the fridge for 3 to 4 days. This dish also freezes well—just place it in a sturdy freezer bag and it'll keep for 3 to 4 months.

NUTRITION INFORMATION

Serving size: 1 serving; **Calories:** 359; **Carbohydrates:** 48 g; **Protein:** 13 g; **Fat:** 12 g

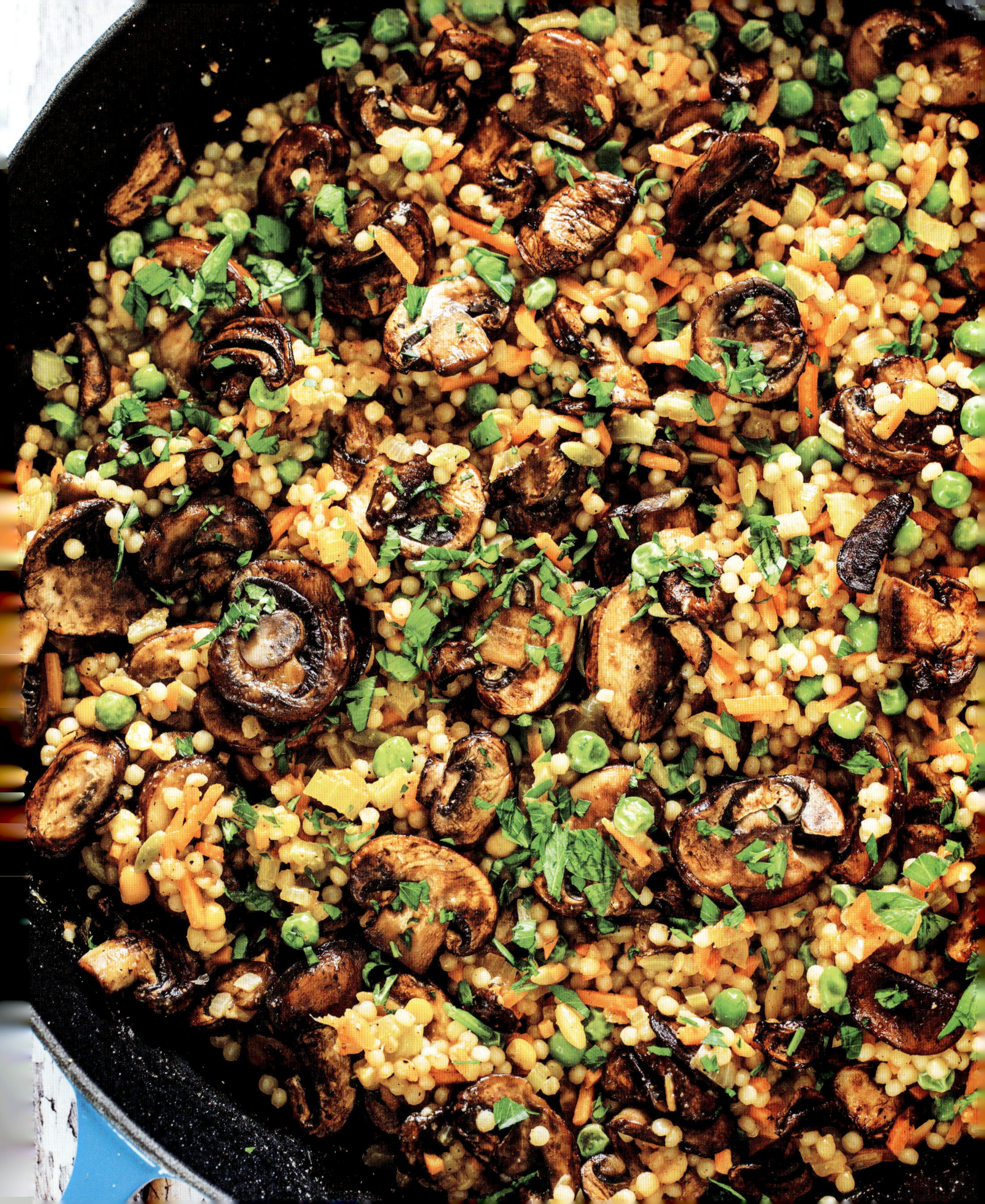

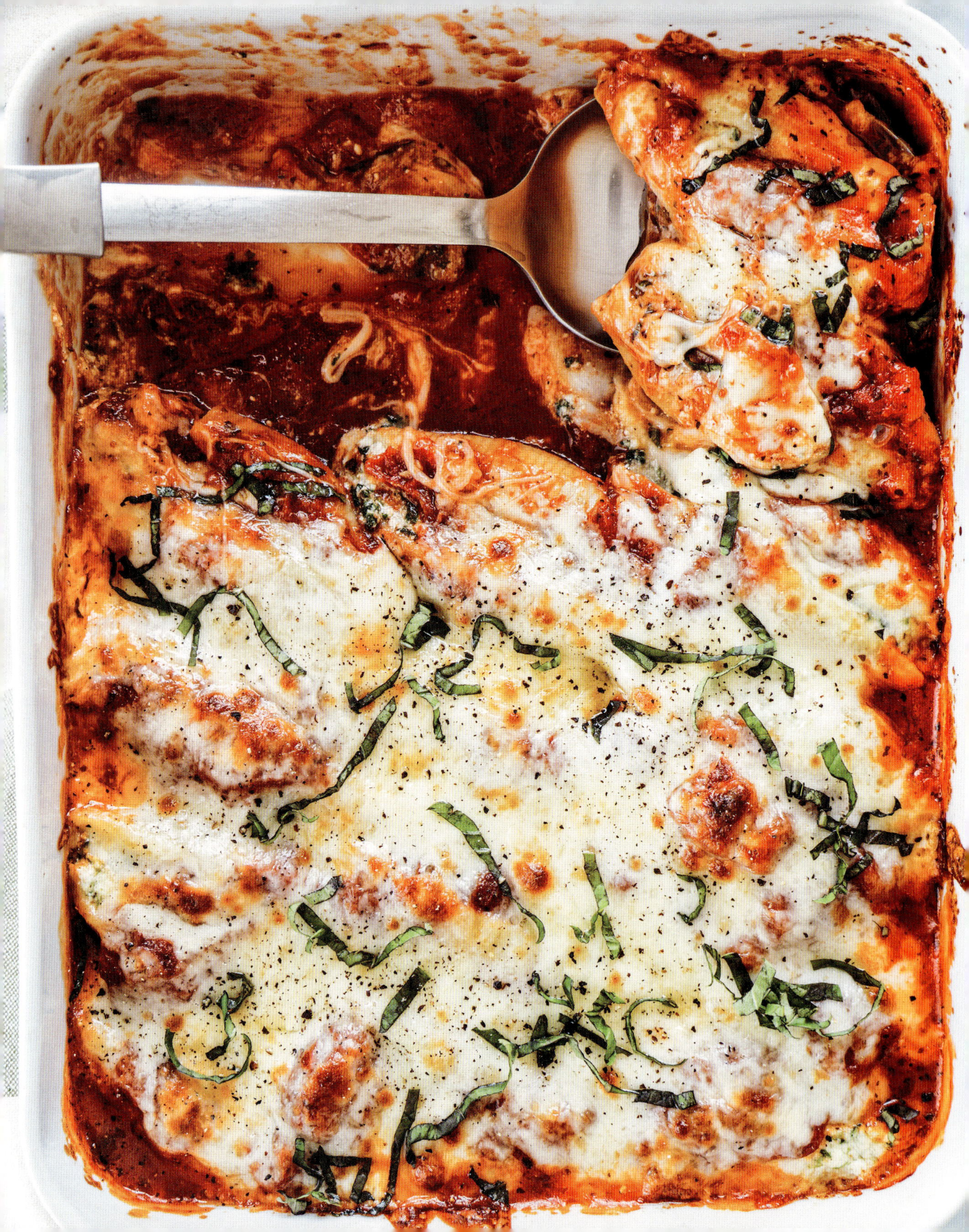

SPINACH AND RICOTTA-STUFFED SHELLS

PREP TIME: 30 MINUTES
COOK TIME: 30 MINUTES
TOTAL TIME: 1 HOUR
SERVES: 9

12 oz (336 g) jumbo pasta shells
1 cup (156 g) frozen chopped spinach, thawed
2 cups (246 g) ricotta cheese
4 oz (112 g) grated Parmesan cheese
1 large egg
½ tsp salt, or as needed
½ tsp black pepper, plus more as needed (see Recipe Notes)
1 (24-oz [720-ml]) jar marinara sauce
2 cups (224 g) shredded mozzarella cheese
Chopped fresh basil, as needed

Comfort food at its finest: easy, saucy shells stuffed with a ricotta, spinach and Parmesan filling. They're perfect to throw together on a weeknight and impressive enough to serve to guests.

Preheat the oven to 400°F (204°C).

In a large pot of heavily salted boiling water, cook the pasta shells according to the package's instructions until they're al dente. Make sure to stir the shells often, as they may stick together. Drain the shells in a strainer and rinse the shells well with cold water.

Squeeze out as much excess water from the spinach as you can.

In a large bowl, mix together the ricotta cheese, Parmesan cheese, spinach, egg, salt and black pepper. Transfer the filling to a large freezer bag or piping bag. Snip the corner of the freezer bag or the tip of the piping bag to a 1-inch (3-cm) diameter.

Pour half of the marinara in a 9 x 13–inch (27 x 39–cm) baking dish. Using the piping bag, fill each shell with about 2 tablespoons (30 g) of the cheese and spinach mixture. Place each stuffed shell in the baking dish on top of the sauce. Pour the remaining half of the marinara sauce over the shells and top them with the mozzarella cheese.

Bake the stuffed shells for 20 to 25 minutes, until the mozzarella is bubbly. Increase the oven's temperature to broil and broil the shells for 2 to 5 minutes, or until the cheese is browned.

Garnish the stuffed shells with the basil and additional black pepper.

RECIPE NOTES

Freshly ground black pepper is best in this dish.

Transfer leftover baked shells to airtight containers and refrigerate them for 3 to 5 days.

Freeze the stuffed shells in a tightly sealed dish for up to 1 month. When you are ready to serve the shells, take the dish out of the freezer the night before and thaw the shells in the refrigerator. Bake the shells according to the recipe's instructions.

NUTRITION INFORMATION

Serving size: 2 shells; **Calories:** 390; **Carbohydrates:** 36 g; **Protein:** 23 g; **Fat:** 17 g

BAKED MAC AND CHEESE

PREP TIME: 15 MINUTES
COOK TIME: 30 MINUTES
TOTAL TIME: 45 MINUTES
SERVES: 8

2½ cups (350 g) elbow macaroni
4 tbsp (60 g) unsalted butter
¼ cup (30 g) all-purpose flour
½ tsp salt
¼ tsp black pepper
3 cups (720 ml) lukewarm milk
2 cups (226 g) shredded provolone cheese
4 cups (480 g) shredded sharp Cheddar cheese, divided (see Recipe Note)
1 tbsp (15 ml) Worcestershire sauce
½ tsp smoked paprika

I couldn't write this book and not include my recipe for baked mac and cheese. What's not to love about mac and cheese? Decadent, creamy macaroni with the most incredible cheese sauce—this is soul food!

Preheat the oven to 350°F (177°C).

Boil the macaroni according to the package's instructions. Drain it and set it aside.

While the macaroni is cooking, melt the butter in a large oven-safe skillet or Dutch oven over medium heat. Whisk in the flour and cook the mixture for 1 to 2 minutes, until it is lightly browned. This will remove the raw taste of the flour. Whisk in the salt and black pepper.

Add the milk, either all at once or a bit a time, and whisk the mixture to remove any lumps.

Add the provolone cheese and 2 cups (240 g) of the Cheddar cheese and whisk until the cheese sauce is smooth. Add the Worcestershire sauce and stir well. Taste the sauce for seasoning and adjust it as necessary.

Increase the heat to medium-high and cook the sauce for about 5 minutes, until it starts to thicken and bubble. Turn off the heat.

Add the macaroni to the skillet and stir it until it is combined with the sauce. Top the mac and cheese with the remaining 2 cups (240 g) of Cheddar cheese. Sprinkle the smoked paprika over the cheese.

Bake the mac and cheese for 15 minutes, until the top starts to brown and the sauce is bubbly.

Serve the mac and cheese while it's warm.

RECIPE NOTE

If you like a crunchy topping on your mac and cheese, combine 1 cup (60 g) of panko breadcrumbs, 3 tablespoons (45 ml) of melted butter and ¼ teaspoon of salt. Sprinkle this mixture over the macaroni and cheese and bake it as instructed. If you are using this crunchy topping, add all 4 cups (480 g) of the Cheddar cheese to the sauce.

NUTRITION INFORMATION

Serving size: 1 serving; **Calories:** 628; **Carbohydrates:** 41 g; **Protein:** 31 g; **Fat:** 36 g

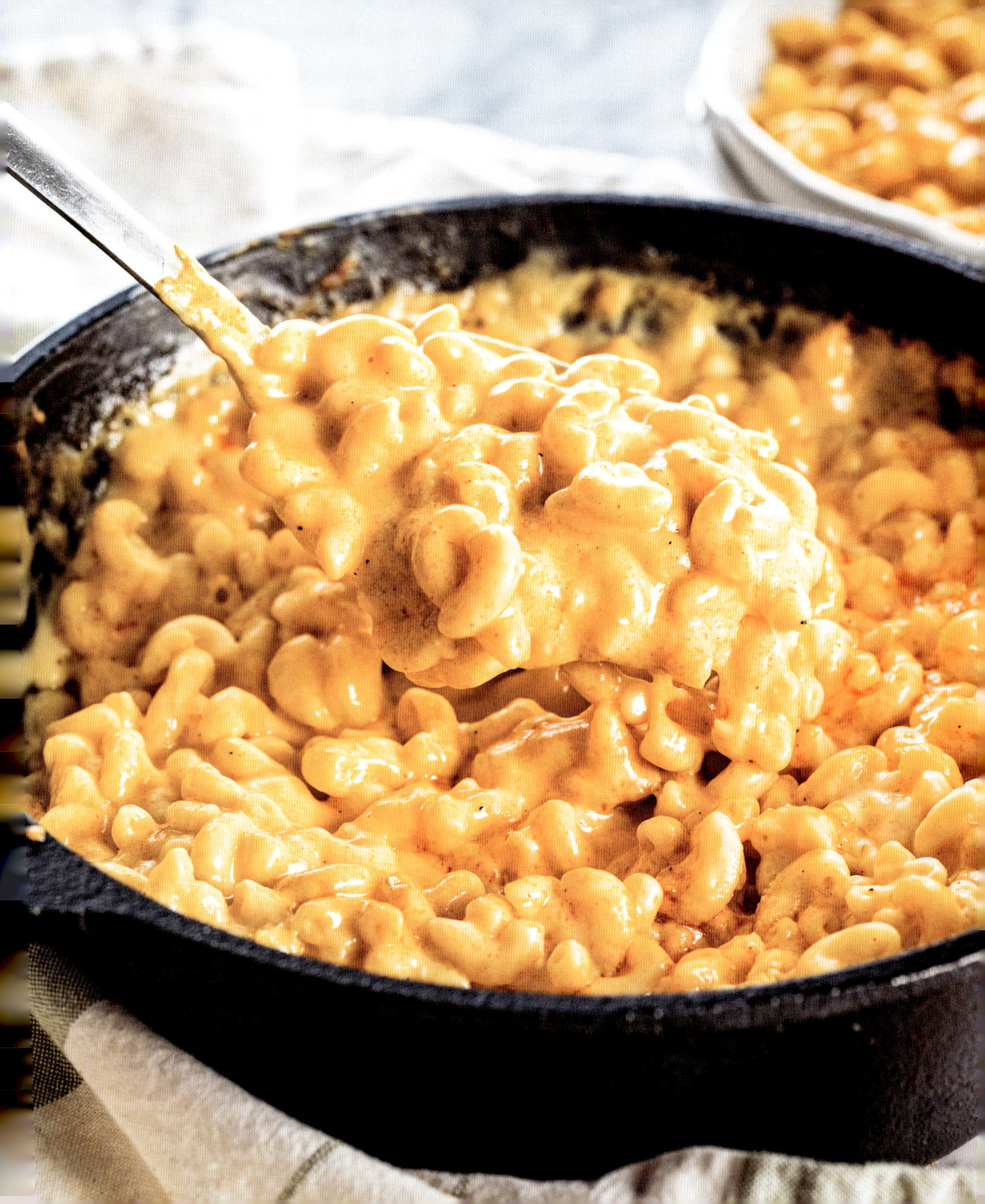

ARUGULA AND BASIL PESTO RISOTTO WITH SAUTÉED MUSHROOMS

PREP TIME: 10 MINUTES
COOK TIME: 35 MINUTES
TOTAL TIME: 45 MINUTES
SERVES: 6

ARUGULA AND BASIL PESTO

4 cloves garlic
1 cup (24 g) fresh basil leaves
2 cups (60 g) baby arugula
¼ cup (60 ml) olive oil
¼ cup (30 g) walnuts
Salt, as needed
Black pepper, as needed

RISOTTO

5 cups (1.2 L) low-sodium chicken broth
2 tbsp (30 ml) olive oil
2 tbsp (30 g) unsalted butter
1 onion, chopped
1½ cups (315 g) arborio rice
1 cup (240 ml) dry white wine
Salt, as needed
Black pepper, as needed

Risotto is the epitome of Italian home cooking and comfort food. Learn to make this simple pesto risotto with sautéed mushrooms for a rich and comforting meal!

To make the arugula and basil pesto, combine the garlic, basil, arugula, oil, walnuts, salt and black pepper in a food processor or blender. Process the ingredients until the pesto is smooth. Taste the pesto for seasoning and adjust it with additional salt and black pepper as needed.

To make the risotto, bring the broth to a simmer in a large pot over low heat.

In a large Dutch oven or skillet over medium heat, combine the oil and butter. When the butter has melted and is hot, add the onion and cook it for about 5 minutes, stirring it occasionally, until it is soft and translucent.

Add the rice to the Dutch oven and stir it, so that the rice is coated in the oil mixture. Cook the rice for 2 minutes, until all the oil is absorbed by the rice.

Stir in the wine, making sure to scrape any bits from the bottom of the Dutch oven if necessary. Cook the rice for 1 to 2 minutes, stirring it constantly, until most of the wine is absorbed by the rice.

Stir in 1 ladle of the broth and cook the mixture until most of the broth is absorbed by the rice. Repeat this process by adding 1 ladle of broth at a time. The whole process should take about 20 minutes, until you run out of broth and the rice is cooked through.

After about 20 minutes of this continuous process, add the pesto to the Dutch oven, stir the risotto and season it with the salt and black pepper. Set the risotto aside.

SAUTÉED MUSHROOMS

1 tbsp (15 ml) olive oil

4 cups (304 g) chopped white button mushrooms

½ tsp red pepper flakes

½ tsp garlic powder

Salt, as needed

Black pepper, as needed

Grated Parmesan cheese, as needed for sprinkling (optional)

To make the sautéed mushrooms, heat the oil in a medium skillet over medium-high heat. Add the mushrooms, red pepper flakes, garlic powder, salt and black pepper. Sauté the mushrooms for about 5 minutes, stirring them occasionally, or until they are browned to your liking.

To serve, spoon the risotto into serving bowls or plates and top each portion with the sautéed mushrooms. Sprinkle each serving with the Parmesan cheese (if using).

RECIPE NOTES

The risotto will last in the refrigerator for up to 5 days. To reheat the risotto, use the microwave and stir the risotto every 15 to 20 seconds. If the microwave isn't an option, you can reheat it in a skillet or saucepan over medium heat. Feel free to add a splash or two of chicken broth or water to prevent the risotto from drying out.

While it isn't ideal to freeze risotto, you can if you need it to last longer than 5 days. Make sure the risotto has fully cooled down to room temperature before storing it in an airtight container. It'll last 2 to 3 months in the freezer.

Let the risotto thaw overnight in the fridge before reheating it. Keep in mind that after freezing and thawing, the risotto will have a much softer texture. You'll have to be careful when reheating so as to not break up the grains of rice.

NUTRITION INFORMATION

Serving size: 1 serving; **Calories:** 348; **Carbohydrates:** 22 g; **Protein:** 11 g; **Fat:** 29 g

PASTA

WE'RE FINALLY AT MY FAVORITE CHAPTER IN THE ENTIRE BOOK.
Pasta is my comfort food, so I'm excited to share with you recipes such as my Pasta Primavera (page 188) and Creamy Carbonara (page 179). Pasta is a great food because it tastes amazing and is very cost-effective. Plus it can solve your breakfast-to-dinner problems easily. I mean, I'm sure we've all had cold pasta for breakfast—I know I have on numerous occasions.

With this chapter, my goal is to make pasta shine, and I hope to show you that sometimes you need less than a handful of ingredients to achieve something delicious like my Easy Spaghetti Bolognese (page 203) or Aglio e Olio (page 187). When you have good ingredients, they do the work for you.

I'm not sharing a recipe for homemade pasta in this chapter because I want to include recipes that are fairly quick to make; however, if you're interested in learning, I have a recipe on the blog that teaches you how to make your own pasta. It's very easy, but it is a bit time-consuming. Here, we'll just focus on some delicious recipes that are perfect for busy weeknights and special occasions alike.

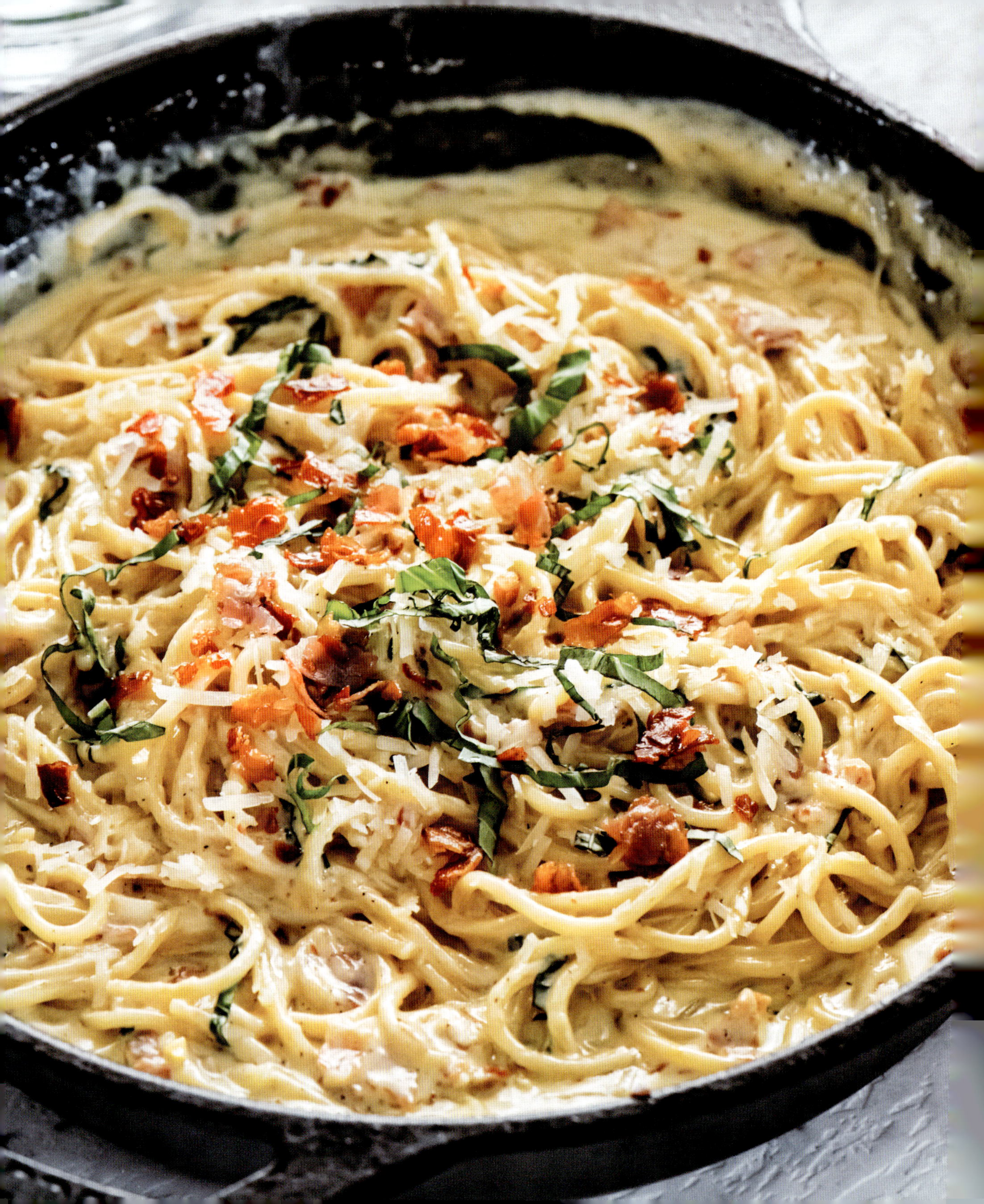

CREAMY CARBONARA

I wanted to start with this recipe because it's by far the most popular on my blog. It's not an authentic carbonara—a true carbonara doesn't have cream—but it's my version for a creamy and cheesy carbonara with crispy pancetta. So good and so easy to make.

PREP TIME: 5 MINUTES
COOK TIME: 25 MINUTES
TOTAL TIME: 30 MINUTES
SERVES: 4

8 oz (224 g) spaghetti
6 oz (168 g) pancetta, chopped
2 cups (480 ml) half-and-half (see Recipe Notes)
2 large egg yolks
1½ cups (270 g) grated Parmesan cheese (see Recipe Notes), plus more as needed
1 tsp black pepper (see Recipe Notes)
Salt, as needed
4 tbsp (12 g) chopped fresh basil

Bring a large pot of salted water to a boil over high heat. Add the spaghetti and cook it according to the package's instructions. Drain the spaghetti and set it aside.

Add the pancetta to a large skillet over medium-low heat. Sauté the pancetta for about 8 minutes, until it is crisp. Using a slotted spoon, transfer the pancetta to a medium bowl.

Add the half-and-half to the skillet and bring it to a simmer. Whisk the egg yolks into the half-and-half. Whisk in the Parmesan cheese. Stir in the black pepper. Taste the sauce for salt and season it with salt if needed.

Add the cooked spaghetti, pancetta and basil to the skillet and toss well to combine the ingredients.

Garnish the carbonara with more Parmesan cheese if desired and serve the pasta immediately.

RECIPE NOTES

Half-and-half is 12 percent fat. Heavy cream can also be used. It is also called heavy whipping cream because it's whipping cream with a milk fat content between 36 and 40 percent.

Freshly grated Parmesan cheese is best in this dish.

Freshly ground black pepper is best in this dish.

Store any leftovers in an airtight container in the fridge for 3 to 4 days. Make sure to refrigerate the carbonara within 2 hours of cooking.

NUTRITION INFORMATION

Serving size: 1 serving; **Calories:** 721; **Carbohydrates:** 49 g; **Protein:** 31 g; **Fat:** 43 g

CREAMY GOAT CHEESE PASTA

PREP TIME: 5 MINUTES
COOK TIME: 20 MINUTES
TOTAL TIME: 25 MINUTES
SERVES: 4

12 oz (336 g) penne
2 tbsp (30 g) unsalted butter
2 cloves garlic, minced
6 oz (168 g) soft goat cheese
1 cup (240 ml) half-and-half
¼ cup (6 g) fresh basil leaves, sliced chiffonade (see Recipe Notes)
¼ tsp salt, or as needed
½ tsp black pepper, or as needed
2 tbsp (30 ml) fresh lemon juice
Zest from 1 lemon
1 cup (180 g) grated Parmesan cheese
2 tbsp (6 g) chopped fresh parsley

This creamy goat cheese pasta, made in one pot, will be ready to devour in fewer than 30 minutes! Creamy goat cheese, basil and parsley: This is the easiest way to marry homemade and gourmet.

Cook the penne in salted water until it is al dente according to the package's instructions. Reserve 1 cup (240 ml) of the pasta water.

Melt the butter in a large skillet over medium-high heat. Add the garlic and sauté it for 30 to 60 seconds, just until it becomes aromatic. Add the goat cheese and half-and-half and stir to combine the ingredients. Whisk the mixture until it is smooth.

Reduce the heat to medium. Add the penne and ½ cup (120 ml) of the reserved pasta water to the skillet. Stir well to coat the pasta. Let it simmer in the sauce for 1 to 2 minutes.

If you'd like a thinner sauce, add more of the pasta water as needed. Mix in the basil, then season the sauce with the salt and black pepper. Add the lemon juice and zest. Turn off the heat and stir in the Parmesan cheese.

Garnish the pasta with the parsley and serve it.

RECIPE NOTES

To chiffonade the basil, stack the basil leaves, starting with the largest to the smallest. Roll the leaves tightly lengthwise. Starting from the pointy end of the leaves, slice the basil all the way down the roll.

Transfer any leftovers to an airtight container and keep it in the fridge for 2 to 3 days. Reheat the pasta either in the microwave or on the stove over medium heat. Stir the pasta often and add a splash of water or cream if you find the sauce is too thick.

NUTRITION INFORMATION

Serving size: 1 serving; **Calories:** 661; **Carbohydrates:** 68 g; **Protein:** 30 g; **Fat:** 29 g

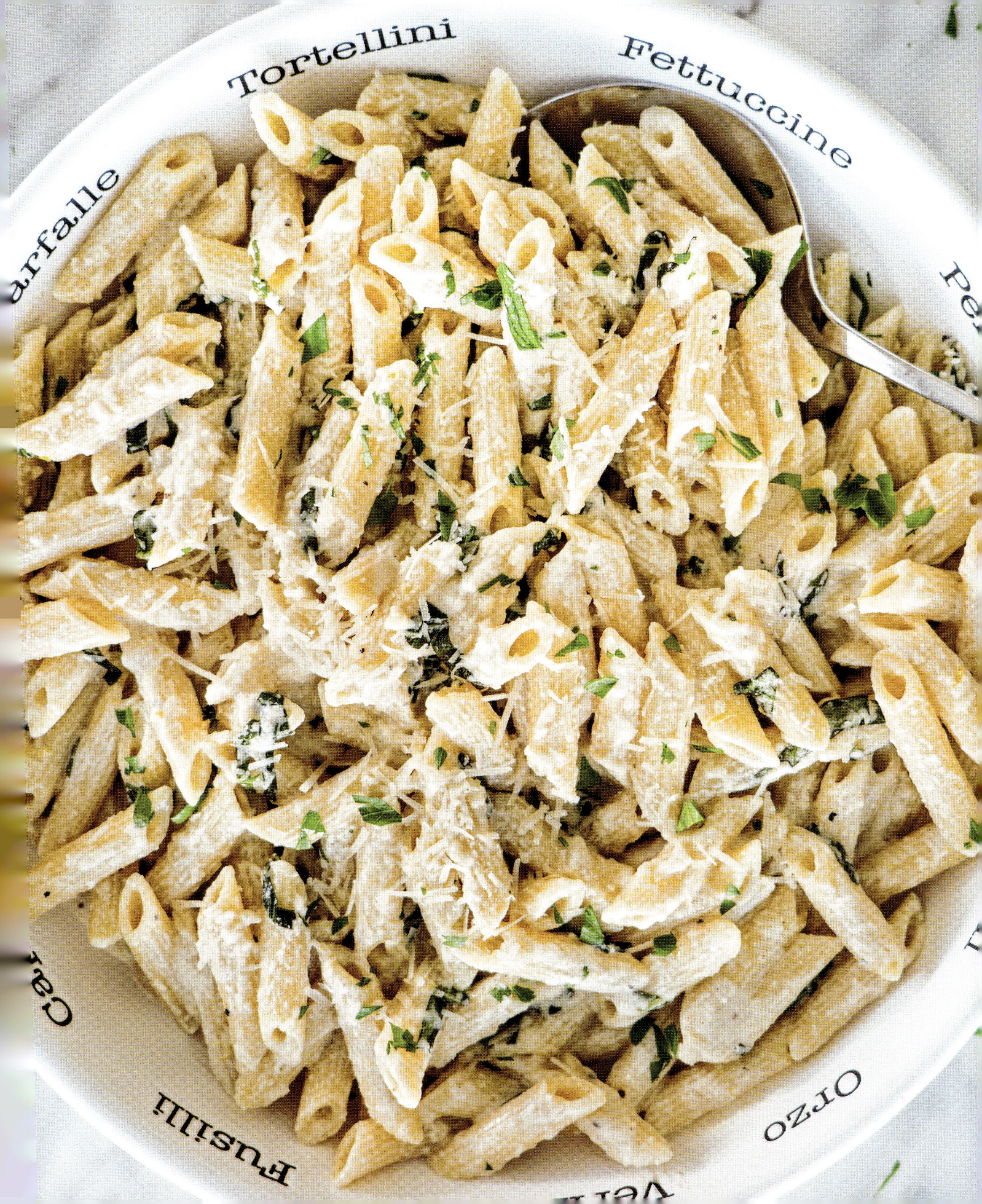
Tortellini
Fettuccine
Orzo
Fusilli

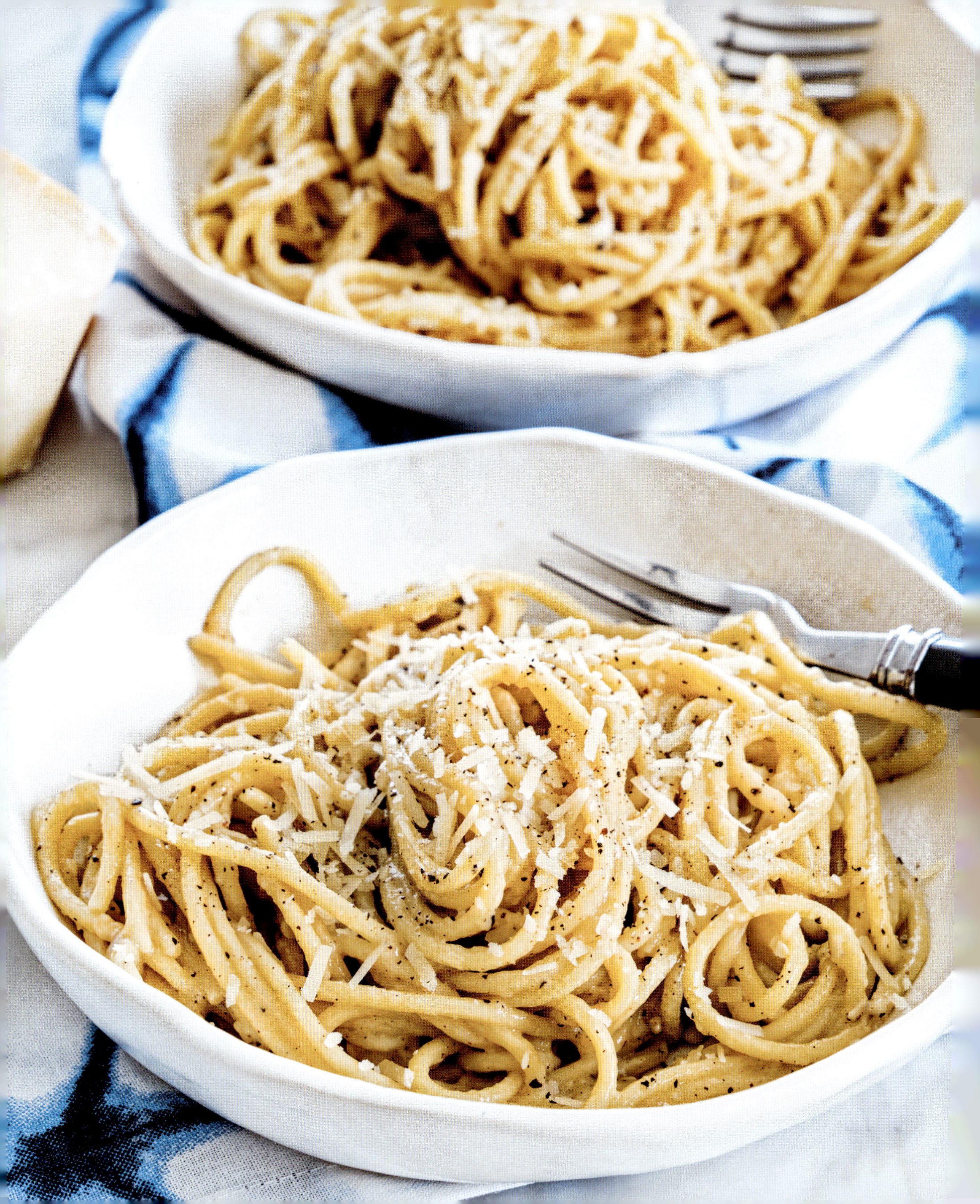

CACIO E PEPE

PREP TIME: 5 MINUTES
COOK TIME: 15 MINUTES
TOTAL TIME: 20 MINUTES
SERVES: 3

8 oz (334 g) pasta (I recommend bucatini or spaghetti)

4 tbsp (60 g) unsalted butter, cubed

1 tsp black pepper, plus more as needed (see Recipe Notes)

1½ cups (270 g) grated Parmesan, pecorino or Grana Padano cheese, divided (see Recipe Notes)

NUTRITION INFORMATION

Serving size: 1 serving; **Calories:** 614; **Carbohydrates:** 58 g; **Protein:** 28 g; **Fat:** 29 g

Cacio e pepe is a classic, authentic Italian dish that truly shows that with just four ingredients you can have a beautiful meal. Cacio e pepe literally translates to "cheese and pepper," which is what this dish is all about. This is a perfect example of letting the ingredients do the work for you.

Fill a large pot with water and generously salt it, using at least 1 to 2 tablespoons (15 to 30 g) of salt. Bring the water to a boil, then add the pasta and cook it for 8 to 9 minutes, until it is barely al dente. Do not overcook the pasta, as it will continue cooking in the sauce. Reserve 1 to 1½ cups (240 to 360 ml) of the pasta water. Drain the pasta.

When the pasta has been cooking for 5 minutes, start the sauce. Melt the butter in a large skillet over medium-high heat. Add the black pepper and sauté it for 1 minute. This will cause the black pepper to "bloom" and deepen its flavor. Add about ¾ cup (180 ml) of the reserved pasta water to the skillet. It will immediately bubble up. Stir it to combine it with the butter. Remove the skillet from the heat.

Add the pasta and about 1 cup (180 g) of the Parmesan cheese. Toss everything together well and add the remaining ¼ to ¾ cup (60 to 180 ml) of pasta water if the pasta starts looking a little dry. Sprinkle the pasta with the remaining ½ cup (90 g) of Parmesan cheese and more black pepper.

RECIPE NOTES

Use freshly ground black pepper. Do not use pre-ground black pepper, as freshly ground makes a world of difference. The pepper should be toasted in the butter. Don't just add it to the finished dish—you want to toast it with that butter to ensure the flavor is as deep as possible.

Use the best cheese that you can afford. This dish is all about the cheese and black pepper, so you want to make sure you're using a good sharp Parmesan cheese or Pecorino Romano. Be sure to grate it yourself—don't buy pre-grated cheese for this dish.

The pasta water is the secret to this recipe. Not only is pasta water a magic ingredient in this dish, but it really is what makes the sauce creamy. Don't reserve the pasta water too early; we want to make sure there's enough starch in the water, as it is the secret to a rich and saucy consistency. Also, don't be stingy with the water, use the full 1½ cups (360 ml) of it, if needed.

Store any leftovers in an airtight container in the fridge for up to 3 days.

PESTO SHRIMP ASPARAGUS PASTA

PREP TIME: 15 MINUTES
COOK TIME: 15 MINUTES
TOTAL TIME: 30 MINUTES
SERVES: 6

PESTO
½ cup (68 g) pine nuts
2 oz (56 g) fresh basil leaves
½ cup (90 g) grated Parmesan cheese
¼ cup (60 ml) olive oil
3 cloves garlic
¼ tsp salt, or as needed
¼ tsp black pepper, or as needed

PASTA
10 oz (280 g) spaghetti or pasta of choice
12 oz (336 g) large shrimp, peeled and deveined
Salt, as needed
Black pepper, as needed
2 tbsp (30 ml) olive oil, divided
1 lb (448 g) asparagus, trimmed
1 cup (240 ml) heavy cream
1 cup (150 g) cherry tomatoes, halved
¼ cup (45 g) grated Parmesan cheese, plus more as needed

NUTRITION INFORMATION
Serving size: 1 serving; **Calories:** 639; **Carbohydrates:** 43 g; **Protein:** 27 g; **Fat:** 41 g

This is a great pasta recipe—especially if you're short on time—because you can either use my pesto recipe or you can use store-bought pesto. But even if you choose to make your own, this dinner is still ready in just 30 minutes.

To make the pesto, you may choose to toast the pine nuts, which will give the pesto a nutty and creamy flavor. To do this, place the pine nuts in a small skillet over medium heat. Toast the pine nuts for about 2 minutes; make sure to watch them closely, as they can burn quickly.

In a food processor, combine the pine nuts, basil, Parmesan cheese, oil, garlic, salt and black pepper. Pulse the ingredients a few times, but don't overprocess the pesto, as the consistency should not be completely smooth. Taste the pesto for seasonings and add more salt and black pepper if needed.

To make the pasta, cook it in salted water according to the package's instructions.

Meanwhile, place the shrimp in a large bowl and add 1 to 2 tablespoons (15 to 30 g) of the pesto. Toss the shrimp until they are all coated in the pesto. Season the shrimp with the salt and black pepper.

Heat 1 tablespoon (15 ml) of the oil in a large skillet over medium heat. Add the shrimp and cook them for about 2 minutes per side, until the shrimp turn pink and are slightly crispy.

Remove the shrimp from the skillet and transfer them to a plate. Add the remaining 1 tablespoon (15 ml) of oil to the skillet, then add the asparagus. Cook the asparagus for about 2 minutes, just until it becomes a bit tender. Add the heavy cream to the skillet and bring it to a boil. Stir in the remaining pesto. Turn off the heat and add the pasta, tomatoes and Parmesan cheese. Toss the ingredients to combine them.

Garnish the pasta with additional Parmesan cheese if desired. Serve the pasta warm.

RECIPE NOTES

If you don't own a food processor, you can use a blender to make the pesto. If you choose to blend the pesto, I recommend chopping the basil and mincing the garlic before adding them to the blender.

If you're using store-bought pesto for this recipe, start with about 4 tablespoons (60 g) and add more if needed.

Store any leftovers in an airtight container in the fridge for no more than 3 or 4 days.

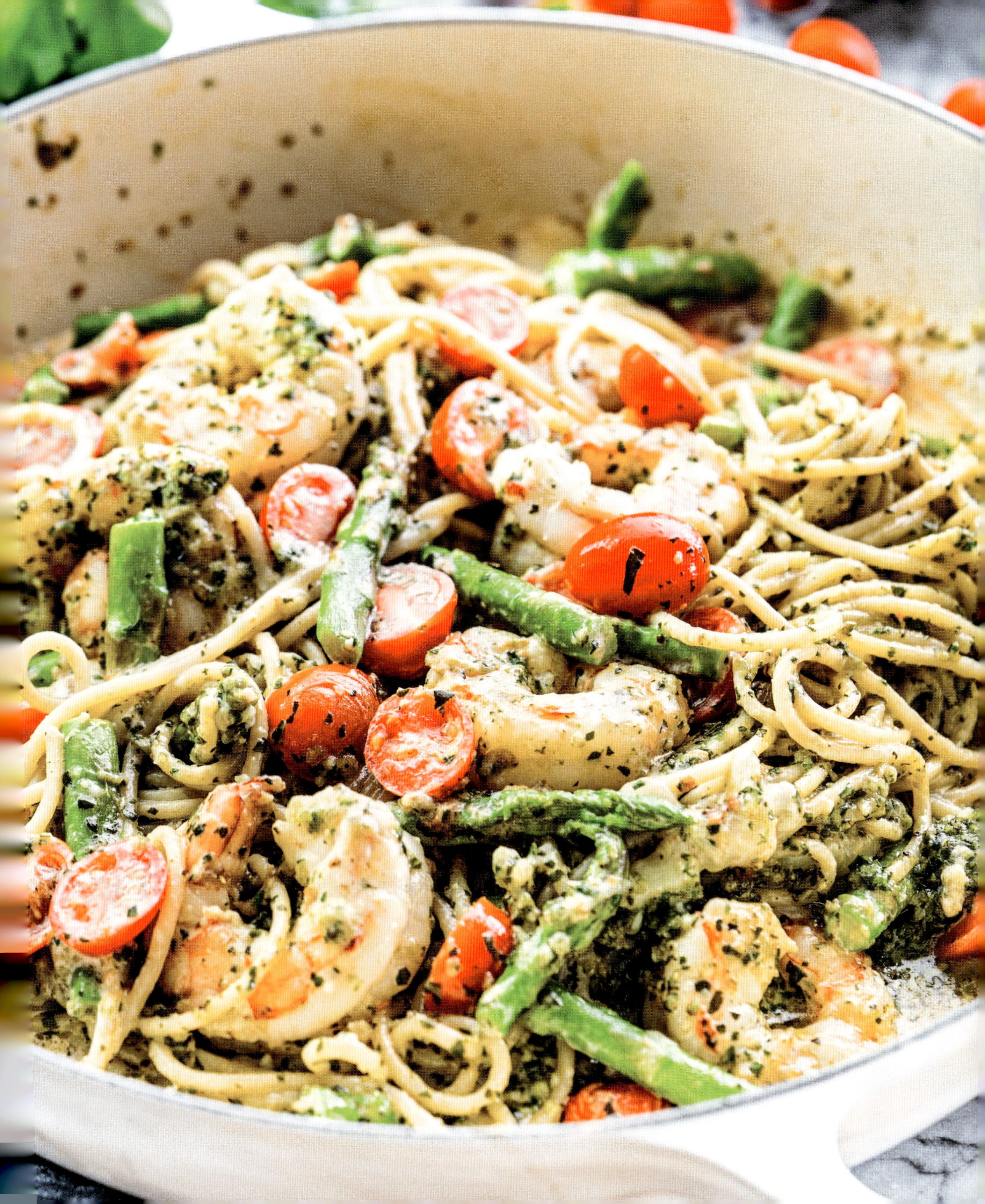

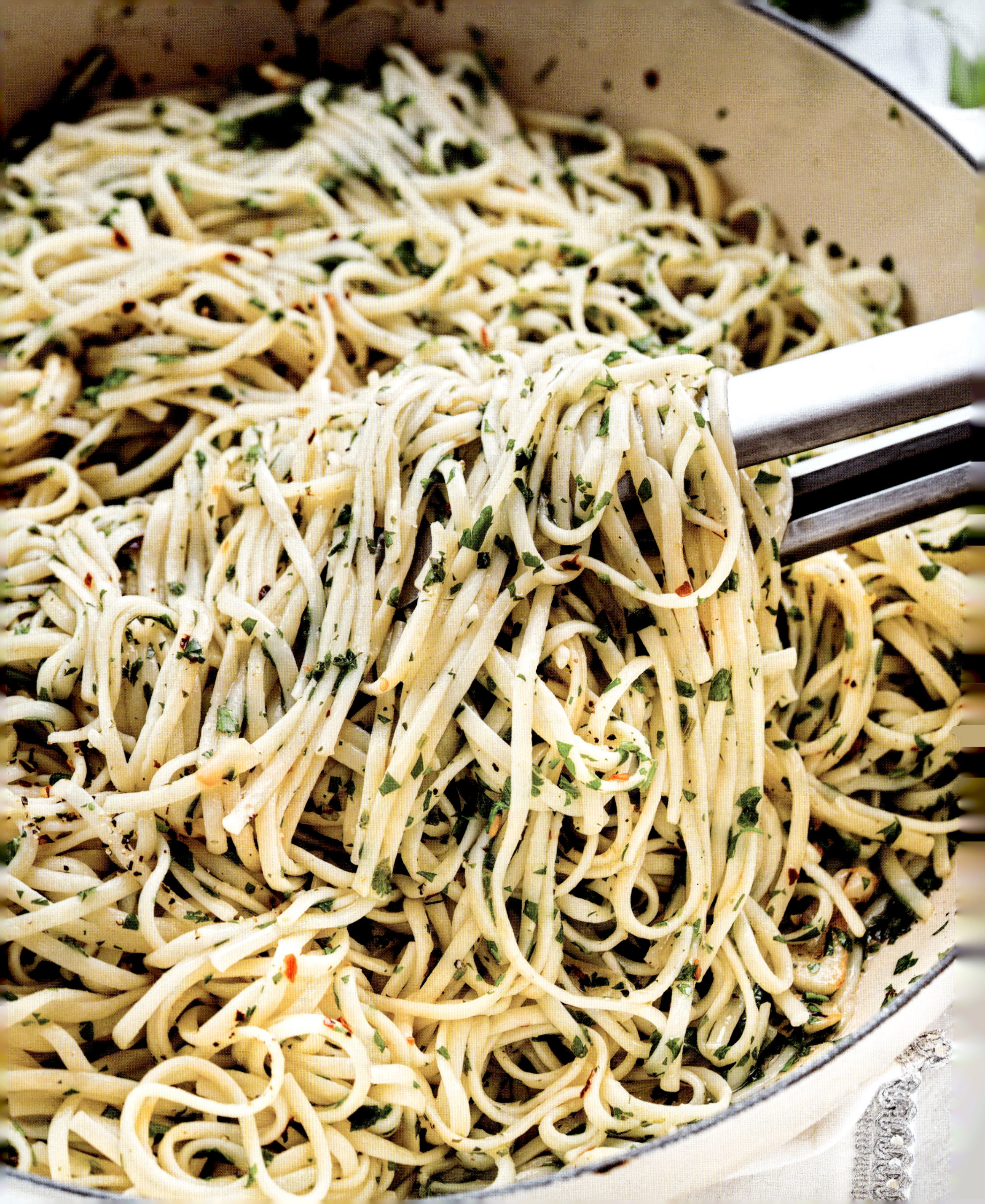

AGLIO E OLIO

PREP TIME: 5 MINUTES
COOK TIME: 15 MINUTES
TOTAL TIME: 20 MINUTES
SERVES: 6

1 lb (448 g) linguini or pasta of choice (see Recipe Notes)
¾ cup (180 ml) olive oil
1 bulb garlic, peeled and sliced
2 tsp (6 g) red pepper flakes
½ tsp salt, or as needed
½ tsp black pepper, or as needed
½ cup (24 g) chopped fresh parsley
½ cup (90 g) grated Parmesan cheese (optional; see Recipe Notes)
Fresh lemon juice, as needed (optional)

Aglio e olio *simply means "garlic and olive oil." This is a traditional dish from Naples made with just a handful of simple ingredients; it truly is more than the sum of its parts.*

Bring a large pot of heavily salted water to a boil. Add the linguini and cook it for about 10 minutes, until it is al dente. Drain the pasta and reserve 1 cup (240 ml) of the pasta water.

Meanwhile, heat the oil in a large, deep skillet or sauté pan over medium heat.

Add the garlic and red pepper flakes and stir them into the oil. Cook them for about 1 minute, until the garlic is a light golden brown. Season the mixture with the salt and black pepper.

Reduce the heat to medium-low and add the cooked pasta and parsley and toss the pasta to coat it in the sauce. If the pasta is too dry, add about ½ cup (120 ml) of the reserved pasta water. Add more of the pasta water, a little at a time, until the sauce reaches the desired consistency. On the other hand, if the pasta is too saucy, cook it for about 1 additional minute, or until the pasta absorbs some of the sauce.

Garnish the pasta with the Parmesan cheese (if using) and lemon juice (if using) prior to serving it.

RECIPE NOTES

Any long pasta—such as spaghetti, linguini or fettuccine—can be used in this dish.

Freshly grated Parmesan cheese is best in this dish.

NUTRITION INFORMATION

Serving size: 1 serving; **Calories:** 572; **Carbohydrates:** 56 g; **Protein:** 14 g; **Fat:** 32 g

PASTA PRIMAVERA

The word primavera *means "springtime" in Italian. In the era before seasonal cooking was customary, pasta primavera was the recipe to order for the best and brightest of spring vegetables. This warm penne is bursting with lots of fresh vegetables and plenty of Parmesan cheese.*

PREP TIME: 15 MINUTES
COOK TIME: 15 MINUTES
TOTAL TIME: 30 MINUTES
SERVES: 4

10 oz (280 g) penne
2 tbsp (30 ml) olive oil
1 onion, chopped
1 lb (448 g) asparagus, trimmed and cut into 2" (6-cm) pieces
2 cups (132 g) sliced white button or cremini mushrooms
1 zucchini, sliced into half-moons
1 carrot, shredded
2 cups (300 g) cherry tomatoes, halved
4 cloves garlic, minced
1 tbsp (3 g) Italian seasoning
½ tsp salt
¼ tsp black pepper
¼ tsp red pepper flakes
1 cup (180 g) grated Parmesan cheese, divided (see Recipe Notes)
1 lemon, cut into wedges

Cook the penne according to the package's instructions. Drain the pasta and reserve ½ cup (120 ml) of the pasta water.

Meanwhile, heat the oil in a large skillet over medium-high heat. Add the onion and cook it for 2 to 3 minutes, until it has softened.

Add the asparagus, mushrooms and zucchini and cook them for about 5 minutes, until they are tender.

Add the carrot, tomatoes, garlic, Italian seasoning, salt, black pepper and red pepper flakes. Stir the vegetables and cook them for 1 minute, until the tomatoes begin to soften.

Stir in the penne, ½ cup (90 g) of the Parmesan cheese and some of the reserved pasta water as needed to thin the sauce.

Top the pasta primavera with the remaining ½ cup (90 g) of Parmesan cheese and lemon wedges.

RECIPE NOTES

Freshly grated Parmesan cheese is best in this dish.

Leftovers can be stored in an airtight container in the refrigerator for 3 to 5 days.

To freeze the pasta primavera, transfer the pasta to an airtight container and store it in the freezer for up to 3 months.

NUTRITION INFORMATION

Serving size: 1 serving; **Calories:** 512; **Carbohydrates:** 73 g; **Protein:** 24 g; **Fat:** 15 g

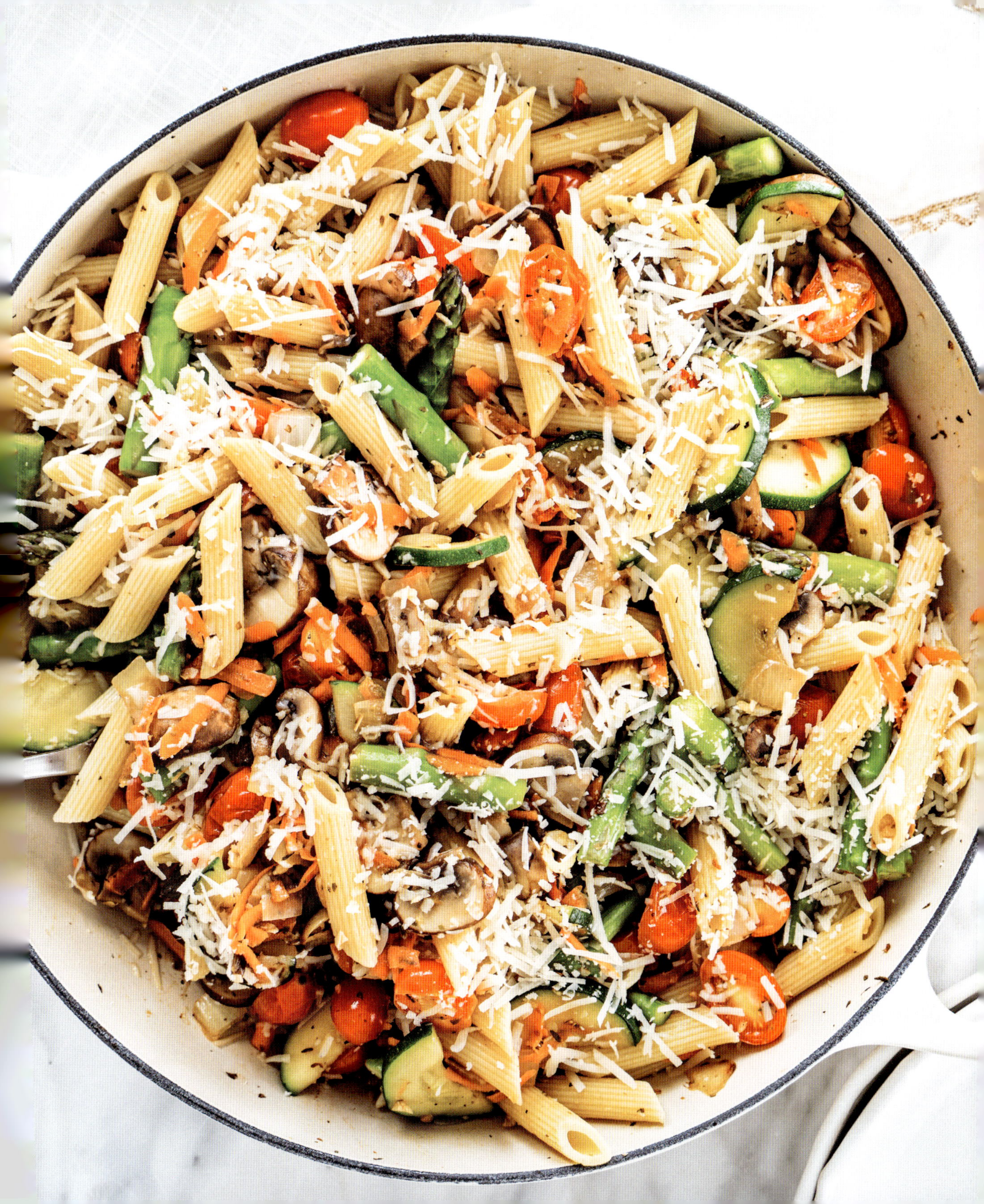

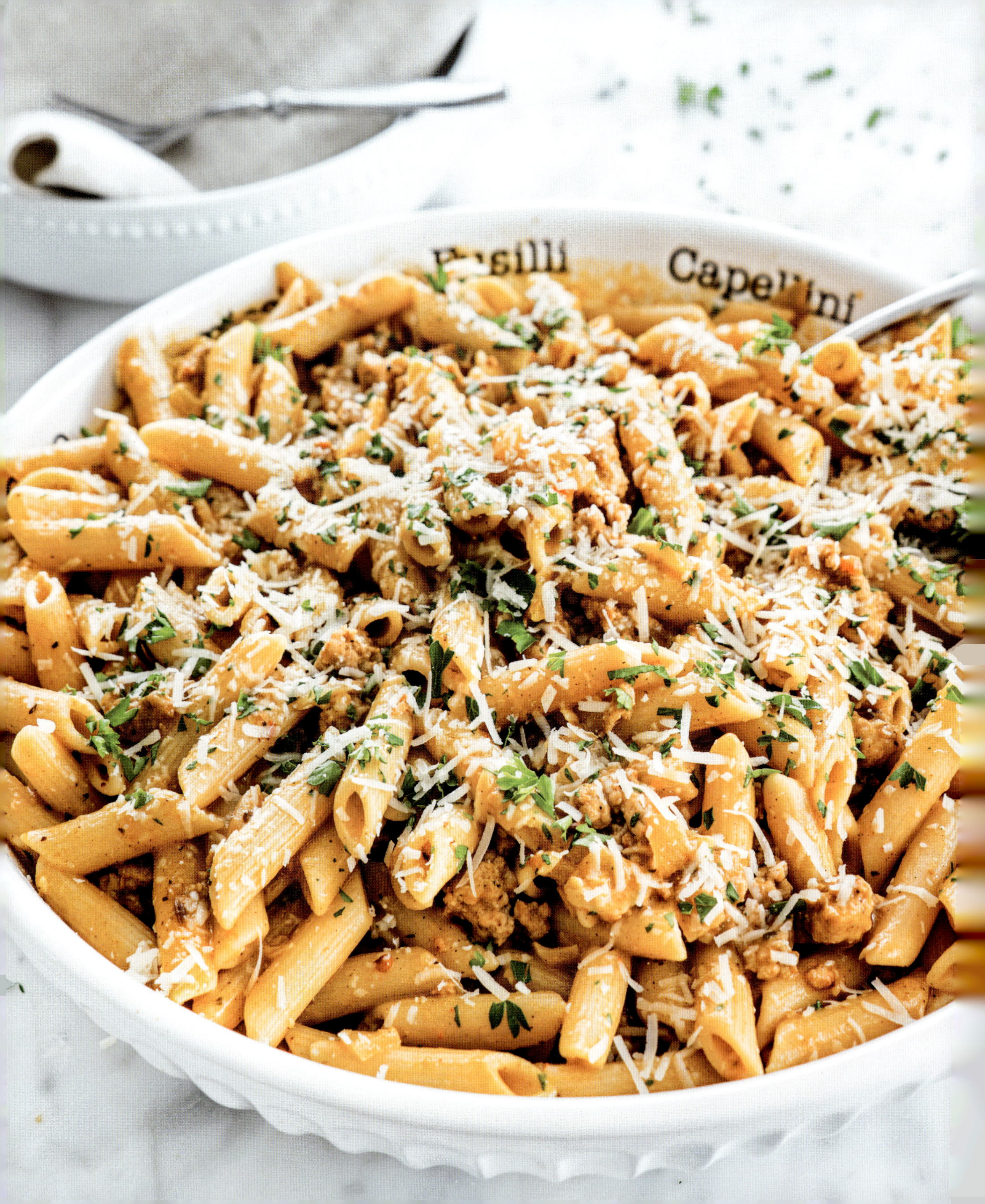
Capellini

PUMPKIN AND SAUSAGE PASTA

This Pumpkin and Sausage Pasta is the perfect comforting fall meal! A delicious and creamy sauce with sausage and pumpkin: The flavors in this dish are incredible. You will want to make this not only during pumpkin season but year-round too.

PREP TIME: 10 MINUTES
COOK TIME: 20 MINUTES
TOTAL: 30 MINUTES
SERVES: 6

1 lb (448 g) pasta of choice
1 tbsp (15 ml) olive oil
1 lb (448 g) mild Italian sausage, casings removed
1 onion, chopped
3 cloves garlic, minced
½ tsp ground nutmeg
¼ tsp ground cinnamon
1 dried bay leaf
½ tsp dried oregano
½ tsp salt, or as needed
½ tsp black pepper, or as needed
1 cup (240 ml) white wine
1 cup (240 ml) low-sodium chicken broth
1 cup (245 g) canned pumpkin
½ cup (120 ml) heavy cream
1 cup (180 g) grated Parmesan cheese (see Recipe Notes)
1 tbsp (3 g) chopped fresh parsley

Cook the pasta in salted water according to the package's instructions. Drain the pasta and set it aside.

Meanwhile, heat the oil in a large skillet or cast-iron pan over medium heat. Add the sausage and cook it for about 5 minutes, breaking it into smaller pieces with a wooden spoon as it browns.

Add the onion and garlic and sauté the mixture for 3 to 5 minutes, or until the onion is tender.

Add the nutmeg, cinnamon, bay leaf, oregano, salt, black pepper and wine. Cook the mixture for about 2 minutes, until the wine is reduced by half. Add the broth, pumpkin and heavy cream. Stir to combine the ingredients and allow the sauce to come to a bubble. Reduce the heat to low and simmer the sauce for about 5 minutes, until it has thickened. Remove the bay leaf from the sauce.

Add the pasta to the skillet and toss it with the sauce. Cook the pasta and sauce for about 1 minute. Stir in the Parmesan cheese and parsley and serve the pasta.

RECIPE NOTES

Freshly grated Parmesan cheese is best in this dish.

Let the pasta cool before storing it. It will stay fresh for 3 to 5 days in an airtight container in the fridge. Frozen, this pasta dish will last for 2 to 3 months—just be sure to let it thaw fully in the fridge before reheating it.

NUTRITION INFORMATION

Serving size: 1 serving; **Calories:** 761; **Carbohydrates:** 65 g; **Protein:** 29 g; **Fat:** 39 g

CREAMY GARLIC-PARMESAN ORZO

PREP TIME: 5 MINUTES
COOK TIME: 10 MINUTES
TOTAL TIME: 15 MINUTES
SERVES: 6

2 tbsp (30 ml) olive oil
4 tbsp (60 g) unsalted butter
1 onion, chopped
4 cloves garlic, minced
2 cups (280 g) orzo
½ tsp salt, or as needed
¼ tsp black pepper, or as needed
2 cups (480 ml) low-sodium chicken broth
2 cups (480 ml) half-and-half (see Recipe Notes)
1½ cups (270 g) Parmesan cheese (see Recipe Notes)
2 tbsp (6 g) chopped fresh parsley

Talk about quick and easy comfort food! While this dish could be a side to any protein, such as my Beer Can Chicken (page 12), I prefer this as a meal on its own because it's cheesy and creamy and really hits the spot.

In a large skillet over medium-high heat, combine the oil and butter. Heat the two for about 30 seconds, until the butter melts. Stir in the onion and garlic and cook them for about 2 minutes, until the onion softens and the garlic becomes aromatic.

Push the onion and garlic to the side of the skillet. Add the orzo to the skillet and cook it for about 2 minutes in the oil-butter mixture, so that it starts to toast lightly—this will give it a nutty flavor.

Season the orzo with the salt and pepper, then stir in the broth and half-and-half. Bring the mixture to a boil, then reduce the heat down to medium-low. Cover the skillet with a lid and cook the orzo for 5 minutes, until it has a firm, chewy texture.

Remove the skillet's lid and stir in the Parmesan cheese and parsley.

Serve the orzo immediately.

RECIPE NOTES

Half-and-half is equal parts whole milk and light cream, and is 10 to 12 percent fat, which is usually less than light cream.

Freshly grated Parmesan cheese is best in this dish.

This dish is quite versatile. Add more nutrition to it by adding spinach, broccoli, mushrooms, peas or asparagus. You can also add some protein by adding chicken—make sure you add it when you cook the onion to give it enough time to cook fully.

Store this dish in an airtight container in the fridge for up to 3 to 4 days. Unfortunately, this cream-based pasta dish doesn't thaw well after being frozen, so I don't recommend storing it in the freezer.

NUTRITION INFORMATION

Serving size: 1 serving; **Calories:** 518; **Carbohydrates:** 44 g; **Protein:** 20 g; **Fat:** 29 g

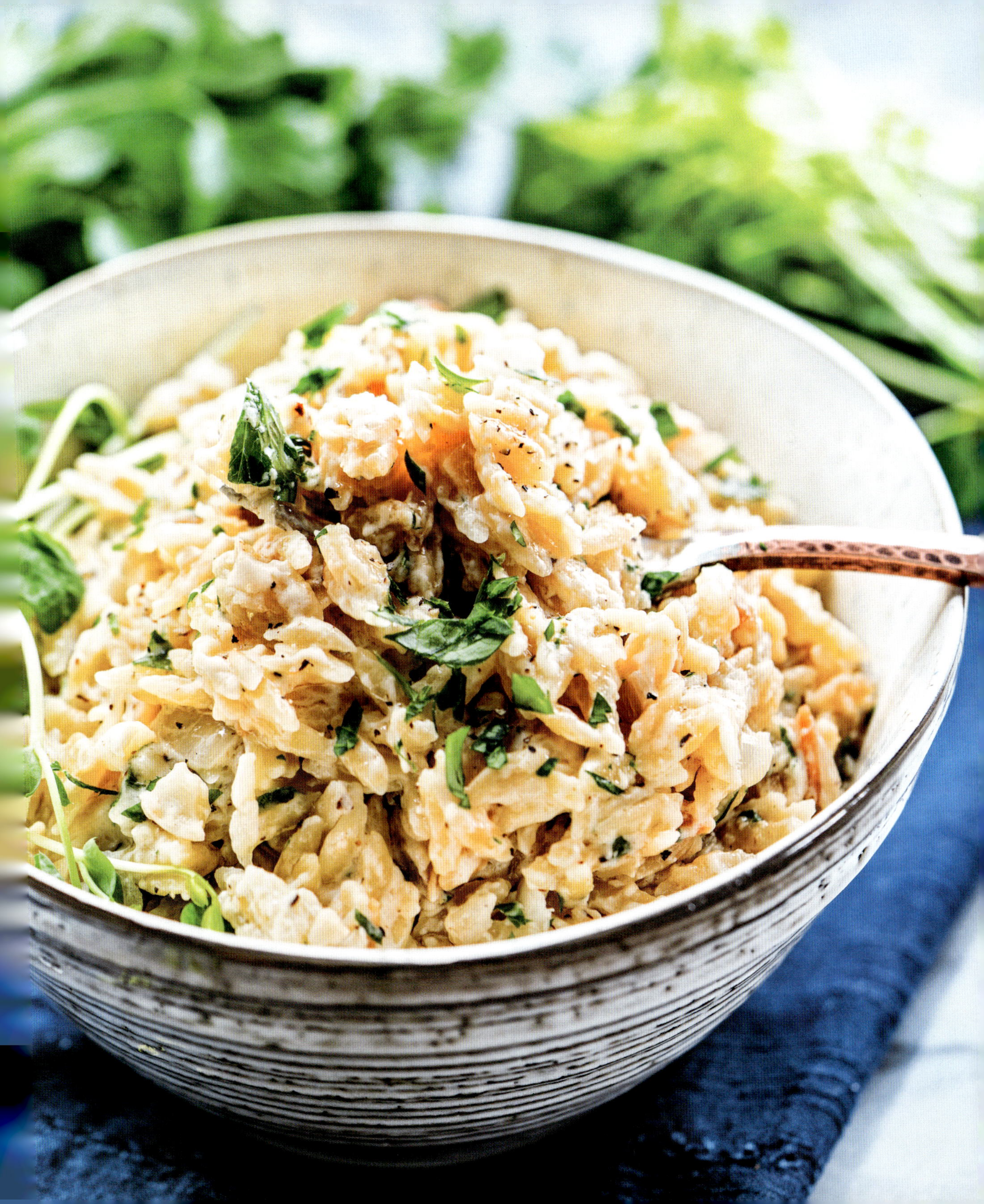

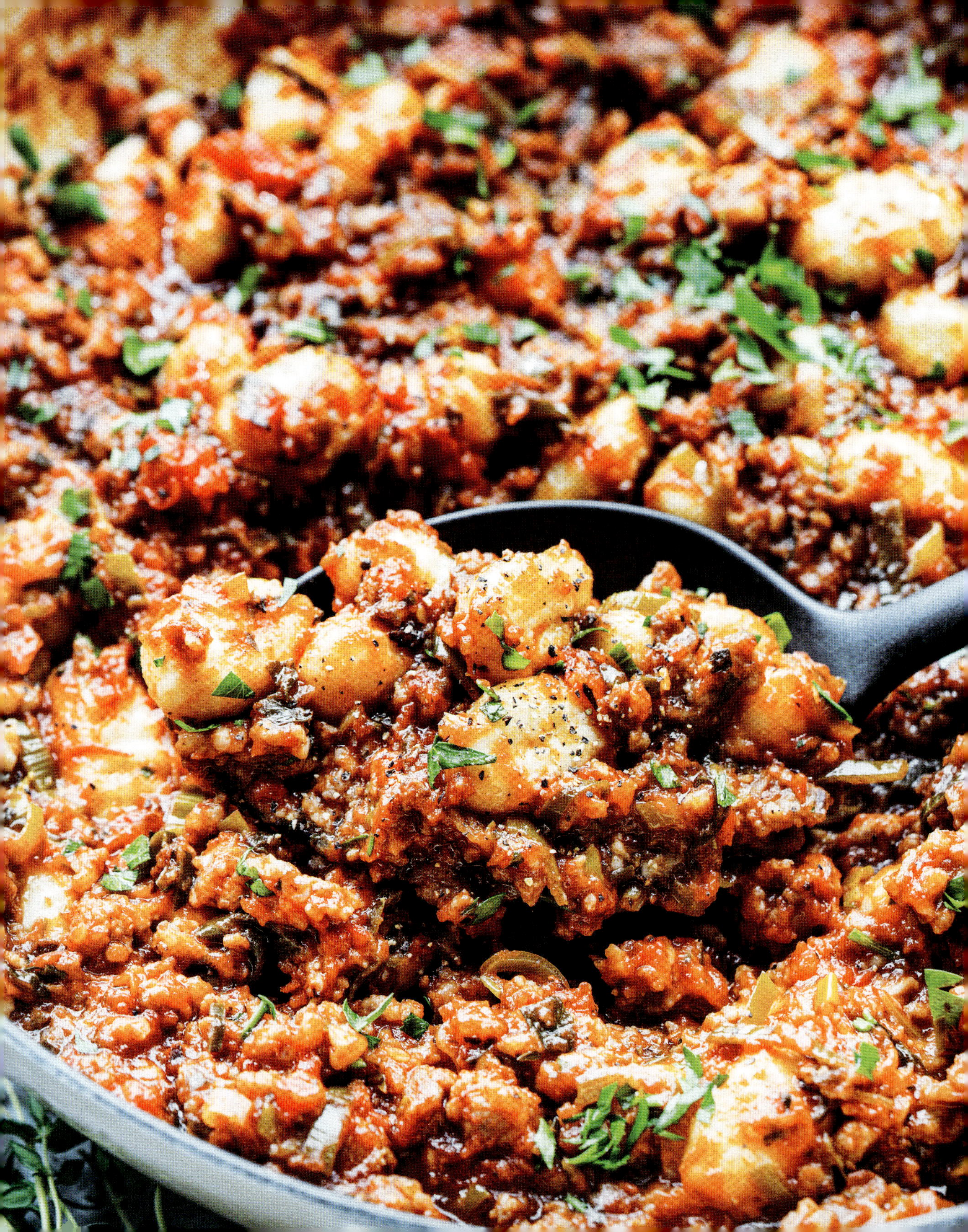

SAUSAGE AND LEEK RAGU GNOCCHI

PREP TIME: 5 MINUTES
COOK TIME: 30 MINUTES
TOTAL TIME: 35 MINUTES
SERVES: 4

1 tbsp (15 ml) olive oil
12 oz (336 g) mild Italian sausage, casings removed
1 leek, chopped (see Recipe Notes)
1 tsp chopped fresh thyme
2 tbsp (6 g) chopped fresh parsley
2 cloves garlic, minced
¼ tsp salt, or as needed
¼ tsp black pepper, or as needed
¼ tsp red pepper flakes
1 (28-oz [784-g]) can crushed tomatoes
1 lb (448 g) potato gnocchi
Grated Parmesan cheese, as needed (optional; see Recipe Notes)

This is a rich, flavorful and comforting meal that's great for any night of the week. The ragu is slowly cooked until it's thick and hearty, then it's served atop soft and fluffy potato gnocchi.

Heat the oil in a large skillet over medium heat. Add the Italian sausage and cook it for 3 to 5 minutes, breaking it up with a wooden spoon as it cooks, until it is no longer pink.

Add the leek, thyme, parsley, garlic, salt, black pepper and red pepper flakes and stir to combine the ingredients. Cook the mixture for 3 minutes, until the leek softens.

Stir in the tomatoes. Bring the sauce to a boil, then reduce the heat to low and simmer the sauce for about 20 minutes, until it thickens and reduces. There should be no liquid left; it should be a thick sauce.

While the sauce is reducing, cook the gnocchi according to the package's instructions.

Add the gnocchi to the sauce and stir them into the sauce. Garnish the gnocchi with the Parmesan cheese (if using). Serve the dish while it's warm.

RECIPE NOTES

Leeks have a mild onion flavor. They can be substituted with green onions or white onions.

Freshly grated Parmesan cheese is best in this dish.

This ragu will work with other types of pastas as well. If you use another type of pasta, reduce the ragu slightly, so that the sauce will cling to the pasta.

You can store this dish in a shallow airtight container in the fridge for 3 to 4 days. Just be sure to allow it to fully cool before placing it in the fridge.

You can freeze this dish as well! Hold off on adding the gnocchi until you're ready to eat it. Freeze the ragu in a shallow airtight container once it has fully cooled. Allow the ragu to thaw overnight in the fridge before reheating it on the stove and incorporating the gnocchi.

NUTRITION INFORMATION

Serving size: 1 serving; **Calories:** 590; **Carbohydrates:** 59 g; **Protein:** 20 g; **Fat:** 32 g

CHEESY CHICKEN AND BROCCOLI PASTA

This is a great one-pot dish—all you have to do is boil the pasta in a delicious creamy sauce with chicken and finish it off with fresh broccoli and lots of cheese. It is easy to make and always a crowd-pleaser.

Heat the oil in a large skillet over medium-high heat. Add the chicken to the skillet and season it with the salt and black pepper. Cook the chicken for about 5 minutes, until it is cooked through and is starting to brown.

Add the onion and garlic and cook the mixture for 2 minutes, until the onion softens a bit.

Add the pasta, broth and milk and bring the mixture to a boil. Reduce the heat to low, stir the pasta, cover the skillet and simmer the pasta for 15 minutes, stirring it occasionally, until the pasta is fully cooked.

Uncover the pot and stir in the broccoli. Cook the pasta and broccoli for 2 minutes, until all the liquid evaporates. Stir in the nutmeg and Cheddar cheese. Taste the pasta for seasoning and add additional salt and black pepper if needed.

Serve the pasta while it is warm.

PREP TIME: 5 MINUTES
COOK TIME: 25 MINUTES
TOTAL TIME: 30 MINUTES
SERVES: 6

1 tbsp (15 ml) olive oil
1 lb (448 g) boneless, skinless chicken breasts, cut into bite-sized pieces
½ tsp salt, plus more as needed
½ tsp black pepper, plus more as needed
1 onion, chopped
4 cloves garlic, minced
8 oz (224 g) pasta (I recommend penne, shells or rigatoni)
1 cup (240 ml) low-sodium chicken broth
2 cups (480 ml) milk
2 cups (170 g) small broccoli florets
¼ tsp ground nutmeg
2 cups (240 g) shredded Cheddar cheese

RECIPE NOTES

This dish can be stored in an airtight container in the fridge for 3 to 5 days. You can freeze this dish for up to 3 months in an airtight container.

To reheat the pasta, remove it from its airtight container and place it in a baking dish, cover the baking dish with aluminum foil and bake the pasta at 350°F (177°C) for 20 to 30 minutes, until it's heated through.

NUTRITION INFORMATION

Serving size: 1 serving; **Calories:** 476; **Carbohydrates:** 38 g; **Protein:** 35 g; **Fat:** 20 g

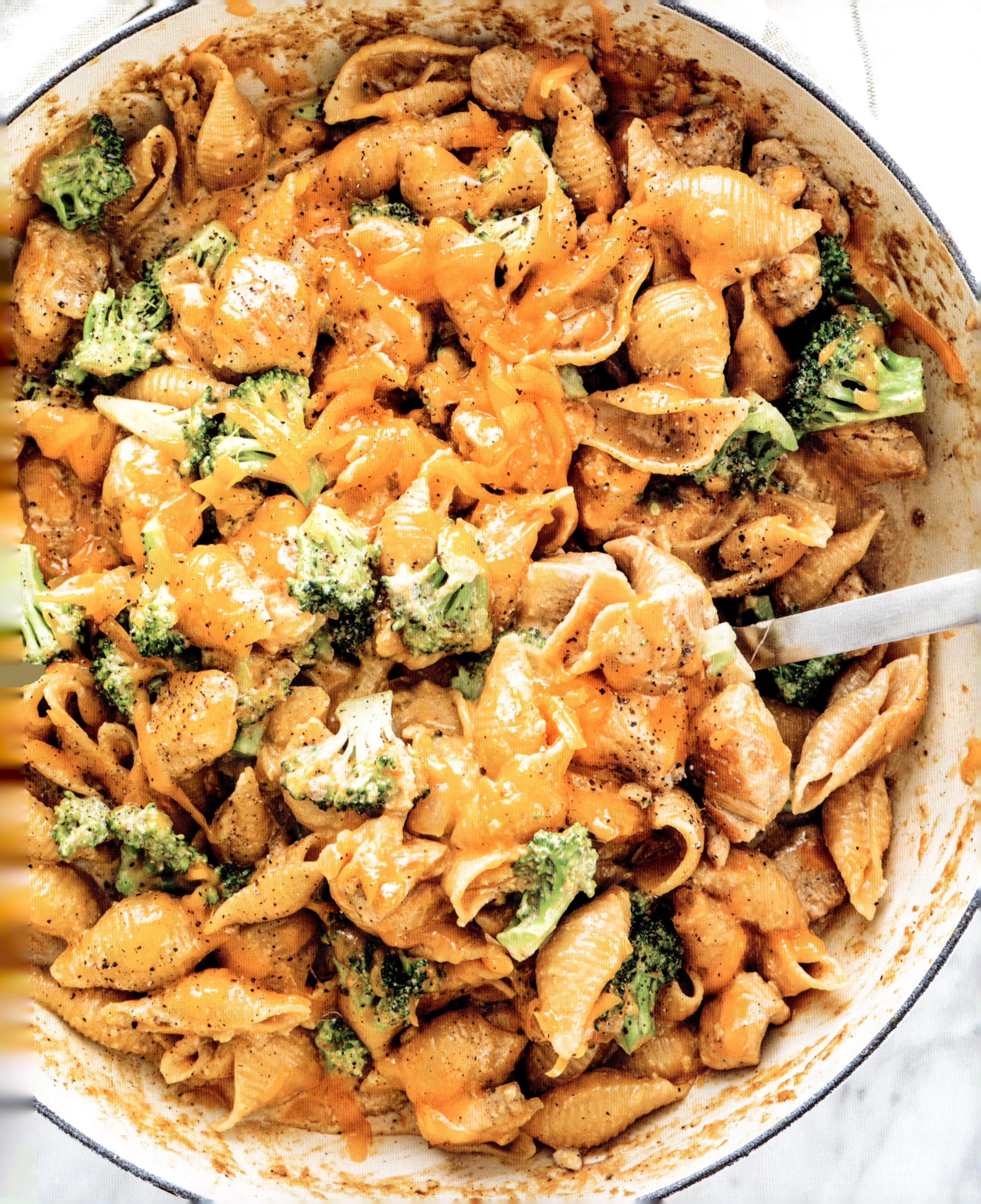

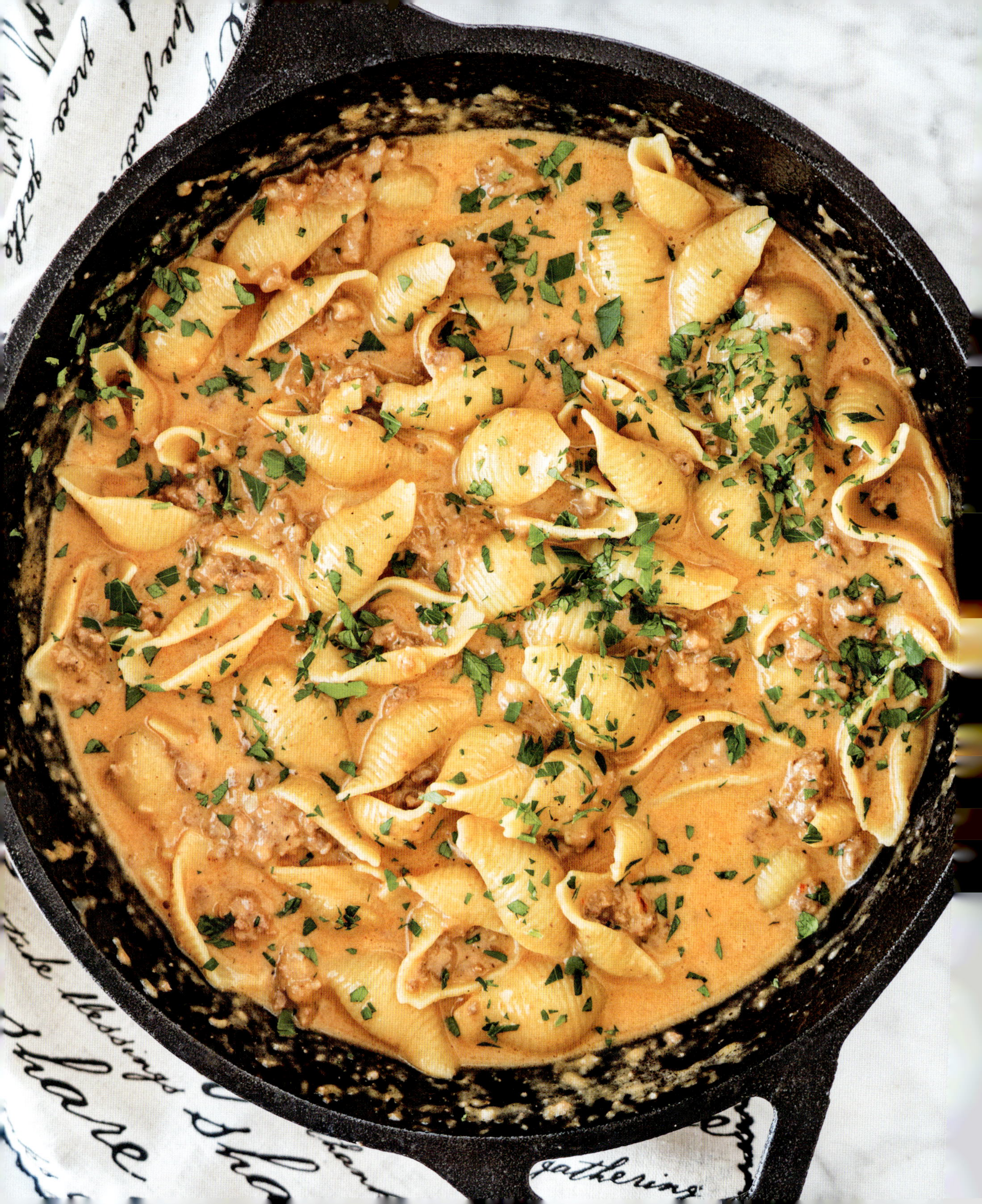

THREE-CHEESE HAMBURGER HELPER

PREP TIME: 5 MINUTES
COOK TIME: 30 MINUTES
TOTAL TIME: 35 MINUTES
SERVES: 6

1 lb (448 g) extra lean ground beef (see Recipe Notes)
1 tbsp (15 g) ketchup
1 tsp Dijon mustard
1 tbsp (15 ml) hot sauce (optional; see Recipe Notes)
1 tsp onion powder
3 cloves garlic, minced
¼ tsp salt, or as needed
¼ tsp black pepper, or as needed
8 oz (224 g) elbow or shell pasta
3½ cups (840 ml) low-sodium beef broth
½ cup (60 g) sour cream
1 cup (120 g) shredded Cheddar cheese
1 cup (112 g) shredded mozzarella cheese
1 cup (113 g) shredded Monterey Jack cheese
1 tbsp (3 g) chopped fresh parsley

Talk about a childhood favorite! This is so much better than anything you'll ever find in a box. It's a homemade twist that is packed full of beef and three different cheeses. What's not to love?

In a large skillet over medium heat, cook the beef for about 5 minutes, until it is no longer pink and starts to brown. Drain off any excess fat if needed.

Add the ketchup, mustard, hot sauce (if using), onion powder, garlic, salt and black pepper and stir everything together.

Stir in the pasta and broth. Bring the mixture to a boil, then reduce the heat to low. Cook the pasta for 15 to 20 minutes, or until it is cooked through and most of the sauce is absorbed.

Stir in the sour cream, then stir in the Cheddar cheese, mozzarella cheese and Monterey Jack cheese. Cook the pasta for 30 to 60 seconds, until the cheeses melt.

Garnish the pasta with the parsley and serve.

RECIPE NOTES

You can use ground chicken or turkey to reduce the fat content.

Sriracha works well in this recipe.

This dish is also delicious the next day—store it in an airtight container in the fridge for 3 to 4 days. You can freeze this recipe too; it'll stay fresh for up to 3 months in an airtight container.

NUTRITION INFORMATION

Serving size: 1 serving; **Calories:** 529; **Carbohydrates:** 31 g; **Protein:** 36 g; **Fat:** 28 g

THE BEST CHILI MAC AND CHEESE

PREP TIME: 10 MINUTES
COOK TIME: 25 MINUTES
TOTAL TIME: 35 MINUTES
SERVES: 8

1 tbsp (15 ml) olive oil
1 lb (448 g) extra lean ground beef
1 onion, chopped
3 cloves garlic, minced
¼ tsp cayenne pepper
1 tsp ground cumin
1 tbsp (9 g) chili powder
1 tsp salt
1 tsp black pepper
1 cup (170 g) black beans, drained and rinsed
1 cup (170 g) kidney beans, drained and rinsed
1 (28-oz [784-g]) can diced tomatoes, undrained
4 cups (960 ml) low-sodium chicken broth
10 oz (280 g) elbow pasta (see Recipe Notes)
2 cups (240 g) shredded Cheddar cheese, divided
2 tbsp (6 g) chopped fresh parsley

This dish is two great comfort foods all in one pot! Delicious and hearty, quick and comforting, this is the dinner that's going to become everyone's favorite. A favorite of mine, it's one of those meals that makes me want to curl up by the fire with a bowl and just relax.

Heat the oil in a large saucepan or Dutch oven over medium-high heat. Add the beef and cook it for about 5 minutes, until it is no longer pink. Drain any excess fat if needed.

Stir in the onion and garlic and cook the mixture for about 3 minutes, or until the onion softens and becomes translucent and the garlic is aromatic.

Add the cayenne pepper, cumin, chili powder, salt and black pepper and stir the ingredients to combine them. Add the black beans, kidney beans, tomatoes and their juice, broth and pasta. Stir everything together and bring the mixture to a boil. Reduce the heat to low and bring the pasta to a simmer. Cover the saucepan and cook the pasta for 9 to 12 minutes, or until the pasta is al dente.

Stir in 1 cup (120 g) of the Cheddar cheese, then sprinkle the remaining 1 cup (120 g) of Cheddar cheese over the top of the chili mac and cheese. Cover the saucepan and allow the chili mac and cheese to cook for about 1 minute, just until the cheese melts.

Garnish the chili mac and cheese with the parsley and serve.

RECIPE NOTES

The elbow macaroni can be replaced with any shape of pasta.

Store any leftovers in an airtight container in the refrigerator for up to 4 days. If you are freezing this recipe, allow the dish to fully cool in a shallow container before storing it in the freezer for up to 3 months.

NUTRITION INFORMATION

Serving size: 1 serving; **Calories:** 496; **Carbohydrates:** 44 g; **Protein:** 26 g; **Fat:** 23 g

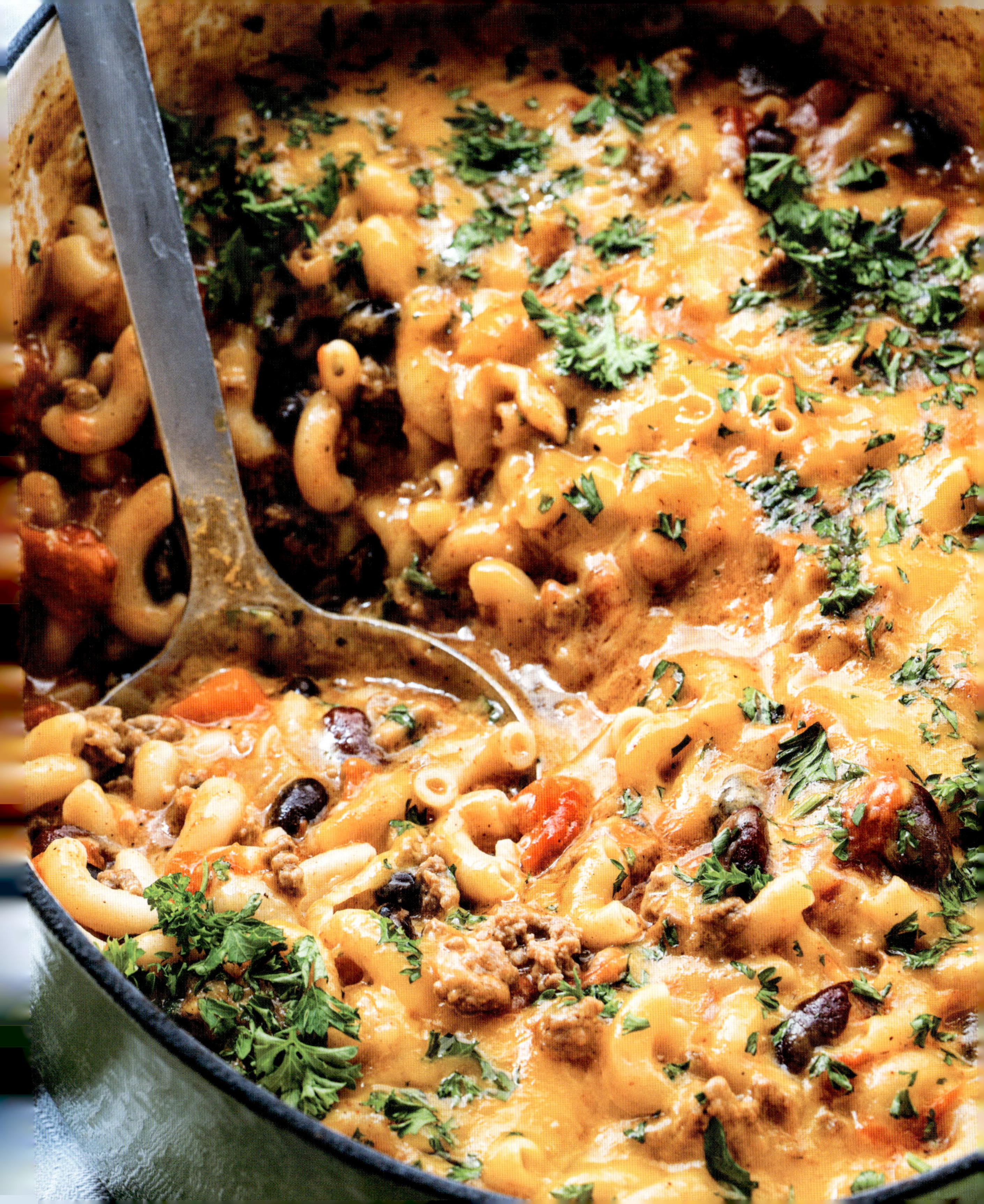

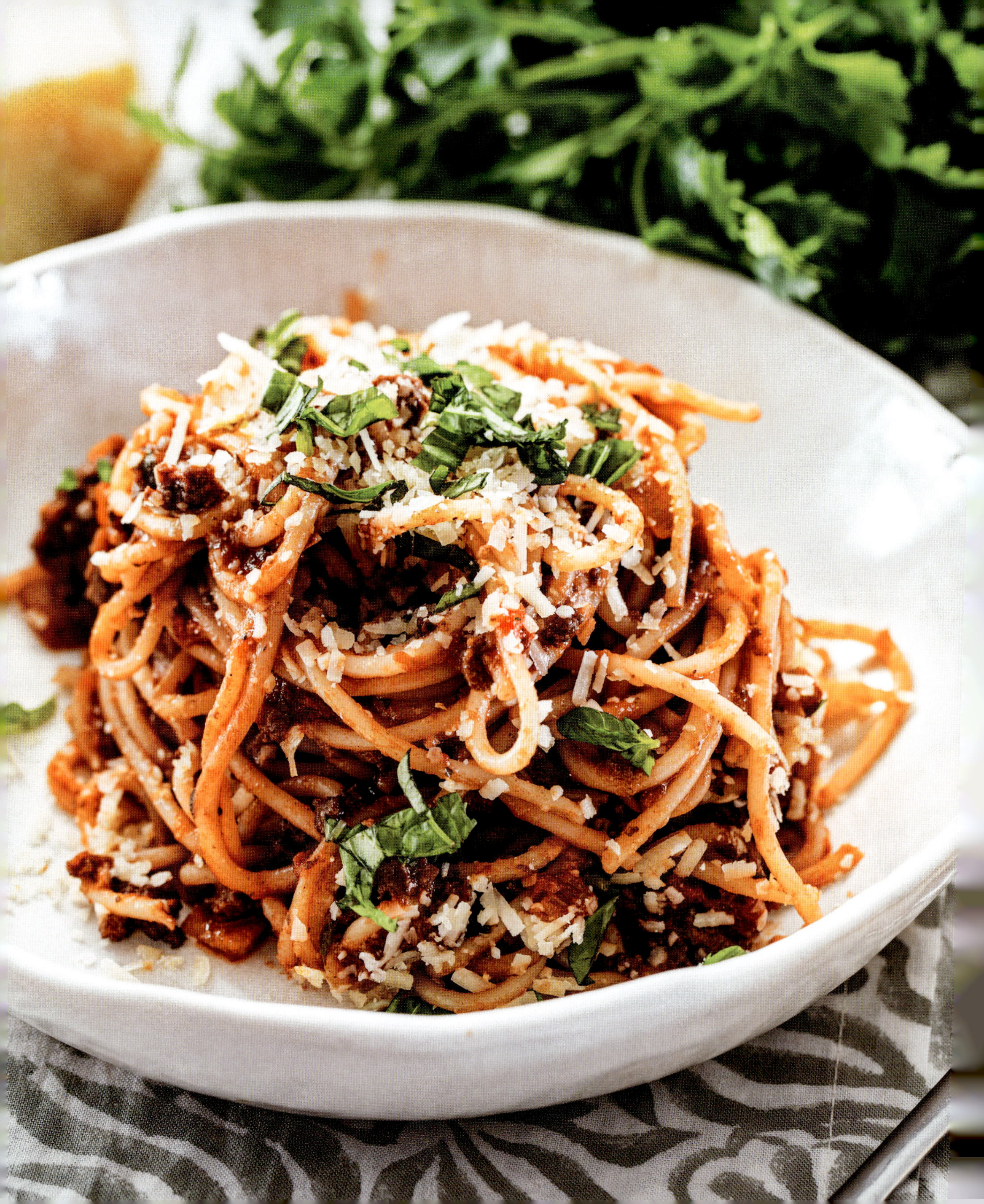

EASY SPAGHETTI BOLOGNESE

Here's another classic Italian meat sauce that is a staple in most families. Before I got married, when I was young and often coming home tired from a long day at work, I loved going next door to my sister's house. She'd make us a big pot of Bolognese—it was the perfect end to a busy day. We added our own twist to the recipe and put feta cheese on it instead of Parmesan—if you're feeling adventurous, you have to try it.

PREP TIME: 10 MINUTES
COOK TIME: 35 MINUTES
TOTAL TIME: 45 MINUTES
SERVES: 6

1 lb (448 g) spaghetti
2 tbsp (30 ml) olive oil
1 lb (448 g) extra lean ground beef
1 onion, chopped
4 cloves garlic, minced
1 tbsp (3 g) dried oregano
¼ tsp red pepper flakes
2 tbsp (30 g) tomato paste
1 cup (240 ml) red wine (see Recipe Notes)
1 (28-oz [784-g]) can crushed tomatoes
4 tbsp (12 g) chopped fresh basil, divided
½ tsp salt, plus more as needed
½ tsp black pepper, plus more as needed
¼ cup (60 ml) heavy cream (optional; see Recipe Notes)
½ cup (90 g) grated Parmesan cheese

Cook the spaghetti in salted water according to the package's instructions. Drain the spaghetti and reserve the pasta water.

Heat the oil in a large pot over medium-high heat. Add the beef and cook it for 3 minutes, breaking it up as it cooks, until it is no longer pink.

Add the onion and garlic and cook the mixture for 3 minutes, until the onion softens. Add the oregano, red pepper flakes and tomato paste and stir the ingredients to combine them. Stir in the wine and cook the mixture for about 5 minutes, until most of the liquid has evaporated.

Add the tomatoes, 2 tablespoons (6 g) of the basil, salt and black pepper. Stir the sauce and bring it to a boil, then reduce the heat to medium-low. Cover the pot and cook the sauce for about 20 minutes.

Stir in the heavy cream (if using) and add additional salt and black pepper if needed. If the sauce is too thick, add some of the pasta water to thin it.

Add the spaghetti to the pot and toss it well to coat it with the sauce. Top the spaghetti with the Parmesan cheese and the remaining 2 tablespoons (6 g) of basil. Serve the spaghetti immediately.

RECIPE NOTES

The flavors of a particular wine will become more concentrated as it cooks. Choose a medium-bodied, dry red wine such as a pinot noir, merlot or Chianti. If you don't want to use red wine, substitute it with beef broth.

I add a bit of heavy cream just to make the sauce creamier, but it can be skipped or replaced with pasta water.

NUTRITION INFORMATION

Serving size: 1 serving; **Calories:** 618; **Carbohydrates:** 72 g; **Protein:** 31 g; **Fat:** 19 g

SPINACH-ARTICHOKE PASTA

PREP TIME: 5 MINUTES
COOK TIME: 15 MINUTES
TOTAL TIME: 20 MINUTES
SERVES: 6

- 8 oz (224 g) penne (see Recipe Notes)
- 2 tbsp (30 ml) olive oil
- 5 oz (140 g) fresh baby or mature spinach, roughly chopped (see Recipe Notes)
- 1 cup (168 g) drained marinated artichoke hearts, roughly chopped
- 8 oz (224 g) cream cheese
- 1 tbsp (9 g) garlic powder
- ¼ tsp salt, or as needed
- ¼ tsp black pepper, or as needed
- 2 cups (480 ml) milk (see Recipe Notes)
- 1 cup (112 g) shredded mozzarella cheese
- ¼ cup (45 g) grated Parmesan cheese

If you love a super creamy and cheesy pasta, then this recipe is for you. It's what cheesy dreams are made of. Plus, you can avoid feeling too guilty about it because I have added some spinach and artichokes—so there, you've got your veggies.

Cook the penne in salted water according to the package's instructions.

Meanwhile, heat the oil in a large saucepan or Dutch oven over medium heat.

Add the spinach and cook it for about 1 minute, until it is wilted. Add the artichoke hearts and cook the vegetables for 1 minute. Add the cream cheese and stir until it has melted and there are no lumps.

Stir in the garlic powder, salt and black pepper. Add the milk and cook the mixture, stirring it occasionally, until it comes to a boil.

Stir in the mozzarella cheese, then add the pasta and mix until the pasta is evenly coated in the sauce.

Sprinkle the pasta with the Parmesan cheese and serve it warm.

RECIPE NOTES

You can use any shape of pasta for this recipe, such as rotini or mini shells.

I use fresh spinach, but frozen will work as well.

I use 2 percent milk for this dish, but you can use any type of milk you have handy.

NUTRITION INFORMATION

Serving size: 1 serving; **Calories:** 428; **Carbohydrates:** 39 g; **Protein:** 17 g; **Fat:** 22 g

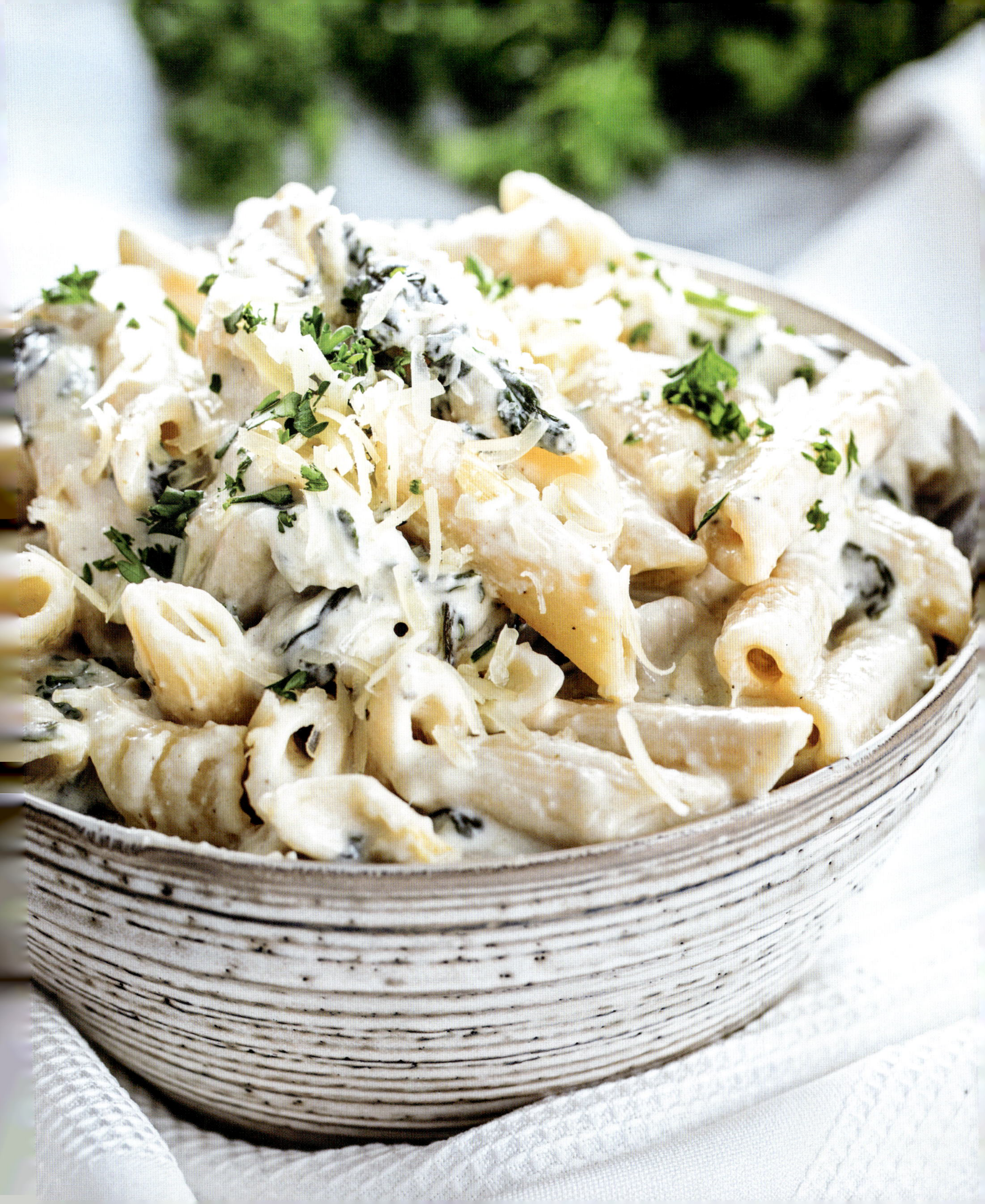

CASSEROLES

WHO DOESN'T LOVE A GOOD CASSEROLE? Casseroles, like my Cabbage Roll Casserole (page 213), are easy to prepare, they're great for make-ahead meals, they're perfect for bringing to potlucks—but best of all, they are comforting and satisfying. Not to mention there's only one pot to clean. How easy is that?

Casseroles are great for leftovers. If you have leftover chicken, beef or any other protein, don't waste it. Make a casserole with it. It saves money and time. Made a big pot of Easy Spaghetti Bolognese (page 203) and have lots left over? Don't throw it out; make a Baked Spaghetti Casserole (page 210).

There are so many uses for leftovers that you can easily turn into casseroles. Of course, my favorite part of a casserole is the topping. I love to load my casseroles with lots of cheese or make them crispy with breadcrumbs, cereals, chips or crackers, as in my Tuna Noodle Casserole (page 214) or Chicken Divan (page 209). Depending on the type of casserole I've baked, I also love to top them with some fresh veggies like tomatoes, avocados, lettuce or green onions—my Chicken Tamale Casserole (page 217) is the perfect casserole to try with fresh toppings.

This chapter focuses on delicious casseroles that are packed with flavor, fresh ingredients and a whole lot of love. These casseroles are beloved on the blog, and I think they are perfect for this book.

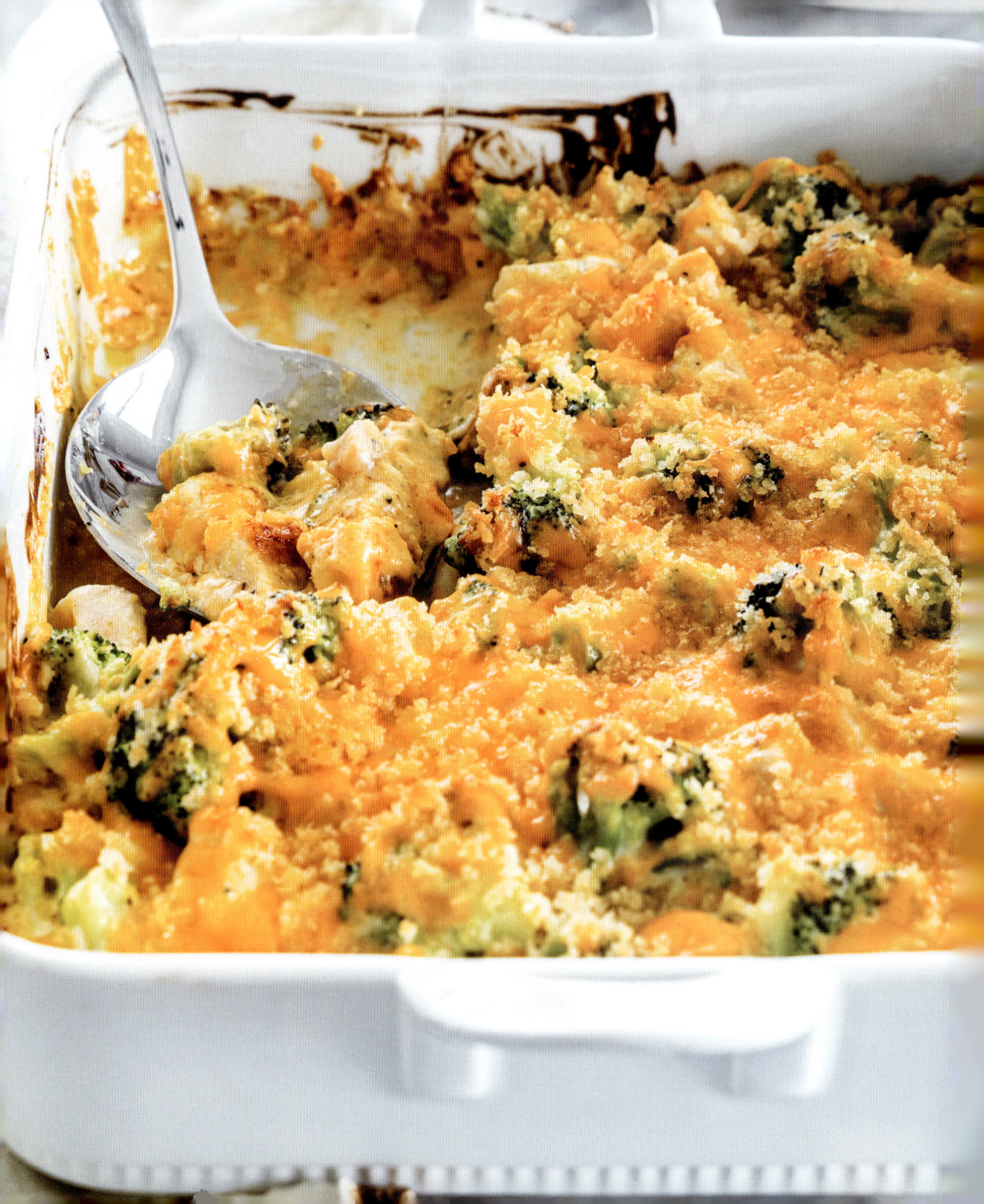

CHICKEN DIVAN

This chicken divan is cheesy, creamy, full of tender broccoli florets and topped with a crunchy panko topping. With 5 minutes of prep, you'll have dinner on the table in just 30 minutes!

PREP TIME: 5 MINUTES
COOK TIME: 25 MINUTES
TOTAL TIME: 30 MINUTES
SERVES: 6

1 lb (448 g) chopped broccoli
2 cups (280 g) cubed cooked chicken
1 (11-oz [308-g]) can condensed cream of chicken soup
½ cup (60 g) sour cream
1½ cups (180 g) shredded Cheddar cheese, divided
⅓ cup (80 ml) milk
¼ tsp salt, or as needed
½ tsp black pepper, or as needed
¼ cup (15 g) panko breadcrumbs
1 tbsp (15 g) butter, melted

Preheat the oven to 450°F (232°C).

Bring a large pot of water to a boil. Add the broccoli and cook it for 3 to 5 minutes, or until it is crisp-tender. Drain the broccoli well.

In a large bowl, combine the chicken, cream of chicken soup, sour cream, 1 cup (120 g) of the Cheddar cheese, milk, salt and black pepper. Stir in the broccoli.

Transfer the casserole mixture to a 9 x 13–inch (27 x 39–cm) baking dish. Top the casserole with the remaining ½ cup (60 g) of Cheddar cheese.

In a small bowl, combine the breadcrumbs and butter. Sprinkle the breadcrumbs over the casserole.

Bake the casserole for 20 minutes, or until it is bubbly.

RECIPE NOTES

To store this recipe, you can wrap your baking dish with foil or transfer the leftovers to an airtight container. Store the casserole in the fridge for 3 to 5 days.

Reheat leftovers either in the microwave or the oven. Preheat the oven to 400°F (204°C). Transfer the leftovers to a baking dish if necessary, cover the casserole with foil and bake it for 8 to 10 minutes, or until it is heated through.

NUTRITION INFORMATION

Serving size: 1 serving; **Calories:** 305; **Carbohydrates:** 14 g; **Protein:** 15 g; **Fat:** 22 g

BAKED SPAGHETTI CASSEROLE

Here's a casserole that's a favorite of kids and adults alike. It boasts the classic Italian flavors that we all know and love in one casserole dish.

PREP TIME: 10 MINUTES
COOK TIME: 55 MINUTES
TOTAL TIME: 1 HOUR, 5 MINUTES
SERVES: 8

12 oz (336 g) spaghetti
1 lb (448 g) ground beef
3 cloves garlic, minced
1 tsp Italian seasoning
Salt, as needed
Black pepper, as needed
1 (24-oz [720-ml]) jar spaghetti sauce
1 (15-oz [420-g]) can diced tomatoes, undrained
2 cups (224 g) shredded mozzarella cheese
⅓ cup (60 g) grated Parmesan cheese (optional)
Chopped fresh basil or parsley, as needed (optional)

Preheat the oven to 350°F (177°C).

Cook the spaghetti in salted water according to the package's instructions. Drain the spaghetti and reserve ½ cup (120 ml) of the pasta water.

In a deep skillet or saucepan over medium heat, cook the beef for 5 minutes, until it is no longer pink. Add the garlic, Italian seasoning, salt and black pepper. Stir the ingredients to combine them and cook the mixture for 30 seconds, until it is aromatic. Add the spaghetti sauce, tomatoes and their juice and reserved pasta water, and stir to combine the ingredients. Simmer the sauce for about 5 minutes.

Stir in the spaghetti. Transfer the spaghetti and sauce to a 9 x 13–inch (27 x 39–cm) baking dish. Top the spaghetti with the mozzarella cheese and Parmesan cheese (if using). Bake the casserole for 30 minutes, until the casserole is heated through.

Garnish the casserole with the basil (if using) and serve.

RECIPE NOTES

Store any leftovers in an airtight container. Cooked spaghetti will last for 3 to 5 days in the refrigerator.

Make sure to refrigerate this casserole after eating it because bacteria will start to grow. Leftovers should be discarded if they are left out for more than 2 hours at room temperature.

NUTRITION INFORMATION

Serving size: 1 serving; **Calories:** 389; **Carbohydrates:** 40 g; **Protein:** 26 g; **Fat:** 14 g

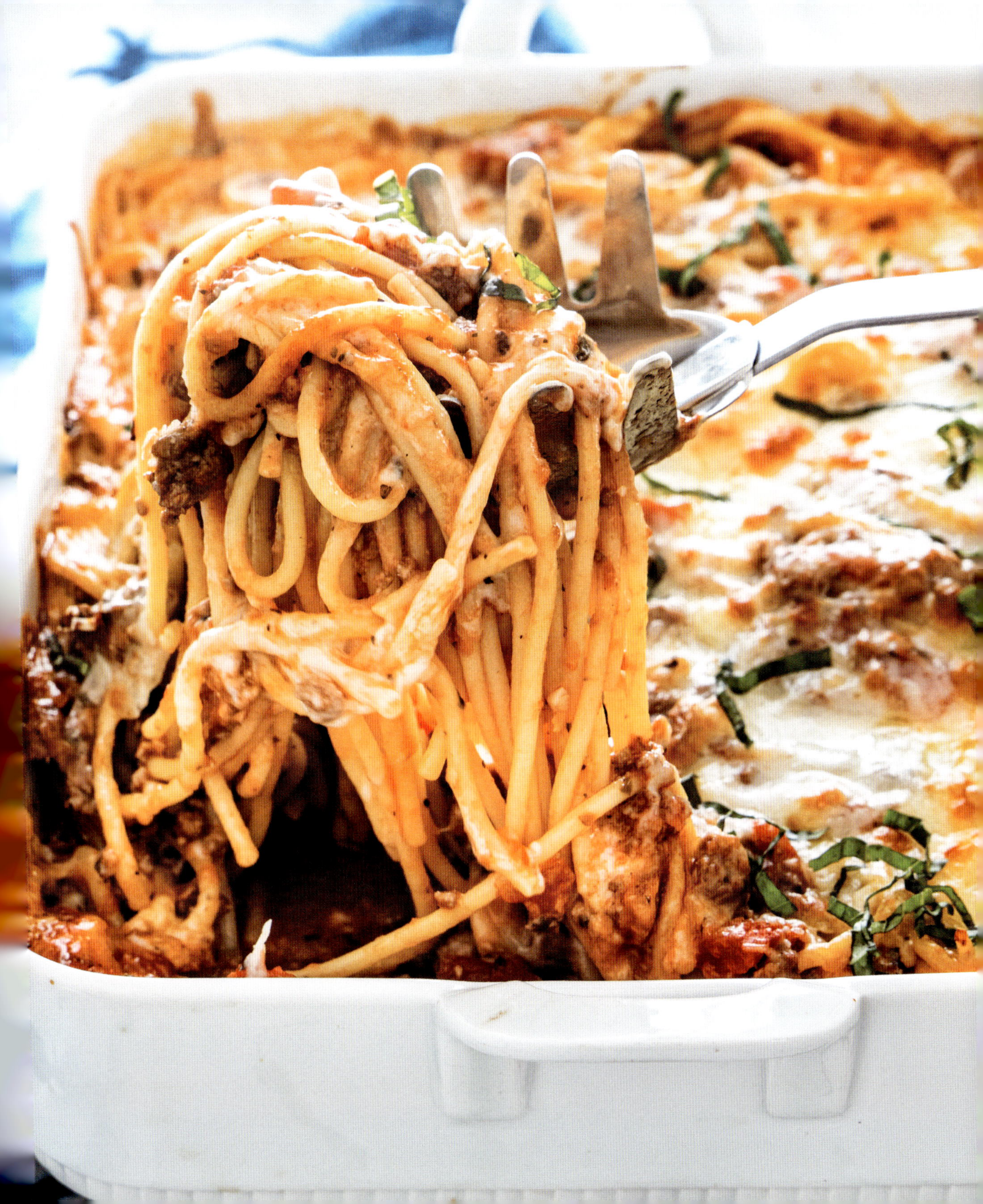

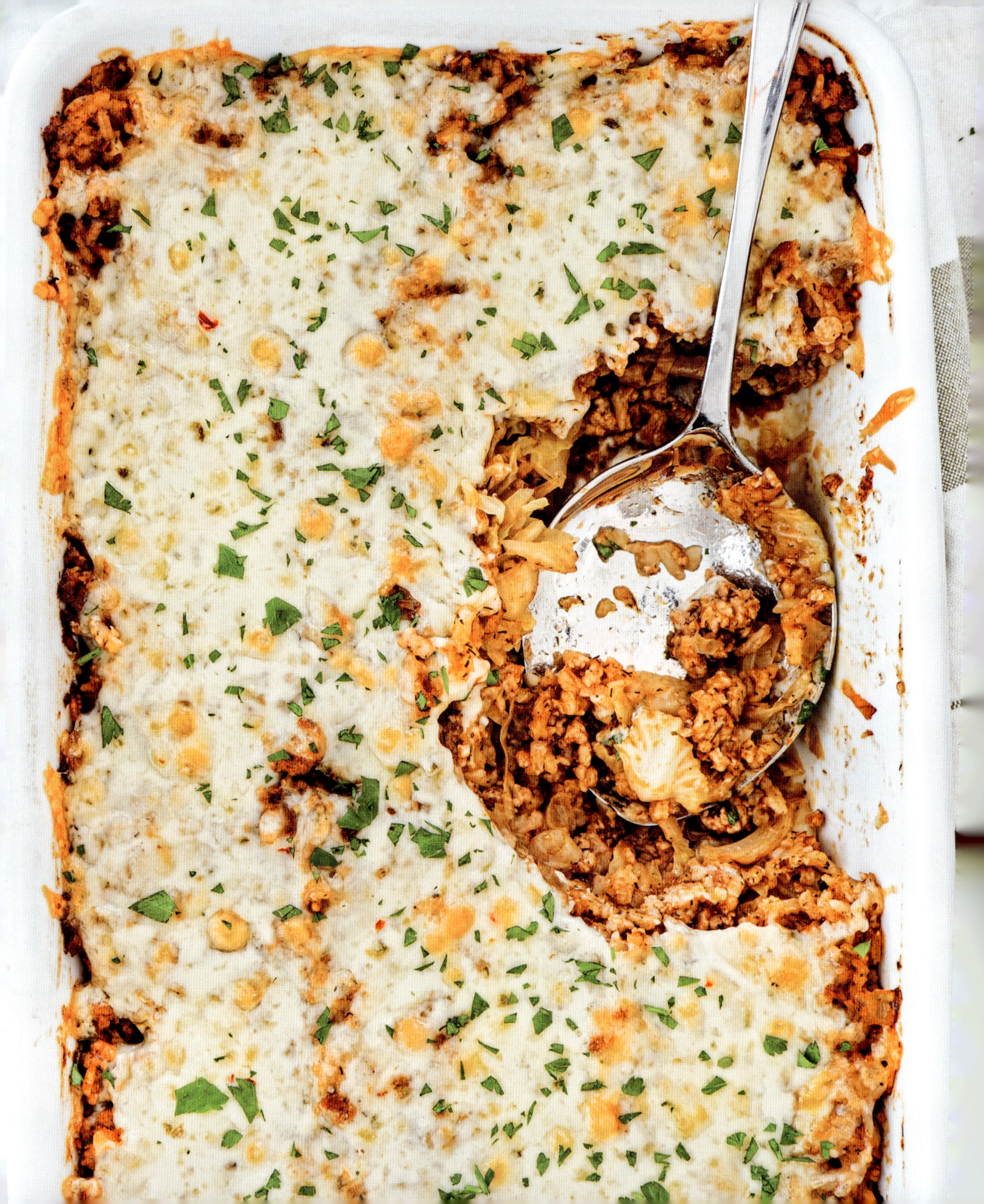

CABBAGE ROLL CASSEROLE

My cabbage roll casserole is layered with a perfectly seasoned pork and rice mixture and tender cabbage. Then it's topped with cheese. It's a comforting meal you can throw together with ease.

PREP TIME: 15 MINUTES
COOK TIME: 1 HOUR, 30 MINUTES
TOTAL TIME: 1 HOUR, 45 MINUTES
SERVES: 9

1 lb (448 g) ground pork
1 onion, chopped
3 cloves garlic, minced
½ tsp salt, or as needed
½ tsp black pepper, or as needed
1 tbsp (3 g) dried dill
1 tsp paprika
1 cup (210 g) rice
1 cup (240 g) crushed tomatoes
4 cups (960 ml) chicken broth
1 tbsp (15 ml) olive oil
1 head cabbage, shredded or roughly chopped
2 cups (226 g) shredded Monterey Jack cheese
1 tbsp (3 g) chopped fresh parsley

In a large skillet over medium heat, cook the pork and onion for 5 minutes, breaking up the meat as it cooks and stirring it occasionally, until the pork is cooked through. Add the garlic, salt, black pepper, dill and paprika. Stir the ingredients together and cook them for 30 seconds. Add the rice, tomatoes and broth. Cook the mixture for 15 minutes, or until the rice is almost cooked and all the liquid has been absorbed.

Meanwhile, heat the oil in a large Dutch oven over medium-low heat. Add the cabbage and cook it for about 5 minutes, stirring it often, until it has softened.

Preheat the oven to 375°F (191°C). Spray a 9 x 13–inch (27 x 39–cm) baking dish with cooking spray.

Layer half of the cabbage on the bottom of the prepared baking dish. Top the cabbage with half of the pork mixture, then add the remaining cabbage. Finally, top the second layer of cabbage with the remaining pork mixture. Cover the casserole with foil.

Bake the casserole for 45 minutes on the middle oven rack. Remove the foil and sprinkle the Monterey Jack cheese over the top of the casserole. Bake the casserole uncovered for another 15 to 20 minutes, or until the cheese is bubbly and slightly browned. Garnish the casserole with parsley and serve.

RECIPE NOTES

Transfer any leftovers to an airtight container or simply cover the baking dish with plastic wrap. Leftovers will keep in the fridge for 3 to 4 days.

Reheat individual servings in the microwave or reheat the casserole, covered with foil, in the oven: Preheat the oven to 350°F (177°C) and bake the casserole for 15 minutes, or until it is heated through.

NUTRITION INFORMATION

Serving size: 1 serving; **Calories:** 350; **Carbohydrates:** 22 g; **Protein:** 19 g; **Fat:** 21 g

TUNA NOODLE CASSEROLE

PREP TIME: 5 MINUTES
COOK TIME: 40 MINUTES
TOTAL TIME: 45 MINUTES
SERVES: 6

12 oz (336 g) egg noodles
15 oz (420 g) tuna in water, drained
1 (11-oz [308-g]) can condensed cream of celery soup
1 cup (240 ml) milk
1 rib celery, chopped
1 cup (134 g) frozen peas
1 cup (150 g) cherry tomatoes, halved
¼ tsp black pepper, plus more as needed
Salt, as needed
¾ cup (42 g) crumbled potato chips

Here's my take on a tuna noodle casserole that's bursting with fresh cherry tomatoes and peas. Not only is this recipe budget-friendly but it requires only five minutes of prep time.

Preheat the oven to 400°F (204°C). Spray a 9 x 13–inch (27 x 39–cm) baking dish with cooking spray.

Cook the egg noodles in salted water according to the package's instructions. Drain the noodles and transfer them to a large bowl.

Add the tuna, cream of celery soup, milk, celery, peas, tomatoes and black pepper to the egg noodles. Stir the ingredients until they are well combined. Season the mixture with the salt and additional black pepper as needed.

Transfer the noodle mixture to the prepared baking dish. Sprinkle the casserole with the potato chips.

Bake the casserole on the middle oven rack for 30 minutes, or until it is heated through.

Serve the casserole warm.

RECIPE NOTE

If stored in an airtight container, tuna casserole can last 2 to 3 days in the refrigerator, which makes it a perfect lunch for the next day!

NUTRITION INFORMATION

Serving size: 1 serving; **Calories:** 426; **Carbohydrates:** 56 g; **Protein:** 25 g; **Fat:** 10 g

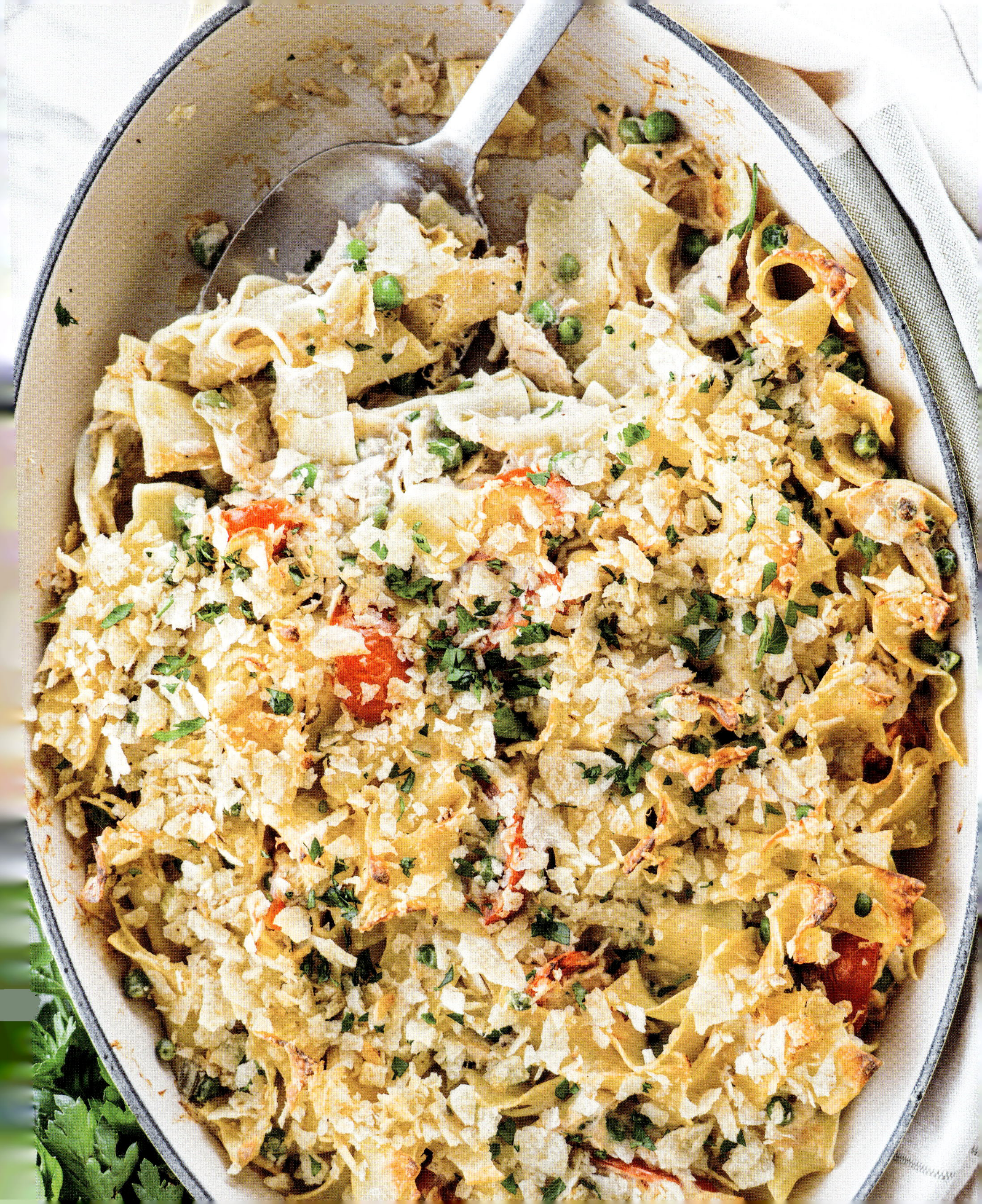

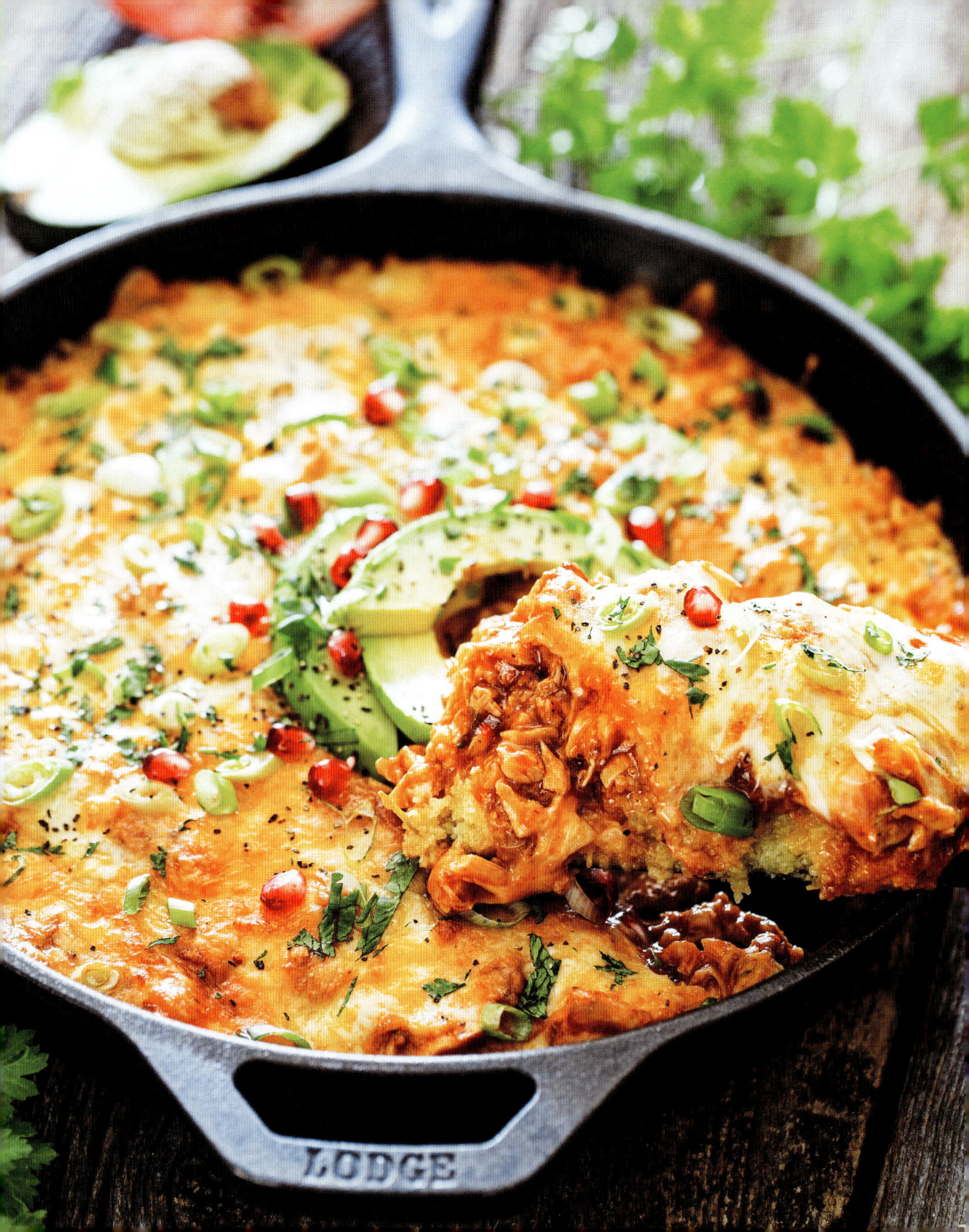
LODGE

CHICKEN TAMALE CASSEROLE

PREP TIME: 10 MINUTES
COOK TIME: 40 MINUTES
TOTAL TIME: 50 MINUTES
SERVES: 8

CORNBREAD CRUST
½ cup (85 g) cornmeal
2 tbsp (24 g) sugar
½ tsp salt
1 tbsp (12 g) baking powder
1 large egg
4 tbsp (60 g) unsalted butter, melted
⅓ cup (80 ml) buttermilk
1 cup (256 g) creamed corn
1 (4-oz [112-g]) can diced green chilies, undrained

TAMALE CASSEROLE
1 (10-oz [300-ml]) can enchilada sauce, divided
2 cups (270 g) shredded cooked white or dark meat chicken
1 cup (113 g) shredded Monterey Jack cheese
1 cup (120 g) shredded Tex-Mex Cheddar cheese

OPTIONAL TOPPINGS
Chopped fresh cilantro
Sliced avocado
Chopped green onions
Pomegranate seeds
Sour cream

Here we have a delicious cornbread crust topped with shredded chicken, enchilada sauce and loads of cheese. This casserole is so good and so comforting.

Preheat the oven to 400°F (204°C). Spray an oven-safe 12-inch (36-cm) skillet or a 9 x 9–inch (27 x 27–cm) baking pan with cooking spray.

To make the cornbread crust, whisk together the cornmeal, sugar, salt and baking powder in a medium bowl. Add the egg, butter and buttermilk and whisk the ingredients well. Stir in the creamed corn and green chilies and their juice. Pour the cornbread mixture into the prepared skillet.

Bake the cornbread crust for 20 to 25 minutes, until a toothpick inserted into the center comes out clean.

When the cornbread is done, poke holes in it with a fork or the end of a wooden spoon.

To make the tamale casserole, mix half of the enchilada sauce with the chicken in a medium bowl. Pour the remaining half of the enchilada sauce over the cornbread crust. Top the cornbread with the chicken, then sprinkle the Monterey Jack cheese and Cheddar cheese evenly over the chicken.

Transfer the skillet to the middle oven rack and bake it for about 15 minutes, or until the cheeses have melted and started to brown on top.

Let the casserole cool for about 5 minutes, then top with any of the optional toppings.

RECIPE NOTES

This dish can be stored in an airtight container in the fridge for 3 to 4 days.

This entire casserole can be popped in the freezer, as long as it's tightly sealed. It can be stored this way for up to 6 months. It needs to thaw out overnight in the fridge when you are ready to eat it. Reheat it in the oven at 350°F (177°C) for 30 minutes.

NUTRITION INFORMATION

Serving size: 1 serving; **Calories:** 295; **Carbohydrates:** 21 g; **Protein:** 13 g; **Fat:** 18 g

CHICKEN GLORIA

Tender chicken smothered in a creamy mushroom sauce then topped with cheese and baked to perfection: What's not to love about this incredible dish?

PREP TIME: 15 MINUTES
COOK TIME: 50 MINUTES
TOTAL TIME: 1 HOUR, 5 MINUTES
SERVES: 6

1 lb (448 g) boneless, skinless chicken breasts, cut in half lengthwise (see Recipe Note)
½ tsp salt, plus more as needed
½ tsp black pepper, plus more as needed
⅓ cup (40 g) all-purpose flour
2 tbsp (30 ml) vegetable oil
1 tbsp (15 g) unsalted butter
8 oz (224 g) cremini mushrooms, sliced
½ cup (120 ml) sherry wine
2 (10-oz [280-g]) cans condensed cream of mushroom soup
6 slices Swiss cheese or Muenster cheese
1 tbsp (3 g) chopped fresh parsley

Preheat the oven to 350°F (177°C).

Season both sides of the chicken with the salt and black pepper.

Place the flour in a shallow dish. Coat both sides of the chicken with flour. Shake off any excess flour from the chicken.

Heat the oil in a large skillet over medium heat. Brown the chicken on both sides, for a total of 5 to 7 minutes. Note that the chicken doesn't have to be cooked through because it will finish cooking in the oven. Transfer the chicken to a 9 x 13–inch (27 x 39–cm) baking dish.

Add the butter to the skillet and melt it over medium-high heat. Add the mushrooms and season them with salt and black pepper. Cook the mushrooms for 5 minutes, until they are golden brown. Stir in the wine and cook the mixture for 2 minutes. Stir in the cream of mushroom soup and cook the sauce until it is heated through.

Pour the mushroom sauce over the chicken and top the sauce with the Swiss cheese, so that the entire casserole is covered with cheese.

Cover the baking dish with foil and bake the casserole for 30 minutes. After 30 minutes, set the oven to broil and remove the foil from the baking dish. Broil the casserole for 2 minutes to brown the cheese, making sure not to burn it.

Garnish the casserole with the parsley and serve.

RECIPE NOTE

Boneless, skinless chicken thighs can be used instead of the chicken breast.

NUTRITION INFORMATION

Serving size: 1 serving; **Calories:** 350; **Carbohydrates:** 13 g; **Protein:** 29 g; **Fat:** 18 g

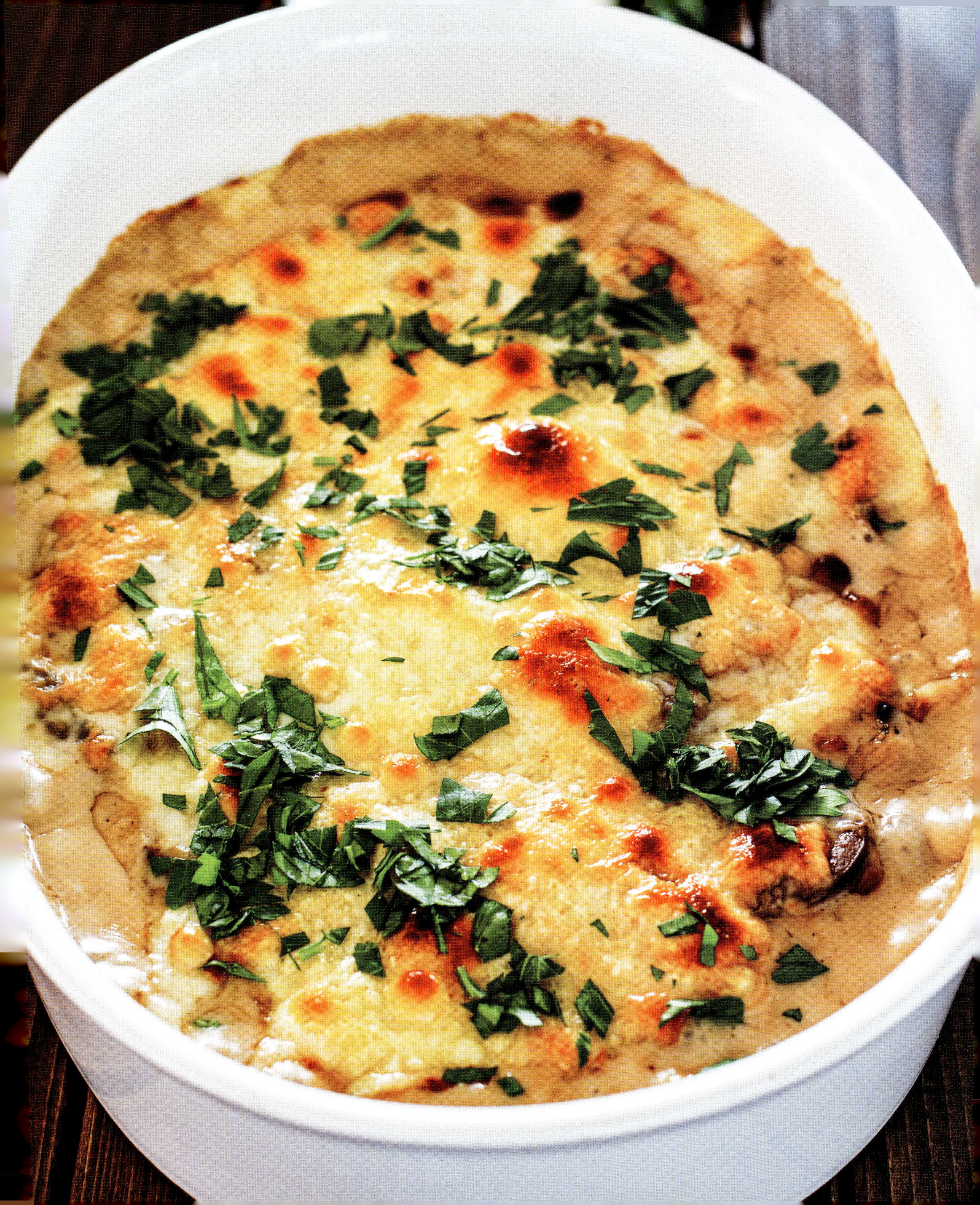

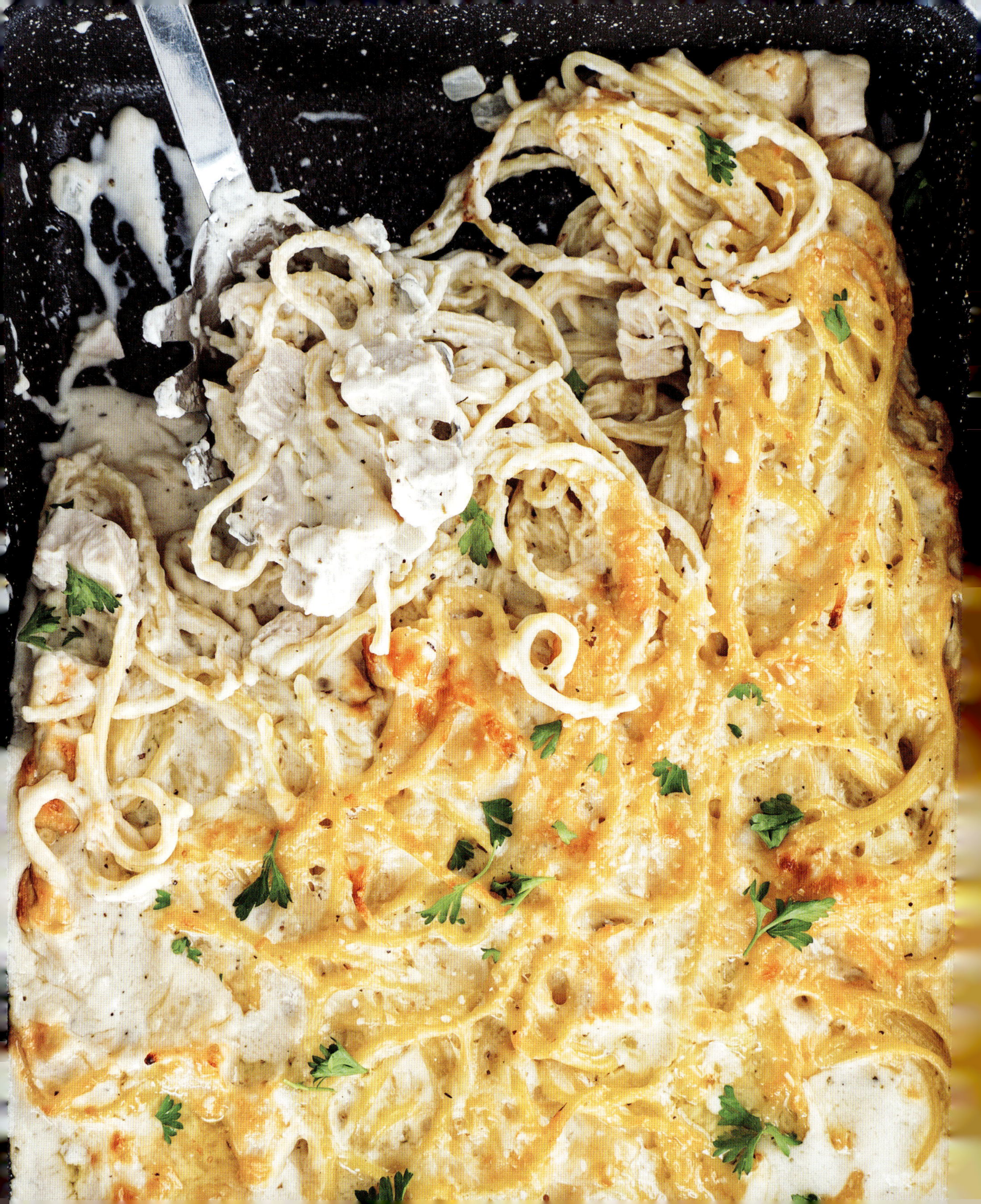

TURKEY TETRAZZINI

This turkey tetrazzini is a heavenly pasta casserole with chunks of turkey smothered in a rich, cheesy and creamy herb-flecked sauce. It's all topped with more cheese and baked until hot and bubbly. It's a dish that's easy to make ahead when you expect a crowd!

PREP TIME: 20 MINUTES
COOK TIME: 1 HOUR, 10 MINUTES
TOTAL TIME: 1 HOUR, 30 MINUTES
SERVES: 8

1 lb (448 g) spaghetti
½ cup (120 g) unsalted butter
2 tbsp (30 ml) olive oil
1 onion, chopped
3 cloves garlic, minced
½ cup (60 g) all-purpose flour
3 cups (720 ml) low-sodium or unsalted chicken broth (see Recipe Notes)
2 cups (480 ml) milk
1 tsp Italian seasoning
Salt, as needed
Black pepper, as needed
8 oz (224 g) cream cheese, at room temperature
2 cups (360 g) grated Parmesan cheese, divided
4 cups (560 g) chopped cooked turkey

Preheat the oven to 350°F (177°C). Spray a 9 x 13–inch (27 x 39–cm) baking dish with cooking spray.

Cook the spaghetti in salted water according to the package's instructions until it is al dente. Drain the spaghetti and transfer it to a large bowl to cool. This will keep the casserole saucy.

While the spaghetti is cooling, heat the butter and oil in a 5-quart (4.8-L) saucepan over medium heat. Add the onion and cook it for about 5 minutes, until it has softened. Stir in the garlic and cook the mixture for 30 seconds, until the garlic is aromatic.

Whisk in the flour and cook the mixture for about 2 minutes. Add the broth, milk, Italian seasoning, salt and black pepper and bring the mixture to a boil. Stir in the cream cheese and 1½ cups (270 g) of the Parmesan cheese. Cook until the cheeses have melted.

Stir in the turkey, then add the cooked spaghetti. Toss the ingredients together until they are well combined. Transfer everything to the prepared baking dish. Top the casserole with the remaining ½ cup (90 g) of Parmesan cheese.

Bake the casserole for 30 to 45 minutes, until it's heated through and the top is starting to brown.

RECIPE NOTES

If you'd like, you can add peas to this casserole. Make sure you add them frozen. You don't have to thaw them—they will cook as the casserole bakes.

Season this dish with salt to taste. I prefer my dishes a bit less salty, which is why I always use no-sodium chicken broth. Go ahead and add as much salt as you prefer.

If you would like to make this recipe ahead, prepare it as instructed and transfer it to the prepared baking dish. Then cover it tightly with a layer of foil and store it in the freezer. Thaw the casserole in the fridge the night before you want to eat it and then bake it as directed when it is time to make dinner!

Store any leftovers in the baking dish, covered with foil, or in an airtight container in the fridge for 3 to 4 days.

To freeze leftovers, store them in an airtight container in the freezer for up to 3 months.

NUTRITION INFORMATION
Serving size: 1 serving; **Calories:** 654; **Carbohydrates:** 57 g; **Protein:** 34 g; **Fat:** 32 g

EASY BEEF LASAGNA

Who doesn't love a meaty and saucy lasagna? This is a classic Italian dish that's warm and comforting. What makes my lasagna special is that I don't cook the noodles—there's plenty of sauce in the casserole to cook the noodles while it's baking.

PREP TIME: 20 MINUTES
COOK TIME: 1 HOUR
TOTAL TIME: 1 HOUR, 20 MINUTES
SERVES: 12

- 1 lb (448 g) ground beef
- 1 onion, diced
- 2 tbsp (6 g) dried oregano, divided
- ½ tsp salt, plus more as needed
- ½ tsp black pepper, plus more as needed
- 1 (24-oz [720-ml]) jar marinara sauce
- 1 cup (240 ml) water
- 15 oz (420 g) ricotta cheese
- 2 large eggs
- ½ cup (90 g) grated Parmesan cheese
- 12 lasagna noodles
- 2 cups (224 g) shredded mozzarella cheese

Preheat the oven to 375°F (191°C).

In a large saucepan or skillet over medium heat, cook the beef for about 5 minutes, until it is no longer pink. Add the onion, 1 tablespoon (3 g) of the oregano, salt and black pepper. Cook the mixture for 3 to 5 minutes, until the onion is translucent.

Add the marinara sauce and water. Stir to combine the ingredients and bring the sauce to a boil. Remove the saucepan from the heat and set it aside.

In a small bowl, combine the ricotta cheese, eggs, Parmesan cheese, remaining 1 tablespoon (3 g) of oregano and additional salt and black pepper. Mix the ingredients well.

Start assembling the lasagna in a 9 x 13–inch (27 x 39–cm) baking dish. Add 2 ladles of the meat sauce to the bottom of the baking dish; this is especially important, since the noodles aren't cooked. Lay 3 lasagna noodles over the meat sauce. Next, add a layer of the ricotta mixture and about ½ cup (56 g) of the mozzarella cheese. Add another 3 lasagna noodles, another layer of the meat sauce, another layer of the ricotta mixture and another layer of mozzarella cheese. Repeat this process until you have 4 layers of noodles, and end with the ricotta mixture and mozzarella cheese.

Bake the lasagna for about 1 hour, or until the noodles are fork-tender.

RECIPE NOTES

Be sure this dish is properly cooled before storing it. It will stay fresh for 3 to 5 days in an airtight container in the fridge. Frozen lasagna will last for 2 to 3 months; just be sure to allow it to thaw fully in the fridge before reheating it in the oven at 350°F (177°C) for 15 minutes.

NUTRITION INFORMATION

Serving size: 1 serving; **Calories:** 333; **Carbohydrates:** 26 g; **Protein:** 22 g; **Fat:** 14 g

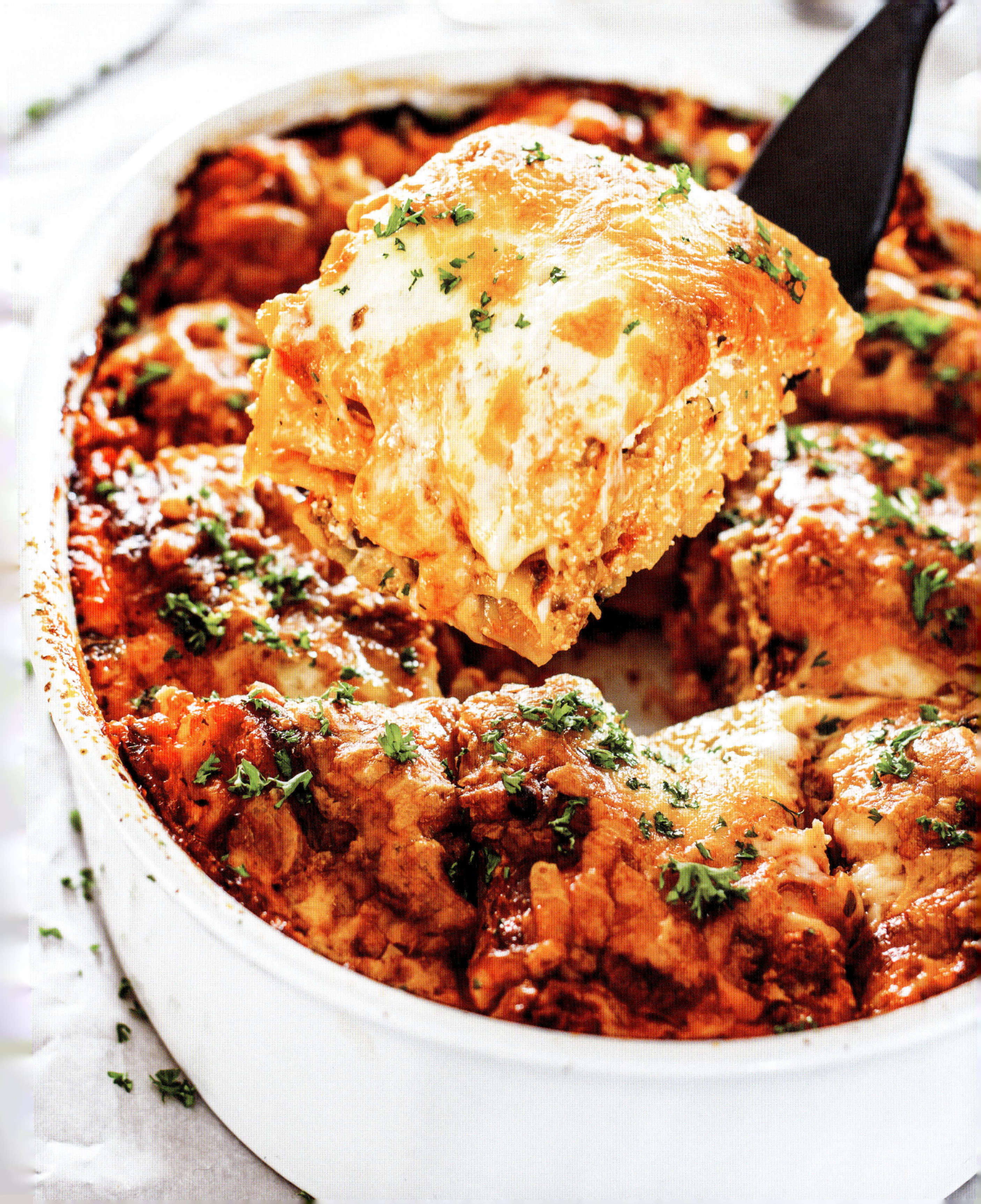

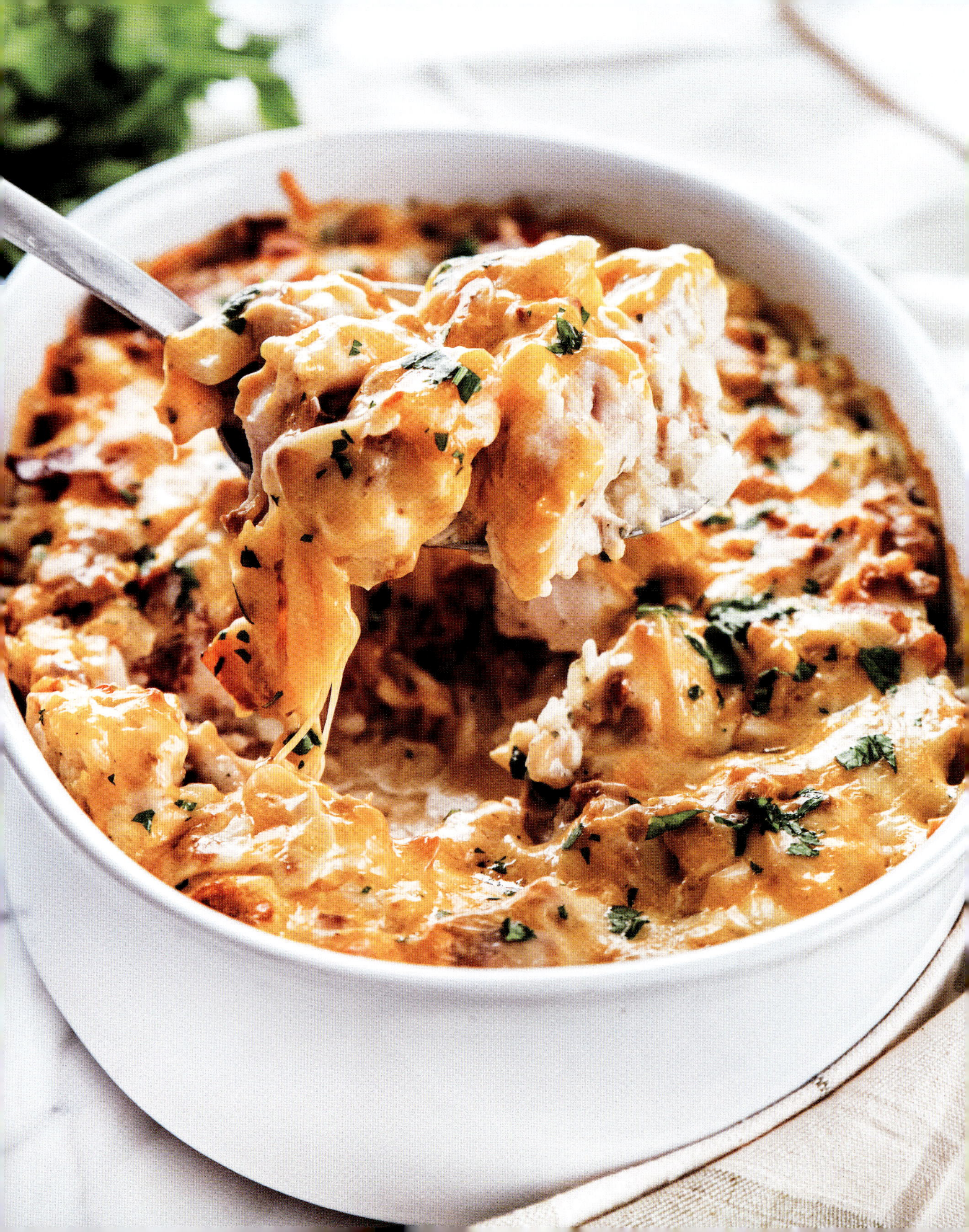

CHICKEN-BACON-RANCH CASSEROLE

PREP TIME: 5 MINUTES
COOK TIME: 1 HOUR
TOTAL TIME: 1 HOUR, 5 MINUTES
SERVES: 12

1 lb (448 g) boneless, skinless chicken breasts, cut into bite-size pieces (see Recipe Notes)

2 tbsp (30 ml) olive oil

3 tbsp (27 g) ranch seasoning and salad dressing mix, divided

1½ cups (315 g) white rice (see Recipe Notes)

1 onion, chopped

2 cloves garlic, minced

8 slices bacon, fried and chopped, divided

2½ cups (600 ml) low-sodium or unsalted chicken broth

½ cup (120 ml) half-and-half

2 cups (240 g) shredded Cheddar cheese

2 tbsp (6 g) chopped fresh parsley

Creamy, cheesy, delicious rice loaded with ranch chicken and bacon: This recipe features all of my favorite things in one casserole!

Preheat the oven to 350°F (177°C).

In a medium bowl, toss the chicken with the oil and 2 tablespoons (18 g) of the ranch seasoning mix. Set the bowl aside.

In a 9 x 13–inch (27 x 39–cm) baking dish, combine the rice, onion, garlic, half of the bacon, broth, half-and-half and the remaining 1 tablespoon (9 g) of ranch seasoning mix. Add the chicken and stir everything together.

Top the casserole with the remaining half of the bacon and the Cheddar cheese. Cover the casserole dish with aluminum foil and bake it for 30 minutes. Remove the foil and bake the casserole for 30 minutes, or until the rice is cooked through.

Garnish the casserole with the parsley and serve.

RECIPE NOTES

I prefer chicken breast in this casserole, but boneless, skinless thighs can be used as well.

I recommend a short-grain rice in this casserole because I like a stickier rice in casseroles, but a longer grain rice would work as well. Brown rice can be used instead of white, but the cooking time will be a bit longer.

Half-and-half has a 10 to 12 percent fat content. Heavy cream can also be used. It is also called heavy whipping cream, because it's whipping cream with a milk fat content of between 36 and 40 percent.

NUTRITION INFORMATION

Serving size: 1 serving; **Calories:** 319; **Carbohydrates:** 22 g; **Protein:** 17 g; **Fat:** 16 g

WHITE CHICKEN ENCHILADAS

These white chicken enchiladas have the easiest cream sauce you could ever make, and it means you're in for delicious, cheesy, gooey, melt-in-your-mouth enchiladas!

PREP TIME: 15 MINUTES
COOK TIME: 35 MINUTES
TOTAL TIME: 50 MINUTES
SERVES: 6

CHICKEN ENCHILADAS
2 chicken breasts, cooked and shredded (see Recipe Note)
1 cup (240 ml) green chili enchilada sauce
2 cups (224 g) shredded mozzarella cheese, divided
6 medium flour tortillas

WHITE SAUCE
2 tbsp (30 g) unsalted butter
2 tbsp (16 g) all-purpose flour
1½ cups (360 ml) low-sodium or unsalted chicken broth
1 (4-oz [112-g]) can diced green chilies, undrained
¾ cup (90 g) sour cream
Salt, as needed
Black pepper, as needed

2 tbsp (6 g) chopped fresh parsley or cilantro

To make the chicken enchiladas, preheat the oven to 350°F (177°C). Spray a 9 x 13–inch (27 x 36–cm) baking dish with cooking spray.

In a medium bowl, combine the chicken, enchilada sauce and 1 cup (112 g) of the mozzarella cheese.

Top 1 tortilla with about ¼ cup (34 g) of the chicken mixture, then roll the tortilla up and place it in the prepared baking dish. Repeat this process with all the tortillas and filling. Set the enchiladas aside.

To make the white sauce, melt the butter in a small saucepan over medium heat. Whisk in the flour. Cook the mixture for 1 minute, then add the broth and whisk the mixture until it is smooth. Cook the sauce for 3 to 5 minutes, until it is thick and bubbly.

Add the green chilies and their juice and the sour cream. Stir the ingredients to incorporate them into the white sauce. Remove the saucepan from the heat. Taste the sauce and season it with the salt and black pepper as necessary.

Pour the sauce over the enchiladas. Top them with the remaining 1 cup (112 g) of mozzarella cheese.

Bake the enchiladas for 22 to 25 minutes, or until the top is light brown and the sauce is bubbly.

Garnish the enchiladas with the parsley or cilantro and serve.

RECIPE NOTE
To make things even quicker and easier, you can use store-bought rotisserie chicken.

NUTRITION INFORMATION
Serving size: 1 enchilada; **Calories:** 374; **Carbohydrates:** 24 g; **Protein:** 21 g; **Fat:** 21 g

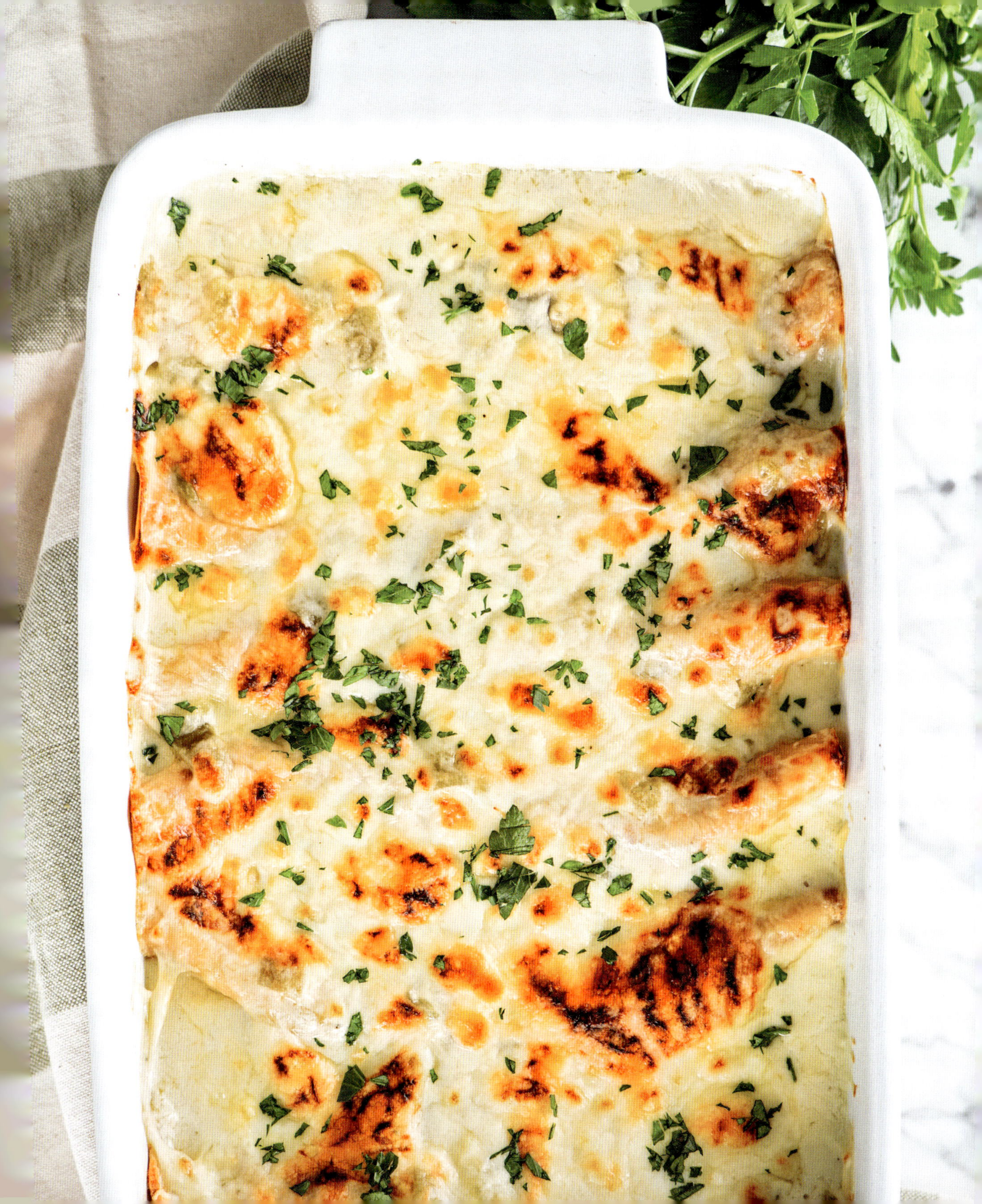

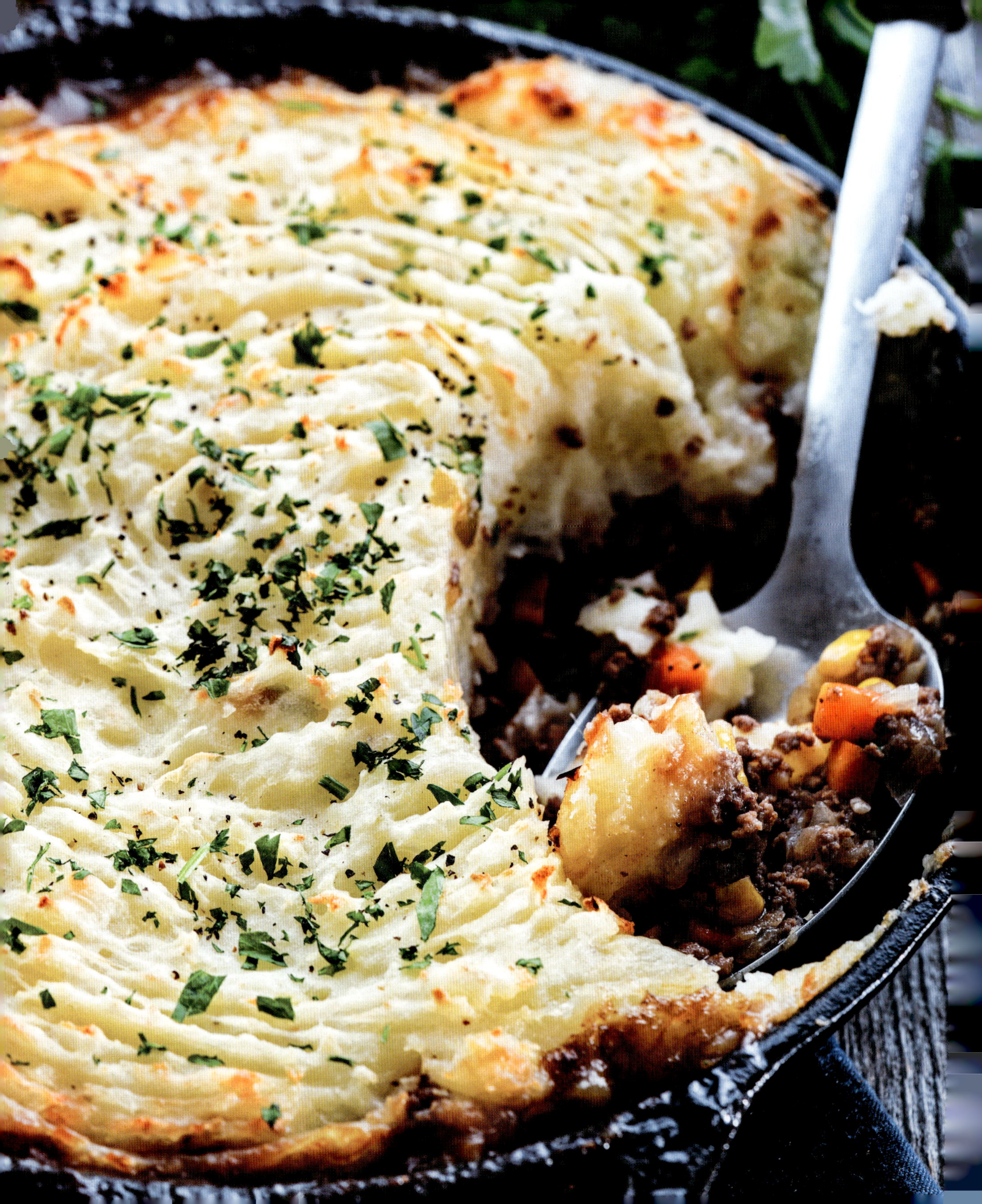

SKILLET SHEPHERD'S PIE

PREP TIME: 15 MINUTES
COOK TIME: 55 MINUTES
TOTAL TIME: 1 HOUR, 10 MINUTES
SERVES: 8

MASHED POTATOES

6 russet or Yukon gold potatoes, peeled and cubed
4 tbsp (60 g) butter, softened
⅔ cup (160 ml) milk
¼ cup (45 g) grated Parmesan cheese
½ tsp salt, or as needed
½ tsp white pepper, or as needed

MEAT MIXTURE

1 tbsp (15 ml) olive oil
1¼ lb (560 g) lean ground beef
½ tsp salt, or as needed
½ tsp black pepper, plus more as needed
1 onion, chopped
1 clove garlic, minced
½ tsp red pepper flakes
2 tbsp (30 ml) Worcestershire sauce
1 (2-oz [56-g]) packet onion soup mix (see Recipe Notes)
1 cup (240 ml) low-sodium beef broth
2 cups (480 g) frozen mixed vegetables (see Recipe Notes)

1 tbsp (3 g) chopped fresh parsley
Black pepper, as needed

This recipe for shepherd's pie, which is also known as cottage pie, is loaded with flavorful beef and veggies, topped with fluffy and creamy mashed potatoes, then baked to perfection—and all in one skillet!

To make the mashed potatoes, cook the potatoes in boiling water for about 15 minutes, or until they are fork-tender.

While the potatoes are cooking, prepare the meat mixture. Heat the oil in a large skillet over medium heat. Add the beef, season it with the salt and black pepper and cook it for about 5 minutes, breaking it up as it cooks, until it's no longer pink.

Add the onion and garlic and cook the mixture for 3 minutes, until the onion softens and becomes translucent. Add the red pepper flakes, Worcestershire sauce, onion soup mix and broth and stir the ingredients to combine them. Stir in the frozen vegetables and cook the meat mixture for 2 minutes. Set the skillet aside.

Preheat the oven to 350°F (177°C).

Drain the potatoes, then transfer them to a large bowl. Add the butter and use a potato masher to mash the potatoes until they are smooth. Add the milk, Parmesan cheese, salt and white pepper and mash the potatoes until they are very smooth. Spread the potatoes over the meat mixture and smooth them with a spoon. Using a fork, create a rustic pattern in the potatoes.

Place the skillet on a large baking sheet. Bake the shepherd's pie for 40 minutes, until it is golden brown on top.

Garnish the shepherd's pie with the parsley and black pepper and serve it warm.

RECIPE NOTES

If you don't have onion soup mix, you can make your own onion soup mix by combining 3 tablespoons (15 g) of minced onion flakes, 2 tablespoons (18 g) of beef bouillon powder, ½ teaspoon of onion powder, ¼ teaspoon of dried parsley, ⅛ teaspoon of ground celery seeds, ½ teaspoon of paprika, salt to taste and black pepper to taste. Use the entire mixture in place of the store-bought onion soup mix in this recipe.

For this recipe, I use a mix of peas, carrots, green beans and corn.

NUTRITION INFORMATION

Serving size: 1 serving; **Calories:** 252; **Carbohydrates:** 14 g; **Protein:** 19 g; **Fat:** 12 g

CASSEROLES

BREAKFAST

I'VE SAID THIS BEFORE MANY TIMES, but breakfast really is my favorite meal of the day. I love it because I can have breakfast for breakfast, brunch, lunch or dinner! Not only that, but breakfast is the most important meal of the day.

Breakfast at my house is never missed. It helps that hubs and I work from home every day, which allows us to have breakfast together every morning. Granted, it's not always a fancy breakfast—there are days when all we have is cereal or oatmeal, and more often than not we have bacon and eggs. But every once in a while, I'll make things like my Dutch Baby Pancake (page 234), Pumpkin-Zucchini Muffins (page 238), Sheet Pan Pancakes (page 249), French Toast (page 245) and other favorites.

Even so, I still don't like to slave in the kitchen for hours making breakfast, which is why I want to share with you my favorite breakfast dishes—after all, I like to make everything as simple as possible.

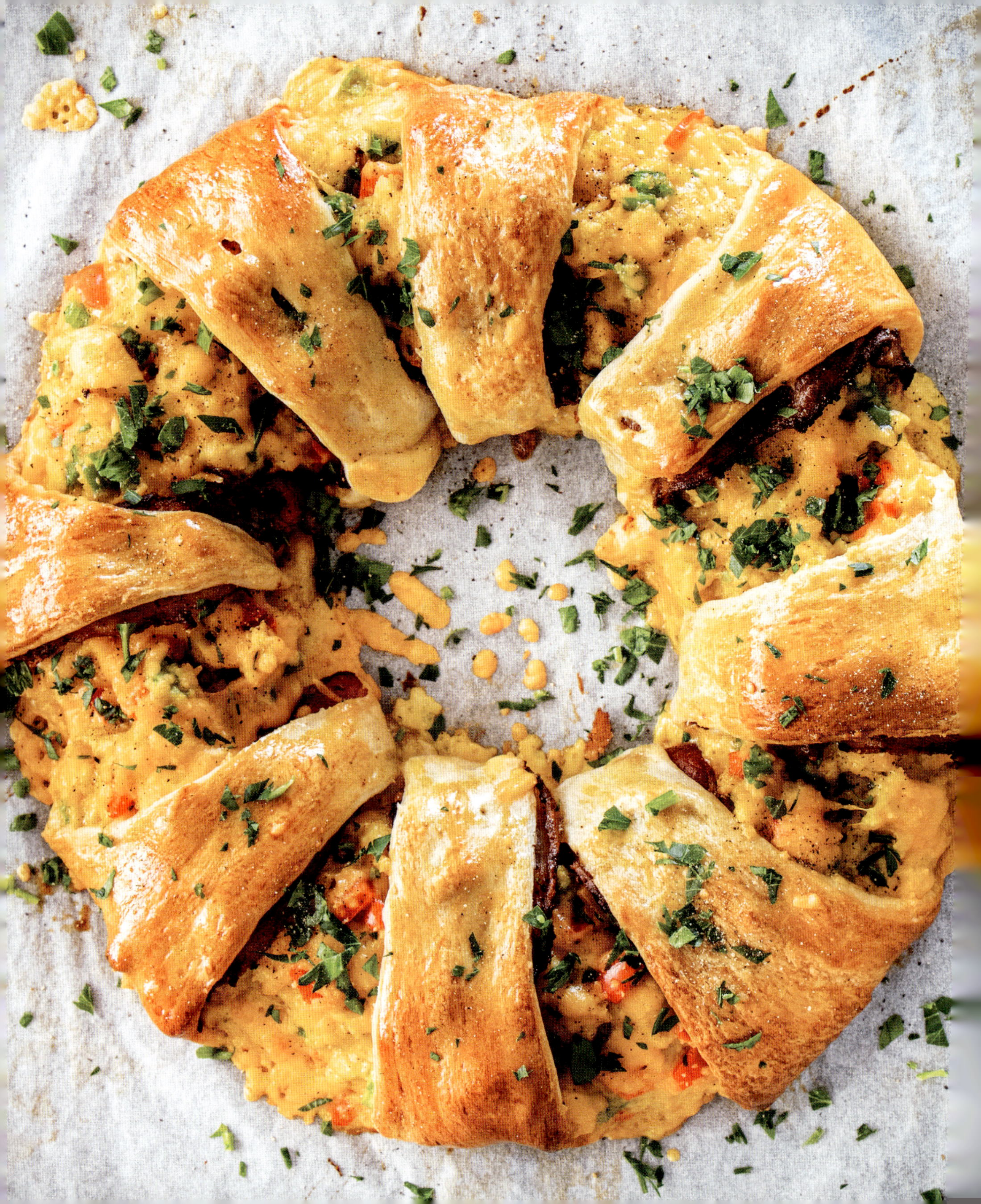

CRESCENT BACON BREAKFAST RING

PREP TIME: 15 MINUTES
COOK TIME: 25 MINUTES
TOTAL TIME: 40 MINUTES
SERVES: 8

6 large eggs, divided
½ red bell pepper, chopped
½ green bell pepper, chopped
¼ tsp salt, or as needed
¼ tsp black pepper, or as needed
1 (8-oz [224-g]) can refrigerated crescent rolls (I recommend Pillsbury™)
8 slices bacon, fried
1 cup (120 g) shredded Cheddar cheese, divided
1 tbsp (3 g) chopped fresh parsley (optional)

This crescent bacon breakfast ring is perfect for a weekend brunch or breakfast. I often make this over the weekend so that I have breakfast to go during the week. I cut it up into slices, wrap the slices in plastic wrap and then refrigerate them. You can eat them cold, or you can pop them into the microwave for a few seconds to warm them up. Either way, this breakfast ring is delicious and loaded with bacon, eggs and cheese!

Preheat the oven to 375°F (191°C). Line a large baking sheet with parchment paper.

In a medium bowl, beat together 5 of the eggs, the red bell pepper, green bell pepper, salt and black pepper. Heat a medium skillet over medium heat. Add the eggs and scramble them for about 5 minutes.

Lay out the crescent rolls like a star on the prepared baking sheet.

Lay a slice of bacon on each crescent roll. Add ½ cup (60 g) of the Cheddar cheese around the ring. Add the scrambled eggs around the ring and top them with the remaining ½ cup (60 g) of Cheddar cheese.

Fold the crescents over. In a small bowl, beat the remaining egg to create an egg wash. Brush the crescent ring with the egg wash.

Bake the crescent ring for 20 minutes, or until the crescents are golden brown.

Garnish the crescent ring with the parsley (if using). Serve the crescent ring warm.

RECIPE NOTES

This can be prepared the night before and refrigerated until you are ready to bake it.

To make it easier to unroll the crescent rolls, do not take the can out of the fridge until you are ready to use the dough.

NUTRITION INFORMATION

Serving size: 1 serving; **Calories:** 299; **Carbohydrates:** 12 g; **Protein:** 11 g; **Fat:** 22 g

DUTCH BABY PANCAKE

I've just recently started making this recipe and it makes me wonder, What have I been waiting for all this time? Not only does it make for a gorgeous presentation but it's also fluffy, delicious and an excellent choice for brunch, lunch or dessert any time of the year.

PREP TIME: 5 MINUTES
COOK TIME: 20 MINUTES
TOTAL TIME: 25 MINUTES
SERVES: 6

3 large eggs, at room temperature
⅔ cup (160 ml) milk, at room temperature
½ cup (60 g) all-purpose flour
¼ tsp salt
1 tsp pure vanilla extract
3 tbsp (45 g) unsalted butter plus 1 tbsp (15 ml) melted unsalted butter, divided
1 tbsp (15 ml) fresh lemon juice
3 cups (450 g) fresh mixed berries
1 tbsp (9 g) powdered sugar

Preheat the oven to 425°F (218°C).

In a blender, combine the eggs, milk, flour, salt and vanilla. Blend the ingredients until the batter is smooth.

In a 10-inch (30-cm) cast-iron skillet, melt the 3 tablespoons (45 g) of butter until it is bubbling. To do this, you may heat the skillet in the preheated oven for about 5 minutes or you may set the skillet over medium heat on the stove and heat the butter for about 2 minutes. If you do this in the oven, be careful handling your skillet, as it will be hot.

Pour the batter into the center of the skillet. Do not mix the batter with the butter. Carefully transfer the skillet back to the oven and bake the Dutch baby pancake for 15 to 20 minutes, until it is puffed and golden.

Remove the skillet from the oven and immediately brush the pancake with the 1 tablespoon (15 ml) of melted butter. Drizzle the lemon juice over the top of the pancake. Add the berries and dust them with the powdered sugar before serving.

RECIPE NOTES

Because Dutch baby pancakes contain dairy and eggs, leftovers will keep for up to 5 days in the fridge, but this recipe is best right after it's made.

You can also freeze your leftover pancake for up to 2 months, but the consistency and texture of it might not be the same.

NUTRITION INFORMATION

Serving size: 1 serving; **Calories:** 209; **Carbohydrates:** 20 g; **Protein:** 6 g; **Fat:** 12 g

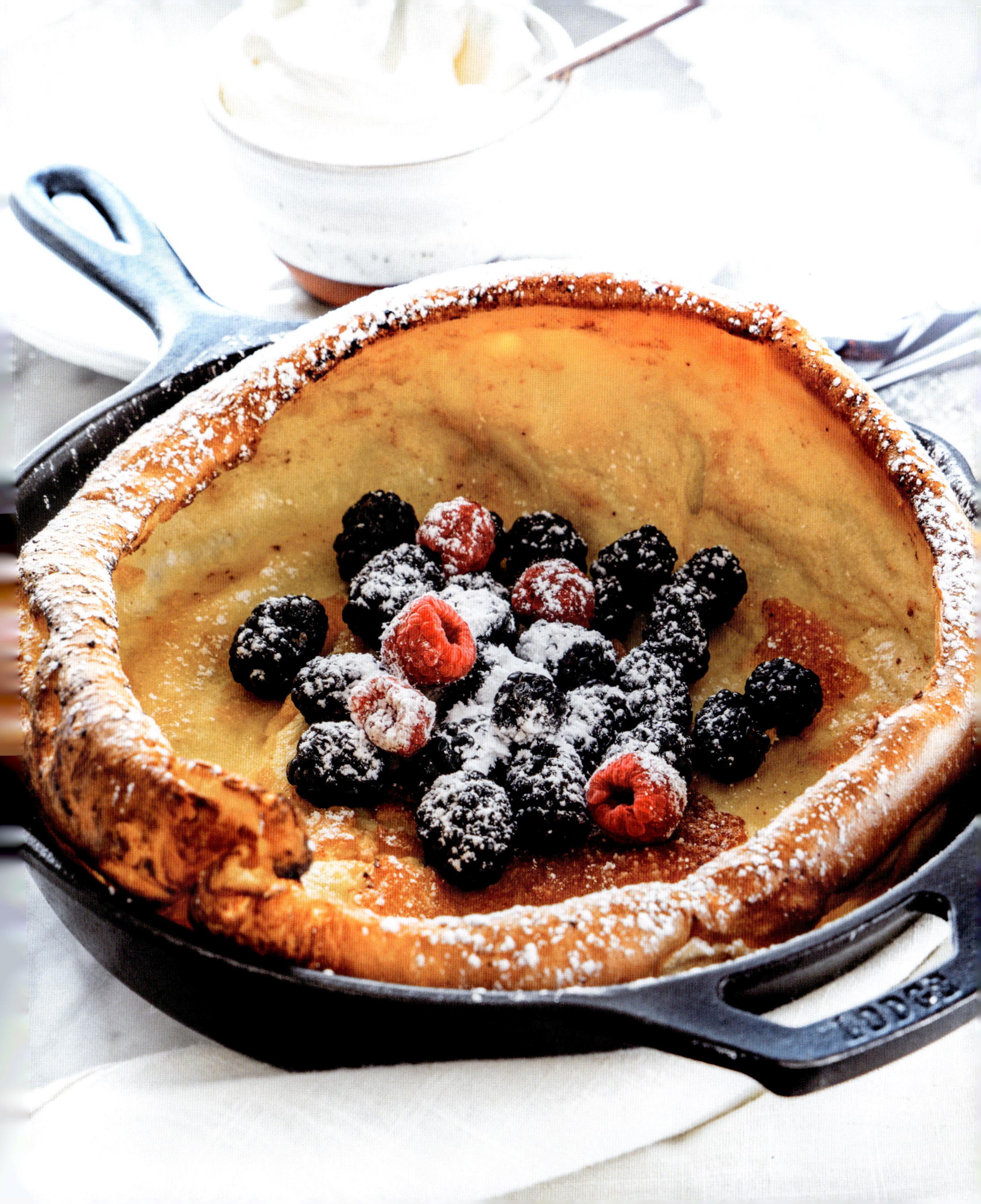
LODGE

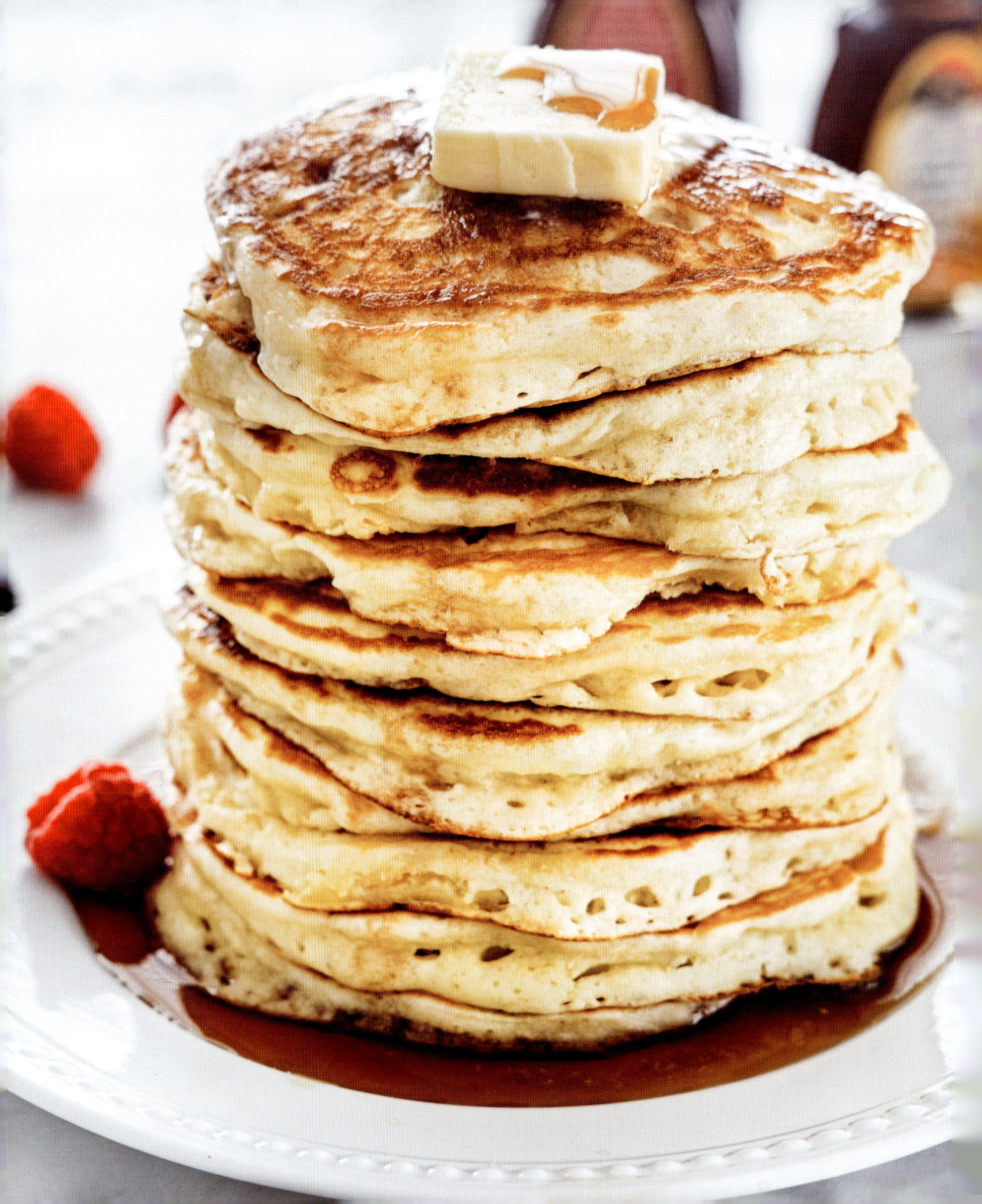

THE BEST BUTTERMILK PANCAKES

PREP TIME: 5 MINUTES
REST TIME: 5 MINUTES
COOK TIME: 25 MINUTES
TOTAL TIME: 35 MINUTES
SERVES: 4

1¼ cups (150 g) all-purpose flour
¼ cup (48 g) sugar
1 tsp baking soda
1 tsp baking powder
½ tsp salt
1½ cups (360 ml) buttermilk
1 large egg
2 tbsp (30 g) unsalted butter, melted

This recipe is a classic, at least in my kitchen. It's a recipe my husband requests at least a couple of times a month, because these are just the best pancakes ever. They are light, fluffy and so simple to make. Top them with a bit of butter, drizzle maple syrup over them and add some fruit preserves if you wish. This recipe is so much better than store-bought pancake mix!

In a large bowl, mix together the flour, sugar, baking soda, baking powder and salt. In a medium bowl, combine the buttermilk, egg and butter. Add the buttermilk mixture to the flour mixture and mix them together using a handheld mixer for about 30 seconds, until they are combined. It's okay if there are lumps; do not overmix the batter. Let the batter rest for about 5 minutes.

Heat a large nonstick skillet or griddle over medium heat. Spray it with cooking spray or brush it with additional melted butter.

Use a measuring cup to pour ⅓ cup (80 ml) of the batter into the skillet and cook the pancake for 1½ to 2 minutes on each side, or until it is golden brown. Transfer the pancake to a plate and repeat this process with the remaining batter.

If you would like to keep the cooked pancakes warm between batches, you can transfer them to a preheated 200°F (93°C) oven.

RECIPE NOTES

You can store these pancakes in an airtight container in the fridge for up to 2 days. Keep in mind that the pancakes will get soggy if they sit around for too long!

To freeze these pancakes, place a piece of wax paper between each pancake and stack them together. Wrap them tightly with aluminum foil and place them in a freezer bag. Properly stored, these pancakes will last for 1 to 2 months in the freezer.

NUTRITION INFORMATION

Serving size: 2 pancakes; **Calories:** 316; **Carbohydrates:** 47 g; **Protein:** 9 g; **Fat:** 10 g

PUMPKIN-ZUCCHINI MUFFINS

I have to tell you how I came to make this recipe. I was watching a Christmas movie, and the mom in the movie was making pumpkin-zucchini muffins. A light went on in my head, and I realized what a great idea that is. The next thing I did was write this recipe—and yes, these muffins are loaded with zucchini and pumpkin and are topped with pepitas. They're incredibly moist and delicious. They'll blow your mind!

PREP TIME: 15 MINUTES
COOK TIME: 30 MINUTES
TOTAL TIME: 45 MINUTES
SERVES: 12

- 2½ cups (300 g) all-purpose flour
- ¾ cup (180 g) packed brown sugar
- 1 tbsp (12 g) baking powder
- 1 tsp salt
- 1 cup (245 g) canned pumpkin
- 1 zucchini, grated and drained
- 1 large egg
- ½ cup (120 g) unsalted butter, melted
- ⅔ cup (160 ml) milk
- 1 tsp pure vanilla extract
- ¼ cup (40 g) toasted pepitas
- 1 tbsp (12 g) turbinado sugar

Preheat the oven to 425°F (218°C). Spray a 12-cavity muffin pan with cooking spray or line the cavities with muffin liners.

In a large bowl, combine the flour, brown sugar, baking powder and salt. Set the flour mixture aside.

In another large bowl, whisk together the pumpkin, zucchini, egg, butter, milk and vanilla.

Add the pumpkin-zucchini mixture to the flour mixture and, using a spatula, mix everything until the flour is moistened; do not overmix the batter, and keep in mind that the batter will be a bit lumpy.

Use an ice cream scoop to spoon the batter into the prepared muffin pan, filling the muffin cavities completely; this way you will get muffins with perfect domes. Top the muffins with the pepitas, then sprinkle them with the turbinado sugar.

Reduce the oven's temperature to 400°F (204°C). Bake the muffins for 25 to 30 minutes, or until they are golden brown.

RECIPE NOTES

Store these muffins in a plastic bag, plastic wrap or an airtight container. They will last at room temperature for 3 days or in your fridge for 1 week. These are extra delicious if you reheat them for about 30 seconds in the microwave before digging in!

To freeze the muffins, wrap them individually with either plastic wrap or foil; or you can place them all in a large freezer bag or airtight container. Reheat them by microwaving them for 1 minute, or until they are heated through.

NUTRITION INFORMATION

Serving size: 1 muffin; **Calories:** 253; **Carbohydrates:** 38 g; **Protein:** 5 g; **Fat:** 10 g

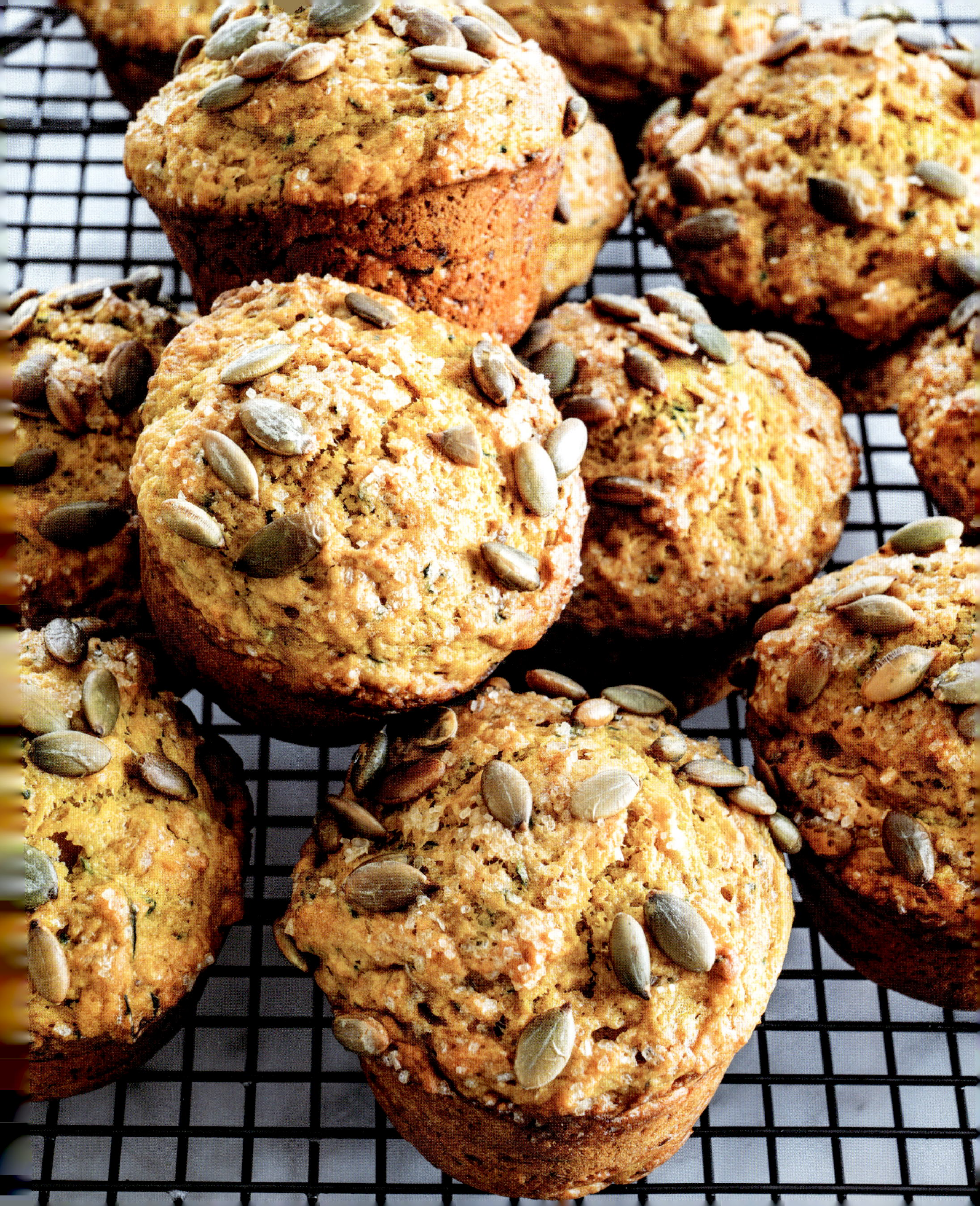

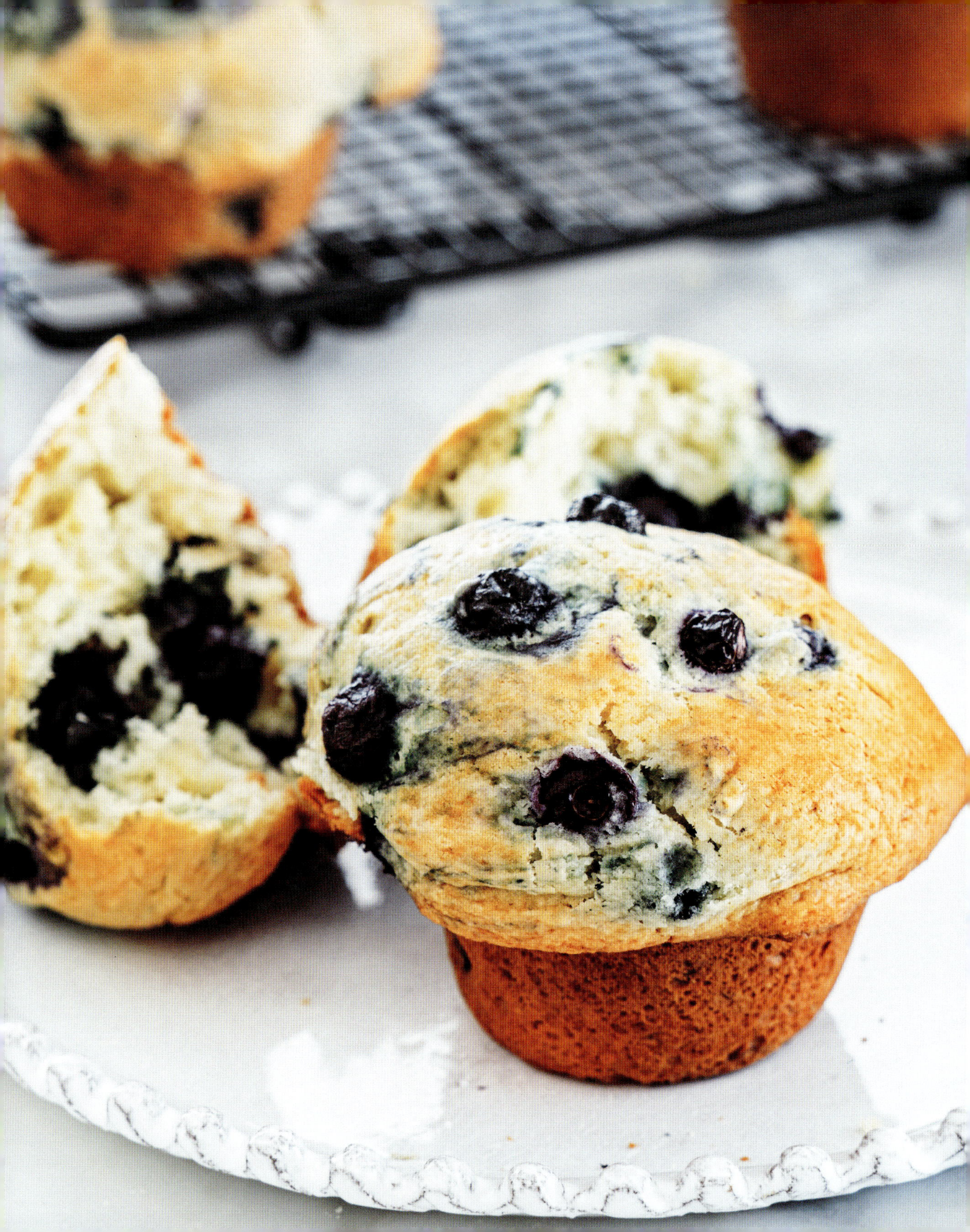

MY FAVORITE BLUEBERRY MUFFINS

While I love all muffins, blueberry muffins are my weakness. They were my breakfast of choice when I was in university. Almost every single morning, I would enjoy a blueberry muffin with a cup of coffee. There's just nothing better. I tried making my own blueberry muffins by using store-bought muffin mix, but they didn't even come close to the real thing. Since then it's been my mission to come up with my very own perfect blueberry muffin recipe, and here it is.

PREP TIME: 10 MINUTES
COOK TIME: 30 MINUTES
TOTAL TIME: 40 MINUTES
SERVES: 12

½ cup (120 g) butter, melted
2 large eggs, beaten
1 cup (192 g) granulated sugar
1 cup (240 ml) milk
2 tsp (10 ml) pure vanilla extract
1 tbsp (15 ml) fresh lemon juice
3 cups (360 g) all-purpose flour, plus more as needed
1 tbsp (12 g) baking powder
½ tsp baking soda
¼ tsp salt
2½ cups (375 g) fresh or frozen blueberries, divided
1 tbsp (12 g) turbinado sugar (optional)

Preheat the oven to 450°F (232°C). Spray a 12-cavity muffin pan with cooking spray or line the cavities with muffin liners.

In the bowl of a stand mixer, combine the butter, eggs and granulated sugar. Beat the ingredients at medium speed until they are well combined. Add the milk, vanilla and lemon juice and mix until the ingredients are combined.

In a large bowl, mix together the flour, baking powder, baking soda and salt. Add the flour mixture to the butter mixture and mix the two slowly until they are fully incorporated. The batter should be quite thick.

In a medium bowl, toss 2 cups (300 g) of the blueberries in a little bit of additional flour, so they don't sink to the bottom of the muffins. Add the blueberries to the batter and use a spatula to incorporate them.

Spoon the batter into the prepared muffin pan, filling the cavities all the way to the top. Use the remaining ½ cup (75 g) of blueberries to top the muffins, then sprinkle the muffins with the turbinado sugar (if using).

Reduce the oven's temperature to 350°F (177°C). Bake the muffins for 20 to 30 minutes, or until a toothpick inserted into the center of a muffin comes out clean.

Allow the muffins to cool in the pan for 10 minutes, then remove and serve them.

RECIPE NOTES

You can store your muffins in a large airtight container or sealable freezer bag. If you want to avoid the classic "plastic taste" that fluffy baked goods can take on, these muffins will store well on a cake plate with a dome.

Your muffins will last for 2 days at room temperature or for 1 week in the fridge.

NUTRITION INFORMATION

Serving size: 1 muffin; **Calories:** 288; **Carbohydrates:** 46 g; **Protein:** 5 g; **Fat:** 10 g

SAUSAGE AND EGG BREAKFAST ROLLS

This recipe came to be as I was trying to think of breakfasts that are perfect for on-the-go mornings. I'm so glad I thought up this recipe, because everyone loves it. Turkey breakfast sausages are wrapped in crescent rolls with scrambled eggs and cheese. These rolls are the perfect on-the-go breakfast—just wrap them and refrigerate them. When you're ready to eat, just pop them in the microwave for a few seconds and you're ready to go!

PREP TIME: 15 MINUTES
COOK TIME: 20 MINUTES
TOTAL TIME: 35 MINUTES
SERVES: 8

6 large eggs, divided
1 tsp butter
2 tbsp (16 g) all-purpose flour
1 (8-oz [224-g]) can refrigerated crescent rolls (I recommend Pillsbury; see Recipe Notes)
2 oz (56 g) shredded Cheddar cheese
8 links turkey breakfast sausage, cooked (see Recipe Notes)
¼ tsp salt, or as needed
¼ tsp black pepper, or as needed

Preheat the oven to 375°F (191°C). Line a large baking sheet with parchment paper or a silicone baking mat.

In a medium bowl, beat 5 of the eggs. Heat the butter in a large nonstick skillet over medium heat. Pour in the beaten eggs. As the eggs begin to set, gently pull the eggs across the skillet using a spatula, forming large, soft curds. Continue pulling, lifting and folding eggs for about 5 minutes, until they have thickened and there is no more visible liquid. Remove the skillet from the heat.

Dust a work surface with the flour. Unroll the crescent dough over the flour. Roll the dough out with a rolling pin if it is uneven. Pinch the dough's seams together if necessary, then cut the dough into 8 rectangles.

Top a rectangle with some of the scrambled eggs, some of the Cheddar cheese and a sausage link. Roll up the rectangle and transfer it to the prepared baking sheet. Repeat this process with the remaining ingredients.

In a small bowl, beat the remaining egg to create an egg wash. Brush each roll with the egg wash, then sprinkle the rolls with the salt and black pepper.

Bake the rolls for 15 minutes, or until they are golden brown.

RECIPE NOTES

You can use puff pastry dough in place of crescent dough.

You can use any type of breakfast sausage that you like.

These can be frozen and reheated in the oven at 400°F (204°C) for 10 to 15 minutes.

NUTRITION INFORMATION

Serving size: 1 roll; **Calories:** 201; **Carbohydrates:** 13 g; **Protein:** 8 g; **Fat:** 12 g

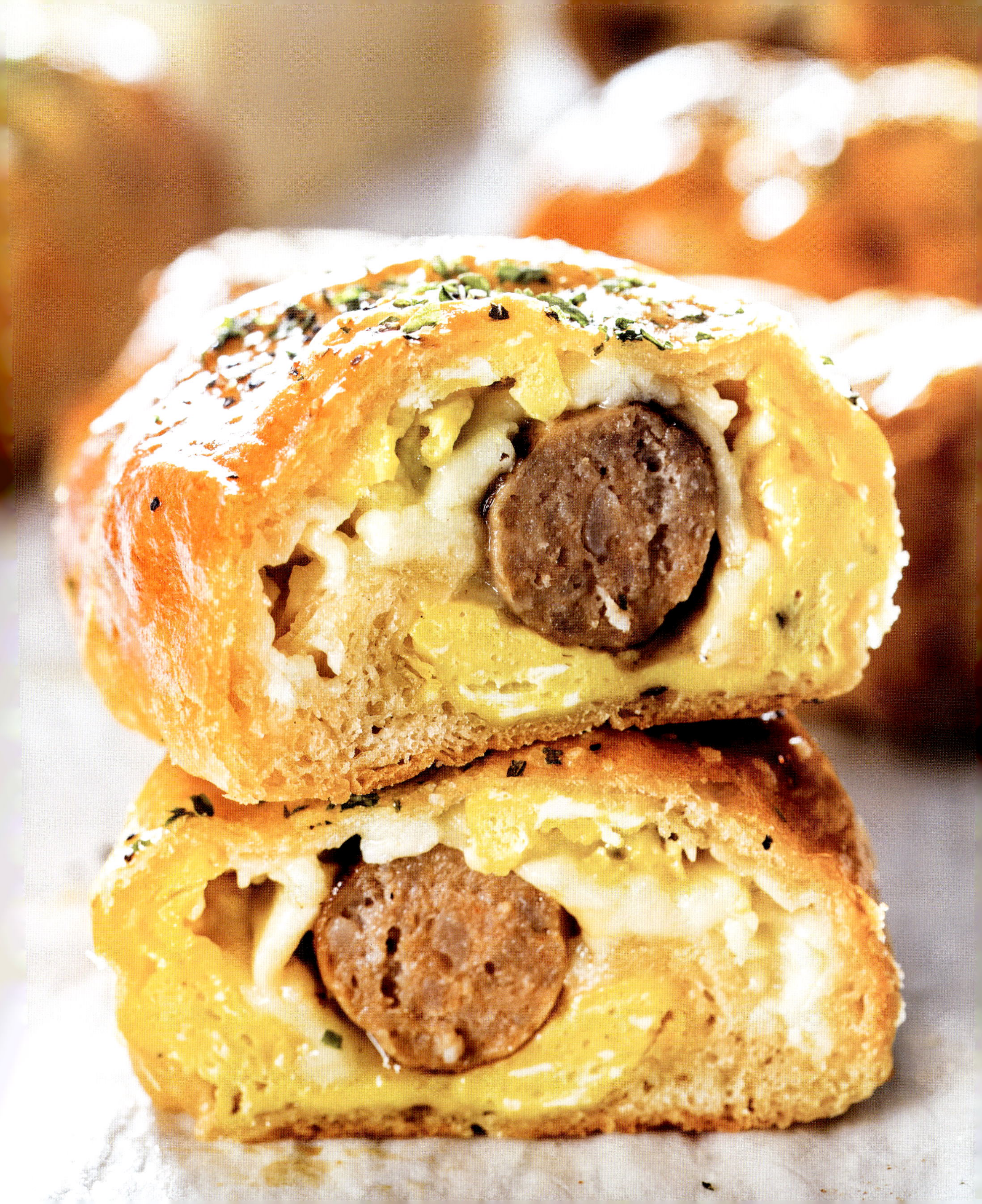

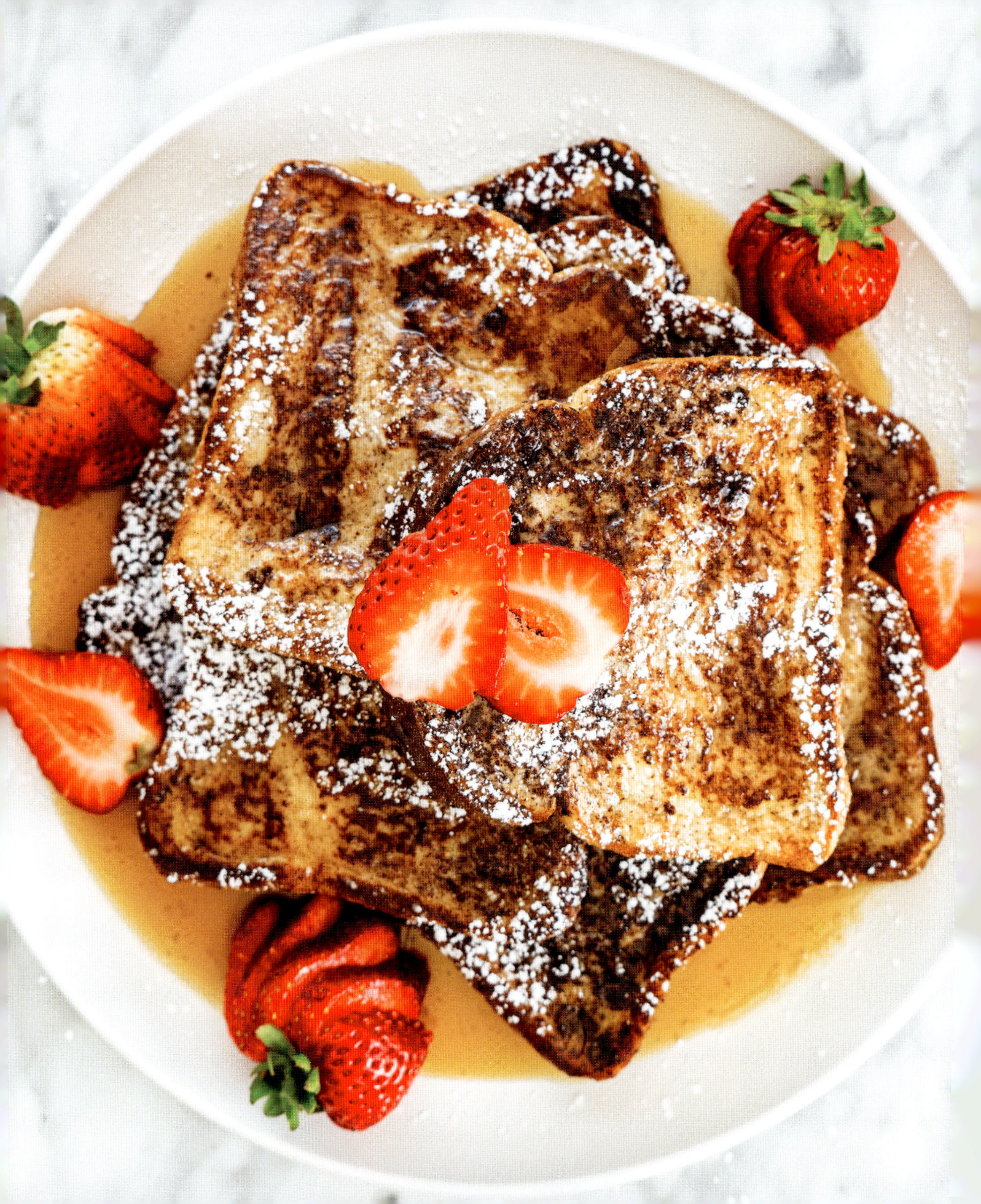

FRENCH TOAST

PREP TIME: 15 MINUTES
COOK TIME: 25 MINUTES
TOTAL TIME: 35 MINUTES
SERVES: 4

4 large eggs
⅔ cup (160 ml) milk
2 tsp (6 g) ground cinnamon
8 thick slices day-old bread
2 tbsp (30 g) butter, plus more as needed
Pure maple syrup, as needed
Fresh strawberries (optional)

French toast is a favorite in my family. It just so happens it's one of my sister's go-to meals whenever we go to a restaurant for breakfast. But what's not to love about thick slices of bread that have been soaked in a mixture of egg, milk and cinnamon then fried in butter and finally served with maple syrup and a dusting of powdered sugar? A great bread for this French toast would be a brioche or a thick slice of Texas toast.

In a medium bowl, beat together the eggs, milk and cinnamon. Pour the mixture into a shallow bowl.

Dip each slice of bread into the egg mixture and allow the bread to soak up some of the mixture.

Melt the butter in a large skillet over medium-high heat. Working in batches, fry the soaked bread for 2 to 3 minutes per side, until it is brown on both sides.

Serve the French toast hot with additional butter, maple syrup and the strawberries (if using).

RECIPE NOTES

Store leftover French toast in the fridge sealed in an airtight container or covered with plastic wrap for up to 2 days. Keep in mind it may get soggy.

To freeze the French toast, cool the French toast and stack each piece separated by a layer of parchment paper. Freeze the French toast in an airtight container for up to 2 months. You can reheat it in the microwave or the toaster when you are ready to eat.

NUTRITION INFORMATION

Serving size: 2 slices; **Calories:** 293; **Carbohydrates:** 31 g; **Protein:** 13 g; **Fat:** 13 g

OVERNIGHT BREAKFAST CASSEROLE

PREP TIME: 15 MINUTES
COOK TIME: 1 HOUR, 15 MINUTES
TOTAL TIME: 1 HOUR, 30 MINUTES
SERVES: 8

12 slices day-old bread, cubed (I recommend challah, brioche or any egg-based bread)
1 tbsp (15 ml) olive oil
1 onion, chopped
1 lb (448 g) Italian sausage, casings removed
1 tsp mustard powder
½ tsp salt, or as needed
½ tsp black pepper, or as needed
1 red bell pepper, finely chopped
3 green onions, chopped
2 cups (240 g) shredded Cheddar cheese, divided
8 large eggs
2 cups (480 ml) milk

Overnight breakfast casseroles are amazing: not only are they crowd-pleasers but they are also cook-pleasers. They are easy to make and a great option for a holiday breakfast or brunch, a special occasion or just an ordinary breakfast. Simply prep this casserole the night before, pop it in the oven in the morning and breakfast is served.

Preheat the oven to 300°F (149°C).

Place the bread cubes on a 13 x 18–inch (39 x 54–cm) baking sheet. Bake the bread for 10 minutes, just enough to dry out the bread but not toast it. Remove the baking sheet from the oven and set it aside.

Heat the oil in a large skillet over medium heat. Add the onion and sausage and cook them for 5 to 7 minutes, breaking up the sausage with a wooden spoon as it cooks, until the onion is soft and the sausage is cooked through. Season the mixture with the mustard powder, salt and black pepper.

Place half of the bread cubes in a 9 x 13–inch (27 x 39–cm) baking dish. Top the bread with half of the onion-sausage mixture. Next, add half of the bell pepper, half of the green onions and 1 cup (120 g) of the Cheddar cheese. Repeat this process with the remaining bread, onion-sausage mixture, bell pepper, green onions and 1 cup (120 g) of the Cheddar cheese.

In a large bowl, whisk together the eggs and milk and pour this mixture evenly over the casserole. Cover the baking dish with aluminum foil and put it in the fridge overnight.

The next morning, preheat the oven to 350°F (177°C) and remove the foil from the baking dish. Bake the casserole for 50 to 55 minutes, until a knife inserted into the center comes out clean. Serve the casserole hot.

RECIPE NOTES

This breakfast casserole will last in an airtight container in the fridge for up to 4 days.

To extend the shelf life of the casserole, I recommend freezing it. Stored properly in an airtight container, it will last anywhere from 3 to 6 months frozen.

NUTRITION INFORMATION

Serving size: 1 serving; **Calories:** 572; **Carbohydrates:** 28 g; **Protein:** 29 g; **Fat:** 38 g

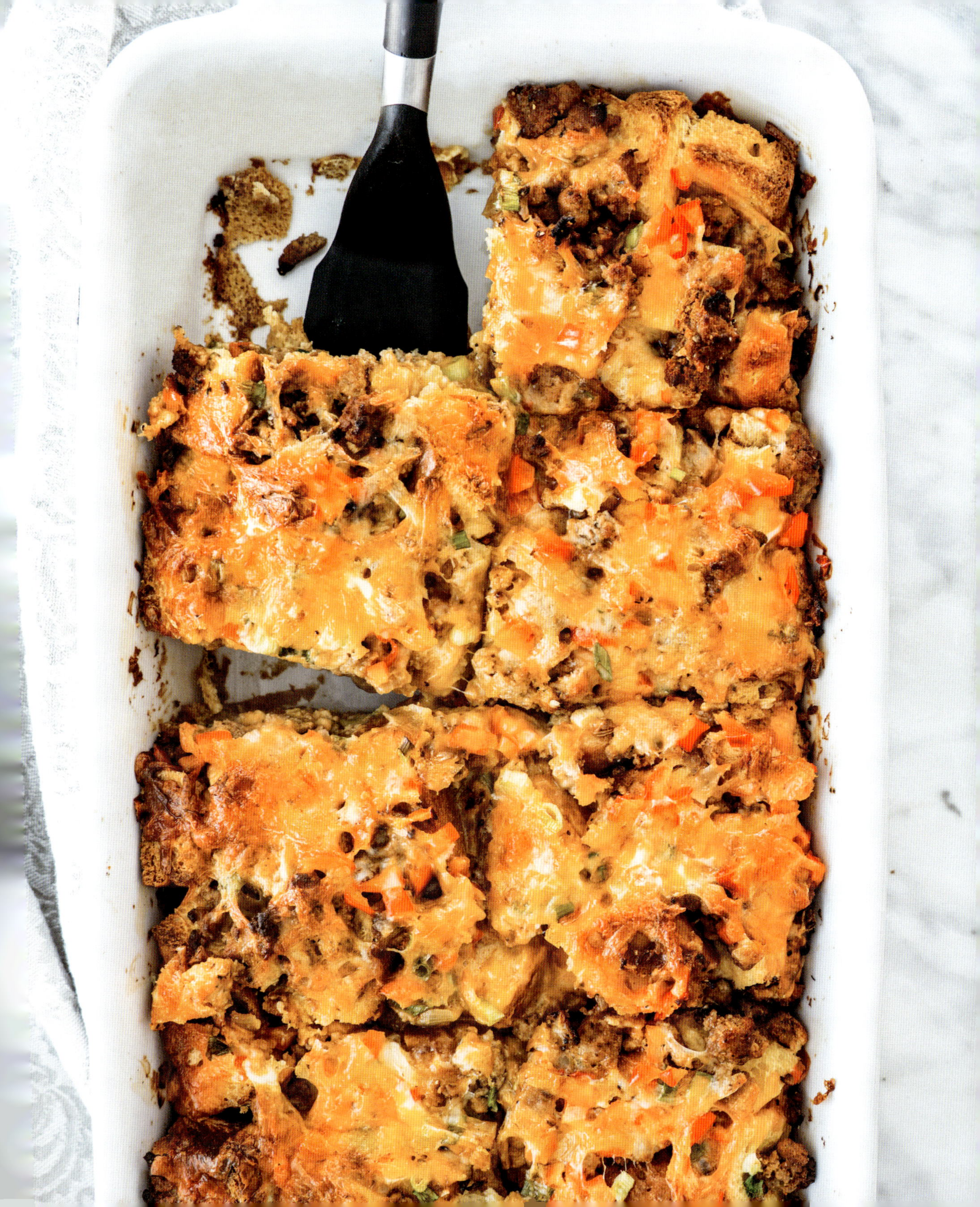

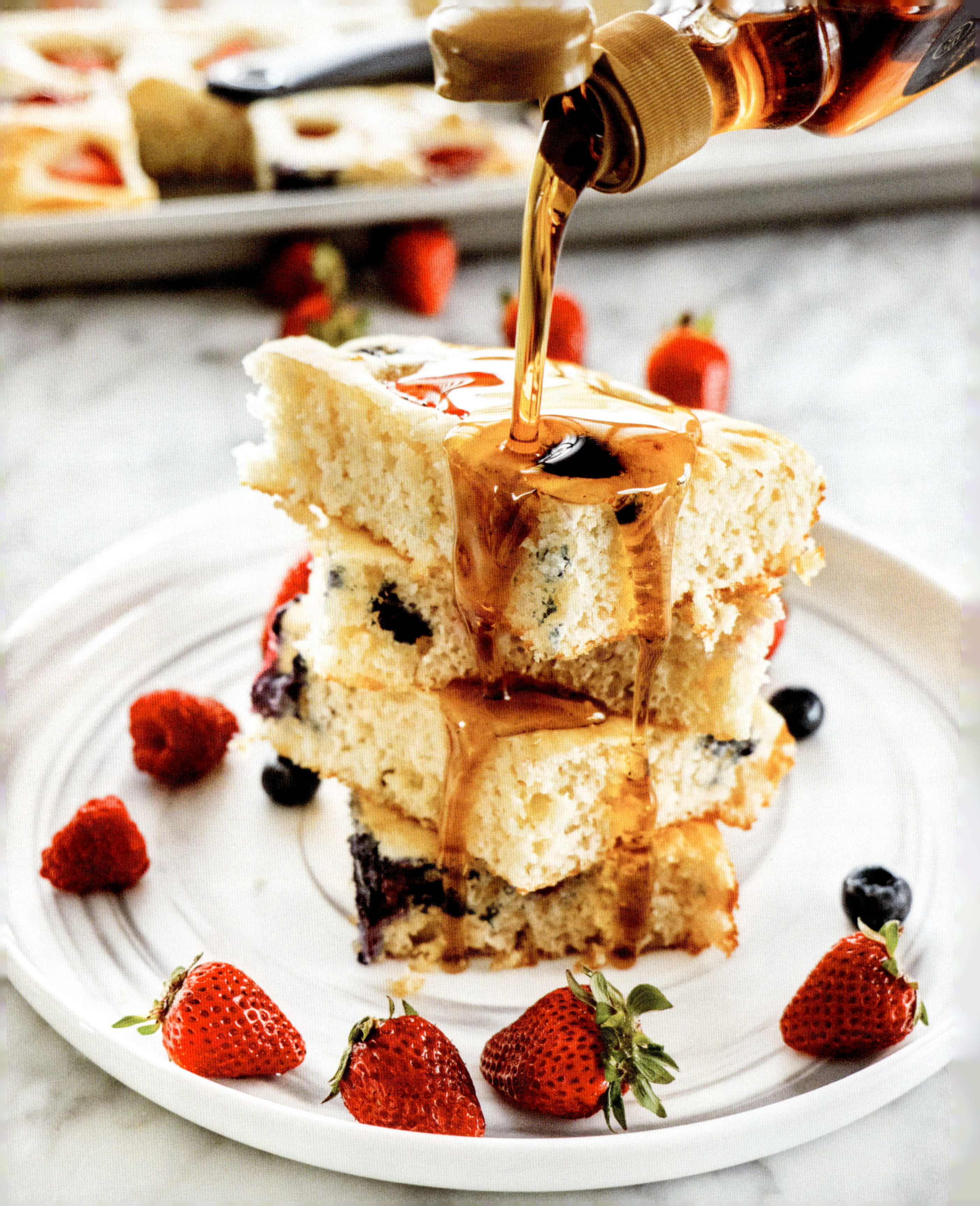

SHEET PAN PANCAKES

PREP TIME: 5 MINUTES
COOK TIME: 15 MINUTES
TOTAL TIME: 20 MINUTES
SERVES: 16

8 tbsp (120 ml) melted butter, divided
2½ cups (300 g) all-purpose flour
3 tbsp (36 g) baking powder
⅓ cup (64 g) sugar
½ tsp salt
2½ cups (600 ml) milk
2 large eggs
2 tsp (10 ml) pure vanilla extract

TOPPINGS
Fruit of choice
Chocolate chips
Pure maple syrup

I was a little skeptical when I decided to make these sheet pan pancakes, but I wanted to try them nonetheless. We're huge pancake fans in my house, and I make them often—but I have to say the part I dislike is cooking them, as it can take a bit of time. With this recipe, I found there was nothing to be scared of: These pancakes turned out wonderful. One sheet pan means one huge pancake that you just cut into pieces, which means you have enough to feed a crowd. Hot, fluffy pancakes for everyone!

Preheat the oven to 425°F (218°C). Brush an 11 x 17–inch (33 x 51–cm) baking sheet with 2 tablespoons (30 ml) of the butter.

In a large bowl, whisk together the flour, baking powder, sugar and salt. In another large bowl, whisk together the milk, eggs, vanilla and remaining 6 tablespoons (90 ml) of butter. Pour the milk mixture into the flour mixture and stir just until there is no more flour visible. It's okay to have some lumps in the batter.

Pour the batter into the prepared baking sheet and even out the top with a spatula. Top the batter with your favorite toppings, such as berries or chocolate chips. Bake the pancake for 12 to 15 minutes, or until the pancake is set, cooked through and golden brown on top.

Take the pancake out of the oven and let it cool for 1 to 2 minutes before slicing and serving it. Serve it with the fruit and maple syrup.

RECIPE NOTES

Leftover pancakes will last in an airtight container in the fridge for up to 5 days. Make sure they've cooled to room temperature before storing them. They'll reheat best in the microwave in 10-second intervals until they are warmed through. You can also reheat them in the oven at 325°F (163°C) for 5 to 10 minutes.

To freeze the pancake, slice the pancake into individual pancakes of your desired size. Line a baking sheet with parchment paper, then place the pancakes on the baking sheet with space between them. Freeze them for 1 to 2 hours, or until they are solid, then transfer them to a large airtight container or freezer bag and freeze them for 1 to 2 months. Let the pancakes thaw at room temperature, then reheat them using your preferred method.

NUTRITION INFORMATION

Serving size: 1 pancake; **Calories:** 172; **Carbohydrates:** 22 g; **Protein:** 4 g; **Fat:** 8 g

HAM AND CHEESE BREAKFAST MUFFINS

These ham and cheese breakfast muffins are the ideal breakfast when you're on the go. They are also the perfect use of leftover holiday ham. However, if you're like me, you always have deli ham in your fridge, so you can make these quite often. Everyone loves them, and they're so easy in the morning. Just pop one in the microwave for a few seconds and breakfast is done.

PREP TIME: 10 MINUTES
COOK TIME: 40 MINUTES
TOTAL TIME: 50 MINUTES
SERVES: 12

2 tbsp (30 ml) olive oil
1 onion, chopped
1 red bell pepper, chopped
1 green bell pepper, chopped
2 cups (420 g) frozen cubed hash brown potatoes
½ tsp black pepper
2 cups (268 g) chopped leftover ham
6 large eggs
¼ cup (60 ml) milk
1 tbsp (15 ml) hot sauce
2 cups (240 g) shredded Cheddar cheese

Preheat the oven to 375°F (191°C). Spray a 12-cavity muffin pan with cooking spray.

Heat the oil in a large skillet over medium heat. Add the onion and cook it for about 2 minutes, until it starts to soften.

Add the red bell pepper, green bell pepper, potatoes and black pepper. Stir everything together and cook the mixture for about 5 minutes, until the potatoes start to brown.

Add the ham and cook the mixture for 1 minute, until the ham is heated through. Transfer this mixture to a large bowl and let it cool for about 5 minutes.

In a smaller bowl, whisk together the eggs, milk and hot sauce. Pour this mixture over the ham mixture. Add the Cheddar cheese and stir everything together.

Using an ice cream scoop, completely fill each muffin cavity with the egg and ham mixture.

Bake the muffins for 25 to 30 minutes, or until they are set and the muffins are golden on top.

Let the muffins cool for 2 minutes in the pan before transferring them to a cooling rack.

RECIPE NOTES

I do not use any additional salt in this recipe because the ham is salty enough for my taste, but feel free to add salt if needed.

Store leftover muffins in an airtight container in the fridge for up to 5 days. To serve the muffins, reheat them in the microwave for 30 seconds.

To freeze the muffins, let them cool completely, then wrap each muffin tightly in plastic wrap and place them in an airtight container in the freezer. To serve the muffins, reheat them in the microwave, frozen and unwrapped, for about 1 minute.

NUTRITION INFORMATION

Serving size: 1 serving; **Calories:** 226; **Carbohydrates:** 9 g; **Protein:** 13 g; **Fat:** 15 g

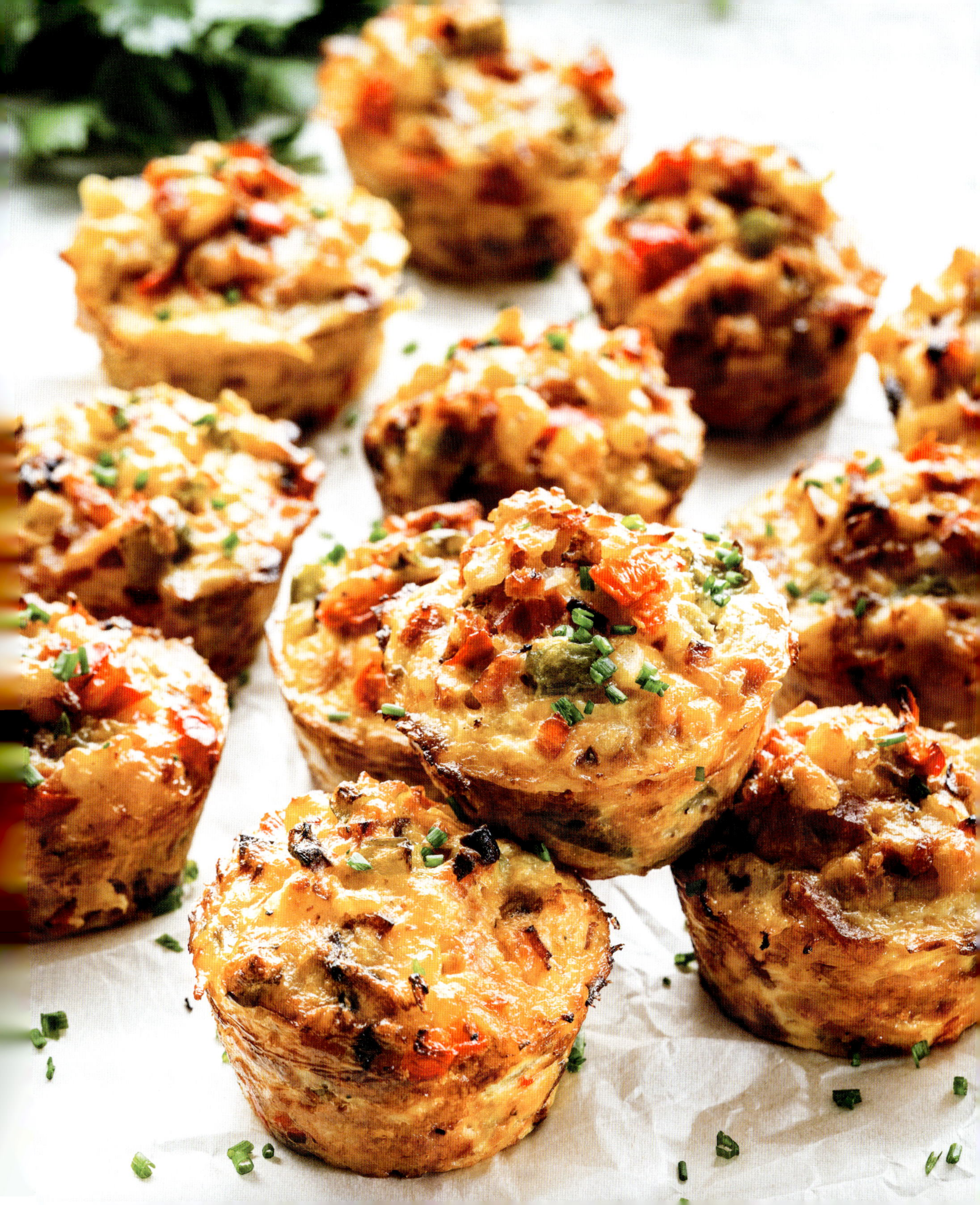

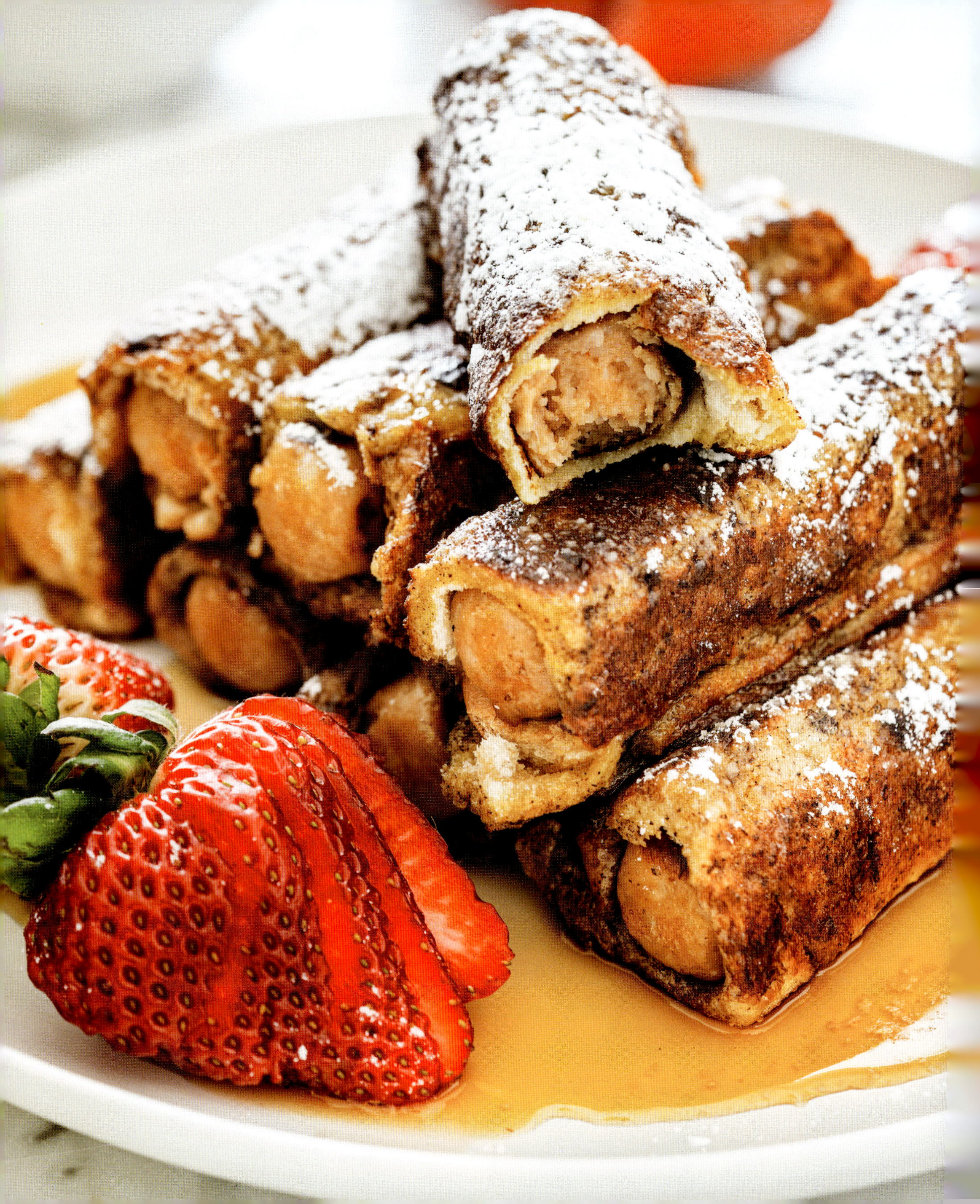

SAUSAGE–FRENCH TOAST ROLL-UPS

PREP TIME: 10 MINUTES
COOK TIME: 20 MINUTES
TOTAL TIME: 30 MINUTES
SERVES: 8

2 large eggs
1 tbsp (15 ml) milk
1 tsp pure vanilla extract
½ tsp ground cinnamon
8 links breakfast sausage
8 slices fresh white sandwich bread
2 tbsp (30 g) unsalted butter
Pure maple syrup, for serving

This is a fun recipe to make with your kids. Not only is it fun to make but it's also fun to eat. With just a few basic ingredients, this is a breakfast or brunch that will be enjoyed by the entire family.

In a large bowl, combine the eggs, milk, vanilla and cinnamon. Set the bowl aside.

Cook the sausages according to the package's instructions.

Roll each slice of bread flat with a rolling pin, then cut off the crusts.

Heat the butter in a large skillet over medium heat.

Place a sausage at the end of each slice of bread and roll the bread up around the sausage. Dip the roll-up into the egg mixture, then fry it on all sides until it is golden brown, about 4 minutes total. Repeat this process with the remaining ingredients.

Serve the roll-ups with the maple syrup.

RECIPE NOTES

Store the roll-ups in an airtight container or large plastic bag in the fridge. They will last for 3 to 4 days.

To freeze the roll-ups, first freeze them on a baking sheet lined with parchment paper, then covered with plastic, for 1 hour. Transfer them to a freezer bag or airtight container, making sure they are separated so they don't all freeze in one block. Freeze the roll-ups for 2 to 3 months.

NUTRITION INFORMATION

Serving size: 1 serving; **Calories:** 290; **Carbohydrates:** 13 g; **Protein:** 25 g; **Fat:** 14 g

BAKED BREAKFAST TAQUITOS

PREP TIME: 10 MINUTES
COOK TIME: 25 MINUTES
TOTAL TIME: 35 MINUTES
SERVES: 16

4 tbsp (60 g) butter, melted, divided
1 lb (448 g) hot Italian sausage, casings removed
1 onion, chopped
3 cloves garlic, minced
½ red bell pepper, chopped
½ green bell pepper, chopped
1 tbsp (9 g) Italian seasoning (optional)
¼ tsp salt, or as needed
¼ tsp black pepper, or as needed
6 large eggs
16 small whole-wheat or white flour tortillas
1 cup (120 g) shredded Cheddar cheese
Salsa, for serving
Sour cream, for serving

NUTRITION INFORMATION

Serving size: 1 taquito; **Calories:** 272; **Carbohydrates:** 17 g; **Protein:** 10 g; **Fat:** 17 g

This is a recipe that's been on the blog for a few years now, and it's one that's quite popular. I love taquitos, especially the breakfast kind. They're baked, which means they are healthier than the fried variety, but even so they are crispy, cheesy and just full of delicious breakfast goodness.

Preheat the oven to 400°F (204°C). Lightly grease a 9 x 13–inch (27 x 39–cm) baking sheet with some of the butter.

In a large skillet over medium heat, cook the sausage for 5 minutes, until it is no longer pink. Drain any excess grease if preferred. Add the onion and garlic and cook the mixture for 5 minutes, until the onion is soft. Add the red bell pepper and green bell pepper and cook the mixture for 1 minute. Season the mixture with the Italian seasoning (if using), salt and black pepper.

In a medium bowl, beat the eggs. Pour the eggs over the sausage mixture and cook the ingredients for 3 to 5 minutes, until the eggs are scrambled.

Lay a tortilla on a work surface. Top the tortilla with 2 tablespoons (30 g) of the sausage-egg mixture. Top the sausage-egg mixture with 1 to 2 tablespoons (8 to 16 g) of the Cheddar cheese. Tightly roll up the tortilla and place it in the prepared baking dish. Brush the taquito with some of the remaining butter. Repeat this process with the remaining filling and tortillas.

Bake the taquitos for about 15 minutes, or until the tortillas are golden and crispy.

Serve the taquitos with the salsa and sour cream.

RECIPE NOTES

Taquitos are best served while they are still warm. If you have leftovers, store them in an airtight container in the fridge for 3 to 5 days. They will get soggy, so to reheat them, place them in a preheated 400°F (204°C) oven for about 10 minutes, or until the taquitos are heated through and they start to crisp up again.

These taquitos are perfect for frozen make-ahead meals. Here's how you freeze them: Bake them for 10 minutes, then let them cool completely. Spread them on a large baking sheet in a single layer and place this baking sheet in the freezer for 1 to 2 hours. After the taquitos have frozen, transfer them to freezer bags or an airtight container. The flash-freezing is required so the taquitos don't stick to one another. Freeze the taquitos for 2 to 3 months. When you are ready to bake them, remove them from the freezer and place them, frozen, on a baking sheet. Bake them at 400°F (204°C) for 10 minutes, or until they are heated through and crispy.

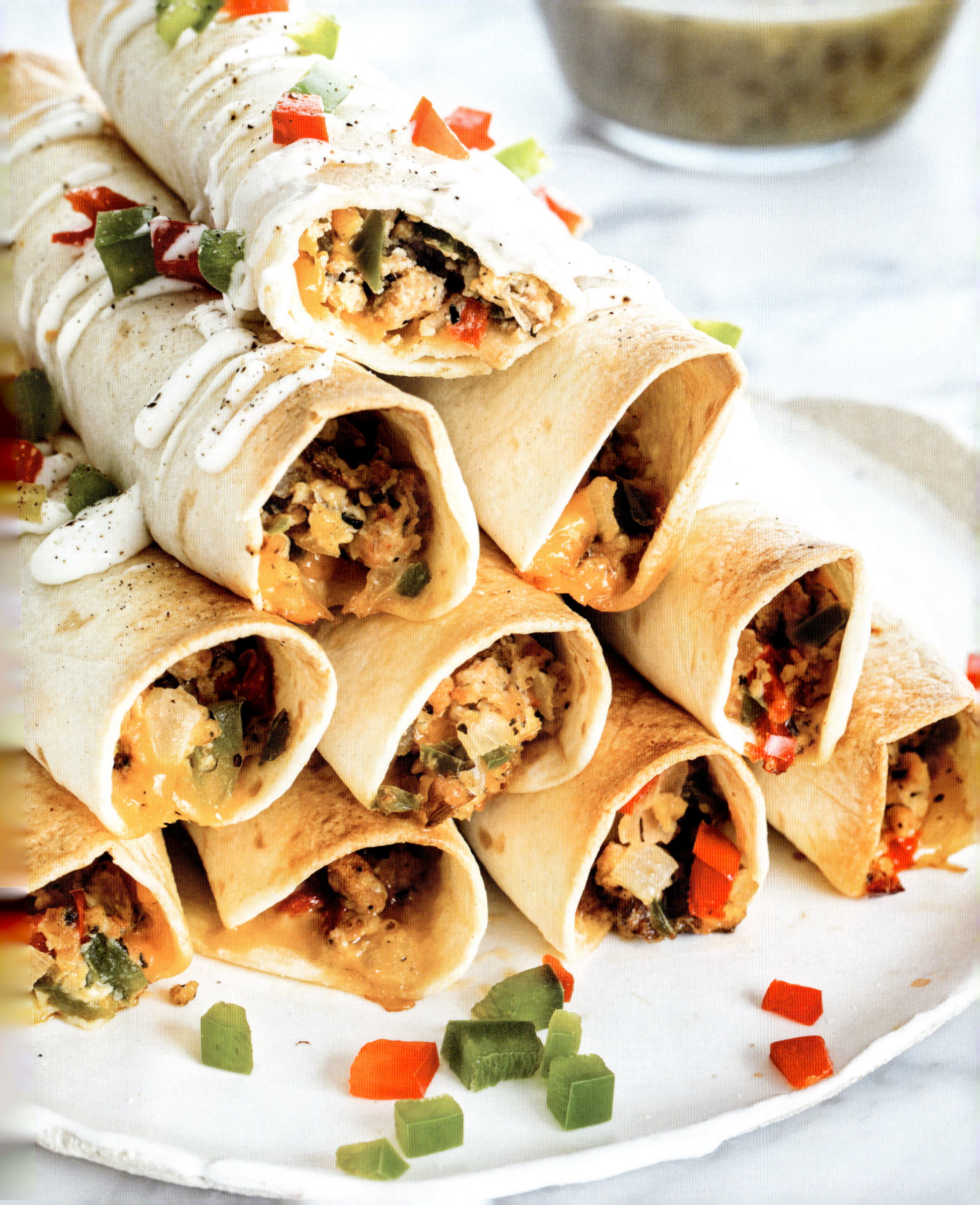

LUNCH

WHEN PICKING WHICH LUNCH RECIPES from my blog to include in this book, I was looking for recipes that are crazy quick to make but still loaded with flavor. When I had my corporate job, lunch usually consisted of boring cafeteria soups and sandwiches. While soups and sandwiches are the ideal lunch meal, life is too short to eat a boring lunch!

I think lunch is often the forgotten meal because of our busy lives, but with a fresh coat of paint, lunch can shine again. I often skipped lunch, then I'd come home and raid the fridge. There's a time and place for that PB&J, but sometimes we just need to devote a little time to that midday meal—having the right lunch will give us that extra boost to continue to be productive in the afternoon and hold us until dinner.

Requiring just a few minutes and a few simple ingredients, lunch has never looked better. Sometimes all you need is a little time to prep ahead: With a bit of creativity, you can trade that boring cafeteria salad for a Quick and Easy Cobb Salad (page 260) or Thai Chicken Salad (page 263). Not only is it cheaper to cook your meals at home but they are also tastier and healthier. Say goodbye to settling for the same dish week after week and mix up your midday meal routine with one of these easy, quick and delicious lunches.

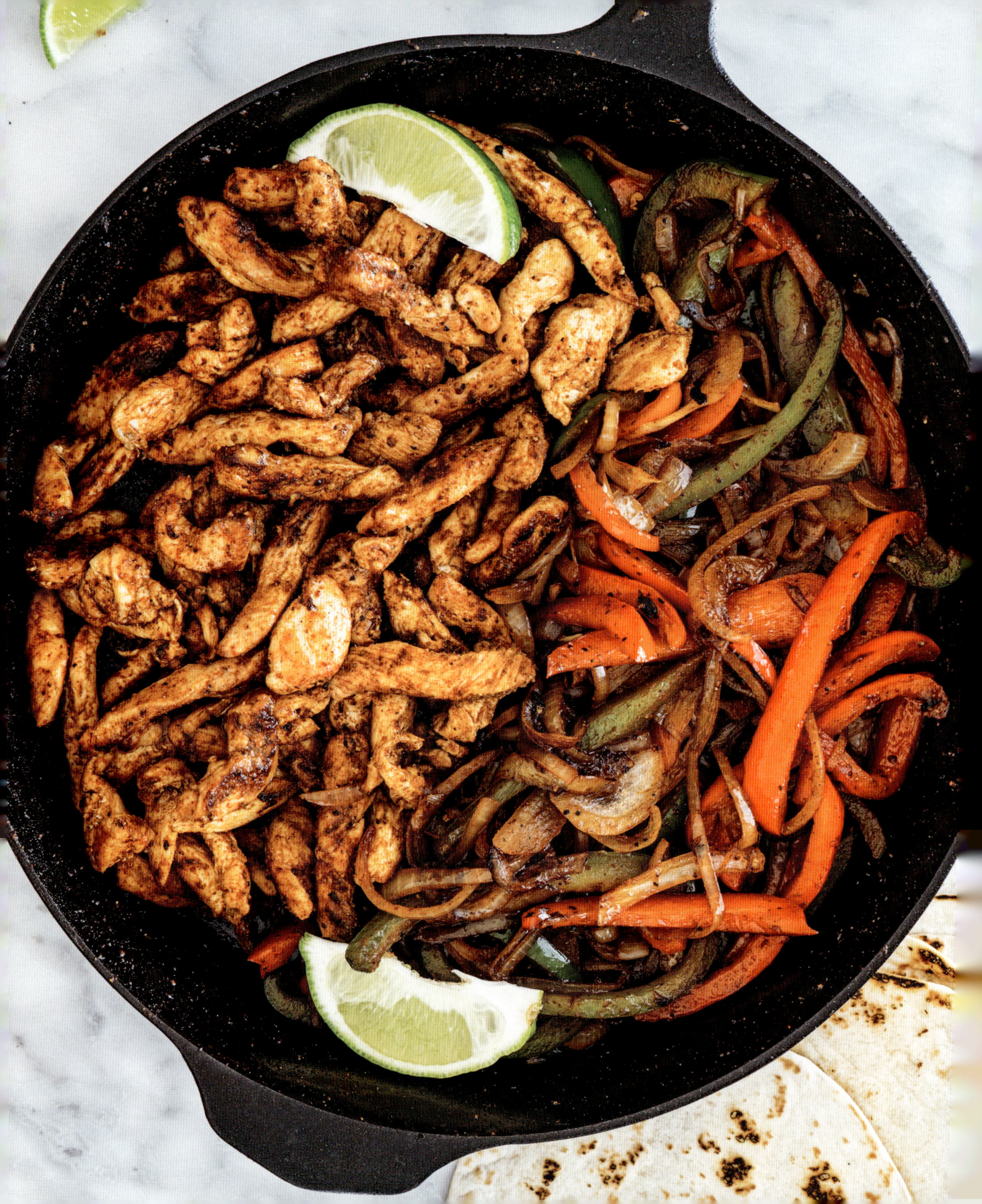

EASY CHICKEN FAJITAS

Chicken fajitas are a classic, and they're incredibly easy to make. They're perfect for lunch or a weeknight meal. Mine include tender pieces of chicken breast, perfectly seasoned with my homemade fajita seasoning, bell peppers and onions, all served on tortillas. I love to serve these with my Homemade Salsa (page 336) and a dollop of sour cream.

PREP TIME: 15 MINUTES
COOK TIME: 20 MINUTES
TOTAL TIME: 45 MINUTES
SERVES: 8

FAJITA SEASONING
1 tbsp (9 g) chili powder
1 tsp ground cumin
1 tsp paprika
¼ tsp cayenne pepper
1 tsp salt
1 tsp black pepper

FAJITAS
2 tbsp (30 ml) olive oil, divided
1 lb (448 g) boneless, skinless chicken breasts, sliced into ½" (13-mm)-thick strips
1 onion, sliced into ¼" (6-mm)-thick strips
1 red bell pepper, sliced into ¼" (6-mm)-thick strips
1 green bell pepper, sliced into ¼" (6-mm)-thick strips
1 jalapeño, chopped (optional)
8 medium tortillas
Homemade Salsa (page 336, optional)
Sour cream (optional)

To make the fajita seasoning, combine the chili powder, cumin, paprika, cayenne pepper, salt and black pepper in a small bowl.

Heat 1 tablespoon (15 ml) of the oil in a large skillet over medium-high heat. Add the chicken to the skillet, sprinkle about half of the fajita seasoning over the chicken and toss it to coat it in the seasoning. Cook the chicken for 5 to 10 minutes, until it's no longer pink and it's slightly charred but not burned. Transfer the chicken to a plate and set it aside.

If the skillet is dry, add the remaining 1 tablespoon (15 ml) of oil. When the oil is hot, add the onion and cook it for 2 minutes, until it's partially translucent. Add the red bell pepper, green bell pepper, jalapeño (if using) and the remaining fajita seasoning and toss everything together. Cook the vegetables for 3 to 5 minutes, until the bell peppers are crisp-tender. Add the chicken back to the skillet and toss it with the vegetables.

Serve the fajitas in the tortillas and top each serving with the Homemade Salsa (if using) and sour cream (if using).

NUTRITION INFORMATION

Serving size: 1 fajita; **Calories:** 274; **Carbohydrates:** 32 g; **Protein:** 18 g; **Fat:** 8 g

QUICK AND EASY COBB SALAD

Stop spending astronomical amounts on salads! With a little prep work, you can have fancy salads, like this gorgeous Cobb salad, for a fraction of the cost. If you prep over the weekend by frying the bacon, boiling the eggs and buying a rotisserie chicken—the leftovers of which you can use in a casserole—all you have to do is assemble your salad the night before you plan to eat it. Your coworkers will envy you when they see you pulling this salad from your lunch box.

PREP TIME: 15 MINUTES
COOK TIME: NONE
TOTAL TIME: 15 MINUTES
SERVES: 6

DRESSING
½ cup (120 ml) olive oil
3 tbsp (45 ml) red wine vinegar
1 tbsp (15 g) Dijon mustard
2 cloves garlic, minced
1 tsp sugar
1 tbsp (3 g) Italian seasoning
½ tsp salt, or as needed
½ tsp black pepper, or as needed

SALAD
1 head romaine lettuce, roughly chopped
2 boneless, skinless chicken breasts, cooked and diced (see Recipe Notes)
1 avocado, thinly sliced
6 slices bacon, fried and chopped
4 oz (112 g) crumbled blue cheese or feta cheese
6 oz (168 g) cherry tomatoes, halved
4 large hard-boiled eggs, sliced

To make the dressing, combine the oil, vinegar, mustard, garlic, sugar, Italian seasoning, salt and black pepper in a medium jar. Secure the jar's lid and shake the jar well to blend the dressing. Set the dressing aside.

To make the salad, spread out the lettuce on a large serving platter, then top the lettuce with the chicken, avocado, bacon, blue cheese, tomatoes and eggs.

Drizzle the dressing over the salad and toss well. Serve it immediately.

RECIPE NOTES

You can use the breast from a rotisserie chicken to save you some time.

Your salad will last anywhere between 1 and 5 days, depending on if you have already dressed the salad. Undressed salad will keep for a few days longer than dressed salad, typically 3 to 5 days. If the salad is already dressed, it's best that day. It might last another day in the fridge, but the lettuce will get soggy.

NUTRITION INFORMATION

Serving size: 1 serving; **Calories:** 501; **Carbohydrates:** 10 g; **Protein:** 22 g; **Fat:** 42 g

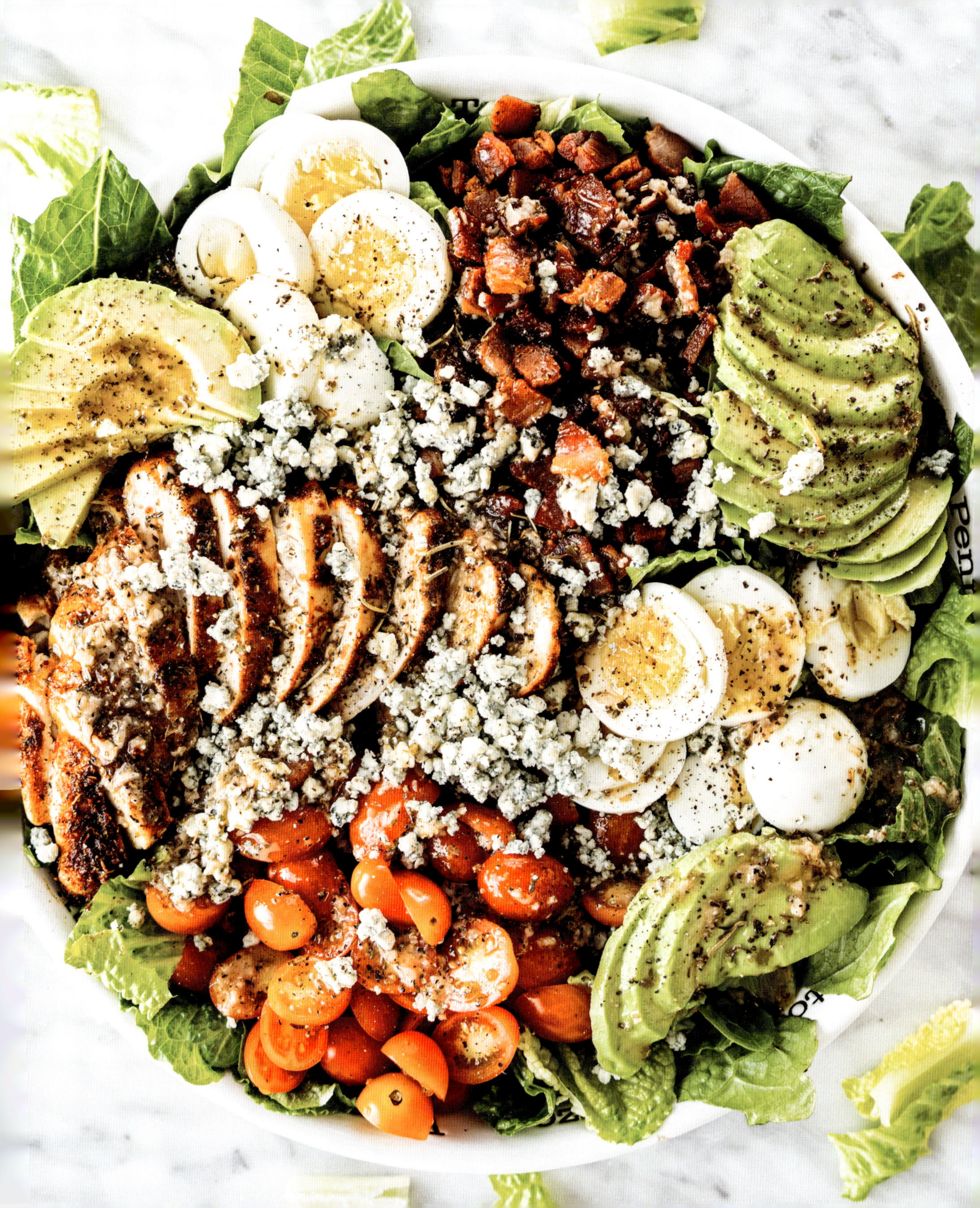

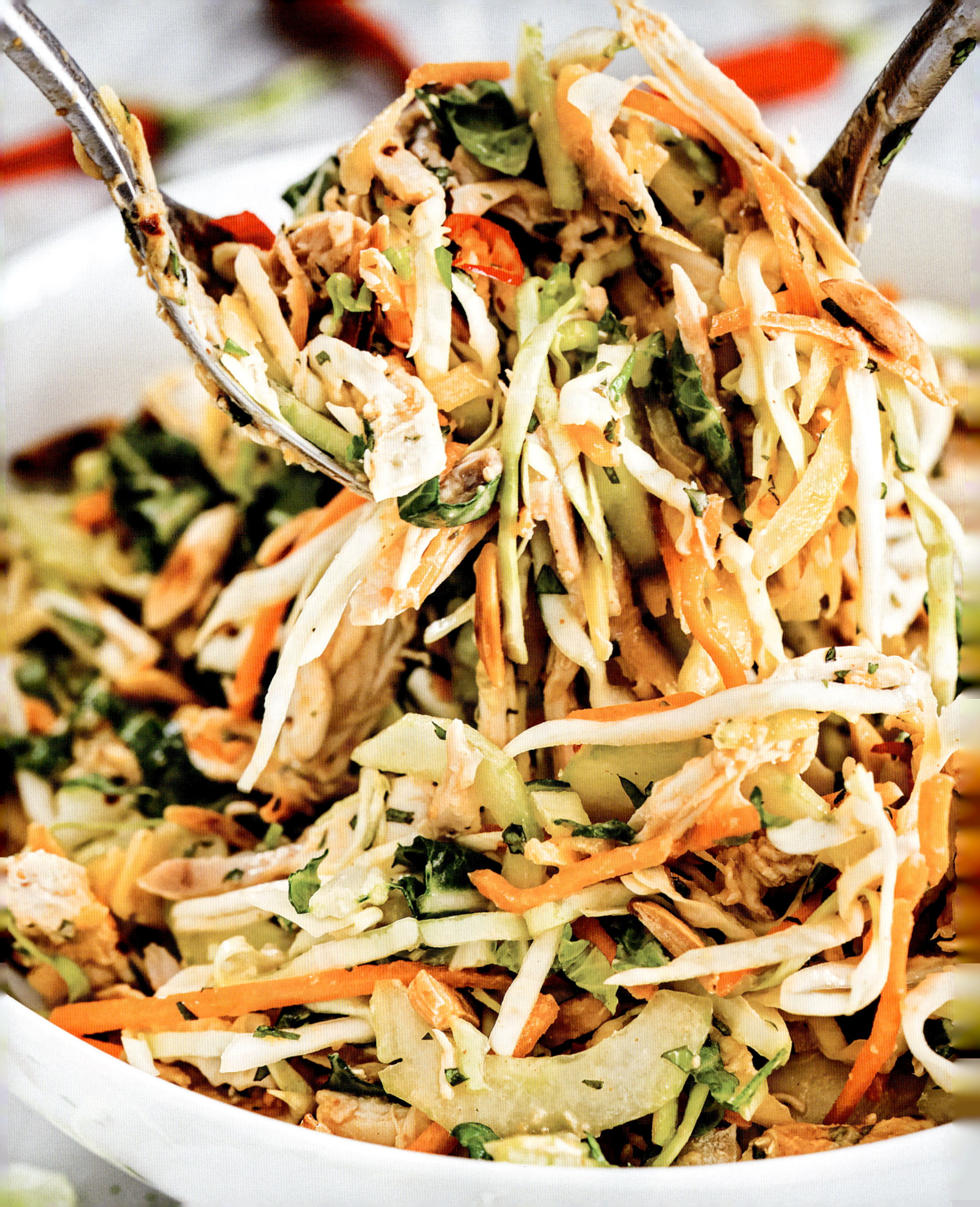

THAI CHICKEN SALAD

This Thai chicken salad has been on my blog for many years, and is very popular with my readers. It features papaya, cabbage, carrots and a spicy peanut dressing. It's a filling and healthy meal on its own. Prep all the salad ingredients the night before, store your dressing in a small Mason jar and then, when you're ready to eat, just toss it all together and enjoy!

PREP TIME: 20 MINUTES
COOK TIME: NONE
TOTAL TIME: 20 MINUTES
SERVES: 8

DRESSING

- 3 tbsp (45 ml) fresh lime juice
- 2 tbsp (30 ml) olive oil
- 2 tbsp (30 ml) low-sodium soy sauce
- 1 tbsp (15 ml) honey
- 2 tbsp (24 g) peanut butter (see Recipe Notes)
- 1 tsp fish sauce
- ¼ tsp red pepper flakes
- ½ tsp chili-garlic sauce

SALAD

- 1 cup (110 g) shredded carrots
- 1 cup (240 g) shredded green papaya
- 1 cup (120 g) peeled, seeded and sliced cucumber
- 2 cups (480 g) bok choy
- 1 red chili pepper, sliced
- 2 chicken breasts, cooked and shredded or cut into small pieces
- ¼ cup (12 g) chopped fresh mint
- ½ cup (55 g) slivered almonds or peanuts
- 3 cups (1 kg) green cabbage

To make the dressing, whisk together the lime juice, oil, soy sauce, honey, peanut butter, fish sauce, red pepper flakes and chili-garlic sauce in a small bowl. Alternatively, combine the ingredients in a small Mason jar, secure the jar's lid and shake the jar until the ingredients form a dressing.

To make the salad, combine the carrots, papaya, cucumber, bok choy, chili pepper, chicken, mint, almonds and cabbage in a large bowl. Add the dressing. Toss everything well and serve the salad.

RECIPE NOTES

If needed, you can microwave the peanut butter for 10 to 15 seconds to soften it for easier mixing.

If you anticipate leftovers, I would leave the dressing off the salad and toss the two together as needed. The veggies tend to get soggy after a day of sitting with the dressing and are not as appetizing.

NUTRITION INFORMATION

Serving size: 1 serving; **Calories:** 166; **Carbohydrates:** 12 g; **Protein:** 10 g; **Fat:** 10 g

EASY THAI STEAK SALAD

This Thai steak salad is a popular one and for good reason. It's loaded with delicious stuff! I'm talking Thai-inspired marinated sirloin steak and a salad that's not only easy to make but also delicious and healthy.

PREP TIME: 15 MINUTES
MARINATING TIME: 4 HOURS
COOK TIME: 15 MINUTES
REST TIME: 10 MINUTES
TOTAL TIME: 4 HOURS, 40 MINUTES
SERVES: 2

STEAK
¼ cup (60 ml) low-sodium soy sauce
2 tbsp (30 ml) molasses
1 tbsp (9 g) minced fresh ginger
3 cloves garlic, minced
1 Thai red chili pepper, chopped
1 tbsp (15 ml) fresh lime juice
1 (8-oz [224-g]) sirloin steak

DRESSING
2 tbsp (30 ml) melted coconut oil
3 tbsp (45 ml) low-sodium soy sauce
1 tsp fish sauce
1 tbsp (15 g) brown sugar
1 Thai red chili pepper, chopped
2 tsp (4 g) lime zest
1 tbsp (15 ml) fresh lime juice

SALAD
4 cups (188 g) lettuce
1 red bell pepper, sliced into long strips
½ English cucumber, sliced
½ cup (24 g) chopped fresh cilantro
¼ cup (12 g) chopped fresh mint
2 tbsp (18 g) peanuts, chopped (optional)

To make the steak, whisk together the soy sauce, molasses, ginger, garlic, chili pepper and lime juice in a small bowl. Pour the marinade into a large ziplock bag, then add the steak. Seal the bag and toss the steak around in the marinade a bit. Place the bag in the fridge and let the steak marinate for 4 hours, or up to overnight. The longer it marinates, the better it will taste.

To prepare the dressing, whisk together the oil, soy sauce, fish sauce, brown sugar, chili pepper, lime zest and lime juice.

Grill the steak to your preferred doneness; I prefer mine medium-rare, so for medium I usually grill it for 7 minutes per side. Let the steak rest for 10 minutes after you have grilled it, then slice the steak across the grain.

To make the salad, toss together the lettuce, bell pepper, cucumber, cilantro and mint. Pour the dressing over the salad and toss it well. Arrange the salad on a platter and place the sliced steak over the salad. Top the salad with the peanuts (if using).

RECIPE NOTES

If you anticipate storing leftovers, use your dressing accordingly. The steak salad will last longer in the fridge, up to 5 days, if it is undressed. No one wants a soggy salad!

To store undressed salad, place it in a large bowl, drape it with a paper towel to help collect moisture and cover the bowl with plastic wrap.

NUTRITION INFORMATION

Serving size: 1 serving; **Calories:** 529; **Carbohydrates:** 46 g; **Protein:** 34 g; **Fat:** 25 g

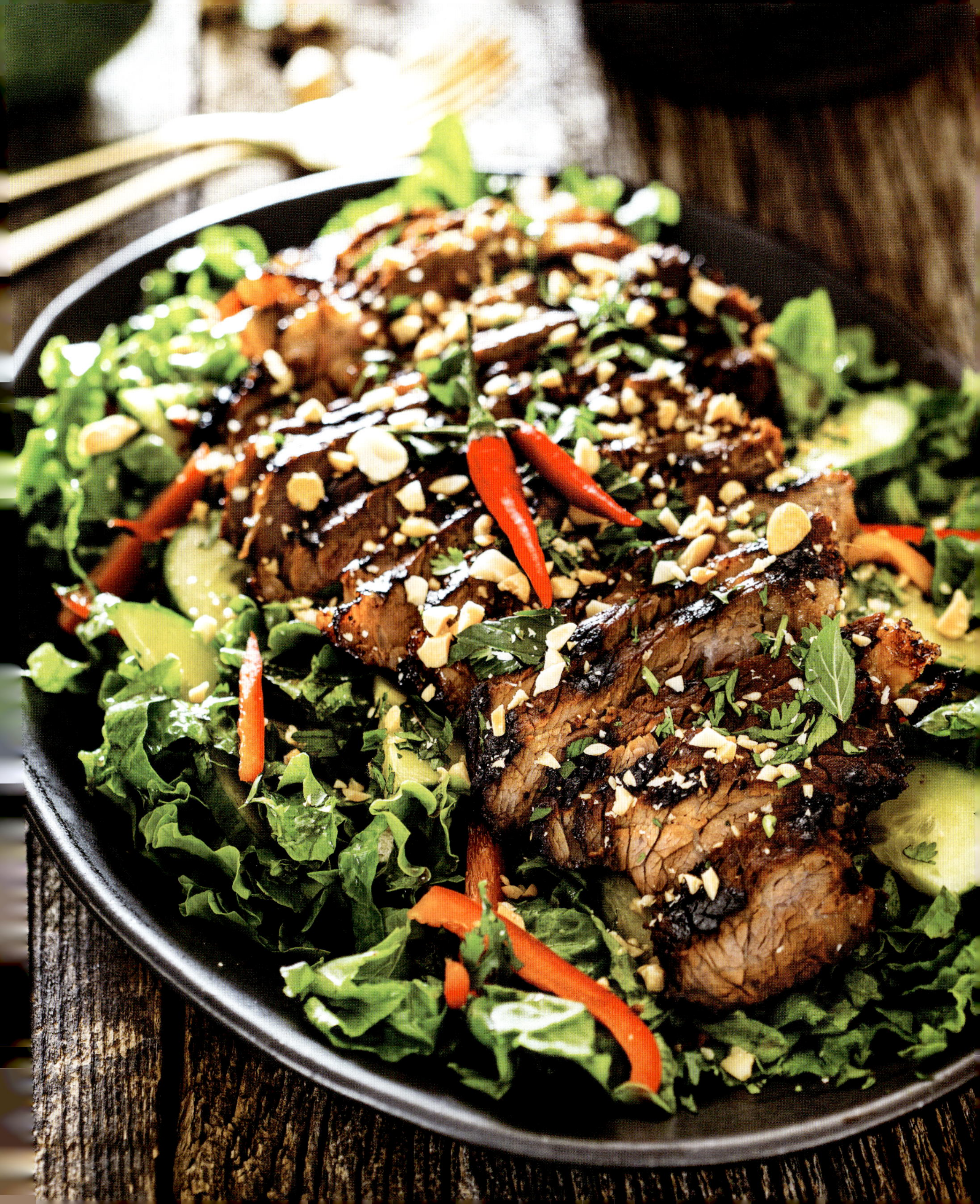

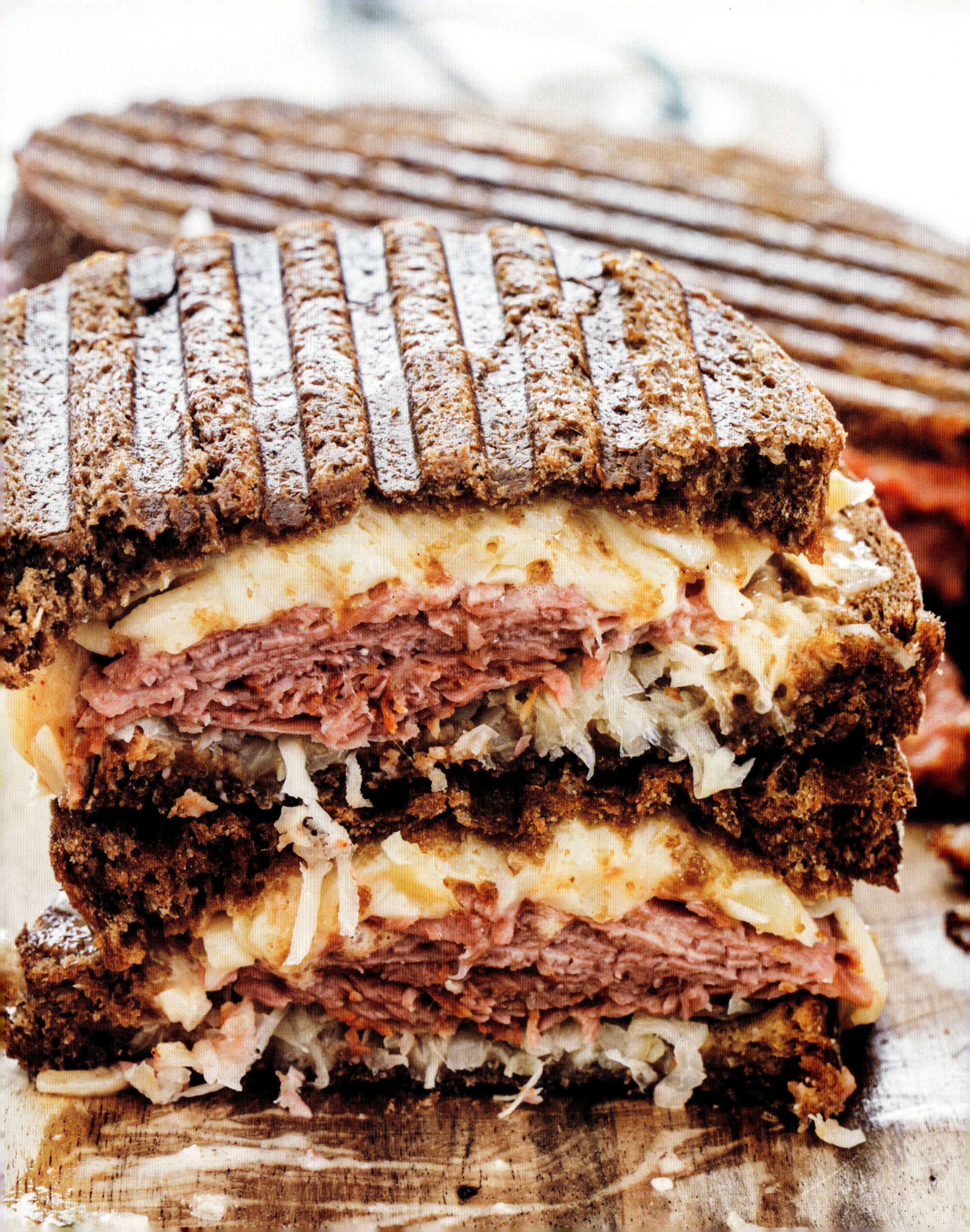

REUBEN SANDWICH

The Reuben is one of my all-time favorite sandwiches. What's not to love? You've got a hot sandwich loaded with corned beef, Swiss cheese, sauerkraut and Thousand Island dressing. This sandwich is undeniably satisfying! If prepping this the night before, store the ingredients separately and assemble your sandwich when you're ready to eat.

PREP TIME: 5 MINUTES
COOK TIME: 10 MINUTES
TOTAL TIME: 15 MINUTES
SERVES: 2

4 slices dark rye bread
1 cup (108 g) shredded Swiss cheese
4 tbsp (60 ml) Thousand Island dressing
8 oz (224 g) corned beef or pastrami, thinly sliced
1 cup (142 g) sauerkraut
4 tbsp (60 g) unsalted butter, softened, divided

Lay out 2 slices of the bread on a cutting board. Top each with ½ cup (54 g) of the Swiss cheese. Drizzle 2 tablespoons (30 ml) of the Thousand Island dressing on each slice, then top each with 4 ounces (112 g) of the corned beef. Place ½ cup (71 g) of the sauerkraut on top of the corned beef, then top each sandwich with another slice of bread. Spread 1 tablespoon (15 g) of the butter on the outside of the top slice of bread.

Heat a large skillet over medium heat. Place both sandwiches in the skillet, buttered side down, and cook the sandwiches for about 3 minutes, until the bottom slice of bread is golden. Spread 1 tablespoon (15 g) of the butter on each of the top slices of bread. Flip the sandwiches and cook them for 2 to 3 minutes, or until the opposite slice of bread is golden.

Serve the sandwiches right away.

NUTRITION INFORMATION

Serving size: 1 sandwich; **Calories:** 931; **Carbohydrates:** 42 g; **Protein:** 38 g; **Fat:** 68 g

MEDITERRANEAN GRILLED CHICKEN SALAD

PREP TIME: 15 MINUTES
MARINATING TIME: 30 MINUTES
COOK TIME: 10 MINUTES
TOTAL TIME: 55 MINUTES
SERVES: 4

MARINADE
¼ cup (60 ml) olive oil
¼ cup (60 ml) fresh lemon juice
1 tbsp (9 g) dried oregano
1 tbsp (9 g) dried basil
3 green onions, chopped
½ tsp salt
¼ tsp black pepper

SALAD
4 boneless, skinless chicken breasts (see Recipe Note)
1 head romaine lettuce, chopped
1 English cucumber, sliced
½ red onion, chopped
1 green bell pepper, chopped
2 cups (300 g) cocktail tomatoes, chopped
½ cup (65 g) Kalamata olives
½ cup (75 g) crumbled feta cheese
1 avocado, sliced

This grilled chicken salad not only boasts Mediterranean flavors but also is a hearty meal that will leave you satisfied. Get ready to enjoy marinated Greek chicken with lots of fresh veggies, all topped with some feta cheese.

DRESSING
¼ cup (60 ml) olive oil
¼ cup (60 ml) lemon juice
1 tsp dried oregano
1 tsp dried basil
¼ tsp salt
¼ tsp black pepper

Hummus, for serving (optional)
Pita chips, for serving (optional)

To make the marinade, whisk together the oil, lemon juice, oregano, basil, green onions, salt and black pepper in a shallow dish.

To make the salad, add the chicken to the marinade and make sure it is fully covered in the marinade. Cover the dish with plastic wrap and refrigerate the chicken for about 30 minutes, or up to 4 hours.

Heat the grill to about 400°F (204°C). In the meantime, make the dressing. In a small bowl, whisk together the oil, lemon juice, oregano, basil, salt and black pepper. Set the dressing aside.

In a large bowl, toss together the lettuce, cucumber, red onion, bell pepper, tomatoes and olives.

Grill the chicken for about 5 minutes per side, or until it is no longer pink and its internal temperature reaches 165°F (74°C). Discard the remaining marinade. Let the chicken cool for about 5 minutes before slicing it into ½-inch (13-mm)-thick slices.

Drizzle the dressing over the salad and toss it well. Add the feta cheese to the salad and mix everything together. Top the salad with the chicken and avocado. Serve it with the hummus (if using) and pita chips (if using) on the side.

RECIPE NOTE
You can bake the chicken breasts at 450°F (232°C) for 20 minutes instead of grilling them.

NUTRITION INFORMATION
Serving size: 1 serving; **Calories:** 575; **Carbohydrates:** 19 g; **Protein:** 30 g; **Fat:** 44 g

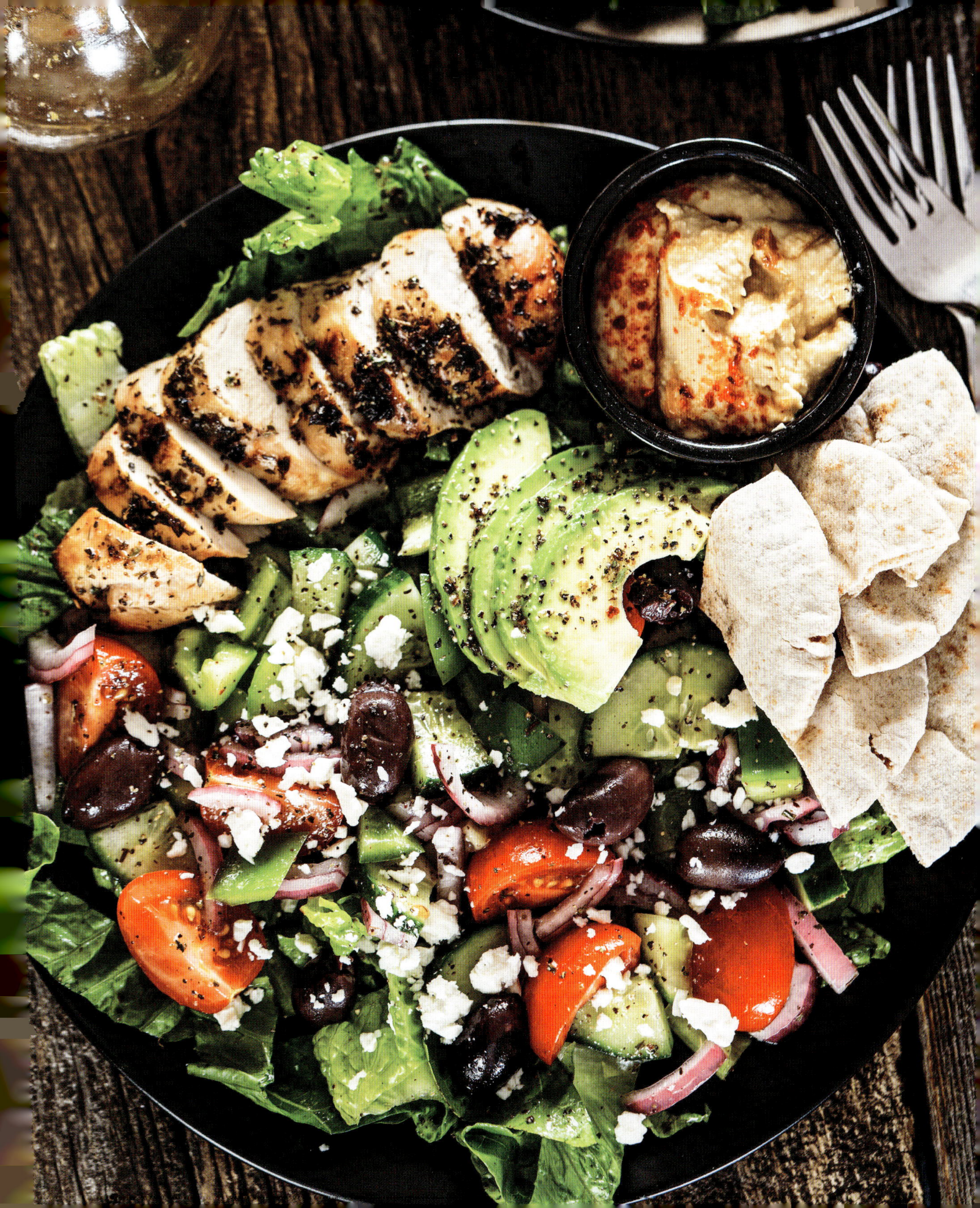

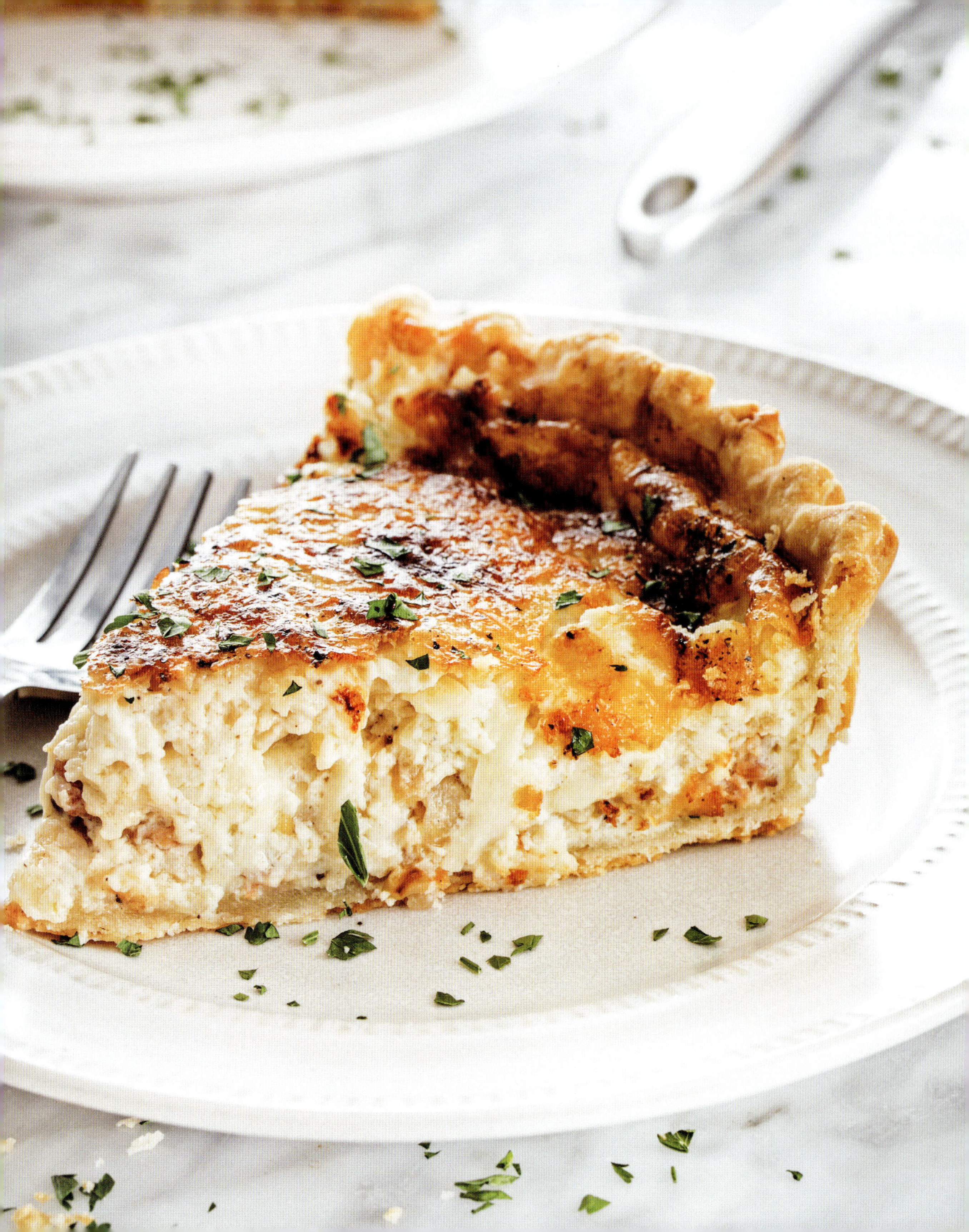

QUICHE LORRAINE

This Quiche Lorraine is such a classic French dish. It's light and fluffy, incredibly cheesy, loaded with bacon and contained in a wonderfully flaky crust. It's surprisingly easy to make and a popular lunch meal. Make it once and enjoy lunch for the rest of the week. Just pop a slice in the microwave and enjoy!

PREP TIME: 30 MINUTES
COOK TIME: 1 HOUR
TOTAL TIME: 1 HOUR, 30 MINUTES
SERVES: 8

- 1 (9" [27-cm]) frozen or fresh pie crust
- 8 strips bacon, chopped
- 1 onion, thinly sliced
- 4 large eggs
- 1½ cups (360 ml) heavy cream
- 1 cup (108 g) shredded Gruyère or Swiss cheese
- ¼ tsp ground nutmeg
- ¼ tsp salt, or as needed
- ¼ tsp black pepper, or as needed
- ½ cup (90 g) grated Parmesan cheese (see Recipe Notes)
- 1 tbsp (3 g) chopped fresh parsley or chives (optional)

Place the pie crust in a deep 9½-inch (29-cm) quiche pan or a shallow 11-inch (33-cm) quiche pan, pressing the crust into the corners of the pan.

Use a rolling pin to roll over the perimeter of the quiche pan to cut the excess dough from the edges. Line the crust with parchment paper and fill it with pie weights or uncooked beans or rice.

Preheat the oven to 425°F (218°C). Bake the crust for 12 to 15 minutes. Remove the pie weights and parchment paper. Reduce the oven's temperature to 375°F (191°C) and bake the crust for 5 minutes.

While the crust is baking, cook the bacon in a large skillet over medium-high heat for about 5 minutes, until the bacon is crisp or done to your liking. Remove the bacon from the skillet and transfer it to a plate lined with paper towels to drain.

Remove all but 1 tablespoon (15 ml) of the bacon drippings from the skillet. Add the onion and cook it for about 5 minutes, until it is translucent and starting to brown.

In a large bowl, whisk together the eggs, heavy cream, Gruyère cheese, nutmeg, salt and black pepper.

Sprinkle the bacon over the bottom of the baked crust, then top the bacon with the cooked onion. Carefully pour the egg mixture over the onion. Top the egg mixture evenly with the Parmesan cheese.

Transfer the quiche to a large baking sheet. Bake the quiche for 35 to 40 minutes, or until the top is golden. The center should be a bit jiggly, but the rest of the quiche should be set.

Garnish the quiche with the parsley (if using) and serve.

NUTRITION INFORMATION

Serving size: 1 serving; **Calories:** 499; **Carbohydrates:** 16 g; **Protein:** 16 g; **Fat:** 41 g

RECIPE NOTES

Freshly grated Parmesan cheese is best in this dish.

Store the quiche in an airtight container in the fridge for 3 to 4 days. You can also freeze it for 3 to 4 months. Because it is a custard, quiche must be refrigerated within 2 hours of cooling.

The best way to reheat this quiche is to cover it with aluminum foil and bake it in an oven preheated to 325°F (163°C) for about 15 minutes.

VIETNAMESE FISH TACOS

I had never had Vietnamese food until we moved to Calgary, so I was excited to try it. I loved it so much that we used to go at least once a week to a Vietnamese restaurant for lunch, which is what inspired me to make these fish tacos. Featuring commonly used ingredients in Vietnamese cooking—like fish sauce, mint and cilantro—these fish tacos are not only incredibly tasty but they are also healthy and refreshing.

PREP TIME: 20 MINUTES
MARINATING TIME: 1 HOUR
COOK TIME: 20 MINUTES
TOTAL TIME: 1 HOUR, 40 MINUTES
SERVES: 6

MARINADE AND FISH
1 tsp ground turmeric
1 tsp minced fresh ginger
2 cloves garlic, minced
1 tsp sugar
1 tsp fish sauce (see Recipe Notes)
1 tbsp (15 ml) fresh lime juice
¼ tsp salt, or as needed
¼ tsp black pepper, or as needed
1½ lb (672 g) skinless halibut fillets, cut into 2" (6-cm) pieces (see Recipe Notes)

SALSA
6 green onions, chopped
½ red onion, chopped
2 cups (150 g) cherry tomatoes, chopped
¼ cup (12 g) chopped fresh basil
¼ cup (12 g) chopped fresh mint
¼ cup (12 g) chopped fresh cilantro
1 tsp fish sauce
2 tbsp (30 ml) fresh lime juice
Salt, as needed
Black pepper, as needed

TACOS
2 tbsp (30 ml) vegetable oil, divided
12 medium tortillas
2 cups (682 g) shredded cabbage
Sriracha sauce, as needed

To make the marinade and fish, combine the turmeric, ginger, garlic, sugar, fish sauce, lime juice, salt and black pepper in a medium bowl. Add the halibut pieces to the bowl and toss them in the marinade, making sure each piece is fully coated. Cover the bowl with plastic wrap and refrigerate it for 1 to 2 hours.

Meanwhile, make the salsa. In a medium bowl, toss together the green onions, red onion, tomatoes, basil, mint, cilantro, fish sauce, lime juice, salt and black pepper. Refrigerate the salsa until you are ready to assemble the tacos.

To make the tacos, heat 1 tablespoon (15 ml) of the oil in a large nonstick skillet over medium heat. Add about half of the halibut pieces and fry them for 2 to 4 minutes per side, until they are light golden brown. Remove the halibut pieces from the skillet and set them aside. Add the remaining 1 tablespoon (15 ml) of oil and repeat the process with the remaining half of the fish.

To assemble the tacos, fill each tortilla with some of the shredded cabbage, then with the halibut. Feel free to flake the fish a bit with a fork if necessary. Top the tacos with the salsa, then drizzle them with some Sriracha sauce.

RECIPE NOTES
Fish sauce can be substituted with low-sodium soy sauce.

You can use any type of whitefish that you prefer or that is available to you.

NUTRITION INFORMATION
Serving size: 2 tacos; **Calories:** 349; **Carbohydrates:** 37 g; **Protein:** 27 g; **Fat:** 10 g

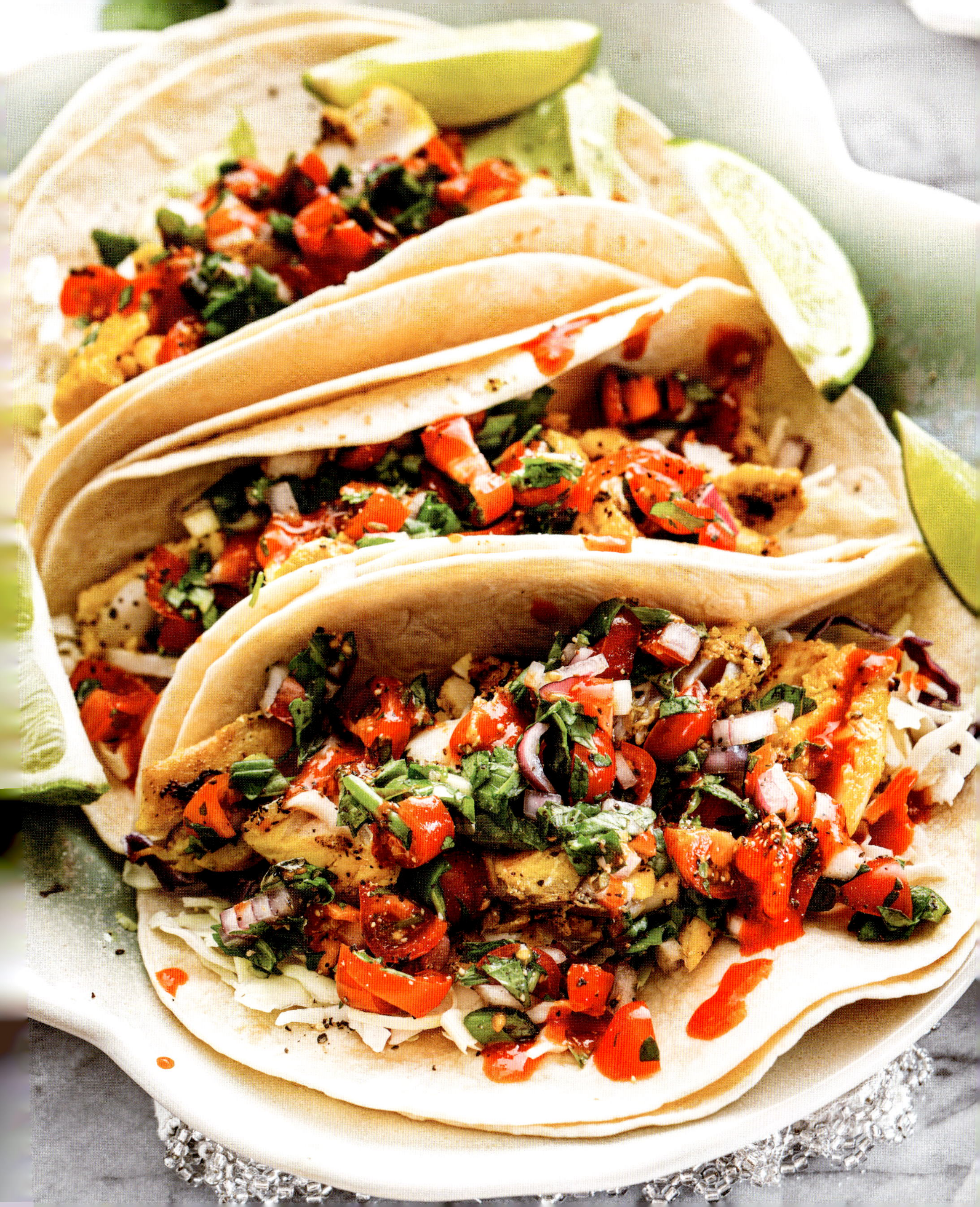

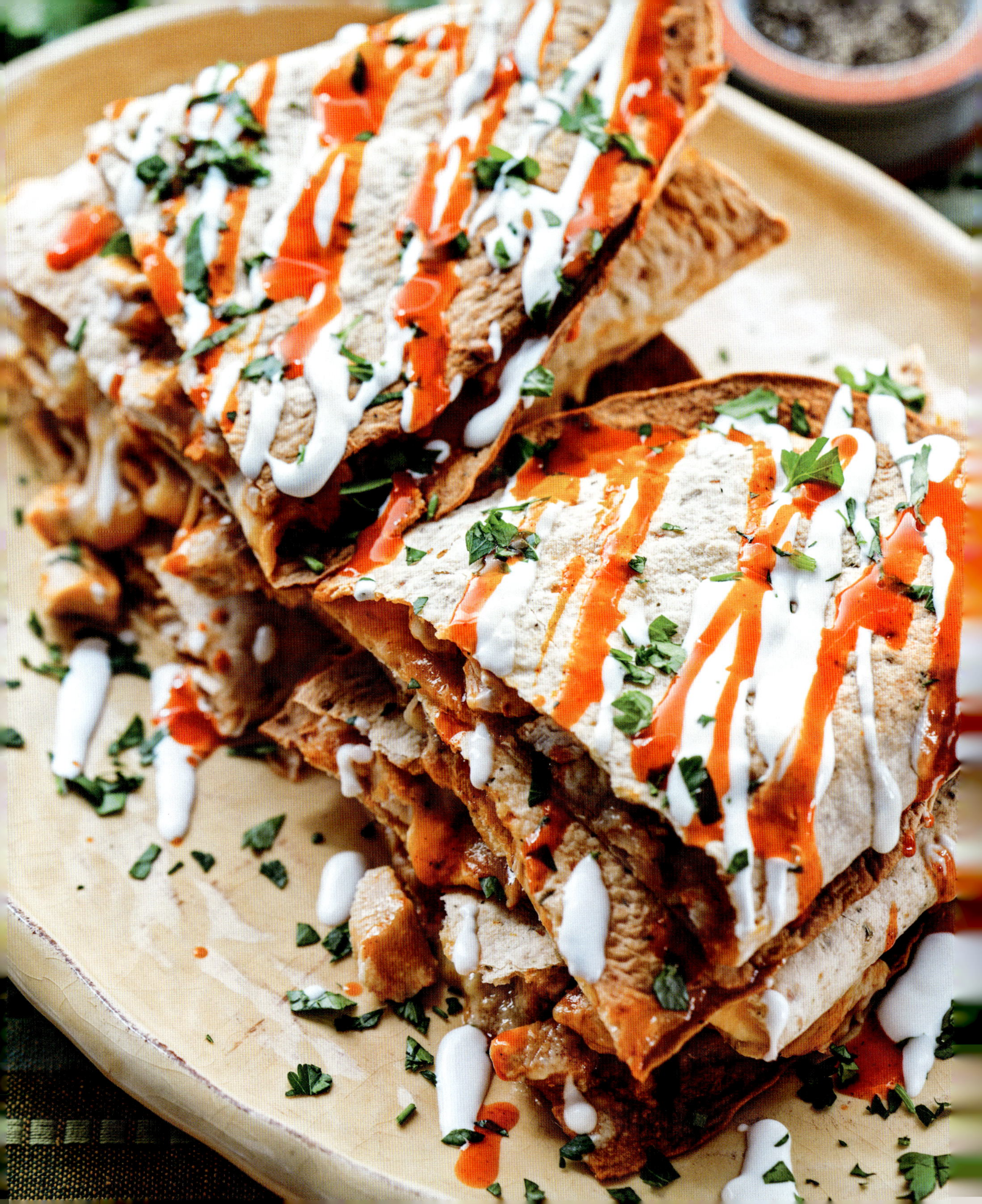

BUFFALO CHICKEN QUESADILLAS

These Buffalo chicken quesadillas will give you the bold flavors of Buffalo chicken wings with gooey melted cheese, all packed in a quesadilla! Quesadillas are a classic lunch dish, and this recipe is quick and simple. Simply make it the night before, let it cool and then store it in an airtight container for the next day. You can pop it in the microwave to heat it up, or if you have an oven around, just heat it at 350°F (177°C) for about 5 minutes.

PREP TIME: 10 MINUTES
COOK TIME: 15 MINUTES
TOTAL TIME: 25 MINUTES
SERVES: 4

2 tbsp (30 ml) olive oil

1 lb (448 g) boneless, skinless chicken breasts, cut into small pieces

¼ tsp salt, or as needed

¼ tsp black pepper, or as needed

¼ cup (60 ml) Buffalo wing sauce, plus more as needed (I recommend Frank's RedHot® brand)

4 large tortillas

½ cup (75 g) crumbled blue cheese

2 cups (240 g) Mexican blend cheese

Sour cream, as needed (optional)

Preheat the oven to 425°F (218°C).

Heat the oil in a large skillet over medium heat. Add the chicken pieces, season them with the salt and black pepper and cook them for about 5 minutes on all sides, until they are no longer pink.

Transfer the chicken to a large bowl. Add the Buffalo wing sauce and toss the chicken pieces well to coat them in the sauce.

Place about one-fourth of the chicken on 1 tortilla and spread it over half of the tortilla. Sprinkle the chicken with 2 tablespoons (18 g) of the blue cheese and about ½ cup (60 g) of the Mexican blend cheese. Fold the tortilla in half and press down gently. Repeat this process with the remaining ingredients.

Place the quesadillas on a large baking sheet. Bake the quesadillas for 8 to 10 minutes, turning them over halfway through the cooking time if necessary in order to ensure both sides are browned and crisp.

Remove the quesadillas from the oven, cut them in half and serve them with the sour cream (if using) or additional Buffalo wing sauce.

RECIPE NOTES

Alternatively, you could grill the quesadillas, use a panini maker or even cook them in a skillet. If you're using a skillet, spray the bottom of the skillet with cooking spray, then place the quesadilla in the skillet and cook for about 3 minutes per side, until it is golden brown.

Store leftover quesadillas in an airtight container in the fridge for up to 3 days. Be sure to reheat them on the stove if you want to prevent the tortillas from getting soggy. If you'd rather freeze the quesadillas, wrap each quesadilla individually in parchment paper and freeze them for up to 4 months.

NUTRITION INFORMATION

Serving size: 1 quesadilla; **Calories:** 542; **Carbohydrates:** 17 g; **Protein:** 43 g; **Fat:** 33 g

PAD THAI

PREP TIME: 20 MINUTES
SOAK TIME: 1 HOUR
COOK TIME: 10 MINUTES
TOTAL TIME: 1 HOUR, 30 MINUTES
SERVES: 4

Pad Thai is my all-time favorite and my go-to dish whenever I eat at a Thai restaurant. However, being a food blogger, I of course had to make my own version. So here I give you a pad Thai with shrimp and tofu that gives you all the flavors and taste of this authentic dish, but in the comfort of your own home!

PAD THAI

- 6 oz (168 g) rice noodles
- 2 shallots, minced
- 3 cloves garlic, minced
- 2 tbsp (10 g) dried shrimp, rinsed and chopped (see Recipe Notes)
- 2 tbsp (14 g) chopped sweet daikon radish
- 8 oz (224 g) firm tofu, cut into small pieces
- 1 tbsp (15 ml) Sriracha sauce
- 1 cup (124 g) fresh bean sprouts
- 1 cup (3" [9-cm]-long) Chinese chives (see Recipe Notes)
- ¼ cup (36 g) roasted peanuts, finely chopped
- 2 to 3 tbsp (30 to 45 ml) peanut oil, divided, plus more as needed
- 1 lb (448 g) shrimp, peeled and deveined
- 2 large eggs

SAUCE

- 2 tbsp (30 g) brown sugar
- ¼ cup (60 g) tamarind paste (see Recipe Notes)
- 2 tbsp (30 ml) fish sauce
- 3 tbsp (45 ml) water

To begin making the pad Thai, place the noodles in a large bowl. Add enough cold water to cover them and let them soak for 1 hour, or until the noodles are pliable but not soft. Drain them well in a colander. They will change from translucent to white.

To make the sauce, whisk together the brown sugar, tamarind paste, fish sauce and water. Set the sauce aside.

Continue making the pad Thai. In a medium bowl, combine the shallots, garlic, dried shrimp, radish, tofu and Sriracha sauce.

In another medium bowl, combine the bean sprouts, Chinese chives and peanuts.

Heat 1 tablespoon (15 ml) of the oil in a medium skillet over high heat. Add the shrimp and cook them for 1 to 2 minutes per side, stirring them frequently, until they turn pink and start to char. Transfer the shrimp to a medium bowl.

Add the remaining 1 to 2 tablespoons (15 to 30 ml) of oil to the skillet. Add the tofu mixture to the skillet and sauté it for about 1 minute. Add the noodles and sauce and toss everything together. Move the noodles to the side of the skillet and add additional oil to the skillet if needed. Add the eggs and break the yolks. Cook the eggs for 30 seconds, then scramble them. Toss everything together.

Add the bean sprouts–Chinese chives mixture to the skillet and toss everything together. Turn off the heat.

TOPPINGS

1 cup (124 g) fresh bean sprouts

1 cup (3" [9-cm]-long pieces) Chinese chives

¼ cup (36 g) roasted peanuts, chopped

Lime wedges

2 tbsp (6 g) chopped fresh cilantro (optional)

Sriracha sauce

To serve the pad Thai, divide it among 2 to 4 plates, depending on the size of the meal you want. Top the stir-fry with the shrimp, then top each serving with the bean sprouts, Chinese chives, peanuts and lime wedges. Serve the pad Thai with the cilantro (if using) and Sriracha sauce on the side.

RECIPE NOTES

Dried shrimp are shrimp that have been sun-dried and shrunk. They are used in a lot of Asian dishes and provide a unique umami taste. They can be found in Asian markets.

Chinese chives (also known as garlic chives) look like regular chives but are much bigger and leafier. They could be considered more of a vegetable than a garnish. They are garlicky in flavor, juicy and crisp in texture. Look for these chives in Asian markets. They can be substituted with regular chives or green onions.

Tamarind paste is a common ingredient used throughout the world. The paste is prepared from tamarind, which is a sticky, sour-tasting fruit that grows in bean-like pods on tamarind trees. Tamarind paste is both sweet and sour, so I recommend substituting it with equal amounts of lime juice and brown sugar.

This pad Thai will keep in an airtight container in the fridge for 3 to 4 days. I don't recommend freezing this dish, as the egg and rice noodles don't thaw well after time in the freezer.

NUTRITION INFORMATION

Serving size: 1 serving; **Calories:** 616; **Carbohydrates:** 58 g; **Protein:** 47 g; **Fat:** 23 g

PAD SEE EW

PREP TIME: 10 MINUTES
SOAK TIME: 1 HOUR
COOK TIME: 10 MINUTES
TOTAL TIME: 1 HOUR, 20 MINUTES
SERVES: 3

STIR-FRY

6 oz (168 g) rice noodles
3 to 4 tbsp (45 to 60 ml) peanut oil, divided
4 cloves garlic, minced
2 large eggs
6 stalks Chinese broccoli (see Recipe Notes)
1 tbsp (15 g) brown sugar

CHICKEN

1 lb (448 g) boneless, skinless chicken breasts, cut into small pieces
1 tsp peanut oil
1 tbsp (15 ml) low-sodium soy sauce

SAUCE

2 tbsp (30 ml) oyster sauce
2 tsp (10 ml) black soy sauce (see Recipe Notes)
½ tbsp (8 ml) fish sauce
1½ tbsp (23 ml) low-sodium soy sauce

Chopped Thai red chilies, for serving (optional)

NUTRITION INFORMATION

Serving size: 1 serving; **Calories:** 634; **Carbohydrates:** 56 g; **Protein:** 33 g; **Fat:** 29 g

This is considered Thai fast food, and trust me when I tell you it is fast. But that doesn't mean it's not delicious, which is what's great about Thai food. This recipe is perfect to make the night before you'll need it—refrigerate it, then just pop it in the microwave for a few seconds when you're ready to eat.

To begin making the stir-fry, place the noodles in a large bowl. Add enough cold water to cover them and let them soak for 1 hour, or until the noodles are pliable but not soft. Drain the noodles well in a colander. They will change from translucent to white.

To make the chicken, place it in a small bowl. Add the oil and low-sodium soy sauce and toss the ingredients together, making sure the chicken is coated in the oil and soy sauce. This seasons the chicken and ensures it will separate nicely when it is cooking.

To make the sauce, combine the oyster sauce, black soy sauce, fish sauce and low-sodium soy sauce in a small bowl. Set the sauce aside.

To continue making the stir-fry, heat 2 tablespoons (30 ml) of the oil in a 14-inch (42-cm) wok over medium-high heat. Add the chicken and cook it for 2 to 3 minutes, just until it is cooked through. Remove the chicken from the wok and set it aside. Wipe away any excess liquid left in the wok with paper towels and return the wok to the heat.

Add the remaining 1 to 2 tablespoons (15 to 30 ml) of oil to the wok, then immediately add the garlic before the oil gets too hot. This will prevent the garlic from burning as soon as it hits the wok. Sauté the garlic for about 30 seconds, just until it is aromatic and turns golden Add the eggs and break the yolks. Cook the eggs, undisturbed, for about 15 seconds before scrambling them for 1 to 2 minutes. Add the Chinese broccoli and toss it to coat it with the oil and the eggs. Cook the mixture for about 15 seconds.

Add the noodles, sauce and brown sugar. Increase the heat to high and toss the noodles to coat them evenly in the sauce. Spread the noodles over the entire surface of the wok and cook them, undisturbed, for about 30 seconds. This will ensure they char slightly, which will give them a toasty flavor. Flip the noodles and again let them cook, undisturbed, for 30 seconds to char the other side. Add the chicken to the noodles and toss everything together.

Remove the pad see ew from the wok, top it with the Thai red chilies (if using) and serve it immediately.

RECIPE NOTES

If you cannot find Chinese broccoli, use broccoli or broccolini.

If you cannot find black soy sauce, you can use dark soy sauce, but it is a bit saltier, so I recommend using about 1 teaspoon.

THE BIG BOOK OF JO'S QUICK & EASY MEALS

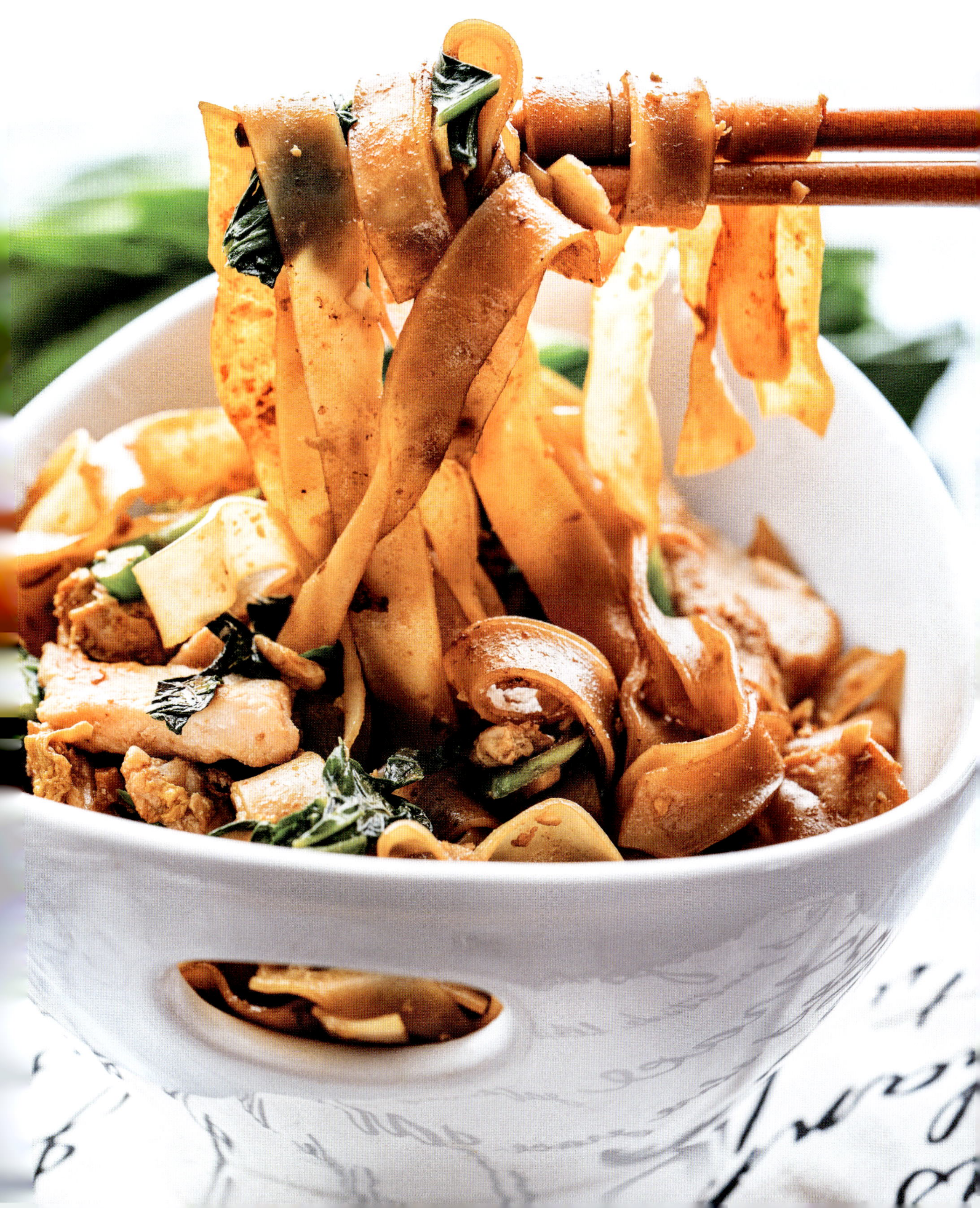

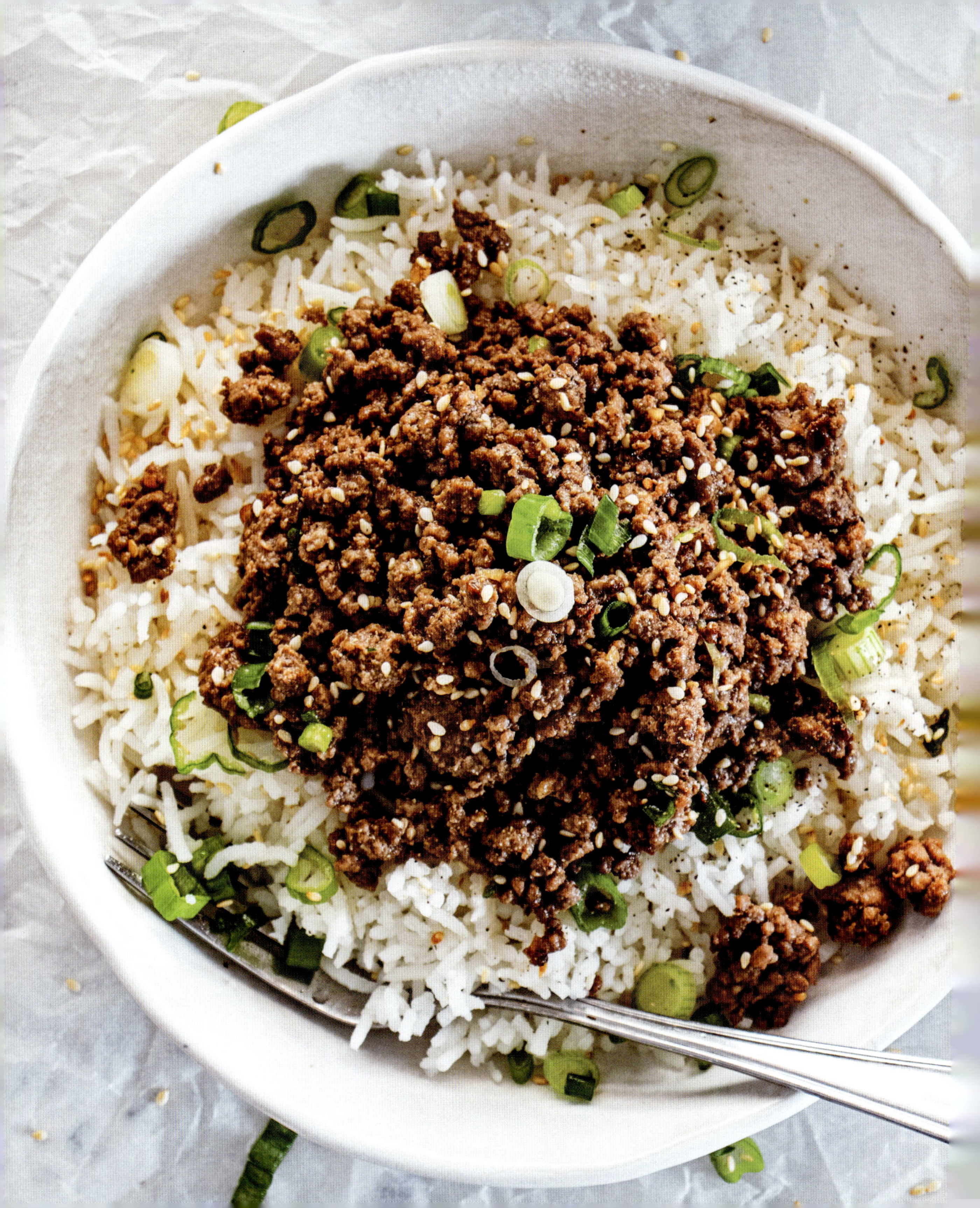

KOREAN BEEF RICE BOWLS

This lunch is as simple as it gets, it's unbelievably delicious and is also pretty healthy. These bowls only take 15 minutes from start to finish, and if you're a fan of Korean cuisine, these rice bowls are for you.

PREP TIME: 5 MINUTES
COOK TIME: 10 MINUTES
TOTAL TIME: 15 MINUTES
SERVES: 4

BOWLS
1 lb (448 g) lean ground beef
3 cloves garlic, minced
1 cup (210 g) rice, cooked

SAUCE
1 tbsp (15 g) packed brown sugar
1 tsp ground ginger
¼ tsp red pepper flakes
¼ cup (60 ml) low-sodium soy sauce
1 tbsp (15 ml) sesame oil

GARNISHES
2 green onions, chopped
1 tbsp (9 g) sesame seeds

In a large skillet over medium heat, cook the beef for about 3 minutes, breaking it apart as it cooks. Stir in the garlic and cook the mixture for 5 minutes, until the beef starts to brown and is no longer pink.

To make the sauce, whisk together the brown sugar, ginger, red pepper flakes, soy sauce and oil in a small bowl. Pour the sauce over the beef. Let the beef simmer in the sauce for 1 minute, stirring it constantly, then remove the beef from the heat.

Garnish the beef with the green onions and sesame seeds. Serve the beef over the rice.

RECIPE NOTES

I prefer to cook my ground beef until it contains some burned bits, then I add the sauce to it. I think the beef has more flavor this way.

Seal this recipe in an airtight container and it'll last in your fridge for 3 to 4 days. If you'd like to freeze this recipe, let it cool completely and then transfer it to freezer bags or an airtight container. It'll last for up to 4 months in the freezer.

NUTRITION INFORMATION

Serving size: 1 serving; **Calories:** 438; **Carbohydrates:** 43 g; **Protein:** 27 g; **Fat:** 16 g

SOUPS

THIS IS ONE OF MY FAVORITE CHAPTERS IN THIS BOOK because soup has always meant comfort to me. I love a bowl of soup any night of the year, not just on a cold winter night or when I'm feeling under the weather. Of course, it helps that I live in Alberta, where we have winter nine months of the year—but trust me, I make soup all summer long too.

Soup means many things to many people because soup is a part of all cultures. We've all grown up with our favorite soups that our parents and grandparents made, like my Instant Pot® Chicken Noodle Soup (page 305). While I was growing up, soup was on our dinner table four or five times a week. Mom always made hearty soups that were full of vegetables and included some sort of protein. In fact, these soups were not starters to our dinners; many times they were the main meal.

The thing I love the most about soups is their simplicity. The base of most soups is made of a mirepoix, which consists of onions, carrots and celery. Regardless of which soup you're making, keep this in mind: If you start with these three ingredients, you can't go wrong. Soups are also the ultimate one-pot meal. Making soup is about as basic as you can get—just throw all the ingredients in one pot and 30 minutes later, you've got soup.

In this chapter, I'm going to share with you a few reader favorites from the blog, some that have been popular for years and some that are newer but quickly moving to the top of the most popular recipes.

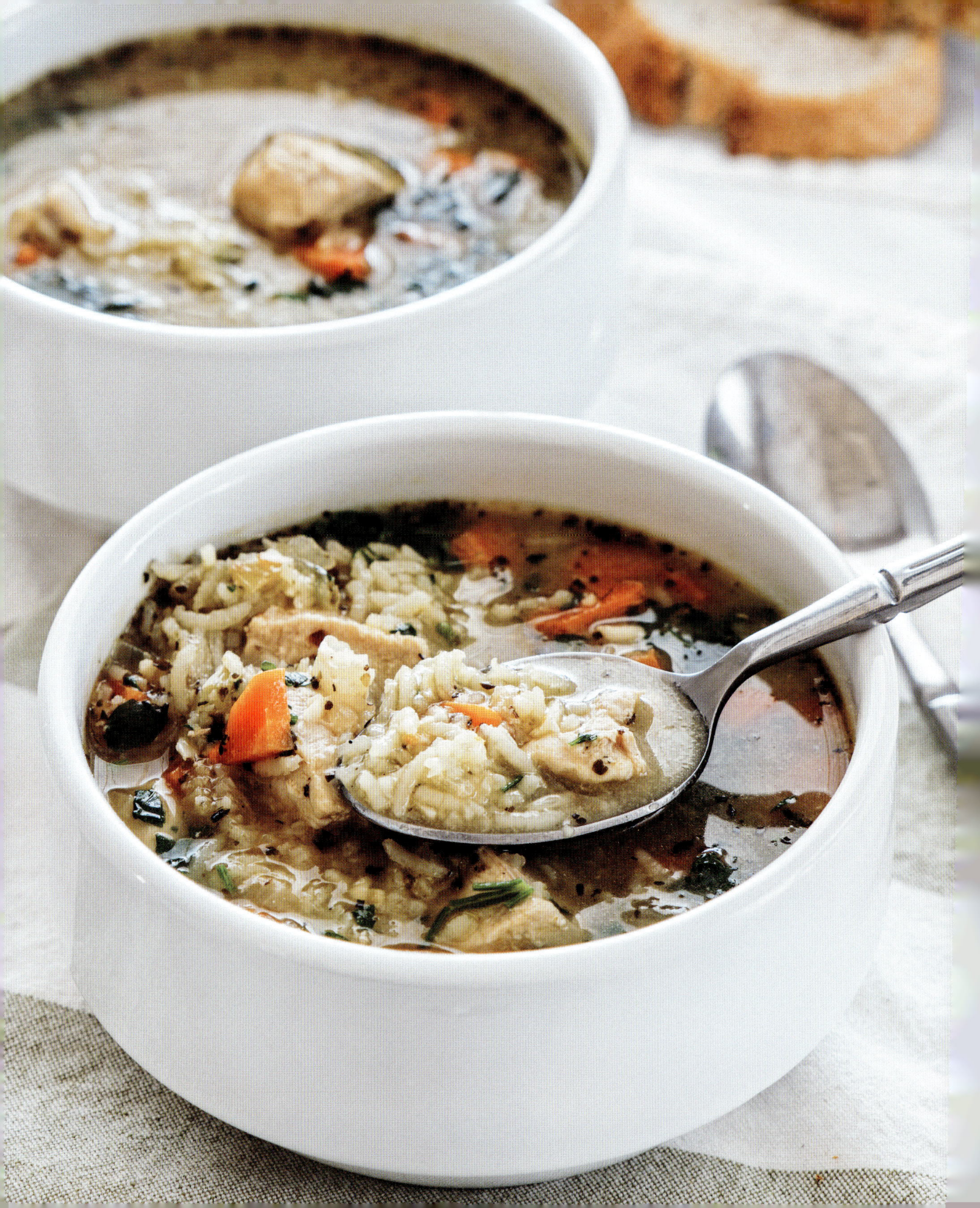

CHICKEN AND RICE SOUP

There are many versions of chicken and rice soup. I have a few on the blog, but here's my favorite. This chicken and rice soup is comforting and loaded with protein, carbs and lots of veggies! It'll leave you warm and filled after just one bowl. It's a simple and fast meal you'll be happy to have in your repertoire for those busy weeknights.

PREP TIME: 15 MINUTES
COOK TIME: 45 MINUTES
TOTAL TIME: 1 HOUR
SERVES: 6

2 tbsp (30 ml) olive oil
1 onion, chopped
3 carrots, chopped
2 ribs celery, chopped
3 cloves garlic, minced
1 lb (448 g) boneless, skinless chicken breasts, cubed
2 dried bay leaves
4 sprigs fresh thyme
1 tsp salt, plus more as needed
½ tsp black pepper, plus more as needed
1 tbsp (9 g) Vegeta seasoning or 1 chicken bouillon cube (optional)
1 cup (210 g) long-grain rice
8 cups (1.9 L) low-sodium chicken broth
1 tbsp (3 g) chopped fresh parsley

Heat the oil in a large Dutch oven or pot over medium heat. Add the onion, carrots and celery and sauté the vegetables for 5 minutes, until the onion is soft and translucent. Add the garlic and sauté the mixture for 30 seconds, until the garlic is aromatic.

Add the chicken, stir to combine the ingredients and cook them for 5 to 7 minutes, until the chicken is no longer pink and is cooked through.

Add the bay leaves, thyme, salt, black pepper, Vegeta (if using), rice and broth. Stir everything together and bring the soup to a boil.

Reduce the heat to medium-low and cook the soup for 25 to 30 minutes, covered, until the rice is tender.

Discard the bay leaves and thyme. Taste the soup for seasoning and add additional salt and black pepper as needed.

Garnish the soup with the parsley and serve it.

RECIPE NOTES

Vegeta is a European vegetable-based seasoning that's used to flavor soups, sauces and stews. Substitute it with a chicken bouillon cube.

Make sure your soup has cooled down to room temperature before storing it. You can leave it in the covered pot or transfer it to an airtight container. Leftovers will last 3 to 4 days in the fridge.

To reheat the soup, microwave it for 30 seconds at a time until it is heated through. You can also reheat in a pot over medium heat. If you've found that the rice has absorbed too much of the liquid and the soup consistency is too thick, add some more chicken broth.

NUTRITION INFORMATION

Serving size: 1 serving; **Calories:** 319; **Carbohydrates:** 35 g; **Protein:** 25 g; **Fat:** 9 g

EASY TORTELLINI SOUP

PREP TIME: 10 MINUTES
COOK TIME: 40 MINUTES
TOTAL TIME: 50 MINUTES
SERVES: 8

1 tbsp (15 ml) olive oil
1 lb (448 g) Italian sausage, casings removed
1 onion, chopped
1 carrot, chopped
2 ribs celery, chopped
4 cloves garlic, minced
1 tbsp (3 g) Italian seasoning
1 tsp salt, or as needed
½ tsp black pepper, or as needed
¼ cup (30 g) all-purpose flour
6 cups (1.4 L) chicken or vegetable broth
1 (15-oz [420-g]) can fire-roasted tomatoes, undrained
2 cups (480 ml) tomato passata
14 oz (392 g) cheese tortellini
2 cups (480 ml) half-and-half
1 cup (30 g) baby spinach, chopped
Grated Parmesan cheese
Chopped fresh basil

This tortellini soup screams comfort food. It's quick and easy and made entirely in one pot. Spicy Italian sausage is romanced by the bright, creamy tomato broth and seasoned to perfection. Don't forget the exquisite bites of cheesy tortellini, which is my favorite part!

Heat the oil in a large Dutch oven over medium heat. Add the Italian sausage and cook it for 3 to 5 minutes, breaking it up with a wooden spoon as it cooks, until it has browned.

Add the onion, carrot and celery and cook the mixture for 5 minutes, stirring it occasionally, until the vegetables are soft.

Add the garlic, Italian seasoning, salt and black pepper and stir to combine the ingredients. Cook the mixture for 30 seconds, stirring it constantly, until the garlic is fragrant.

Sprinkle the flour over everything and stir it into the mixture. Cook the mixture for 1 minute, stirring it occasionally. Gradually add the broth, then add the fire-roasted tomatoes and their juice and the tomato passata. Bring the soup to a boil, then reduce the heat to low and cook it for 15 minutes.

Stir in the cheese tortellini and half-and-half. Cook the soup for 10 more minutes, or until the tortellini is al dente. Stir in the spinach and cook the soup for 2 minutes, until the spinach has wilted.

Garnish the soup with the Parmesan cheese and basil and serve.

RECIPE NOTES

Store any leftover soup in an airtight container in the fridge for 3 to 5 days.

To reheat the soup, microwave it or heat it on the stove.

NUTRITION INFORMATION

Serving size: 1 serving; **Calories:** 534; **Carbohydrates:** 40 g; **Protein:** 23 g; **Fat:** 32 g

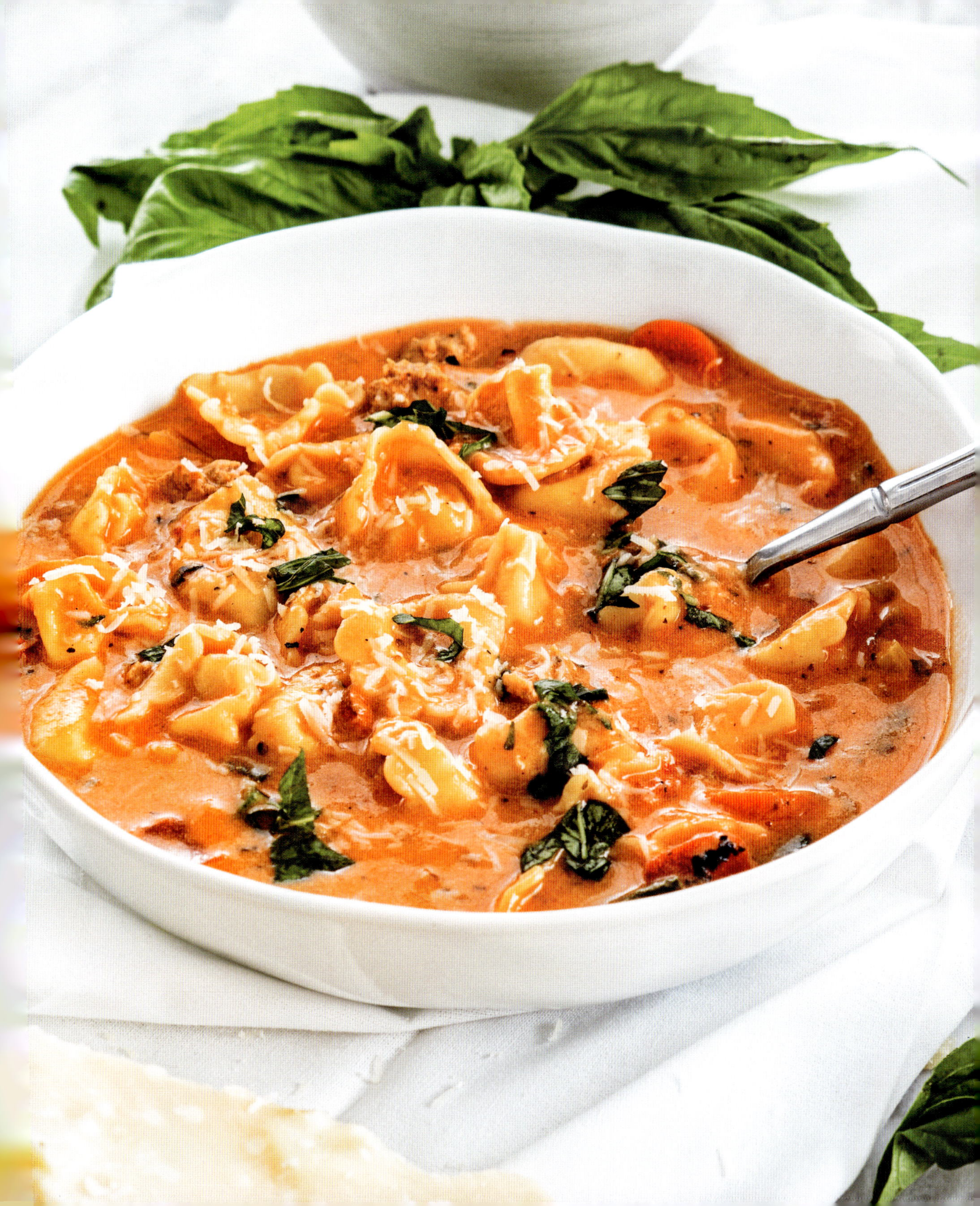

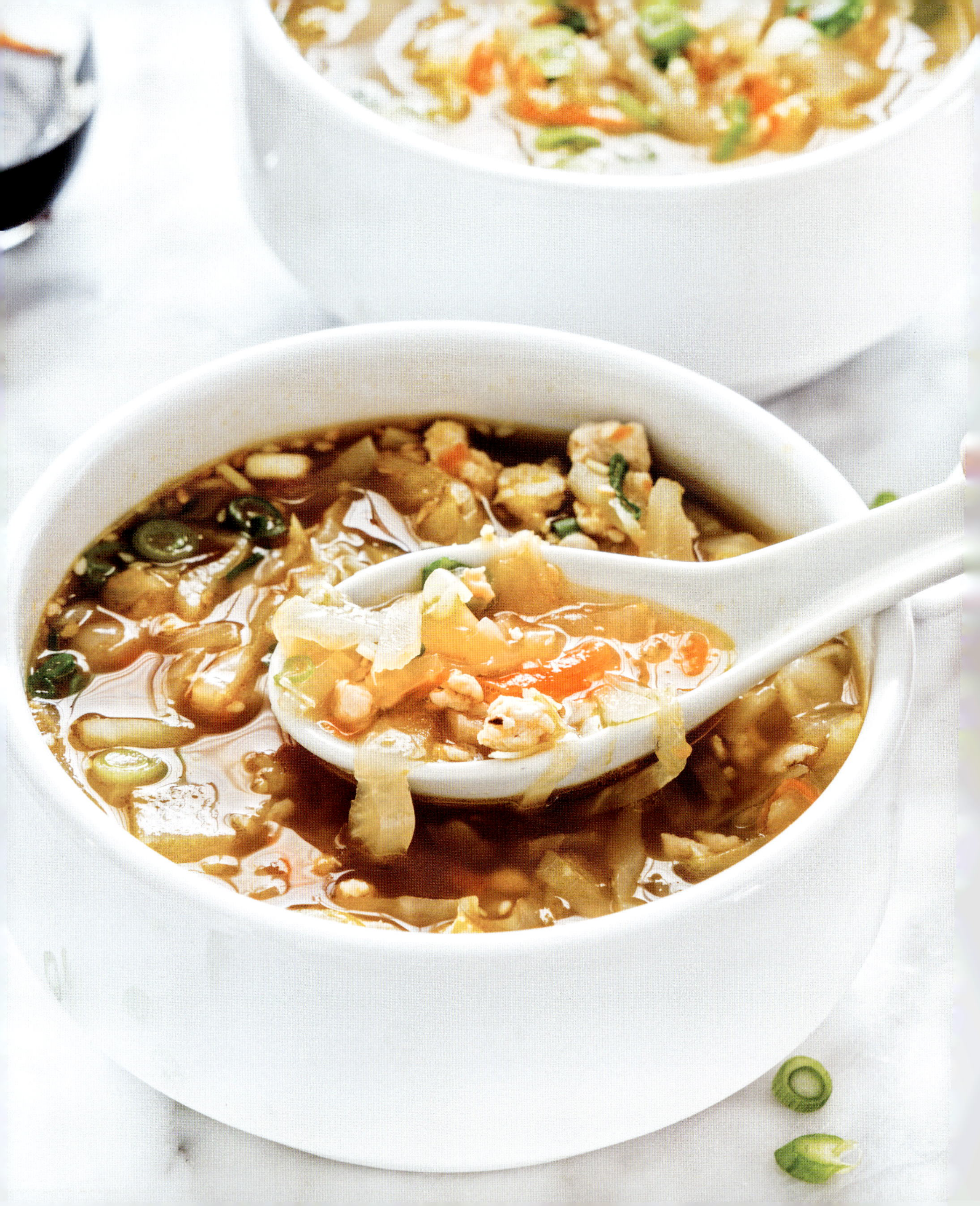

EGG ROLL SOUP

This egg roll soup is what happens when you turn your favorite egg roll into soup! It's a soup that is almost impossible to mess up—it's easy to make, fairly quick and healthy.

PREP TIME: 15 MINUTES
COOK TIME: 35 MINUTES
TOTAL TIME: 50 MINUTES
SERVES: 6

1 lb (448 g) ground chicken
2 tbsp (30 ml) olive oil
1 head green cabbage, shredded
1 onion, chopped
1 carrot, shredded
3 cloves garlic, minced
1 tsp minced fresh ginger
6 cups (1.4 L) low-sodium or unsalted chicken broth
½ tsp salt
1 tsp toasted sesame oil, plus more as needed
2 green onions, chopped
Sriracha sauce, for serving
Soy sauce, for serving

In a large Dutch oven or pot over medium heat, cook the chicken for 5 minutes, or until the chicken is no longer pink.

Add the olive oil to the Dutch oven. When the oil is hot, add the green cabbage, onion, carrot, garlic and ginger and stir to combine the ingredients. Cook the mixture for about 10 minutes, until the cabbage softens.

Stir in the broth, salt, and sesame oil. Reduce the heat to low and simmer the soup for 20 minutes, until the cabbage is completely soft.

Top the soup with the green onions. Serve the soup with the Sriracha sauce, soy sauce and additional sesame oil.

RECIPE NOTES

To maximize the shelf life of this soup, refrigerate it promptly in airtight containers for 3 to 4 days.

You can freeze individual servings of this soup, which is perfect for work lunches. I recommend freezing this in airtight containers or heavy-duty freezer bags. This soup can last in the freezer for 2 to 3 months.

NUTRITION INFORMATION

Serving size: 1 serving; **Calories:** 241; **Carbohydrates:** 14 g; **Protein:** 20 g; **Fat:** 13 g

BEEF STROGANOFF SOUP

This soup takes all the rich and delicious flavors of beef stroganoff and transforms them into a one-pot, 30-minute soup full of tender beef and loads of noodles. This is a great example of a soup that is a meal on its own. Serve it with some toasted crusty bread and you've reached perfection.

PREP TIME: 10 MINUTES
COOK TIME: 20 MINUTES
TOTAL TIME: 30 MINUTES
SERVES: 6

8 oz (224 g) cremini mushrooms
1 tbsp (15 ml) olive oil
1 tbsp (15 g) unsalted butter
1 lb (448 g) sirloin, cut into thin strips
½ tsp salt, plus more as needed
¼ tsp black pepper, plus more as needed
1 onion, chopped
2 cloves garlic, minced
1 tsp Worcestershire sauce
1 tsp smoked paprika
8 cups (1.9 L) low-sodium beef broth
4 oz (112 g) egg noodles (see Recipe Notes)
½ cup (60 g) sour cream (see Recipe Notes)
1 tbsp (3 g) chopped fresh parsley

Trim the bottom of the mushrooms' stems, as they are usually dirty. Slice the mushrooms and set them aside.

Heat the oil and butter in a large Dutch oven over medium-high heat. Add the sirloin and season them with the salt and black pepper. Cook the sirloin for about 5 minutes, until the meat has browned slightly. Using a slotted spoon, transfer the meat to a plate.

Add the mushrooms, onion and garlic to the Dutch oven and stir to combine the vegetables. Sauté them for about 3 minutes, until they soften.

Add the Worcestershire sauce, smoked paprika and broth. Stir everything together, bring the soup to a boil and then return the sirloin to the Dutch oven. Stir in the noodles and cook them for about 8 minutes, or until they are cooked to your liking.

In a small bowl, whisk together the sour cream and about ½ cup (120 ml) of the hot soup. Pour this mixture back into the soup and stir to incorporate it. Taste the soup for seasoning and add additional salt and black pepper as necessary.

Garnish the soup with the parsley and serve.

RECIPE NOTES

Any type of noodle that you like can be used in this recipe. I prefer egg noodles because they hold up well to hot soup without getting soggy.

Greek yogurt or crème fraîche can be substituted for the sour cream if preferred.

This dish will last in an airtight container in the fridge for 3 to 4 days. You can reheat it on the stove or in the microwave.

This dish is perfect for freezing; be sure to freeze only the soup and hold off on the noodles until you're ready to eat it. In a shallow airtight container, this dish will last for 3 to 4 months in the freezer.

NUTRITION INFORMATION

Serving size: 1 serving; **Calories:** 281; **Carbohydrates:** 19 g; **Protein:** 26 g; **Fat:** 12 g

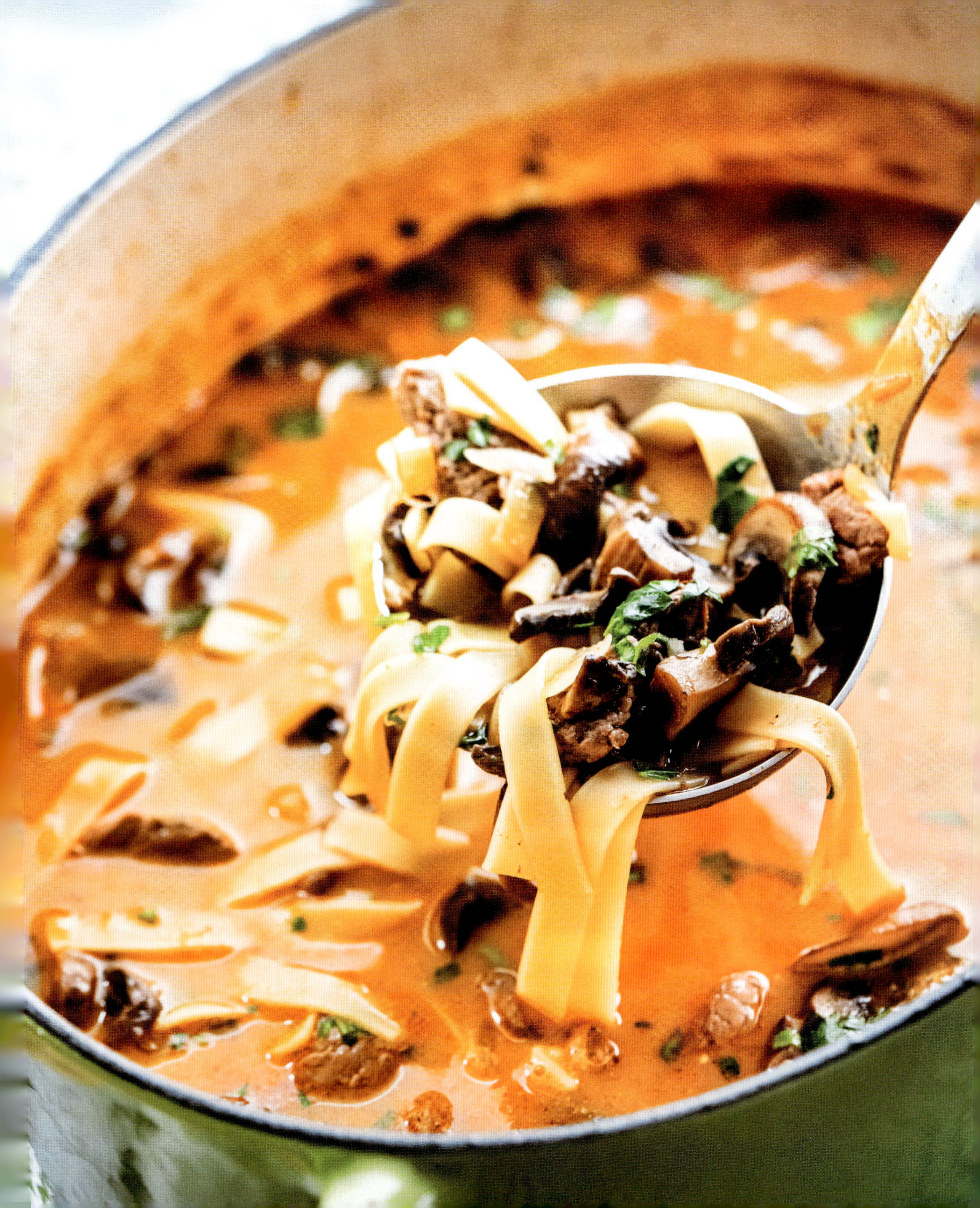

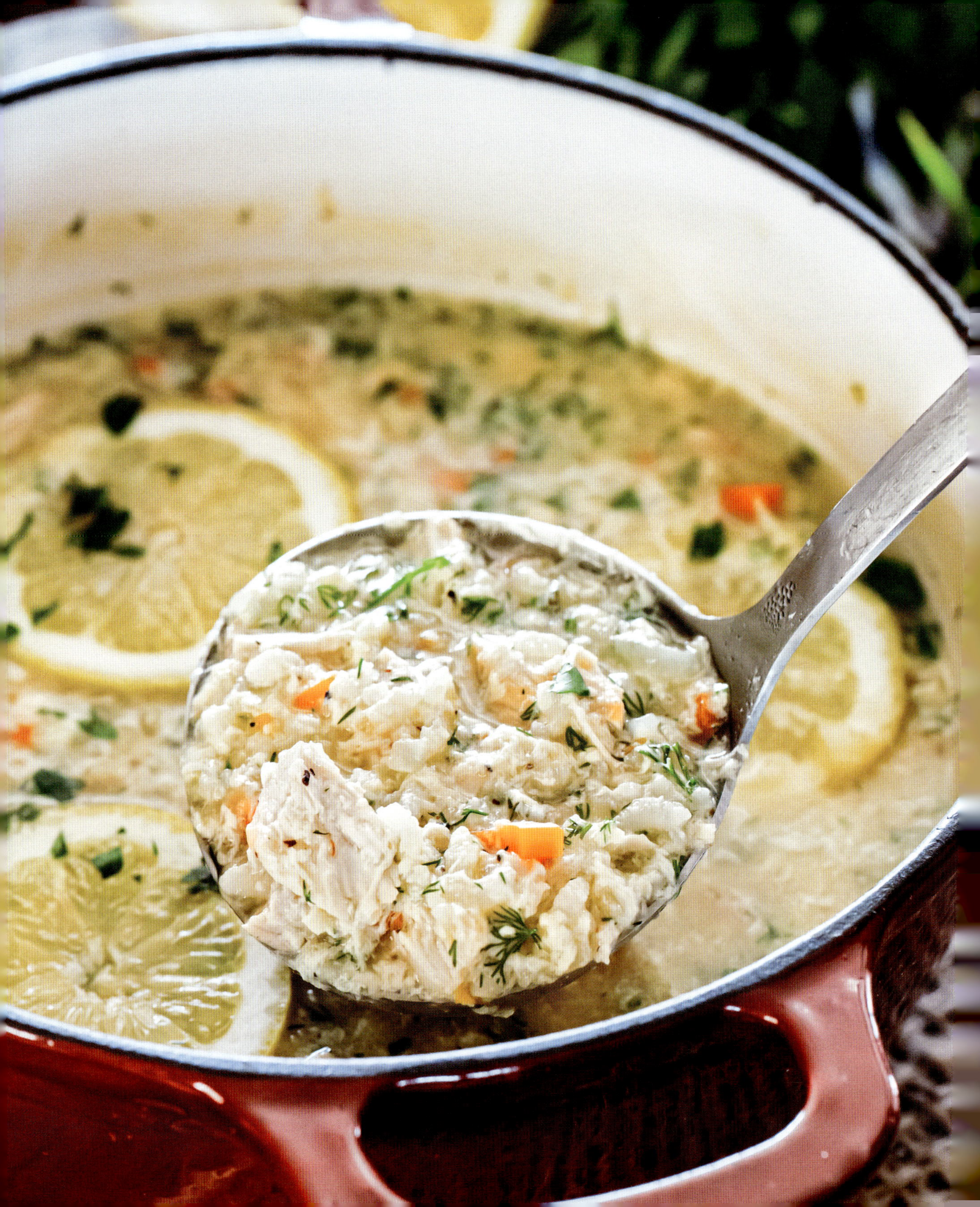

AVGOLEMONO SOUP

The Greeks may not have invented everything, but they did come up with this delicious lemon, rice and chicken soup. Here's a classic Greek soup that's thickened with eggs, loaded with rice and chicken and flavored with lots of lemon. I'm talking hearty, delicious, minimal effort and ready in only 30 minutes!

PREP TIME: 5 MINUTES
COOK TIME: 25 MINUTES
TOTAL TIME: 30 MINUTES
SERVES: 6

1 tbsp (15 ml) olive oil
1 onion, chopped
1 carrot, chopped
½ cup (105 g) arborio rice (see Recipe Notes)
4 cups (960 ml) low-sodium chicken broth
3 large eggs
3 tbsp (45 ml) fresh lemon juice, plus more as needed
2 skinless, boneless chicken breasts, cooked and shredded (see Recipe Notes)
½ tsp salt, or as needed
1 tsp black pepper, or as needed
¼ cup (12 g) chopped fresh dill
Crumbled feta cheese, for serving (optional)
Lemon slices, for serving (optional)

Heat the oil in a large pot or Dutch oven over medium-high heat. Add the onion and carrot and cook them for about 5 minutes, or just until the carrot is tender and the onion is translucent.

Add the rice and broth and bring the soup to a boil. Reduce the heat to low. Simmer the soup for about 15 minutes, or until the rice is cooked through.

Meanwhile, in a small bowl, beat together the eggs and lemon juice.

Add the chicken to the pot. Add a ladle of the soup broth to the egg mixture and stir. Pour the egg mixture into the soup. You will notice the soup thickening up. Season the soup with the salt and black pepper. Add more lemon juice as desired.

Garnish the soup with the dill. Serve it with some feta cheese (if using) and lemon slices (if using).

RECIPE NOTES

Arborio rice is an Italian short-grain rice.

I use cooked small chicken breasts, which I shred with two forks. This yields about 2 cups (270 g) of shredded chicken.

NUTRITION INFORMATION

Serving size: 1 serving; **Calories:** 192; **Carbohydrates:** 18 g; **Protein:** 15 g; **Fat:** 6 g

EGG DROP SOUP

If you're looking for a soup that's super quick, then this soup is for you. Ready in about fifteen minutes and clocking in at only 120 calories a bowl, this Chinese soup is not only simple but also much tastier and healthier than takeout!

PREP TIME: 5 MINUTES
COOK TIME: 10 MINUTES
TOTAL TIME: 15 MINUTES
SERVES: 4

4 cups (960 ml) low-sodium chicken broth
1 tsp low-sodium soy sauce
1 tsp sesame oil
1 tbsp (9 g) cornstarch
2 tbsp (30 ml) water
4 large eggs, beaten
½ tsp salt, or as needed
½ tsp black pepper, or as needed
¼ cup (12 g) chopped fresh chives

In a small saucepan, combine the broth, soy sauce and oil. Bring the mixture to a boil.

In a small bowl, stir together the cornstarch and water until the cornstarch dissolves and creates a slurry. Pour the slurry into the boiling broth.

Gently whisk the broth while you pour in the eggs. Make sure to pour the eggs at a steady pace while whisking the broth continuously. You should see egg ribbons form immediately.

Season the soup with the salt and black pepper. Garnish it with the chives and serve it.

RECIPE NOTES

Store this soup in an airtight container in the fridge for up to 4 days. You may want to add a bit of water to the soup before reheating it in the microwave, as the soup will keep getting thicker as it sits.

Unfortunately, this egg drop soup won't thaw properly after being frozen, so I don't recommend freezing it.

NUTRITION INFORMATION

Serving size: 1 serving; **Calories:** 120; **Carbohydrates:** 5 g; **Protein:** 10 g; **Fat:** 7 g

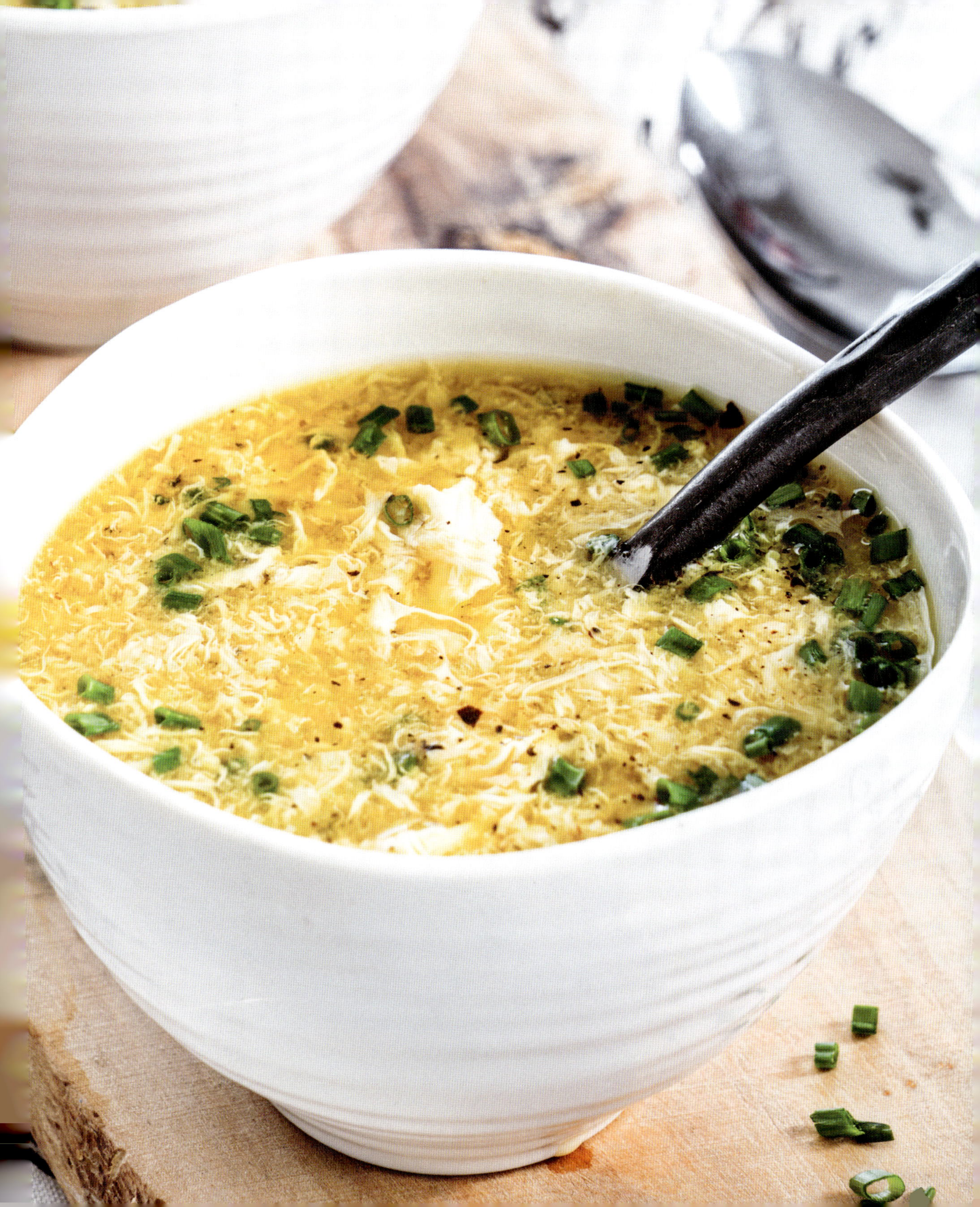

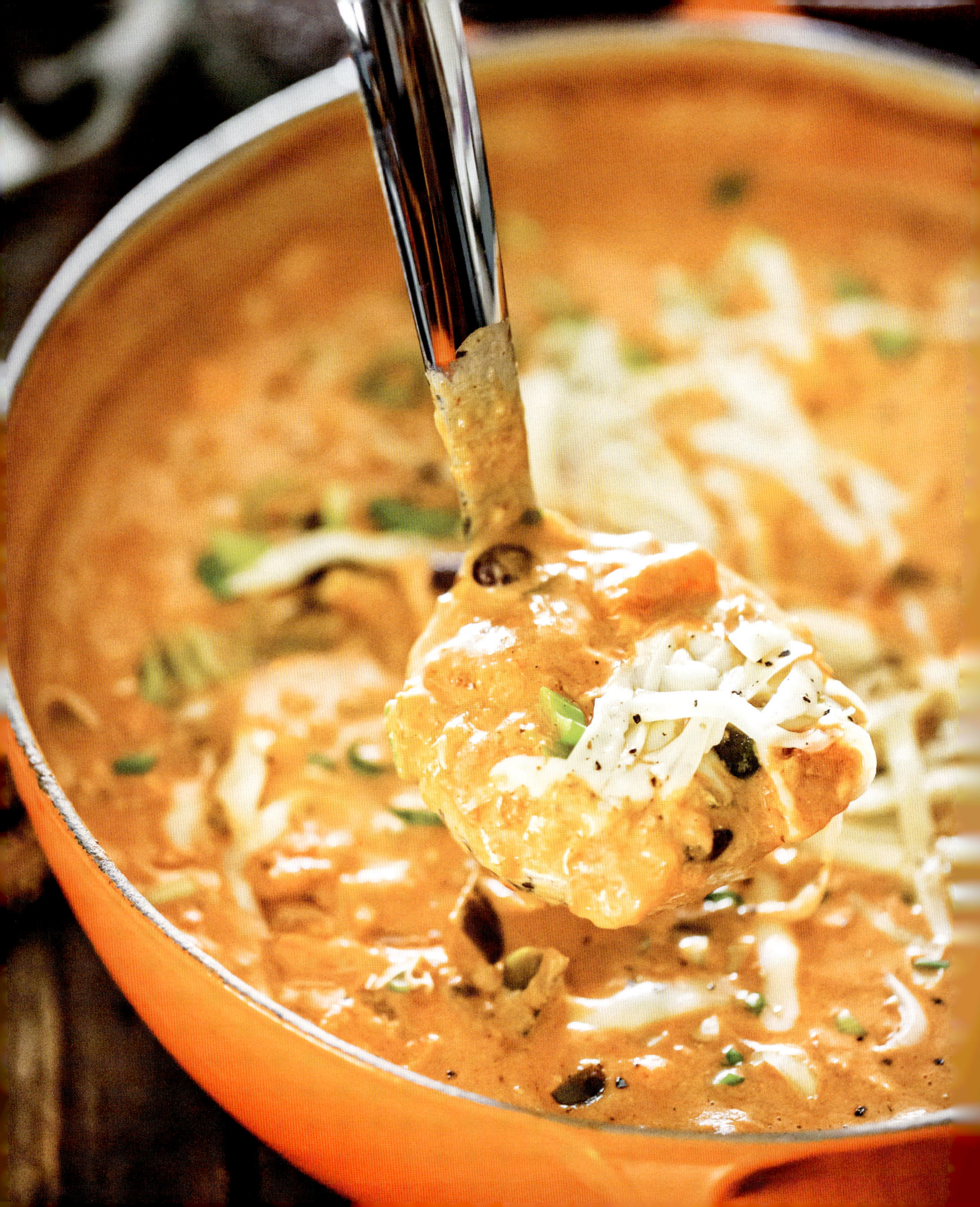

CHEESY CHICKEN ENCHILADA SOUP

PREP TIME: 5 MINUTES
COOK TIME: 25 MINUTES
TOTAL TIME: 30 MINUTES
SERVES: 8

1 tbsp (15 ml) olive oil
1 onion, chopped
1 green bell pepper, chopped
1 (10-oz [300-ml]) can enchilada sauce
8 oz (224 g) cream cheese
1 (15-oz [420-g]) can diced tomatoes, undrained
1 cup (170 g) black beans, drained and rinsed
1 cup (144 g) frozen corn
2 cups (280 g) chopped cooked chicken breast
1 cup (240 ml) chicken broth, plus more as needed
2 green onions, chopped
1 cup (112 g) shredded mozzarella cheese

Here's a fiesta of flavors, full of chunky chicken, savory black beans, sweet corn and juicy diced tomatoes. This is a thick soup with a creamy tomato broth that's soothing, simple to make and full of savory flavor. Serve this with some tortilla chips and you've got a complete meal.

Heat the oil in a large Dutch oven or pot over medium heat. Add the onion and bell pepper and cook them for about 5 minutes, until the onion is soft and translucent.

Add the enchilada sauce and cream cheese. Break down the cream cheese with a wooden spoon and cook the mixture for about 3 minutes, or until the cream cheese has completely melted.

Add the tomatoes and their juice, black beans and corn and stir to combine the ingredients.

Add the chicken and broth, then stir to combine the ingredients. Cook the soup for 10 to 15 minutes, stirring it occasionally, just until the soup is hot but not boiling. If you find the soup is too thick, add a bit more broth.

Remove the soup from the heat and top it with the green onions and mozzarella cheese before serving.

RECIPE NOTES

Store this soup in an airtight container in the fridge for up to 4 days.

To freeze this soup, wait for it to cool down first. Transfer it to an airtight container and freeze it for 3 months.

NUTRITION INFORMATION

Serving size: 1 serving; **Calories:** 359; **Carbohydrates:** 27 g; **Protein:** 24 g; **Fat:** 18 g

ITALIAN WEDDING SOUP

PREP TIME: 10 MINUTES
COOK TIME: 20 MINUTES
TOTAL TIME: 30 MINUTES
SERVES: 6

MEATBALLS
1 lb (448 g) extra lean ground beef (see Recipe Notes)
¼ cup (60 ml) milk
½ cup (90 g) grated Parmesan cheese
½ cup (75 g) breadcrumbs
¼ cup (12 g) chopped fresh parsley
1 large egg
½ tsp salt, or as needed
½ tsp black pepper, or as needed

SOUP
1 tbsp (15 ml) olive oil
1 carrot, chopped
8 cups (1.9 L) low-sodium chicken broth
2 cups (60 g) packed baby spinach, roughly chopped
1 cup (140 g) orzo (see Recipe Notes)
1 tsp salt, or as needed
1 tsp black pepper, or as needed
Grated Pecorino Romano cheese, for serving (see Recipe Notes)

I used to think that this soup was served only at Italian weddings, hence the name. I have since found out that it has nothing to do with weddings. It's said to get its name from the marriage of ingredients—the meat, greens and noodles—because together they are a marriage made in heaven. Regardless of the origin of its name, this soup is quick, simple and always a big hit! I might add that I'm a bit partial to meatball soups, so this one ranks pretty high for me.

To make the meatballs, combine the beef, milk, Parmesan cheese, breadcrumbs, parsley, egg, salt and black pepper in a large bowl. Mix the ingredients well using your hands until they are well incorporated. Shape the meat into meatballs that are ¾ to 1 inch (19 mm to 3 cm) in diameter. Place the meatballs in another large bowl; set it aside.

To make the soup, heat the oil in a large pot or Dutch oven over medium-high heat. Add the carrot and sauté it for 2 minutes, or until it is tender.

Add the meatballs and broth. Bring the mixture to a boil, stirring it occasionally. Stir in the spinach, orzo, salt and black pepper. Reduce the heat to medium-low and cook the soup for 10 to 15 minutes, until the meatballs are cooked through and the orzo is tender.

Ladle the soup into bowls and serve it with the Pecorino Romano cheese.

RECIPE NOTES

When making the meatballs, you can use 8 ounces (224 g) of ground beef and 8 ounces (224 g) of ground pork. You can even use ground chicken or ground turkey for a healthier version.

Instead of orzo, the soup is also sometimes made with acini de pepe.

Freshly grated Pecorino Romano cheese is best in this dish.

You can make the meatballs beforehand and freeze them in a freezer bag until you're ready to use them.

NUTRITION INFORMATION

Serving size: 1 serving; **Calories:** 391; **Carbohydrates:** 31 g; **Protein:** 30 g; **Fat:** 16 g

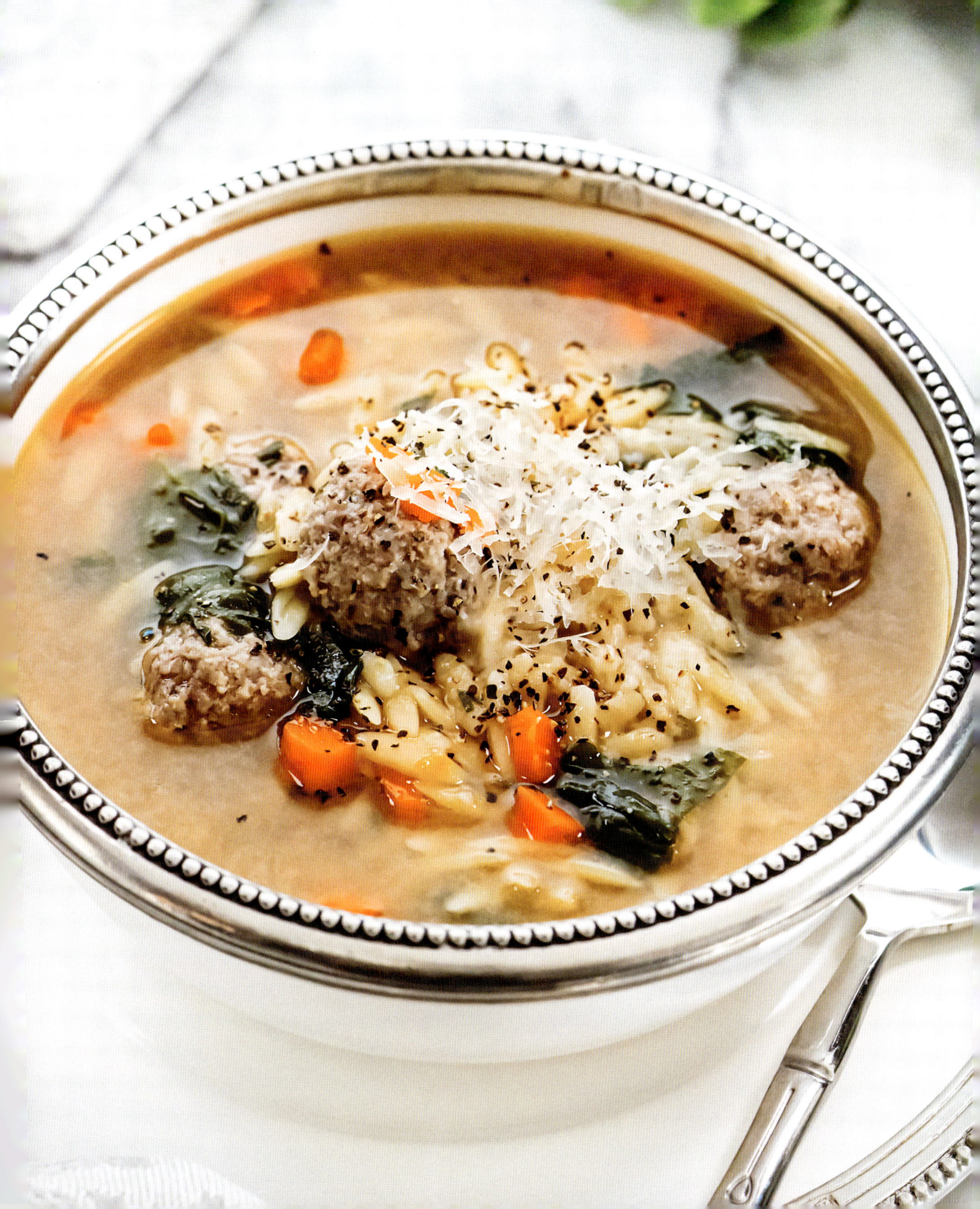

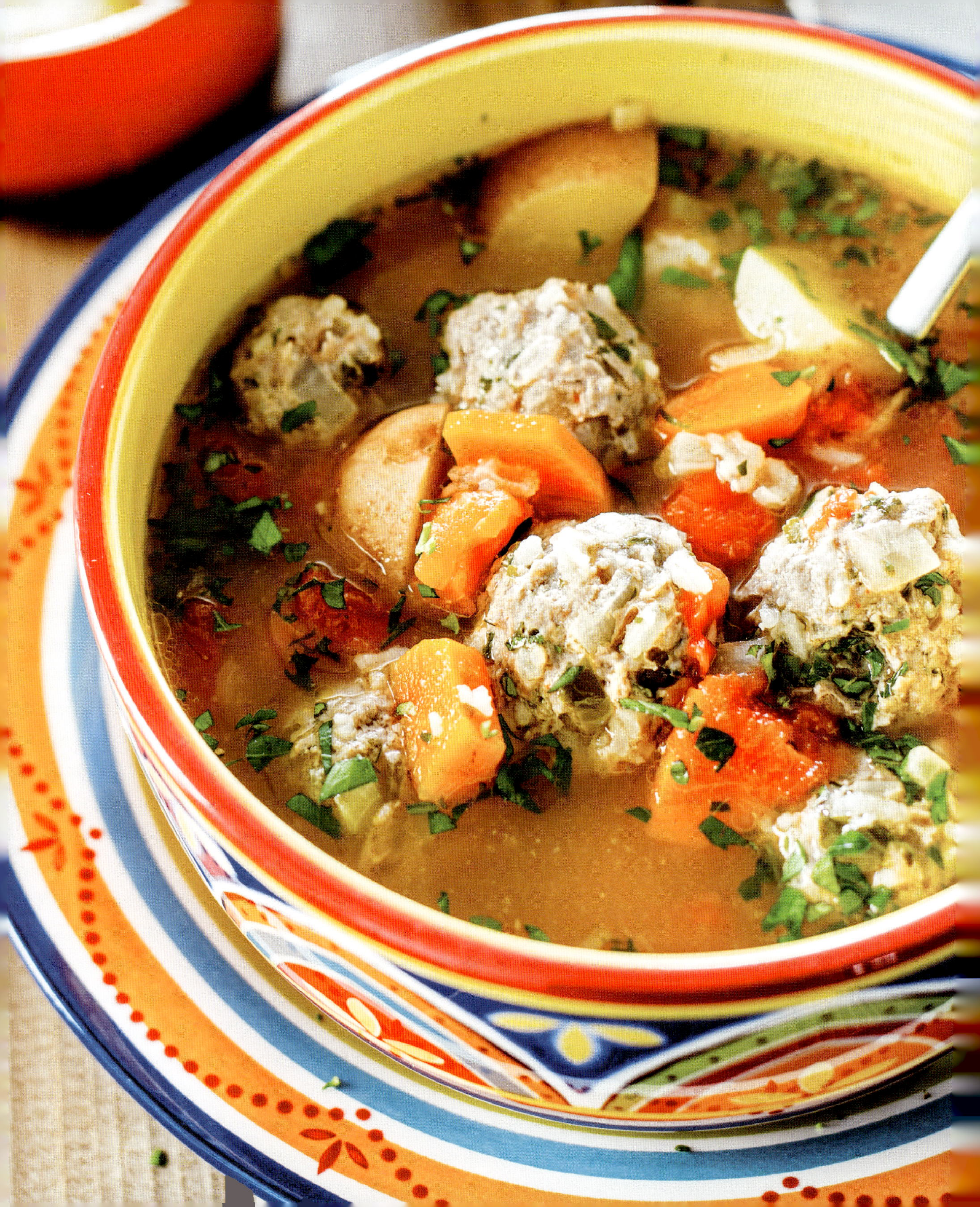

ALBONDIGAS SOUP

Don't let the fancy name of this recipe scare you away. Albondigas simply means "meatballs." This is a traditional Mexican soup, a light broth loaded with vegetables. It is quite light but very hearty. Serve it with a good crusty bread and it can be enjoyed as an entire meal.

PREP TIME: 20 MINUTES
COOK TIME: 30 MINUTES
TOTAL TIME: 50 MINUTES
SERVES: 6

MEATBALLS

1 lb (448 g) extra lean ground beef
2 cloves garlic, minced
½ onion, chopped
½ cup (105 g) long-grain rice (I recommend basmati)
1 large egg, beaten
¼ cup (12 g) chopped fresh mint
¼ cup (12 g) chopped fresh parsley
¼ cup (12 g) chopped fresh oregano or 1 tbsp (3 g) dried oregano
1 tsp ground cumin
½ tsp chili powder
½ tsp salt, or as needed
½ tsp black pepper, or as needed

SOUP

2 tbsp (30 ml) olive oil
½ onion, chopped
3 cloves garlic, minced
1 carrot, chopped
2 potatoes, peeled and chopped into 1" (3-cm) cubes
1 (15-oz [420-g]) can diced tomatoes, undrained
3 cups (720 ml) low-sodium beef broth
3 cups (720 ml) water
Salt, as needed
Black pepper, as needed
⅛ tsp cayenne pepper
1 tbsp (15 ml) fresh lemon juice
2 tbsp (6 g) chopped fresh cilantro
2 tbsp (6 g) chopped fresh parsley

To make the meatballs, combine the beef, garlic, onion, rice, egg, mint, parsley, oregano, cumin, chili powder, salt and black pepper in a large bowl. Mix the ingredients well. Shape the mixture into meatballs that are about 1 inch (3 cm) in diameter. You should get 25 to 30 meatballs. Place the meatballs in the fridge.

To make the soup, heat the oil in a heavy-bottomed 5-quart (4.8-L) pot over medium heat. Add the onion and garlic and cook them for 3 to 5 minutes, being careful not to burn the garlic, until the onion is translucent. Add the carrot and potatoes and cook the mixture for 3 to 5 minutes, until the vegetables are beginning to caramelize.

Add the tomatoes and their juice, broth, water, salt, black pepper and cayenne pepper. Bring the soup to a boil, reduce the heat to low and simmer the soup for about 5 minutes.

Slowly add the meatballs to the pot, one at a time. Slowly stir the soup with a wooden spoon. Cover the pot and cook the soup for 15 minutes, or until the meatballs are cooked through. Add the lemon juice, cilantro and parsley. Taste the soup for seasoning and adjust it as needed prior to serving the soup.

RECIPE NOTE

If you have extra meatballs or don't use them all, you can place them in an airtight container and freeze them until you are ready to use them.

NUTRITION INFORMATION

Serving size: 1 serving; **Calories:** 288; **Carbohydrates:** 21 g; **Protein:** 20 g; **Fat:** 13 g

BEEF AND BARLEY SOUP

If you're looking for a rich, hearty, delicious soup that's loaded with beef, veggies and fiber, then this soup is for you. This recipe for comfort in a bowl will take you a bit longer to get on the dinner table, but that's simply because barley takes a while to cook. But the wait is worth it—you'll love this beef and barley soup.

PREP TIME: 10 MINUTES
COOK TIME: 1 HOUR, 45 MINUTES
TOTAL TIME: 1 HOUR, 55 MINUTES
SERVES: 6

1 lb (448 g) beef stew meat
1 tsp salt, plus more as needed
1 tsp black pepper, plus more as needed
½ cup (60 g) all-purpose flour, plus more as needed
2 tbsp (30 ml) olive oil
1 onion, chopped
1 carrot, chopped
2 ribs celery, chopped
3 cloves garlic, minced
1 tbsp (3 g) chopped fresh oregano or 1 tsp dried oregano
3 tbsp (45 g) tomato paste
4 cups (960 ml) low-sodium beef broth
3 cups (720 ml) water
¾ cup (139 g) barley (see Recipe Notes)
1 tbsp (3 g) chopped fresh parsley

Season the beef with the salt and black pepper. Place the beef in a large ziplock bag and then add the flour. Seal the bag and shake it until each piece of beef is fully covered in flour. Add more flour if needed.

Heat the oil in a large pot or Dutch oven over medium-high heat. Working in batches so as not to overcrowd the pot, add the beef and cook it for 5 minutes, just until the meat starts to brown. Remove the meat from the pot and set it aside.

Add the onion, carrot and celery to the pot. Cook the vegetables for about 5 minutes, stirring them occasionally, until they are soft.

Add the garlic, oregano and tomato paste and stir to combine the ingredients. Return the beef to the pot, then add the broth and water. Season the soup with additional salt and black pepper if needed. Bring the soup to a boil, then reduce the heat to medium and cook the soup for about 45 minutes, stirring it occasionally.

Add the barley and cook the soup for another 30 minutes, stirring it occasionally, or until the barley is tender. If you find that too much liquid has evaporated or the soup is too thick, add more water until you get the desired consistency.

Remove the soup from the heat and garnish it with the parsley before serving it.

RECIPE NOTES

I use pearl barley. If you can't find barley, use rice or couscous instead. Please note that cooking time will change if using rice or couscous. Rice takes about 15 to 25 minutes and couscous about 10 minutes.

If you make this soup ahead of time, add the barley the day you serve it.

This can be made in a slow cooker. Cook it for 4 hours on high or for 8 hours on low.

NUTRITION INFORMATION

Serving size: 1 serving; **Calories:** 339; **Carbohydrates:** 31 g; **Protein:** 28 g; **Fat:** 11 g

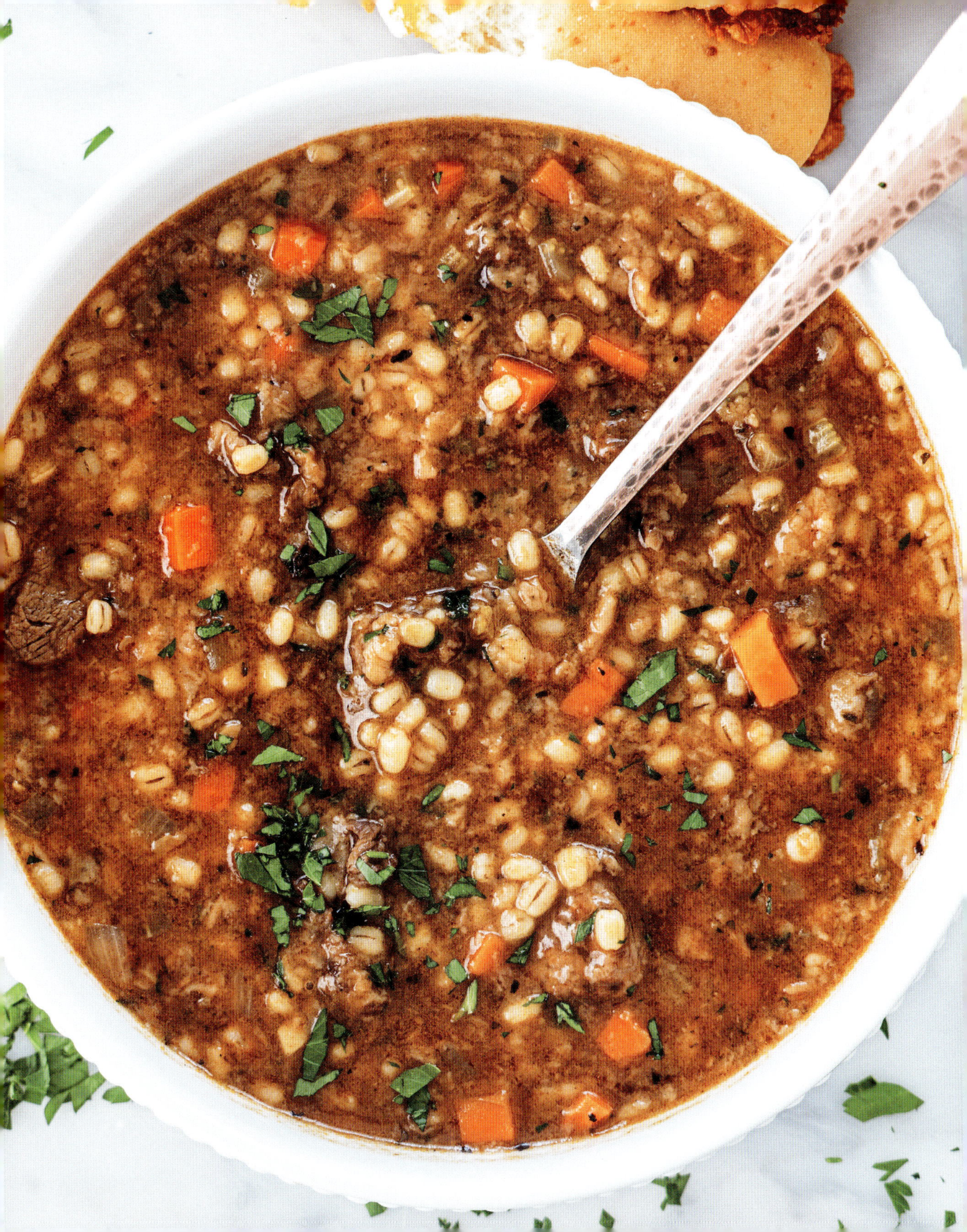

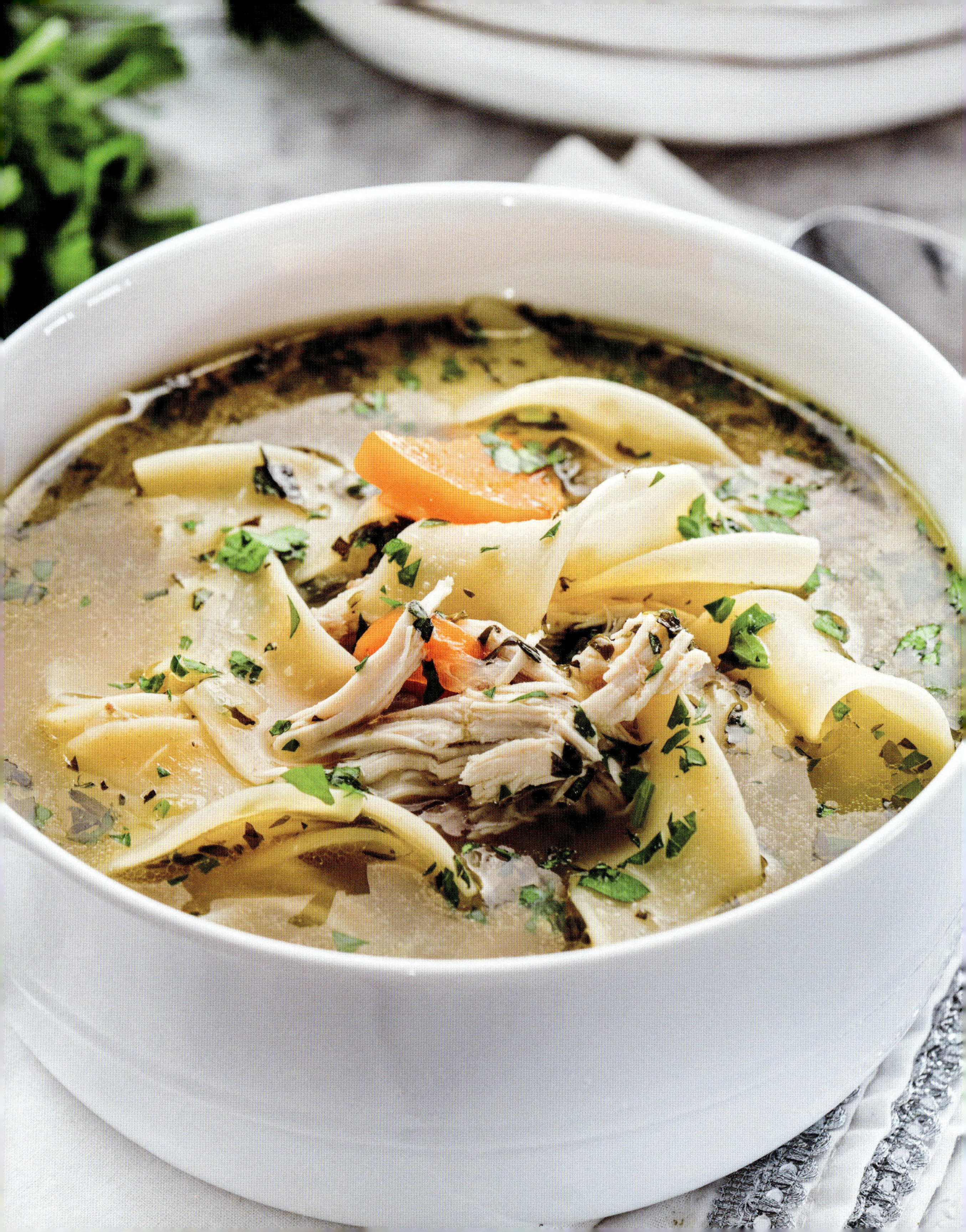

INSTANT POT® CHICKEN NOODLE SOUP

PREP TIME: 5 MINUTES
COOK TIME: 20 MINUTES
NATURAL PRESSURE RELEASE: 10 MINUTES
TOTAL TIME: 35 MINUTES
SERVES: 8

2 tbsp (30 g) unsalted butter
1 onion, chopped
2 carrots, chopped
2 ribs celery, chopped
1 tsp salt, or as needed
1 tsp black pepper, or as needed
1 tsp dried thyme or 1 tbsp (3 g) fresh thyme leaves
1 tbsp (3 g) chopped fresh parsley, plus more as needed
1 tbsp (3 g) chopped fresh oregano or 1 tsp dried oregano
4 cups (960 ml) unsalted chicken broth (see Recipe Notes)
2 lb (896 g) skin-on, bone-in chicken pieces (use at least 1 breast; see Recipe Notes)
4 cups (960 ml) water
5 oz (140 g) egg noodles

NUTRITION INFORMATION

Serving size: 1 serving; **Calories:** 374; **Carbohydrates:** 18 g; **Protein:** 26 g; **Fat:** 21 g

Not only is this the most popular soup on my blog but it's also the most popular soup in my household. Ever since I got my trusted pressure cooker, I've been making this soup on a regular basis. I even make this with a whole chicken, especially if I have a cold. If there's any tip I can give you for this soup, it is to add a dash or three of Sriracha to your bowl. You'll love it!

Turn the Instant Pot to the Sauté setting.

Add the butter and allow it to melt. Add the onion, carrots and celery and sauté the vegetables for 3 minutes, until the onion softens and becomes translucent.

Season the vegetables with the salt and black pepper. Add the thyme, parsley and oregano and stir to combine the ingredients. Pour in the broth. Add the chicken pieces and the water. Secure the lid of the Instant Pot and turn the valve from Vent to Seal. Set the Instant Pot to the Soup setting and set the timer for 7 minutes.

Once the Instant Pot's cycle is complete, wait for about 10 minutes to allow the pressure to release naturally. If you are in a rush, follow the manufacturer's guide for a quick pressure release. Carefully unlock and remove the lid from the Instant Pot.

Remove the chicken pieces from the soup and shred the meat with 2 forks.

Add the egg noodles to the soup and set the Instant Pot to the Sauté setting. Cook the soup, uncovered, for 6 minutes, or until the noodles are cooked.

Turn off the Instant Pot by pressing the Cancel button. Add the shredded chicken back to the Instant Pot. Taste the soup for seasoning and adjust it as necessary. Garnish the soup with additional parsley prior to serving it.

RECIPE NOTES

The chicken broth can be replaced with water.

You can use boneless, skinless chicken breast in this recipe, but cooking the chicken with the skin and bones will give the broth a deeper flavor. Any part of the chicken can be used, as long as you have enough chicken meat to add to the soup after you shred it. You can also use frozen chicken. The cooking time for frozen chicken can vary depending on how big your chicken pieces are, but I would start with 10 to 12 minutes and go from there.

If you plan to freeze the soup, hold off on adding the noodles. Wait to add the noodles until you reheat it. The noodles won't hold up very well after being defrosted and reheated.

CREAMY LOADED POTATO SOUP

PREP TIME: 15 MINUTES
COOK TIME: 25 MINUTES
TOTAL TIME: 40 MINUTES
SERVES: 8

8 slices thick-cut bacon
1 onion, chopped
4 cloves garlic, minced
1 tsp dried basil
1 tsp dried oregano
½ tsp salt, or as needed
½ tsp black pepper, or as needed
½ cup (60 g) all-purpose flour
3 cups (720 ml) low-sodium chicken broth
2 cups (480 ml) heavy cream
6 Yukon gold or russet potatoes, cubed and cooked (see Recipe Notes)
Chopped green onions, for serving
Shredded Cheddar cheese, for serving

Creamy soups may have a bad name, but they don't have to be bad for you. This soup is not too shabby in the calorie department, and it has a lot of other positive attributes: It's easy, relatively quick, rich and creamy, not to mention full of savory flavor. Did I mention bacon? Cheese? Yeah, it's got all that!

In a large skillet over medium heat, cook the bacon for 5 minutes, until it is crispy. Transfer it to a plate lined with paper towels, then crumble it into small pieces. Reserve 2 tablespoons (30 ml) of the rendered bacon fat and discard the rest.

In a large Dutch oven or pot over medium heat, combine the reserved bacon fat and onion. Cook the onion for about 5 minutes, until it is soft and translucent. Add the garlic and cook the mixture for 30 seconds, until the garlic is aromatic. Stir in the basil, oregano, salt and black pepper.

Sprinkle the flour over the mixture and stir to combine the ingredients. Cook the mixture for about 1 minute to get rid of the raw flour taste. Add the broth 1 cup (240 ml) at a time, stirring to remove any lumps. Once all the broth has been added, add the heavy cream all at once. Bring the soup to a boil.

Add the potatoes, reduce the heat to medium-low and cook the soup for 10 minutes, stirring it occasionally. The soup should thicken nicely. Stir in half of the bacon. Taste the soup for seasoning and adjust it as necessary.

Ladle the soup into bowls, top each serving with the remaining bacon and serve the soup with the green onions and Cheddar cheese.

RECIPE NOTES

Add the cubed potatoes to a pot of salted boiling water and cook them for about 15 minutes, until they are fork-tender. Alternatively, bake them in the oven at 425°F (218°C) for about 45 minutes, until they are fork-tender.

Store leftover soup in airtight containers and refrigerate them within 2 hours of cooking. The soup will last for 3 to 4 days in the fridge or for 4 to 6 months in the freezer.

NUTRITION INFORMATION

Serving size: 1 serving; **Calories:** 422; **Carbohydrates:** 27 g; **Protein:** 10 g; **Fat:** 32 g

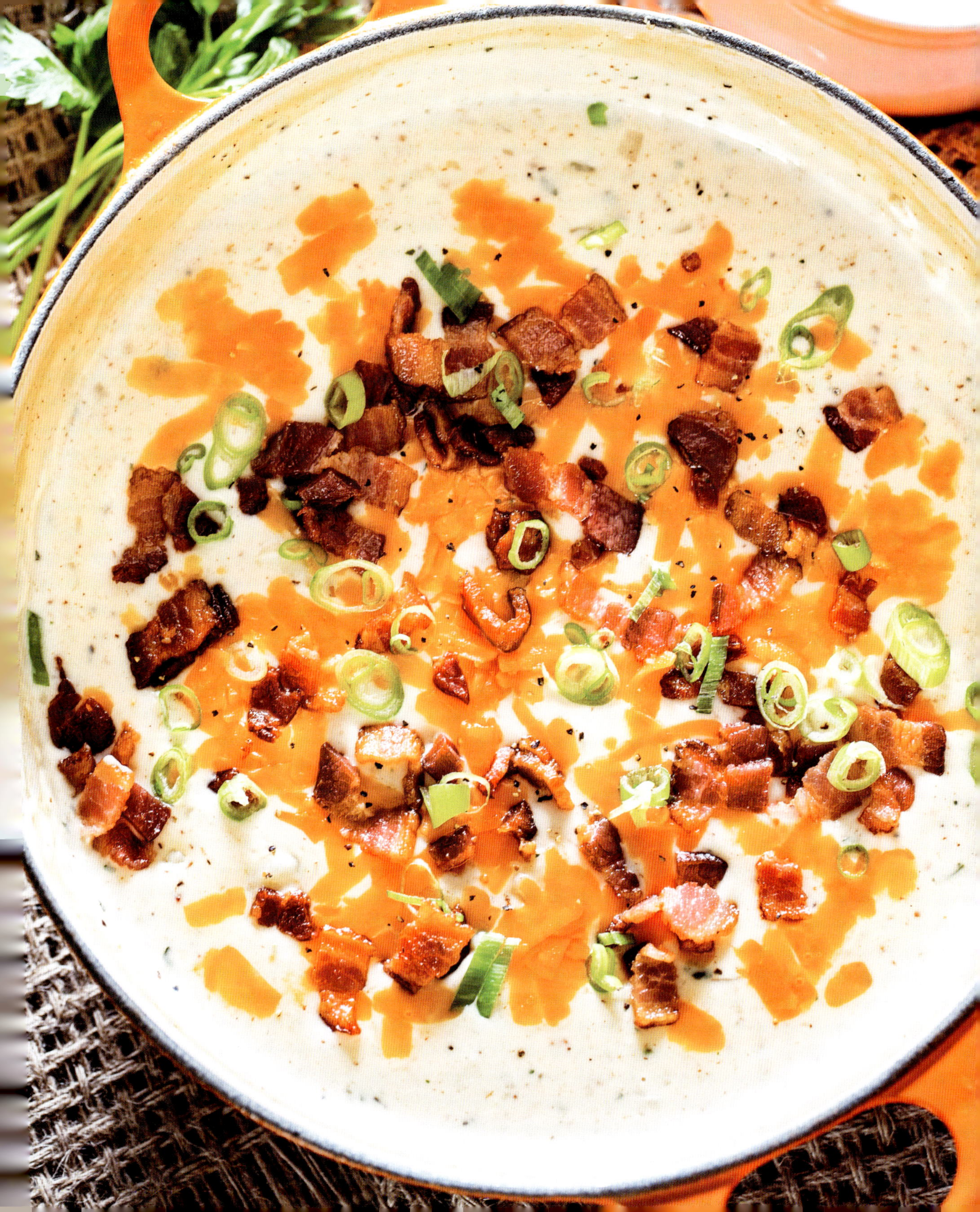

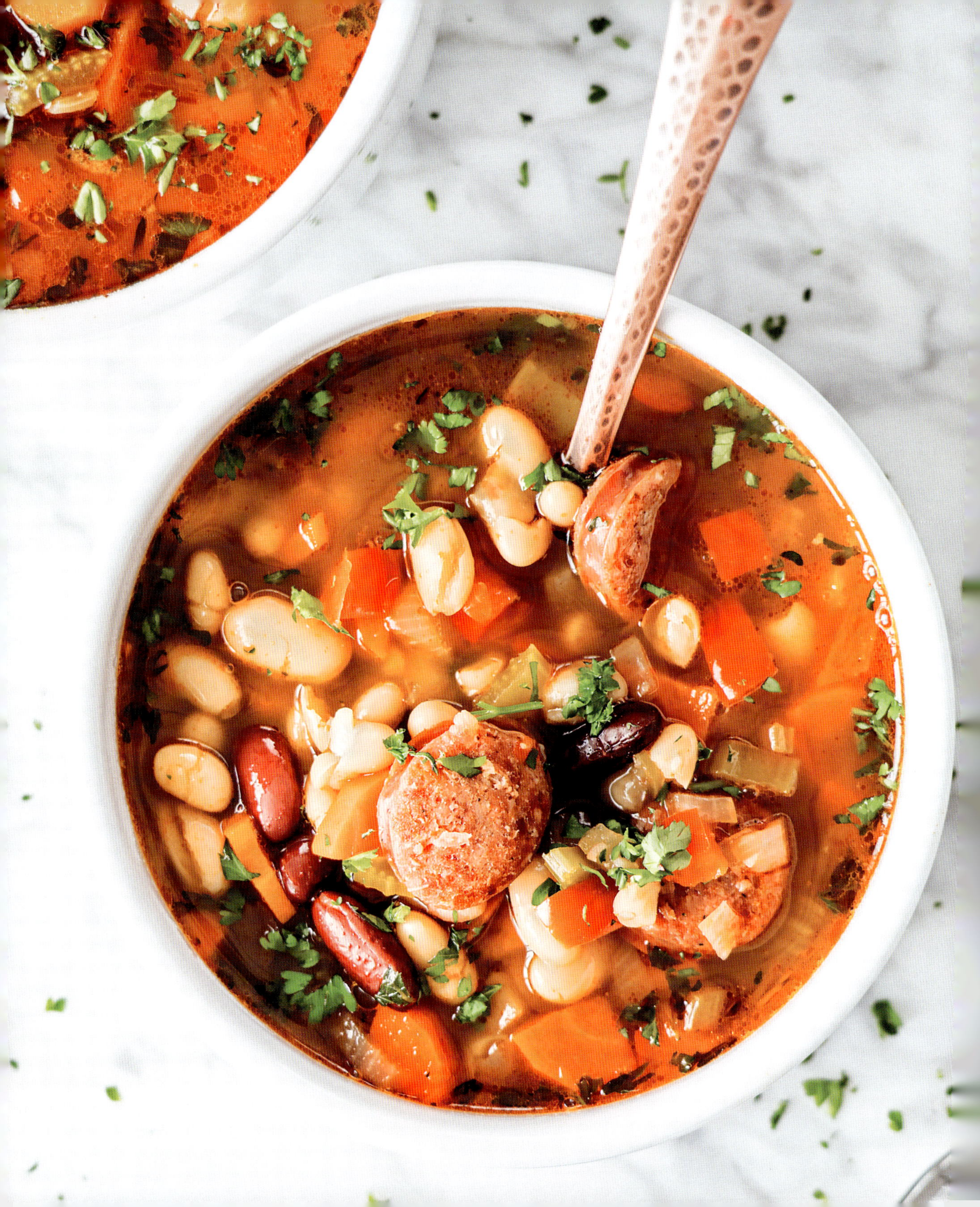

SAUSAGE AND BEAN SOUP

This is what I call a manly soup, a soup my husband loves. It's loaded with veggies, beans and sausage, so it's extra filling. Bursting with bold flavors, it will make your house smell amazing. Serve this with a good crusty bread because you're going to want to dip it in this soup.

PREP TIME: 10 MINUTES
COOK TIME: 45 MINUTES
TOTAL TIME: 55 MINUTES
SERVES: 8

2 tbsp (30 ml) olive oil
10 oz (280 g) sausage of choice (see Recipe Note)
1 onion, chopped
2 carrots, chopped
3 ribs celery, chopped
1 red bell pepper, chopped
1 tsp salt, or as needed
½ tsp black pepper, or as needed
1 tsp smoked paprika
1 tsp chopped fresh thyme
3 cloves garlic, minced
2 dried bay leaves
8 cups (1.9 L) low-sodium or unsalted chicken broth
1 (15-oz [420-g]) can navy beans, drained and rinsed
1 (15-oz [420-g]) can red kidney beans, drained and rinsed
1 (15-oz [420-g]) can cannellini beans, drained and rinsed
1 tbsp (9 g) chopped fresh parsley

Heat the oil in a large Dutch oven or pot over medium heat. Add the sausage and cook it for 5 minutes, until it is browned. If the sausage you're using is fatty, you might need to drain some of the fat.

Add the onion, carrots, celery, bell pepper, salt, black pepper, smoked paprika and thyme. Stir everything together and cook the mixture for about 8 minutes, or until the vegetables soften. Stir in the garlic.

Add the bay leaves and broth. Bring the soup to a boil, then reduce the heat to low. Bring the soup to a simmer, cover the Dutch oven and cook the soup for 20 minutes.

Add the navy beans, kidney beans and cannellini beans to the soup and cook it, uncovered, for 10 minutes, until the beans have warmed through.

Discard the bay leaves. Garnish the soup with the parsley and serve.

RECIPE NOTE

I like to use old-fashioned farmers' sausage in this soup, but there are many types of sausages you can use: Italian sausage, chicken sausage, kielbasa, andouille or any smoked sausage.

NUTRITION INFORMATION

Serving size: 1 serving; **Calories:** 386; **Carbohydrates:** 42 g; **Protein:** 22 g; **Fat:** 15 g

BROCCOLI-CHEESE SOUP

PREP TIME: 5 MINUTES
COOK TIME: 25 MINUTES
TOTAL TIME: 30 MINUTES
SERVES: 8

6 tbsp (90 g) unsalted butter
1 onion, chopped
6 tbsp (48 g) all-purpose flour
2 cups (480 ml) half-and-half (see Recipe Notes)
6 cups (1.4 L) low-sodium chicken broth
1 tsp salt
1 tsp white pepper
¼ tsp ground nutmeg
1 lb (448 g) broccoli florets (see Recipe Notes)
1 cup (140 g) cubed Velveeta (see Recipe Notes)
3 cups (360 g) shredded Cheddar cheese, divided
2 tbsp (6 g) chopped fresh parsley

I'm a sucker for creamy soups, and this soup is near the top of my list. Give me anything that's cheesy and I'll be your best friend for life. I like to fool myself that this is a healthy soup because it has broccoli, but let's face it—this soup is really a cheese sauce with broccoli thrown in. Whatever you want to call it, this soup is utterly addictive.

You may ask why I chose to use Velveeta here, but I'm willing to take all the flak—Velveeta is a must in this soup. Velveeta is what makes this soup creamy, smooth and silky. Yeah, you can replace it with more Cheddar cheese, but Velveeta takes the soup to the next level of creaminess.

Melt the butter in a large Dutch oven over medium heat. Add the onion and cook it for 5 minutes, until it is soft and beginning to brown.

Sprinkle the flour over the onion and gently whisk to combine the ingredients. Cook the mixture for about 2 minutes to remove the raw flour flavor.

Slowly whisk in the half-and-half. Pour in the broth and whisk the mixture to remove any lumps and to scrape away any browned bits from the bottom of the Dutch oven.

Season the soup with the salt, white pepper and nutmeg. Bring the soup to a boil, then add the broccoli. Cook the soup for about 10 minutes, until the broccoli is tender.

Add the Velveeta and 2 cups (240 g) of the Cheddar cheese, stirring the soup constantly until the cheeses have completely melted. Taste the soup for seasoning and adjust it as necessary.

Top the soup with the remaining 1 cup (120 g) of Cheddar cheese and garnish it with the parsley.

RECIPE NOTES

Half-and-half, also known as half cream, is a blend of equal parts whole milk and light cream. It averages 10 to 12 percent fat.

You can use precut fresh or frozen broccoli florets.

If you don't want to use Velveeta, you can substitute it with more Cheddar or Monterey Jack cheese. Note that Velveeta will make the soup creamier and smoother.

If preferred, you can puree the broccoli in the soup for a thicker texture; I prefer the bigger florets in the soup.

Store leftover soup in the fridge for up to 3 days. Reheat it over low heat to avoid scorching it.

NUTRITION INFORMATION

Serving size: 1 serving; **Calories:** 427; **Carbohydrates:** 13 g; **Protein:** 19 g; **Fat:** 33 g

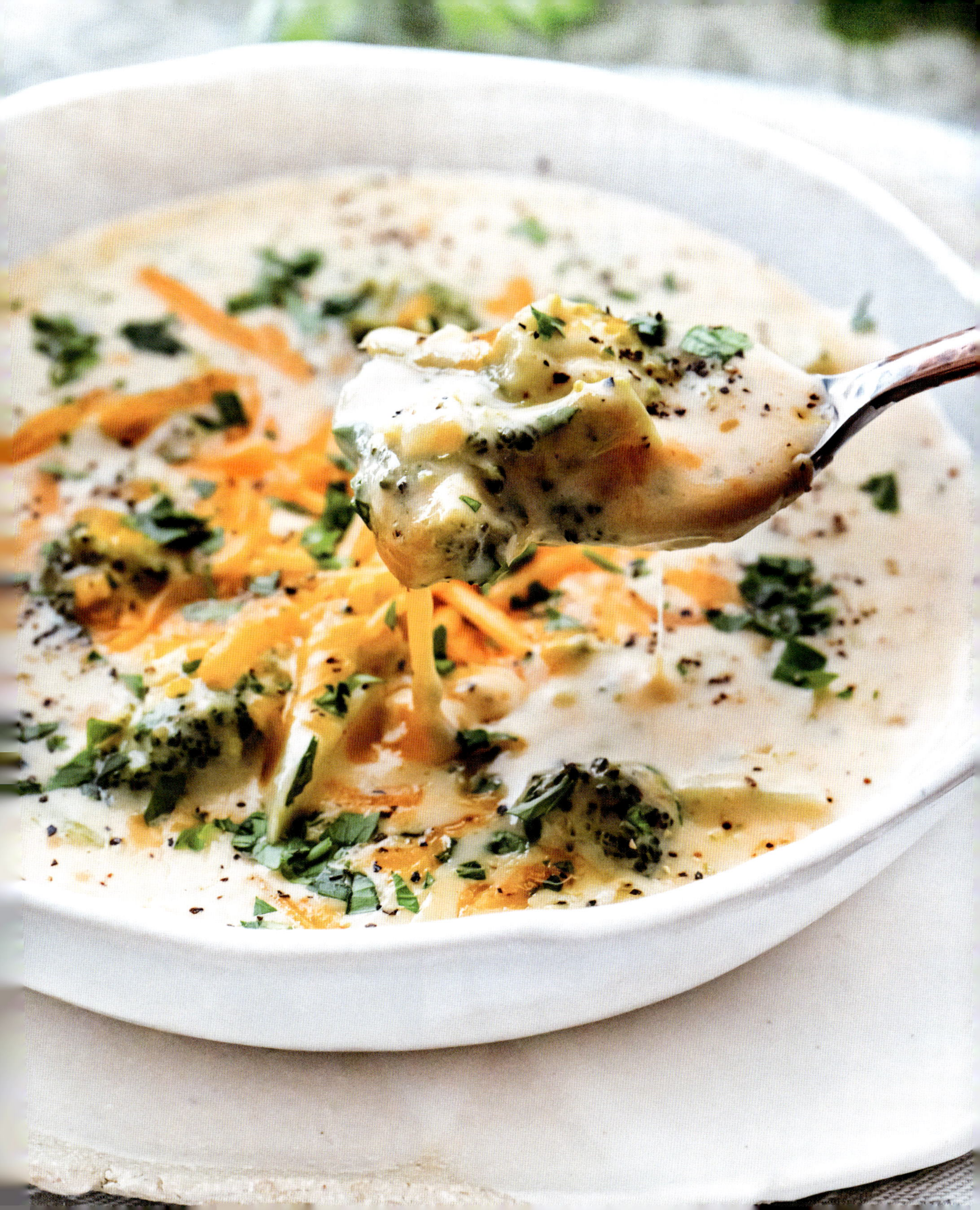

STARTERS

A MEAL ISN'T THE SAME WITHOUT A FANTASTIC STARTER. Starters are the key to not only a good dinner but a good party, whether you're hosting friends or family, watching a game or celebrating a special event.

When I was in college, I'd have some friends over and we'd make only appetizers like Easy Bruschetta (page 316) or Pico de Gallo (page 320)—we didn't need dinner! We'd nibble on a bunch of appetizers with some great cocktails and that was how we rolled. As an adult—I do consider myself an adult sometimes—when I host a dinner party, I actually serve the dinner as well, but I never skip the starter course.

Starters are a great way to entertain your guests: Even if your dinner isn't done cooking, you can keep them entertained and satisfied with some tasty starters. You can even make most starters ahead of time, like my Taco Meatball Ring (page 327) or Homemade Salsa (page 336), which really makes it a breeze when hosting a party. I love starters so much that I never serve just one appetizer. Sometimes I go all out and make three or four different kinds. Don't worry, I'm not crazy—I don't make them all the same day. Nope, I prep them all before. I want to enjoy the party too, not just cook in the kitchen!

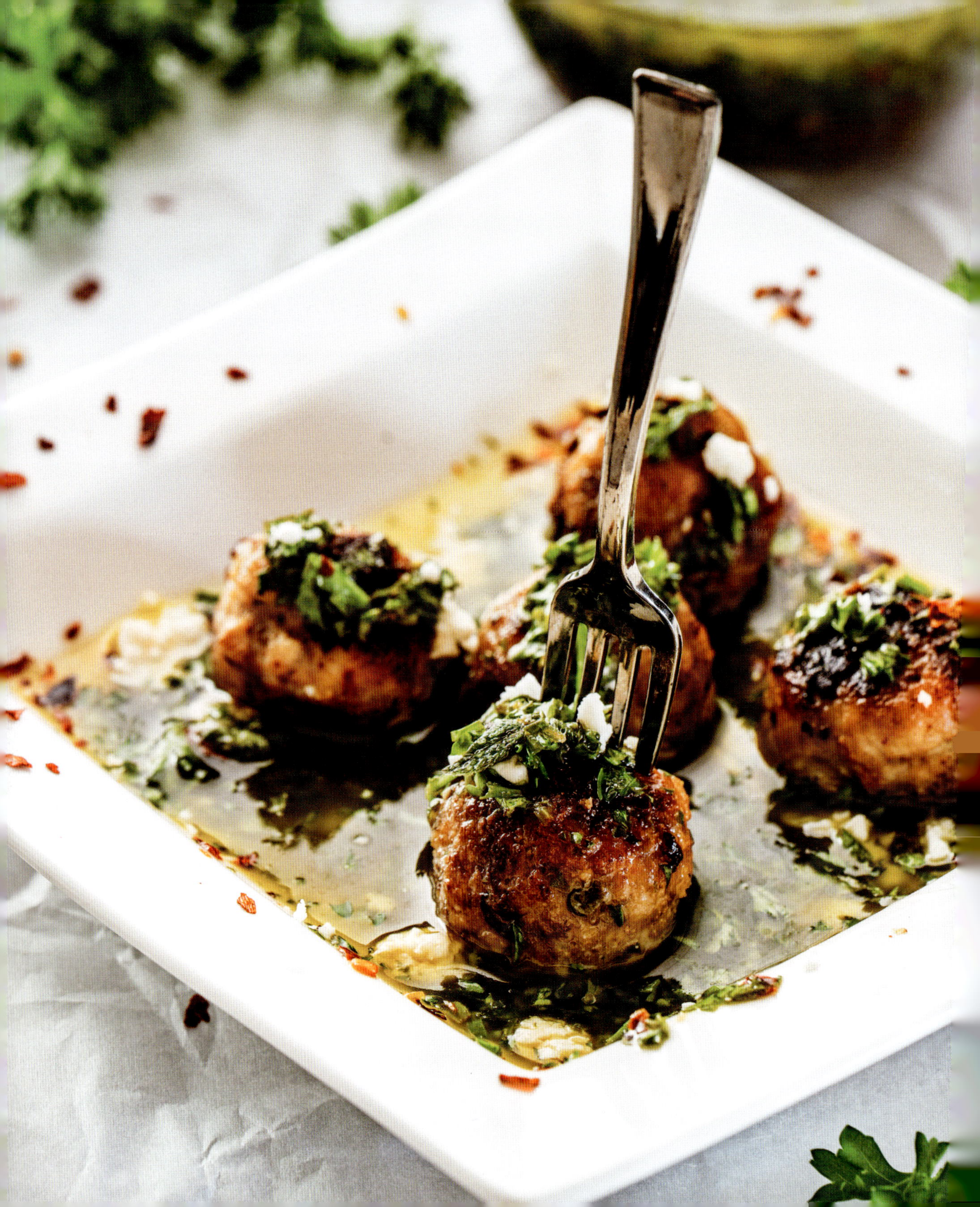

CHIMICHURRI MEATBALLS

If you follow my blog, you know how much I love meatballs. I have dozens of meatball recipes. Pairing these meatballs with chimichurri sauce and a bit of feta cheese was a no-brainer.

PREP TIME: 30 MINUTES
COOK TIME: 15 MINUTES
TOTAL TIME: 45 MINUTES
SERVES: 16

CHIMICHURRI SAUCE
½ cup (24 g) minced fresh curly-leaf parsley
½ cup (120 ml) olive oil
¼ cup (60 ml) red wine vinegar
1 tbsp (3 g) chopped fresh oregano
½ tsp red pepper flakes
1 tbsp (15 ml) fresh lemon juice
½ tsp salt
½ tsp black pepper (see Recipe Notes)

MEATBALLS
1 lb (448 g) ground pork (see Recipe Notes)
8 oz (224 g) ground beef
½ cup (30 g) panko breadcrumbs
2 green onions, minced
3 cloves garlic, minced
½ tsp salt
½ tsp black pepper
1 large egg
3 tbsp (45 ml) vegetable oil
½ cup (75 g) crumbled feta cheese

To make the chimichurri sauce, whisk together the parsley, olive oil, vinegar, oregano, red pepper flakes, lemon juice, salt and black pepper in a medium bowl. Let the chimichurri sauce sit at room temperature until the meatballs are ready.

To make the meatballs, combine the pork, beef, breadcrumbs, green onions, garlic, salt, black pepper and egg in a large bowl.

Form the meat mixture into about 48 (1-inch [3-cm]) meatballs.

Heat the vegetable oil in a large skillet over medium heat. Working in batches so as not to overcrowd the skillet, fry the meatballs for about 7 minutes, until they are golden all around.

To assemble the appetizer, pour about half of the chimichurri sauce on the bottom of a serving platter, then transfer the meatballs to the platter. Top the meatballs with the remaining chimichurri sauce and garnish them with the feta cheese.

RECIPE NOTES

Freshly ground black pepper is best in this dish.

These meatballs can be made with any type of ground meat that you prefer.

If you don't want to fry the meatballs, you can bake them. Place them on a baking sheet lined with parchment paper and bake them at 400°F (204°C) for 20 to 25 minutes, or until they are done to your liking.

Refrigerate any leftovers in an airtight container for 3 or 4 days.

NUTRITION INFORMATION

Serving size: 3 meatballs; **Calories:** 214; **Carbohydrates:** 3 g; **Protein:** 9 g; **Fat:** 18 g

EASY BRUSCHETTA

PREP TIME: 15 MINUTES
COOK TIME: 5 MINUTES
TOTAL TIME: 20 MINUTES
SERVES: 6

1 baguette, cut in ½" (13-mm)-thick slices

2 cups (360 g) finely chopped tomatoes (see Recipe Notes)

2 cloves garlic, minced

¼ onion, finely chopped

6 leaves fresh basil, finely chopped

½ cup (90 g) grated Parmesan cheese (see Recipe Notes)

¼ tsp salt, plus more as needed

½ tsp black pepper, plus more as needed

3 tbsp (45 ml) olive oil

¼ cup (60 ml) balsamic reduction (optional; see Recipe Notes)

Oh, bruschetta! In my opinion, it's one of the best things to ever come out of Italy. Yes, there are pizzas and pastas, but nothing beats a good bruschetta over a piece of crusty baguette. A good Italian bruschetta is made with Italian tomatoes, such as Roma or cherry tomatoes, and some great cheese. For my recipe, I chose a freshly grated, high-quality Parmesan cheese. It is also customary to top bruschetta with a balsamic vinegar, balsamic reduction or even some good olive oil, but because there's olive oil in my bruschetta, I recommend a balsamic reduction.

Preheat the oven to broil. Place the baguette slices on a large baking sheet. Place the baguette slices under the broiler and toast them for 1 to 2 minutes per side, until they are golden. Set the baguette slices aside.

In a medium bowl, toss together the tomatoes, garlic, onion, basil, Parmesan cheese, salt, black pepper and oil. Taste the bruschetta for seasoning and adjust it with additional salt and black pepper if needed.

Top the toasted baguette slices with the bruschetta and drizzle the balsamic reduction (if using) over the bruschetta.

RECIPE NOTES

Usually, Roma or cherry tomatoes are used in bruschetta. You can also use heirloom tomatoes.

Freshly grated Parmesan cheese is best in this dish.

Balsamic reduction is a glaze made from balsamic vinegar. You can usually buy balsamic reduction, which is often found with the vinegars and oils. To make your own balsamic reduction, place about ½ cup (120 ml) of balsamic vinegar in a small saucepan over medium-high heat. Bring the vinegar to a boil, then reduce heat to low and let the vinegar simmer for about 10 minutes, stirring it occasionally, or until it reduces enough to coat the back of a spoon. Let the balsamic reduction cool before using it.

If preferred, prior to toasting the bread, you could brush both sides of the baguette slices with a bit of olive oil and season them with some salt and black pepper.

Store leftover bruschetta by itself in an airtight container in the refrigerator for up to 3 days. Do not leave bruschetta at room temperature for more than 2 hours.

NUTRITION INFORMATION

Serving size: 1 serving; **Calories:** 220; **Carbohydrates:** 23 g; **Protein:** 7 g; **Fat:** 10 g

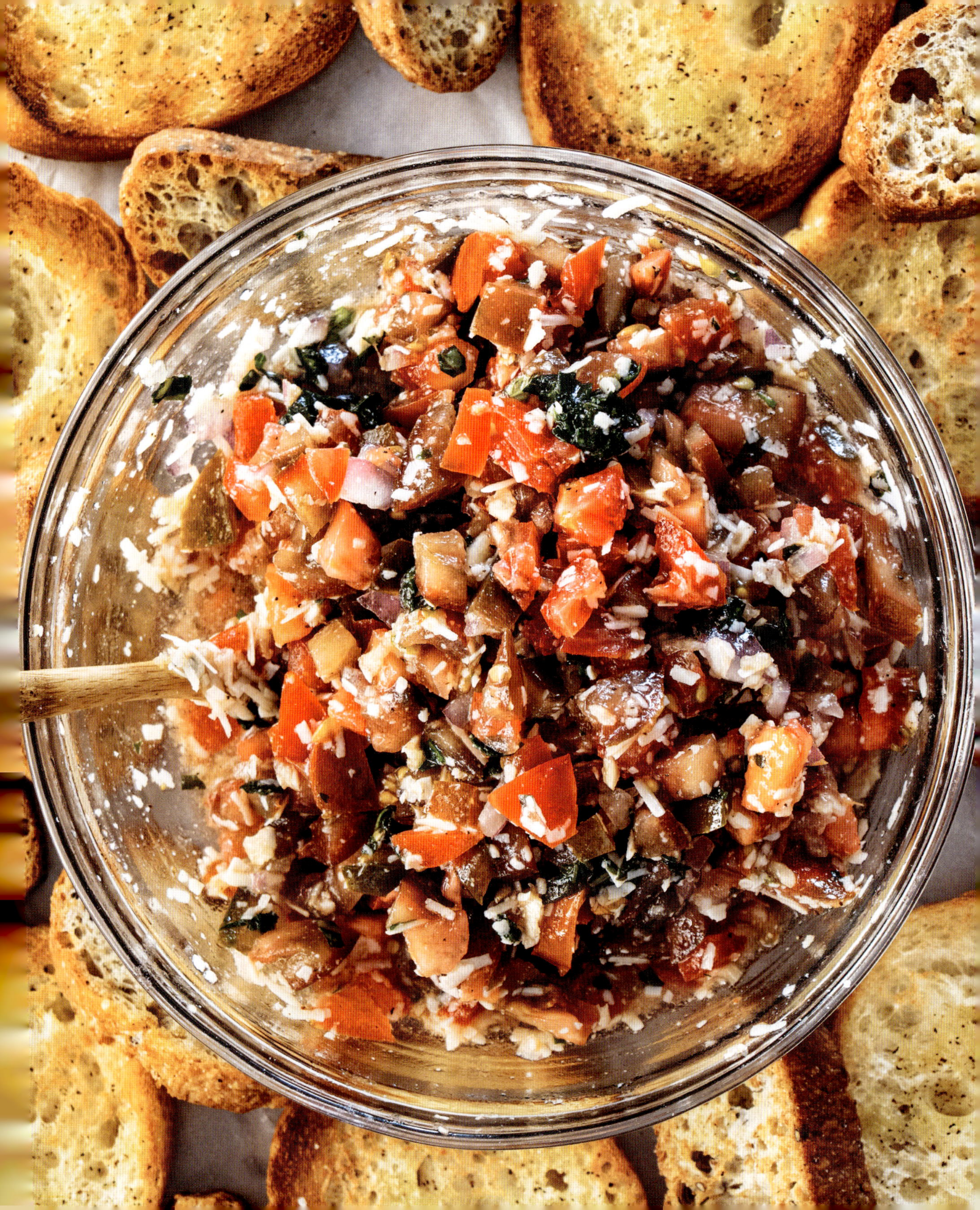

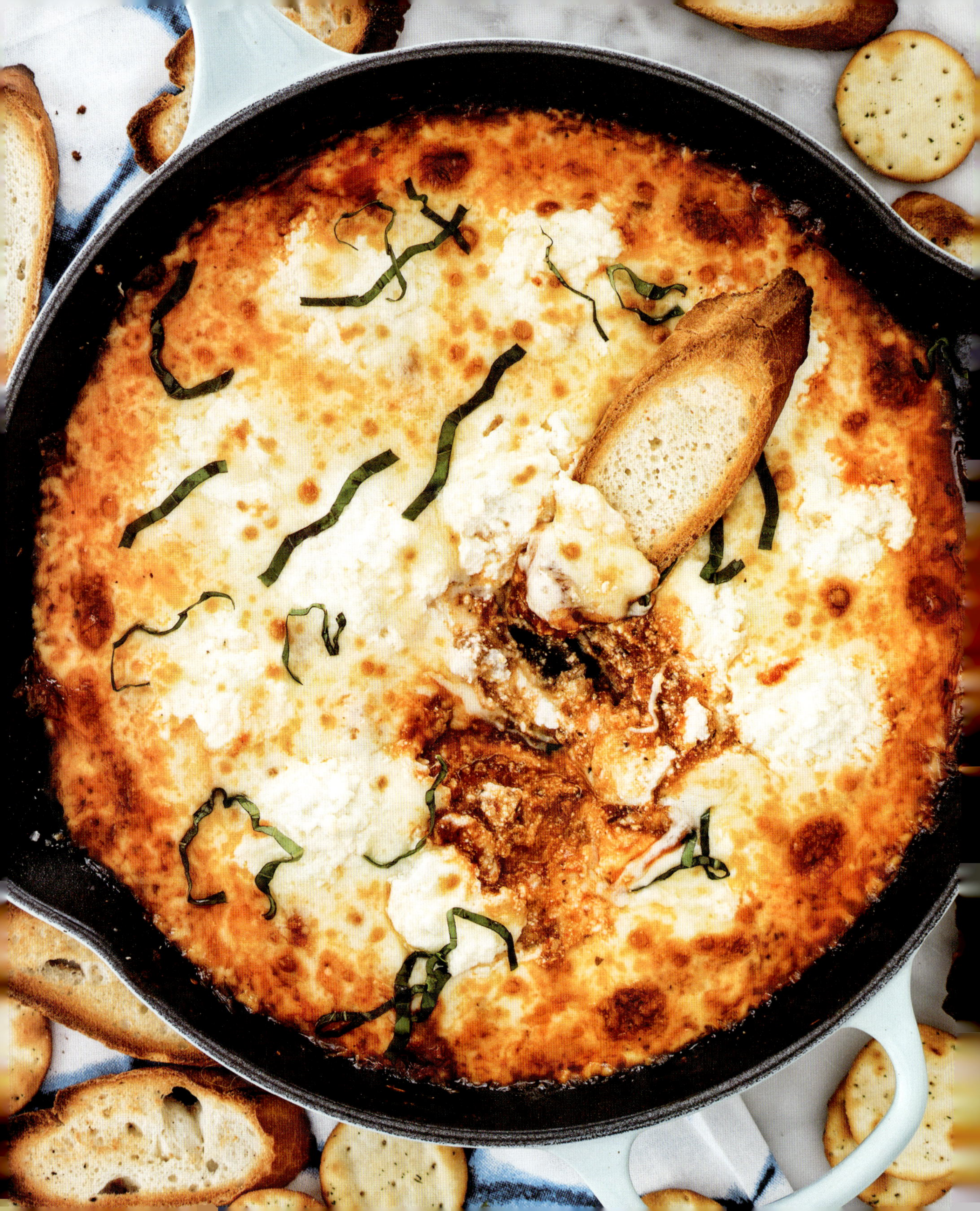

LASAGNA DIP

PREP TIME: 10 MINUTES
COOK TIME: 30 MINUTES
TOTAL TIME: 40 MINUTES
SERVES: 6

8 oz (224 g) Italian sausage, casings removed
2 cloves garlic, minced
1 tsp Italian seasoning
2 cups (480 ml) marinara sauce
Salt, as needed
Black pepper, as needed
1 cup (123 g) ricotta cheese
2 cups (224 g) shredded mozzarella cheese
¼ cup (45 g) grated Parmesan cheese
3 leaves fresh basil, chopped
Baguette slices or crackers, for serving

Who doesn't love lasagna? I honestly don't know of anyone. Even my picky husband, who is not a fan of pasta, loves lasagna. But when you take the delicious meat sauce and cheese that go into lasagna and turn them into a dip, well, you've got a masterpiece. This dip so good, you won't be able to stop yourself from eating it. I recommend digging in with some toasted baguette slices or your favorite crackers.

Preheat the oven to 450°F (232°C).

In a large, oven-safe skillet over medium heat, cook the sausage for 5 to 7 minutes, breaking it up with a wooden spoon as it cooks, until the meat is no longer pink. Add the garlic and Italian seasoning. Stir to combine the ingredients and cook them for 30 seconds.

Add the marinara sauce and stir it into the sausage mixture. Taste the meat sauce for seasoning and adjust it with salt and black pepper as needed. Bring the meat sauce to a simmer, reduce the heat to low and cook the sauce for 5 minutes. Remove it from the heat.

Top the meat sauce with dollops of the ricotta cheese all over. Sprinkle the mozzarella cheese over the meat sauce and ricotta. Sprinkle the Parmesan cheese over everything.

Bake the dip for 15 minutes, until the cheeses melt and are bubbly.

Garnish dip with chopped basil and serve it with the baguette slices.

RECIPE NOTES

Let the dip cool and transfer it to an airtight container. If there is lots of dip left over, you can keep it in the skillet and cover it well with plastic wrap. The dip will keep well in the fridge for up to 3 days.

You can reheat the dip in the skillet in an oven preheated to 400°F (204°C) for about 10 minutes, or until it is heated through.

NUTRITION INFORMATION

Serving size: 1 serving; **Calories:** 352; **Carbohydrates:** 7 g; **Protein:** 21 g; **Fat:** 27 g

PICO DE GALLO

PREP TIME: 20 MINUTES
COOK TIME: NONE
REST TIME: 10 MINUTES
TOTAL TIME: 30 MINUTES
SERVES: 8

8 Roma tomatoes, seeds removed and diced into ¼" (6-mm) pieces
½ red onion, diced into ¼" (6-mm) pieces
1 jalapeño, diced into small pieces
¼ cup (12 g) finely chopped fresh cilantro
¼ cup (60 ml) fresh lime juice
½ tsp salt, or as needed
½ tsp black pepper, or as needed

I love inviting my friends over for lunch and cooking for them. One of my favorite things to cook is Mexican food—everyone loves it, and it's easy to make. This pico de gallo is an appetizer I make for these gatherings with my friends. It's fresh, healthy and a great starter.

In a medium bowl, combine the tomatoes, onion, jalapeño and cilantro. Pour in the lime juice, then season the mixture with the salt and black pepper. Toss everything together until the ingredients are well combined and let the pico de gallo rest for at least 10 minutes before serving it.

RECIPE NOTES

Store the pico de gallo in an airtight container in the fridge for 3 days. As excess liquid collects, drain it off and refresh your pico de gallo with a spritz of lime juice and some more seasoning. I don't recommend freezing this recipe. The fresh ingredients will get soggy and lose their shape after thawing.

NUTRITION INFORMATION

Serving size: 1 serving; **Calories:** 17; **Carbohydrates:** 4 g; **Protein:** 1 g; **Fat:** 1 g

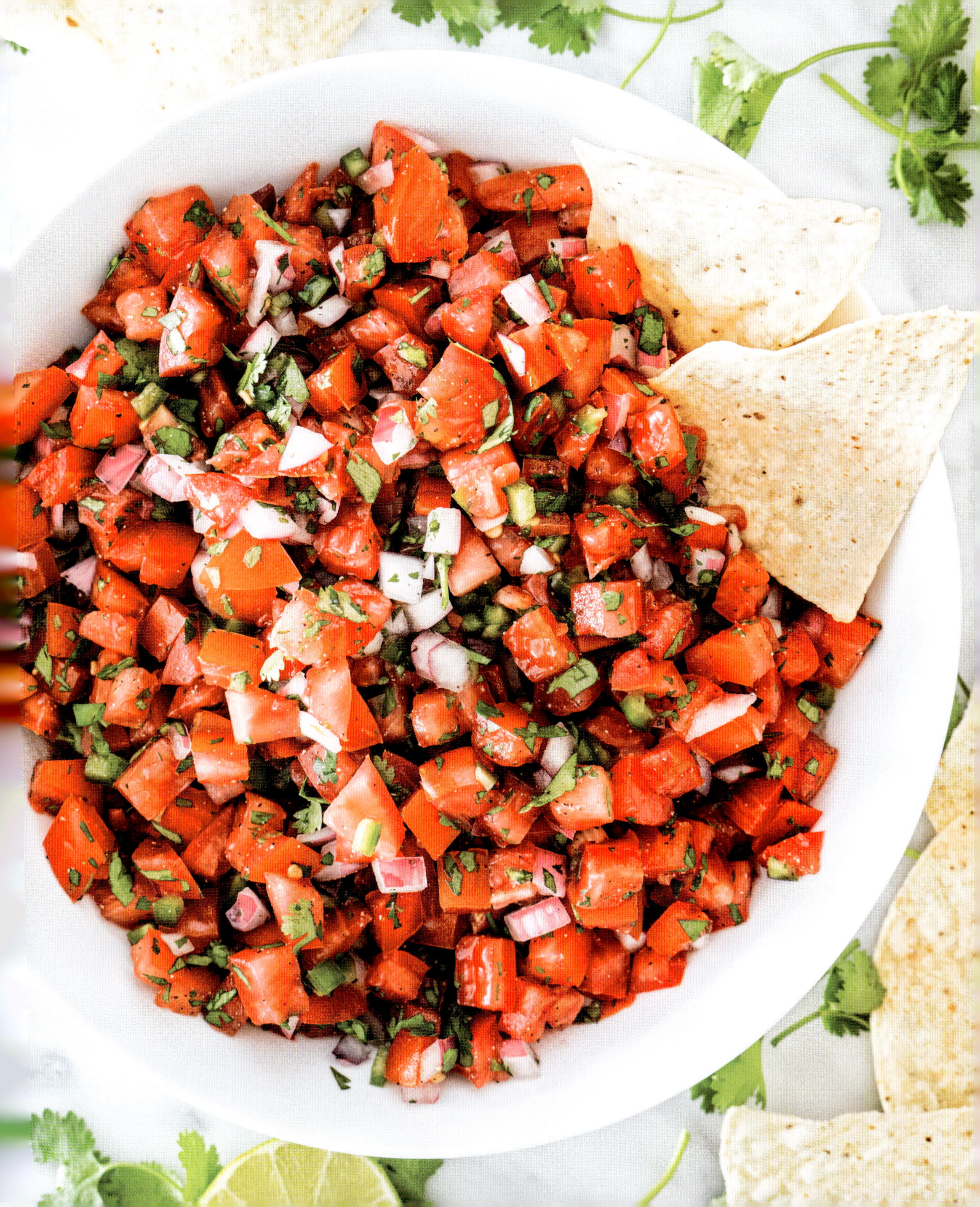

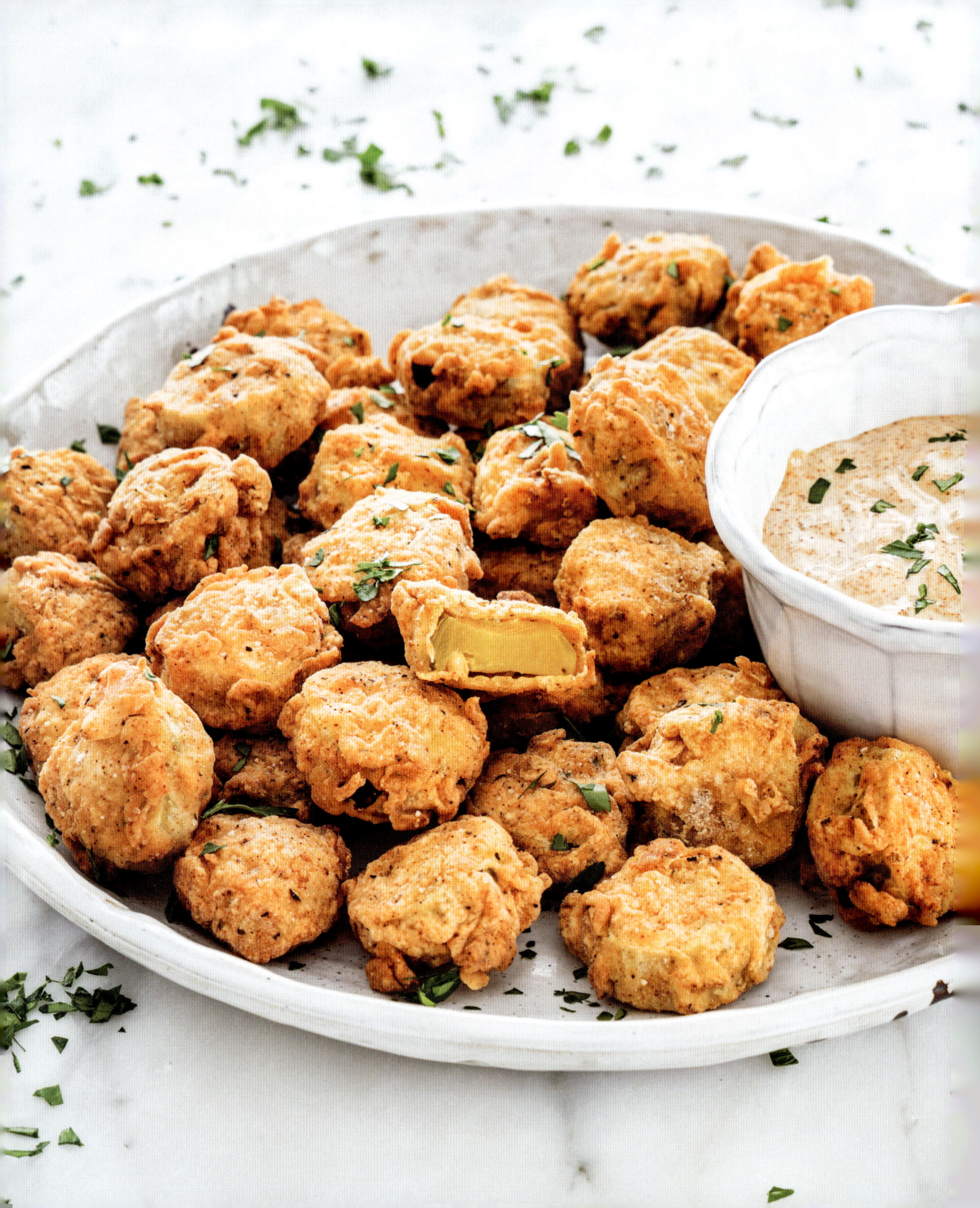

FRIED PICKLES

If you've never had fried pickles, you're in for a treat! They make for a great snack or starter, and they're popular in the South. Now we can all be Southerners—or at least enjoy Southern food, right?

PREP TIME: 15 MINUTES
COOK TIME: 10 MINUTES
TOTAL TIME: 25 MINUTES
SERVES: 4

Vegetable oil, as needed
1 cup (120 g) all-purpose flour
½ tsp salt, or as needed
½ tsp black pepper, or as needed
1 tsp paprika
½ tsp Italian seasoning
¼ tsp cayenne pepper
½ cup (120 ml) buttermilk
1 large egg
2 cups (306 g) sliced dill pickles, drained
Ranch dressing, for serving

Fill a 5-quart (4.8-L) Dutch oven with 2 to 3 inches (6 to 9 cm) of the vegetable oil. Heat the oil to 375°F (191°C). This should take about 10 minutes.

Meanwhile, combine the flour, salt, black pepper, paprika, Italian seasoning and cayenne pepper in a medium bowl. In another medium bowl, whisk together the buttermilk and egg.

Dredge the pickles through the flour mixture, then through the buttermilk mixture and finally through the flour mixture again. Carefully transfer about 5 of the battered pickles to the hot oil and fry them for 1 to 2 minutes, until they are golden brown. Repeat this step with the remaining ingredients.

Serve the warm fried pickles with the ranch dressing.

RECIPE NOTE
Leftover fried pickles will keep in an airtight container in the fridge for 2 to 3 days.

NUTRITION INFORMATION
Serving size: 1 serving; **Calories:** 225; **Carbohydrates:** 16 g; **Protein:** 5 g; **Fat:** 16 g

VEGETARIAN STUFFED MUSHROOMS

These vegetarian stuffed mushrooms are probably the first appetizer I shared on my blog. I remember my mom teaching me how to make these when I was a kid, so needless to say these are one of my favorites. They're incredibly easy to make, they're healthy and they're so much fun to eat. Just pop one in your mouth and enjoy!

PREP TIME: 15 MINUTES
COOK TIME: 25 MINUTES
TOTAL TIME: 40 MINUTES
SERVES: 10

40 white button mushrooms, stems removed and reserved
2 tbsp (30 ml) olive oil
1 red bell pepper, chopped
¼ cup (80 g) chopped roasted red bell pepper
½ onion, chopped
3 green onions, chopped
1 tsp dried oregano
½ tsp salt, or as needed
¼ tsp black pepper, or as needed
¼ cup (12 g) chopped fresh parsley
6 tbsp (54 g) breadcrumbs
4 tbsp (44 g) grated Parmesan cheese

Preheat the oven to 400°F (204°C).

While the oven is preheating, chop half of the mushrooms' stems. Discard the remaining half of the stems. Set the chopped stems aside.

Place the mushrooms stem side down on a large baking sheet. Bake the mushrooms for about 5 minutes, until they release their juices. Place the mushrooms stem side down on paper towels to soak up any additional liquid.

Heat the oil in a large skillet over medium heat. Add the mushroom stems, red bell pepper, roasted red bell pepper, onion, green onions, oregano, salt and black pepper. Sauté the mixture for about 5 minutes, until the red bell pepper and onion are tender.

Transfer the stuffing to a large bowl and let it cool slightly. Add the parsley, breadcrumbs and Parmesan cheese and mix well.

Place the mushrooms stem side up on the baking sheet and fill them generously with the stuffing.

Bake the mushrooms for 15 minutes, until the stuffing is golden.

Serve the mushrooms warm.

RECIPE NOTES

Leftover stuffed mushrooms can be refrigerated in an airtight container for up to 4 days.

You can also prepare these mushrooms the day before and bake them right before serving them.

NUTRITION INFORMATION

Serving size: 4 mushrooms; **Calories:** 85; **Carbohydrates:** 9 g; **Protein:** 4 g; **Fat:** 4 g

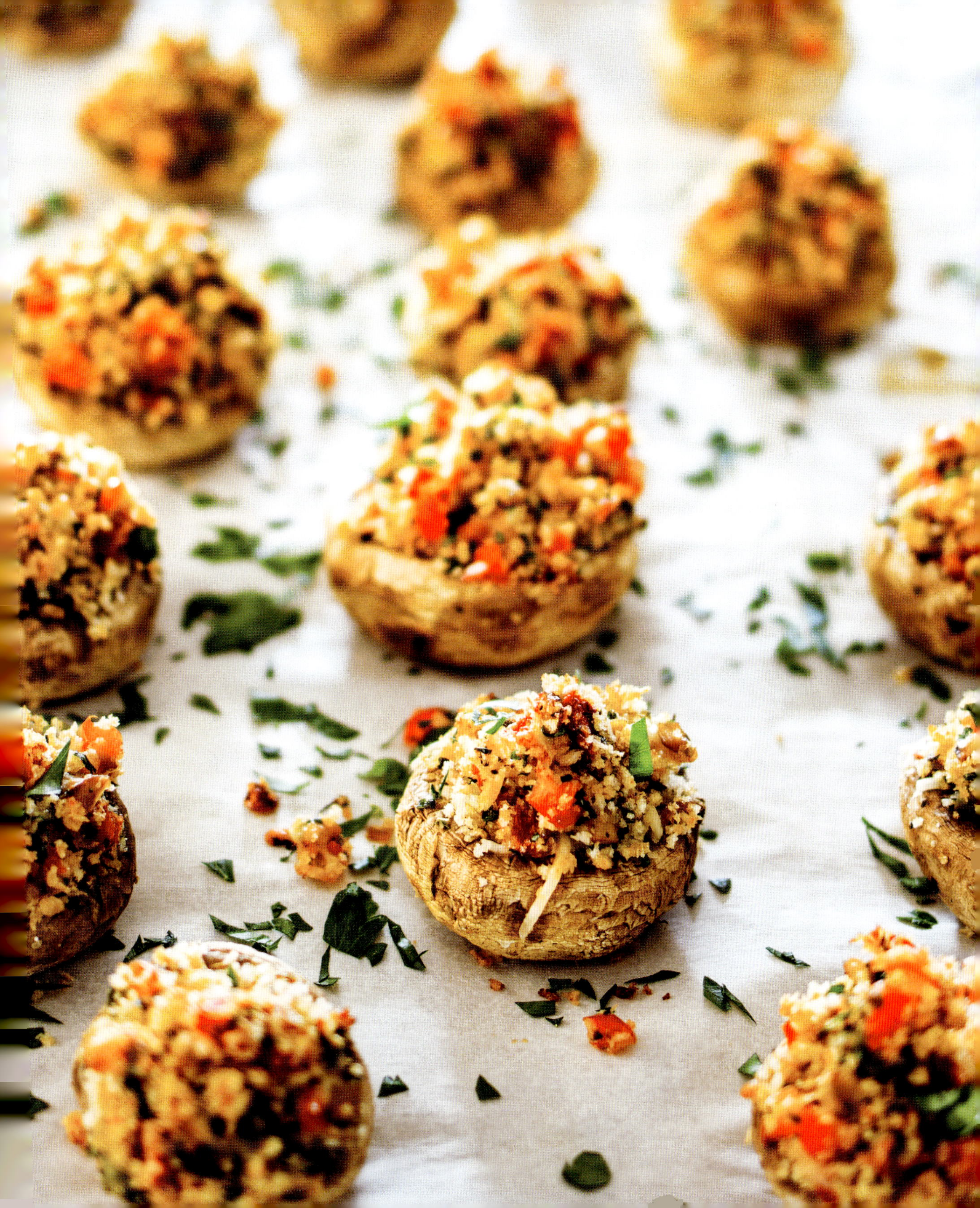

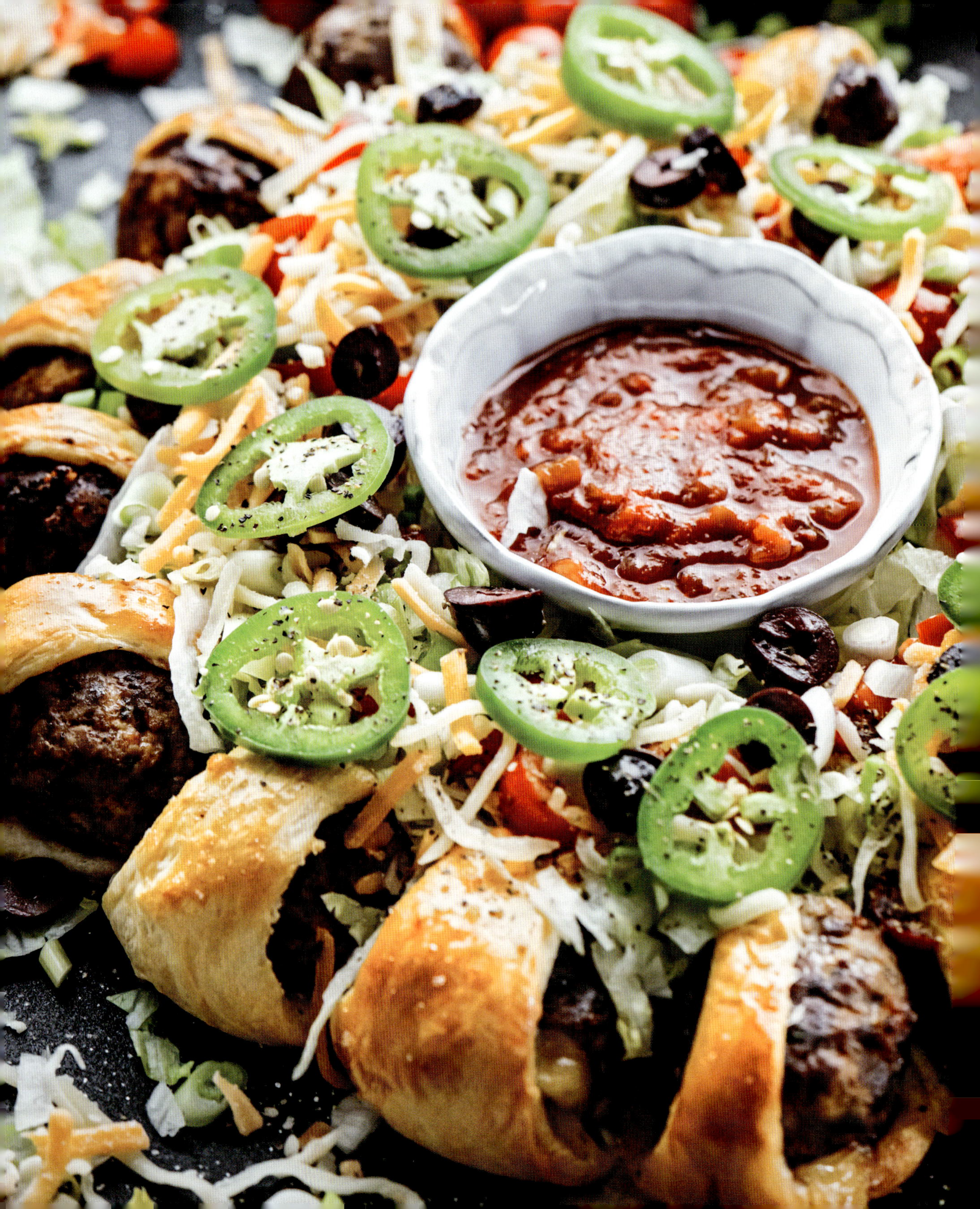

TACO MEATBALL RING

Let's take a minute to appreciate the beauty that is this taco meatball ring. Look at those giant meatballs stuffed with Monterey Jack cheese, wrapped in crescent dough, baked to perfection, then topped with all your favorites. Let's be honest: Who would say no to this?

PREP TIME: 30 MINUTES
COOK TIME: 30 MINUTES
TOTAL TIME: 1 HOUR
SERVES: 16

MEATBALLS

12 oz (336 g) ground pork
12 oz (336 g) ground beef
1 large egg
1 tbsp (15 ml) Sriracha sauce or hot sauce of choice
1 tbsp (9 g) Tex-Mex seasoning
1 tbsp (9 g) taco seasoning
½ tsp salt, or as needed
¼ tsp black pepper, or as needed
½ cup (30 g) panko breadcrumbs
¼ cup (12 g) chopped fresh parsley
4 oz (112 g) Monterey Jack cheese, cut into ½" (13-mm) cubes
2 tbsp (30 ml) vegetable oil

CRESCENT RING

2 (8-oz [224-g]) cans refrigerated crescent rolls
1 large egg white, beaten

OPTIONAL ACCOMPANIMENTS

½ head iceberg lettuce, shredded
1 cup (150 g) cherry tomatoes, quartered
4 green onions, chopped
½ cup (60 g) shredded Cheddar cheese
¼ cup (33 g) black olives, sliced
1 jalapeño, sliced
Sour cream, for serving
Salsa, for serving

To make the meatballs, mix together the pork, beef, egg, Sriracha sauce, Tex-Mex seasoning, taco seasoning, salt, black pepper, breadcrumbs and parsley in a large bowl.

Form the meat mixture into 16 (1½-inch [5-cm]) meatballs, sticking a cube of the Monterey Jack cheese in each meatball and ensuring the cheese is fully enclosed in the meat mixture. Heat the oil in a large skillet over medium heat. Add all the meatballs to the skillet and fry them for about 7 minutes, until they are golden brown all around.

Preheat the oven to 350°F (177°C). Line a large baking sheet or a large pizza pan with parchment paper.

To make the crescent ring, arrange the crescent rolls on the prepared baking sheet, forming a ring with the pointed ends facing the edges of the baking sheet. To make this easier, put a small bowl in the center and arrange the crescent rolls with the wide ends overlapping around the bowl.

Place a meatball on a crescent roll and fold the pointed end of the dough over the meatball and pinch the pointed end together with the wider end of the crescent roll. Repeat this process with all the meatballs and dough.

Brush the egg white over the crescent dough. Bake the meatball ring for 20 minutes, or until it is golden brown.

Transfer the ring to a serving platter or a large cutting board. Fill the center of the meatball ring with the optional accompaniments and serve with the sour cream and salsa.

RECIPE NOTE

You should get 16 large meatballs from this, but if you have any meat left over, form it into meatballs, fry the meatballs and serve them separately.

NUTRITION INFORMATION

Serving size: 1 serving; **Calories:** 170; **Carbohydrates:** 3 g; **Protein:** 11 g; **Fat:** 12 g

AVOCADO-SHRIMP SALSA

If you're looking for a quick starter, this dish fits the bill. The only cooking involved is cooking the shrimp in a bit of butter, then chopping them and tossing them with the other ingredients. That's all that's required to enjoy this delicious avocado-shrimp salsa. Get your favorite tortilla chips or crackers and snack away.

PREP TIME: 15 MINUTES
COOK TIME: 5 MINUTES
TOTAL TIME: 20 MINUTES
SERVES: 10

SHRIMP

1 tbsp (15 g) butter
1 lb (448 g) large shrimp, shells removed and deveined
¼ tsp salt, or as needed
¼ tsp black pepper, or as needed
2 tbsp (30 ml) fresh lemon juice

SALSA

2 avocados, chopped
1 cup (180 g) chopped tomatoes
1 English cucumber, chopped
⅓ cup (50 g) chopped red onion
⅓ cup (16 g) chopped fresh cilantro

DRESSING

⅓ cup (80 ml) fresh orange juice
2 tbsp (30 ml) fresh lime juice
1 tsp garlic powder
2 cloves garlic, minced
1 tsp salt
1 tsp black pepper

To make the shrimp, melt the butter in a large skillet over medium-high heat. Add the shrimp, season them with the salt and black pepper and cook them for 2 minutes. Flip the shrimp and cook them on the opposite side for 1 minute, until they are pink. Drizzle the lemon juice all over the shrimp and toss them to coat them in the lemon juice.

Remove the shrimp from the skillet and chop them into small pieces. Add the chopped shrimp to a large bowl.

To make the salsa, add the avocados, tomatoes, cucumber, onion and cilantro to the chopped shrimp.

To make the dressing, whisk together the orange juice, lime juice, garlic powder, garlic, salt and black pepper in a small bowl. Pour the dressing over the avocado-shrimp salsa. Toss everything together well. Serve the salsa immediately.

RECIPE NOTES

Because avocados brown quickly when they are exposed to air, this salsa is best served fresh. If you want it to last longer, mix everything together except the avocadoes and add them just before serving the salsa.

NUTRITION INFORMATION

Serving size: 1 serving; **Calories:** 72; **Carbohydrates:** 4 g; **Protein:** 9 g; **Fat:** 1 g

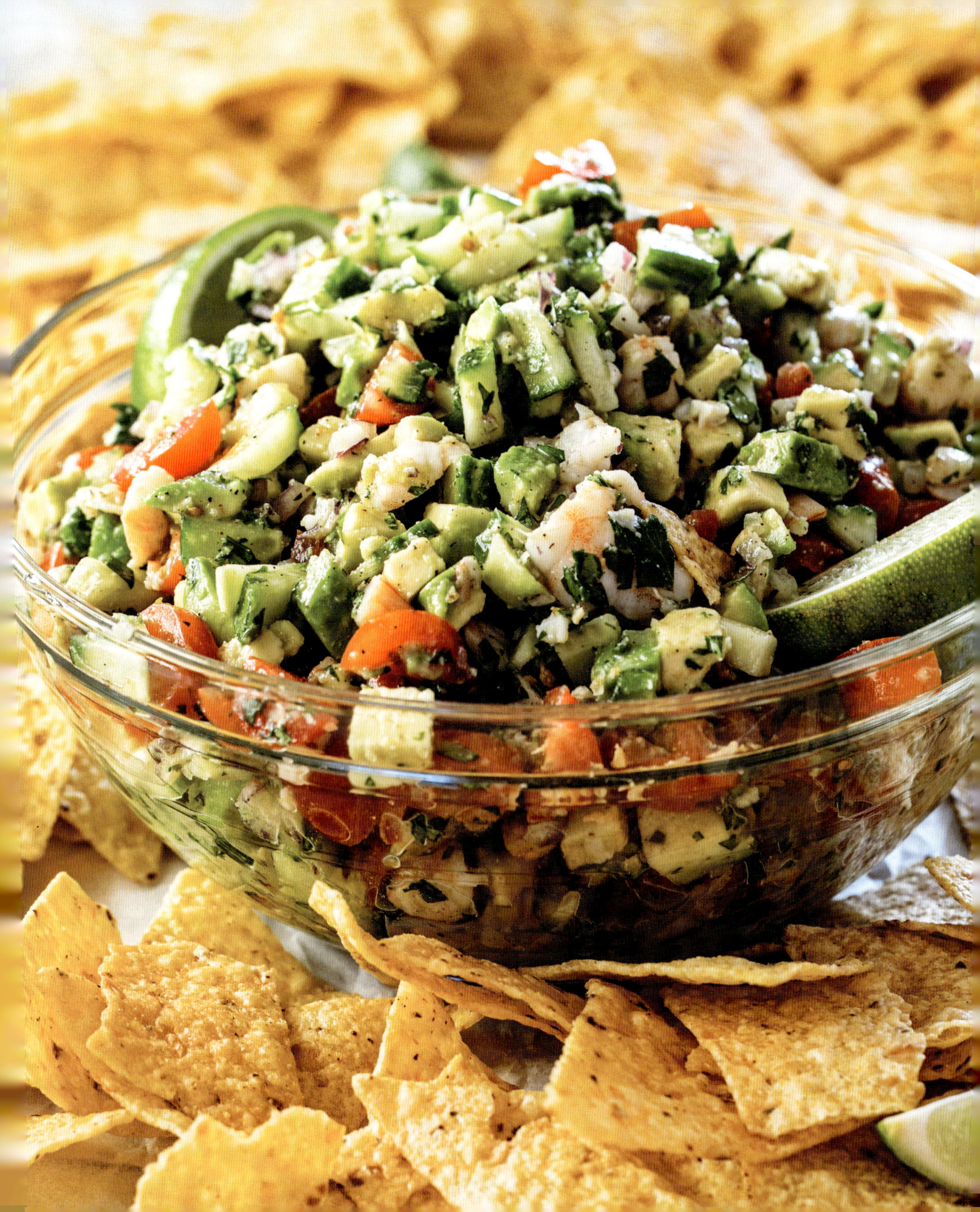

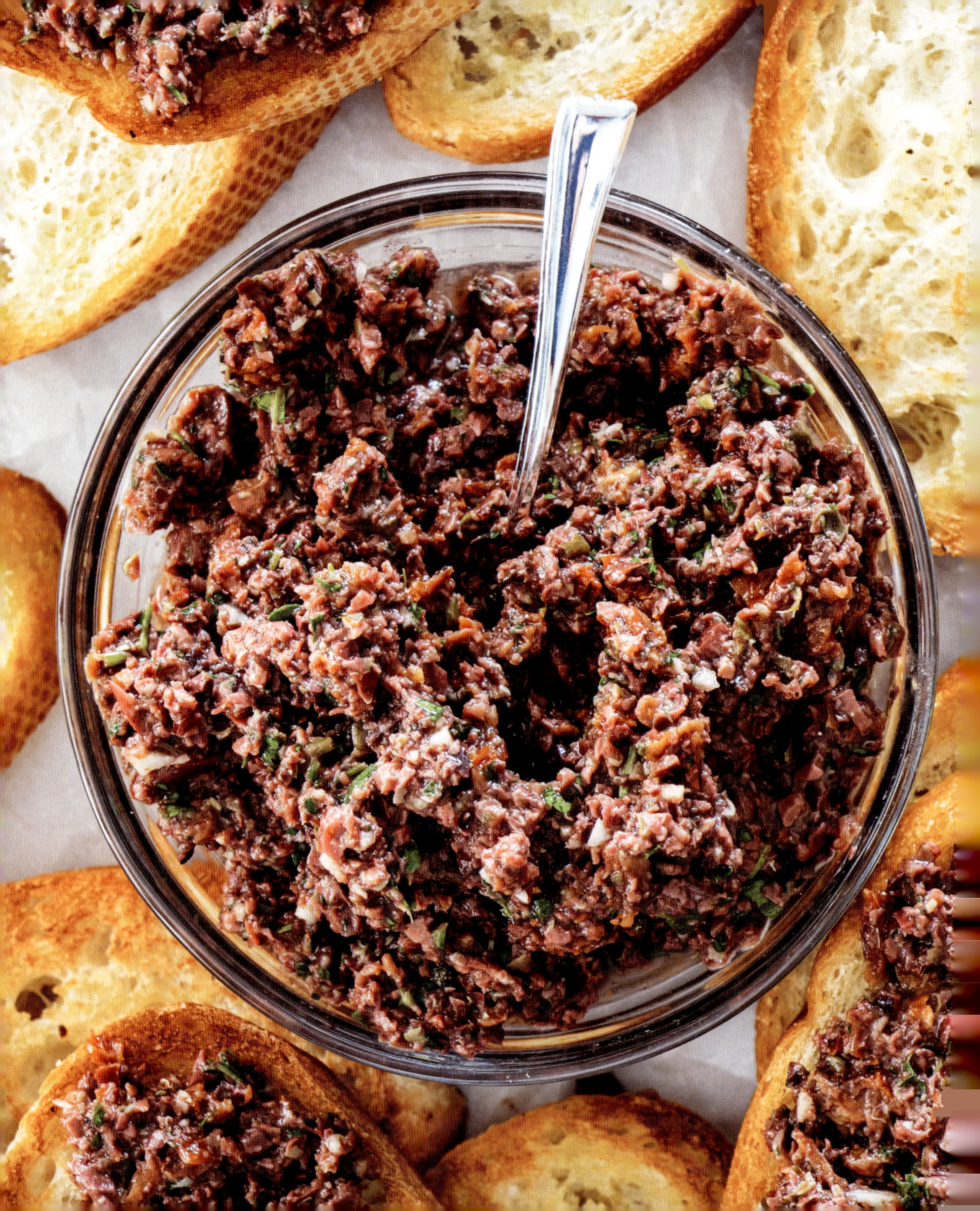

OLIVE TAPENADE

I can't believe there are people in the world who don't like olives. But if you're like me and love Kalamata olives, then you will love this spread. Just pop all the ingredients in a food processor and you're good to go!

PREP TIME: 5 MINUTES
COOK TIME: NONE
TOTAL TIME: 5 MINUTES
SERVES: 8

1 cup (130 g) Kalamata olives
¼ cup (60 g) oil-packed sun-dried tomatoes, oil reserved
¼ cup (12 g) chopped fresh parsley
5 cloves garlic
1 tbsp (9 g) capers, drained
2 tbsp (30 ml) fresh lemon juice
½ tsp black pepper, or as needed

In a food processor, combine the olives, tomatoes and 2 tablespoons (30 ml) of their oil, parsley, garlic, capers, lemon juice and black pepper. Pulse until the ingredients form a coarse puree or reach the desired texture.

Serve the tapenade as a dip or condiment.

RECIPE NOTES

Tapenade can be stored in an airtight container or jar in the refrigerator for up to 3 days. Make sure to bring it back to room temperature before serving it. If you place the tapenade in freezer containers, you can freeze it for up to 3 months.

NUTRITION INFORMATION

Serving size: 1 serving; **Calories:** 46; **Carbohydrates:** 4 g; **Protein:** 1 g; **Fat:** 3 g

CHILE CON QUESO

This classic dip is much easier to make than you might think. It makes enough to feed a crowd, so it's perfect for all types of gatherings. If you're looking for a dip that's not only delicious but spicy, silky and super cheesy, then this chile con queso is for you. You know what makes it silky? It's that Velveeta cheese. Don't knock it until you try it!

PREP TIME: 10 MINUTES
COOK TIME: 15 MINUTES
TOTAL TIME: 25 MINUTES
SERVES: 8

1 tbsp (15 ml) olive oil
8 oz (224 g) extra lean ground beef (see Recipe Notes)
1 tsp chili powder
1 red onion, diced
1 clove garlic, minced
1 (4-oz [112-g]) can diced green chilies, undrained
1 jalapeño, seeds removed and chopped
1 (15-oz [420-g]) can fire-roasted tomatoes, undrained
1 cup (220 g) evaporated milk (see Recipe Notes)
1 cup (140 g) cubed Velveeta (see Recipe Notes)
2½ cups (283 g) shredded Monterey Jack cheese, divided
1 tbsp (3 g) chopped fresh cilantro
Tortilla chips, for serving

Preheat the oven to broil.

Heat the oil in a large cast-iron or oven-safe skillet over medium-high heat. Add the beef to the skillet, season it with the chili powder and cook it for about 5 minutes, breaking it up as it cooks, until it is no longer pink.

Stir in the onion and garlic and cook the mixture for 2 minutes, or until the onion softens and becomes translucent.

Add the green chilies and their juice, jalapeño and tomatoes and their juice and stir to combine the ingredients. Bring the mixture to a simmer, then reduce the heat to medium-low.

Add the evaporated milk and Velveeta and cook the mixture for 2 minutes, or until the Velveeta melts. Stir in 2 cups (226 g) of the Monterey Jack cheese and cook the mixture for 1 minute, until the cheese melts.

Turn off the heat. Sprinkle the remaining ½ cup (57 g) of Monterey Jack cheese over the top of the chile con queso. Broil it for about 5 minutes, or until it is browned and bubbly, watching it closely so it doesn't burn.

Garnish the chile con queso with the cilantro and serve it with the tortilla chips.

RECIPE NOTES

If you prefer a meatless option, skip the beef. Just sauté the onion and garlic in the olive oil and then continue with the recipe as it is written.

Why use evaporated milk? It's used in this dip to provide extra creaminess and body without the fat of real cream.

I use Velveeta because if you want a truly silky queso, Velveeta is the way to go; however, feel free to use any shredded cheese you prefer, such as Monterey Jack, Cheddar or any other great melting cheese.

NUTRITION INFORMATION

Serving size: 1 serving; **Calories:** 323; **Carbohydrates:** 10 g; **Protein:** 22 g; **Fat:** 20 g

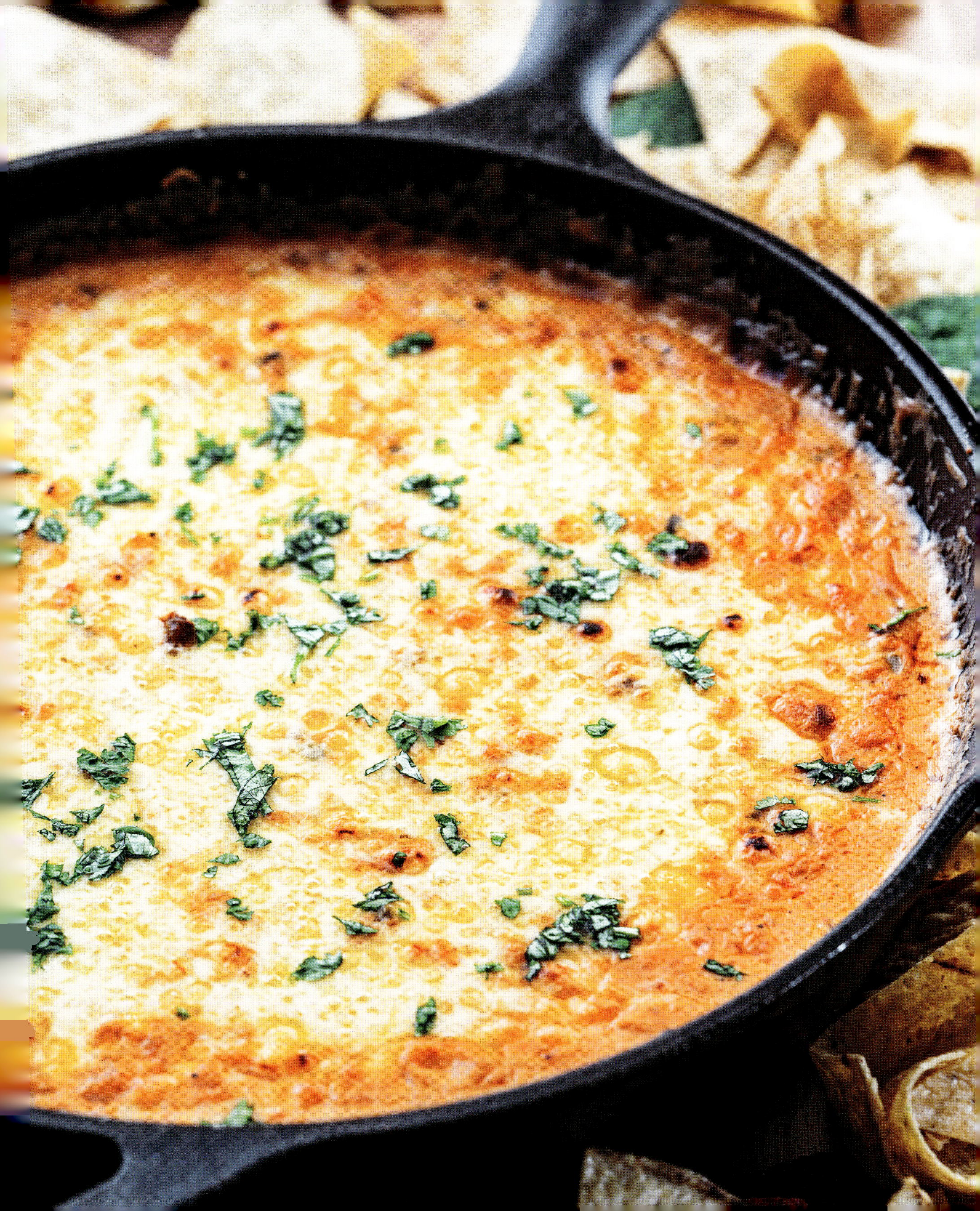

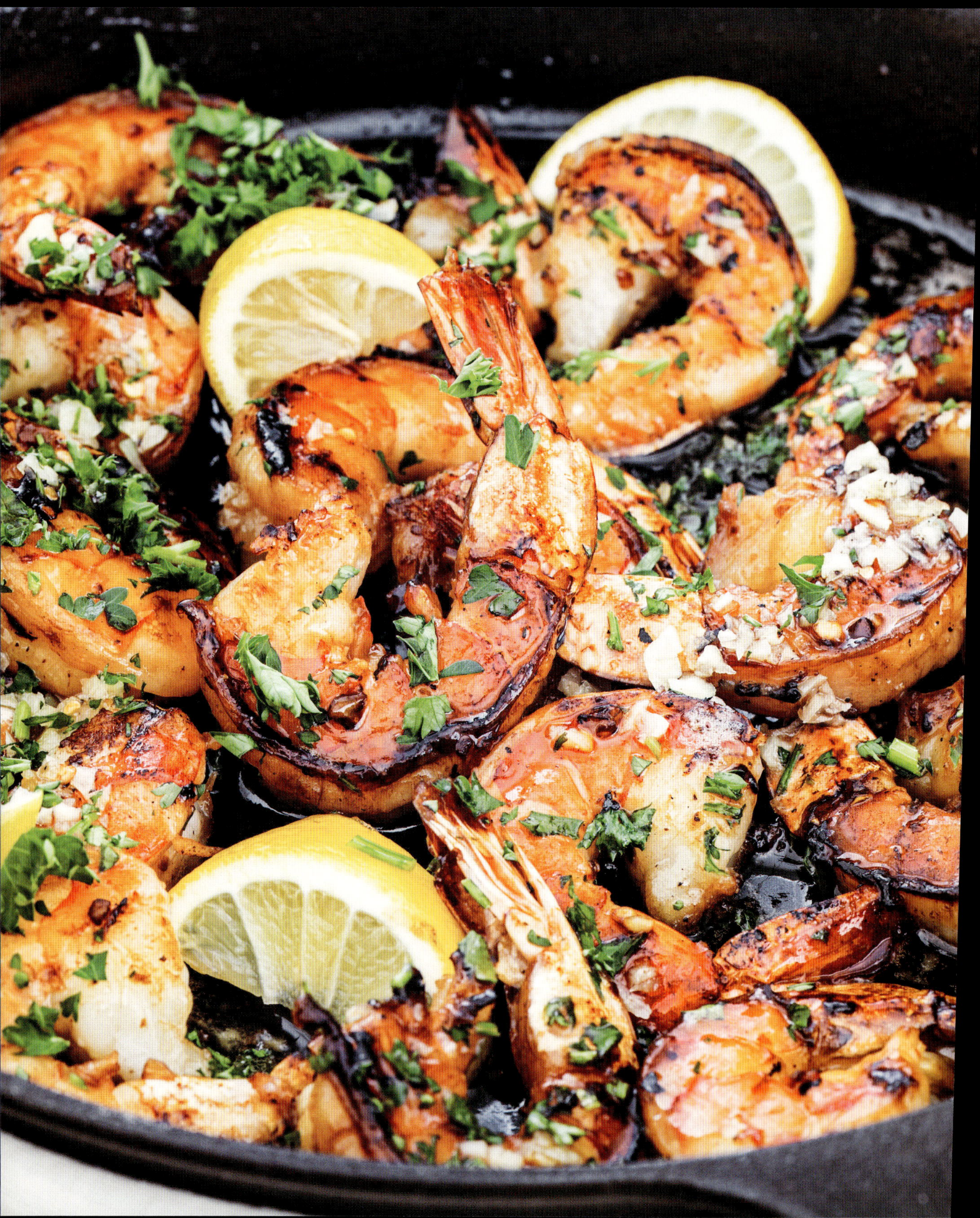

HONEY-GARLIC SHRIMP

PREP TIME: 5 MINUTES
COOK TIME: 10 MINUTES
TOTAL TIME: 15 MINUTES
SERVES: 4

6 tbsp (90 g) unsalted butter
4 cloves garlic, minced
2 tbsp (30 ml) fresh lemon juice
¼ cup (60 ml) honey
¼ tsp red pepper flakes
¼ tsp salt, or as needed
¼ tsp black pepper, or as needed
1½ lb (672 g) tail-on shrimp, peeled and deveined
2 tbsp (6 g) chopped fresh parsley
1 lemon, cut into wedges

Talk about a quick appetizer! Fifteen minutes is all you need to make these amazing honey-garlic shrimp. Requiring just a handful of ingredients and no marinating, it's really a no-fail recipe. I'll tell you a little secret: Unfortunately, a few years back, I became allergic to shrimp out of the blue. So whenever I make any of my quick shrimp recipes for guests, I always make the same version with chicken. If you've got friends or family with shellfish allergies, chicken is a great alternative. The only thing that changes is the cooking time, as chicken takes a bit longer to cook.

Melt the butter in a large skillet over medium-high heat. Once the butter has melted completely, cook it for 1 minute. Watch it closely so it doesn't burn.

Stir in the garlic and cook it for 30 seconds, watching it closely so it doesn't burn.

Add the lemon juice, honey, red pepper flakes, salt and black pepper and stir the ingredients together. Cook the mixture for 1 minute, until it has thickened slightly.

Pour about three-fourths of the butter mixture into a cup or bowl and set it aside. Leave the remaining one-fourth of the butter mixture in the skillet.

Working in batches so as not to overcrowd the skillet, sear the shrimp for about 2 minutes per side, just until they turn pink and are no longer opaque.

Once all the shrimp have been cooked, add them all back to the skillet and pour the reserved butter sauce over the shrimp. Garnish the shrimp with the parsley and remove the skillet from the heat.

Serve the shrimp with the lemon wedges.

RECIPE NOTES

This honey-garlic shrimp is best served right away. However, if you have leftovers, store the shrimp in an airtight container in the fridge for 3 or 4 days.

This recipe is great served over a bed of basmati or jasmine rice. The shrimp are also delicious served with a salad. If you're looking to keep it low-carb, try serving this dish over cauliflower fried rice.

NUTRITION INFORMATION

Serving size: 1 serving; **Calories:** 402; **Carbohydrates:** 21 g; **Protein:** 35 g; **Fat:** 19 g

HOMEMADE SALSA

Fresh ingredients and lots of flavor: That's what this salsa is all about. While it's much easier to buy store-bought salsa, this recipe is perfect to make in the summer when tomatoes are in abundance. And no matter how much easier it is to buy a jar of salsa, homemade is always best. And you know what else? It really only takes 25 minutes of hands-on time to make this great salsa. Not to mention you will have bragging rights!

PREP TIME: 10 MINUTES
COOK TIME: 15 MINUTES
CHILLING TIME: 2 HOURS
TOTAL TIME: 2 HOURS, 25 MINUTES
SERVES: 6

8 Roma tomatoes, halved
2 onions, quartered
6 cloves garlic, peeled
1 (4-oz [112-g]) can mild diced green chilies, undrained
½ cup (24 g) fresh cilantro stems and leaves
2 tbsp (30 ml) fresh lime juice (see Recipe Notes)
½ tsp salt, or as needed
½ tsp black pepper, or as needed

Preheat the oven to 350°F (177°C).

Place the tomatoes, onions and garlic on a large baking sheet. Roast them for 15 minutes, or just until the onions and tomatoes start to get a little char on them. Remove the baking sheet from the oven and let the vegetables cool for about 5 minutes.

Combine the tomatoes, onions, garlic, green chilies and their juice, cilantro, lime juice, salt and black pepper in a food processor. Pulse a few times until the ingredients reach your desired consistency.

Pour the salsa in a bowl or airtight container. Cover the bowl with plastic wrap or secure the container's lid and refrigerate the salsa for 2 to 4 hours before serving.

RECIPE NOTES

To add more spiciness to the salsa, add 1 or 2 jalapeños or your favorite hot peppers to the baking sheet and roast them along with the tomatoes, onions and garlic.

For a tangier salsa, add more fresh lime juice.

This salsa will last for 5 to 7 days in the fridge or for 3 to 4 months in the freezer.

NUTRITION INFORMATION

Serving size: 1 serving; **Calories:** 33; **Carbohydrates:** 7 g; **Protein:** 1 g; **Fat:** 0 g

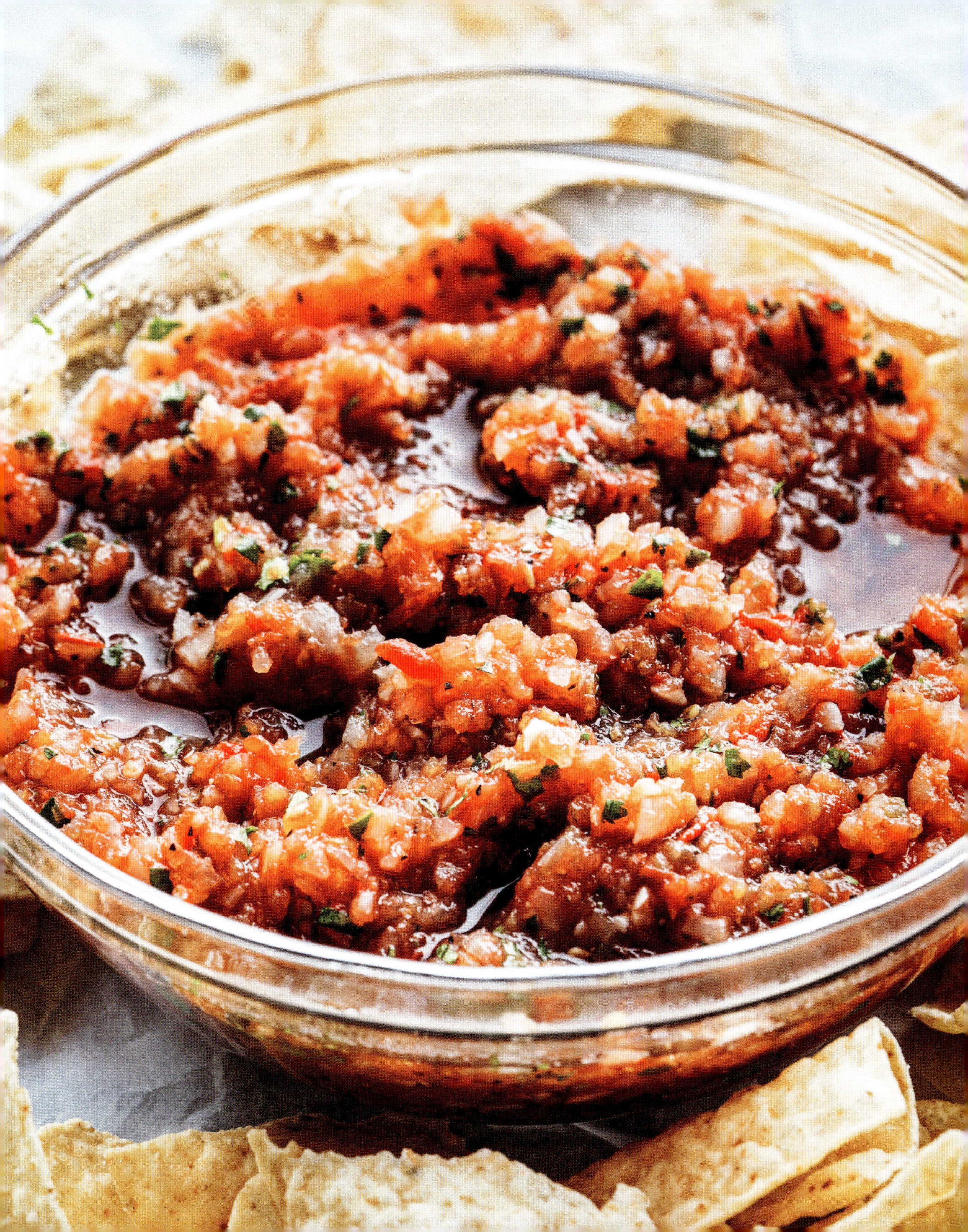

SALADS

LONG AGO, I looked at salads as something I would have only in January or February when I formed a new resolution to start eating healthy. I used to look at salads as boring, just some lettuce with dressing. But since I've grown up and started food blogging, I've been making salads that are worth eating and enjoying.

Salads don't have to be boring; not only can they be nutritious but they can also be tasty and filling, like my Fattoush Salad (page 362) or my Mexican Street Corn Salad (page 353). They can also be a meal on their own, especially if they're paired with a protein, like my Kale and Quinoa Salad with Lemon Vinaigrette (page 361) or my Waldorf Salad (page 354).

With the right ingredients and the right dressings, salads can outshine any other meal. In this chapter, I'm sharing with you some hearty pasta salads, some great classic salads and some traditional salads like Tabbouleh Salad (page 341) and Greek Salad (page 342).

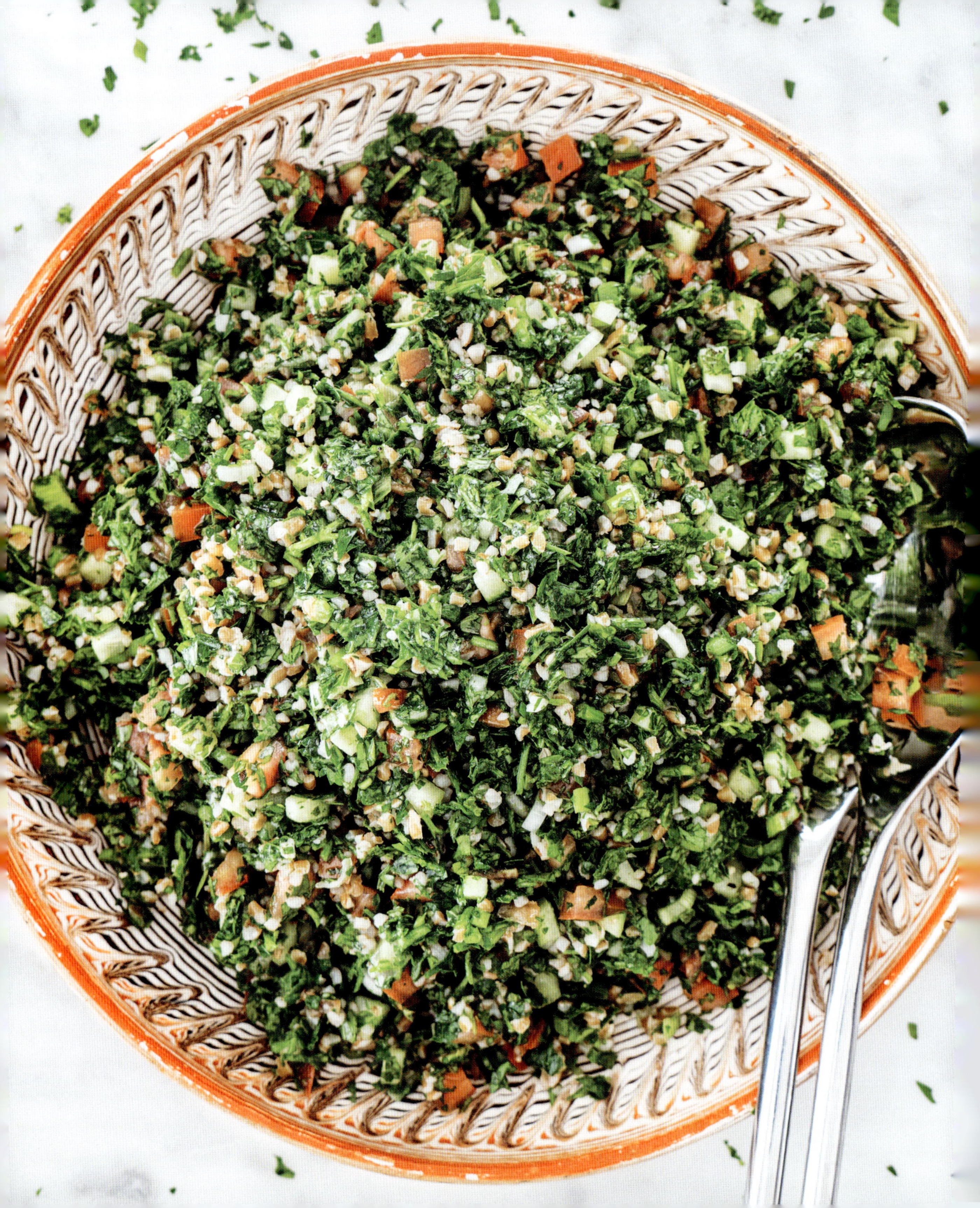

TABBOULEH SALAD

This is a traditional Middle Eastern salad featuring bulgur wheat, tomatoes, cucumber and loads of parsley and mint. The dressing is a simple one featuring lemon juice and olive oil.

PREP TIME: 10 MINUTES
COOK TIME: 5 MINUTES
TOTAL TIME: 15 MINUTES
SERVES: 4

1 cup (240 ml) water
½ cup (70 g) bulgur wheat
3 bunches fresh parsley, chopped (see Recipe Notes)
½ cup (24 g) chopped fresh mint
⅓ cup (80 ml) olive oil
⅓ cup (80 ml) fresh lemon juice
1 cup (180 g) seeded and finely chopped tomatoes
½ cup (67 g) seeded and finely chopped English cucumber
3 green onions, finely chopped
Salt, as needed
Black pepper, as needed

In a small pot over high heat, bring the water to a boil. Add the bulgur and cover the pot. Reduce the heat to low and simmer the bulgur for about 5 minutes, stirring it occasionally. Let the bulgur cool to room temperature.

Combine the parsley and mint in a food processor. Pulse it until the herbs are chopped very small, being careful to not turn them into a paste.

Transfer the bulgur to a large bowl. Add the herb mixture, oil, lemon juice, tomatoes, cucumber, green onions, salt and black pepper. Toss the salad well and serve it.

RECIPE NOTES

I like to use a salad spinner to clean the parsley. I first cut out most of the big stems, then I place the parsley in a salad spinner to wash it out, just in case there are bugs or dirt. The salad spinner is great for drying out parsley. After removing the parsley from the salad spinner, you can chop the parsley by hand using a very sharp knife if you do not have a food processor.

You can store leftover tabbouleh salad in an airtight container in the refrigerator for up to 2 days. If your salad has too much dressing or too much liquid, make sure to drain any excess before refrigerating it.

NUTRITION INFORMATION

Serving size: 1 serving; **Calories:** 254; **Carbohydrates:** 21 g; **Protein:** 4 g; **Fat:** 19 g

GREEK SALAD

A classic salad loaded with cucumbers, tomatoes, feta cheese and olives, this dish comes complete with a homemade Greek salad dressing. And it's ready in just ten minutes!

PREP TIME: 10 MINUTES
COOK TIME: NONE
TOTAL TIME: 10 MINUTES
SERVES: 4

DRESSING

2 cloves garlic, minced
¼ cup (60 ml) red wine vinegar
¼ cup (60 ml) olive oil
2 tbsp (30 ml) fresh lemon juice
1 tbsp (3 g) dried oregano
½ tsp black pepper
1½ tsp (6 g) sugar

SALAD

1 English cucumber, cubed
1 red onion, roughly chopped (see Recipe Notes)
1 green bell pepper, chopped
2 cups (300 g) cocktail tomatoes, halved or quartered (see Recipe Notes)
1½ cups (225 g) crumbled or cubed feta cheese
¾ cup (98 g) Kalamata olives (see Recipe Notes)

To make the dressing, whisk together the garlic, vinegar, oil, lemon juice, oregano, black pepper and sugar in a small bowl. Alternatively, combine the ingredients in a blender and blend them for about 30 seconds, until they are well combined. Finally, you may also combine the ingredients in a small jar, secure the jar's lid and shake the jar vigorously to form the dressing.

To make the salad, place the cucumber, onion, bell pepper, tomatoes, feta cheese and olives in a large bowl. Pour the dressing over the salad ingredients. Toss the salad well and serve it immediately.

RECIPE NOTES

If you don't like raw onions, you can do a quick pickle. Slice the onion, then place it in a medium bowl. Add 1 teaspoon of sugar, ¼ teaspoon of salt and ¼ cup (60 ml) of distilled white vinegar or apple cider vinegar. Stir the ingredients to combine them. Cover the bowl and refrigerate the pickled onions for about 30 minutes. These onions are great to use on sandwiches or other salads.

Cocktail tomatoes are a smaller variety of tomatoes, although they are larger than a cherry or grape tomato. They pack a very juicy bite. However, any type of tomatoes will work in this salad.

Kalamata olives are best for a classic Greek salad. They're a large black or brown variety of olive that's very meaty, and they're usually preserved in wine vinegar or olive oil. I highly recommend using Kalamata olives for this salad—they make all the difference.

Store leftover salad in an airtight container in the fridge for up to 2 days. Greek salad is one of the few salads that will actually still taste good, if not better, the next day—the tomatoes and cucumbers marinate in the dressing and all the flavors have the chance to develop.

NUTRITION INFORMATION

Serving size: 1 serving; **Calories:** 352; **Carbohydrates:** 14 g; **Protein:** 9 g; **Fat:** 29 g

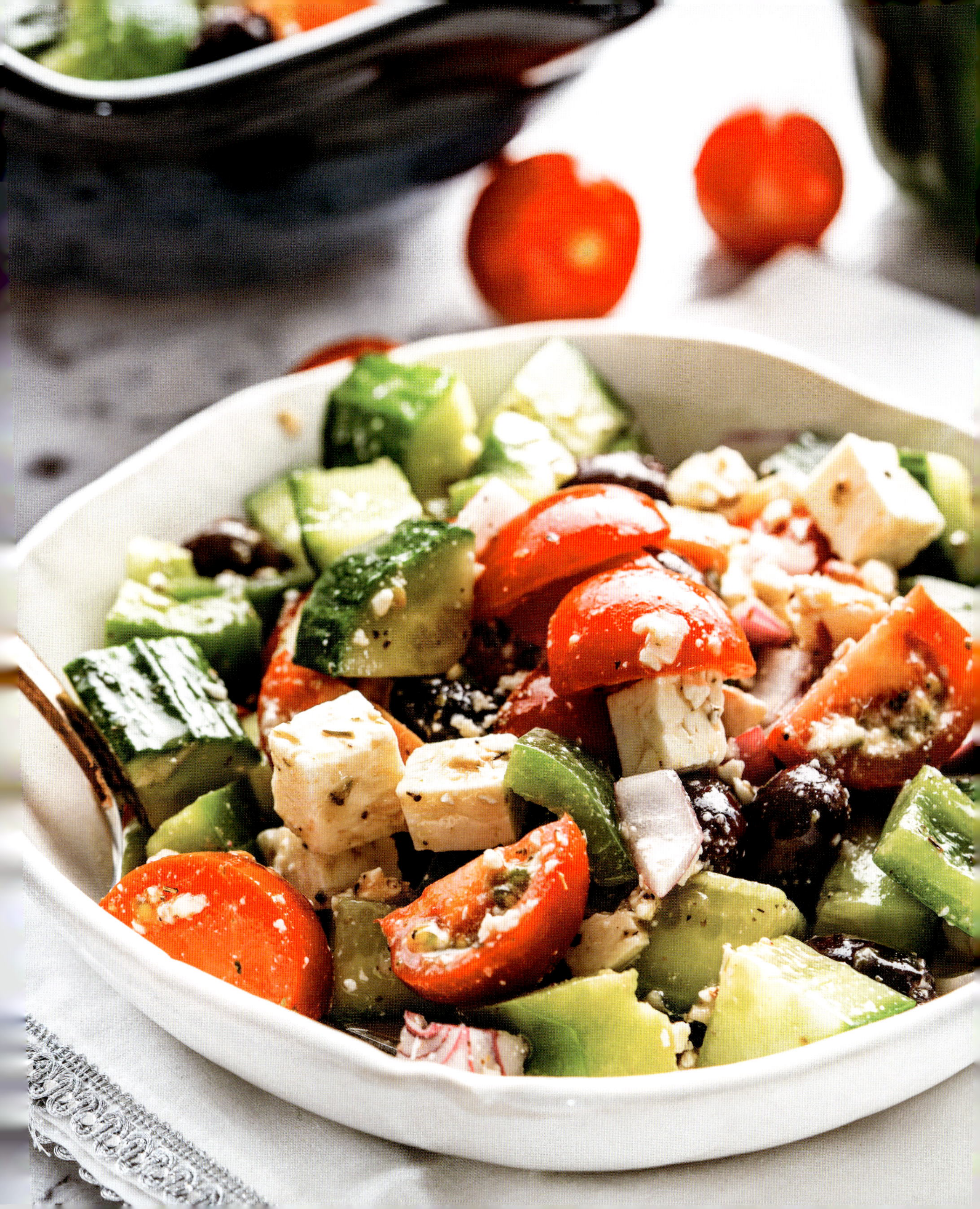

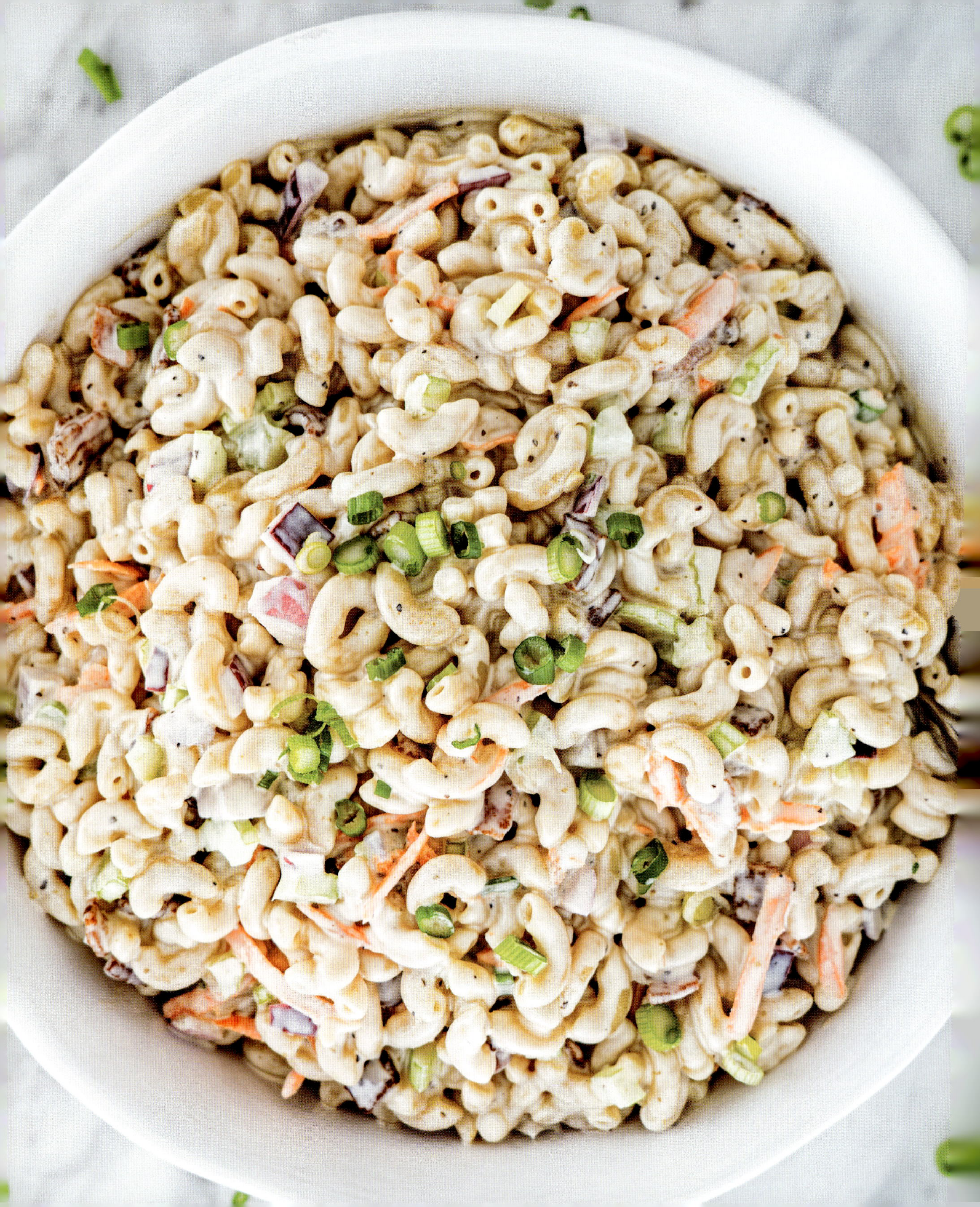

MACARONI SALAD

What's more classic than a macaroni salad? My version features lots of fresh and crunchy veggies, a homemade creamy dressing and my secret ingredient: bacon!

PREP TIME: 10 MINUTES
COOK TIME: 10 MINUTES
TOTAL TIME: 20 MINUTES
SERVES: 10

SALAD
- 4 cups (560 g) elbow macaroni
- ½ cup (50 g) diced celery
- ½ cup (75 g) diced red onion
- 8 slices bacon, fried and chopped
- ½ carrot, shredded
- 1 tbsp (3 g) thinly sliced green onion, divided

DRESSING
- 1½ cups (360 g) mayonnaise
- 1 tsp mustard powder
- 1 tbsp (12 g) sugar
- 2 tbsp (30 ml) apple cider vinegar
- ⅓ cup (40 g) sour cream
- 1 tsp salt, or as needed
- 1 tsp black pepper, or as needed

To make the salad, cook the macaroni in salted water according to the package's instructions, usually about 10 minutes. Drain the macaroni and rinse it well with cold water.

Meanwhile, make the dressing. In a small bowl, whisk together the mayonnaise, mustard powder, sugar, vinegar, sour cream, salt and black pepper.

Combine the macaroni, celery, red onion, bacon, carrot, ½ tablespoon (2 g) of the green onion and the prepared dressing in a large bowl. Toss the salad well.

Garnish the salad with the remaining ½ tablespoon (1 g) of green onion and serve cold.

RECIPE NOTES

This salad will stay good for 3 to 5 days stored in an airtight container in the fridge. It's a perfect recipe for making ahead! I find that when the ingredients have a chance to mingle, the salad gets even more delicious.

If you plan on serving this salad for guests or bringing it to a potluck, it will be okay for 2 hours at room temperature. After 2 hours, you should put it back in the fridge.

NUTRITION INFORMATION

Serving size: 1 serving; **Calories:** 537; **Carbohydrates:** 45 g; **Protein:** 10 g; **Fat:** 35 g

CREAMY CUCUMBER SALAD

Get ready for a creamy cucumber salad with red onion, dill and lots of feta cheese that's fast and refreshing! I love this salad because it's perfect for picnics, barbecues or potlucks.

To make the dressing, mix together the yogurt, mayonnaise, vinegar, sugar, salt and black pepper in a small bowl. Set the dressing aside.

To make the salad, combine the cucumbers, onion, dill, feta cheese and dressing in a large bowl. Toss the salad well. Garnish it with more dill and feta and serve.

PREP TIME: 10 MINUTES
COOK TIME: NONE
TOTAL TIME: 10 MINUTES
SERVES: 6

DRESSING
½ cup (143 g) plain Greek yogurt
¼ cup (60 g) mayonnaise
2 tbsp (30 ml) distilled white vinegar
1 tsp sugar
¼ tsp salt, or as needed
½ tsp black pepper, or as needed

SALAD
2 English cucumbers, seeds removed and sliced
1 red onion, thinly sliced
¼ cup (12 g) chopped fresh dill, plus more as needed
½ cup (75 g) crumbled feta cheese, plus more as needed

RECIPE NOTES
Store leftovers in the fridge in an airtight container. While the salad will last for 5 to 7 days in the fridge, it's best enjoyed within a few days. The longer everything sits together, the more moisture is drawn from the cucumbers.

NUTRITION INFORMATION
Serving size: 1 serving; **Calories:** 133; **Carbohydrates:** 7 g; **Protein:** 5 g; **Fat:** 10 g

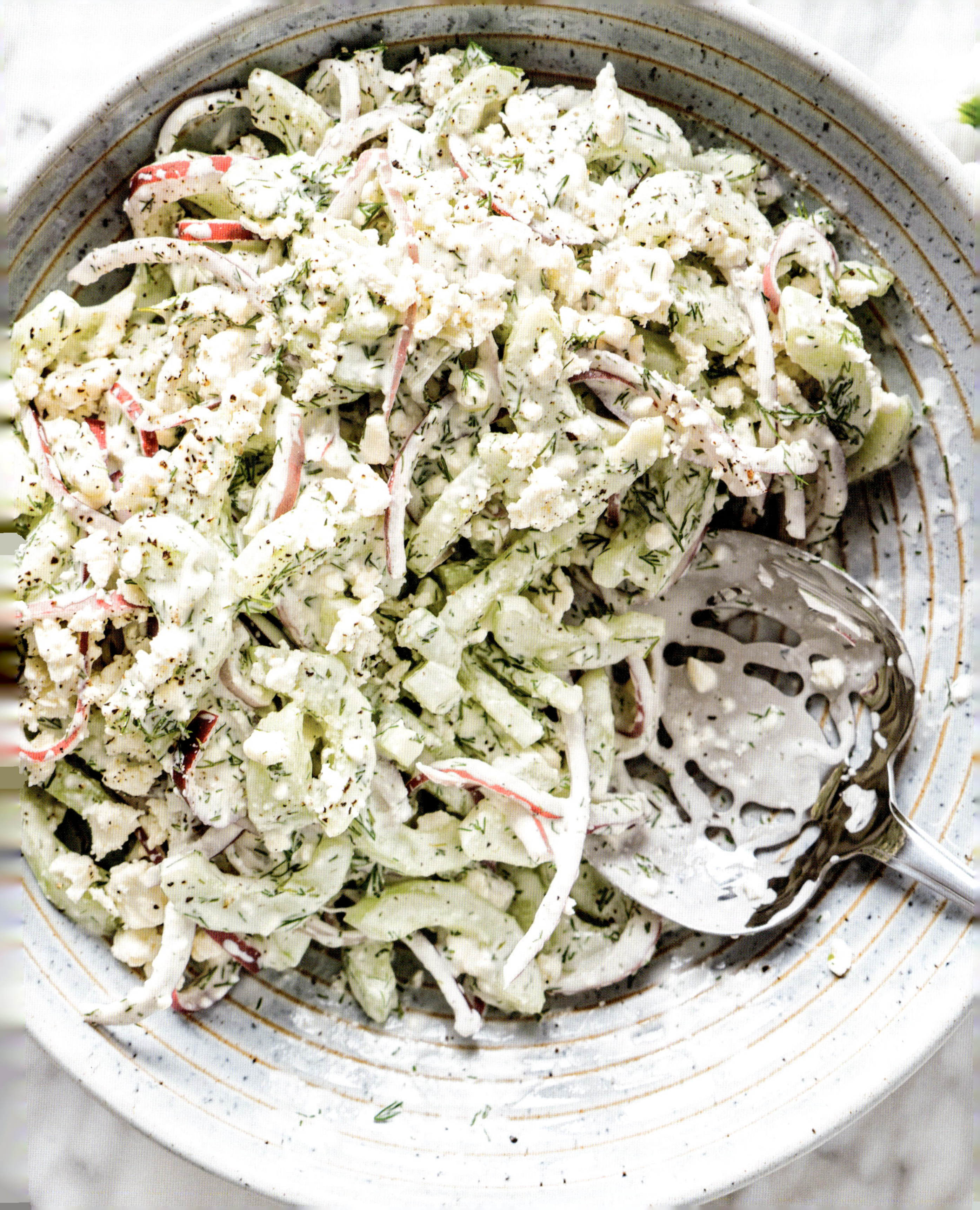

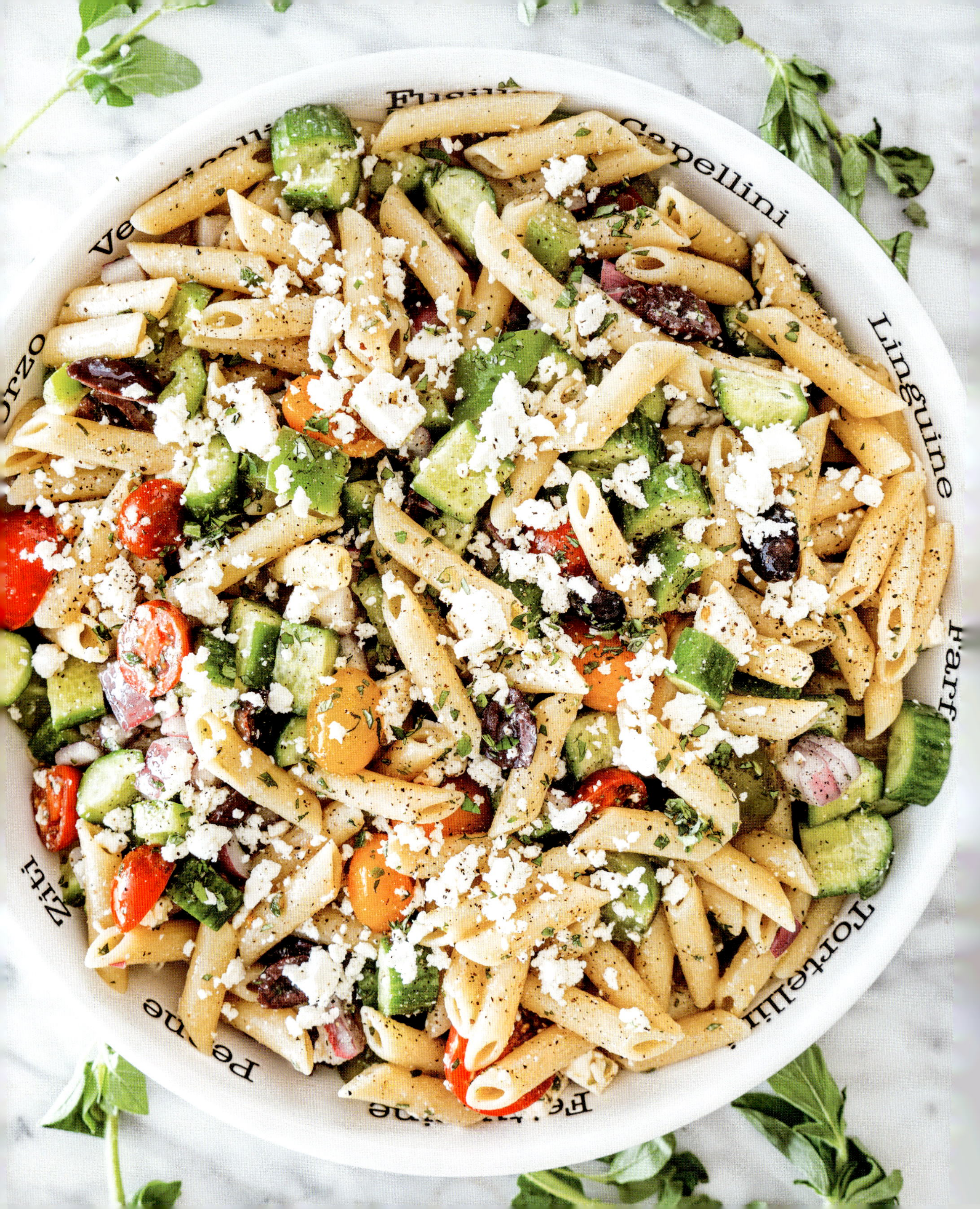
Capellini
Linguine
Tortellini
Ziti

GREEK PASTA SALAD

I love a good Greek salad, but when it's paired with pasta, it's a match made in heaven. This salad comes complete with a fresh and bright homemade dressing.

PREP TIME: 15 MINUTES
COOK TIME: 10 MINUTES
TOTAL TIME: 25 MINUTES
SERVES: 8

SALAD

12 oz (336 g) penne or pasta of choice

2 cups (266 g) chopped cucumber, cut into bite-sized pieces

2 cups (300 g) grape tomatoes, cut into bite-sized pieces

1 green bell pepper, cut into bite-sized pieces

½ cup (65 g) olives, cut into bite-sized pieces (I recommend Kalamata olives)

½ red onion, chopped

½ cup (75 g) crumbled feta cheese, plus more as needed

DRESSING

¼ cup (60 ml) red wine vinegar

⅓ cup (80 ml) olive oil

2 tbsp (30 ml) lemon juice

½ tsp garlic powder

1 tbsp (3 g) chopped fresh oregano or 1 tsp dried oregano, plus more as needed

½ tsp salt, or as needed

½ tsp black pepper, plus more as needed

To make the salad, cook the penne in salted water according to the package's instructions, usually about 10 minutes. Drain the penne and rinse it with cold water until it is completely cool. Transfer the penne to a large bowl.

To the penne, add the cucumber, tomatoes, bell pepper, olives, onion and feta cheese.

To make the dressing, combine the vinegar, oil, lemon juice, garlic powder, oregano, salt and black pepper in a medium Mason jar. Secure the jar's lid and shake the jar vigorously until the dressing is mixed well.

Pour the dressing over the salad and toss it well.

Garnish the salad with additional feta cheese, oregano and black pepper.

RECIPE NOTES

I don't recommend freezing this salad, as the veggies and pasta will get soggy and fall apart after thawing.

To store leftovers in the refrigerator, place the salad in an airtight container and refrigerate it for up to 4 days.

NUTRITION INFORMATION

Serving size: 1 serving; **Calories:** 295; **Carbohydrates:** 37 g; **Protein:** 8 g; **Fat:** 13 g

ITALIAN PASTA SALAD

This is a cold pasta salad that's easy to put together and comes with a refreshing dressing. It's great for potlucks, picnics or family gatherings.

PREP TIME: 15 MINUTES
COOK TIME: 10 MINUTES
CHILLING TIME: 1 HOUR
TOTAL TIME: 1 HOUR, 25 MINUTES
SERVES: 12

SALAD
1 lb (448 g) penne, elbow macaroni, fusilli or rotini
Olive oil, as needed
1 green bell pepper, chopped
1 cup (150 g) cherry tomatoes, halved or quartered
8 oz (224 g) salami, thickly sliced or cut into small pieces
8 oz (224 g) mini bocconcini (see Recipe Notes)
½ red onion, finely chopped
8 oz (224 g) spicy salami, thickly sliced or cut into small pieces
8 oz (224 g) Monterey Jack cheese, cut into small cubes (see Recipe Notes)
½ cup (65 g) Kalamata olives, sliced

ITALIAN DRESSING
2 cloves garlic, minced
2 tbsp (6 g) chopped fresh parsley
2 tbsp (6 g) chopped fresh oregano or 1 tbsp (3 g) dried oregano
2 tbsp (6 g) chopped fresh basil or 1 tbsp (3 g) dried basil
¼ tsp red pepper flakes
½ cup (120 ml) olive oil
3 tbsp (45 ml) white wine vinegar
2 tbsp (30 ml) lemon juice
½ tsp salt, or as needed
1 tsp black pepper, or as needed

Cook the pasta in heavily salted water according to the package's directions, usually about 10 minutes. Drain the pasta, but do not rinse it; instead, transfer it to a large bowl and add a little oil to it to prevent it from sticking together.

To the pasta, add the bell pepper, tomatoes, salami, bocconcini, onion, spicy salami, Monterey Jack cheese and olives. Toss the salad well.

To make the Italian dressing, whisk together the garlic, parsley, oregano, basil, red pepper flakes, oil, vinegar, lemon juice, salt and black pepper in a small bowl. Alternatively, combine the ingredients in a medium Mason jar, secure the jar's lid and shake the jar vigorously to form the dressing. The dressing should emulsify a bit; this will ensure the pasta will absorb the dressing.

Pour the dressing over the pasta and toss it well. Chill the pasta salad for at least 1 hour before serving it.

RECIPE NOTES

If you cannot find mini bocconcini, regular mozzarella, cut into cubes, can be used as well.

You can substitute the Monterey Jack cheese with a marble Jack cheese or sharp Cheddar cheese.

For 1 pound of pasta, you will need about 2 gallons (3.8 L) of water. Make sure to salt your water well; I recommend using at least 2 tablespoons (30 g) of salt.

Store any leftover salad in an airtight container in the fridge for 2 to 3 days. This salad is even better the next day.

NUTRITION INFORMATION

Serving size: 1 serving; **Calories:** 512; **Carbohydrates:** 31 g; **Protein:** 21 g; **Fat:** 33 g

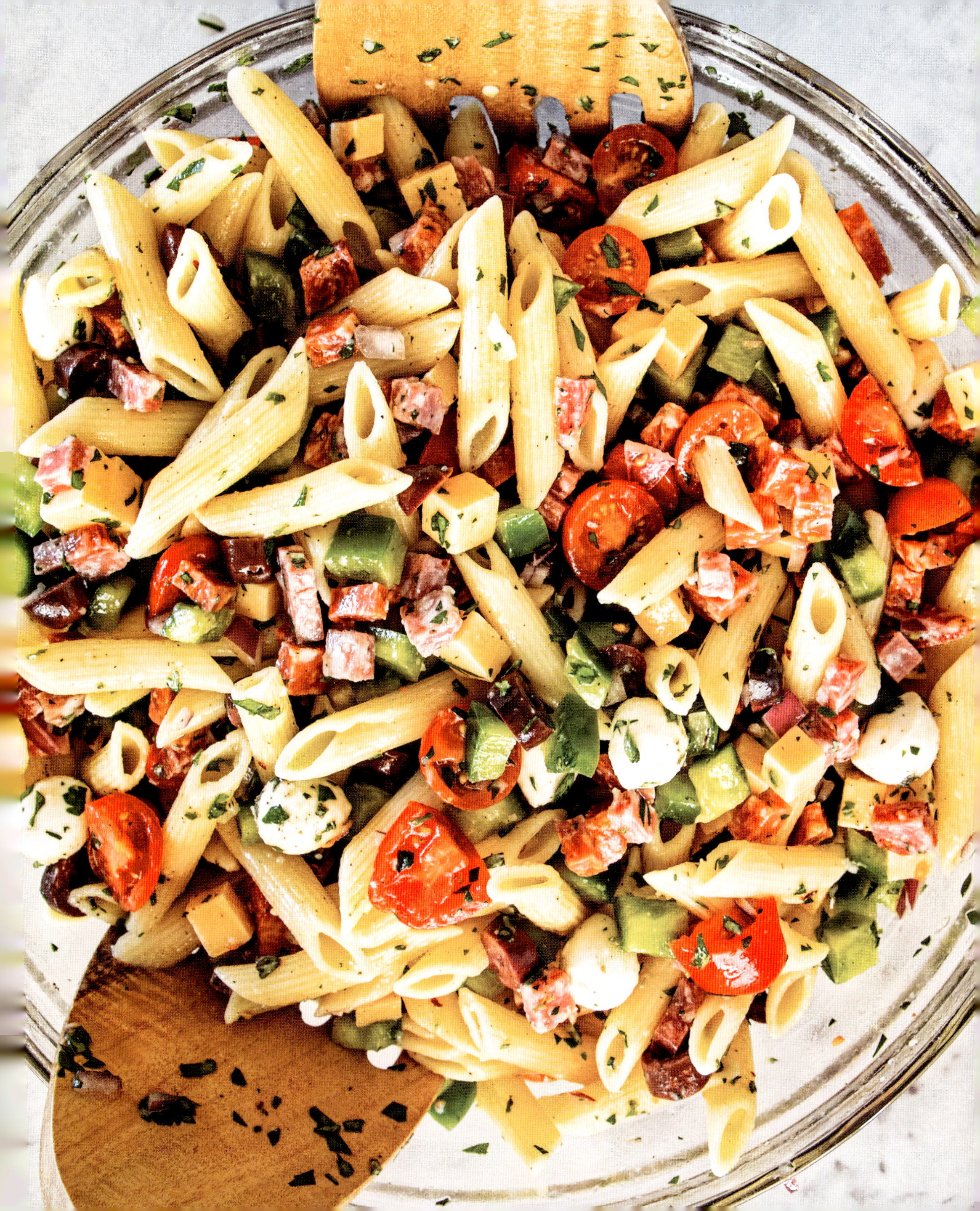

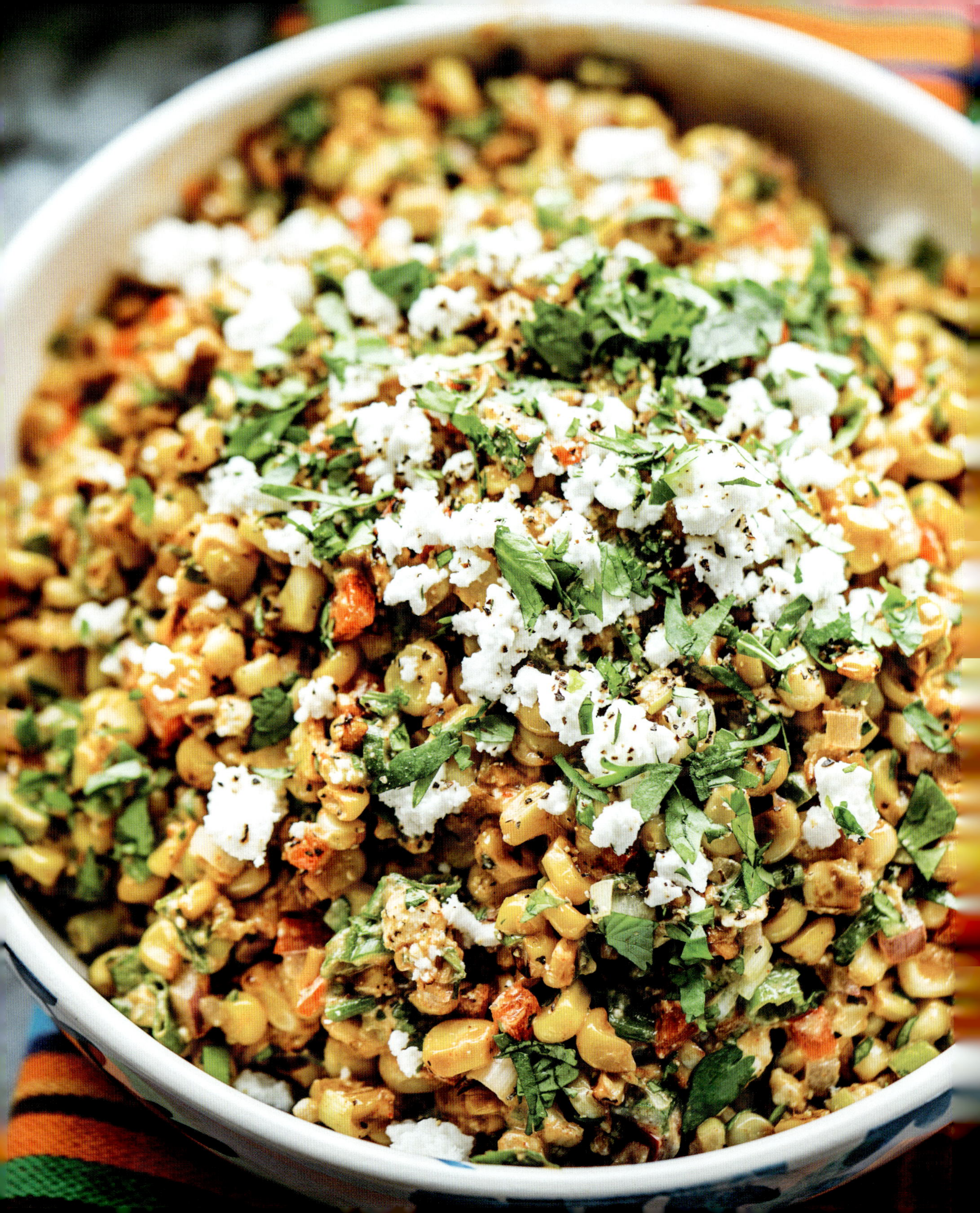

MEXICAN STREET CORN SALAD

PREP TIME: 10 MINUTES
COOK TIME: 10 MINUTES
TOTAL TIME: 20 MINUTES
SERVES: 4

1 tbsp (15 ml) olive oil

4 cups (616 g) fresh, canned or frozen corn (see Recipe Notes)

½ red bell pepper, chopped

½ red onion, finely chopped

½ cup (24 g) chopped fresh cilantro, plus more as needed

6 green onions, chopped

1 jalapeño, diced

½ avocado, chopped

¼ cup (60 ml) fresh lime juice, plus more as needed

½ tsp ground cumin

½ tsp smoked paprika

¼ tsp salt, plus more as needed

¼ tsp black pepper, plus more as needed

2 tbsp (16 g) sour cream or plain Greek yogurt

2 tbsp (30 g) mayonnaise

½ cup (75 g) crumbled cotija cheese, plus more as needed (see Recipe Notes)

Also known as esquites, this salad is smoky, spicy, tangy and incredibly delicious. If you love corn on the cob, then this salad is for you. I include additional veggies in this salad, such as bell peppers, onions and jalapeños. I also add lots of cheese.

Heat the oil in a large skillet over high heat. Add the corn and stir it. Cook it for 3 to 5 minutes, or until it starts to char. If you are using frozen corn, you will need to cook it for 5 to 7 minutes.

Transfer the corn to a large bowl and let it cool for 2 minutes.

Add the bell pepper, red onion, cilantro, green onions, jalapeño, avocado, lime juice, cumin, smoked paprika, salt, black pepper, sour cream, mayonnaise and cotija cheese. Stir everything together until the ingredients are well combined. Taste the salad for seasoning and adjust it as needed with additional lime juice, salt and black pepper.

Garnish the salad with additional cilantro and cotija cheese if preferred, then serve.

RECIPE NOTES

You will need approximately 5 ears of corn to end up with 4 cups (616 g) of fresh corn kernels. If you use canned corn, drain it well. If you use frozen corn, there's no need to thaw it.

While this recipe calls for cotija cheese, I usually use feta cheese, as cotija can be difficult to find.

Store the salad in an airtight container in the fridge for 3 to 4 days. I don't recommend freezing this dish.

NUTRITION INFORMATION

Serving size: 1 serving; **Calories:** 344; **Carbohydrates:** 39 g; **Protein:** 9 g; **Fat:** 20 g

WALDORF SALAD

Here's a classic salad packed with chicken, apples, pears, grapes and a delicious homemade dressing. It's crunchy, it's creamy, it's brilliant!

PREP TIME: 15 MINUTES
COOK TIME: NONE
TOTAL TIME: 15 MINUTES
SERVES: 4

- 1 tbsp (15 ml) fresh lemon juice
- ¼ cup (71 g) plain Greek yogurt
- ¼ cup (60 g) low-fat mayonnaise
- 1 Granny Smith apple, chopped (see Recipe Notes)
- 1 Bosc pear, peeled, cored and diced (see Recipe Notes)
- 1 cup (150 g) seedless grapes, halved
- 2 ribs celery, chopped
- 1 cup (140 g) chopped cooked chicken breast
- ¼ cup (38 g) raisins
- ¼ cup (30 g) walnuts, chopped
- ½ tsp salt, or as needed
- ¼ tsp black pepper, or as needed
- 1 head romaine lettuce, chopped

In a small bowl, whisk together the lemon juice, yogurt and mayonnaise.

In a large bowl, toss together the apple, pear, grapes, celery, chicken, raisins and walnuts. Pour the dressing over the salad and toss it well. Season the salad with the salt and black pepper.

Serve the salad over the romaine lettuce.

RECIPE NOTES

I use a Granny Smith apple for this recipe, but you can use whichever type you like.

Bosc pears can be found at most grocery stores. They are browner in color than a regular green pear. You can use whichever type you prefer.

You can also make sandwiches with this salad and turn it into a chicken salad sandwich with your favorite bread or fresh croissants.

Refrigerate this salad—minus the romaine lettuce—in an airtight container for 3 to 5 days.

NUTRITION INFORMATION

Serving size: 1 serving; **Calories:** 305; **Carbohydrates:** 31 g; **Protein:** 11 g; **Fat:** 16 g

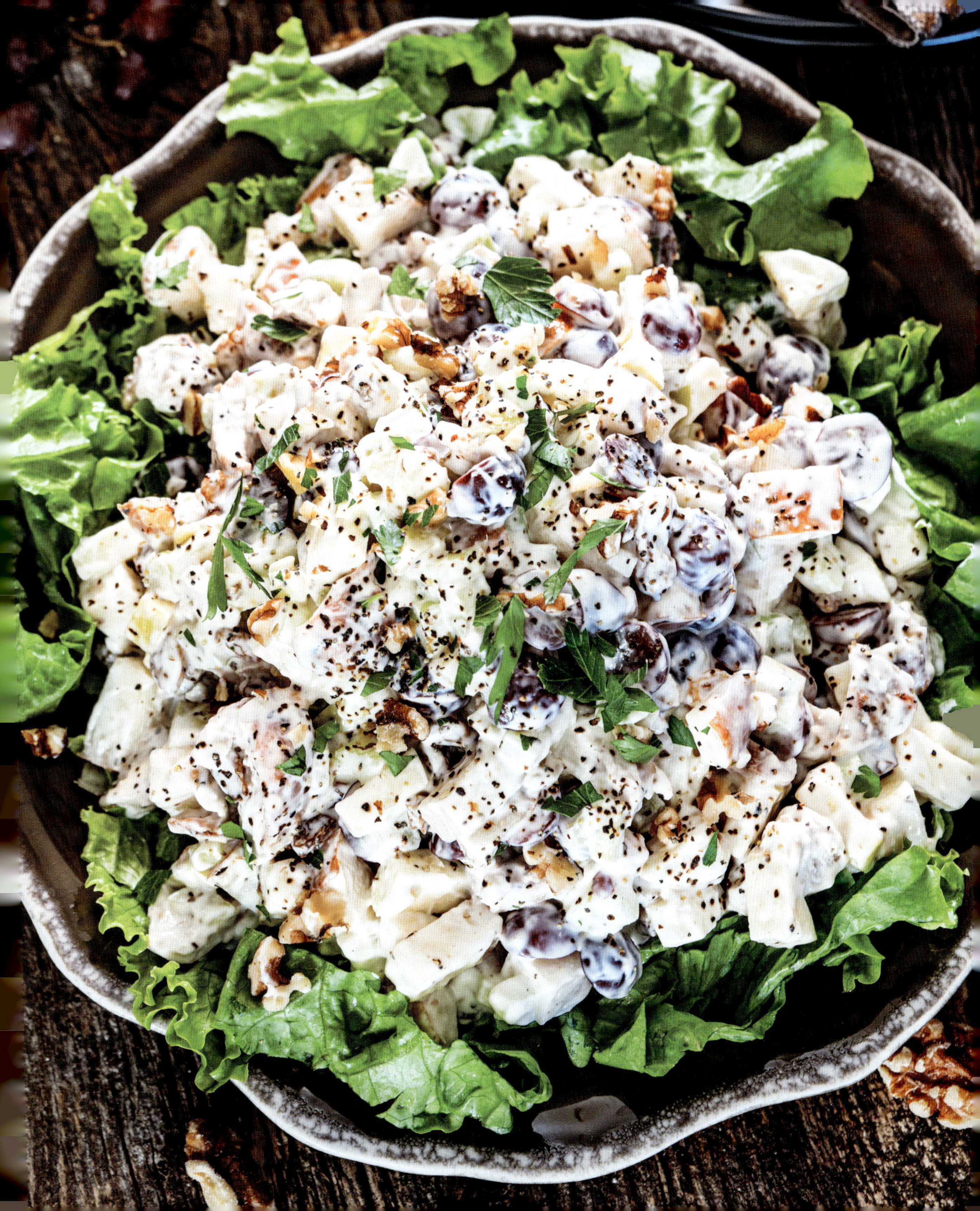

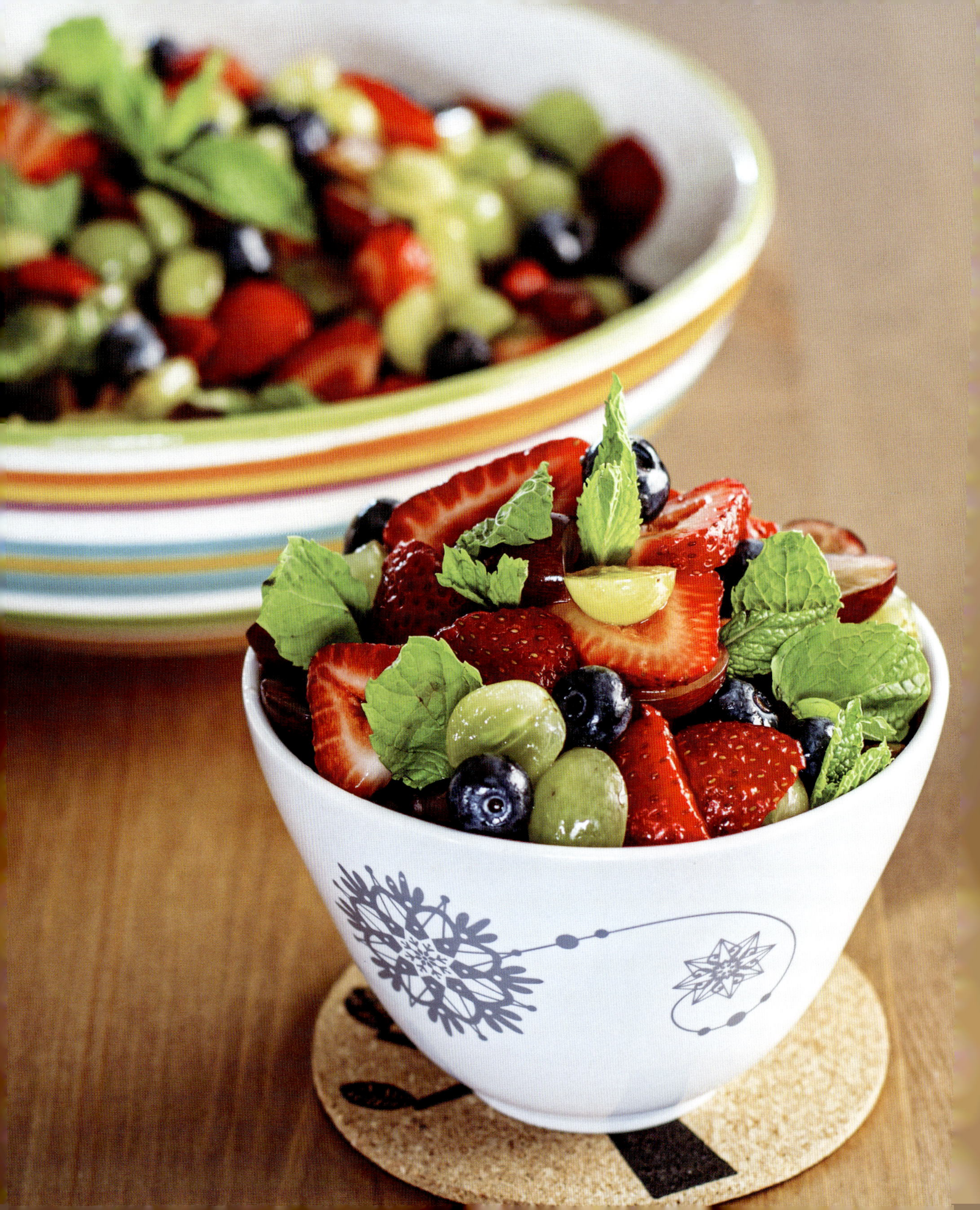

SUMMER FRUIT SALAD WITH LEMON DRESSING

PREP TIME: 20 MINUTES
COOK TIME: 5 MINUTES
CHILLING TIME: 1 HOUR
TOTAL TIME: 1 HOUR, 25 MINUTES
SERVES: 8

¼ cup (48 g) sugar
¾ cup (180 ml) water
2 tbsp (12 g) lemon zest
3 tbsp (45 ml) fresh lemon juice
2 cups (300 g) seedless red grapes, halved
2 cups (300 g) seedless green grapes, halved
2 cups (300 g) fresh blueberries
2 cups (332 g) sliced strawberries
Chopped fresh mint, as needed

This recipe is an oldie but a goody. It's been on the blog since almost the beginning. You'll love this refreshing fruit salad with a delicious lemon dressing.

In a small saucepan over medium heat, combine the sugar, water, lemon zest and lemon juice. Bring the mixture to a boil and cook for 5 minutes, until the sauce begins to thicken. Let the dressing cool to room temperature and then refrigerate it for about 1 hour, until it is chilled.

In a big bowl, toss together the red grapes, green grapes, blueberries and strawberries. Add the mint and pour the dressing over the fruits just before serving the salad.

RECIPE NOTE
Store any leftover fruit salad in an airtight container in the refrigerator for 3 to 5 days.

NUTRITION INFORMATION
Serving size: 1 serving; **Calories:** 110; **Carbohydrates:** 28 g; **Protein:** 1 g; **Fat:** 0 g

TACO PASTA SALAD

PREP TIME: 15 MINUTES
COOK TIME: 15 MINUTES
CHILLING TIME: 1 HOUR
TOTAL TIME: 1 HOUR, 30 MINUTES
SERVES: 16

- 1 lb (448 g) pasta (I recommend penne or shells)
- 1 lb (448 g) ground beef
- 3 tbsp (27 g) taco seasoning
- 1 cup (144 g) canned corn, drained, or frozen corn, thawed
- 1 (15-oz [420-g]) can black beans, drained and rinsed
- 2 cups (300 g) grape tomatoes
- 2 cups (94 g) shredded iceberg lettuce
- ½ cup (65 g) black olives, sliced
- 2 cups (240 g) shredded Cheddar cheese or Mexican blend cheese
- 1½ cups (360 ml) French dressing
- 2 cups (52 g) crushed nacho cheese Doritos®

The photo for this salad doesn't do it justice. This salad is loaded with everything you'd want to see on your taco and more. Doritos and French dressing are musts!

Cook the pasta in salted water according to the package's instructions. Drain the pasta and rinse it well with cold water. Set the pasta aside.

In a large skillet over medium-high heat, cook the beef for 5 to 7 minutes, until it is brown and crumbly. Drain the fat and mix in the taco seasoning.

In a large bowl, combine the pasta, beef, corn, black beans, tomatoes, lettuce, olives, Cheddar cheese, French dressing and Doritos. Toss the salad well. Chill the salad for about 1 hour prior to serving it.

RECIPE NOTES

Store any leftovers in an airtight container in the fridge for 3 to 4 days.

I don't recommend storing this recipe in the freezer. Because of the water content of the veggies and cooked pasta, the dish will become soggy after thawing.

NUTRITION INFORMATION

Serving size: 1 serving; **Calories:** 470; **Carbohydrates:** 47 g; **Protein:** 18 g; **Fat:** 24 g

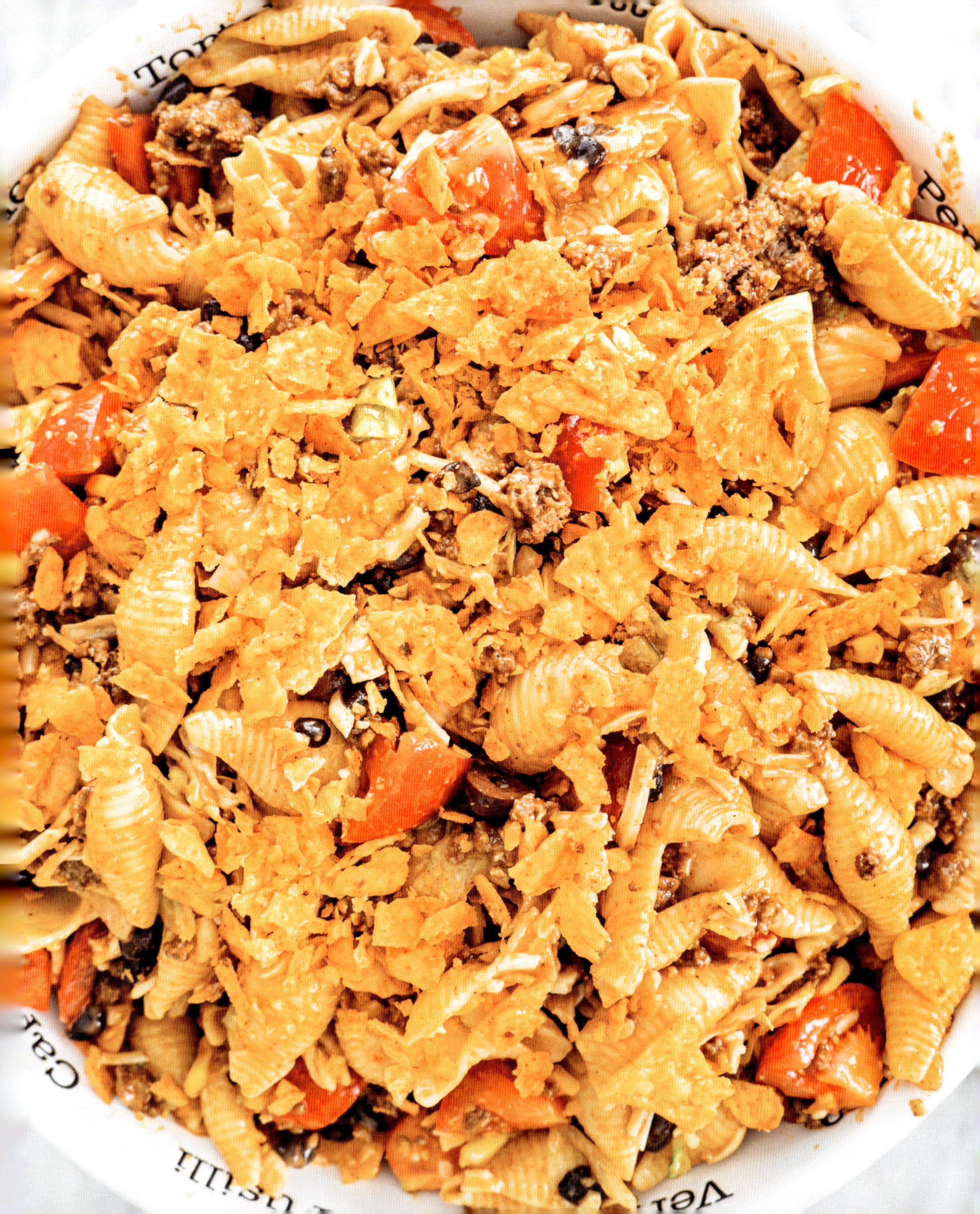

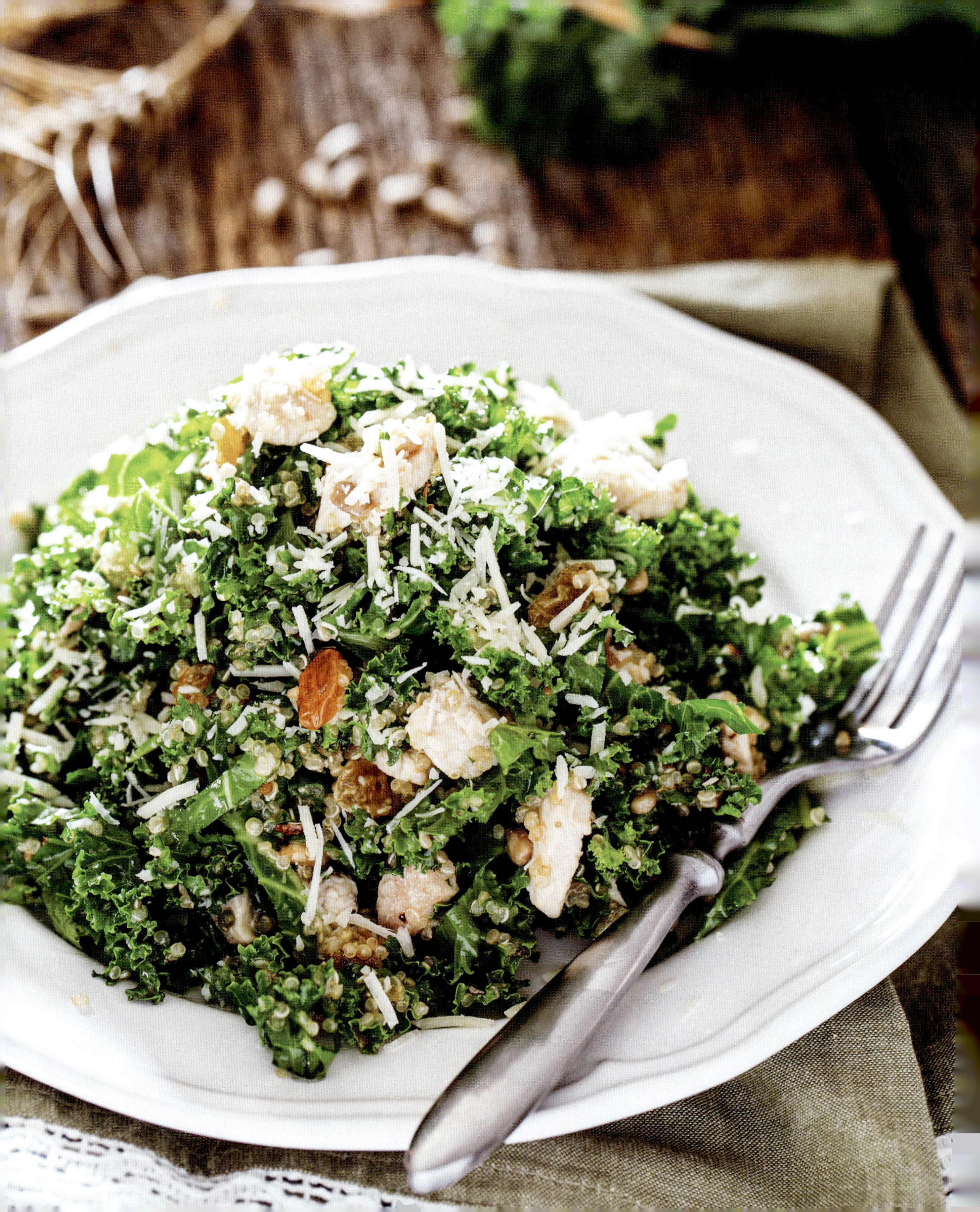

KALE AND QUINOA SALAD WITH LEMON VINAIGRETTE

PREP TIME: 20 MINUTES
COOK TIME: 25 MINUTES
TOTAL TIME: 45 MINUTES
SERVES: 4

SALAD
½ cup (85 g) quinoa
1 cup (240 ml) water
1 tbsp (15 ml) olive oil
1 lb (448 g) boneless, skinless chicken breasts, chopped into small pieces
½ tsp salt, or as needed
1 tsp black pepper, or as needed
½ tsp garlic powder
5 cups (335 g) finely chopped kale
¼ cup (35 g) sunflower seeds
¼ cup (38 g) golden raisins

LEMON VINAIGRETTE
¼ cup (60 ml) olive oil
¼ cup (60 ml) fresh lemon juice
2 cloves garlic, minced
½ tsp salt, plus more as needed
½ tsp black pepper, plus more as needed
1 tsp dried oregano
1 tsp honey

¼ cup (45 g) grated Parmesan cheese (see Recipe Notes)

Chunks of tender chicken, sweet raisins, savory Parmesan cheese and fatty sunflower seeds rest on a bed of bright, fresh kale and earthy quinoa in this delicious recipe. Paired with a stunning homemade lemon vinaigrette, this simple salad is the perfect healthy lunch.

To make the salad, combine the quinoa and water in a small saucepan over medium-high heat. Bring the quinoa to a boil, cover the saucepan and reduce the heat to low. Simmer the quinoa for about 15 minutes, until it is tender. If there's any water left in the saucepan, drain it from the quinoa.

While the quinoa is cooking, prepare the chicken. Heat the oil in a large skillet over medium-high heat. Add the chicken pieces and season them with the salt, black pepper and garlic powder. Cook the chicken for about 8 minutes, until it is no longer pink and it's just starting to brown. Remove the chicken from the skillet and let it cool.

In a large bowl, toss together the kale, chicken, quinoa, sunflower seeds and raisins.

To make the lemon vinaigrette, whisk together the oil, lemon juice, garlic, salt, black pepper, oregano and honey in a small bowl. Taste the vinaigrette for seasoning and adjust it with additional salt and black pepper as necessary.

Pour the vinaigrette over the kale salad and toss it well. Sprinkle the Parmesan cheese over the salad before serving it.

RECIPE NOTES
Freshly grated Parmesan cheese is best in this dish.

The beauty of this kale and quinoa salad is that it will absorb the flavor of the lemon vinaigrette over time, tasting even better the next day! Covered and stored in the fridge, it will keep for 3 to 5 days.

NUTRITION INFORMATION
Serving size: 1 serving; **Calories:** 514; **Carbohydrates:** 33 g; **Protein:** 35 g; **Fat:** 28 g

FATTOUSH SALAD

This fattoush salad is a delicious Lebanese salad with pita bread, mint and a special spice called sumac. It is fresh, loaded with tantalizing herbs and so good for you!

PREP TIME: 20 MINUTES
COOK TIME: 5 MINUTES
TOTAL TIME: 25 MINUTES
SERVES: 4

- 2 tbsp (30 ml) olive oil
- 2 pita breads, torn into small pieces
- 1 English cucumber, chopped
- 1 green bell pepper, chopped
- 3 tomatoes, finely chopped
- 6 green onions, chopped
- ½ cup (58 g) radishes
- ⅓ cup (16 g) chopped fresh parsley
- 2 tbsp (6 g) finely chopped fresh mint
- ¼ cup (60 ml) olive oil
- ¼ cup (60 ml) fresh lemon juice
- ¼ tsp salt, or as needed
- ½ tsp black pepper, or as needed
- 1 tbsp (9 g) ground sumac

Heat the olive oil in a large skillet over medium-high heat. Add the pieces of pita bread and fry them for 1 to 2 minutes, until they are golden brown and crispy.

In a large bowl, combine the cucumber, bell pepper, tomatoes, green onions, radishes, parsley and mint.

In a small bowl, whisk together the oil, lemon juice, salt, black pepper and sumac, until the dressing is thick.

Add the dressing and pita chips to the salad. Toss the salad well and serve it.

RECIPE NOTES

If you would prefer baked pita chips, toss the pieces of pita bread with 1 tablespoon (15 ml) olive oil, ½ teaspoon sumac, salt as needed and black pepper as needed. Place the pita pieces on a large baking sheet and broil them for 2 minutes, until the pita chips are crispy.

This salad can be stored in an airtight container in the fridge for 3 to 4 days, but be sure to store the pita chips separately to prevent them from getting soggy. Unfortunately, defrosted tomatoes tend to be very mushy when eaten raw, so I don't recommend freezing this salad.

NUTRITION INFORMATION

Serving size: 1 serving; **Calories:** 244; **Carbohydrates:** 26 g; **Protein:** 4 g; **Fat:** 14 g

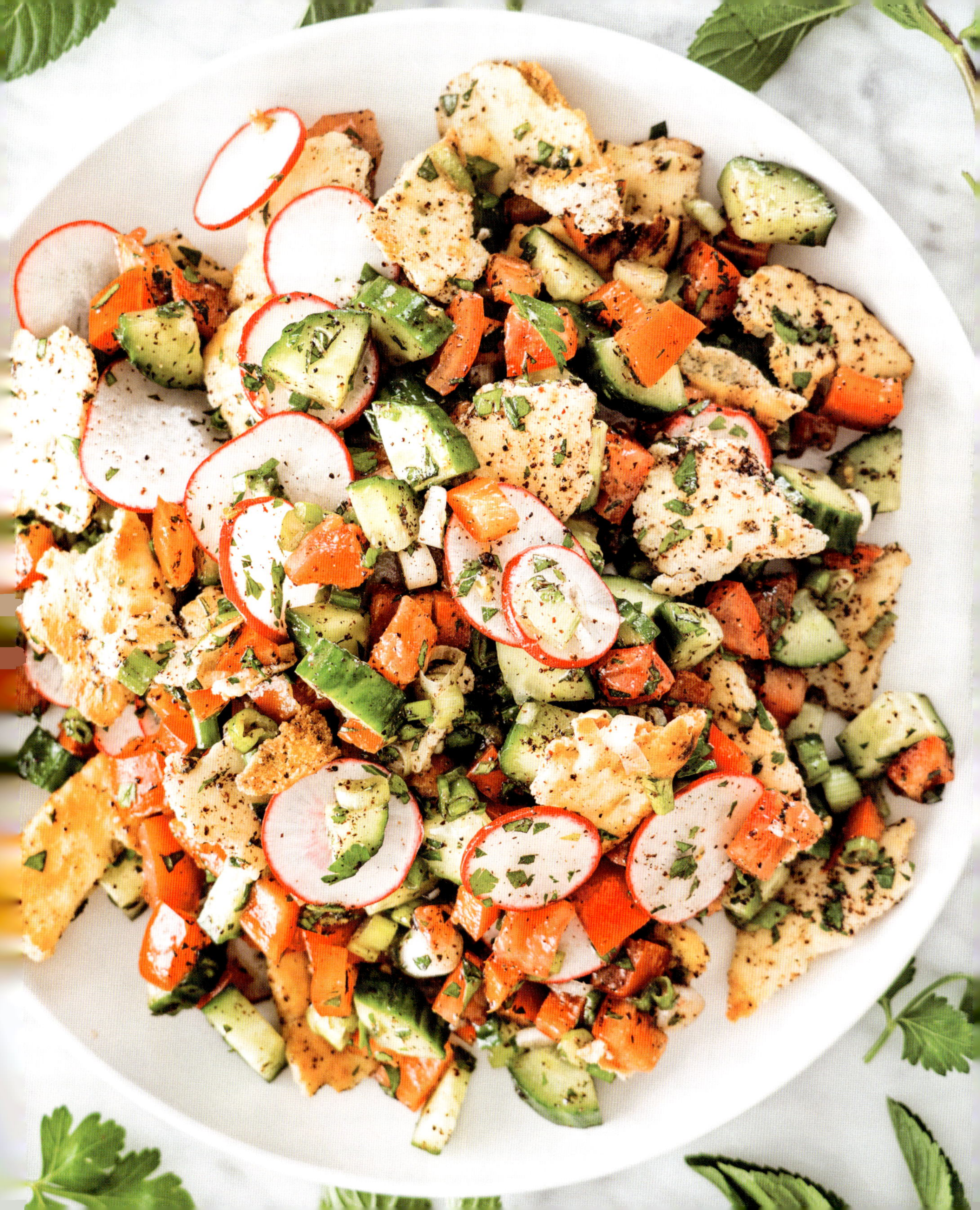

SIDES

NO MEAL IS COMPLETE WITHOUT A GOOD SIDE DISH. What's meatloaf without Mashed Potatoes (page 383)? What's a roasted chicken without some Brandy-Glazed Carrots (page 379) on the side? Side dishes are more important than we give them credit for!

To be honest, my idea of the perfect meal includes some sort of protein surrounded by a few sides. I love a good pork roast with some White Beans with Bacon and Herbs (page 375) or some Skillet Green Beans (page 367) on the side.

Whether your preferred side is roasted veggies, rice, potatoes, beans or polenta, I've got you covered. This chapter focuses on sides that are not only popular on my blog but are favorites in my household.

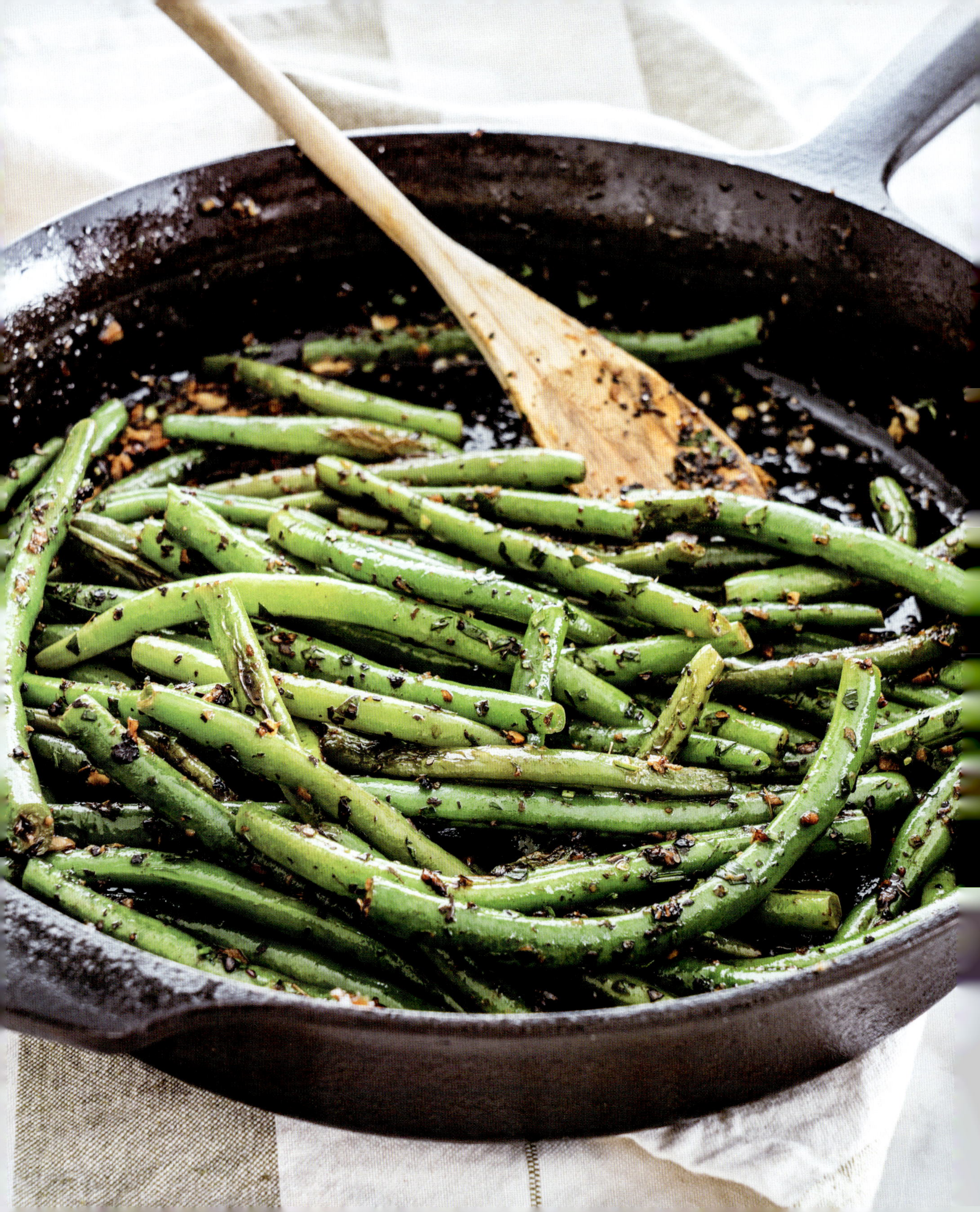

SKILLET GREEN BEANS

This simple recipe for green beans with lemon and garlic is ready in 25 minutes and goes great with any meal. It can't get simpler than a handful of ingredients in one pan—you're going to love these green beans!

PREP TIME: 5 MINUTES
COOK TIME: 20 MINUTES
TOTAL TIME: 25 MINUTES
SERVES: 4

2 tbsp (30 g) butter
4 cloves garlic, minced
1 lb (448 g) fresh green beans
2 tsp (2 g) Italian seasoning
¼ tsp red pepper flakes (optional)
¼ tsp salt, or as needed
¼ tsp black pepper, or as needed
¼ cup (60 ml) low-sodium or unsalted chicken broth
2 tbsp (30 ml) fresh lemon juice
1 tbsp (3 g) chopped fresh parsley

Melt the butter in a large skillet over medium heat. Add the garlic and sauté it for about 30 seconds, or until it is aromatic.

Stir in the green beans, Italian seasoning, red pepper flakes (if using), salt, black pepper and broth. Cover the skillet and cook the green beans for 10 to 12 minutes, stirring them occasionally.

Uncover the skillet, reduce the heat to medium-low and cook the green beans for 2 to 3 minutes, just until they start to char. Stir in the lemon juice, garnish the green beans with the parsley and serve.

RECIPE NOTES

Stored in an airtight container in the fridge, these green beans will last for 3 to 4 days.

These green beans also freeze really well, so if you'd like to extend the shelf life of the beans, store them in an airtight container in the freezer for 4 to 6 months.

NUTRITION INFORMATION

Serving size: 1 serving; **Calories:** 97; **Carbohydrates:** 10 g; **Protein:** 3 g; **Fat:** 6 g

PERFECT THYME SKILLET POTATOES

PREP TIME: 5 MINUTES
COOK TIME: 20 MINUTES
TOTAL TIME: 25 MINUTES
SERVES: 4

2 tbsp (30 ml) olive oil
2 tbsp (30 g) unsalted butter
1 tbsp (3 g) chopped fresh thyme
2 lb (896 g) baby potatoes, halved
½ tsp salt, or as needed
¼ tsp black pepper, or as needed

Crispy on the outside, incredibly creamy on the inside and prepared in a skillet in less than 30 minutes, these potatoes are sure to please everyone.

Heat the oil and butter in a large skillet over medium heat. When the oil is hot and the butter is melted, add the thyme and stir it. This will help infuse the thyme aroma into the oil and butter.

Arrange the potatoes in the skillet, interior side down, and cook them for about 10 minutes, or until they are brown and crispy.

Turn the potatoes over and cover the skillet with a lid. Cook the potatoes for 8 to 10 minutes, or until they are fork-tender. Season them with the salt and black pepper.

Remove the potatoes from the skillet and serve them.

RECIPE NOTES

I prefer to use a cast-iron skillet for this recipe.

You can store your potatoes in an airtight container in the fridge for up to 1 week. Cooked potatoes also freeze really well. If you store them in an airtight container, they will last in the freezer for 10 to 12 months.

NUTRITION INFORMATION

Serving size: 1 serving; **Calories:** 289; **Carbohydrates:** 40 g; **Protein:** 5 g; **Fat:** 13 g

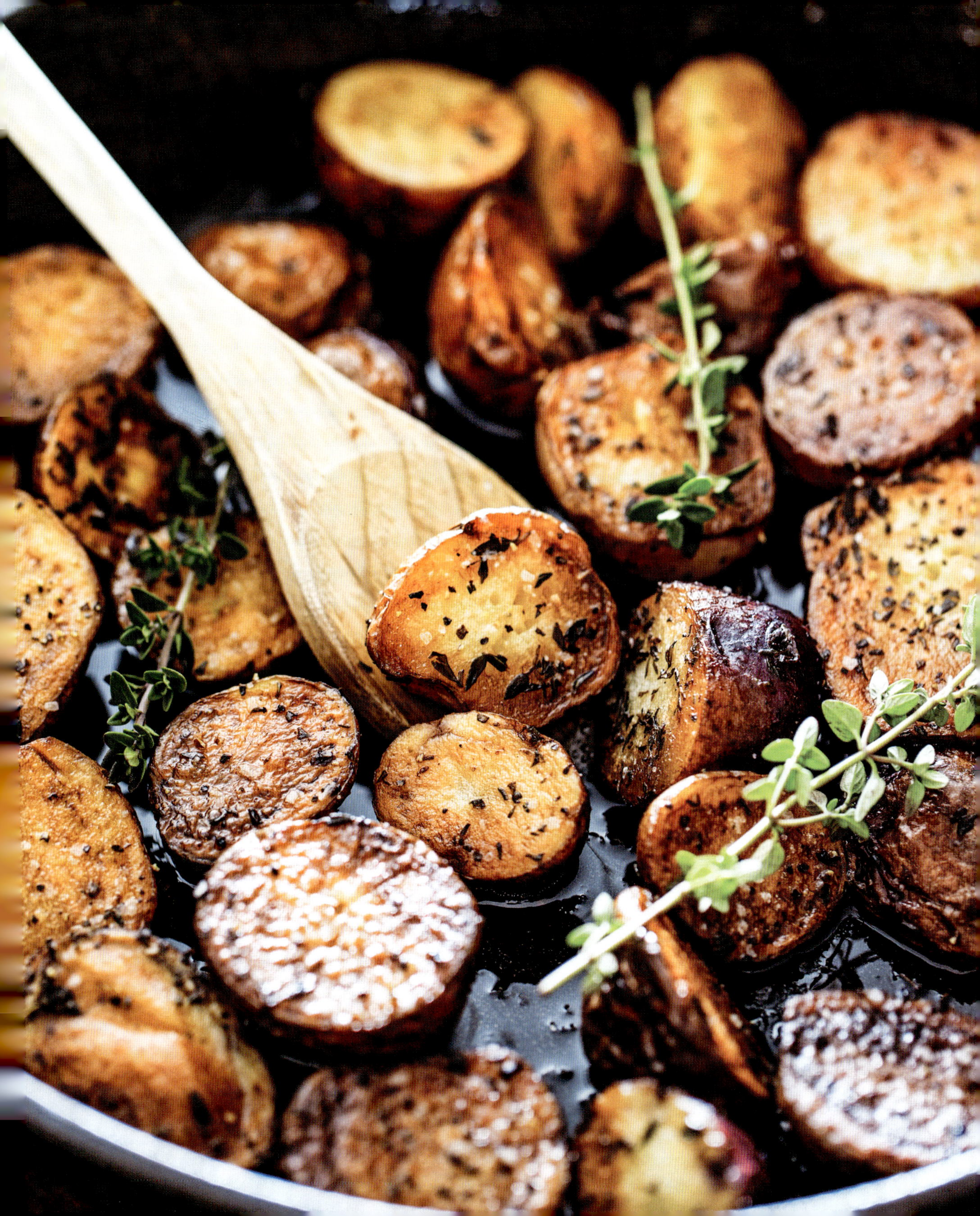

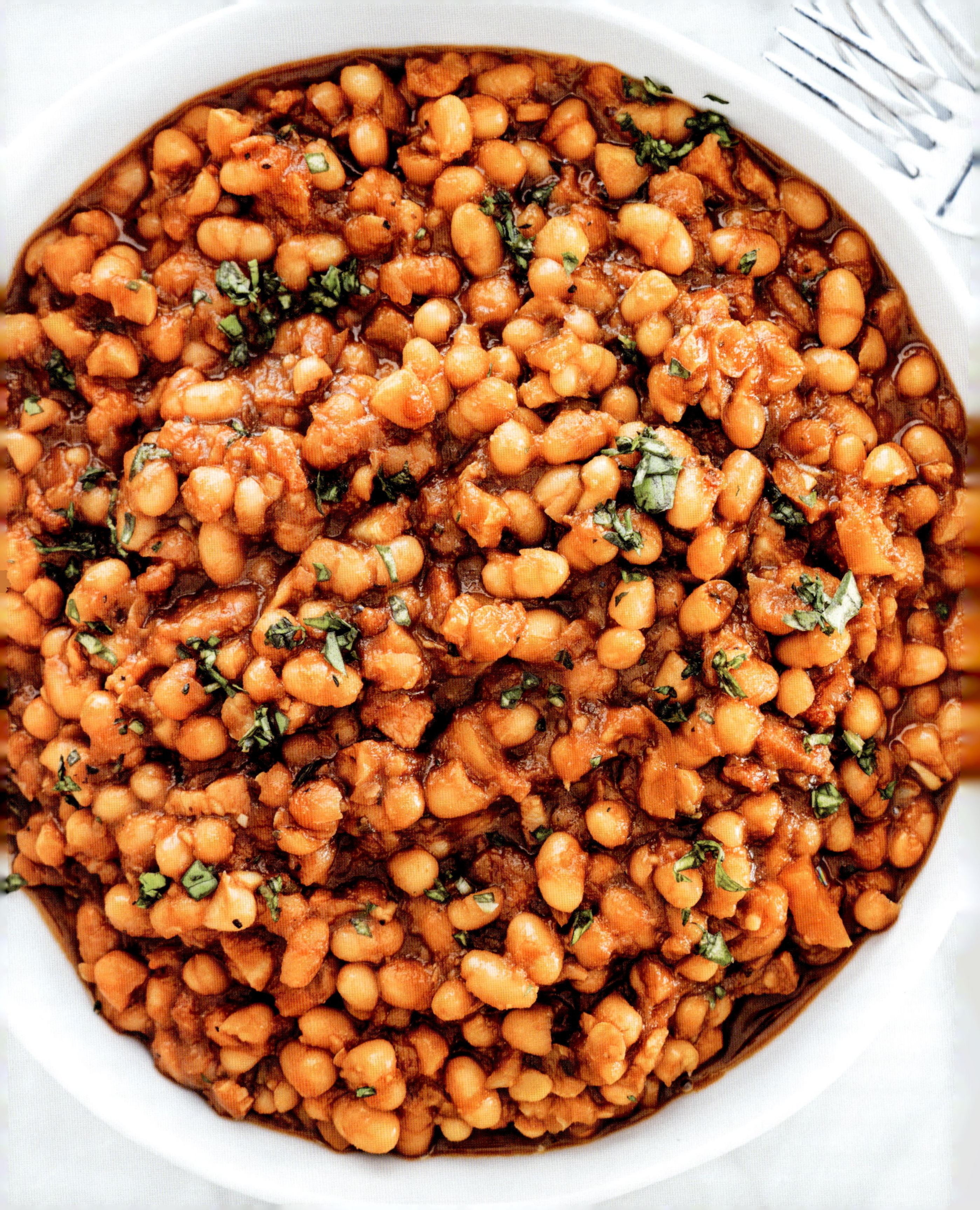

INSTANT POT® BAKED BEANS

I love this recipe because of its simplicity. Pork and beans are combined with a range of flavors, from garlic and rosemary to mustard and ketchup—all in one pot! The aroma this dish puts off is unreal, and the best part is that there is nothing complicated about it.

PREP TIME: 10 MINUTES
COOK TIME: 15 MINUTES
NATURAL PRESSURE RELEASE: 15 MINUTES
TOTAL: 40 MINUTES
SERVES: 8

1 cup (240 g) ketchup
¼ cup (60 ml) molasses
1 tbsp (9 g) mustard powder
1 tbsp (3 g) chopped fresh rosemary
1 tsp Worcestershire sauce
½ tsp salt, or as needed
½ tsp black pepper, or as needed
4 slices thick-cut bacon, chopped
1 onion, chopped
3 cloves garlic, minced
1 bell pepper (any color), chopped
3 (15-oz [420-g]) cans navy beans, drained and rinsed
½ cup (120 ml) low-sodium beef, chicken or vegetable broth

In a medium bowl, whisk together the ketchup, molasses, mustard powder, rosemary, Worcestershire sauce, salt and black pepper. Set the sauce aside.

Set the Instant Pot to the Sauté function. Add the bacon, onion, garlic and bell pepper. Cook the mixture, uncovered, for about 6 minutes, or until the bacon begins to crisp. Turn off the Instant Pot by pressing Cancel and drain any excess fat if necessary.

Stir the beans into the bacon mixture. Pour the broth and sauce over the beans, but do not stir them. Secure the lid of the Instant Pot and turn the valve from Vent to Seal. Select Manual or Pressure Cook and cook the beans at high pressure for 8 minutes. When the cooking is complete, allow for a natural pressure release, which can take anywhere from 10 to 15 minutes.

Once the pressure has been released, unlock and remove the lid. Stir the beans and serve them warm.

RECIPE NOTES

The reason we do not mix the beans with the sauce is because this helps keep things that might scorch from touching the bottom.

These baked beans will last in the fridge for 3 to 4 days when stored in an airtight container. They also freeze well; if stored in an airtight container, they will last in the freezer for 4 to 6 months.

NUTRITION INFORMATION

Serving size: 1 serving; **Calories:** 354; **Carbohydrates:** 61 g; **Protein:** 16 g; **Fat:** 6 g

OLD-FASHIONED GREEN BEANS

PREP TIME: 5 MINUTES
COOK TIME: 20 MINUTES
TOTAL TIME: 25 MINUTES
SERVES: 4

10 strips bacon, cut into ¼" (6-mm) pieces
2 tbsp (30 ml) low-sodium soy sauce
2 tbsp (30 g) packed brown sugar
½ cup (120 ml) water
1½ lb (672 g) fresh green beans
⅛ tsp salt, or as needed
¼ tsp black pepper, or as needed

I love making this dish with fresh green beans and lots of bacon. I add soy sauce and brown sugar for that sweet and salty combination so many of us love.

In a large skillet over medium heat, cook the bacon for about 5 minutes, until it is crispy and most of the fat has rendered.

Add the soy sauce, brown sugar and water to the skillet and stir to combine the ingredients. Bring the mixture to a boil.

Add the green beans and toss them to coat them in the sauce. Reduce the heat to medium-low, cover the skillet and simmer the green beans for 15 minutes, or until they are crisp-tender.

Season the green beans with the salt and black pepper and serve them.

RECIPE NOTES

This recipe is very versatile and can be made with different types of vegetables. Try it on carrots, broccolini, asparagus, peas or whatever your favorite vegetables are!

This dish will store well in an airtight container in the fridge for 3 to 4 days. These beans will also freeze well. Store them in an airtight container in the freezer for 4 to 6 months.

NUTRITION INFORMATION

Serving size: 1 serving; **Calories:** 309; **Carbohydrates:** 19 g; **Protein:** 10 g; **Fat:** 22 g

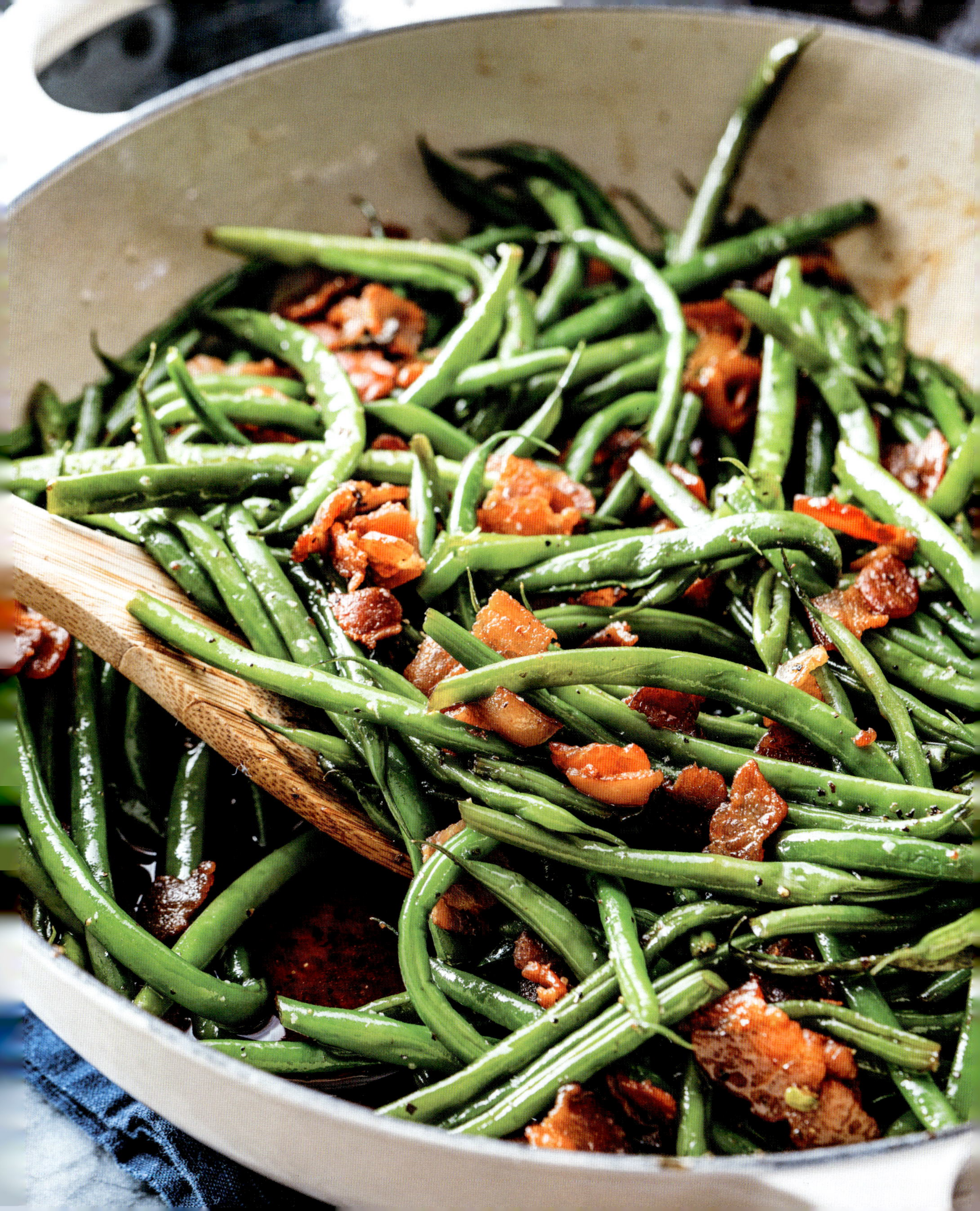

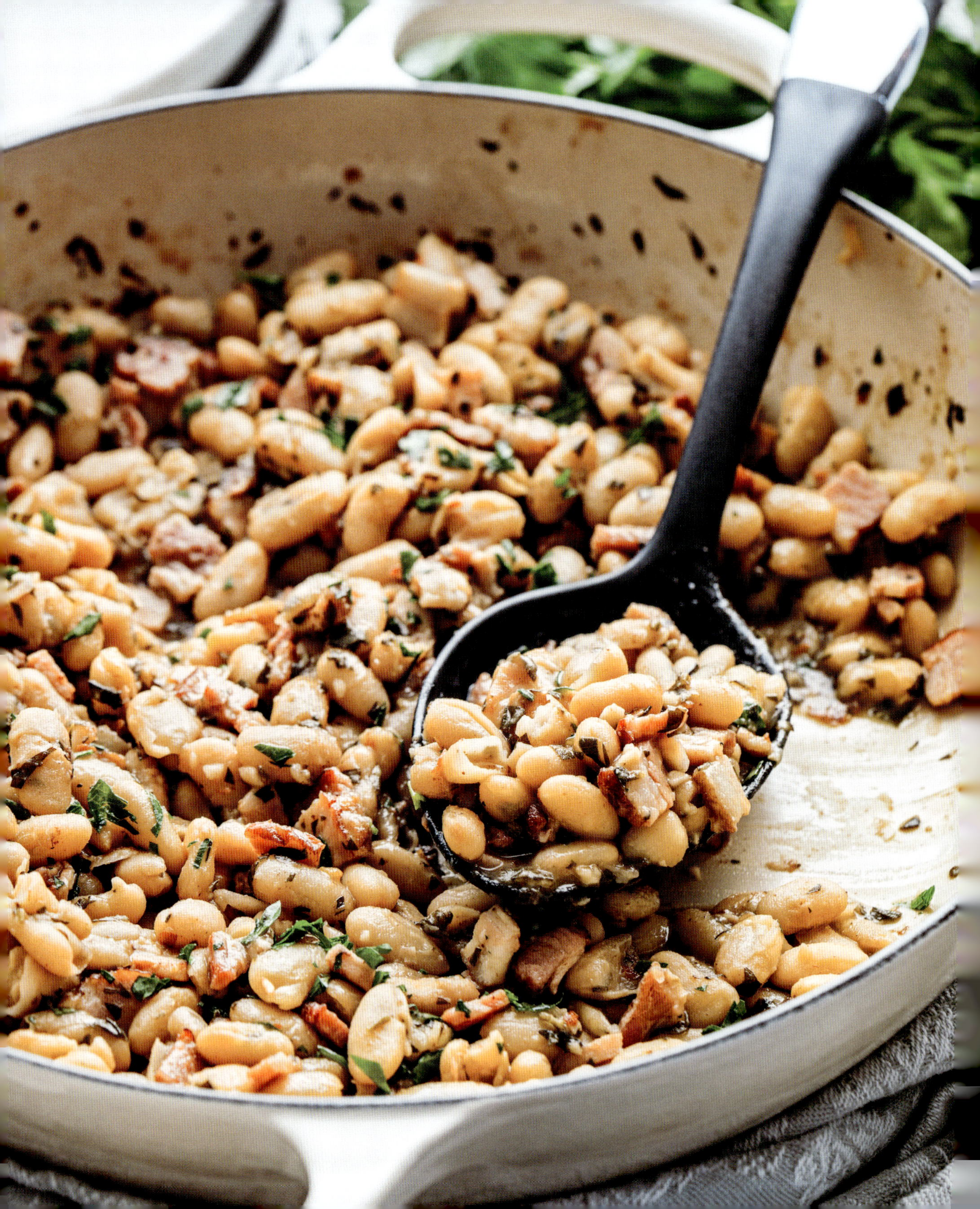

WHITE BEANS WITH BACON AND HERBS

PREP TIME: 5 MINUTES
COOK TIME: 25 MINUTES
TOTAL TIME: 30 MINUTES
SERVES: 8

8 slices bacon, chopped
4 cloves garlic, minced
1½ tbsp (5 g) chopped fresh basil
1½ tbsp (5 g) chopped fresh rosemary
3 tbsp (9 g) chopped fresh parsley, divided
½ tsp red pepper flakes
2 tbsp (30 ml) red wine vinegar
2½ cups (600 ml) low-sodium chicken broth, plus more as needed, divided
2 (15-oz [420-g]) cans cannellini beans, drained and rinsed (see Recipe Notes)
½ tsp salt, or as needed
½ tsp black pepper, or as needed

What's not to love about beans and bacon? Loaded with yummy fresh herbs, this recipe for beans and bacon goes perfectly with any kind of roast or pork chops.

In a large skillet or Dutch oven over medium-high heat, cook the bacon for about 3 minutes, until it is crispy.

Stir in the garlic, basil, rosemary, 2 tablespoons (6 g) of the parsley and the red pepper flakes. Cook the mixture for about 30 seconds, until the garlic is aromatic.

Add the vinegar and ½ cup (120 ml) of the broth and stir to deglaze the skillet. All the brown bits should come up from the bottom of the skillet.

Add the beans and the remaining 2 cups (480 ml) of the broth. The broth should barely cover the beans; if there is not enough broth in the skillet, add more as needed. Season the beans with the salt and black pepper.

Reduce the heat to low and simmer the beans for 15 to 20 minutes, or until most of the liquid has evaporated. Taste the beans for seasoning and adjust as necessary.

Garnish the beans with the remaining 1 tablespoon (3 g) of parsley and serve them warm.

RECIPE NOTES

You can also make this with dried beans. To do so, soak them in water overnight. Follow the rest of the instructions, keeping in mind that they will take longer to cook—about 1 hour over medium heat.

This dish will store well in an airtight container in the fridge for 3 to 4 days. These beans will also freeze well. Store them in an airtight container in the freezer for 4 to 6 months.

NUTRITION INFORMATION

Serving size: 1 serving; **Calories:** 226; **Carbohydrates:** 25 g; **Protein:** 11 g; **Fat:** 9 g

ROASTED RED PEPPERS

I grew up with this recipe, and it is one of my favorite Romanian dishes. These red peppers are grilled until they are charred, then they are peeled and tossed in an incredible garlic sauce. My family eats these as a side dish, but they are great in sauces, salads, dips or sandwiches!

PREP TIME: 15 MINUTES
COOK TIME: 20 MINUTES
TOTAL TIME: 35 MINUTES
SERVES: 4

6 sweet pointed red peppers
4 cloves garlic, minced
2 tbsp (30 ml) olive oil
¼ cup (60 ml) cold water
Salt, as needed
1 tbsp (3 g) chopped fresh parsley

Preheat the grill to medium-high heat. Add the peppers and cook them for 20 minutes, until they are charred and blistered on all sides. Set them aside to cool until they can be handled safely.

To peel the peppers, cut their tops off, then peel away the blistered skin. Slice the peppers lengthwise and remove the seeds. I find this easier to do under running water, as it cleans them thoroughly and quickly.

In a medium bowl, whisk together the garlic, oil, water and salt. Toss the peppers with the sauce. Garnish the peppers with the parsley and serve.

RECIPE NOTES

To store the peppers, keep them, along with the garlic sauce, in an airtight container or a jar in the fridge. They will last for 5 to 6 days. The longer they get to sit and soak up that sauce, the better they'll taste!

These peppers will last for about 1 year in the freezer. You can store them with or without the sauce.

NUTRITION INFORMATION

Serving size: 1 serving; **Calories:** 143; **Carbohydrates:** 16 g; **Protein:** 3 g; **Fat:** 8 g

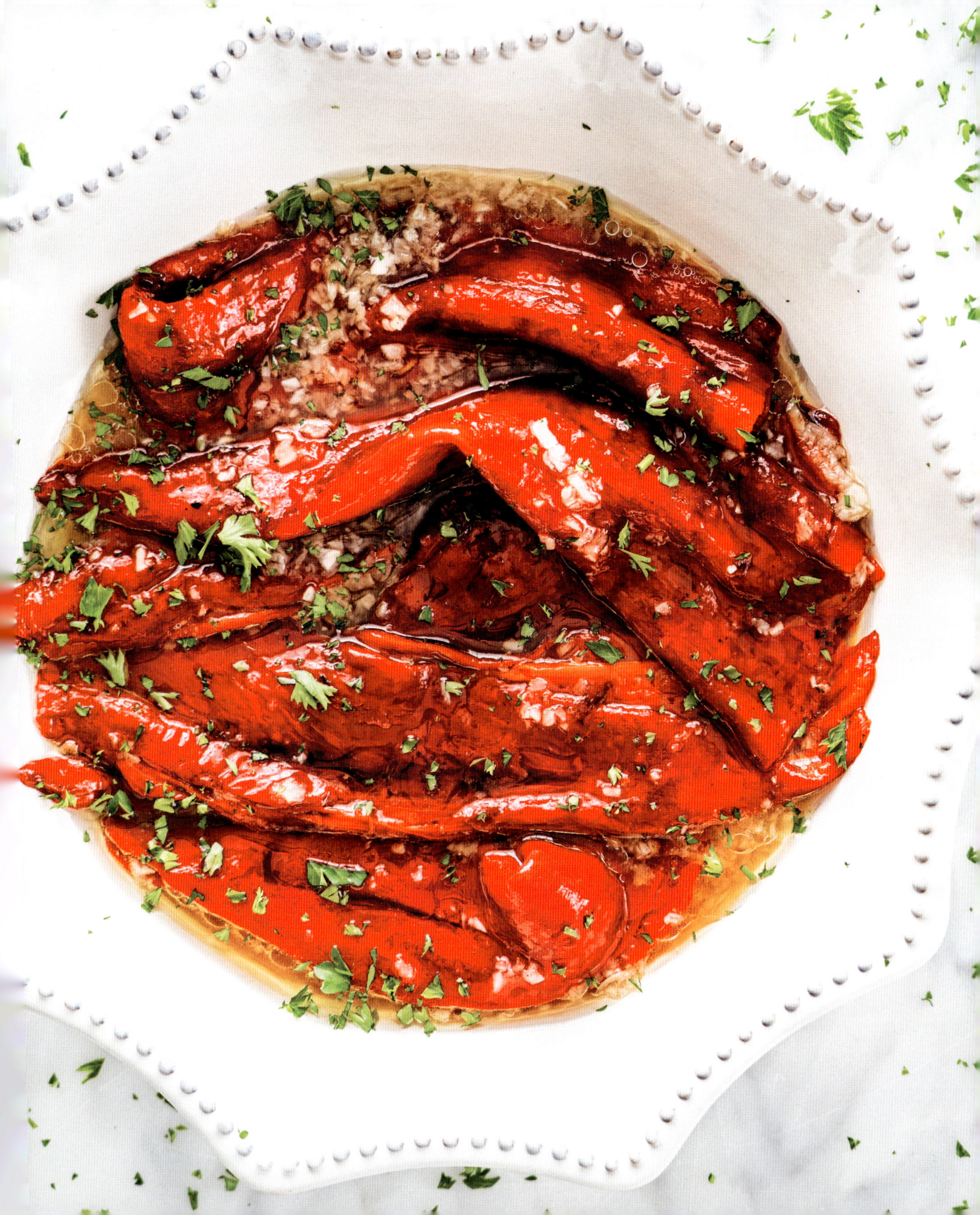

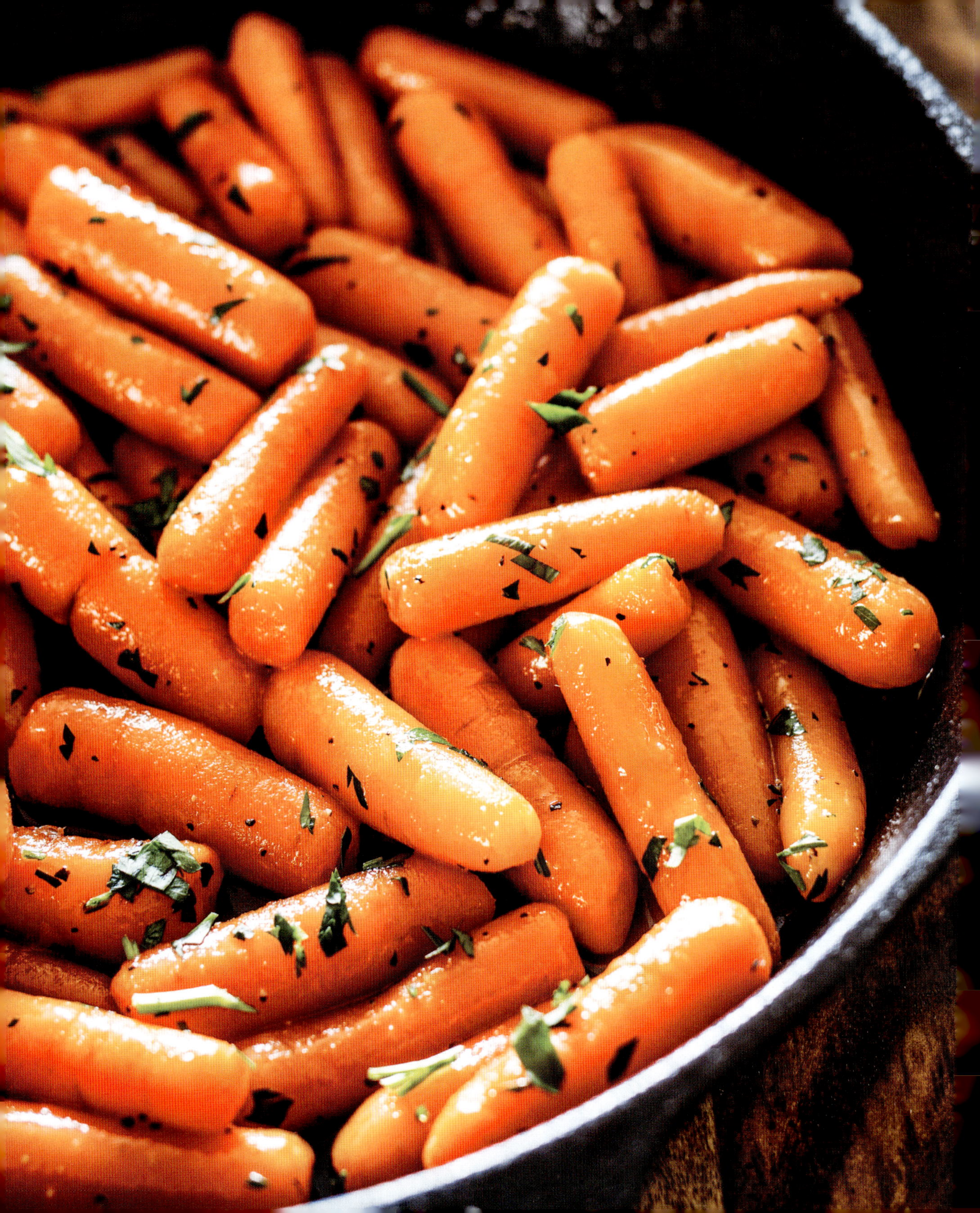

BRANDY-GLAZED CARROTS

PREP TIME: 5 MINUTES
COOK TIME: 20 MINUTES
TOTAL TIME: 25 MINUTES
SERVES: 8

Water, as needed
2 lb (896 g) baby carrots
½ cup (120 g) unsalted butter
¼ cup (60 ml) honey
¼ cup (60 ml) brandy
1 tbsp (3 g) chopped fresh parsley
¼ tsp salt, or as needed
¼ tsp black pepper, or as needed

What I love most about these carrots is how elegant they are: They're colorful, shiny and scrumptious. Although these are the perfect side dish for your holiday dinner, I wouldn't hesitate to make these any time of the year for any occasion.

In a large skillet over high heat, bring ½ inch (13 mm) of water to a boil. Add the carrots, cover the skillet and cook for about 15 minutes, until they are crisp-tender. Drain the carrots and set them aside.

In the same skillet over medium heat, combine the butter and honey and allow the butter to melt. Stir in the brandy and bring the mixture to a boil. Cook the mixture for 2 to 3 minutes, until it has reduced to about ½ cup (120 ml).

Add the carrots and parsley to the glaze. Season the carrots with the salt and black pepper. Cook the carrots until they are heated through, then serve.

RECIPE NOTE

Store any leftover glazed carrots in an airtight container in the fridge for 3 to 5 days.

NUTRITION INFORMATION

Serving size: 1 serving; **Calories:** 191; **Carbohydrates:** 18 g; **Protein:** 0 g; **Fat:** 11 g

MUSHROOM RISOTTO

This mushroom risotto is rich, creamy, cheesy and made with salty bacon and earthy mushrooms. While this classic dish is usually enjoyed in restaurants with a high price tag, I've created this risotto with basic ingredients and foolproof instructions. Time to treat yourself!

PREP TIME: 10 MINUTES
COOK TIME: 45 MINUTES
TOTAL TIME: 55 MINUTES
SERVES: 6

5 cups (1.2 L) low-sodium chicken broth
4 sprigs fresh thyme
8 slices bacon, cut into ¼" to ½" (6- to 13-mm) pieces
1 tbsp (15 ml) olive oil (optional)
1 white onion, diced
8 oz (224 g) cremini mushrooms, sliced
¼ tsp salt, plus more as needed
½ tsp black pepper, plus more as needed
2 cloves garlic, minced
1½ cups (315 g) arborio rice (see Recipe Notes)
½ cup (120 ml) white wine
½ cup (90 g) grated Parmesan cheese (see Recipe Notes)
1 tbsp (3 g) chopped fresh parsley

NUTRITION INFORMATION

Serving size: 1 serving; **Calories:** 421; **Carbohydrates:** 47 g; **Protein:** 15 g; **Fat:** 18 g

Combine the broth and thyme sprigs in a medium pot over medium heat. Once the broth comes to a simmer, reduce the heat to low to keep it hot but barely simmering.

In a large Dutch oven over medium-high heat, cook the bacon for 5 to 7 minutes, until it is crispy. Remove the bacon from the Dutch oven with a slotted spoon. Leave the bacon fat in the Dutch oven.

Add the oil to the bacon fat if needed—I usually have enough fat rendered from the bacon that I don't need to use it. Add the onion, mushrooms, salt and black pepper. Cook the mixture for 5 minutes, stirring it often, until the onion is translucent and the mushrooms are browned. Stir in the garlic and cook the mixture for 30 seconds.

Add the rice, stir to combine the ingredients, then pour in the wine. Reduce the heat to medium-low and let the rice cook for 2 minutes, or until it has absorbed the wine. Add 1 cup (240 ml) of the hot broth, avoiding the thyme sprigs, and stir the rice. Cook the rice for 4 to 5 minutes, stirring it occasionally, until the liquid has been mostly absorbed. Repeat this step until the rice is tender and you have used all the broth, which should take 20 to 25 minutes.

Stir in the bacon and Parmesan cheese. Taste the risotto for seasoning and add more salt and black pepper if needed. Garnish the risotto with the parsley and serve it.

RECIPE NOTES

Arborio rice is also known as risotto rice.

Freshly grated Parmesan cheese is best in this dish.

Stored in the refrigerator, this risotto will last for up to 5 days. To reheat the risotto, microwave it and stir it every 15 to 20 seconds. If the microwave isn't an option, you can reheat it in a skillet or saucepan over medium heat. Feel free to add a splash or two of chicken broth or water to avoid the risotto drying out.

While it isn't ideal to freeze risotto, you can if you need it to last longer than 5 days. Make sure the risotto has fully cooled down to room temperature before storing it in an airtight container. It'll last for 2 to 3 months in the freezer. Let the risotto thaw overnight in the fridge before reheating. Keep in mind that after freezing and thawing, the risotto will have a much softer texture. You'll have to be careful when reheating so as to not break up the grains of rice.

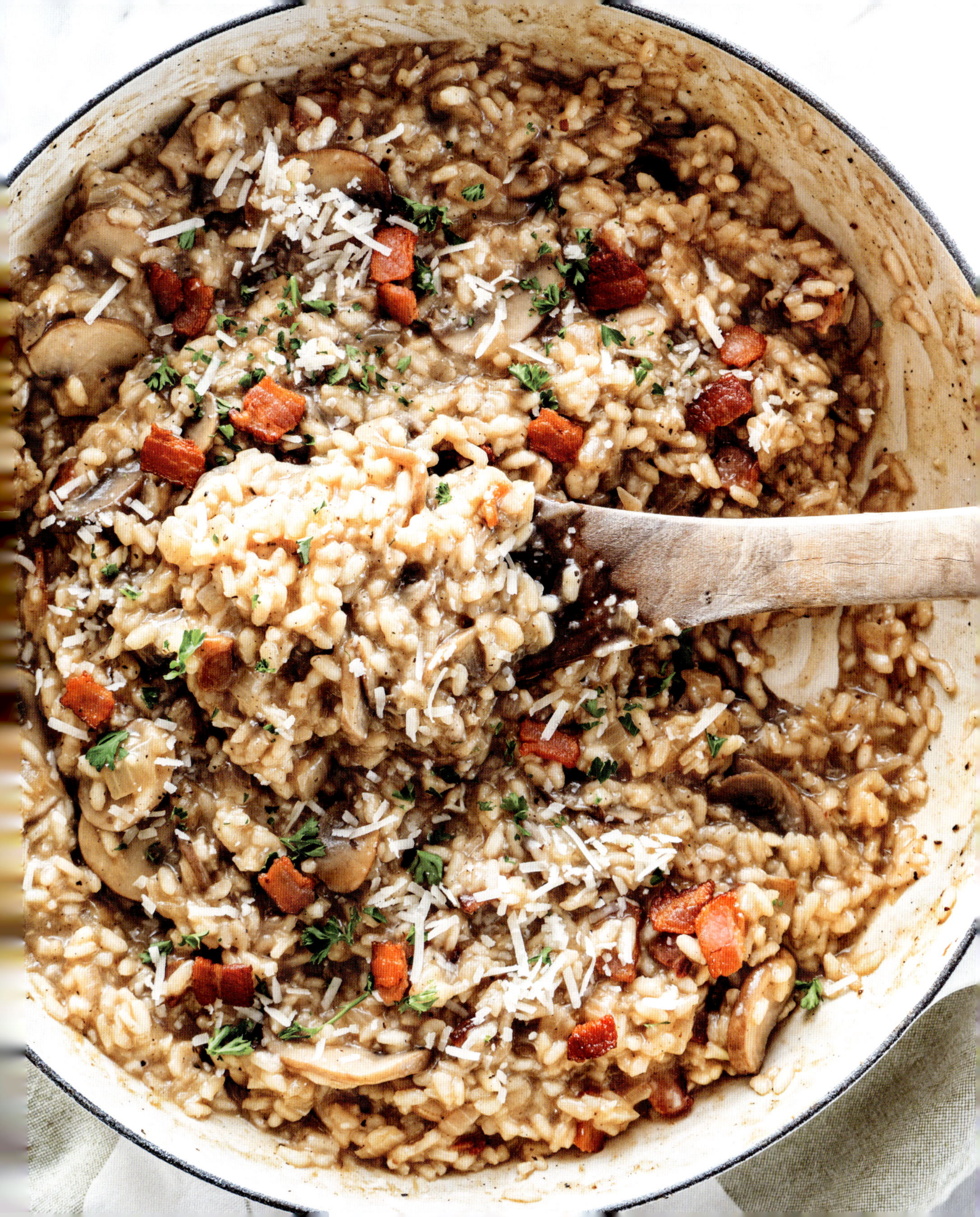

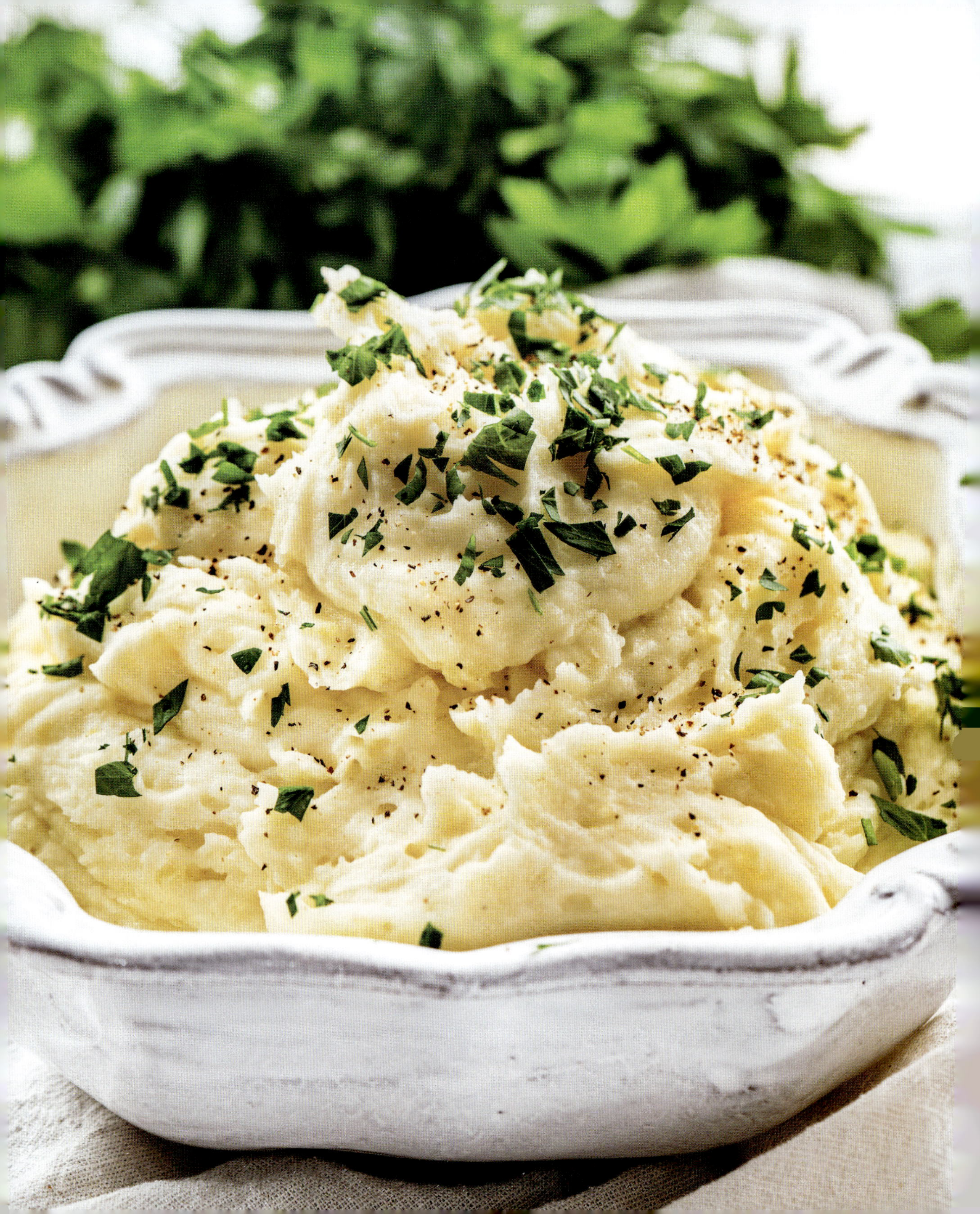

MASHED POTATOES

This is my mom's recipe for fluffy mashed potatoes. To get them fluffy, she uses a mixer to whip them. They're delicious, creamy and buttery!

PREP TIME: 15 MINUTES
COOK TIME: 20 MINUTES
TOTAL TIME: 35 MINUTES
SERVES: 8

4 lb (1.8 kg) potatoes, peeled and cubed (see Recipe Notes)
1 tsp salt, plus more as needed
4 tbsp (60 g) unsalted butter, at room temperature
1 cup (240 ml) half-and-half or milk
½ tsp white or black pepper

Place the potatoes in a large pot and fill the pot with enough cold water to fully cover the potatoes. Add the salt to the water and stir to dissolve the salt.

Bring the potatoes to a boil over high heat, then reduce the heat to medium and cook the potatoes for about 15 minutes, or until they are fork-tender.

Drain the potatoes and transfer them to the bowl of a stand mixer fitted with the whisk attachment. Mix the potatoes on medium speed until they are mashed. Add the butter, half-and-half and white pepper.

Mix the potatoes until they are smooth and fluffy and the ingredients have been fully combined. Taste the potatoes for seasoning and add more salt if needed.

RECIPE NOTES

I use Yukon gold potatoes, but russet potatoes would work as well. Make sure all the potatoes are cut into equal size pieces so that they all cook at the same time.

Store any leftovers in an airtight container in the refrigerator for 3 to 5 days.

Freeze the mashed potatoes in an airtight container or freezer bag for up to 10 months.

NUTRITION INFORMATION

Serving size: 1 serving; **Calories:** 222; **Carbohydrates:** 29 g; **Protein:** 6 g; **Fat:** 9 g

CREAMY GARLIC-PARMESAN MUSHROOMS

PREP TIME: 10 MINUTES
COOK TIME: 20 MINUTES
TOTAL TIME: 30 MINUTES
SERVES: 6

3 tbsp (45 g) unsalted butter
2 tbsp (30 ml) olive oil
2 lb (896 g) cremini mushrooms, halved (see Recipe Notes)
¼ tsp salt, or as needed
½ tsp black pepper, or as needed
3 cloves garlic, minced
1½ cups (360 ml) heavy cream (see Recipe Notes)
¾ cup (135 g) grated Parmesan cheese, divided (see Recipe Notes)
2 tbsp (6 g) chopped fresh parsley

My favorite way to serve these creamy mushrooms is on a bed of fluffy Mashed Potatoes (page 383), over spaghetti or over grilled steak. They really are incredible and versatile.

Heat the butter and oil in a large skillet over medium-high heat until the butter has melted.

Add the mushrooms, salt and black pepper and sauté them for about 15 minutes, until they are brown and tender.

Add the garlic and cook the mixture for 30 seconds, until the garlic is aromatic. Stir in the heavy cream and ½ cup (90 g) of the Parmesan cheese and cook the mushrooms until the sauce is bubbly and has thickened slightly. Taste the mushrooms and sauce for seasoning and adjust it as necessary.

Garnish the mushrooms with the remaining ¼ cup (45 g) of Parmesan cheese and parsley. Serve the mushrooms immediately.

RECIPE NOTES

I use cremini mushrooms, which are usually brown in color and are a more mature version of the white button mushroom, so the flavor is similar. Because of this similarity, white button mushrooms can be used as well.

Heavy cream is also called heavy whipping cream because it's whipping cream with a milk fat content of between 36 and 40 percent. Half-and-half, which has a fat content of 10 to 12 percent, can also be used for a lighter version of this recipe.

Freshly grated Parmesan cheese is best in this dish.

For a dairy-free option, use almond milk or rice milk instead. Add about 1 tablespoon (9 g) of cornstarch to thicken the sauce and use dairy-free butter.

Store any leftovers in an airtight container in the refrigerator for 3 to 4 days. Make sure to refrigerate the mushrooms within 2 hours of cooking them.

Freeze these mushrooms in an airtight container or heavy-duty freezer bags for 4 to 6 months.

NUTRITION INFORMATION

Serving size: 1 serving; **Calories:** 382; **Carbohydrates:** 9 g; **Protein:** 9 g; **Fat:** 35 g

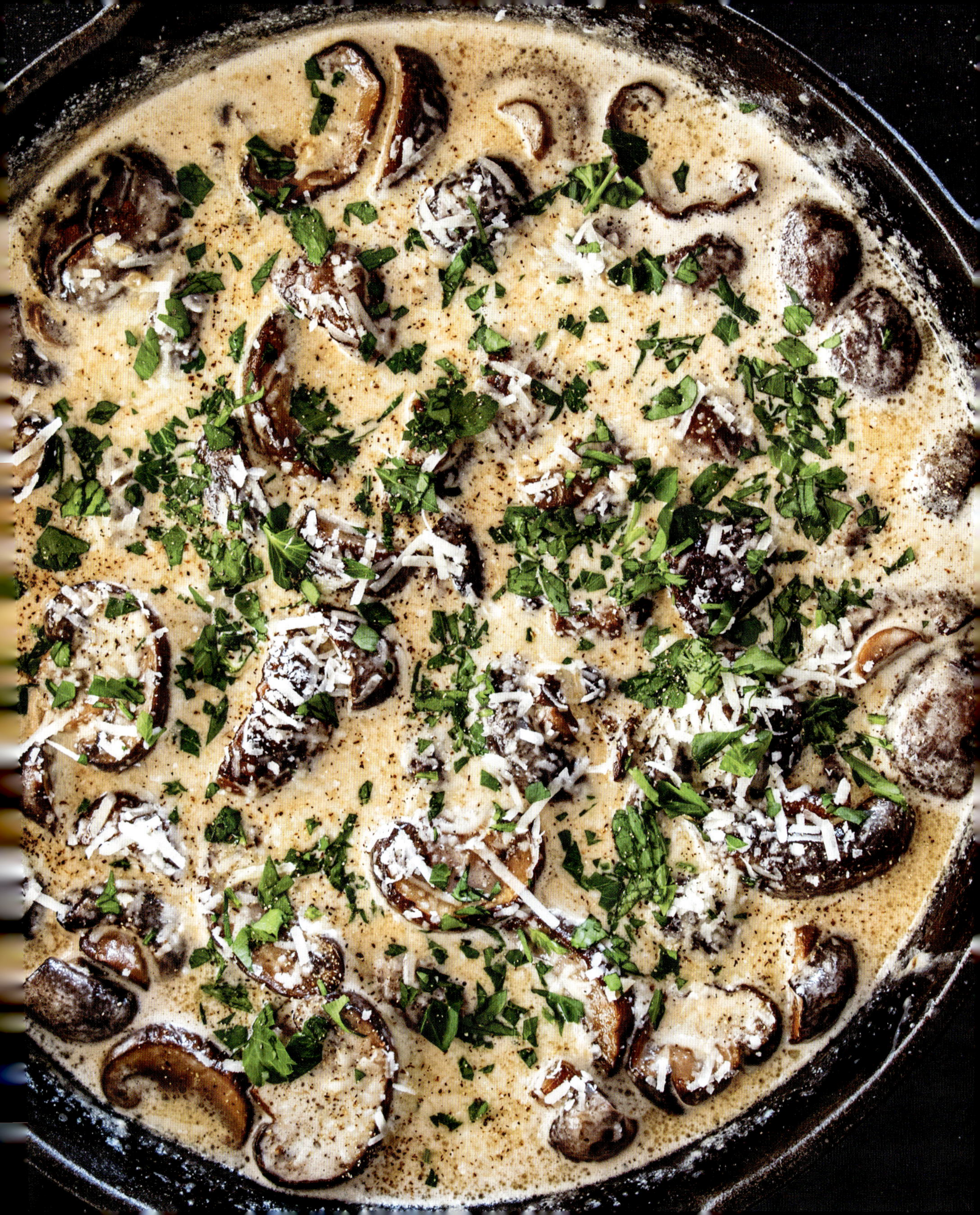

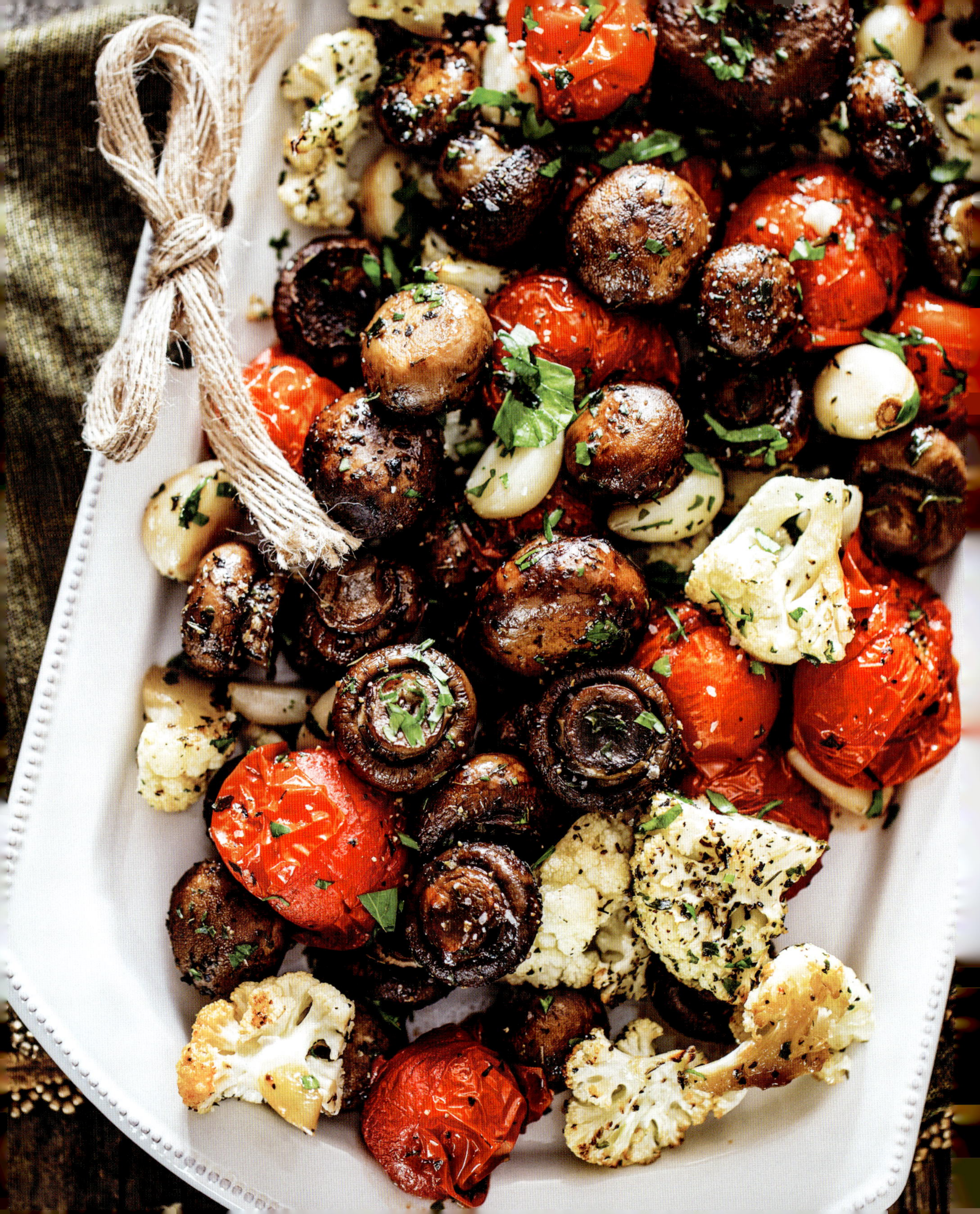

ITALIAN ROASTED VEGGIES

PREP TIME: 10 MINUTES
COOK TIME: 30 MINUTES
TOTAL TIME: 40 MINUTES
SERVES: 6

1 lb (448 g) cremini mushrooms
2 cups (460 g) small cauliflower florets
2 cups (300 g) cocktail tomatoes
12 cloves garlic, peeled
2 tbsp (30 ml) olive oil
1 tbsp (3 g) Italian seasoning (see Recipe Notes)
Salt, as needed
Black pepper, as needed
1 tbsp (3 g) chopped fresh parsley

I love roasted veggies, and in this side dish I included all my favorite veggies, which I seasoned with Italian seasoning and some salt and pepper. In my opinion, the tomatoes make this dish. I love using whole cocktail tomatoes—as you bite into them, you experience an explosion of flavor!

Preheat the oven to 400°F (204°C).

In a large bowl, combine the mushrooms, cauliflower, tomatoes and garlic. Drizzle the vegetables with the oil, then add the Italian seasoning, salt and black pepper. Toss the vegetables until the ingredients are well combined.

Transfer the vegetables to a large baking sheet. Roast the vegetables for 20 to 30 minutes, or until the mushrooms are golden brown and the cauliflower is fork-tender.

Garnish the vegetables with the parsley before serving them.

RECIPE NOTES

If you do not have Italian seasoning, you can use equal amounts of dried basil, dried oregano, dried rosemary and dried thyme.

This recipe is so easy to make and store! Just refrigerate the veggies in an airtight container and they'll stay fresh for up to 1 week.

NUTRITION INFORMATION

Serving size: 1 serving; **Calories:** 87; **Carbohydrates:** 9 g; **Protein:** 3 g; **Fat:** 4 g

CREAMY POLENTA

When I was a young girl, my mom told me all the time that in Romania, when a young girl learns to make polenta, she's ready to get married. I learned to make it at a young age because polenta was and still is very common in our household. Now, I did get married, but it probably had nothing to do with learning how to make polenta. Or did it?

PREP TIME: 5 MINUTES
COOK TIME: 25 MINUTES
TOTAL TIME: 30 MINUTES
SERVES: 4

4 cups (960 ml) water
1 tsp salt, plus more as needed
1 cup (170 g) cornmeal
4 tbsp (60 g) unsalted butter
½ cup (90 g) grated Parmesan cheese
Black pepper, as needed

In a large saucepan or Dutch oven over high heat, combine the water and salt. Bring the water to a boil.

Gradually whisk in the cornmeal. Whisk the cornmeal constantly until it is smooth and beginning to thicken. Reduce the heat to medium-low and cook the cornmeal for about 25 minutes, stirring it often, until it is tender and thick but still creamy and it pulls cleanly away from the saucepan.

Stir in the butter and Parmesan cheese. Season the polenta with the salt and black pepper, then serve it.

RECIPE NOTE

Store leftover polenta in an airtight container or wrapped in aluminum foil or plastic wrap in the fridge for up to 5 days.

NUTRITION INFORMATION

Serving size: 1 serving; **Calories:** 303; **Carbohydrates:** 29 g; **Protein:** 9 g; **Fat:** 17 g

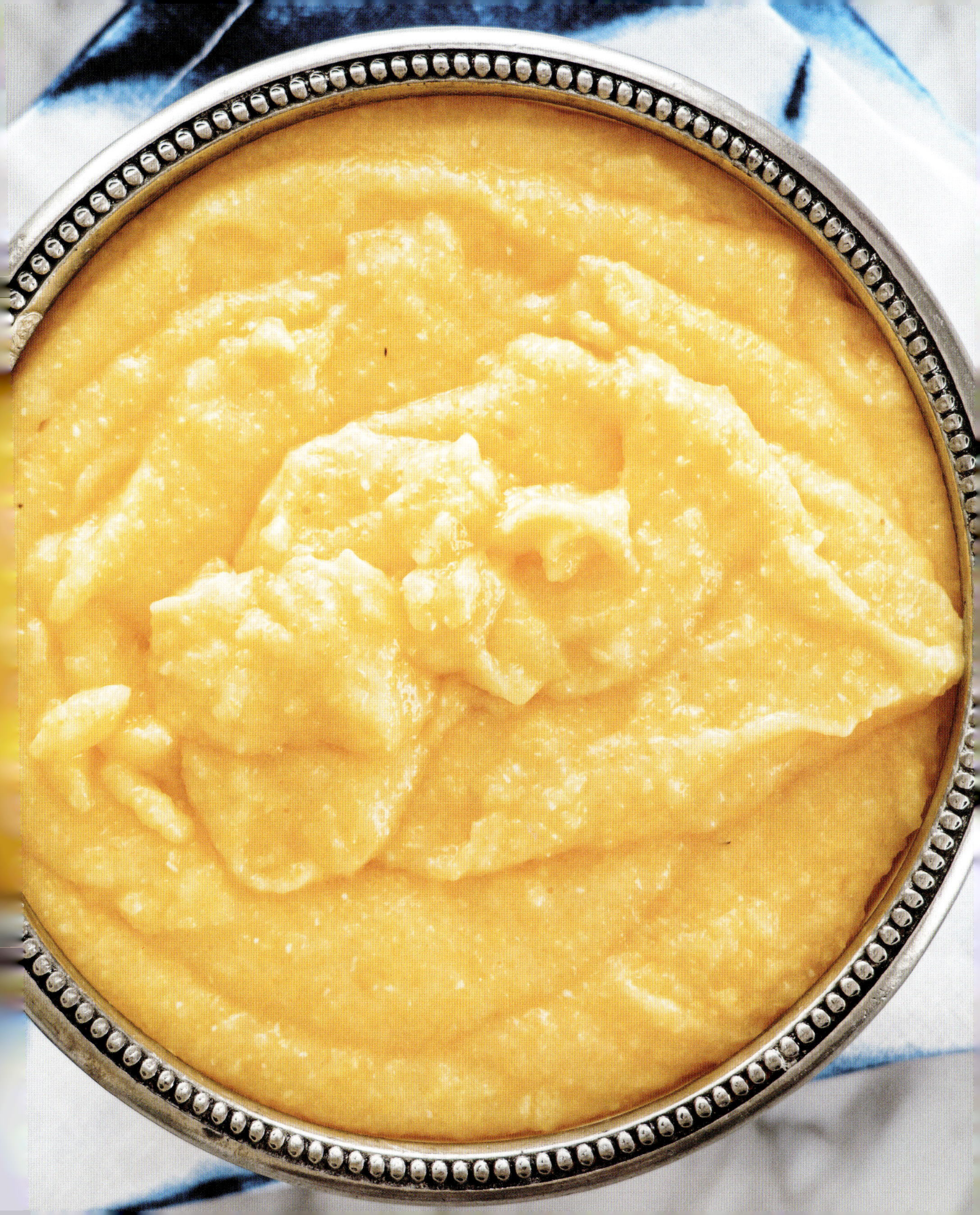

BREADS AND ROLLS

BAKING HAS ALWAYS BEEN MY NUMBER ONE PASSION. For as long as I remember, I've always loved to bake: cookies, breads, rolls, cakes, muffins, scones, you name it. Even before cooking, there was always baking for me.

I've always said that baking is therapeutic. There's nothing more satisfying than seeing your dough rise beautifully and then turning that dough into something delicious. Not to mention that the smell of bread baking in your oven is incredible—it's better than any perfume.

In the following pages, I want to show you that baking can be easy and may just require a little practice. I've included in this book a few recipes for breads and rolls that are not only my favorites but also my readers' favorites.

WORKING WITH YEAST

There are many reasons why dough doesn't rise. Here's my list of possible reasons that you should keep in mind when baking with yeast:

- **The yeast is dead.** This is probably the reason 90 percent of the time. I know it's frustrating, but if the yeast is old, your dough will not rise and you'll end up with a brick of bread. Make sure you store yeast properly. Yeast is a living organism; over time, it will lose activity, even if you've never opened the jar or package.

- **The water is too hot.** Yes, yeast loves a warm environment, which is why we usually add lukewarm water or milk to dough. However, if that water or milk is too hot, it will kill the yeast. For yeast, the ideal water temperature is anywhere from 95 to 105°F (35 to 41°C).

- **The environment is inhospitable.** If your room is too cold, this could prevent dough from rising. Yeast loves a warm and draft-free environment. If your oven has a Proof function, use it. The Proof function preheats the oven to 100°F (38°C), creating a warm but not hot environment for dough to rise nicely. If your oven doesn't have this function, I still recommend that you use the oven. What I usually do is preheat the oven to 200°F (93°C) or to its lowest setting. Once it reaches that temperature, turn off the oven and place the dough inside to rise. This will speed up the proofing process tremendously.

- **The dough does not have enough time to rise.** Patience is key. Sometimes dough may take 2 to 3 hours to rise properly and sometimes it can take 30 to 40 minutes. Just give it some more time—if the yeast is good, it will do its job.

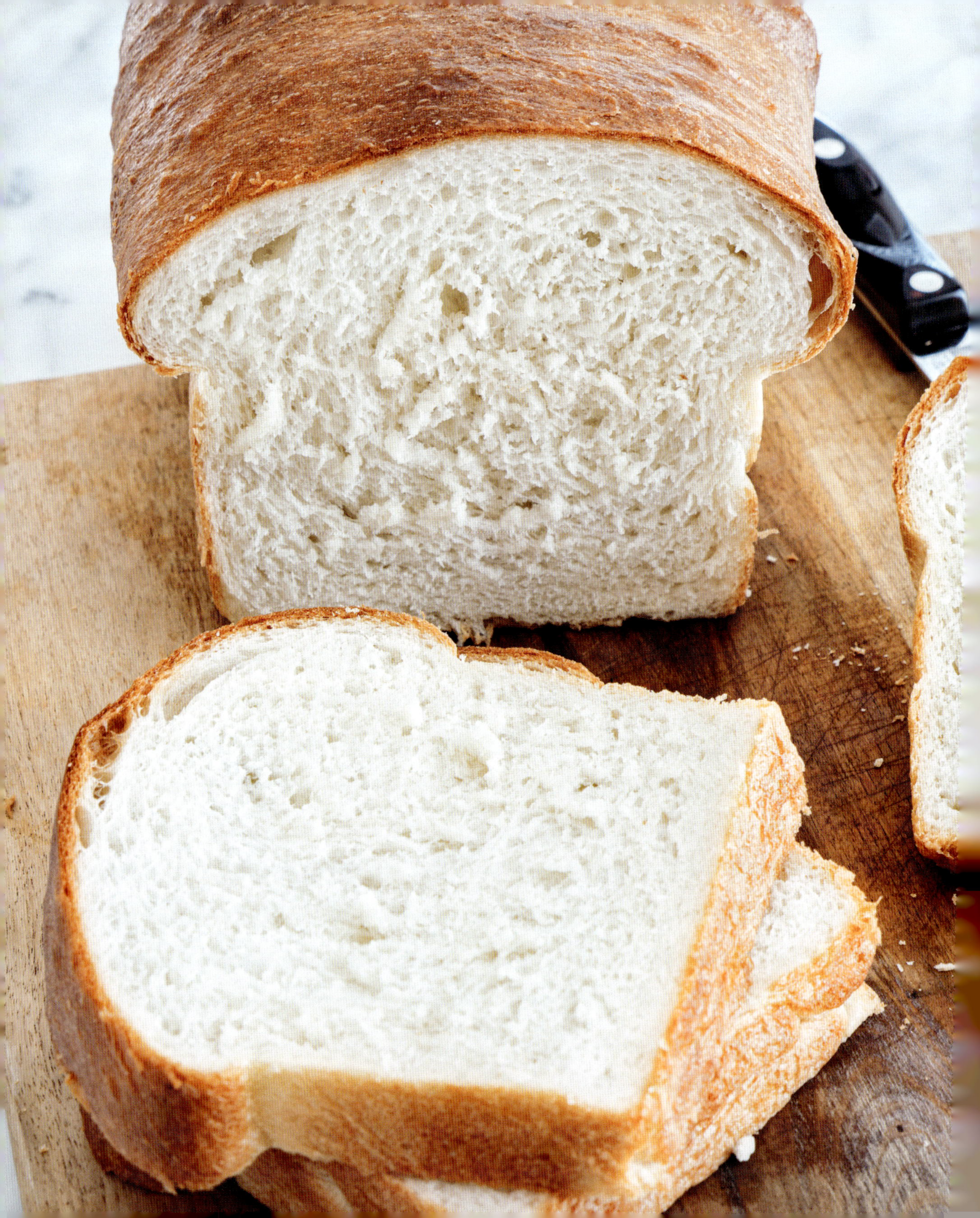

WHITE BREAD

A simple white bread is probably the most common thing you'll ever want to bake in your kitchen—it's perfect for sandwiches and everyone loves a good white bread. Now you can make it all from scratch with just a few baking ingredients and a bit of time.

PREP TIME: 15 MINUTES
REST TIME: 1 HOUR, 50 MINUTES
COOK TIME: 35 MINUTES
TOTAL TIME: 2 HOURS, 40 MINUTES
SERVES: 10

2¼ tsp (7 g) instant yeast
½ cup (120 ml) plus 1⅓ cups (320 ml) lukewarm water, divided
2 tbsp (24 g) sugar
2 tsp (10 g) salt
2 tbsp (30 g) unsalted butter, at room temperature and cubed, plus more as needed
5 cups (600 g) all-purpose flour, divided, plus more as needed
Melted unsalted butter, as needed

In the bowl of a stand mixer fitted with the dough hook, combine the yeast, ½ cup (120 ml) of the water and the sugar. Stir the ingredients and let the mixture rest for 5 minutes.

Add the remaining 1⅓ cups (320 ml) of water, salt, room-temperature butter and 4 cups (480 g) of the flour to the yeast mixture. Mix the ingredients on low speed for 7 to 10 minutes, until the dough comes cleanly away from the sides of the bowl. Add the remaining 1 cup (120 g) of flour, 2 tablespoons (16 g) at a time, as needed. The dough should be soft but not sticky.

Place the dough in a large, lightly greased bowl and cover it with plastic wrap. Place the bowl in a warm spot. Let the dough rest until it doubles in size, which usually takes about 1 hour.

Lightly dust a clean work surface with flour. Grease a 5 x 9–inch (15 x 27–cm) loaf pan with additional room-temperature butter.

Gently punch down the dough with your fist to get rid of some of the air. Transfer the dough to the prepared work surface and press it down with your fingers to remove some of the air pockets. Using your hands, pat down the dough into a 9 x 12–inch (27 x 36–cm) rectangle, then roll it up jelly-roll style. Place the dough in the prepared loaf pan. Place the pan in a warm, draft-free environment and let the dough rest until it doubles in size again, which should take 30 to 45 minutes.

Preheat the oven to 400°F (204°C) and position the oven rack on the lowest setting. Brush the loaf with the melted butter. Bake the bread for 30 to 35 minutes, rotating it halfway through the baking time, until it is golden brown and an instant-read thermometer inserted into the center of the loaf reads 195°F (91°C).

Remove the loaf from the oven and immediately brush it with more melted butter. Allow the bread to cool in the loaf pan for 10 minutes, then transfer it to a cooling rack. Let the bread cool completely before slicing it.

RECIPE NOTE

Store the bread at room temperature, wrapped tightly in plastic wrap, for up to 4 days.

NUTRITION INFORMATION

Serving size: 1 slice; **Calories:** 247; **Carbohydrates:** 46 g; **Protein:** 6 g; **Fat:** 4 g

TWO-INGREDIENT DOUGH

This is one of my favorite doughs because no yeast is required. It requires only two ingredients, and you can make anything with it. Think dinner rolls, pretzel bites, flatbread, even pizza!

PREP TIME: 20 MINUTES
COOK TIME: 25 MINUTES
TOTAL TIME: 45 MINUTES
SERVES: 8

2 cups (240 g) self-rising flour
2 cups (570 g) plain Greek yogurt

In the bowl of a stand mixer fitted with the dough hook, combine the flour and yogurt. Mix the ingredients on medium speed until the dough comes together and comes cleanly away from the sides of the bowl, which may take up to 7 minutes. If you don't have a stand mixer, combine the ingredients in a large bowl and mix them together with a wooden spoon or spatula until they are just combined. Use your hands to knead the dough for 7 to 10 minutes, until it is smooth and comes together.

To make dinner rolls with this dough, generously dust a work surface with flour. Transfer the dough to the floured work surface. Cut the dough into 8 equal pieces using a dough cutter or a sharp knife, then roll each piece into a roll. Using a sharp knife, make 2 small incisions on the top of each roll that are about ¼ inch (6 mm) deep; this step is purely to make the dinner rolls look nicer. Grease a 12-inch (36-cm) cast-iron or oven-safe skillet with butter. Place the rolls in the prepared skillet. Bake them at 350°F (177°C) for about 25 minutes, until they are golden brown.

RECIPE NOTES

If your dough is too sticky, add more flour, 1 tablespoon (8 g) at a time, until the dough is smooth and workable.

If you'd like to make this dough ahead of time, tightly wrap the dough with plastic wrap. You can also cut it up into portions and wrap them individually. The dough will last for 3 days in the refrigerator or for 1 month in the freezer.

Whether you've stored the dough in the freezer or fridge, let it slowly warm up to room temperature, still wrapped, before using it.

NUTRITION INFORMATION

Serving size: 1 serving; **Calories:** 142; **Carbohydrates:** 24 g; **Protein:** 9 g; **Fat:** 1 g

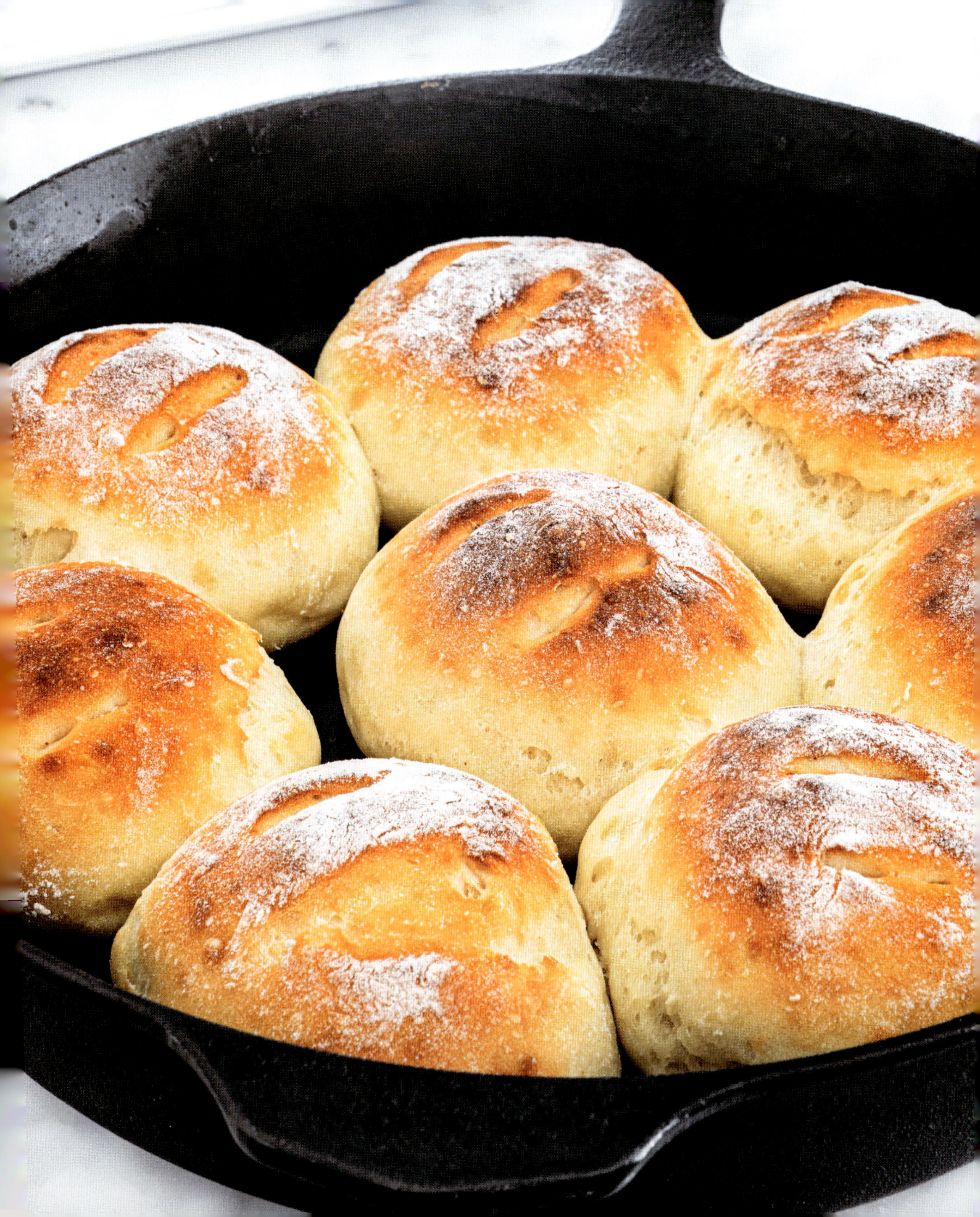

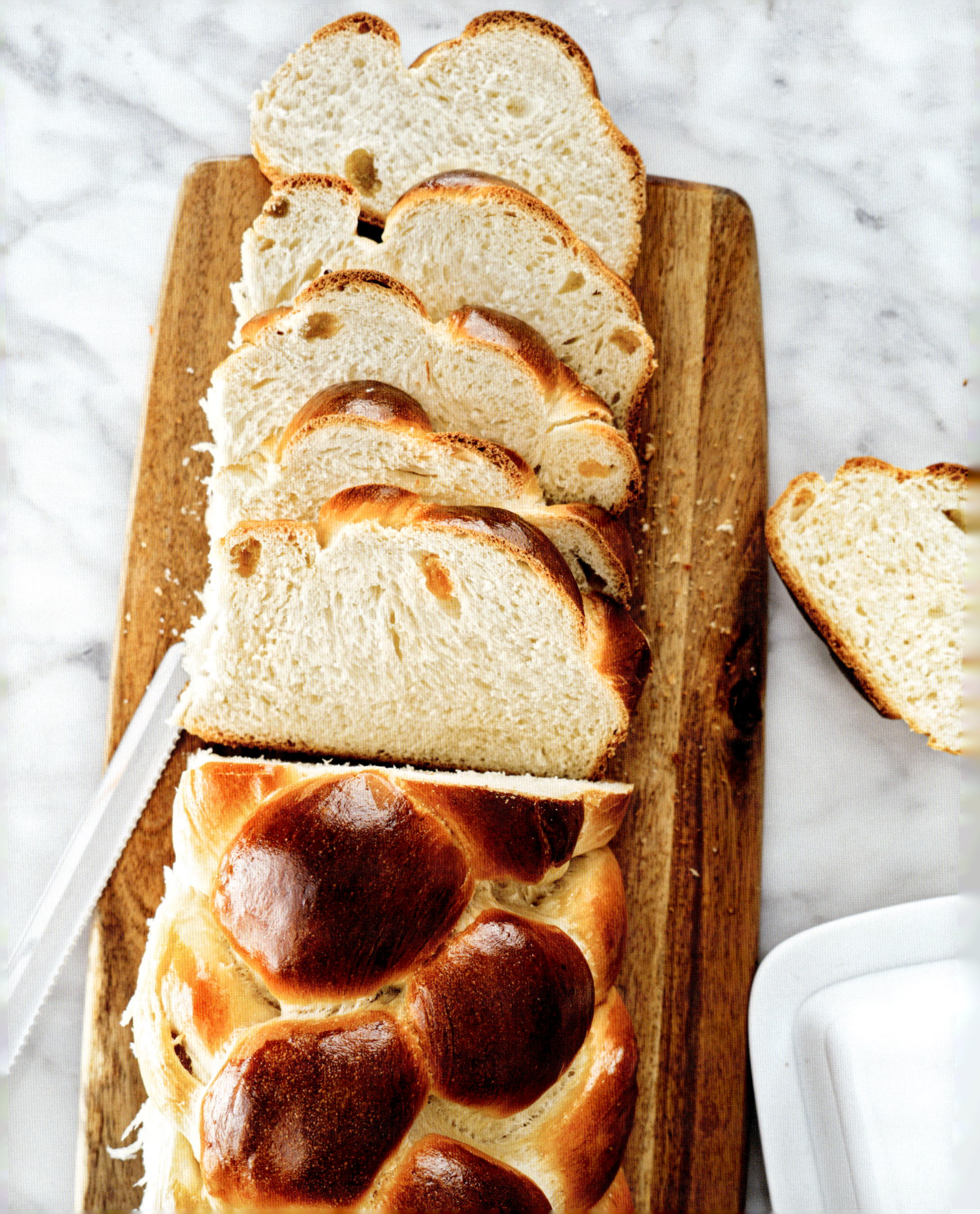

RAISIN BREAD

PREP TIME: 15 MINUTES
REST TIME: 1 HOUR, 40 MINUTES
COOK TIME: 30 MINUTES
TOTAL: 2 HOURS, 25 MINUTES
SERVES: 24

YEAST MIXTURE
4 tsp (12 g) active dry yeast
4 tsp (16 g) sugar
1 large egg, beaten
¾ cup (180 ml) milk, warmed to 110°F (43°C)

RAISINS
1 cup (150 g) raisins
¼ cup (60 ml) rum or orange juice

DOUGH
1 tbsp (6 g) lemon zest
2 tbsp (30 ml) fresh lemon juice
1 cup (240 ml) milk, warmed to 110°F (43°C)
4 tbsp (60 g) unsalted butter, melted
¼ cup (60 ml) vegetable oil
1 cup (192 g) sugar
5 large eggs
1 tsp pure vanilla extract
1 tsp salt
6 cups (720 g) all-purpose flour, plus more as needed

EGG WASH
1 large egg

NUTRITION INFORMATION
Serving size: 1 slice; **Calories:** 242; **Carbohydrates:** 39 g; **Protein:** 6 g; **Fat:** 6 g

Toasted raisin bread slathered with butter and jam and paired with a good cup of coffee is my ideal breakfast. This raisin bread reminds me of a brioche bread because of its stunning braided design. Not only will this raisin bread impress your guests with its delicious taste but with its beautiful design as well.

To make the yeast mixture, combine the yeast, sugar, egg and milk in the bowl of a stand mixer fitted with the paddle attachment. Mix the ingredients on low speed to fully incorporate them. Let the mixture rest in a warm place for about 10 minutes, until it froths up.

Meanwhile, prepare the raisins. Soak the raisins in the rum for 10 minutes. If you are in a rush, you can warm up the rum to make this process happen faster. Drain the raisins and set them aside.

To make the dough, add the lemon zest, lemon juice, milk, butter, oil, sugar, eggs, vanilla and salt to the yeast mixture. Mix the ingredients on medium speed until they are well combined.

Fit the stand mixer with the dough hook. Add 2 cups (240 g) of the flour to the mixer's bowl and mix the ingredients on low speed until they are well combined. Repeat this step with the remaining 4 cups (480 g) of flour, mixing on low speed between 2-cup (240-g) additions of flour. This process should take about 5 minutes, and the dough should be soft and sticky. Add the raisins.

Spray a large bowl with cooking spray. Place the dough in the bowl and lightly spray the dough itself with cooking spray. Cover the bowl with plastic wrap. Let the dough rest in a warm, draft-free environment until it has doubled in size, which usually takes 40 to 60 minutes. Once the dough has doubled in size, punch it down to release some of the air.

Divide the dough in half in order to create 2 (6-stranded) braided loaves. Cut each dough half into 6 pieces and roll each piece into strips that are about 12 inches (36 cm) long. Start by pinching all 6 ropes of dough together at one end. Organize them by setting the 2 outermost ropes off to each side, with the other 4 ropes in pairs. Cross the 2 outer strands, keeping them off to the side. Bring the outer left strand to the center, then bring the second strand from the right over to the outer left. Bring the outer right strand to the center, then bring the second strand from the left over to the outer right. Repeat this process until you have no dough left. Pinch the ends together. Repeat this process with the other half of the dough.

Preheat the oven to 400°F (204°C). While the oven is preheating, place the loaves on a large baking sheet. Let them rest in a warm, draft-free environment for about 30 minutes, until they have doubled in size.

To make the egg wash, beat the egg in a small bowl. Brush the loaves all over with the egg wash. Bake the bread for 30 minutes, or it is until golden brown.

SLOW COOKER BREAD

PREP TIME: 15 MINUTES
REST TIME: 10 MINUTES
COOK TIME: 2 HOURS, 15 MINUTES
TOTAL TIME: 2 HOURS, 40 MINUTES
SERVES: 10

1⅓ cups (320 ml) lukewarm water
1 tbsp (12 g) sugar
1 tbsp (9 g) active dry yeast
1 tsp salt
3 cups (360 g) all-purpose flour, plus more as needed
½ cup (90 g) grated Parmesan cheese (optional)

This recipe came to be because I received a lot of comments and emails asking if I could write a bread recipe for the slow cooker. I had never thought about it before, and of course I'm always up for a challenge. The great thing about this bread is that you just make the dough; you don't even have to let the dough rise because the slow cooker provides an ideal environment for dough to rise slowly. Keep in mind that the loaf won't get the nice golden color on top that the oven produces—if you're going for that, you'll need to brown the loaf a bit in the oven.

Preheat the slow cooker on high heat. Line the slow cooker with parchment paper. Cover the slow cooker with its lid.

In the bowl of a stand mixer fitted with the dough hook, combine the water, sugar and yeast. Let the mixture rest for about 10 minutes, until the yeast becomes frothy. Add the salt, flour and Parmesan cheese (if using). Mix the ingredients on low speed until they are well incorporated and the dough comes cleanly away from the sides of the bowl.

Lightly flour a work surface. Transfer the ball of dough to the prepared work surface. Knead the dough about 5 times, until it is smooth. Form the dough into a ball and place it in the preheated slow cooker. Cover the slow cooker with its lid.

Bake the bread for 2 hours, checking on it occasionally.

Preheat the oven to 450°F (232°C). Remove the bread and parchment paper from the slow cooker and place them on a large baking sheet. Bake the bread for 10 to 15 minutes, until the top has browned.

RECIPE NOTES

Homemade bread is not going to last as long as store-bought bread. Store it in an airtight plastic bag in a cool, dry place for 2 to 3 days. Also keep in mind that heat and humidity will cause the bread to mold.

NUTRITION INFORMATION

Serving size: 1 slice; **Calories:** 162; **Carbohydrates:** 30 g; **Protein:** 6 g; **Fat:** 2 g

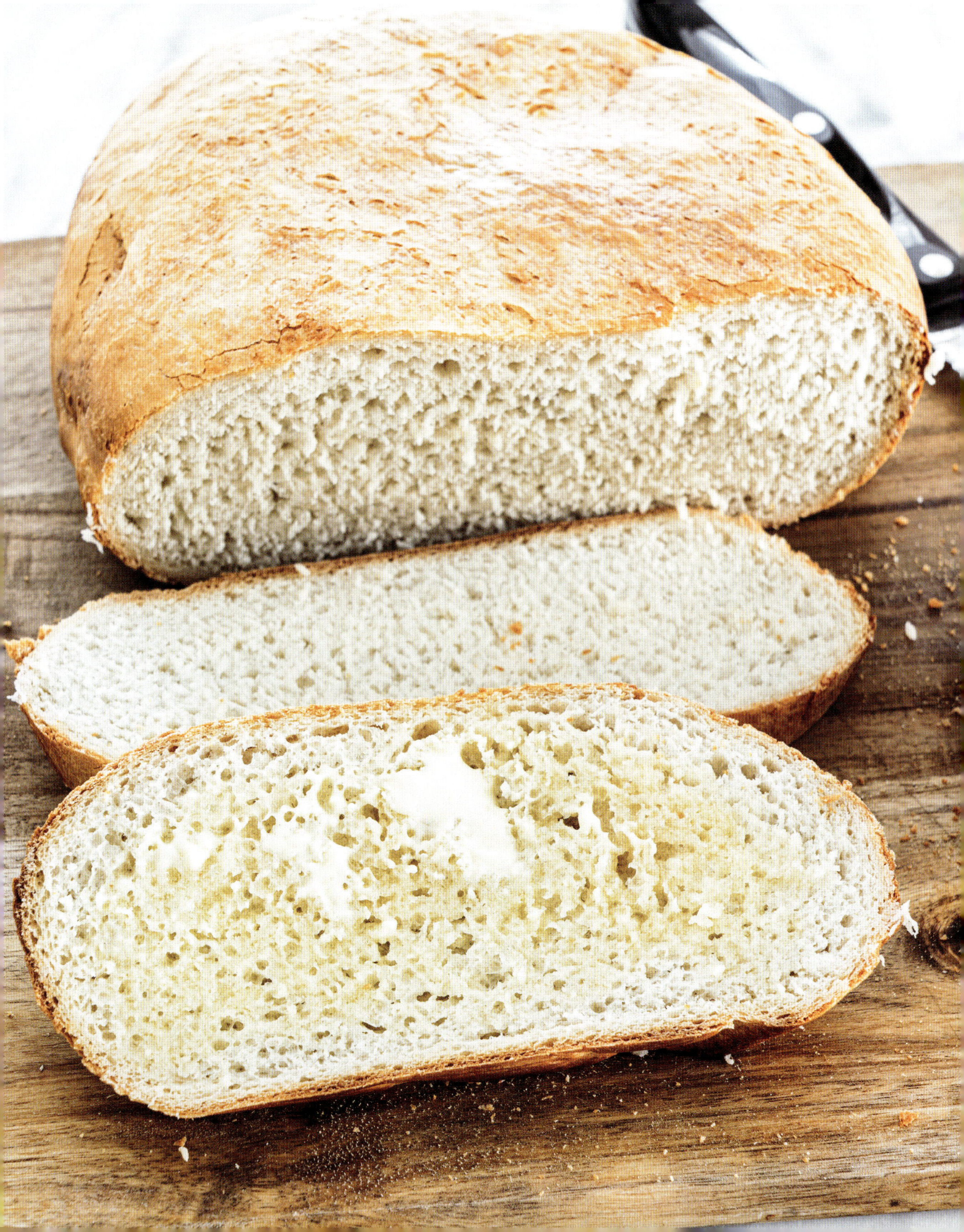

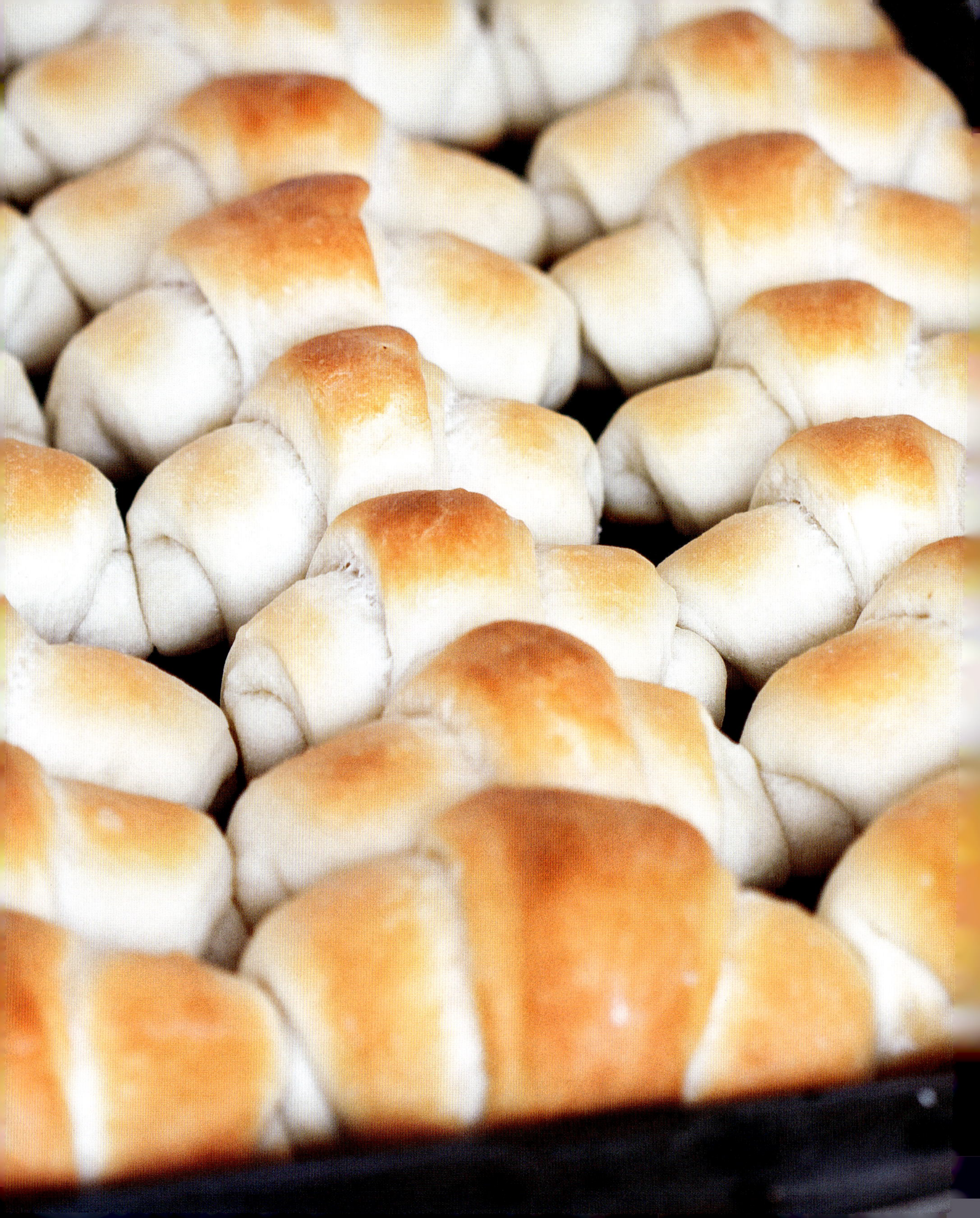

DINNER CRESCENTS

I'm a sucker for hot breads and rolls—or anything baked, really. Which is why I love these dinner crescents. They're buttery, soft and delicious. This is a classic milk dough recipe that's perfect for these crescents.

PREP TIME: 20 MINUTES
REST TIME: 1 HOUR, 15 MINUTES
COOK TIME: 20 MINUTES
TOTAL TIME: 1 HOUR, 55 MINUTES
SERVES: 24

1 cup (240 ml) lukewarm water
1 tbsp (9 g) active dry yeast
¾ cup (180 ml) milk
¼ cup (48 g) sugar
¾ cup (180 g) unsalted butter, divided, plus more as needed
1 large egg
4 to 5 cups (480 to 600 g) all-purpose flour, divided
½ tbsp (8 g) salt

In a small bowl, combine the water and yeast. Stir the yeast a little. Let it rest for 10 to 15 minutes, until it foams.

In a medium microwave-safe bowl, combine the milk, sugar and ¼ cup (60 g) of the butter. Microwave this mixture for about 1 minute, until the butter melts. Whisk the mixture, so that the butter melts completely. Let the milk cool until it is just warm to the touch. Whisk in the egg.

In the bowl of a stand mixer fitted with the dough hook, combine 4 cups (480 g) of the flour and salt. Add the milk mixture and the yeast mixture to the flour. Mix the ingredients on slow speed for 2 minutes. The dough is ready when it comes cleanly away from the sides of the bowl. If the dough is too sticky, add the remaining 1 cup (120 g) of flour, about ¼ cup (30 g) at a time, until the dough comes cleanly away from the sides of the bowl while mixing.

Place the dough in a large oiled bowl. Cover the bowl with a clean, damp kitchen towel or plastic wrap. Let the dough rest until it has doubled in size, which usually takes at least 30 minutes.

Once the dough is ready, grease a 10 x 15–inch (30 x 45–cm) baking sheet with butter. Punch down the dough to let the air out. Cut it into 2 pieces. Roll each piece into a circle about 14 inches (42 cm) in diameter. Divide ¼ cup (60 g) of the butter between the dough circles, spreading the butter across the dough. Using the pizza cutter, cut the dough circles into quarters first, then cut each quarter into thirds to make a total of 12 pieces per circle. Roll up each piece to form a crescent.

Place the rolls on the prepared pan. Let the rolls rest until the edges touch and they have almost doubled in size, which usually takes at least 30 minutes.

Preheat the oven to 350°F (177°C).

Bake the crescents for 15 to 20 minutes, until they are golden brown. Melt the remaining ¼ cup (60 g) of butter and brush the rolls with it while they are still warm.

NUTRITION INFORMATION

Serving size: 1 roll; **Calories:** 144; **Carbohydrates:** 19 g; **Protein:** 3 g; **Fat:** 6 g

RECIPE NOTES

You can store these rolls wrapped in foil or plastic wrap right on your counter for up to 5 days. You can also freeze them. Place them separately on a baking sheet and freeze them before transferring them to a freezer bag or airtight container. They will last for up to 6 months in the freezer and can be thawed on the counter when you are ready to eat them.

CLASSIC DINNER ROLLS

We all need a classic dinner roll recipe in our baking repertoire, and my recipe is a no-fail version that requires very little effort to make. I've made these rolls on numerous occasions and every time I do, they're gone immediately! These rolls are even great as hamburger buns, and if your family doesn't like sesame seeds, you can top them with poppy seeds, rolled oats or sunflower seeds.

PREP TIME: 30 MINUTES
REST TIME: 1 HOUR, 45 MINUTES
COOK TIME: 30 MINUTES
TOTAL TIME: 2 HOURS, 45 MINUTES
SERVES: 16

2½ tsp (8 g) active dry yeast or instant yeast

⅓ cup (64 g) plus 1 tbsp (12 g) sugar, divided

1 cup (240 ml) milk, warmed to between 95 and 105°F (35 and 41°C)

8 tbsp (120 g) unsalted butter, melted

3 large egg yolks

1 tsp salt

4 cups (480 g) all-purpose flour, plus more as needed

1 large egg white, lightly beaten

2 tbsp (18 g) poppy seeds (optional)

2 tbsp (18 g) sesame seeds (optional)

In the bowl of a stand mixer fitted with the dough hook, combine the yeast, 1 tablespoon (12 g) of the sugar and the milk. Gently whisk the ingredients together and allow the mixture to rest for 10 to 15 minutes, until it is frothy.

Add the butter, remaining ⅓ cup (64 g) of sugar, egg yolks, salt and flour to the yeast mixture. Mix the ingredients together on low speed until they are incorporated. Increase the speed to medium-high and knead the dough for 5 minutes. The dough should be slightly sticky but still soft to the touch.

Place the dough in a large, lightly greased bowl and cover the bowl with plastic wrap. Let the dough rest for 45 to 60 minutes, until it has doubled in size. If you are using instant yeast, see the Recipe Notes regarding this step.

Lightly grease a 9 x 13–inch (27 x 39–cm) baking dish with cooking spray or butter.

Lightly dust a work surface with flour. Transfer the dough to the prepared work surface, then press it down so that it deflates. Shape the dough into a ball, but do not knead it. Divide the dough in 16 equal pieces. To shape each piece into a roll, flatten it with your palm or fingers. Fold it up into a ball by pinching the sides together, then turn it over and roll it briefly. Place the roll, smooth side up, in the prepared baking dish. Cover the baking dish with plastic wrap or a clean kitchen towel. Let the dough rest again for 30 minutes, until it has doubled in size.

Preheat the oven to 375°F (191°C). Uncover the baking dish and brush the rolls with the egg white. Sprinkle the rolls with the poppy seeds (if using) or sesame seeds (if using). Bake the rolls for 30 minutes, or until they are golden brown.

NUTRITION INFORMATION

Serving size: 1 roll; **Calories:** 216; **Carbohydrates:** 29 g; **Protein:** 5 g; **Fat:** 8 g

RECIPE NOTES

If you are using instant yeast, no proofing is required. Simply add the yeast along with the rest of the ingredients.

Let the rolls cool completely before storing them. Wrap each roll tightly in plastic wrap. You may also store the rolls in a ziplock bag. If you use a ziplock bag, push out all the excess air from inside, as the air will dry out the bread. You can keep the rolls at room temperature for 2 to 3 days. If you refrigerate them, they will dry out faster.

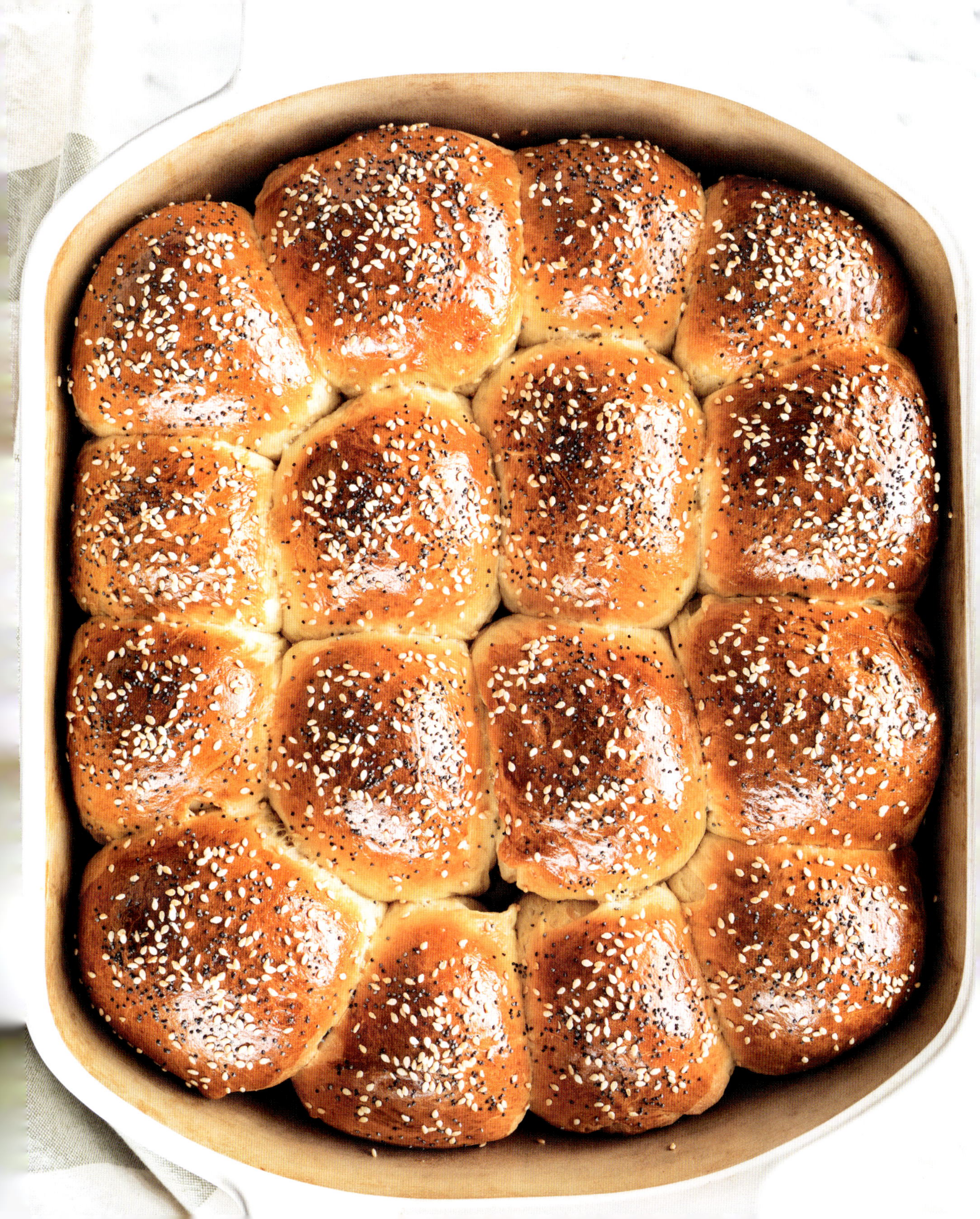

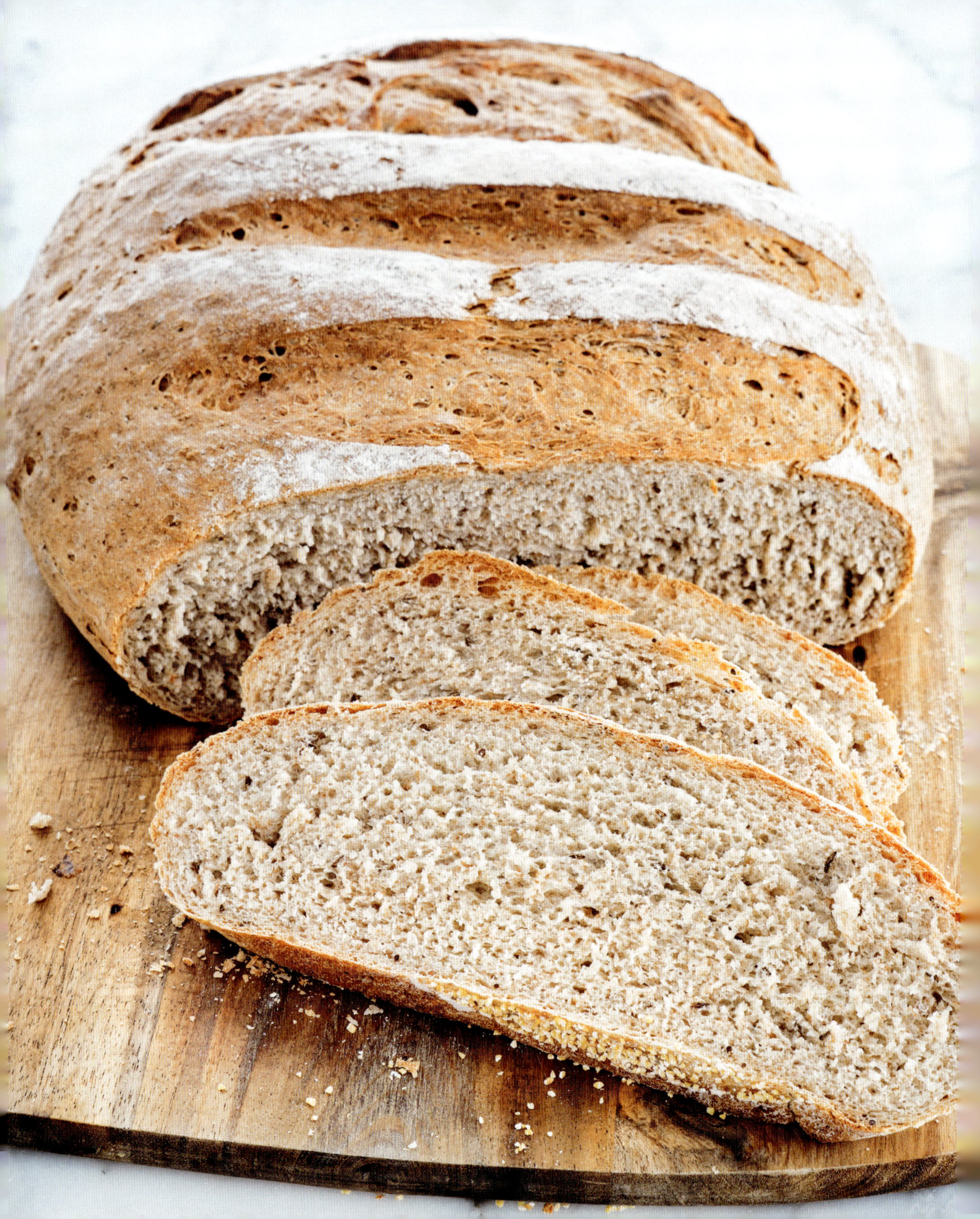

RYE BREAD

PREP TIME: 10 MINUTES
REST TIME: 1 HOUR, 30 MINUTES
COOK TIME: 30 MINUTES
TOTAL: 2 HOURS, 10 MINUTES
SERVES: 12

3 cups (720 ml) lukewarm water, divided
1½ tbsp (14 g) active dry yeast
2 tbsp (30 g) brown sugar
1½ tsp (8 g) salt
2 tbsp (14 g) caraway seeds
2 tbsp (30 ml) vegetable oil
1½ cups (135 g) rye flour, plus more as needed
3 cups (360 g) all-purpose flour, divided (see Recipe Notes)
2 tbsp (22 g) cornmeal

Rye bread is such an easy bread to make at home—all you really need is rye flour and all-purpose flour. You can even replace some of the all-purpose flour with whole-wheat flour for a healthier alternative. This recipe gives you a beautiful rustic loaf, with lots of fiber and aromatic caraway, which is a staple in rye breads.

In the bowl of a stand mixer fitted with the dough hook, combine 2 cups (480 ml) of the water and yeast. Stir the ingredients and let the mixture rest for 5 to 10 minutes, until it is frothy.

Add the brown sugar, salt, caraway seeds, oil, rye flour and 2½ cups (300 g) of the all-purpose flour. Mix the ingredients on medium speed until they are smooth. Add the remaining ½ cup (60 g) of all-purpose flour and mix on medium speed for about 5 minutes, until the dough is firm and comes cleanly away from the sides of the bowl.

Spray a large bowl with cooking spray. Place the dough in the bowl, spritz the top of the dough with cooking spray and cover the bowl with a clean kitchen towel. Let the dough rest in a warm, draft-free environment for 30 to 40 minutes, or until it has doubled in size.

Line a medium baking sheet with parchment paper. Sprinkle the parchment paper with the cornmeal.

Punch down the dough and form it into a ball by pulling the dough from the center to its underside. Repeat this step 4 or 5 times. Sprinkle some additional rye flour over the dough. Cut a few slashes in the top of the dough with a sharp knife. Place the dough ball on the prepared baking sheet. Let it rest in a warm, draft-free environment for 30 to 40 minutes, or until it has doubled in size.

Preheat the oven to 425°F (218°C). Place a shallow metal baking pan—do not use glass, as glass will break—on the lower rack in the oven. Transfer the baking sheet to the middle rack of the oven. Pour the remaining 1 cup (240 ml) of water in the baking pan on the lower rack.

Bake the bread for 30 minutes, until it is crusty and golden brown.

NUTRITION INFORMATION

Serving size: 1 slice; **Calories:** 200; **Carbohydrates:** 38 g; **Protein:** 6 g; **Fat:** 3 g

RECIPE NOTES

You can mix the all-purpose flour with whole-wheat flour: Use 1 cup (130 g) of whole-wheat flour and 2 cups (240 g) of all-purpose flour.

You can also place the loaf of bread in a Dutch oven to bake; if doing so, make sure to preheat the Dutch oven first.

Allow the bread to cool to room temperature before storing it. Keep your loaf in a bread box, large freezer bag, airtight container or domed cake plate to ensure it doesn't go stale. It'll last for 3 to 4 days at room temperature or 6 to 9 days in the fridge.

BUTTERMILK BISCUITS

This is one of my all-time favorite recipes from my blog. These buttermilk biscuits are simply perfect. They're flaky, buttery and melt-in-your-mouth delicious! They're easy to make from scratch and—best of all—they're ready in only 25 minutes!

PREP TIME: 10 MINUTES
COOK TIME: 15 MINUTES
TOTAL TIME: 25 MINUTES
SERVES: 12

4 cups (480 g) all-purpose flour, plus more as needed
1 tsp salt
1 tbsp (12 g) baking powder
2 tsp (8 g) baking soda
¾ cup (180 g) unsalted butter, chilled and cut into pieces
1¾ cups (420 ml) buttermilk
1 large egg, beaten

Preheat the oven to 450°F (232°C).

In a large bowl, mix together the flour, salt, baking powder and baking soda.

Add the butter to the flour mixture. Using a pastry cutter or 2 knives, cut the butter into the flour mixture until it resembles a coarse meal. Stir in the buttermilk until the dough is just moist. Knead the dough about 5 times, until it starts to come together.

Dust a work surface with flour. Transfer the dough to the prepared work surface and knead it 2 more times, or just until it comes together fully. Don't overwork the dough, as the butter will begin to melt.

Roll out the dough until it is ½ to ¾ inch (13 to 19 mm) in thickness. Cut out the biscuits with a 2-inch (6-cm) biscuit cutter. You should get about 12 biscuits. Place the biscuits on a large baking sheet and brush them with the beaten egg. Alternatively, you can also place the biscuits in a 12-inch (36-cm) buttered oven-safe skillet.

Bake the biscuits for 10 to 15 minutes, or until they are golden.

RECIPE NOTES

Covered and stored at room temperature, these biscuits will stay fresh for up to 3 days. They also freeze well; just be sure to freeze them spaced evenly on a baking sheet before placing them in a freezer bag or airtight container. They will stay fresh for up to 3 months in the freezer.

NUTRITION INFORMATION

Serving size: 1 biscuit; **Calories:** 281; **Carbohydrates:** 34 g; **Protein:** 6 g; **Fat:** 13 g

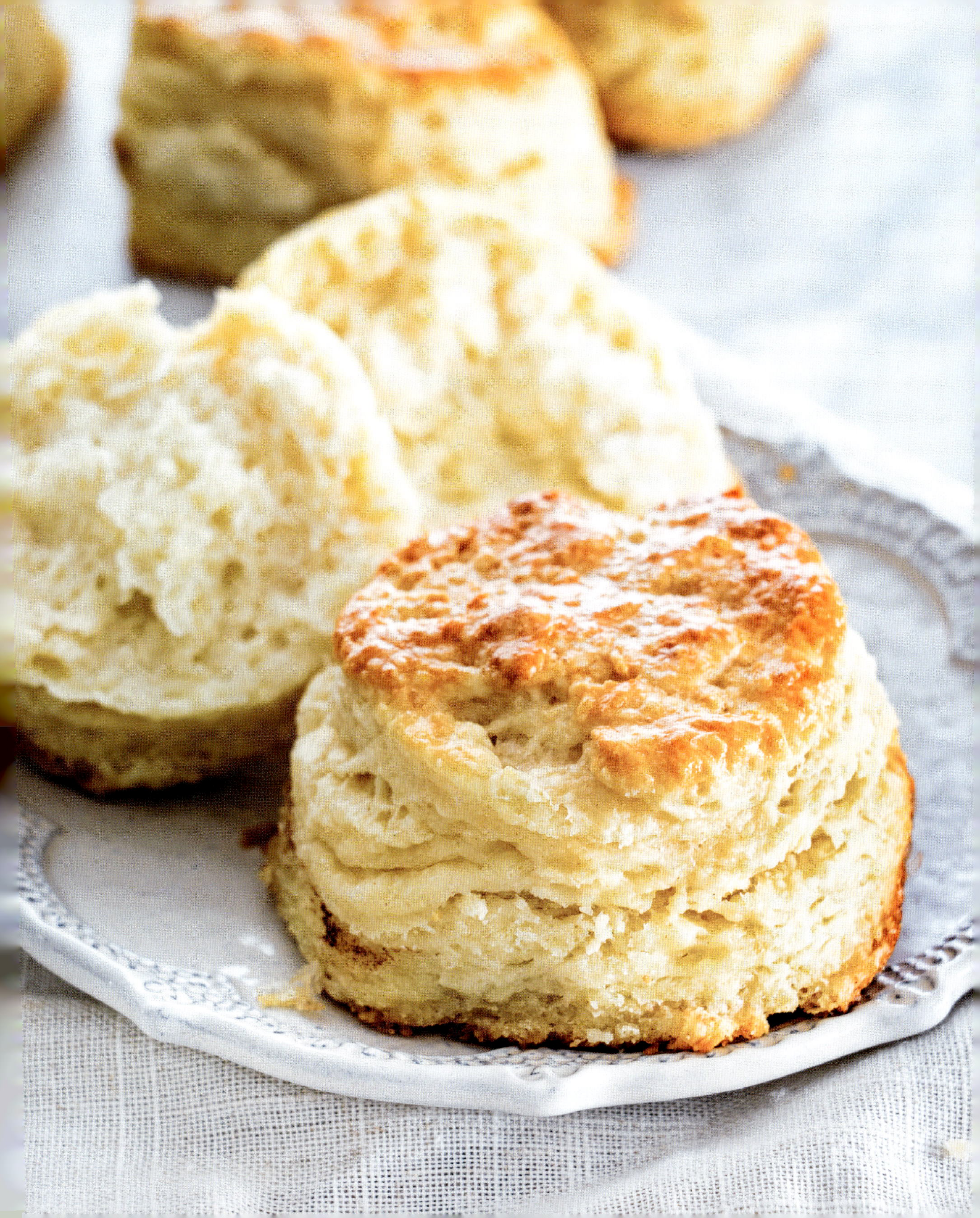

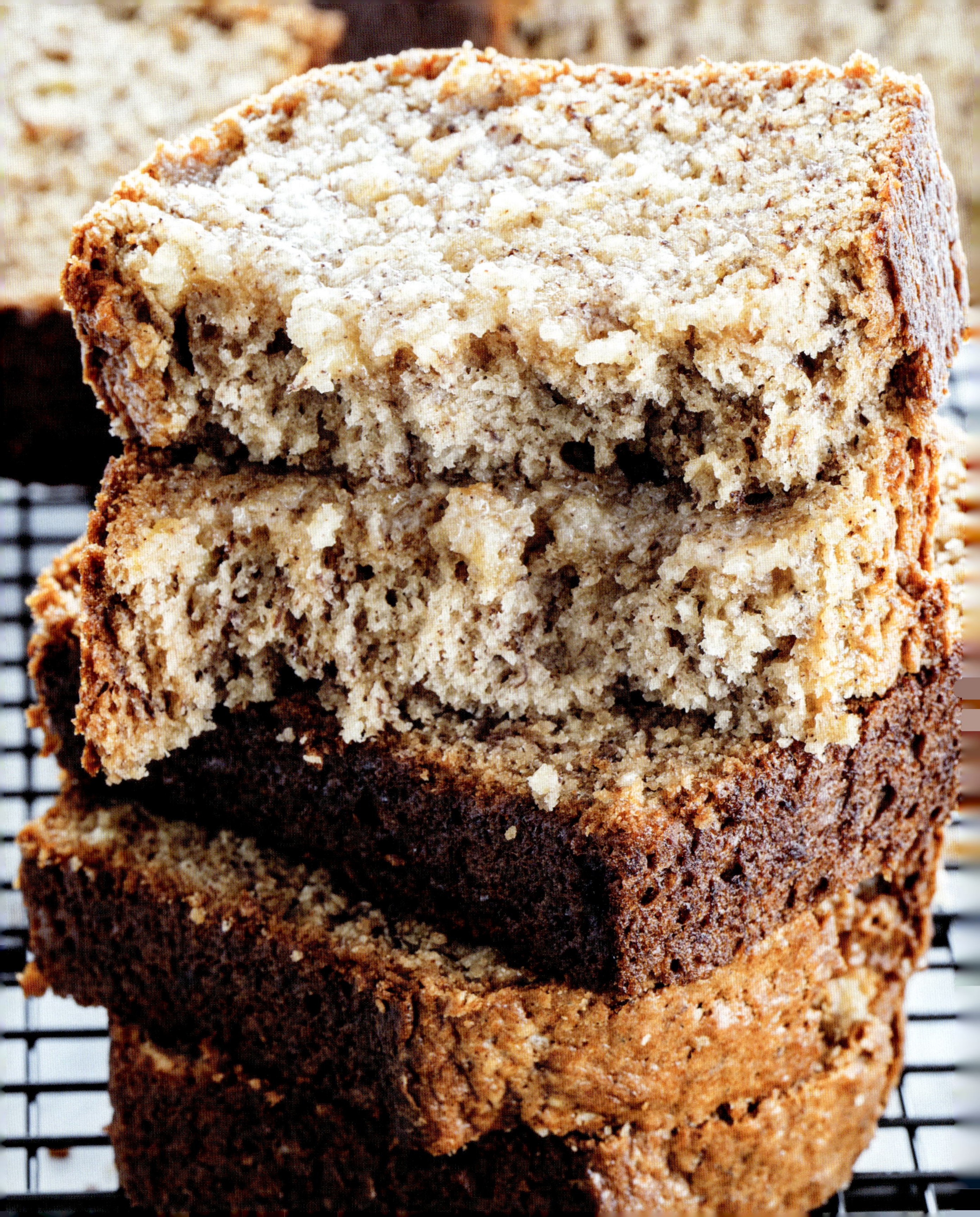

EASY BANANA BREAD

I've been making this banana bread for decades, and every single time it comes out perfect. Whenever I have some ripe bananas, I make this bread. I even think that sometimes we don't eat the bananas, just so I have a reason to make this bread. It truly is a no-fail recipe, and no mixer is needed to make this fabulous banana bread.

PREP TIME: 10 MINUTES
COOK TIME: 1 HOUR
TOTAL TIME: 1 HOUR, 10 MINUTES
SERVES: 12

- 3 ripe bananas, mashed (see Recipe Notes)
- ½ cup (96 g) granulated sugar
- ½ cup (120 g) brown sugar
- ⅓ cup (80 g) unsalted butter, softened
- 1 large egg
- 1 tsp baking soda
- 1 tsp baking powder
- 2 cups (240 g) all-purpose flour
- 1 tsp pure vanilla extract
- 1 tsp ground cinnamon
- ¼ cup (30 g) sour cream
- ⅛ tsp salt

Preheat the oven to 350°F (177°C). Generously grease a 5 x 12–inch (15 x 36–cm) or 5 x 9–inch (15 x 27–cm) loaf pan, or spray it with cooking spray.

In a large bowl, whisk together the bananas, granulated sugar, brown sugar, butter, egg, baking soda, baking powder, flour, vanilla, cinnamon, sour cream and salt. Use a spatula to scrape down the sides of the bowl if needed.

Transfer the bread batter to the prepared loaf pan. Bake the banana bread for 45 to 60 minutes, or until a toothpick inserted into the center comes out clean.

Allow the bread to cool for 5 minutes in the loaf pan, then transfer the bread to a cooling rack and let it come to room temperature. Slice the bread and serve it.

RECIPE NOTES

The key to a good banana bread is ripened bananas. The riper they get, the better the flavor and color of your banana bread. Don't fear a brown banana.

Wrap this bread tightly with plastic wrap or store it in an airtight container. It will last on your counter for 3 days, or in the fridge for about 1 week. I love to microwave my slices of banana bread for 20 to 30 seconds to soften them, especially if the bread has been in the fridge.

You can freeze banana bread. Freeze the whole loaf or individual slices. Wrap the loaf or the individual slices extremely well with plastic wrap, even if they're being stored in an airtight container. The bread will give off some moisture, which can cause freezer burn without the plastic wrap. The bread will last in the freezer for 3 to 4 months. Let it thaw completely at room temperature.

NUTRITION INFORMATION

Serving size: 1 slice; **Calories:** 230; **Carbohydrates:** 40 g; **Protein:** 3 g; **Fat:** 6 g

NO-KNEAD SKILLET BREAD

PREP TIME: 10 MINUTES
REST TIME: 1 HOUR, 40 MINUTES
COOK TIME: 45 MINUTES
TOTAL: 2 HOURS, 35 MINUTES
SERVES: 12

2 cups (480 ml) lukewarm water
2¼ tsp (7 g) instant yeast
3½ cups (420 g) all-purpose flour
1 tsp salt, or as needed
2 cups (240 g) shredded Cheddar cheese

The no-knead bread recipe I shared on the blog years ago has become one of my most popular recipes. The problem with that recipe is that it takes too long for the dough to work its magic, which is why I came up with this recipe. In a fraction of the time and with only five ingredients, you can have this skillet bread, which is soft on the inside and deliciously crusty on the outside. I make this version with some Cheddar cheese, but feel free to add your favorite cheese or even some jalapeño peppers—you'll love it!

In a large bowl, mix together the water and yeast. Set this yeast mixture aside for 10 minutes.

In a separate large bowl, mix together the flour, salt and cheese until the ingredients are well combined. Add the flour mixture to the yeast mixture. Using a wooden spoon or spatula, mix the dough until everything is well combined. Cover the dough with a kitchen towel and set it aside to rest for about 1 hour, or until it has doubled in size.

Generously oil a 10-inch (30-cm) oven-safe skillet, including the sides (see the Recipe Notes). Use a spatula to loosen the dough from the bowl and transfer the dough to the prepared skillet. Use the spatula to even out the dough, so that it fills the skillet. Cover the skillet with another clean kitchen towel and set the dough aside to rest for another 30 minutes, until its volume has increased by about 75 percent.

Preheat the oven to 450°F (232°C). Bake the bread for 30 to 45 minutes, or until the top is golden brown. Let the bread cool in the skillet for 10 minutes. Carefully remove it from the skillet, transfer it to a cutting board and allow it to cool fully before slicing it.

RECIPE NOTES

I use a 10-inch (30-cm) cast-iron skillet to make this recipe. If you use a smaller skillet, the loaf will end up taller. If you use a bigger one, the loaf will end up thinner.

You can make this bread without cheese for a plain loaf. You can also get creative: Spices, garlic, onion, hot peppers and dried fruit are all great examples of ingredients you can use in your bread.

NUTRITION INFORMATION

Serving size: 1 slice; **Calories:** 211; **Carbohydrates:** 28 g; **Protein:** 8 g; **Fat:** 6 g

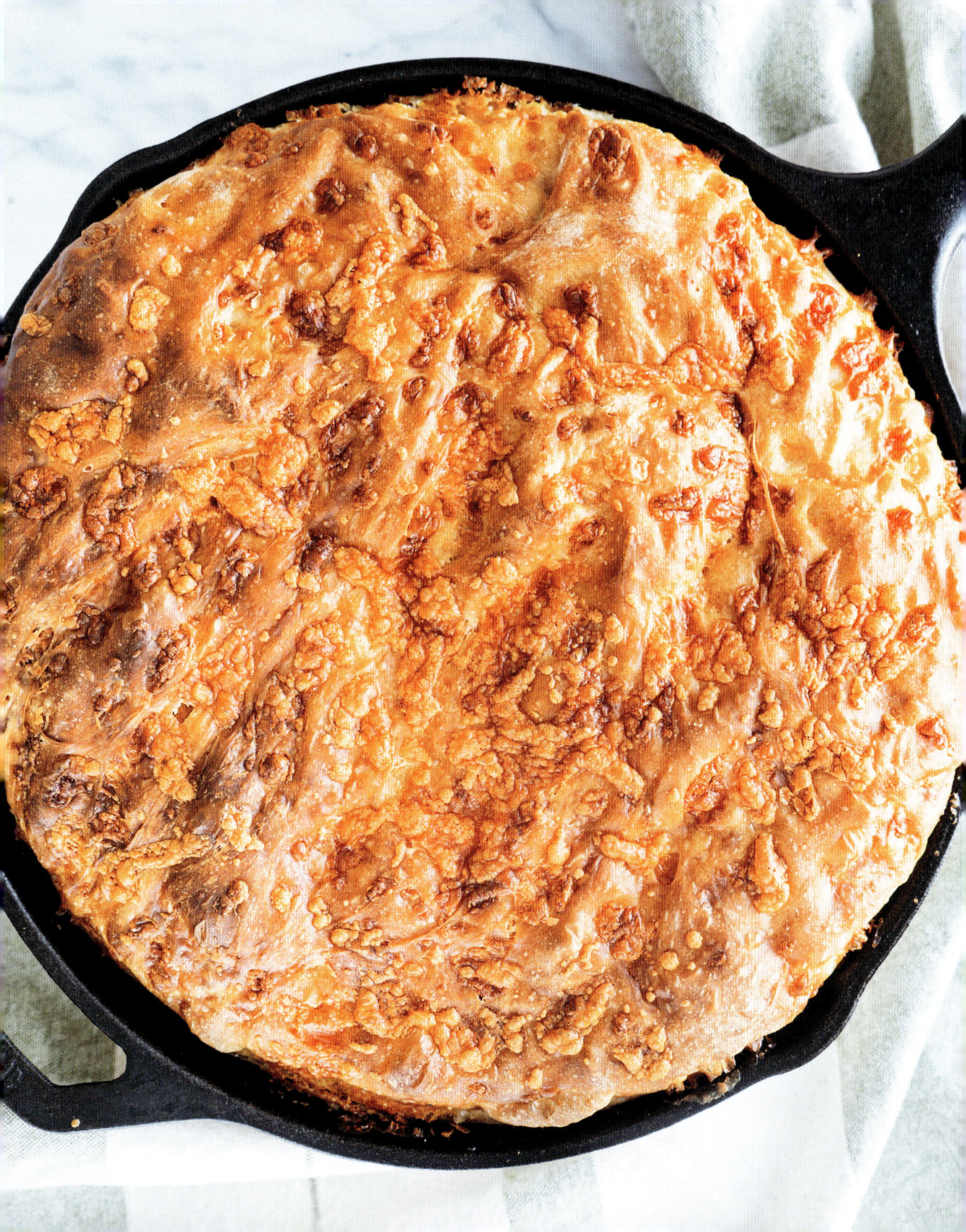

DESSERTS

IN THIS CHAPTER, I share my favorite simple desserts that anyone can make, such as cookies, galettes, trifles or turnovers. They all use easy-to-find ingredients and don't require a lot of effort or time.

If you follow my blog, you know that while I love to bake, I'm not a huge dessert maker. I don't usually make fancy cakes and cupcakes or any sort of posh desserts. Who's got time for that? Even though I love my dessert—I have a sweet tooth like no other—I still love simplicity. Which is why when I make something sweet, I want to make sure it's easy and fairly quick to make and that I have all the ingredients I need in my pantry.

I love to take shortcuts whenever possible, so you'll often see me using things like puff pastry to make Quick Apple Turnovers (page 424), premade biscuit dough to whip up Cinnamon Cream Cheese Pockets (page 416) or even premade pie crusts to create Churro Apple Pie Cookies (page 415). Why not? I love taking the easy way out. I'll still make the dessert delicious by making a part of it from scratch—I'm just not a fan of slaving in my kitchen all day long.

Rest assured that even if you don't have the time or don't want to spend a lot of money on crazy ingredients, you can still have your cake and eat it too!

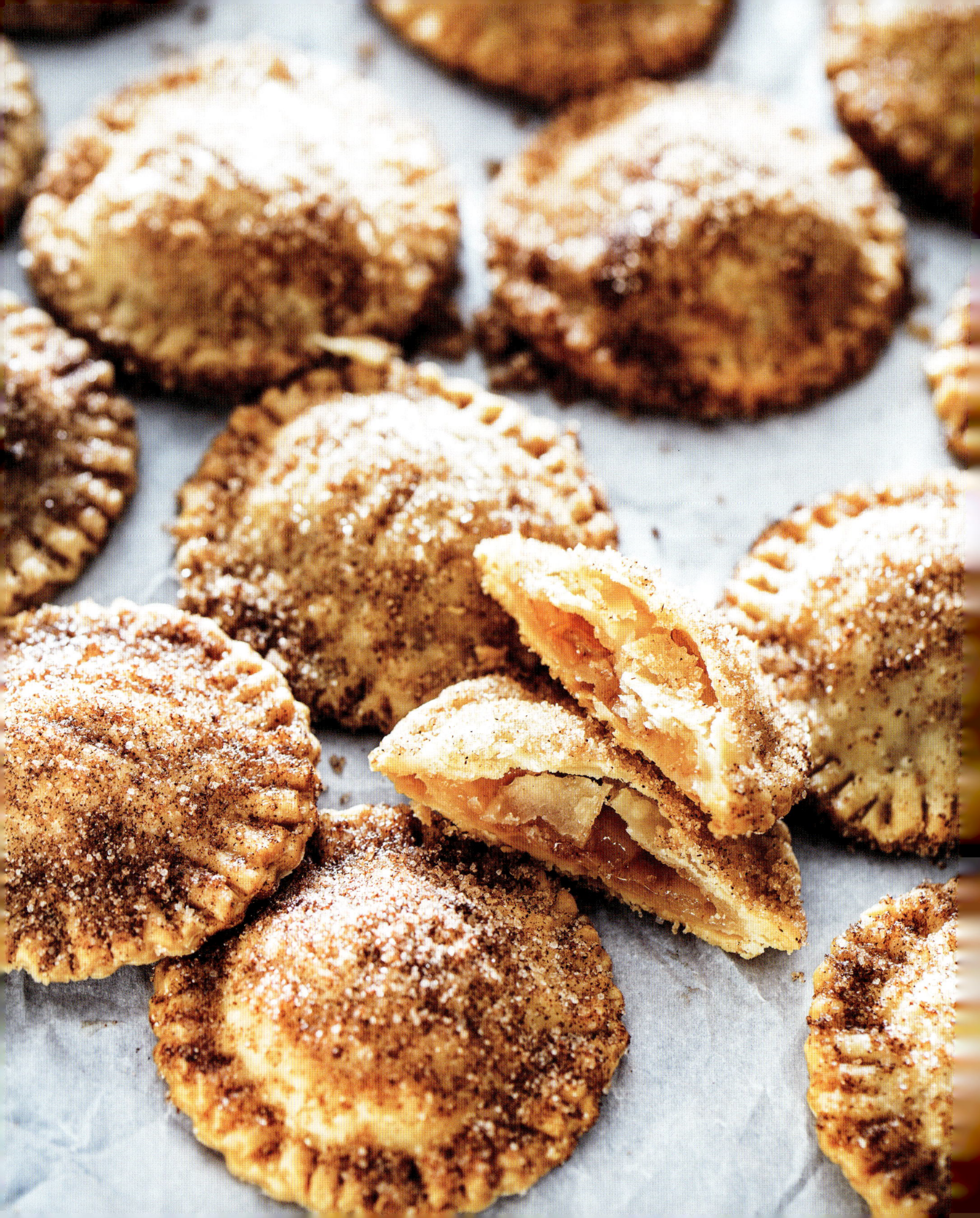

CHURRO APPLE PIE COOKIES

PREP TIME: 30 MINUTES
COOK TIME: 25 MINUTES
TOTAL TIME: 55 MINUTES
SERVES: 24

All-purpose flour, as needed
2 (2-count) packages Pillsbury refrigerated pie crusts
1 cup (125 g) roughly chopped apple pie filling
1 cup (192 g) sugar
1 tbsp (9 g) ground cinnamon
8 tbsp (120 g) butter, melted

I came up with this recipe when I was going through my churro phase. I'm so glad I did, because they're delicious and cute little apple pies, churro style!

Preheat the oven to 350°F (177°C). Line a medium baking sheet with parchment paper.

Lightly dust a work surface with flour. Roll out each pie crust, one at a time, just enough to straighten it out since it comes in a roll. It should be about 14 inches (42 cm) in diameter once it has been rolled out. Using a 2-inch (6-cm) cookie cutter, cut each pie crust into about 12 rounds for a total of about 48 rounds. Discard any remaining pie crust or keep it to reroll and use again.

Place 1 teaspoon of the apple pie filling in the center of 24 of the pastry rounds. Don't use too much apple pie filling, because it will overflow. Brush the edges of each of these rounds with a bit of water, then top each one with the remaining pastry rounds. Press the edges of the pastry with a fork to seal them. Using a sharp knife, cut a small slit into the top of each cookie.

Place the cookies on the prepared baking sheet and bake them for 20 to 25 minutes, or until they are golden brown.

On a shallow plate, mix together the sugar and cinnamon.

Let the cookies cool for about 2 minutes, then brush each cookie with the melted butter. Roll each cookie through the cinnamon sugar.

These cookies would be great with other pie fillings, such as pumpkin, cherry, chocolate and so on.

Store these cookies in an airtight container in the fridge for 3 to 4 days.

RECIPE NOTES

I discard the remaining dough after cutting the dough with the cookie cutter. If you reuse the remaining dough, you will end up with a lot more cookies.

If you make these cookies the day before you want to serve them, reheat them in the oven at 350°F (177°C) for 5 minutes.

NUTRITION INFORMATION

Serving size: 1 cookie; **Calories:** 221; **Carbohydrates:** 29 g; **Protein:** 2 g; **Fat:** 11 g

CINNAMON CREAM CHEESE POCKETS

PREP TIME: 20 MINUTES
COOK TIME: 10 MINUTES
TOTAL TIME: 30 MINUTES
SERVES: 20

8 oz (224 g) cream cheese, softened
1 cup (144 g) powdered sugar, divided
1 tsp pure vanilla extract
2 (10-count) cans refrigerated biscuits
Vegetable oil, as needed
½ cup (96 g) granulated sugar
2 tsp (6 g) ground cinnamon

I first had these when I visited my local coffee shop and tried their version. I was in love, and I knew that I had to make my own at home. Here's my simplified version using store-bought biscuits as a shortcut. These are really addictive!

In a medium bowl, beat the cream cheese with a handheld mixer until it is smooth. Add ½ cup (72 g) of the powdered sugar and the vanilla, and beat the ingredients until they are mostly combined. Scrape down the sides of the bowl and add the remaining ½ cup (72 g) of powdered sugar. Beat the mixture for about 2 minutes, until it is creamy.

Roll out a biscuit until it is about ¼ inch (6 mm) thick. Spoon or pipe about 1½ tablespoons (23 g) of the cream cheese mixture into the middle of the biscuit. Fold the edges over and pinch them together, then press a fork around the edges to ensure they are fully sealed. Repeat this process with the remaining biscuits and cream cheese mixture.

In a large pot, heat 2 inches (6 cm) of the oil to 350°F (177°C). Working in batches so as not to overcrowd the pot, fry the cream cheese pockets for 1 to 2 minutes. Flip them and fry them for 1 to 2 minutes, or until they are golden brown. Remove them from the oil with a slotted spoon and transfer them to a large bowl lined with paper towels.

In a medium bowl, stir together the sugar and cinnamon. While the pockets are still warm, but not too hot to touch, roll them through the cinnamon sugar to coat them. Allow them to cool for 10 to 15 minutes before serving them.

RECIPE NOTES

These tasty little treats will keep in an airtight container in the fridge for 3 to 4 days.

To make this recipe in advance, you can assemble the pockets and freeze them for up to 1 month. Place the pockets on a baking sheet and transfer the baking sheet to the freezer. Freeze the pockets for about 1 hour. After an hour, wrap the pockets in plastic wrap, then place them back in the freezer.

You may also freeze these treats after baking them. Let them cool completely, then wrap each one in plastic wrap and freeze them. Thaw the pockets and warm them in the oven at 350°F (177°C) for about 10 minutes.

NUTRITION INFORMATION

Serving size: 1 pocket; **Calories:** 235; **Carbohydrates:** 35 g; **Protein:** 4 g; **Fat:** 9 g

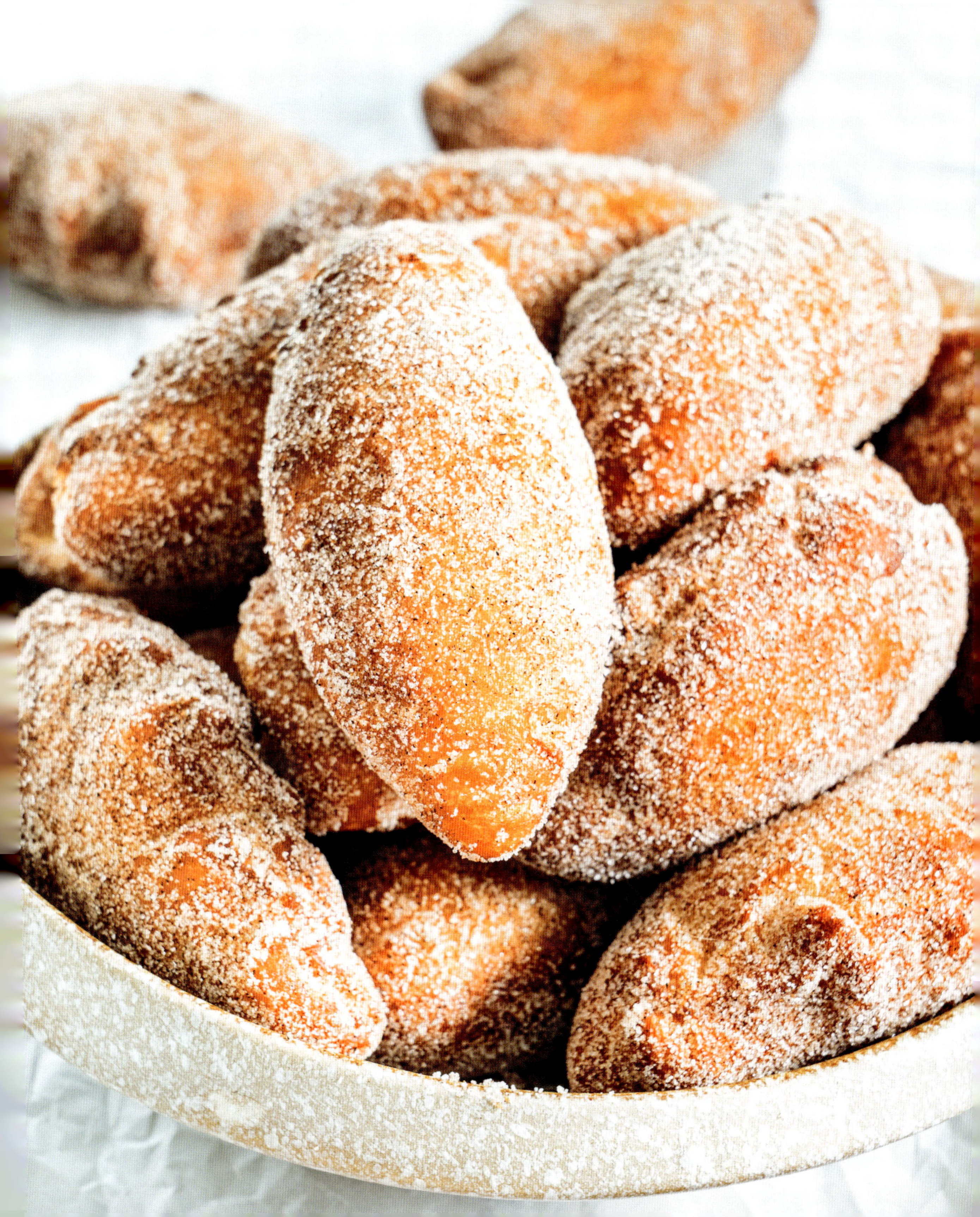

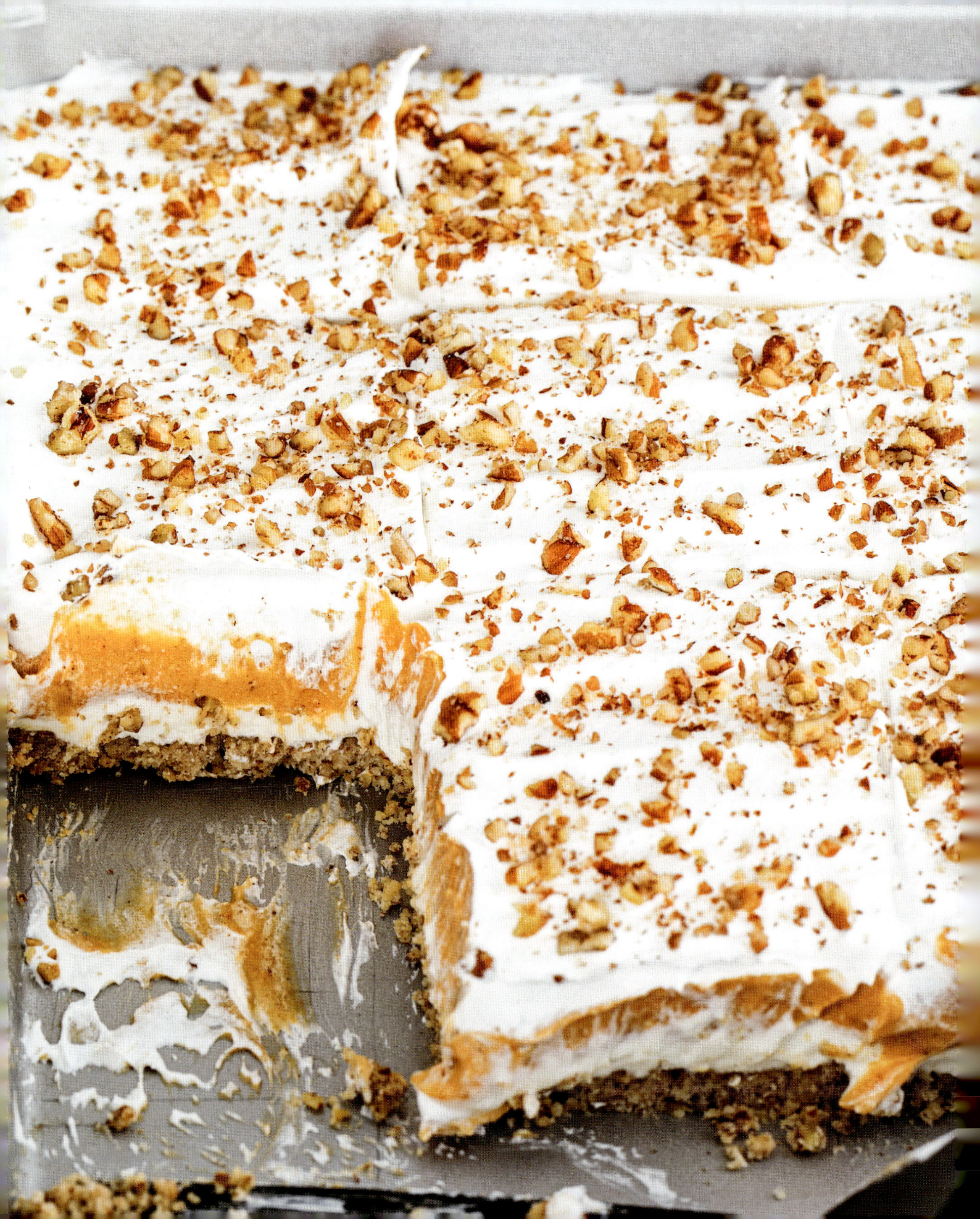

PUMPKIN DELIGHT

This dessert is truly luscious! I'm talking a buttery pecan crust, a spiced pudding layer and a cream cheese layer topped with whipped cream and chopped pecans. That's all I have to say.

PREP TIME: 40 MINUTES
COOK TIME: 20 MINUTES
CHILLING TIME: 3 HOURS
TOTAL TIME: 4 HOURS
SERVES: 12

CRUST
2 cups (198 g) pecan halves
3 tbsp (36 g) granulated sugar
½ cup (120 g) unsalted butter, melted
1 cup (120 g) all-purpose flour

CREAM CHEESE LAYER
8 oz (224 g) cream cheese
1 cup (144 g) powdered sugar
1 cup (60 g) whipped topping or whipped cream

PUMPKIN LAYER
1 (5-oz [140-g]) box instant vanilla pudding
2½ cups (600 ml) milk
1 (15-oz [420-g]) can pumpkin
1 tsp pumpkin pie spice
3 cups (180 g) whipped topping or whipped cream, divided

To make the crust, preheat the oven to 350°F (177°C). Spray a 9 x 13–inch (27 x 39–cm) baking dish with cooking spray.

Place the pecans in a food processor and pulse until the pecans are chopped. Reserve about ¼ cup (30 g) of the chopped pecans for topping the dessert. Do not remove the remaining chopped pecans from the food processor.

Add the granulated sugar, butter and flour to the food processor and pulse a few times, until the ingredients are combined. Press the crust mixture into the prepared baking dish.

Bake the crust for 20 minutes. Let the crust cool completely before proceeding.

To make the cream cheese layer, place the cream cheese in a large bowl and mix it with a handheld mixer until it has softened. Add the powdered sugar and mix until the ingredients are smooth. Fold in the whipped topping. Set the cream cheese layer aside.

To make the pumpkin layer, prepare the vanilla pudding according to the package's instructions with the exception of using 2½ cups (600 ml) of milk rather than the 3 cups (720 ml) listed on the package. This will produce a firmer pudding.

Add the pumpkin, pumpkin pie spice and 1 cup (60 g) whipped topping to the pudding and fold everything together until the ingredients are well combined. Once the crust has cooled completely, spread the cream cheese layer evenly over the crust. Next, spread all of the pumpkin mixture evenly over the cream cheese layer. Top the pumpkin layer with the remaining 2 cups (120 g) whipped topping, then sprinkle the whipped topping with the reserved chopped pecans.

Chill the pumpkin delight in the fridge for at least 3 hours prior to serving to allow it to set.

RECIPE NOTE
Although the instant vanilla pudding mix instructions ask for 3 cups (720 ml) of milk, I use 2½ cups (600 ml) instead, because I want a firmer pudding for the layers. However, feel free to use 3 cups (720 ml) of milk if you prefer a softer pudding.

NUTRITION INFORMATION
Serving size: 1 serving; **Calories:** 434; **Carbohydrates:** 47 g; **Protein:** 6 g; **Fat:** 25 g

MINI BLUEBERRY GALETTES

A galette is a rustic French tart with hand-folded edges. Here's my version of mini galettes filled with fresh blueberries.

Preheat the oven to 400°F (204°C). Line 2 medium baking sheets with parchment paper.

In a medium bowl, combine the blueberries, granulated sugar, cornstarch, lemon zest and lemon juice. Set the blueberries aside.

Lightly dust a work surface with flour. Roll out each pie crust on the prepared work surface until it is flat. Using a bowl or cookie cutter that is 4 to 5 inches (12 to 15 cm) in diameter, cut 3 rounds in each pie crust by pressing down on the bowl or running a knife around it. Reroll the remaining dough. You should be able to get 1 more pie crust round from each rerolled pie crust. Each pie crust should yield 4 rounds for a total of 16 rounds.

Spoon 1 to 2 tablespoons (9 to 18 g) of the blueberry mixture on the center of a pie crust round. Fold up the dough over the filling of each galette, but do not cover the filling completely.

Place the galettes on the prepared baking sheets, with 8 galettes per baking sheet. Brush each galette with the beaten egg, then sprinkle each one with the turbinado sugar.

Bake the galettes for 30 to 35 minutes, or until they are golden brown. Garnish the galettes with the mint (if using). Serve them warm with the whipped cream (if using).

PREP TIME: 20 MINUTES
COOK TIME: 35 MINUTES
TOTAL TIME: 55 MINUTES
SERVES: 16

1 lb (448 g) fresh blueberries
¼ cup (48 g) granulated sugar
2 tbsp (18 g) cornstarch
Zest of 1 lemon
Juice of 1 lemon
All-purpose flour, as needed
2 (2-count) packages Pillsbury refrigerated pie crusts (see Recipe Notes)
1 large egg, beaten
1 tbsp (12 g) turbinado sugar (see Recipe Notes)
Torn or roughly chopped fresh mint leaves, as needed (optional)
Whipped cream or vanilla ice cream, for serving (optional)

RECIPE NOTES

If your pie crust has come down to room temperature, place the baking sheets with the unbaked galettes in the fridge for about 30 minutes, so that the dough gets cold again; otherwise, your galettes might open up during baking and you'll end up with a mess.

If you can't find turbinado sugar, coconut sugar would be a great replacement.

To prepare these in advance, assemble the galettes by filling them and folding the crusts' edges. Freeze them up to 1 month. First, place the galettes on the baking sheets and place the baking sheets in the freezer. Freeze the galettes for about 1 hour. After an hour, wrap the galettes in plastic wrap, then place them back in the freezer. You may also freeze the galettes after baking them. Let them cool completely, then wrap each one in plastic wrap and freeze them. Thaw them and warm them in the oven at 350°F (177°C) for about 15 minutes, or until the crust crisps again.

NUTRITION INFORMATION

Serving size: 1 galette; **Calories:** 295; **Carbohydrates:** 39 g; **Protein:** 2 g; **Fat:** 15 g

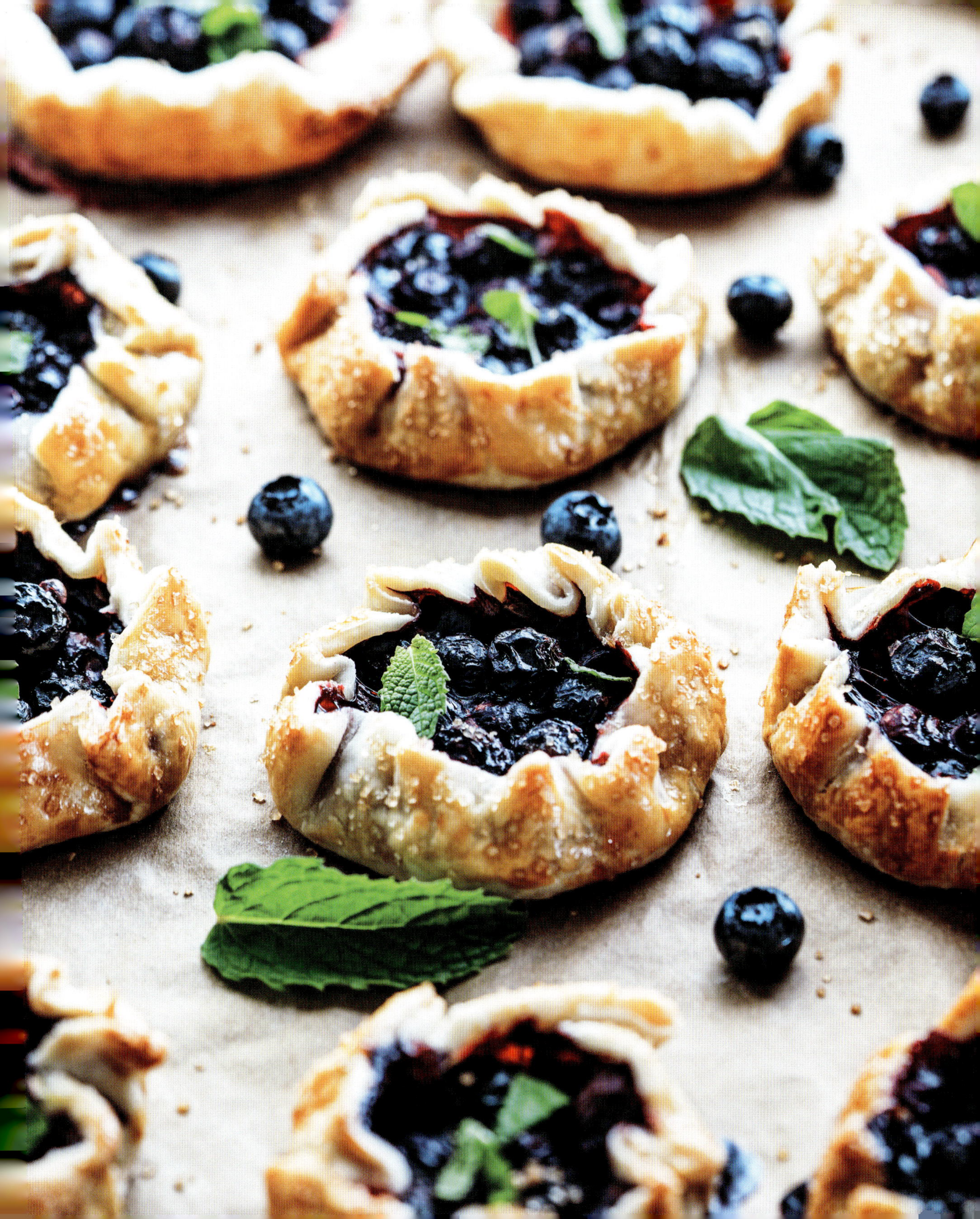

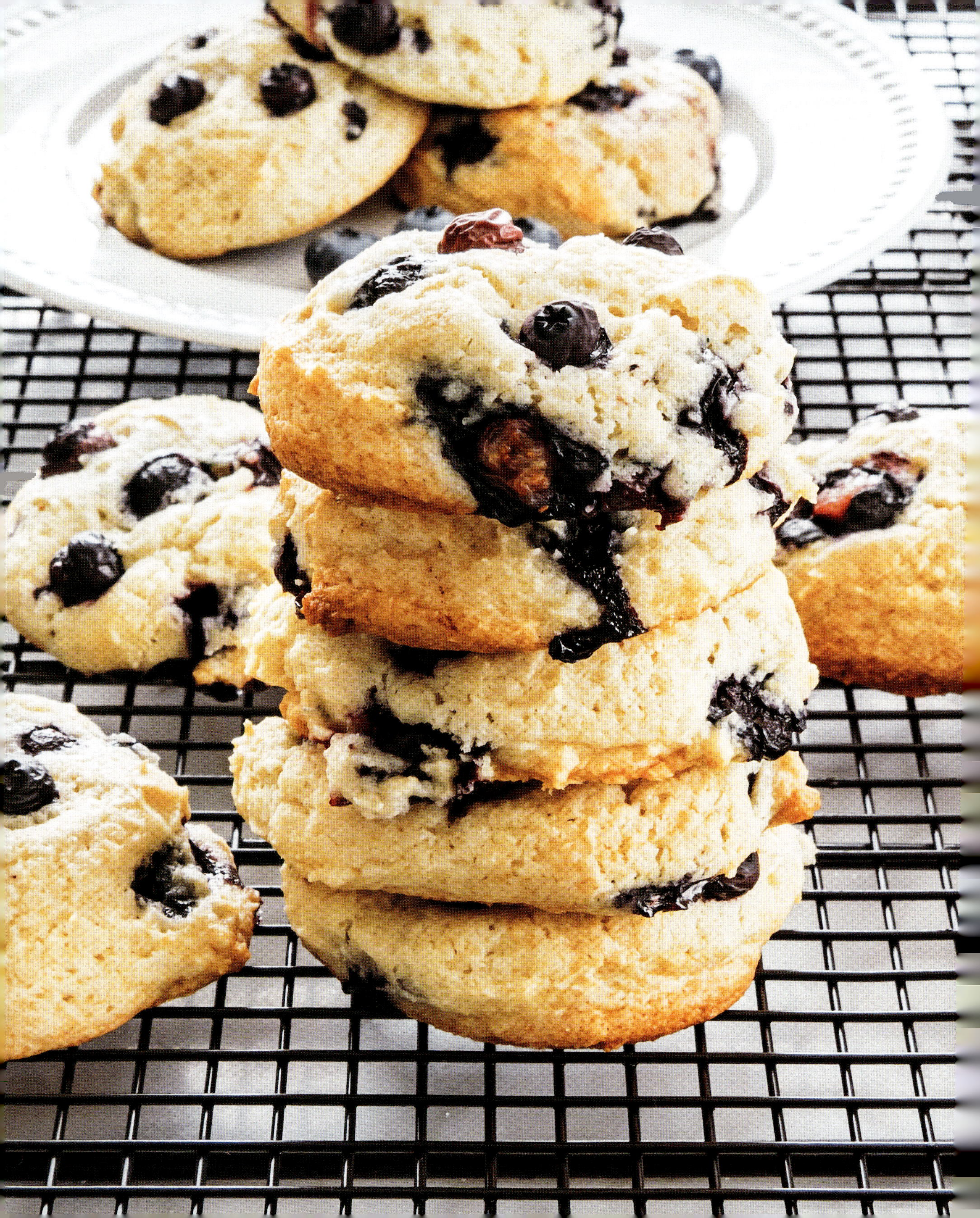

BLUEBERRY CHEESECAKE COOKIES

PREP TIME: 20 MINUTES
COOK TIME: 20 MINUTES
TOTAL TIME: 40 MINUTES
SERVES: 22

2 cups (240 g) all-purpose flour
1 tsp baking powder
½ tsp baking soda
¼ tsp salt
1 cup (192 g) sugar
¾ cup (180 g) unsalted butter, softened
4 oz (112 g) cream cheese, at room temperature
1 large egg
2 tsp (10 ml) pure vanilla extract
⅓ cup (40 g) sour cream
1½ cups (225 g) fresh blueberries

These cookies are soft, fluffy and almost cake-like. They're bursting with fresh blueberries and are perfect in the morning with a good cup of coffee. Cheesecake and blueberries all in one cookie—what's not to love?

Preheat the oven to 350°F (177°C). Line 2 medium baking sheets with parchment paper.

In a medium bowl, whisk together the flour, baking powder, baking soda and salt. Set the flour mixture aside.

In a large bowl, use an electric mixer to beat together the sugar, butter and cream cheese for about 2 minutes, until the mixture is light and fluffy. Add the egg, vanilla and sour cream, and mix the ingredients until they are well combined.

Add the flour mixture to the creamed mixture and stir until the two are just combined. Do not overmix the dough.

Gently fold in the blueberries. Place 1½-tablespoon (23-g)-sized balls of dough on the prepared baking sheets about 2 inches (6 cm) apart.

Bake the cookies for 15 to 18 minutes, just until the bottoms of the cookies begin to brown. Cool on the baking sheets for 5 minutes, then transfer them to a wire rack to cool completely.

RECIPE

This recipe will yield 22 to 24 cookies.

To store leftover cookies, cool them completely, then transfer the cookies to an airtight container or ziplock bag. Place a piece of white bread in the cookie container to keep them fresh. Store the cookie container at room temperature for 3 to 5 days.

These blueberry cheesecake cookies are perfect for freezing. You can either wrap them individually or place them together in an airtight container or ziplock bag. They will last in the freezer for 3 months. Thaw the cookies in their packaging at room temperature for 15 minutes, then place them on a plate to come to room temperature.

NUTRITION INFORMATION

Serving size: 1 cookie; **Calories:** 160; **Carbohydrates:** 20 g; **Protein:** 2 g; **Fat:** 8 g

QUICK APPLE TURNOVERS

When I was a teenager, I worked in a bakery. Apple turnovers were my favorite thing to eat there. Here's my simplified version with puff pastry and a homemade apple filling.

PREP TIME: 20 MINUTES
COOK TIME: 30 MINUTES
TOTAL TIME: 50 MINUTES
SERVES: 8

2 tbsp (30 g) unsalted butter
8 Golden Delicious or Granny Smith apples, peeled, cored and shredded or sliced
1 tsp ground cinnamon
2 tbsp (30 g) packed brown sugar
All-purpose flour, as needed
2 sheets puff pastry (see Recipe Notes)
1 large egg, beaten
Caramel sauce or powdered sugar, for garnish

Melt the butter in a medium skillet over medium heat. Add the apples, cinnamon and brown sugar. Cook the apples for about 10 minutes, until all the juice from the apples has evaporated and the apples are cooked through. Let the filling cool for about 5 minutes.

Preheat the oven to 400°F (204°C). Line a large baking sheet with parchment paper.

Dust a work surface with the flour. Roll out each sheet of puff pastry and cut it into 4 pieces that are 5 x 5 inches (15 x 15 cm).

Place about one-eighth of the apple mixture on each piece of pastry, then fold the pastry around the filling. You can fold the pastry as a triangle or as a rectangle. Brush some of the beaten egg around the edges of the pastry, then seal the edges with a fork.

Brush the turnovers with more of the beaten egg. Cut 2 slits in the top of each turnover.

Bake the turnovers for 15 to 20 minutes, or until they are golden brown.

Serve drizzled with caramel sauce or sprinkled with powdered sugar.

RECIPE NOTES

I use store-bought puff pastry in this recipe. You can definitely make your own if you'd like. You can also use any pie pastry if that's more convenient for you.

To freeze these turnovers, allow them to cool and do not ice them or sprinkle them with powdered sugar. Line a baking sheet with parchment paper and arrange the turnovers in a single layer. Place the baking sheet in the freezer and flash-freeze the turnovers for about 1 hour. After they are frozen, wrap each turnover in plastic wrap or aluminum foil, then place them in a freezer bag and store them in the freezer for up to 1 month. Reheat foil-wrapped turnovers at 325°F (163°C) for 15 minutes, or until they are heated through. Alternatively, you can remove the foil and microwave the turnovers for 1 minute.

NUTRITION INFORMATION

Serving size: 1 turnover; **Calories:** 477; **Carbohydrates:** 56 g; **Protein:** 5 g; **Fat:** 27 g

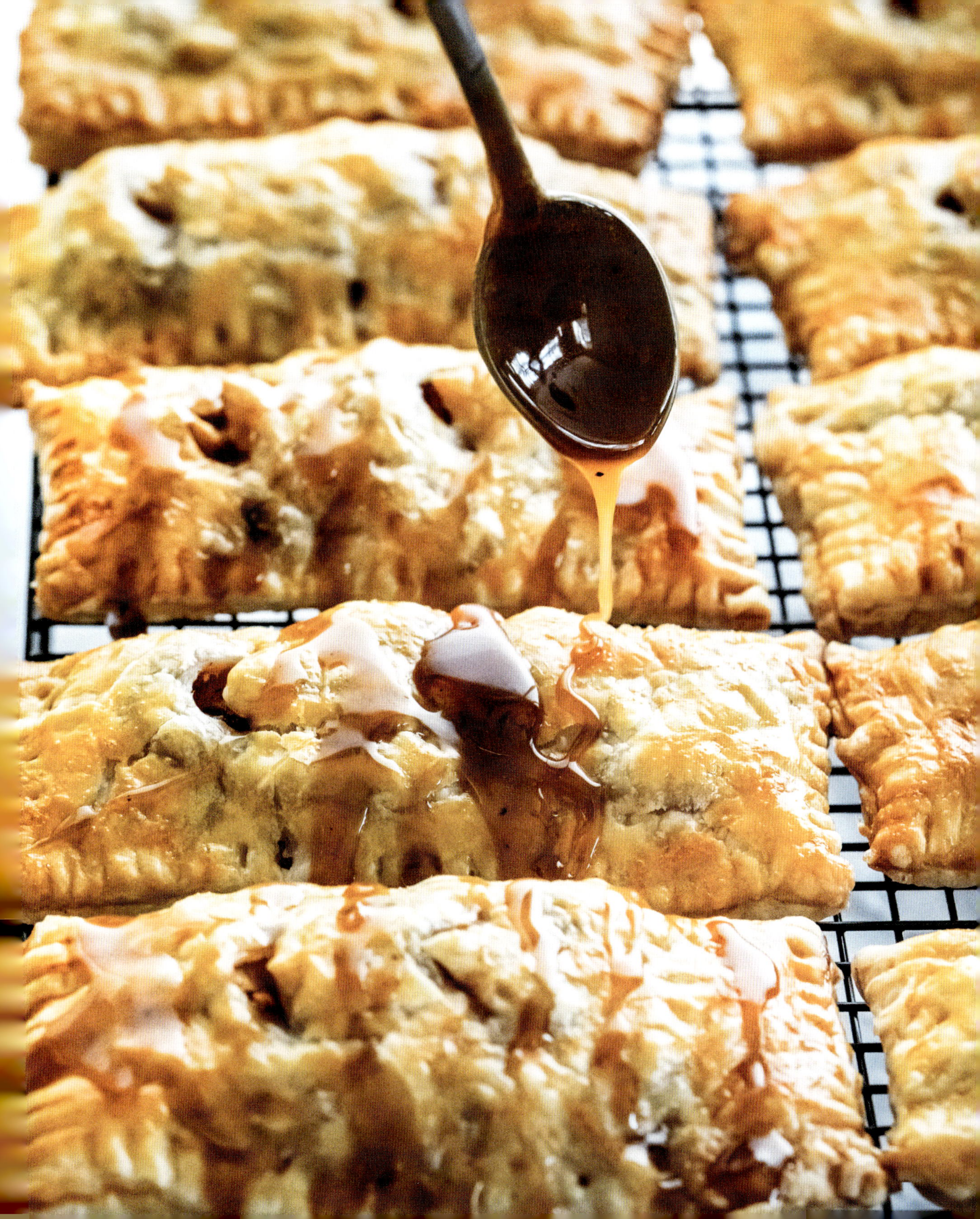

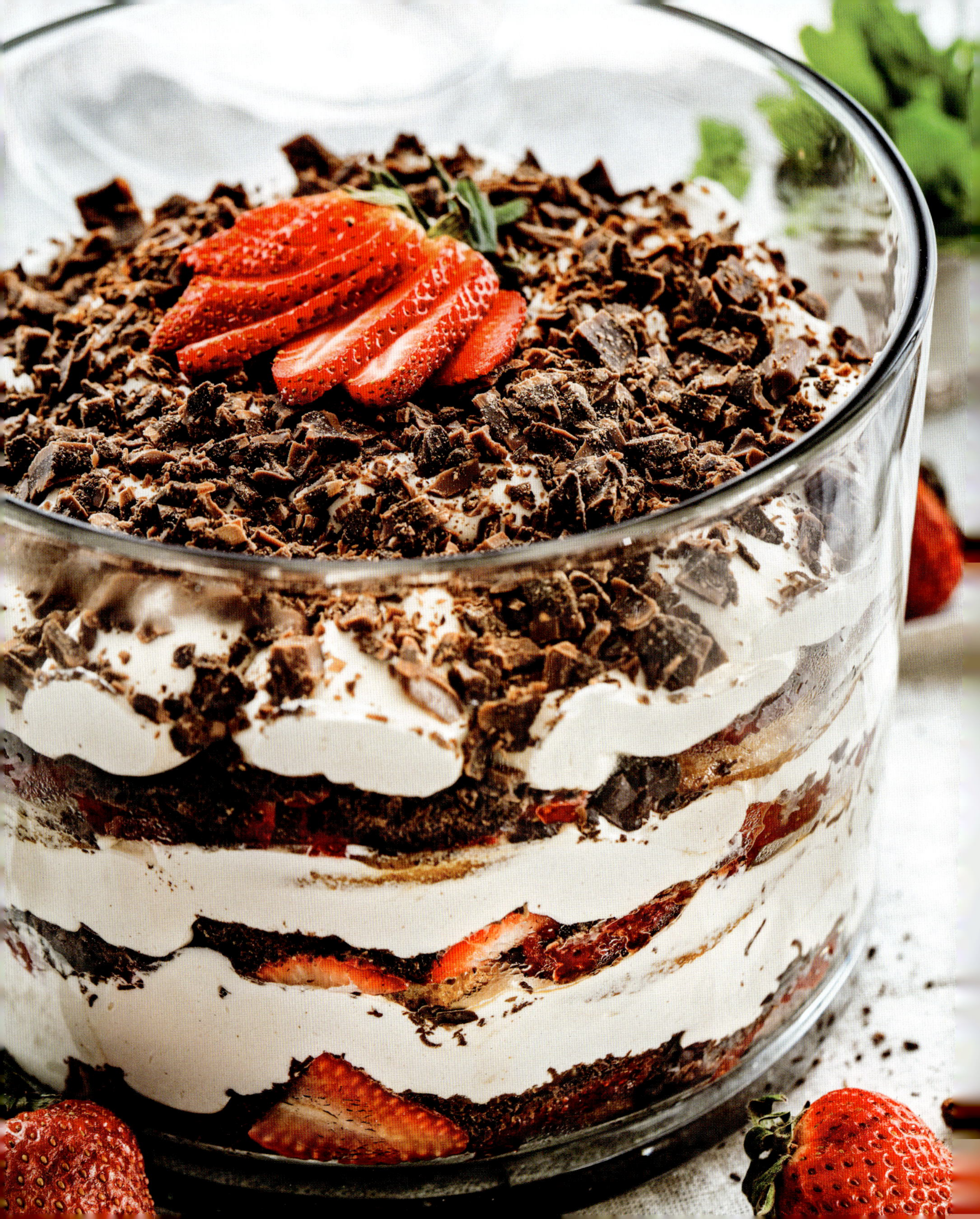

STRAWBERRY TIRAMISU TRIFLE

This strawberry tiramisu trifle is a classic dessert that gets a berry twist thanks to lots of strawberries, chocolate and a fabulous mascarpone and pudding cream. And if you're a lover of traditional tiramisu, don't worry—it's still packed with lots of coffee flavor!

PREP TIME: 30 MINUTES
CHILLING TIME: 4 HOURS
TOTAL TIME: 4 HOURS, 30 MINUTES
SERVES: 12

4 cups (576 g) fresh strawberries
1½ cups (360 ml) cold milk
1 (3-oz [84-g]) package instant vanilla pudding
8 oz (224 g) mascarpone cheese
2 cups (480 ml) instant coffee or brewed coffee, at room temperature, divided
2 cups (120 g) whipped topping or whipped cream
3 oz (84 g) ladyfingers
6 oz (168 g) bittersweet chocolate, grated or shaved

Set aside 1 strawberry for garnish. Remove the stems of the remaining strawberries, then slice them.

In a large bowl, whisk together the milk and pudding for 2 minutes. Refrigerate the mixture for 2 minutes.

In a large bowl, use a handheld mixer to beat the mascarpone cheese until it is smooth. Gradually beat in 2 tablespoons (30 ml) of the coffee. Beat in the pudding. Fold in the whipped topping.

Note that you will need to dip both sides of the ladyfingers in the remaining coffee as you are layering the trifle; do not dip them ahead of time. Line the bottom of a 3-quart (2.9-L) trifle dish or glass serving bowl with one-third of the coffee-dipped ladyfingers. Top them with one-third of the sliced strawberries, chocolate and mascarpone mixture. Repeat this process, creating 3 layers of each element, finishing the trifle with the mascarpone mixture and chocolate.

Garnish the top of the trifle with the reserved strawberry.

Refrigerate the trifle for at least 4 hours, or up to overnight, prior to serving.

RECIPE NOTES

If you make this trifle a day or two ahead of time, wait to garnish it with the reserved strawberry until right before you serve it.

If you don't like vanilla pudding, use whichever type is your favorite. The flavor of the trifle will change, but it will still be good.

If you'd like to make an adult version of this cake, try dipping the ladyfingers in a coffee liqueur, dark rum or sweet sparkling wine.

You can store this recipe, covered, in the fridge for up to 3 days. I don't recommend freezing this dish, as once it thaws the ladyfingers will be too mushy. Enjoy this trifle within the first few days of whipping it up and you'll thank me later!

NUTRITION INFORMATION

Serving size: 1 serving; **Calories:** 287; **Carbohydrates:** 30 g; **Protein:** 5 g; **Fat:** 16 g

BLUEBERRY CAKE

This is a fluffy and decadent little cake. It's perfect for serving after a big meal or enjoying with a steaming cup of coffee for breakfast.

PREP TIME: 20 MINUTES
COOK TIME: 50 MINUTES
TOTAL TIME: 1 HOUR, 10 MINUTES
SERVES: 8

CAKE
¾ cup (180 g) unsalted butter, softened
¾ cup (144 g) plus 1½ tbsp (18 g) granulated sugar, divided
½ tsp salt
2 tsp (10 ml) pure vanilla extract
3 large egg yolks
2¼ cups (270 g) all-purpose flour
2 tsp (8 g) baking powder
⅔ cup (160 ml) milk

BLUEBERRIES
2¼ cups (338 g) fresh blueberries
1½ tbsp (12 g) all-purpose flour

MERINGUE
3 large egg whites
⅓ cup (64 g) granulated sugar

Powdered sugar, as needed (optional)

To make the cake, preheat the oven to 350°F (177°C). Grease a 9-inch (27-cm) round baking pan or a 9 x 9–inch (27 x 27–cm) baking pan.

In a large bowl, use a handheld mixer to cream together the butter and ¾ cup (144 g) of the granulated sugar for 2 to 3 minutes, until the mixture is fluffy. Mix in the salt and vanilla. Add the egg yolks to the sugar mixture and beat for about 2 minutes, until it is creamy.

In a medium bowl, combine the flour and baking powder. Add the flour mixture and the milk to the creamed mixture and mix until the ingredients are well combined.

To prepare the blueberries, place the blueberries in a medium bowl and toss them with the flour, ensuring they are coated. Fold the blueberries into the cake batter.

To make the meringue, in a medium bowl, use a handheld mixer to beat the egg whites for 4 to 5 minutes, until soft peaks form. Add the granulated sugar, 1 tablespoon (12 g) at a time, and beat the mixture for 1 to 2 minutes, until stiff peaks form. Fold the meringue whites into the cake batter.

Pour the batter into the prepared baking pan. Sprinkle the top with the remaining 1½ tablespoons (18 g) of granulated sugar.

Bake the cake for 50 minutes, or until a toothpick inserted into the center comes out clean.

Let the cake cool in the pan for 5 minutes, then transfer it to a cooling rack to finish cooling. Dust the cake with the powdered sugar (if using) and serve it.

RECIPE NOTES

Store the cake on a covered cake plate at room temperature. Don't refrigerate it, as it may dry out and the coldness can dull the flavor. If you have a covered cake plate, your cake will keep just fine for 5 days. If you don't have a covered cake plate, use a bowl—such as the bowl from a salad spinner—to cover the cake.

To freeze this cake, let it cool completely. Cut the cake into individual slices, then wrap each one in plastic wrap and place them in a freezer bag. Freeze the slices for up to 1 month.

NUTRITION INFORMATION

Serving size: 1 slice; **Calories:** 470; **Carbohydrates:** 65 g; **Protein:** 8 g; **Fat:** 20 g

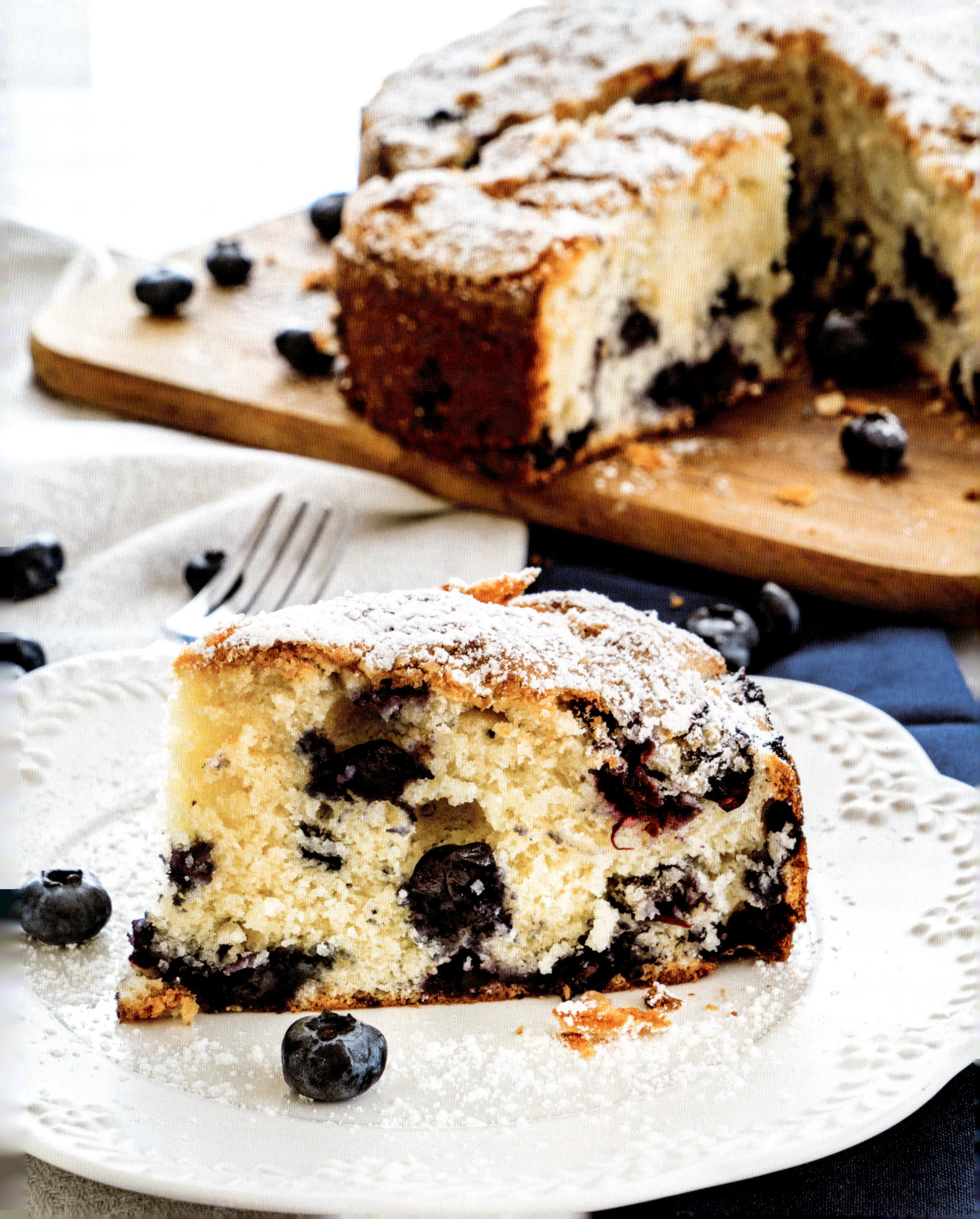

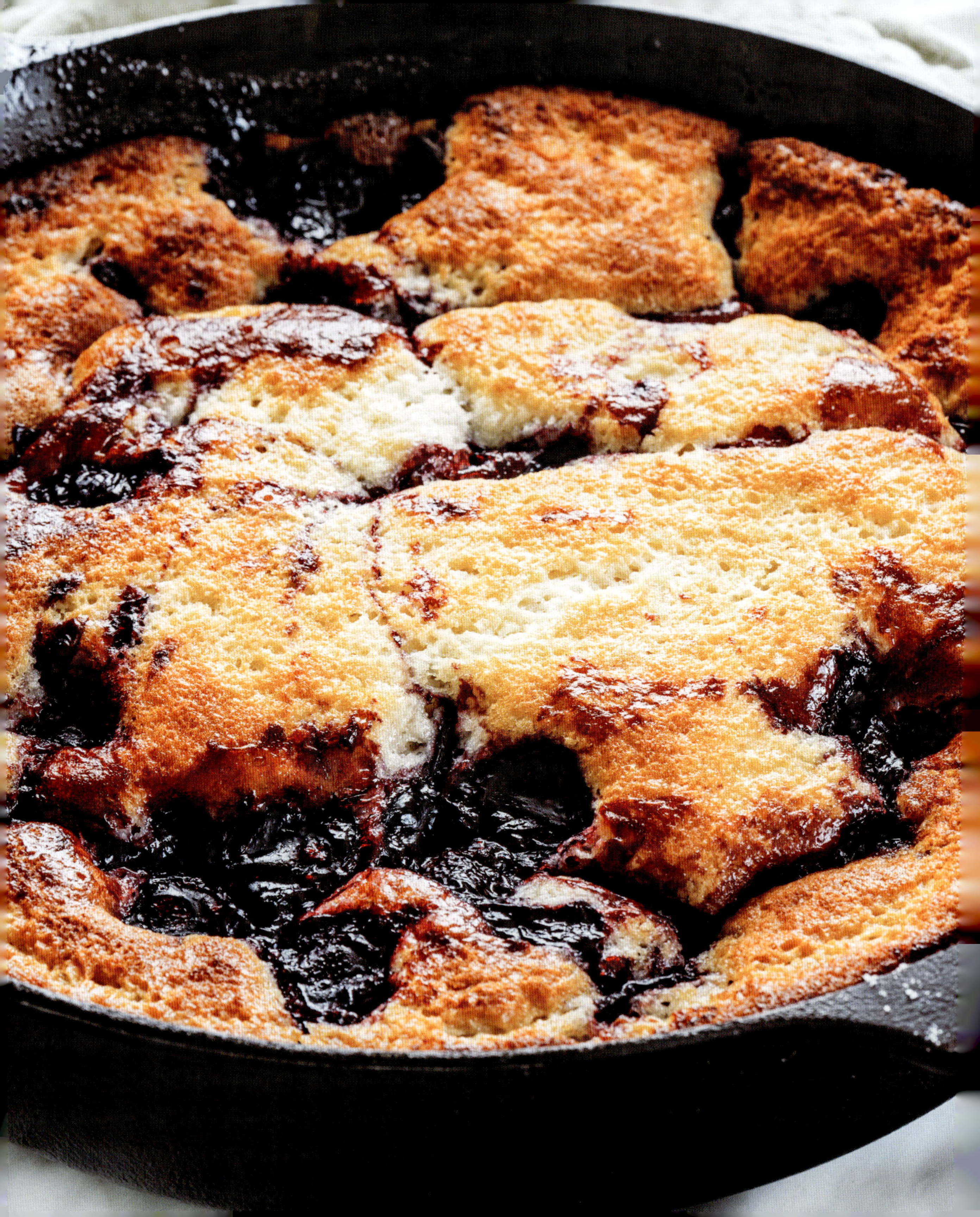

CHERRY COBBLER

This easy homemade cherry cobbler recipe is made with fresh cherries and a soft topping. Served with a scoop of ice cream, it'll be at the top of your dessert go-to list!

PREP TIME: 15 MINUTES
COOK TIME: 45 MINUTES
TOTAL TIME: 1 HOUR
SERVES: 8

FILLING

2 lb (896 g) fresh cherries, pitted and halved
½ cup (96 g) sugar
2 tbsp (18 g) cornstarch
2 tbsp (30 ml) fresh lemon juice
⅛ tsp salt

BATTER

1 cup (120 g) all-purpose flour
1 cup (192 g) sugar
1 tbsp (12 g) baking powder
¼ tsp salt
1 large egg
¾ cup (180 ml) milk
½ cup (120 g) unsalted butter

Preheat the oven to 375°F (191°C).

To make the filling, combine the cherries, sugar, cornstarch, lemon juice and salt in a medium saucepan over medium heat. Cook the cherries for about 5 minutes, stirring them occasionally, until the sauce thickens slightly.

To make the batter, mix together the flour, sugar, baking powder, salt, egg and milk in a large bowl until the ingredients are smooth.

Melt the butter in a large oven-safe skillet over medium heat. Remove the skillet from the heat. Pour the batter into the skillet.

Spoon the filling over the batter in an even layer. Reduce the oven temperature to 350°F (177°C). Bake the cobbler for 40 to 45 minutes, or until the topping is golden brown.

RECIPE NOTES

This cobbler will last for 4 to 5 days in the fridge. You can store it in an airtight container or right in the skillet to avoid making a mess. If you leave it in the skillet, make sure it has cooled fully, then cover it well with plastic wrap or foil. Reheating it in the microwave works best, but you can also reheat it in the oven at 325°F (163°C) for about 15 minutes, or until it is heated through.

You can also store your cobbler in the freezer for 6 to 8 months. If you keep it in the skillet, make sure to wrap it well with a layer of plastic wrap and a layer of foil to prevent freezer burn. Let the cobbler thaw overnight in the fridge before reheating it. Keep in mind that because it has thawed, the cobbler will be a bit more watery.

NUTRITION INFORMATION

Serving size: 1 serving; **Calories:** 407; **Carbohydrates:** 72 g; **Protein:** 4 g; **Fat:** 13 g

APPLE FRITTERS

These apple fritters are incredibly easy to make, with a simple batter that whips up in seconds. Just fry them, dust them with a bit of powdered sugar and enjoy!

PREP TIME: 10 MINUTES
COOK TIME: 20 MINUTES
TOTAL TIME: 30 MINUTES
SERVES: 30

Canola oil or vegetable oil, as needed
2 cups (240 g) all-purpose flour
2½ tsp (10 g) baking powder
2 tsp (6 g) cinnamon
1 tsp salt
2 large eggs
½ cup (96 g) granulated sugar
2 tbsp (30 g) unsalted butter, melted
¾ cup (180 ml) milk
2 tsp (10 ml) pure vanilla extract
3 to 4 apples, peeled, cored and finely chopped (see Recipe Notes)
Powdered sugar, as needed (optional)

Heat a large pot of the oil to 375°F (191°C).

In a large bowl, mix together the flour, baking powder, cinnamon and salt. In a small bowl, whisk together the eggs and granulated sugar. Add the butter, milk and vanilla to the egg mixture.

Add the egg mixture to the flour mixture and stir them together using a wooden spoon or a spatula. Fold in the apples, so that everything is well incorporated.

Working in batches so as not to overcrowd the pot, use a large cookie scoop to very carefully drop balls of the batter directly into the hot oil. It's best to let them drop slowly and as closely to the oil as you can to avoid splashes. Fry the fritters for 2 to 3 minutes total, until they are browned. Use a chopstick or skewer to flip the fritters and fry the opposite side. Keep a close eye on them, as they can burn quickly.

Use a slotted spoon to transfer the apple fritters from the oil to a large bowl or plate lined with paper towels.

Sprinkle the fritters with the powdered sugar (if using) and serve them warm.

RECIPE NOTES

I use Granny Smith apples for this recipe. Honeycrisp apples would also work. These types of apples are great for this dish because they don't get mushy and are able to hold their form after being fried!

This recipe will yield about 30 fritters, depending on their size.

Wherever you keep these apple fritters, make sure to store them in an airtight container so they don't dry out. They will last for 2 days at room temperature, 1 week in the fridge and 2 to 3 months in the freezer. If you freeze them, thaw them by leaving them at room temperature for a few hours, until they're soft.

NUTRITION INFORMATION

Serving size: 1 fritter; **Calories:** 89; **Carbohydrates:** 13 g; **Protein:** 1 g; **Fat:** 3 g

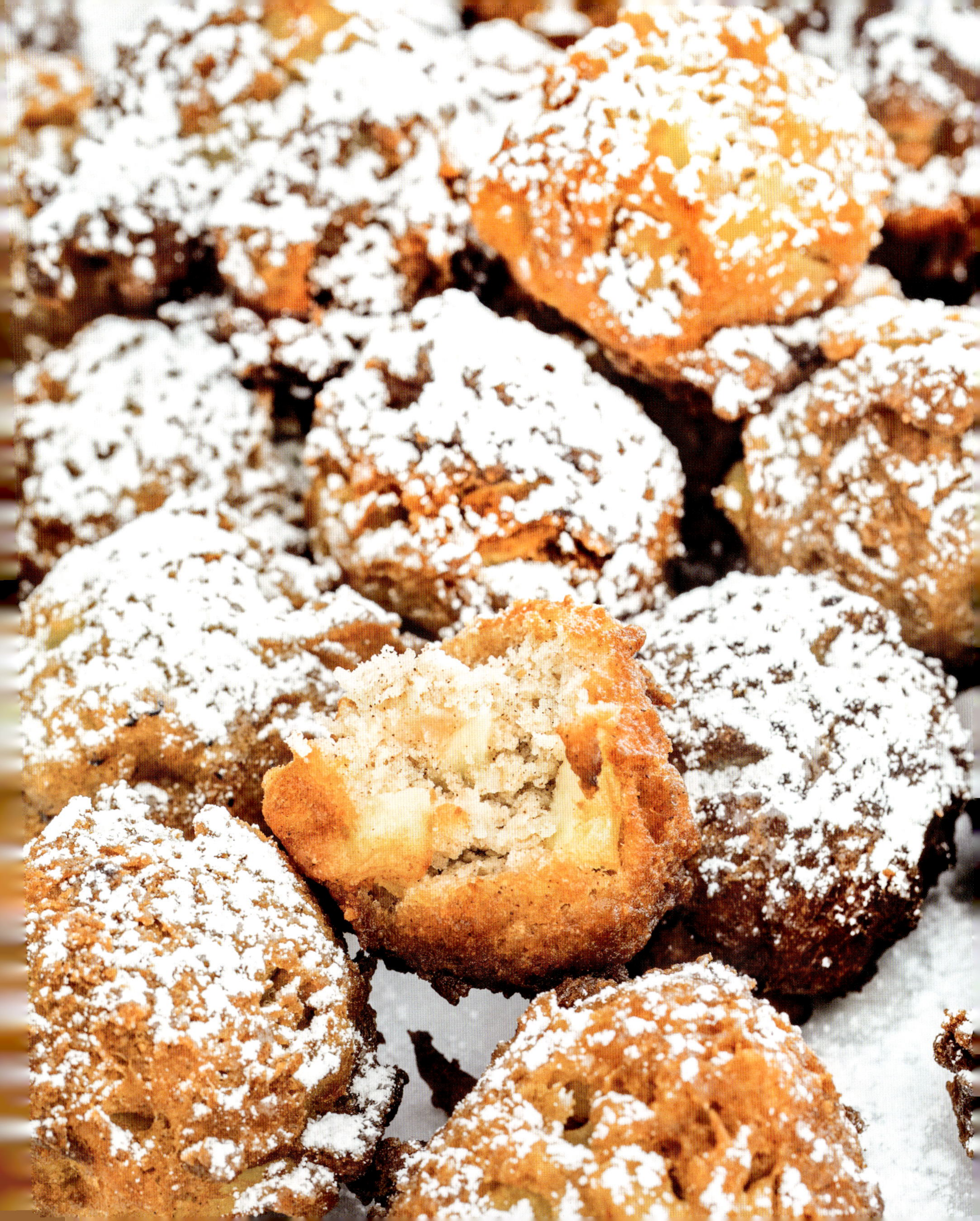

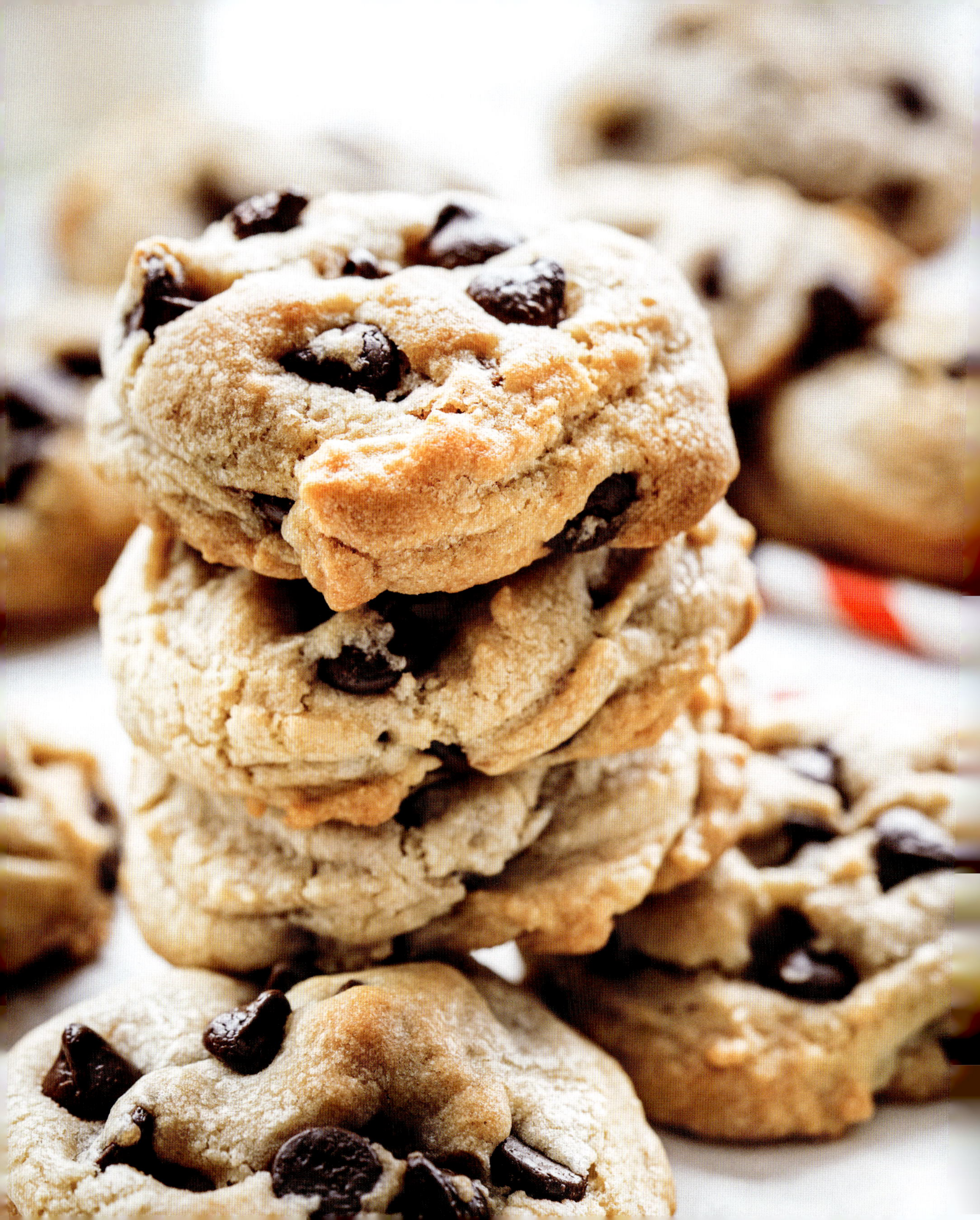

BEST EVER CHOCOLATE CHIP COOKIES

PREP TIME: 10 MINUTES
COOK TIME: 30 MINUTES
TOTAL TIME: 40 MINUTES
SERVES: 50

¾ cup (180 g) packed brown sugar
¾ cup (144 g) granulated sugar
1 cup (240 g) unsalted butter, melted (see Recipe Notes)
2 large eggs
1 tsp pure vanilla extract
1 tsp baking soda
¼ tsp salt
2¾ cups (330 g) all-purpose flour
2 cups (360 g) semisweet chocolate chips

NUTRITION INFORMATION

Serving size: 1 cookie; **Calories:** 120; **Carbohydrates:** 16 g; **Protein:** 1 g; **Fat:** 5 g

I once received a Christmas card from a friend and inside the Christmas card was this wonderful chocolate chip cookie recipe, titled "Best Ever Chocolate Chip Cookies." Ever since then, this has been my go-to recipe for chocolate chip cookies. They really are the best.

Preheat the oven to 375°F (191°C). Line a medium baking sheet with parchment paper or leave it ungreased.

In a large bowl or the bowl of a stand mixer fitted with the paddle attachment, beat together the brown sugar, granulated sugar and butter for 3 to 5 minutes, until the mixture is creamy.

Add the eggs, vanilla, baking soda and salt to the bowl and beat the mixture for about 30 seconds on low speed until the ingredients are well incorporated.

Add the flour and mix it into the sugar and egg mixture until crumbles form. Add the chocolate chips and use a spatula to mix them throughout the dough.

You can use a small ice cream scoop to scoop out cookie dough balls, or you can use your hands to roll the dough into balls, depending on how big you want your cookies to be. Place the cookies on the prepared baking sheet. This recipe yields about 50 cookies, so if you can bake only one batch of cookies at a time, place the remaining cookie dough in the fridge until you are ready to make the next batch and repeat this step to make the cookie dough balls.

Bake the cookies for 9 to 11 minutes per batch, or until they are barely golden around the edges. Do not overbake these cookies.

Let the cookies cool on the baking sheet for about 15 minutes, then transfer them to a wire rack to finish cooling.

RECIPE NOTES

Melt the butter in the microwave for 30 to 40 seconds, until it's almost entirely melted but not hot. I find that if I use softened butter the cookies will not spread enough, while melting the butter will produce the perfect cookie every time.

If you find that the dough is too sticky, add a little more flour. You should be able to form some dough into a ball with your hands.

Store these cookies in an airtight container. They will stay soft and chewy for 2 to 3 weeks at room temperature. You can also freeze them. Place them unwrapped in an airtight container, or wrap them individually with plastic wrap and then place them in an airtight container. They will keep in the freezer for 3 months.

ANGEL BERRY TRIFLE

This angel berry trifle is perfect for the holidays, but it's also a great dessert to bring to potlucks. With angel food cake, vanilla cream and lots of fresh berries, this is an impressive dessert that's also simple to make.

PREP TIME: 30 MINUTES
COOK TIME: NONE
TOTAL TIME: 30 MINUTES
SERVES: 12

1 (1-oz [28-g]) package sugar-free instant vanilla pudding
1½ cups (360 ml) milk
1 cup (245 g) vanilla yogurt
6 oz (168 g) cream cheese (I recommend whipped cream cheese)
½ cup (60 g) sour cream
3 cups (180 g) whipped topping, divided
1 prepared angel food cake, cubed (see Recipe Notes)
2 cups (332 g) chopped fresh strawberries
2 cups (300 g) fresh raspberries
2 cups (300 g) fresh blackberries

In the bowl of a stand mixer fitted with the whisk attachment, mix together the pudding and milk for 2 minutes, or until the pudding is firm. Transfer the pudding to a medium bowl and set it aside.

In the bowl of the stand mixer, combine the yogurt, cream cheese and sour cream and beat the ingredients for about 1 minute, until they are smooth. Fold in the pudding and 1 cup (60 g) of the whipped topping.

Place one-third of the angel food cake cubes in a 4-quart (3.8-L) trifle bowl. Top the cake cubes with one-third of the pudding mixture, 1 cup (60 g) of the whipped topping and one-third of the berries. Repeat these layers one more time: one-third of the cake, one-third of the pudding mixture, the remaining 1 cup (60 g) of whipped topping and one-third of the berries. Finally, top the trifle with the remaining one-third of the cake, the remaining one-third of the pudding and the remaining one-third of the berries.

Serve the trifle immediately or chill it in the refrigerator.

NUTRITION INFORMATION

Serving size: 1 serving; **Calories:** 265; **Carbohydrates:** 34 g; **Protein:** 6 g; **Fat:** 12 g

RECIPE NOTES

I buy a prepared angel food cake for this dessert, but you can make your own and use that instead.

Make sure to store this trifle in the refrigerator; because it has a lot of dairy, you don't want to leave it at room temperature for too long. This trifle will last for up to 3 days in the refrigerator.

ABOUT THE AUTHOR

JOANNA CISMARU is a full-time blogger, recipe developer, photographer and videographer for her popular food blog, Jo Cooks. Before blogging, she worked in the IT world for more than fifteen years in high-stress jobs. She started blogging as an escape and through it she discovered her love for cooking and baking. Although she always enjoyed cooking and helping her mom in the kitchen, she never did a lot of cooking at home—but she was secretly dreaming about making extravagant meals.

Throughout the development of her blog, Joanna shared many of her family's recipes while discovering her passion for cooking and baking. Because she was still working full time at her day job, Joanna was always looking for simple and quick meals that still offered delicious flavors. She let go of her fears and experimented in her kitchen day in and day out, and in no time her passion developed into a full-time career of living her dream.

Joanna is a great example of the truism that if you are passionate enough about something and you continue with it no matter what, your dreams will come true.

Joanna and her husband, Remo, live outside of Calgary, Alberta, Canada. Joanna's blog can be found online at www.jocooks.com.

INDEX

apples
    Apple Fritters, 432
    Churro Apple Pie Cookies, 415
    Quick Apple Turnovers, 424
    Waldorf Salad, 354
artichokes: Spinach-Artichoke Pasta, 204
arugula
    Arugula and Basil Pesto Risotto with Sautéed Mushrooms, 174–175
    Blue Cheese Burgers with Crispy Fried Onions, 75
asparagus
    Pasta Primavera, 188
    Pesto Shrimp Asparagus Pasta, 184
avocado
    Avocado-Shrimp Salsa, 328
    Guacamole, 115
    Mediterranean Grilled Chicken Salad, 268
    Mexican Street Corn Salad, 353
    Quick and Easy Cobb Salad, 260
    Steak Tacos, 55
    Taco Lasagna, 68

bacon
    Chicken-Bacon-Ranch Casserole, 225
    Creamy Loaded Potato Soup, 306
    Crescent Bacon Breakfast Ring, 233
    Instant Pot Baked Beans, 371
    Macaroni Salad, 345
    Mushroom Risotto, 380
    Old-Fashioned Green Beans, 372
    Quiche Lorraine, 271
    Quick and Easy Cobb Salad, 260
    White Beans with Bacon and Herbs, 375
Banana Bread, Easy, 409
Barley Soup, Beef and, 302
beans. *See also* green beans
    The Best Chili Mac and Cheese, 200
    Cheesy Chicken Enchilada Soup, 297
    Instant Pot Baked Beans, 371
    Sausage and Bean Soup, 309
    Taco Pasta Salad, 358

    White Beans with Bacon and Herbs, 375
beef
    Albondigas Soup, 301
    Baked Spaghetti Casserole, 210
    Beef and Barley Soup, 302
    Beef Stroganoff Soup, 290
    Beef Tenderloin, 80
    Beef Tips with Gravy, 59
    The Best Chili Mac and Cheese, 200
    Blue Cheese Burgers with Crispy Fried Onions, 75
    Carne Asada, 79
    Chile con Queso, 332
    Chimichurri Meatballs, 315
    Easy Beef and Broccoli Stir-Fry, 63
    Easy Beef Lasagna, 222
    Easy Meatloaf, 67
    Easy Spaghetti Bolognese, 203
    Easy Swiss Steak, 56
    Easy Thai Steak Salad, 264
    Garlic Butter Steak Bites, 64
    Ginger Beef, 72
    Instant Pot Beef Burgundy, 60

    Italian Stuffed Peppers, 76
    Italian Wedding Soup, 298
    Korean Beef Rice Bowls, 281
    Matambre (Argentinean Stuffed Flank Steak), 71
    Pan-Seared Steak, 52
    Reuben Sandwich, 267
    Salisbury Steak, 51
    Skillet Lasagna, 83
    Skillet Shepherd's Pie, 229
    Steak Tacos, 55
    Taco Lasagna, 68
    Taco Meatball Ring, 327
    Three-Cheese Hamburger Helper, 199
bell pepper
    Baked Breakfast Taquitos, 254
    Cheesy Chicken Enchilada Soup, 297
    Crescent Bacon Breakfast Ring, 233
    Easy California Quinoa Salad, 156
    Easy Chicken Fajitas, 259
    Easy Thai Steak Salad, 264

437

Easy Tomato and Chickpea Salad, 163
Fattoush Salad, 362
Greek Pasta Salad, 349
Greek Salad, 342
Grilled Vegetable Quesadillas, 159
Ham and Cheese Breakfast Muffins, 250
Italian Pasta Salad, 350
Italian Stuffed Peppers, 76
Matambre (Argentinean Stuffed Flank Steak), 71
Mediterranean Grilled Chicken Salad, 268
Mexican Street Corn Salad, 353
Overnight Breakfast Casserole, 246
Pork Fajitas, 115
Roasted Chicken and Vegetables, 15
Sausage and Bean Soup, 309
Spanish Chicken and Rice, 43
Taco Lasagna, 68
Tofu Drunken Noodles, 155
Vegetarian Stuffed Mushrooms, 324

berries
Angel Berry Trifle, 436
Blueberry Cake, 428
Blueberry Cheesecake Cookies, 423
Dutch Baby Pancake, 234
Mini Blueberry Galettes, 420
My Favorite Blueberry Muffins, 241
Strawberry Tiramisu Trifle, 427
Summer Fruit Salad with Lemon Dressing, 357

biscuits
Buttermilk Biscuits, 406
Cinnamon Cream Cheese Pockets, 416

black beans. *See* beans
blackberries. *See* berries
blueberries. *See* berries

bread. *See also* rolls
Easy Banana Bread, 409
Easy Bruschetta, 316
Fattoush Salad, 362
French Toast, 245
No-Knead Skillet Bread, 410
Overnight Breakfast Casserole, 246
Raisin Bread, 397
Rye Bread, 405
Sausage–French Toast Roll-Ups, 253
Slow Cooker Bread, 398
Two-Ingredient Dough, 394
White Bread, 393

broccoli
Broccoli-Cheese Soup, 310
Cheesy Chicken and Broccoli Pasta, 196
Chicken Divan, 209
Easy Beef and Broccoli Stir-Fry, 63
Pad See Ew, 278
Tofu Drunken Noodles, 155

bruschetta
Bruschetta Chicken, 11
Easy Bruschetta, 316
Burgers with Crispy Fried Onions, Blue Cheese, 75

cabbage
Cabbage Roll Casserole, 213
Egg Roll Soup, 289
Thai Chicken Salad, 263

cake
Angel Berry Trifle, 436
Blueberry Cake, 428
cannellini beans. *See* beans

carrots
Brandy-Glazed Carrots, 379
Chicken and Rice Soup, 285
Egg Roll Soup, 289
Instant Pot Chicken Noodle Soup, 305
Italian Wedding Soup, 298
Macaroni Salad, 345
Pasta Primavera, 188
Sausage and Bean Soup, 309
Thai Chicken Salad, 263
cauliflower: Italian Roasted Veggies, 387

cheese
Baked Breakfast Taquitos, 254
Baked Mac and Cheese, 172
Baked Spaghetti Casserole, 210
The Best Chili Mac and Cheese, 200
Blue Cheese Burgers with Crispy Fried Onions, 75
Broccoli-Cheese Soup, 310
Bruschetta Chicken, 11
Buffalo Chicken Quesadillas, 275
Cabbage Roll Casserole, 213
Cacio e Pepe, 183
Chanterelle Mushrooms with Tagliatelle, 164
Cheese and Prosciutto–Stuffed Chicken Breasts, 47
Cheesy Chicken and Broccoli Pasta, 196
Cheesy Chicken Enchilada Soup, 297
Cheesy Zucchini Quiche, 167
Chicken-Bacon-Ranch Casserole, 225
Chicken Divan, 209
Chicken Gloria, 218
Chicken Tamale Casserole, 217
Chile con Queso, 332
Creamy Carbonara, 179
Creamy Garlic-Parmesan Mushrooms, 384
Creamy Garlic-Parmesan Orzo, 192
Creamy Goat Cheese Pasta, 180
Crescent Bacon Breakfast Ring, 233
Easy Beef Lasagna, 222
Easy Bruschetta, 316
Easy Tomato and Chickpea Salad, 163
Grilled Vegetable Quesadillas, 159
Ham and Cheese Breakfast Muffins, 250

Italian Pasta Salad, 350
Lasagna Dip, 319
Mediterranean Grilled Chicken Salad, 268
No-Knead Skillet Bread, 410
Overnight Breakfast Casserole, 246
Quiche Lorraine, 271
Quick and Easy Cobb Salad, 260
Reuben Sandwich, 267
Sausage and Egg Breakfast Rolls, 242
Skillet Lasagna, 83
Spinach and Ricotta–Stuffed Shells, 171
Spinach-Artichoke Pasta, 204
Taco Lasagna, 68
Taco Meatball Ring, 327
Taco Pasta Salad, 358
Three-Cheese Hamburger Helper, 199
Turkey Tetrazzini, 221
White Chicken Enchiladas, 226
Cherry Cobbler, 431

chicken
Avgolemono Soup, 293
Beer Can Chicken, 12
Bruschetta Chicken, 11
Buffalo Chicken Quesadillas, 275
Cheese and Prosciutto–Stuffed Chicken Breasts, 47
Cheesy Chicken and Broccoli Pasta, 196
Cheesy Chicken Enchilada Soup, 297
Chicken and Mushrooms in Creamy Dill Sauce, 44
Chicken and Rice Soup, 285
Chicken-Bacon-Ranch Casserole, 225
Chicken Divan, 209
Chicken Drumsticks with Beluga Lentils, 28
Chicken Francese, 36
Chicken Gloria, 218
Chicken Kiev, 32
Chicken Stroganoff, 35
Chicken Tamale Casserole, 217
Coconut Chicken Curry, 27
Easy Chicken Fajitas, 259
Egg Roll Soup, 289
fully cooked, 9
Garlic and Paprika Chicken, 39
Garlic Butter Chicken, 24
Instant Pot Chicken Noodle Soup, 305
Kale and Quinoa Salad with Lemon Vinaigrette, 361
Korean Fried Chicken, 23
Lemon Chicken Piccata, 16
Mediterranean Grilled Chicken Salad, 268
Oven-Baked Chicken Thighs, 31
Oven-Roasted Chicken Shawarma, 40
Pad See Ew, 278
Quick and Easy Cobb Salad, 260
Roasted Chicken and Vegetables, 15
Roasted Cornish Hens, 20
Spanish Chicken and Rice, 43

Spatchcock Chicken, 19
Thai Chicken Salad, 263
thawing frozen, 9
Waldorf Salad, 354
washing raw, 9
White Chicken Enchiladas, 226
Chickpea Salad, Easy Tomato and, 163

chilies
Chicken Tamale Casserole, 217
Chile con Queso, 332
Chili-Garlic Shrimp, 141
Easy Thai Steak Salad, 264
Homemade Salsa, 336
Thai Chicken Salad, 263

chocolate
Best Ever Chocolate Chip Cookies, 435
Strawberry Tiramisu Trifle, 427
Cobbler, Cherry, 431

coconut
Coconut Chicken Curry, 27
Coconut Shrimp Curry, 134
Easy California Quinoa Salad, 156
Cod, Lemon-Butter Baked, 146

cookies
Best Ever Chocolate Chip Cookies, 435
Blueberry Cheesecake Cookies, 423
Churro Apple Pie Cookies, 415

corn
Chicken Tamale Casserole, 217
Mexican Street Corn Salad, 353
Taco Pasta Salad, 358
Tofu Drunken Noodles, 155
Cornish Hens, Roasted, 20

cornmeal
Chicken Tamale Casserole, 217
Creamy Polenta, 388
Couscous Pilaf with Sautéed Mushrooms, 168
Crab Cakes, Easy, 122

cucumber
Avocado-Shrimp Salsa, 328
Creamy Cucumber Salad, 346
Easy Thai Steak Salad, 264
Easy Tomato and Chickpea Salad, 163
Fattoush Salad, 362
Greek Pasta Salad, 349
Greek Salad, 342
Mediterranean Grilled Chicken Salad, 268
Tabbouleh Salad, 341
Thai Chicken Salad, 263

curries
Coconut Chicken Curry, 27
Coconut Shrimp Curry, 134

dips and spreads
Avocado-Shrimp Salsa, 328
Chile con Queso, 332
Guacamole, 115
Homemade Salsa, 336
Lasagna Dip, 319
Olive Tapenade, 331
Pico de Gallo, 320
dough. *See also* bread
Two-Ingredient Dough, 394

dressings
- Italian Dressing, 350
- Lemon Vinaigrette, 361

egg noodles. *See* noodles

eggs
- Avgolemono Soup, 293
- Baked Breakfast Taquitos, 254
- Cheesy Zucchini Quiche, 167
- Crescent Bacon Breakfast Ring, 233
- Egg Drop Soup, 294
- Ham and Cheese Breakfast Muffins, 250
- Matambre (Argentinean Stuffed Flank Steak), 71
- Overnight Breakfast Casserole, 246
- Pad See Ew, 278
- Pad Thai, 276–277
- Quiche Lorraine, 271
- Quick and Easy Cobb Salad, 260
- Sausage and Egg Breakfast Rolls, 242

enchiladas
- Cheesy Chicken Enchilada Soup, 297
- White Chicken Enchiladas, 226

fajitas
- Easy Chicken Fajitas, 259
- Pork Fajitas, 115

Fattoush Salad, 362

fish
- Baked Lemon-Garlic Halibut, 125
- Baked Lemon-Pepper Salmon, 130
- Cilantro-Lime Salmon, 121
- Easy Tuna Salad, 137
- Firecracker Salmon, 145
- Honey-Garlic Salmon and Veggies Sheet Pan Dinner, 133
- Honey Mustard Salmon, 149
- Lemon-Butter Baked Cod, 146
- Maple and Mustard–Glazed Salmon, 150
- Sole Meunière, 138
- Tuna Noodle Casserole, 214
- Vietnamese Fish Tacos, 272

French Toast, 245
- Sausage–French Toast Roll-Ups, 253

Fritters, Apple, 432

fruit. *See also* specific types
- Summer Fruit Salad with Lemon Dressing, 357
- Waldorf Salad, 354

Galettes, Mini Blueberry, 420

garlic
- Aglio e Olio, 187
- Baked Lemon-Garlic Halibut, 125
- Chili-Garlic Shrimp, 141
- Creamy Garlic-Parmesan Mushrooms, 384
- Creamy Garlic-Parmesan Orzo, 192
- Garlic and Paprika Chicken, 39
- Garlic Butter Chicken, 24
- Garlic Butter Steak Bites, 64
- Garlic Sauce, 40
- Honey-Garlic Pork Loin, 96
- Honey-Garlic Salmon and Veggies Sheet Pan Dinner, 133
- Honey-Garlic Shrimp, 335
- Lemon-Garlic Pork Roast, 99
- Lemon-Garlic Scallops, 142
- Rosemary-Garlic Pork Roast, 95

Gnocchi, Sausage and Leek Ragu, 195

gravy
- Beef Tips with Gravy, 59
- chicken, 12, 19
- Onion-Mushroom Gravy, 51
- Pan-Seared Pork Chops with Gravy, 103

Greek Pasta Salad, 349
Greek Salad, 342

green beans
- Honey Mustard Pork Tenderloin, 91
- Old-Fashioned Green Beans, 372
- Skillet Green Beans, 367

Guacamole, 115

halibut
- Baked Lemon-Garlic Halibut, 125
- Vietnamese Fish Tacos, 272

Ham and Cheese Breakfast Muffins, 250

honey
- Baked Honey-Glazed Pork Ribs, 88
- Honey-Garlic Pork Loin, 96
- Honey-Garlic Salmon and Veggies Sheet Pan Dinner, 133
- Honey-Garlic Shrimp, 335
- Honey Mustard Pork Tenderloin, 91
- Honey Mustard Salmon, 149
- Honey-Soy Shrimp, 126

Instant Pot
- Instant Pot Baked Beans, 371
- Instant Pot Barbecue Pork Ribs, 108
- Instant Pot Chicken Noodle Soup, 305

Italian Pasta Salad, 350

Kale and Quinoa Salad with Lemon Vinaigrette, 361
Korean Fried Chicken, 23

lasagna
- Easy Beef Lasagna, 222
- Lasagna Dip, 319
- Skillet Lasagna, 83

Leek Ragu Gnocchi, Sausage and, 195

lemon
- Avgolemono Soup, 293
- Baked Lemon-Garlic Halibut, 125
- Baked Lemon-Pepper Salmon, 130
- Chicken Francese, 36

Kale and Quinoa Salad with Lemon Vinaigrette, 361
Lemon-Butter Baked Cod, 146
Lemon Chicken Piccata, 16
Lemon-Garlic Pork Roast, 99
Lemon-Garlic Scallops, 142
lentils: Chicken Drumsticks with Beluga Lentils, 28

Macaroni Salad, 345
mango: Easy California Quinoa Salad, 156

meatballs
- Albondigas Soup, 301
- Chimichurri Meatballs, 315
- Italian Wedding Soup, 298
- Taco Meatball Ring, 327

Mexican Street Corn Salad, 353

muffins
- Ham and Cheese Breakfast Muffins, 250
- My Favorite Blueberry Muffins, 241
- Pumpkin-Zucchini Muffins, 238

mushrooms
- Arugula and Basil Pesto Risotto with Sautéed Mushrooms, 174–175
- Beef Stroganoff Soup, 290
- Chanterelle Mushrooms with Tagliatelle, 164
- Chicken and Mushrooms in Creamy Dill Sauce, 44
- Chicken Gloria, 218
- Chicken Stroganoff, 35
- Couscous Pilaf with Sautéed Mushrooms, 168
- Creamy Garlic-Parmesan Mushrooms, 384
- Grilled Vegetable Quesadillas, 159
- Instant Pot Beef Burgundy, 60
- Italian Roasted Veggies, 387
- Mushroom Risotto, 380
- Pasta Primavera, 188
- Salisbury Steak, 51
- Tofu Drunken Noodles, 155
- Vegetarian Stuffed Mushrooms, 324

noodles. *See also* pasta
- Beef Stroganoff Soup, 290
- Instant Pot Chicken Noodle Soup, 305
- Pad See Ew, 278
- Pad Thai, 276–277
- Sesame Noodles, 160
- Tofu Drunken Noodles, 155
- Tuna Noodle Casserole, 214

Olive Tapenade, 331

onions
- Blue Cheese Burgers with Crispy Fried Onions, 75
- Onion-Mushroom Gravy, 51
- pickling, 342

orzo
- Creamy Garlic-Parmesan Orzo, 192
- Italian Wedding Soup, 298

Pad See Ew, 278
Pad Thai, 276–277

pancakes
- The Best Buttermilk Pancakes, 237
- Dutch Baby Pancake, 234
- Sheet Pan Pancakes, 249

pancetta: Creamy Carbonara, 179
papaya: Thai Chicken Salad, 263

pasta. *See also* noodles
- Aglio e Olio, 187
- Baked Mac and Cheese, 172
- Baked Spaghetti Casserole, 210
- The Best Chili Mac and Cheese, 200
- Cacio e Pepe, 183
- Chanterelle Mushrooms with Tagliatelle, 164
- Cheesy Chicken and Broccoli Pasta, 196
- Creamy Carbonara, 179
- Creamy Garlic-Parmesan Orzo, 192
- Creamy Goat Cheese Pasta, 180
- Easy Beef Lasagna, 222
- Easy Spaghetti Bolognese, 203
- Easy Tortellini Soup, 286
- Greek Pasta Salad, 349
- Italian Pasta Salad, 350
- Italian Wedding Soup, 298
- Macaroni Salad, 345
- Pasta Primavera, 188
- Pesto Shrimp Asparagus Pasta, 184
- Pumpkin and Sausage Pasta, 191
- Sausage and Leek Ragu Gnocchi, 195
- Skillet Lasagna, 83
- Spinach and Ricotta–Stuffed Shells, 171
- Spinach-Artichoke Pasta, 204
- Taco Lasagna, 68
- Taco Pasta Salad, 358
- Three-Cheese Hamburger Helper, 199
- Turkey Tetrazzini, 221

pastrami: Reuben Sandwich, 267
pears: Waldorf Salad, 354

peas
- Couscous Pilaf with Sautéed Mushrooms, 168
- Easy Tomato and Chickpea Salad, 163
- Tuna Noodle Casserole, 214

pecans
- Easy Tuna Salad, 137
- Pumpkin Delight, 419

pesto
- Arugula and Basil Pesto, 174–175
- Pesto Shrimp Asparagus Pasta, 184

Pickles, Fried, 323
Pico de Gallo, 320
pine nuts: Pesto Shrimp Asparagus Pasta, 184
Polenta, Creamy, 388

pork. *See also* bacon; sausage
- Baked Honey-Glazed Pork Ribs, 88

INDEX 439

Braised Pork in Sweet Soy Sauce, 116
Cabbage Roll Casserole, 213
Chimichurri Meatballs, 315
Easy Meatloaf, 67
Grilled Tomahawk Pork Chops, 111
Honey-Garlic Pork Loin, 96
Honey Mustard Pork Tenderloin, 91
Instant Pot Barbecue Pork Ribs, 108
Italian Breaded Pork Chops, 100
Lemon-Garlic Pork Roast, 99
Mustard-Balsamic Pork Chops, 92
Pan-Seared Pork Chops with Gravy, 103
Perfect Pork Tenderloin, 87
Pork Fajitas, 115
Pork Schnitzel, 104
Quick and Easy Pork Sausages, 112
Ranch Pork Chops and Potatoes, 107
Rosemary-Garlic Pork Roast, 95
Taco Meatball Ring, 327
potatoes
    Albondigas Soup, 301
    Creamy Loaded Potato Soup, 306
    Ham and Cheese Breakfast Muffins, 250
    Honey Mustard Pork Tenderloin, 91
    Mashed Potatoes, 383
    Perfect Thyme Skillet Potatoes, 368
    Ranch Pork Chops and Potatoes, 107
    Roasted Chicken and Vegetables, 15
    Skillet Shepherd's Pie, 229
poultry. *See* chicken; turkey
Prosciutto–Stuffed Chicken Breasts, Cheese and, 47
pudding
    Angel Berry Trifle, 436
    Pumpkin Delight, 419
    Strawberry Tiramisu Trifle, 427
pumpkin
    Pumpkin and Sausage Pasta, 191
    Pumpkin Delight, 419
    Pumpkin-Zucchini Muffins, 238
quesadillas
    Buffalo Chicken Quesadillas, 275
    Grilled Vegetable Quesadillas, 159
quiche
    Cheesy Zucchini Quiche, 167
    Quiche Lorraine, 271
quinoa
    Easy California Quinoa Salad, 156
    Kale and Quinoa Salad with Lemon Vinaigrette, 361

radishes: Fattoush Salad, 362

raisins
    Easy Tuna Salad, 137
    Kale and Quinoa Salad with Lemon Vinaigrette, 361
    Raisin Bread, 397
    Waldorf Salad, 354
raspberries. *See* berries
red peppers. *See also* bell pepper
    Roasted Red Peppers, 376
Reuben Sandwich, 267
ribs
    Baked Honey-Glazed Pork Ribs, 88
    Instant Pot Barbecue Pork Ribs, 108
rice
    Albondigas Soup, 301
    Arugula and Basil Pesto Risotto with Sautéed Mushrooms, 174–175
    Avgolemono Soup, 293
    Cabbage Roll Casserole, 213
    Chicken and Rice Soup, 285
    Italian Stuffed Peppers, 76
    Korean Beef Rice Bowls, 281
    Mushroom Risotto, 380
    Spanish Chicken and Rice, 43
rolls
    Buttermilk Biscuits, 406
    Classic Dinner Rolls, 402
    Dinner Crescents, 401
    Sausage and Egg Breakfast Rolls, 242
    Two-Ingredient Dough, 394
Rye Bread, 405

salads
    Creamy Cucumber Salad, 346
    Easy California Quinoa Salad, 156
    Easy Tomato and Chickpea Salad, 163
    Easy Tuna Salad, 137
    Fattoush Salad, 362
    Greek Pasta Salad, 349
    Greek Salad, 342
    Italian Pasta Salad, 350
    Kale and Quinoa Salad with Lemon Vinaigrette, 361
    Macaroni Salad, 345
    Mediterranean Grilled Chicken Salad, 268
    Mexican Street Corn Salad, 353
    Quick and Easy Cobb Salad, 260
    Summer Fruit Salad with Lemon Dressing, 357
    Tabbouleh Salad, 341
    Taco Pasta Salad, 358
    Thai Chicken Salad, 263
    Waldorf Salad, 354
salami: Italian Pasta Salad, 350
Salisbury Steak, 51
salmon
    Baked Lemon-Pepper Salmon, 130
    Cilantro-Lime Salmon, 121
    Firecracker Salmon, 145
    Honey-Garlic Salmon and Veggies Sheet Pan Dinner, 133
    Honey Mustard Salmon, 149

Maple and Mustard–Glazed Salmon, 150
salsa
    Avocado-Shrimp Salsa, 328
    Homemade Salsa, 336
Sandwich, Reuben, 267
sauces
    Barbecue Sauce, 108
    Chimichurri Sauce, 315
    Curry Sauce, 134
    Firecracker Sauce, 145
    Honey Mustard Sauce, 149
    Lemon-Butter Sauce, 146
    Lemon-Garlic Sauce, 142
    White Sauce, 226
    Yogurt Sauce, 80
sauerkraut: Reuben Sandwich, 267
sausage
    Baked Breakfast Taquitos, 254
    Easy Tortellini Soup, 286
    Lasagna Dip, 319
    Overnight Breakfast Casserole, 246
    Pumpkin and Sausage Pasta, 191
    Quick and Easy Pork Sausages, 112
    Sausage and Bean Soup, 309
    Sausage and Egg Breakfast Rolls, 242
    Sausage and Leek Ragu Gnocchi, 195
    Sausage–French Toast Roll-Ups, 253
Scallops, Lemon-Garlic, 142
seafood. *See also* fish
    Chili-Garlic Shrimp, 141
    Coconut Shrimp Curry, 134
    Easy Crab Cakes, 122
    Honey-Garlic Shrimp, 335
    Honey-Soy Shrimp, 126
    Lemon-Garlic Scallops, 142
    Pesto Shrimp Asparagus Pasta, 184
    Spicy New Orleans Shrimp, 129
Sesame Noodles, 160
shrimp
    Avocado-Shrimp Salsa, 328
    Chili-Garlic Shrimp, 141
    Coconut Shrimp Curry, 134
    Honey-Garlic Shrimp, 335
    Honey-Soy Shrimp, 126
    Pad Thai, 276–277
    Pesto Shrimp Asparagus Pasta, 184
    Spicy New Orleans Shrimp, 129
snap peas: Tofu Drunken Noodles, 155
Sole Meunière, 138
soups
    Albondigas Soup, 301
    Avgolemono Soup, 293
    Beef and Barley Soup, 302
    Beef Stroganoff Soup, 290
    Broccoli-Cheese Soup, 310
    Cheesy Chicken Enchilada Soup, 297
    Chicken and Rice Soup, 285
    Creamy Loaded Potato Soup, 306
    Easy Tortellini Soup, 286

Egg Drop Soup, 294
    Egg Roll Soup, 289
    Italian Wedding Soup, 298
    Sausage and Bean Soup, 309
spinach
    Easy Tortellini Soup, 286
    Italian Wedding Soup, 298
    Spinach and Ricotta–Stuffed Shells, 171
    Spinach-Artichoke Pasta, 204
squash: Grilled Vegetable Quesadillas, 159
steak. *See* beef
strawberries
    Angel Berry Trifle, 436
    Strawberry Tiramisu Trifle, 427
    Summer Fruit Salad with Lemon Dressing, 357
sun-dried tomatoes
    Cheese and Prosciutto–Stuffed Chicken Breasts, 47
    Olive Tapenade, 331

Tabbouleh Salad, 341
tacos
    Steak Tacos, 55
    Taco Lasagna, 68
    Taco Meatball Ring, 327
    Taco Pasta Salad, 358
    Vietnamese Fish Tacos, 272
Tiramisu Trifle, Strawberry, 427
tofu
    Pad Thai, 276–277
    Tofu Drunken Noodles, 155
trifles
    Angel Berry Trifle, 436
    Strawberry Tiramisu Trifle, 427
tuna
    Easy Tuna Salad, 137
    Tuna Noodle Casserole, 214
turkey
    Sausage and Egg Breakfast Rolls, 242
    Turkey Tetrazzini, 221

vegetables. *See also specific types*
    Grilled Vegetable Quesadillas, 159
    Italian Roasted Veggies, 387
    Roasted Chicken and Vegetables, 15
    Skillet Shepherd's Pie, 229

Waldorf Salad, 354

yeast, 391
Yogurt Sauce, 80

zucchini
    Cheesy Zucchini Quiche, 167
    Grilled Vegetable Quesadillas, 159
    Honey-Garlic Salmon and Veggies Sheet Pan Dinner, 133
    Pasta Primavera, 188
    Pumpkin-Zucchini Muffins, 238